T0142043

Lecture Notes in Computer Science 13002

More information about this subseries at http://www.springer.com/series/7412

Nadia Magnenat-Thalmann · Victoria Interrante ·
Daniel Thalmann · George Papagiannakis ·
Bin Sheng · Jinman Kim ·
Marina Gavrilova (Eds.)

Advances in Computer Graphics

38th Computer Graphics International Conference, CGI 2021
Virtual Event, September 6–10, 2021
Proceedings

 Springer

Editors
Nadia Magnenat-Thalmann
University of Geneva
Carouge, Switzerland

Nanyang Technological University
Singapore, Singapore

Daniel Thalmann
EPFL
Lausanne, Switzerland

Bin Sheng
Shanghai Jiao Tong University
Shanghai, China

Marina Gavrilova
University of Calgary
Calgary, AB, Canada

Victoria Interrante ⓘ
University of Minnesota
Minneapolis, MN, USA

George Papagiannakis
University of Crete
Heraklion, Crete, Greece

Jinman Kim
University of Sydney
Sydney, NSW, Australia

ISSN 0302-9743   ISSN 1611-3349 (electronic)
Lecture Notes in Computer Science
ISBN 978-3-030-89028-5   ISBN 978-3-030-89029-2 (eBook)
https://doi.org/10.1007/978-3-030-89029-2

LNCS Sublibrary: SL6 – Image Processing, Computer Vision, Pattern Recognition, and Graphics

This Springer imprint is published by the registered company Springer Nature Switzerland AG
The registered company address is: Gewerbestrasse 11, 6330 Cham, Switzerland

Preface

Welcome to the Lecture Notes in Computer Science (LNCS) proceedings of the 38th Computer Graphics International conference (CGI 2021). CGI is one of the oldest international conferences in computer graphics in the world. It is the official conference of the Computer Graphics Society (CGS), a long-standing international computer graphics organization. The CGI conference has been held annually in many different countries across the world and gained a reputation as one of the key conferences for researchers and practitioners to share their achievements and discover the latest advances in computer graphics. As with CGI 2020, this year, CGI 2021 was held fully virtual due to the ongoing COVID-19 pandemic. It was organized online by the MIRALab of the University of Geneva.

This CGI 2021 LNCS proceedings is composed of 53 papers. We accepted 18 papers that were reviewed highly in the CGI TVC track from over 100 submissions, and we received 64 papers for the LNCS track, accepting an additional 35 full papers. To ensure the high quality of the publication, each paper was reviewed by at least three experts in the field and the authors of accepted papers were asked to revise the paper according to the review comments prior to publication.

The proceedings also feature papers from the ENGAGE 2021 Workshop, which focused specifically on important aspects of geometric algebra including surface construction, robotics, encryption, qubits, and expression optimization. The workshop has been part of CGI conference since 2016.

We would like to express our deepest gratitude to all the Program Committee members and external reviewers who have provided timely and high quality reviews. We would also like to thank all the authors for contributing to the conference by submitting their work.

September 2021

Nadia Magnenat Thalmann
Victoria Interrante
Daniel Thalmann
Bin Sheng
Jinman Kim
George Papagiannakis
Marina Gavrilova

Organization

Conference Chairs

Nadia Magnenat Thalmann   University of Geneva, Switzerland
Victoria Interrante   University of Minnesota, USA

LNCS Program Chairs

Bin Sheng   Shanghai Jia Tong University, China
Jinman Kim   The University of Sydney, Australia

TVC Program Chairs

George Papagiannakis   University of Crete, Greece
Daniel Thalmann   EPFL, Switzerland

LNCS Publication Chair

Marina Gavrilova   University of Calgary, Canada

Program Committee

Ahmad Karambakhsh   Shanghai Jiao Tong University, China
Anum Masood   COMSATS University Islamabad, Pakistan
Aouaidjia Kamel   Algerian Space Agency, Algeria
Chuanyan Hao   Nanjing University of Posts and Telecommunications, China
Huisi Wu   Shenzhen University, China
Ibraheem Alhashim   KAUST, Saudi Arabia
Jian Zhu   Guangdong University of Technology, China
Makoto Okabe   Shizuoka University, Japan
Masahiro Toyoura   University of Yamanashi, Japan
Masaki Oshita   Kyushu Institute of Technology, Japan
Meng Yang   Beijing Forestry University, China
Nicolas Ray   Inria Nancy, France
Norimasa Yoshida   Nihon University, Japan
Parag Chaudhuri   Indian Institute of Technology Bombay, India
Roberto Grosso   Friedrich-Alexander-Universität Erlangen-Nürnberg, Germany
Sudhir Mudur   Concordia University, Canada

Gregory Slabaugh	Queen Mary University of London, UK
Oh-Young Song	Sejong University, South Korea
Charlie Wang	Delft University of Technology, The Netherlands
Keze Wang	Sun Yat-sen University, China
Franz-Erich Wolter	Leibniz University of Hannover, Germany
Chunxia Xiao	Wuhan University, China
Junfeng Yao	Xiamen University, China
Jianmin Zheng	Nanyang Technological University, Singapore
Yiannis Aloimonos	University of Maryland, USA
Andreas Aristidou	University of Cyprus, Cyprus
Loic Barthe	IRIT - Université de Toulouse, France
Bedrich Benes	Purdue University, USA
Y. Cai	Nanyang Technological University, Singapore
Jian Chang	Bournemouth University, UK
Falai Chen	University of Science and Technology of China, China
Renjie Chen	University of Science and Technology of China, China
David Coeurjolly	CNRS – LIRIS, France
Frederic Cordier	Université de Haute-Alsace, France
Naser Damer	Fraunhofer Institute for Computer Graphics Research, Germany
Zhigang Deng	University of Houston, USA
Parris Egbert	Brigham Young University, USA
Bin Fan	University of Science and Technology Beijing, China
Ioannis Fudos	University of Ioannina, Greece
Issei Fujishiro	Keio University, Japan
Xifeng Gao	Florida State University, USA
Marina Gavrilova	University of Calgary, Canada
Enrico Gobbetti	CRS4 Visual Computing, Italy
Laurent Grisoni	Lille University of Science and Technology, France
Yunqing Guan	Singapore Institute of Technology, Singapore
Stefan Guthe	TU Darmstadt, Germany
Eckhard Hitzer	International Christian University, Japan
Ruizhen Hu	Shenzhen University, China
Kei Iwasaki	Wakayama University, Japan
Prem Kalra	IIT Delhi, India
Daniel Keim	University of Konstanz, Germany
Hyungseok Kim	Konkuk University, South Korea
George Alex Koulieris	Durham University, UK
Arjan Kuijper	TU Darmstadt, Germany
Di Lin	Shenzhen University, China
Ligang Liu	University of Science and Technology of China, China
Xiaoyang Mao	University of Yamanashi, Japan
Bochang Moon	GIST, South Korea
Shigeo Morishima	Waseda University, Japan
Luciana Nedel	UFRGS, Brazil
Junyong Noh	Korea Advanced Institute of Science and Technology, South Korea

Contents

Computer Animation

Temporal Parameter-Free Deep Skinning of Animated Meshes 3
Anastasia Moutafidou, Vasileios Toulatzis, and Ioannis Fudos

The Impact of Animations in the Perception of a Simulated Crowd 25
Elena Molina, Alejandro Ríos, and Nuria Pelechano

Computer Vision

Virtual Haptic System for Shape Recognition Based on Local Curvatures 41
Guillem Garrofé, Carlota Parés, Anna Gutiérrez, Conrado Ruiz Jr,
Gerard Serra, and David Miralles

Stable Depth Estimation Within Consecutive Video Frames 54
Fei Luo, Lin Wei, and Chunxia Xiao

Progressive Multi-scale Reconstruction for Guided Depth Map
Super-Resolution via Deep Residual Gate Fusion Network 67
Yang Wen, Jihong Wang, Zhen Li, Bin Sheng, Ping Li, Xiaoyu Chi,
and Lijuan Mao

SE_EDNet: A Robust Manipulated Faces Detection Algorithm 80
Chaoyang Peng, Lihong Yao, Tanfeng Sun, Xinghao Jiang,
and Zhongjie Mi

PointCNN-Based Individual Tree Detection Using LiDAR Point Clouds 89
Wenyuan Ying, Tianyang Dong, Zhanfeng Ding, and Xinpeng Zhang

Variance Weight Distribution Network Based Noise Sample Learning
for Robust Person Re-identification 101
Xiaoyi Long, Ruimin Hu, and Xin Xu

Monocular Dense SLAM with Consistent Deep Depth Prediction 113
Feihu Yan, Jiawei Wen, Zhaoxin Li, and Zhong Zhou

3D Shape-Adapted Garment Generation with Sketches 125
Yijing Chen, Chuhua Xian, Shuo Jin, and Guiqing Li

Geometric Computing

Light-Weight Multi-view Topology Consistent Facial Geometry
and Reflectance Capture 139
  Penglei Ji, Hanchao Li, Luyan Jiang, and Xinguo Liu

Real-Time Fluid Simulation with Atmospheric Pressure Using Weak Air
Particles 151
  Tian Sang, Wentao Chen, Yitian Ma, Hui Wang, and Xubo Yang

Human Poses and Gestures

Reinforcement Learning for Quadruped Locomotion 167
  Kangqiao Zhao, Feng Lin, and Hock Soon Seah

Partially Occluded Skeleton Action Recognition Based on Multi-stream
Fusion Graph Convolutional Networks 178
  Dan Li and Wuzhen Shi

Social-Scene-Aware Generative Adversarial Networks for Pedestrian
Trajectory Prediction 190
  Binhao Huang, Zhenwei Ma, Lianggangxu Chen, and Gaoqi He

Image Processing

Cecid Fly Defect Detection in Mangoes Using Object Detection
Frameworks 205
  Maria Jeseca C. Baculo, Conrado Ruiz Jr, and Oya Aran

Twin-Channel Gan: Repair Shape with Twin-Channel Generative
Adversarial Network and Structural Constraints 217
  Zhenjiang Du, Ning Xie, Zhitao Liu, Xiaohua Zhang, and Yang Yang

CoPaint: Guiding Sketch Painting with Consistent Color and Coherent
Generative Adversarial Networks 229
  Shiqi Jiang, Chenhui Li, and Changbo Wang

Multi-Stream Fusion Network for Multi-Distortion Image
Super-Resolution 242
  *Yang Wen, Yupeng Xu, Bin Sheng, Ping Li, Lei Bi, Jinman Kim,
  Xiangui He, and Xun Xu*

Generative Face Parsing Map Guided 3D Face Reconstruction Under
Occluded Scenes 252
  Dapeng Zhao and Yue Qi

Compact Double Attention Module Embedded CNN for Palmprint
Recognition 264
*Yongmin Zheng, Lunke Fei, Wei Jia, Jie Wen, Shaohua Teng,
and Imad Rida*

M2M: Learning to Enhance Low-Light Image from Model to Mobile FPGA ... 276
Ying Chen, Wei Wang, Wei Hu, and Xin Xu

Character Flow Detection and Rectification for Scene Text Spotting 288
Beiji Zou, Wenjun Yang, Kaiwen Li, Enquan Huang, and Shu Liu

A Deep Learning Method for 2D Image Stippling 300
Zhongmin Xue, Beibei Wang, and Lei Ma

Medical Imaging

In Silico Heart Versatile Graphical Interface with Systole and Diastole
Phases Customizable for Diversified Arrhythmias Simulations 315
*C. M. G. Godoy, M. C. Selusniacki, V. S. dos Santos, C. C. Godoy,
G. M. dos Santos, and R. C. Coelho*

ADD-Net:Attention U-Net with Dilated Skip Connection and Dense
Connected Decoder for Retinal Vessel Segmentation 327
Dongjin Huang, Hao Guo, and Yue Zhang

BDFNet: Boundary-Assisted and Discriminative Feature Extraction
Network for COVID-19 Lung Infection Segmentation 339
*Hui Ding, Qirui Niu, Yufeng Nie, Yuanyuan Shang, Nianzhe Chen,
and Rui Liu*

A Classification Network for Ocular Diseases Based on Structure Feature
and Visual Attention 354
*Yang Wen, Yupeng Xu, Kun Liu, Bin Sheng, Lei Bi, Jinman Kim,
Xiangui He, and Xun Xu*

Physics-Based Simulation

DSNet: Dynamic Skin Deformation Prediction by Recurrent Neural
Network 365
Hyewon Seo, Kaifeng Zou, and Frederic Cordier

Curvature Analysis of Sculpted Hair Meshes for Hair Guides Generation 378
Florian Pellegrin, Andre Beauchamp, and Eric Paquette

Synthesizing Human Faces Using Latent Space Factorization and Local
Weights 398
    Minyoung Kim and Young J. Kim

CFMNet: Coarse-to-Fine Cascaded Feature Mapping Network for Hair
Attribute Transfer 406
    *Zhifeng Xie, Guisong Zhang, Chunpeng Yu, Jiaheng Zheng,
    and Bin Sheng*

Rendering and Textures

Dynamic Shadow Synthesis Using Silhouette Edge Optimization 421
    *Jihong Wang, Zhen Li, Saba Ghazanfar Ali, Bin Sheng, Ping Li,
    Xiaoyu Chi, Jinman Kim, and Lijuan Mao*

DDISH-GI: Dynamic Distributed Spherical Harmonics Global Illumination 433
    *Julius Ikkala, Petrus Kivi, Joel Alanko, Markku Mäkitalo,
    and Pekka Jääskeläinen*

Simplicity Driven Edge Refinement and Color Reconstruction in Image
Vectorization 452
    *Zheng Zhang, Junhao Zhao, Shiqing Xin, Shuangmin Chen,
    Yuanfeng Zhou, Changhe Tu, and Wenping Wang*

Temporal-Consistency-Aware Video Color Transfer 464
    Shiguang Liu and Yu Zhang

An Improved Advancing-front-Delaunay Method for Triangular Mesh
Generation 477
    *Yufei Guo, Xuhui Huang, Zhe Ma, Yongqing Hai, Rongli Zhao,
    and Kewu Sun*

Robotics and Vision

Does Elderly Enjoy Playing Bingo with a Robot? A Case Study
with the Humanoid Robot Nadine 491
    *Nidhi Mishra, Gauri Tulsulkar, Hanhui Li, Nadia Magnenat Thalmann,
    Lim Hwee Er, Lee Mei Ping, and Cheng Siok Khoong*

Resilient Navigation Among Dynamic Agents with Hierarchical
Reinforcement Learning 504
    Sijia Wang, Hao Jiang, and Zhaoqi Wang

Visual Analytics

MeshChain: Secure 3D Model and Intellectual Property management
Powered by Blockchain Technology 519
Hunmin Park, Yuchi Huo, and Sung-Eui Yoon

Image Emotion Analysis Based on the Distance Relation of Emotion
Categories via Deep Metric Learning 535
Guoqin Peng, Hao Zhang, and Dan Xu

How Much Do We Perceive Geometric Features, Personalities
and Emotions in Avatars? 548
*Victor Araujo, Bruna Dalmoro, Rodolfo Favaretto, Felipe Vilanova,
Angelo Costa, and Soraia Raupp Musse*

High-Dimensional Dataset Simplification by Laplace-Beltrami Operator 568
Chenkai Xu and Hongwei Lin

VR/AR

Characterizing Visual Acuity in the Use of Head Mounted Displays 589
Vladimir Soares da Fontoura and Anderson Maciel

Effects of Different Proximity-Based Feedback on Virtual Hand Pointing
in Virtual Reality 608
Yujun Lu, BoYu Gao, Huawei Tu, Weiqi Luo, and HyungSeok Kim

Virtual Scenes Construction Promotes Traditional Chinese Art Preservation 621
Hui Liang, Fanyu Bao, Yusheng Sun, Chao Ge, and Jian Chang

A Preliminary Work: Mixed Reality-Integrated Computer-Aided Surgical
Navigation System for Paranasal Sinus Surgery Using Microsoft
HoloLens 2 633
Sungmin Lee, Hoijoon Jung, Euro Lee, Younhyun Jung, and Seon Tae Kim

Engage

Algorithms for Multi-conditioned Conic Fitting in Geometric Algebra
for Conics 645
Pavel Loučka and Petr Vašík

Special Affine Fourier Transform for Space-Time Algebra Signals 658
Eckhard Hitzer

On Explicit Formulas for Characteristic Polynomial Coefficients
in Geometric Algebras 670
    Kamron Abdulkhaev and Dmitry Shirokov

Unified Expression Frame of Geodetic Stations Based on Conformal
Geometric Algebra 682
    Zhenjun Yan, Zhaoyuan Yu, Yun Wang, Wen Luo, Jiyi Zhang, Hong Gao,
    and Linwang Yuan

Never 'Drop the Ball' in the Operating Room: An Efficient Hand-Based
VR HMD Controller Interpolation Algorithm, for Collaborative,
Networked Virtual Environments 694
    Manos Kamarianakis, Nick Lydatakis, and George Papagiannakis

The Rules of 4-Dimensional Perspective: How to Implement Lorentz
Transformations in Relativistic Visualization 705
    Andrew J. S. Hamilton

Author Index 719

Computer Animation

Temporal Parameter-Free Deep Skinning
of Animated Meshes

Anastasia Moutafidou, Vasileios Toulatzis, and Ioannis Fudos[⊠]

University of Ioannina, Ioannina, Greece
fudos@uoi.gr

Abstract. In computer graphics, animation compression is essential for efficient storage, streaming and reproduction of animated meshes. Previous work has presented efficient techniques for compression by deriving skinning transformations and weights using clustering of vertices based on geometric features of vertices over time. In this work we present a novel approach that assigns vertices to bone-influenced clusters and derives weights using deep learning through a training set that consists of pairs of vertex trajectories (temporal vertex sequences) and the corresponding weights drawn from fully rigged animated characters. The approximation error of the resulting linear blend skinning scheme is significantly lower than the error of competent previous methods by producing at the same time a minimal number of bones. Furthermore, the optimal set of transformation and vertices is derived in fewer iterations due to the better initial positioning in the multidimensional variable space. Our method requires no parameters to be determined or tuned by the user during the entire process of compressing a mesh animation sequence.

Keywords: Animation · Skinning · Deep learning

1 Introduction

Nowadays an animator may produce a realistic character animation by following either of the two modern workflows:

i rigging a static mesh (i.e. define a bone structure and associate the bones with the mesh vertices by weight painting), apply transformations to bones along a time line, correct erroneous deformations by adding bones, introduce additional per frame deformations to simulate non linear effects, or

ii use recent developments of computer vision and tracking techniques to derive mesh sequences that are reconstructed by markerless capture or by motion capture with dense markers (see e.g. [10]).

Electronic supplementary material The online version of this chapter (https:// doi.org/10.1007/978-3-030-89029-2_1) contains supplementary material, which is available to authorized users.

Both workflows produce sequences of animated meshes. These mesh animation sequences must subsequently be converted to a representation that allows for streaming and editing. To this end, a first step is to use compression.

With the evolution of cloud based graphics applications, a compression approach such as Linear Blend Skinning is a necessity for efficiently storing and using animation sequences. Compression is performed by producing an approximation of the animation that consists of an initial pose and a number of transformations that describe each subsequent pose by a deformation of a surface part.

Linear blend skinning (LBS) [24] is a time and space efficient mesh deformation technique where mesh vertices are influenced by a set of bones. In spite of several limitations that have been addressed in the literature [10], LBS-based approaches are significant in the animation industry due to their simplicity and straightforward GPU implementation.

There exists a variety of approaches for compression using clustering techniques, most of which are based on geometric features of vertices over time. We introduce a novel deep learning approach that uses a training set of successfully fully rigged animated models to produce a skinning model. Given a new animated mesh sequence, the trained network derives pseudo-bones and weights. There is no limit on the number of vertices, faces and frames given as input. There is just an upper limit on the number of bones for all animations. A single trained network can be used to predict weights for any animation sequence.

We also improve the efficiency of the least square optimization of transformations and weights that is commonly used to reduce the approximation error by employing conjugate gradient optimization that is suitable for multidimensional systems.

While previous skinning approaches use a predetermined number of bones and several other tuning parameters, our approach is parameter free. An appropriate set of bones is derived based on similar successfully rigged animations of the training dataset. In our method there is no need for preprocessing (scaling, rotation or translation) for the geometry of the input, since we only use vertex trajectories, so only the relative movement of the vertex is taken into account. To evaluate our approach, we use both mesh sequences that are derived from rigged and animated characters and benchmark mesh sequences from available animation sequence datasets. Our experimental evaluation shows that our approach outperforms previous approaches in terms of both compression rate and approximation error for all datasets.

The mesh clustering derived by our method can also be used to create a skeletal rig since it yields segmentations that correspond to the influence of bones on mesh vertices. Therefore, the output of our methods can be easily converted to a fully rigged animated character and used in subsequent phases of animation editing and rendering.

2   Related Work

Although there is a lot of research on skinning of animated models, the use of deep learning techniques for skinning has not been explored thoroughly.

Elastiface [30] indicate that an animated character can be quite complex and that managing and processing needs cumbersome human intervention and a significant amount of computationally intensive tasks. Moreover techniques such as cross-parameterization [17] or procedures that can convert an animated character into an animation sequence have high memory and space requirements. So there is a need for different procedures that can produce animated models in a compressed form without being provided with a skeleton or skin specification [11].

In the context of animation compression, James and Twigg [11] were the first to explore the use of LBS to approximately reproduce articulated characters as a function of their bone movement. Extending this work, Kavan et al. [12, 13] presented a dual quaternion skinning scheme that can compute approximations for highly-deformable animations by suggesting that uniformly selected points on the mesh can act as bones. Both of them are enhance their final skinned approximation by exploiting EigenSkin [18]. FESAM [14] introduced an algorithm that optimizes all of the skinning parameters in an iterative manner. While FESAM offers high-quality reproduction results, is limited to download-and-play scenarios, since they do not use information about topology and the location of proxy joints is occluded once the optimization process kicks in.

[28] introduces a pose-to-pose skinning technique that exploits temporal coherence that enables the full spectrum of applications supported by previous approaches in conjunction with a novel pose editing of arbitrary animation poses, which can be smoothly propagated through the subsequent ones generating new deformed mesh sequences.

[19] approaches a set of example poses by defining a constrained optimization problem for deriving weights and transformations which yields better results in terms of error. In our method we ensure convexity by an additional equation for each vertex and a non negative least square solver. Then we employ linear solvers and update the weights and the bone transformations successively.

On the other hand, there are techniques that can create a plausible skeleton for a mesh model either by exploiting the movement of vertices to perform mesh segmentation [5], by exploiting the mesh structure by performing constrained Laplacian smoothing [2], or by analyzing the mesh structure of a set of several sparse example poses [8]. Recently, [21] presented a method that first produces a large number of plausible clusters, then reconstructs mesh topology by removing bones and finally performs an iterative optimization for joints, weights and bone transformations.

[22] and [29] predicts a set of vertex weights based on the morphology of a static mesh, by previously training with static meshes and their corresponding weights from animated characters. [7] presents a method for automatically rigging a static mesh by matching the mesh against a set of morphable models. Our method predicts weights based on the vertex trajectories by training with the motion of the vertices over time and the corresponding weights from animated characters and is not restricted by the morphology of the static mesh.

[4] tries to capture non linear deformations that are used in conjunction with a linear system and an underlying skeleton by employing a deep learning technique to determine the non linear part. [23] captures better nonlinear deformations by including in the animation pipeline a light weight neural network (NNWarp) that is known for its rich expressivity of nonlinear functions.

3   Temporal Deep Skinning

Skinning is based on the core idea that character skin vertices are deformed based on the motion of skeletal bones. One or more weights are assigned to each vertex that represent the percentage of influence vertices receive from each bone. With this approach we can reproduce an animation sequence based on a reference pose, the vertex weights and a set of transformations for every frame and bone.

Figure 1 in Appendix A illustrates the concept of our *Temporal Deep Skinning* method (or simply *Deep Skinning* for short) and the details of our method.

We restrict each vertex to have no more than six weights so as to be compatible with the existing animation pipelines [13]. For simple gaming characters, usually four weights per vertex are enough, but six weights per vertex can be used to correct artifacts or capture local deformations with pseudo bones. In our comparative evaluation we have implemented all previous methods with six weights as well, so as to conduct an objective comparison. The derived six (or less) weights per vertex correspond to the six highest probability predictions of the network. We then normalize these weights which are already in $[0, 1]$ to sum to 1 (coefficients of a convex combination). Since probability prediction of a vertex towards a specific bone cluster represents similarity to a training example, this is naturally translated to influence of the bone on the vertex.

Subsequently, we perform optimization to minimize the least square error between the original and approximated mesh frames. We do so by optimizing weights and transformations in an iterative manner.

3.1   Training and Test Datasets

The network is trained on a training set using a supervised learning method. Training dataset consists of input vector pairs that represent the motion of each vertex through all frames and the corresponding output vector of labels which determines whether a vertex is influenced by a specific bone. The input vector size is $(3 \cdot F)$, where 3 represents the x, y, z coordinates of a vertex and F the number of frames for the specific animation and the output consists of B_{max} labels, where B_{max} is the maximum number of bones. The current network model is fed with the training dataset and produces a result, which is then compared with the label vector, for each input vector in the training set. Based on the result of the comparison and the specific learning algorithm being used, the parameters of model are adjusted (supervised learning).

We have used two types of training datasets, one that consists of human character animations and one consisting of animal character animations. The animal dataset contains 32 animated animal characters with an average number of 12k vertices each, an average number of 3 animations per character and an average number of 195 frames per animation. The human dataset contains 35 animated human characters with an average number of 10k vertices each, 1 animation per character, and an average number of 158 frames per animation.

Successively, the fitted network model is used to predict the response of observations in a second smaller dataset called the validation set. This set provides an unbiased evaluation of the model and has been used to tune the hyperparameters of the network. Figure 3 indicates the average time that we need for training using LSTM or CNN networks (Sect. 3.4). After a complete training session, we export the trained network model so that we can use it in our Temporal Deep Skinning method to predict bones and weights for a given animation sequence.

For the test dataset that is used in the experiments we have used a set of human and animal models that are not included in the training datasets. The efficiency of our algorithm has been tested with more than 20 human and animal models to ensure generalization and accuracy. For example the testing dataset includes four animations Spider-man (27,030 Vertices & 28Frames), Man-Walking (15,918 Vertices & 32 Frames), Fox (1,728 Vertices & 400 Frames) and Lizard (29,614 Vertices & 75 Frames). Note that all dataset models are extracted from FBX animations which means that are fully animated with skeletal rigs, skinning information and transformations. The skeletal information is only used for comparison with the outcome of our method.

3.2 Transformation and Weight Optimization

Approximating an animation sequence to produce a more succinct representation is common in the case of articulated models and is carried out through a process called *skinning*.

For every vertex v_i that is influenced by a bone j, a weight w_{ij} is assigned. For skeletal rigs the skeleton and skin of a mesh model is given in a predetermined pose also known as bind or rest pose. The rigging procedure blends the skeleton with skin which is given by the rest pose of the model. Each transformation is the concatenation of a *bind matrix* that takes the vertex into the local space of a given *bone* and a transformation matrix that moves the bone to a new position.

In LBS the new position of vertex $v'^{\,p}_i$ at pose (frame) p is given by Eq. 1. This approach corresponds to using proxy bones instead of the traditional hierarchical bone structure on rigid or even on deformable models [13].

$$v'^{\,p}_i = \sum_{j=1}^{B} w_{ij} \cdot T_j^p \cdot v_i \tag{1}$$

In this equation, v_i represents the position of the vertex in rest pose, w_{ij} the weight by which bone j influences vertex v_i and T_j^p is the transformation that is applied to bone j during frame p. Figure 2 in the Appendix A summarizes the successive weight and transformation optimization that aims at reducing the approximation error for all frames.

Computing a good initial set of weights is a key step for the final result. In temporal deep skinning, a neural network provides the proxy bones and initial weights that are appropriate for an animation sequence. After that, we perform a successive optimization to find weights and proxy bone transformations. Both problems are formulated as least squares optimization problems that minimize the quantity given in Eq. 2.

$$\sum_{i=1}^{N} \|v'^{p}_i - v^p_i\|^2 \tag{2}$$

where v^p_i denotes the coordinates of the original vertex in pose p, v'^p_i is the approximation based on deep skinning and N is the number of vertices in the model. For the following, the number of vertices is N, the number of frames is P and the number of proxy bones is B. To solve the weight optimization problem, we formulate the system $Ax = b$, where matrix A is a $3PN \times 6N$ (where 6 is 6 the maximum bone number) matrix constructed by combining the rest-pose vertex positions and the corresponding transformations, x is a $6N$ vector of unknowns that contains the weights and b is a known $3PN$ vector that consists of the original (target) vertex coordinates in all frames. In the case of finding the optimal weights we include the convexity coefficient requirement as an extra equation per vertex (so A becomes $(3P+1)N \times 6N$ and b becomes $(3P+1)N$).

Finally, to solve the transformation optimization problem we formulate a linear system that consists of 3N equations, the unknowns of which are the (3×4) elements of the transformation matrices T^p_j of each bone j and frame p. This sums to $12BP$ unknowns. The system can be expressed as $Ax = b$, where A is a $3N \times 12BP$ known matrix constructed by combining the rest-pose vertex positions and the corresponding vertex weights. Moreover b is a known $3N$ vector that contains the original (target) vertex coordinates.

To avoid reverting into non linear solvers we alternatively optimize weights and transformations separately. In terms of optimization [28] uses NNLS (non negative least square) optimization for enforcing the convexity condition of the weights. We express the convexity by a separate equation per vertex which is closer to the approach adopted by [14]. [28] suggests that 5 iterations are enough, whereas [14] employs 15 iterations. We have performed experiments for up to 50 iterations and our conclusion is that after 5 iterations there is no significant error improvement. To perform the optimization problem we have employed conjugate gradient optimization which works better on multidimensional variable spaces and can be carried out efficiently on the GPU.

3.3   Measuring the Error

We used three different types of measures to calculate error of the approximation methods. The first two measures are standard measures used in [11, 13] and [14].

Next, we introduce a novel error measure, namely the *max average distance (MaxAvgDist)* given by Eq. 5) which is a novel quality metric that reflects better the visual quality of the result.

So, based on (Appendix A) we have three types of error estimation to evaluate the performance of our method. These metrics besides the visualization part, will be the basis for all the experiments that will substantiate the effectiveness of the Deep Skinning.

3.4   Building and Tuning a Neural Network for Weight Prediction

Network Structure. Our method adopts a supervised learning approach to leverage the power of neural networks on multiple class classification. Consequently, we utilize a neural network instead of using clustering techniques (unsupervised learning) to obtain better initial weights and bones for skinning. We have experimented with a variety of neural network models that can be efficiently trained to detect vertex motion patterns and mesh geometry characteristics and use similarities among them for clustering vertices into bones and determining weights implicitly through the influence of bones on the mesh surface. We have chosen networks that perform well in sequence learning (Appendix B).

All networks take as input an arbitrarily large sequence that represents the trajectory of a vertex, i.e. the (x, y, z) position at each frame, and predict the bone weights for this vertex.

Hyper Parameters Tuning. The most essential parameters during training are (i) the effectiveness and efficiency trade off of the batch-size and (ii) the smallest number of epochs that yields maximum accuracy and minimum loss and error. We have determined the batch-size in a two-fold manner. Firstly, we have used a validation test of the vertices (20% of the examples of the training set) in all frames so as to monitor the accuracy and loss of each network model during and after training. Secondly, we have determined the best batch-size based on the skinning error of a validation dataset that consists of additional examples that do not belong to the training set.

Figures 8 and 9 illustrate the loss and accuracy values that our network models achieved with several batch sizes. For loss we utilized the binary cross-entropy function given by Eq. 7, since we have a multi-label problem (a vertex may belong to multiple bones). Figures 10, 11 illustrate $DisPer$, $ERMS$ and $MaxAvgDist$ measures with the validation dataset.

So, for the CNN case of Fig. 10 it is apparent that there is no significant difference for the quantitative error measures (DisPer, RMS). Therefore the batch-size should be determined by the qualitative metric (MaxAvgDist) and the actual visual outcome. Consequently, based on MaxAvgDist that reflects more effectively the visual result we propose and use as the most efficient batch-size 4096 training examples. Furthermore, for the LSTM case, from Fig. 11 we conclude that the network exhibits similar behavior to the CNN. Therefore we select a batch-size of 4096 samples for training our LSTM model as well.

4   Experimental Evaluation of Deep Skinning

One of the main contributions of our work is that it expresses a combinatorial optimization problem with constraints as a classification problem and then proposes a method to solve it using deep learning techniques. For that reason, we have conducted a thorough experimental study to substantiate the effectiveness of our method based on the resulting error. Figures of all the images and the details of the developed method are included in the Appendix C.

4.1   Quantitative Results

In this section we present quantitative results for the Temporal Deep Skinning algorithm. We have conducted several experiments with multiple neural network structures to derive the top three choices of classification networks that fit best our training data with generalization capability.

The fitting part of our method optimizes weights and transformations (Weight Fitting-WF & Transformation Fitting-TF in Figs. 10, 11, 12, 13, 17) alternatively using a linear optimizer for five iterations. After five iterations we have observed that there is practically no improvement of the error for any of the methods. For each iteration the error metrics are computed and registered for every fitting case separately. Additionally, the initial error values in the plots below are the actual errors computed with the weights that each neural network produces.

Figures 12 and 13 provide a comparative evaluation of our method with the most competent skinning approach FESAM [14]. The original FESAM algorithm follows three steps of optimization with the first step being the process of optimizing the initial pose something that is not compatible with the traditional animation pipelines. For that reason this step is not included in our experiments and subsequently we use the FESAM-WT approach with two steps (weight and transformation optimization). More specifically, we evaluate the performance of our approach with distortion and RMS errors for the three top networks as compared to FESAM-WT. Based on Fig. 12a and Fig. 12b we conclude that LSTM 4096 performs overall better among the three prevalent networks on animal characters. We have performed the same experiments with the same test sets using decimated versions of our animation characters (50% and 20% decimation) and we have obtained the same results with differences only in the fourth decimal place.

The behavior of our method on human characters is illustrated in Figs. 13a and 13b. We conclude that CNN 4096 is the most appropriate network structure in comparison with the other two. Table 1 is a comparison of our method with other similar methods producing LBS schemes with pseudo bones when presented with several benchmark animation sequences from literature.

Finally, Fig. 14 shows the speed up that we have achieved in the fitting time by using the conjugate gradient method which is more efficient in multi dimensional problems such as the ones that we are solving ($12BP$ variables for transformations, and $6N$ variables for weights).

4.2 Visual Quality Evaluation Results

In computer graphics qualitative results (visual and otherwise) is an important means of assessing a novel method. In this section we present three processes for assessing the visual quality of temporal deep skinning.

Quality Measure Evaluation. We use the MaxAvgDist quality assessment measure that indicates how far in terms of visual quality the generated frames are from the original frame sequence (see Sect. 3.3). Low measure values correspond to high quality animation.

Figure 16 suggests that Temporal Deep Skinning yields results with better quality measure as compared to FESAM-WT. The results of Figs. 15a and 15b confirm the quantitative results. Specifically, the LSTM network for animals and the CNN for humans are the most appropriate choices quantitatively and qualitatively.

Visualization-Based Evaluation. As an additional assessment criterion for our method we provide an illustration of the visual outcome. By using the term visual outcome, we refer to the approximated output frames as compared to the frames of original 3D model. After conducting several experiments we have observed that our approach seems to approximate better the original model. In every case there is a noticeable difference between temporal deep skinning and FESAM-WT. To this end, a demonstration video is also provided as supplementary material.

Figure 16 illustrates the differences of the two approximation methods as compared to the original model animation. Several frames have been selected with noticeable structural flaws.

Error visualization techniques can provide an insight for the parts where errors occur. We use the turbo colormap [25] to represent the error per vertex which is color blind friendly. This error is the distance in a particular frame of the approximated vertex from the original one. Figure 18 illustrates the per vertex error in a particular frame for deep skinning and FESAM_WT.

Lighting Quality Evaluation. Finally, we offer the results of evaluating the average distortion of normal vectors. The normal distortion measure (see Sect. 3.3) shows how close the normal vectors of the approximated sequence are to the normal vectors of the original animation sequence. This determines how the approximated character will behave in an lighting model as compared to the original animated character. The results of Fig. 17 exhibit an average error of 0.01 radians for human characters and an average error of 0.05 radians for animal characters.

4.3 Discussion and Applications

We have presented a method called *Temporal Deep Skinning* that feeds an animation sequence with no underlying skeleton or rigging/skinning information to a pre-trained neural network to generate an approximated compressed skinning model with pseudo-bones.

Moreover, we have developed a post processing tool that using the compressed skinning model with pseudo bones and per frame transformations obtained by temporal deep skinning produces the corresponding hierarchical skeleton, skinning data and transformations. More specifically, using the mesh clustering derived by our method, the pseudo bones and transformations we produce a fully animated character model. This is accomplished by the following steps: (i) perform weight regularization and derive disjoint vertex clusters that are influenced by each bone, (ii) based on the neighboring clusters export the joints of the entire model (the structure of the skeleton) [20] and (iii) finally perform joint location adjustment by geometric constraints and a simple recalculation of orientation and rotation for each of the joints that yields their final position [3]. Figure 19a illustrates the original and approximated representation of a 3D model. This animated model consisting of 14,007 vertices and 4,669 faces was approximated by the deep skinning algorithm with 24 bone clusters and up to six weights per vertex.

Figure 19b presents the computed bones and weights for an animation sequence. This animation sequence consists of 48 different frames from the horse-gallop sequence. After the Deep Skinning algorithm we were able to extract 19 bone clusters and up to six weights per vertex. Subsequently, we have produced a fully animated character.

Finally, Table 2 in (Appendix C) provides a comparison of our method with four methods that produce actual skeletal rigs.

For the horse gallop model our method approximates the sequence by using 26 bones and achieves a smaller $ERMS$ error as compared to all previous methods. For the samba model our method uses 17 bones and outperforms all previous methods.

5   Conclusions

We have introduced a novel approach that derives pseudo-bones and weights for an animated sequence using deep learning on a training set of fully rigged animated characters. We have experimented with a variety of neural network models that can efficiently be trained to detect vertex motion patterns and mesh geometry characteristics and exploit similarities among them for clustering vertices into bones and determining weights implicitly through the influence of bones on the mesh surface. Our method does not require setting or tuning any parameters regarding the mesh structure or the kinematics of the animation.

Based on a comparative evaluation, we conclude that the approximation error of our method is always smaller than the error of previous approaches that are compatible with existing animation pipelines.

A   Appendix A

We build an appropriate neural network model that classifies each vertex by capturing mesh geometry and vertex kinematics. Then we use a set of human and animal animations to train the neural network model. We achieve this by using as input features the trajectories of all vertices and as output the weights that represent how each vertex is influenced by a bone. The output weight is conceived by the network as the probability of a bone to influence the corresponding vertex. Subsequently, we provide as input to our network arbitrary mesh animation sequences and predict their weights. From the per vertex classifier we determine the number of bones and the weights for each vertex.

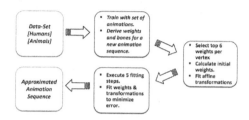

Fig. 1. Temporal Deep Skinning workflow.

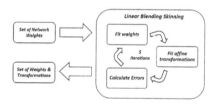

Fig. 2. Deep Skinning optimization workflow for weights and transformations.

The first error measure is the percentage of deformation known as *distortion percentage (DisPer)*.

$$DisPer = 100 \cdot \frac{\|A_{orig} - A_{Approx}\|_F}{\|A_{orig} - A_{avg}\|_F}. \qquad (3)$$

where $\| \cdot \|_F$ is the Frobenius matrix metric. In Eq. 3 A_{orig} is a $3NP$ matrix which consists of the real vertex coordinates in all frames of the model. Similarly, A_{Approx} has all the approximated vertex coordinates and matrix A_{avg} contains in each column, the average of the original coordinates in all frames. [14] replaces 100 by 1000 and divides by the surrounding sphere diameter. Sometimes this measure tends to be sensitive to the translation of the entire character, therefore we use a different measure that is invariant to translation. The *root mean square*

(ERMS) error measure in Eq. 4 is an alternative way to express distortion with the difference that we use $\sqrt{3NP}$ in the denominator so as to obtain the average deformation per vertex and frame during the sequence. $3NP$ is the total number of elements in the A_{orig} matrix. [21] uses as denominator the diameter of the bounding box multiplied by $\sqrt{NP}$.

$$ERMS = 100 \cdot \frac{\|A_{orig} - A_{Approx}\|_F}{\sqrt{3NP}} \tag{4}$$

Max distance denotes the largest vertex error in every frame. So this measure represents the average of max distances over all frames.

$$MaxAvgDist = \frac{1}{P} \sum_{f=1}^{P} \max_{i=1,\ldots,N} \|v_{orig}^{f,i} - v_{Approx}^{f,i}\| \tag{5}$$

Finally, we introduce an additional measure that characterizes the *normal distortion - (NormDistort)* and is used to measure the different behavior of two animation sequences during rendering. We compute the average difference between the original and the approximated face normals by the norm of their cross product that equals to the sine of the angle between the two normal vectors. Therefore for a model with F faces and P frames, where $NV^{i,j}$ is the normal vector of face j at frame i, Eq. 6 computes the normal distortion measure.

$$NormDistort = sin^{-1}(\frac{1}{FP} \sum_{i=1}^{P} \sum_{j=1}^{F} \|NV_{orig}^{i,j} \times NV_{Approx}^{i,j}\|) \tag{6}$$

B   Appendix B

Fig. 3. Training time for LSTM & CNN networks (Sect. 3.4).

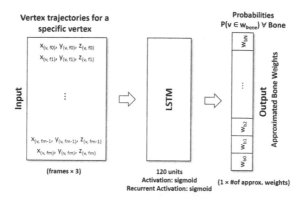

Fig. 4. LSTM-network.

The first network that we propose as the first step and mean of animation compression is a Recurrent Neural Network (RNN).

The type of RNN network used is a Long Short-term Memory network firstly introduced by [9] (LSTM), which consists of units made up of a cell remembering time inconstant data values, a corresponding forget cell, an input and an output gate being responsible of controlling the flow of data in and out of the remembering component of it Fig. 4. Thus, utilization of many network units for LSTM construction (120 units used) produces a network that is able yo predict weights even for models with a large number of bones. Regarding the activation functions we used (i) an alternative for the activation function (cell and hidden state) by using *sigmoid* instead of *tanh* and (ii) the default for the recurrent activation function (for input, forget and output gate) which is *sigmoid*. The main reason of using the *sigmoid* function instead of the hyperbolic tangent is that our training procedure involves the network deciding per vertex whether it belongs or not to the influence range of a bone. This results in higher efficacy and additionally makes our model learn more effectively.

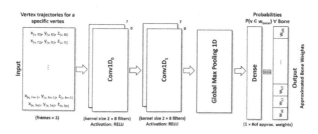

Fig. 5. CNN-network.

The second network that we have used successfully is a feed-forward network called Convolutional Neural Network (CNN) [15] that uses convolutional operations to capture patterns in order to determine classes mainly in image classification problems. CNNs are additionally able to be used in classification of sequence data with quite impressive results. On top of the two convolutional layers utilized, we have also introduced a global max-pooling layer (down-sampling layer) and a simple dense layer so that we have the desirable number of weights for each proxy bone, as it is illustrated in Fig. 5. In the two convolutional layers (Conv1D) used we utilize 8 filters of kernel size 2. The number of filters and kernel size have been determined experimentally. However, CNN with small kernel size is working efficiently and it is a reasonable network option on capturing animation sequences due to its capturing capabilities of almost minor transitions from one frame to the next one which is a consequence of small vertex movements within a two consecutive frames interval Fig. 6.

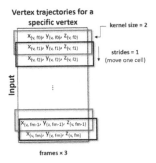

Fig. 6. Convolutional kernel & strides representation given an animation sequence input. Blue is used to highlight the previous step of computations (convolutions of input data with filter) and red the next step. In this manner, a Conv1D layer is capable of capturing vertex trajectories in an animation sequence. (Color figure online)

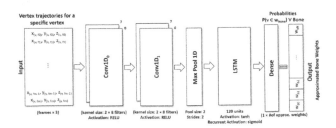

Fig. 7. Hybrid-network.

The last network that we have considered for completeness is a hybrid neural network (Fig. 7) that is a combination of the two aforementioned networks with some modifications. Unfortunately, the hybrid network does not perform equally well as its counterparts but it still derives comparable results.

$$L(y, y_{pred}) = -\frac{1}{N} \sum_{i=0}^{N} ((1-y) \cdot log(1 - y_{pred}) + y \cdot log(y_{pred})) \qquad (7)$$

where y are the real values (1: belongs to a bone or 0: does not) and y_{pred} are the predicted values. Binary cross-entropy measures how far in average a prediction is from the real value for every class. To this end, we also used binary accuracy which calculates the percentage of matched prediction-label pairs the 0/1 threshold value set to 0.5. What we have inferred by these plots is that for CNN there is no reason to increase the batch-size higher than 4096 owing to the fact that accuracy and loss values tend to be almost identical after increasing batch-size from 2048 samples to 4096. Likewise, for the LSTM case (see Fig. 9) we observe that batch-size 2048 is the best option. From Figs. 8 and 9 we infer that we should use at least 20 epochs for training. After that the improvement of loss and accuracy is negligible but as we observed occasional overfitting is alleviated by increasing further the number of epochs.

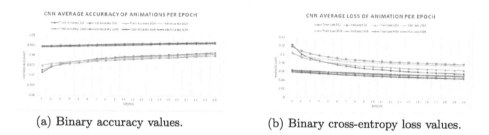

(a) Binary accuracy values.   (b) Binary cross-entropy loss values.

Fig. 8. Average per epoch Accuracy & Loss for CNN.

C   Appendix C

The entire method was developed[1] using Python and Tensorflow under the Blender 2.79b scripting API. The training part runs on a system with an NVIDIA

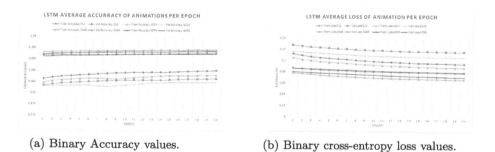

(a) Binary Accuracy values.   (b) Binary cross-entropy loss values.

Fig. 9. Average per epoch Accuracy & Loss for LSTM.

---

[1] Source code available here: https://github.com/AnastasiaMoutafidou/Deep Skinning.

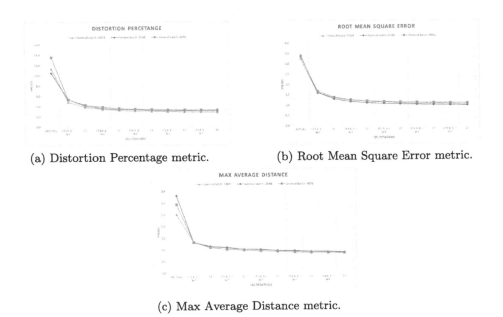

(a) Distortion Percentage metric.

(b) Root Mean Square Error metric.

(c) Max Average Distance metric.

Fig. 10. Error Metrics for batch-size tuning in CNN.

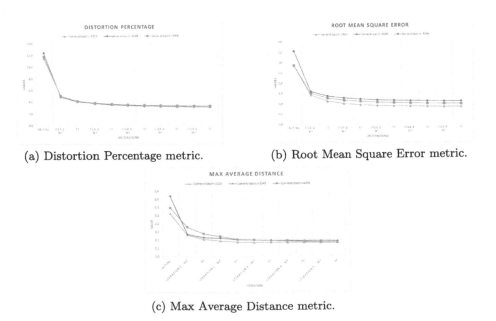

(a) Distortion Percentage metric.

(b) Root Mean Square Error metric.

(c) Max Average Distance metric.

Fig. 11. Error Metrics for batch-size tuning in LSTM.

GeForce RTX 2080Ti GPU with 11 GB GDDR6 RAM. We trained our network models with Adam Optimizer [16], *learningRate* = 0.001 for 20–100 *epochs* with *batchSize* = 4096 over a training data-set that incorporates 60 animated character models of different size in terms of number of vertices, animations and frames per animation. We have inferred that 20 *epochs* are usually enough to have our method converging in terms of the error metrics and most importantly towards an acceptable visual outcome. However to obtain better RMS and distortion errors without over-fitting 100 *epochs* is a safe choice independently of the training set size. Furthermore, with this choice of batch-size we overcome the over-fitting problem that was apparent by observing the Max Average Distance metric and was manifested by locally distorted meshes.

The rest of our algorithm (prediction and optimization) was developed and ran on a commodity computer equipped with an Intel Core i7-4930K 3.4 GHz processor with 48 Gb under Windows 10 64-bit operating System. In addition, the FESAM algorithm was developed and ran on the same system.

Images for the experiments section.

Table 1. Comparative evaluation of our method versus Method I [11], Method II [13], Method III [14], Method IV [26], Method V [1].

Approximation error ERMS														
Input data			Our method		Method I		Method II		Method III		Method IV		Method V		Compression rate
Dataset	N	F	Bones	ERMS	Bones	ERMS	Bones	ERMS	Bones	ERMS	Bones	ERMS	Bones	ERMS	OURS	I-IV
Horse-gallop	8,431	48	26	0.15	30	2.3(0.3)	30	4.9(2.9)	30	1.3	30	2.4	–	2E-5	92.5	92.3
Elephant-gallop	42,321	48	18	0.35	25	2.6(0.5)	25	15(6.5)	25	1.4	25	2.3	–	6E-5	93.59	93.51
Camel-gallop	21,887	48	16	0.22	23	3.1(0.5)	23	4.7(2.2)	23	1.4	23	2.8	–	2E-4	93.45	93.33
Samba	9,971	175	17	0.60	30	8.6(3.6)	30	11.4(6)	30	1.5	30	4	–	0.2	97.6	97.4

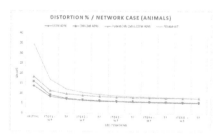

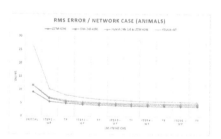

(a) Distortion percentage error metric for animal characters.

(b) Root mean square error metric for animals.

Fig. 12. Quantitative error results for animal characters.

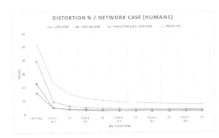

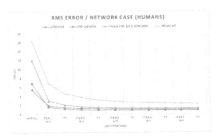

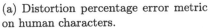

(a) Distortion percentage error metric on human characters.

(b) Root mean square error metric on human characters.

Fig. 13. Quantitative error results for human characters.

More specifically, presents a comparison of our method on four benchmark animation sequences, that were not produced by fully animated rigs, with all previous combinations of LBS, quaternion-based and SVD methods. N is the number of Vertices, F is the number of frames and the number in round brackets is the result of the method combined with SVD. Our method derives better results in terms of both error and compression rate as compared to methods I–IV. Method V is only cited for reference since it only obtains compression and is not compatible with any of the standard animation pipelines.

Table 2. Comparison between temporal deep skinning and four methods. Specifically method A [21], Method B [27], Method C [6], Method D [8].

Input sata			Approximation Error ERMS														
			Our method			Method A			Method B			Method C			Method D		
Dataset	N	F	Bones	ERMS	CRP	Bones	ERMS	CRP	Bones	ERMS	CRP	Bones	ERMS	CRP	Bones	ERMS	CRP
Horse-gallop	8,431	48	26	0.15	92.5	27	0.19	92.4	27	0.44	92.4	27	1.10	92.4	27	0.88	92.4
Samba	9,971	175	17	0.60	97.6	22	0.63	97.4	22	1.29	97.4	22	1.57	97.4	22	1.79	97.4

Fig. 14. Speed up of fitting time by using the conjugate gradient optimization method.

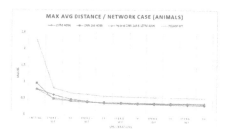

(a) Max average distance on animal characters.

(b) Max average distance on human characters.

Fig. 15. Qualitative error metric $MaxAvgDistr$ results for humans and animals.

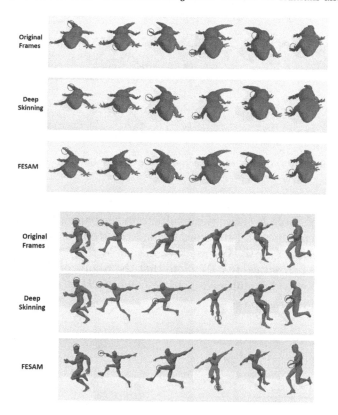

Fig. 16. Visual comparison of Deep Skinning, FESAM-WT and the original frames for two models.Six frames have been selected in which structural flaws are marked by small circles.

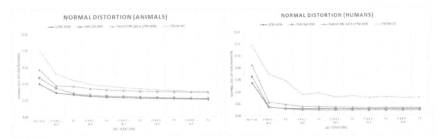

(a) Normal distortion on animal characters.

(b) Normal distortion on human characters.

Fig. 17. Qualitative normal distortion metric results for humans and animals.

Fig. 18. Distance error comparison in a particular frame between Deep Skinning and FESAM-WT.

In this case of Table 2 we cite the results from the papers since such methods are difficult to reproduce and this goes beyond the scope of this paper. For two models (*horse gallop* and *samba*) we have measured the *ERMS* error and the compression rate percentage (CRP). Note that the results of [21] were converted to our ERMS metric by multiplying by $\frac{D}{\sqrt{3}}$, where D is the diagonal of the bounding box of the rest pose.

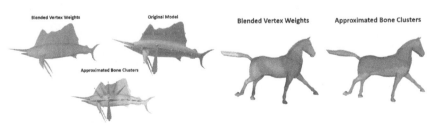

(a) Original and approximate representation for a Sailfish.

(b) Approximate bone clusters and vertex weights for an animation sequence.

Fig. 19. Original and approximate representations.

References

1. Alexa, M., Müller, W.: Representing animations by principal components. Comput. Graph. Forum **19**, 411–418 (2000)
2. Au, O.K.C., Tai, C.L., Chu, H.K., Cohen-Or, D., Lee, T.Y.: Skeleton extraction by mesh contraction. ACM Trans. Graph. **27**(3), 44:1–44:10 (2008)
3. Avril, Q., et al.: Animation setup transfer for 3D characters. In: Proceedings of the 37th Annual Conference of the European Association for Computer Graphics, EG '16, pp. 115–126. Eurographics Association, Goslar (2016)
4. Bailey, S.W., Otte, D., Dilorenzo, P., O'Brien, J.F.: Fast and deep deformation approximations. ACM Trans. Graph. **37**(4), 1–12 (2018)
5. De Aguiar, E., Theobalt, C., Thrun, S., Seidel, H.P.: Automatic conversion of mesh animations into skeleton-based animations. Comput. Graph. Forum **27**(2), 389–397 (2008)
6. De Aguiar, E., Theobalt, C., Thrun, S., Seidel, H.P.: Automatic conversion of mesh animations into skeleton-based animations. Comput. Graph. Forum **27**, 389–397 (2008)
7. Feng, A., Casas, D., Shapiro, A.: Avatar reshaping and automatic rigging using a deformable model. In: Proceedings of the 8th ACM SIGGRAPH Conference on Motion in Games, MIG '15, pp. 57–64. Association for Computing Machinery, New York (2015). https://doi.org/10.1145/2822013.2822017
8. Hasler, N., Thormählen, T., Rosenhahn, B., Seidel, H.P.: Learning skeletons for shape and pose. In: Proceedings of the 2010 ACM SIGGRAPH Symposium on Interactive 3D Graphics and Games, I3D '10, pp. 23–30. Association for Computing Machinery, New York (2010). https://doi.org/10.1145/1730804.1730809
9. Hochreiter, S., Schmidhuber, J.: Long short-term memory. Neural Comput. **9**(8), 1735–1780 (1997)
10. Jacobson, A., Deng, Z., Kavan, L., Lewis, J.P.: Skinning: real-time shape deformation. In: ACM SIGGRAPH 2014 Courses, SIGGRAPH '14. Association for Computing Machinery, New York (2014). https://doi.org/10.1145/2614028.2615427
11. James, D.L., Twigg, C.D.: Skinning mesh animations. In: ACM SIGGRAPH 2005 Papers, SIGGRAPH '05, pp. 399–407. Association for Computing Machinery, New York (2005)
12. Kavan, L., Collins, S., Žára, J., O'Sullivan, C.: Skinning with dual quaternions. In: Proceedings of the 2007 Symposium on Interactive 3D Graphics and Games, I3D '07, pp. 39–46. Association for Computing Machinery, New York (2007). https://doi.org/10.1145/1230100.1230107
13. Kavan, L., McDonnell, R., Dobbyn, S., Žára, J., O'Sullivan, C.: Skinning arbitrary deformations. In: Proceedings of the 2007 Symposium on Interactive 3D Graphics and Games, I3D '07, pp. 53–60. Association for Computing Machinery, New York (2007)
14. Kavan, L., Sloan, P.P., O'Sullivan, C.: Fast and efficient skinning of animated meshes. Comput. Graph. Forum **29**, 327–366 (2010)
15. Khan, A., Sohail, A., Zahoora, U., Qureshi, A.S.: A survey of the recent architectures of deep convolutional neural networks (2019)
16. Kingma, D.P., Ba, J.: Adam: a method for stochastic optimization (2014)
17. Kraevoy, V., Sheffer, A.: Cross-parameterization and compatible remeshing of 3d models. In: ACM SIGGRAPH 2004 Papers, SIGGRAPH '04, pp. 861–869. ACM, New York (2004)

18. Kry, P.G., James, D.L., Pai, D.K.: Eigenskin: real time large deformation character skinning in hardware. In: Proceedings of the 2002 ACM SIGGRAPH/Eurographics Symposium on Computer Animation, SCA '02, pp. 153–159. Association for Computing Machinery, New York (2002)
19. Le, B.H., Deng, Z.: Smooth skinning decomposition with rigid bones. ACM Trans. Graph. **31**(6), 199:1–199:10 (2012)
20. Le, B.H., Deng, Z.: Smooth skinning decomposition with rigid bones. ACM Trans. Graph. 31(6) (2012). https://doi.org/10.1145/2366145.2366218
21. Le, B.H., Deng, Z.: Robust and accurate skeletal rigging from mesh sequences. ACM Trans. Graph. 33(4) (2014). https://doi.org/10.1145/2601097.2601161
22. Liu, L., Zheng, Y., Tang, D., Yuan, Y., Fan, C., Zhou, K.: Neuroskinning: automatic skin binding for production characters with deep graph networks. ACM Trans. Graph. **38**(4), 1–12 (2019)
23. Luo, R., et al.: Nnwarp: neural network-based nonlinear deformation. IEEE Trans. Vis. Comput. Graph. **26**(4), 1745–1759 (2020)
24. Magnenat-Thalmann, N., Laperrière, R., Thalmann, D.: Joint-dependent local deformations for hand animation and object grasping. In: Proceedings on Graphics Interface '88, pp. 26–33. Canadian Information Processing Society, CAN (1989)
25. Mikhailov, A.: Turbo, An Improved Rainbow Colormap for Visualization, Google AI Blog (2019)
26. Sattler, M., Sarlette, R., Klein, R.: Simple and efficient compression of animation sequences. In: Proceedings of the 2005 ACM SIGGRAPH/Eurographics Symposium on Computer Animation, SCA '05, pp. 209–217. Association for Computing Machinery, New York (2005)
27. Schaefer, S., Yuksel, C.: Example-based skeleton extraction. In: Proceedings of the Fifth Eurographics Symposium on Geometry Processing, SGP '07, pp. 153–162. Eurographics Association, Goslar (2007)
28. Vasilakis, A.A., Fudos, I., Antonopoulos, G.: Pps: pose-to-pose skinning of animated meshes. In: Proceedings of the 33rd Computer Graphics International, CGI '16, pp. 53–56. ACM, New York (2016)
29. Xu, Z., Zhou, Y., Kalogerakis, E., Landreth, C., Singh, K.: RigNet: neural rigging for articulated characters. ACM Trans. Graphi. **39**(4), article no. 58, 58:1–58:14 (2020)
30. Zell, E., Botsch, M.: Elastiface: matching and blending textured faces. In: Proceedings of the Symposium on Non-Photorealistic Animation and Rendering, NPAR '13, pp. 15–24. ACM, New York (2013)

The Impact of Animations in the Perception of a Simulated Crowd

Elena Molina(✉), Alejandro Ríos(✉), and Nuria Pelechano(✉)

Universitat Politècnica de Catalunya, Barcelona, Spain
arios@cs.upc.edu, npelechano@cs.upc.edu
https://www.cs.upc.edu/~arios/

Abstract. Simulating virtual crowds is an important challenge in many areas such as games and virtual reality applications. A lot of effort has been dedicated to improving pathfinding, collision avoidance, or decision making, to achieve more realistic human-like behavior. However, crowd simulation will be far from appearing realistic as long as virtual humans are limited to walking animations. Including animation variety could greatly enhance the plausibility of the populated environment. In this paper, we evaluated to what extend animation variety can affect the perceived level of realism of a crowd, regardless of the appearance of the virtual agents (bots vs. humanoids). The goal of this study is to provide recommendations for crowd animation and rendering when simulating crowds. Our results show that the perceived realism of the crowd trajectories and animations is significantly higher when using a variety of animations as opposed to simply having locomotion animations, but only if we render realistic humanoids. If we can only render agents as bots, then there is no much gain from having animation variety, in fact, it could potentially lower the perceived quality of the trajectories.

Keywords: Perception · Crowd simulation · Character animation

1 Introduction

Virtual environments have been used in many disciplines such as building design, teaching, medicine and simulating dangerous situations or evacuations that would not be reasonable to recreate with real people or materials. Achieving realistic and believable virtual scenarios depends on both the quality of the environment (affected by global illumination, surrounding sound, environmental effects or rendering quality) and the plausibility of the virtual humanoids and crowds. Simulating believable virtual humanoids can be an extremely hard problem, and its complexity rapidly escalates when simulating crowds due to the interactions between virtual humans.

Two important factors must be taken into account: characters' rendering and behavior, as was confirmed by Bailenson et al. [1]. Nowadays, realistic rendering of humanoids can be achieved with details such as wrinkles, the fibers of the

© Springer Nature Switzerland AG 2021
N. Magnenat-Thalmann et al. (Eds.): CGI 2021, LNCS 13002, pp. 25–38, 2021.
https://doi.org/10.1007/978-3-030-89029-2_2

clothes or even the hairs on the arms. However, simulating crowds of highly realistic models with unnatural looking motion can provoke an *Uncanny Valley* effect [18]. The Uncanny Valley tends to appear in crowd simulation when the behavioral response of the characters does not match their appearance, because as the virtual humans look more realistic, we expect them to also behave in a more human like way. Therefore any awkward behavior will be quickly perceived by the user and make the character not likeable.

Existing work in virtual reality to study user response to crowd simulations, has been primarily focused on improving the simulation models of collision avoidance [14], the use of interactions through gestures [11] or gaze to enhance a sense of immersion [19], and studies of proxemics [5].

Crowd simulation has become a mature field of research with many different applications areas. However, crowd simulation models present many difficulties when it comes to validating new models. There are currently two main alternatives for validations: (1) quantitative measurements to compare against existing models or real crowds, or (2) perceptual studies. The former is difficult because there are no standard measurements or perfect models to compare against, and comparing against the real world can also be extremely difficult due to the non-deterministic aspects of human behavior. The later, is also very challenging because humans are not capable of separating the quality of the simulation from other aspects such as appearance, animation artifacts, etc. Therefore, if we want to further enhance the realism of a simulated crowd to populate virtual environments, we may need to put further emphasis on secondary aspects instead of focusing exclusively on improving the local movement of the individuals.

In this work, we want to focus on studying how the characters' appearance and animations can impact the perceived level of realism of a simulated crowd, the quality of the trajectories and the animations. For this purpose we ran experiments of a simulated crowd with the avatars rendered with robotic (bot) or human-like appearance (humanoids), and performing two types of animations: (1) locomotion only, and (2) locomotion combined with animation variety such as gesturing during conversation, waving, using the phone or sitting down. Our main findings are:

- Animation variety with humanoid avatars provides the highest levels of realism.
- Appearance quality only has an impact on realism if we have animation variety, but not if we only use locomotion.
- If only locomotion animations are used, then trajectories are likely to be perceived as being more realistic if we render bots instead of humanoids.

The conclusions of this study are restricted to the specific stimuli that we used for the experiments. However, they provide useful information on what aspects of the appearance and animation can affect the perceptual evaluation of a crowd simulation and thus its plausibility when being used to populate virtual environments.

2   Related Work

2.1   Appearance and Motion of Virtual Humans

Shape, material and rendering style can affect the way users perceive emotions from virtual agents. Zell et al. [29] compared cartoonish, medium and high realistic characters with different materials to analyze the perception of different facial expressions such as sadness, anger, happiness and surprise. Their results showed that shape is the main factor for the perceived realism and that some expressions are perceived more intense with cartoon shapes. Vihanga et al. showed that participants in a virtual reality classroom were more engaged when the lesson was taught by a virtual character rather than a voice-only version [7].

Lighting has been used over the decades in VFX and animation movies to transmit emotions. Wisessing et al. [28] studied whether the brightness and the intensity of light had an effect on the recognition of emotions such as happiness, sadness, anger and fear. Their results showed that brightness intensifies happiness while darker lighting intensifies sadness and that darker conditions did not affect anger or fear.

Several works have studied whether emotional responses of participants are affected by photorealism of virtual avatars [15,25,26]. In the works by Zibrek et al. [32] a single virtual character performed several emotions like sadness, guilt, friendly and unfriendly with different rendering styles (realistic, simple, toon, sketch) and the participants reported their emotional experience through questionnaires. Friendly emotions gave higher scores of perceived realism when having a realistic rendering style instead of a sketch style and the avatar's personality also played an important role on the perception of realism by the participants, meaning that both appearance and behavior must be combined carefully in immersive virtual reality to transmit the desired effect.

Emotional avatars play an important role in videogames, movies and simulations experiences. The better the avatars transmit emotions, the more truthful and realistic will be the experience. Randhaven et al. presented *EVA*, an algorithm to generate virtual agents with different emotions happiness, anger, sadness based on gaze and gait [22]. Their results indicated that avatars showing emotions generated from gait and gaze increased the sense of presence and the overall realism of the simulations.

2.2   Crowd Simulation

Populating virtual environments with convincing crowds has been investigated for decades by the computer graphics community. Including personality traits can further enhance the plausibility of a virtual crowd. The OCEAN personality model [27] has been used in different crowd simulation models (such as HiDAC [6], RVO [9], and Biocrowds [10]) to provide each virtual agent in a crowd with personality traits. These models successfully modify the decision making or local movement parameters, thus resulting in a more heterogeneous crowd simulation, although agents are still limited to showing exclusively locomotion animations.

Emergency simulations have been extensively used to determine whether building facilities like emergency exits are correctly designed, or whether there is a possibility of finding a bottleneck when people run towards an exit. There exists many studies to model the evacuation of virtual crowds in disaster scenarios like fire, earthquakes, flooding, storms or civil disorders [23,24]. Zhao et al. reproduced the 2010 Love Parade disaster using virtual reality to study the behavior of participants and help organizers to avoid this kind of disasters in the future [30].

Pelechano et al. [21], proposed using immersive virtual reality as a platform to evaluate crowd simulation models. This platform allowed them to study the behavior of the participants when interacting with a virtual crowd in a cocktail party scenario. The experiment showed what features of each model could enhance or break presence. Participants did exhibit behaviors that were consistent with the interaction with a real crowd, and their behavioral response indicated that a high level of presence could be achieved in such setup. The system included animations to further enhance the believability of the crowd, but without studying its impact. Bruneau et al. [4] studied the impact that crowd appearance could have on the collision detection maneuvering of a participant walking against a virtual crowd. They showed a crowd of humanoids with casual clothing, with military clothing, and with zombie appearance. Their study found that the avatars appearance affected the local movement of the participant to avoid collisions. Berton et al. [3] studied the trajectories of participants through a dense crowd by including vibrotactile armbands, and found that participants' movement (speed and torso rotation) was affected by the haptic feedback.

Emotional virtual characters is another aspect that has been studied along the literature to produce more realistic crowds. Liu et at. [12] used an emotion contagion model to simulate the evacuation process in a virtual scenario. Their model introduced two states for every individual: normal and evacuating states. The speed of a virtual agent increases when its state changes from normal to evacuating. The state of an agent is also influenced by the state of the surrounding agents in a certain radius. The use of emotion contagion produced simulated behaviors that resembled of those in the real world. Zhou et al. [31] combined both the OCEAN personality traits model with emotion contagion to simulate emergency evacuations.

From the literature review we can conclude that, the presence of dynamic elements in the virtual environment, global illumination and good quality rendering of avatars can have an impact on the participants' response. It seems that the correct combination of realistic appearance and animations in the simulation of virtual avatars could have a high impact on the perception of realism by participants in an immersive virtual reality environment. Therefore, we are interested in exploring to what extend, improving appearance and/or animation can enhance the perceived realism of a virtual crowd.

3   Experiment Design

The goal of the experiment was to study whether the perception of realism of a virtual crowd was affected by the characters appearance and by the variety of animations. For this purpose, we generated a virtual city scene with decorative elements such as benches, fountains, street lamps, signs and trees (see Fig. 3 in the appendix) Five viewpoints were selected to show various aspects of the environment such as wide spaces for the crowd to move, narrow spaces to observe close interactions and sections with benches to see the action of sitting.

3.1   Stimuli Creation

We had two independent variables, which were appearance and animation type, each one with two possible values (Bot/Humanoid and Locomotion/Animation variety). A total of four videos[1] were recorded with the possible combinations between avatar appearance and animation type. In the first video the city was populated with bots extracted from Mixamo ([16]) that blended between walking cycles to move through the city with no other animation than locomotion. In the second video the same bots performed blending between walk cycles combined with other actions such as chatting with other avatars, looking around, sitting down or talking on the phone. In the third and fourth videos the robots were replaced by humanoid avatars extracted from the RocketBox library ([8]) and performed the same animations as the first and second videos. Table 1 shows the labels for each video and Fig. 1 shows screen captures.

Table 1. Labels for the four conditions.

BL	Bots with locomotion only
BA	Bots with animation variety
HL	Humanoids with locomotion only
HA	Humanoids with animation variety

The recorded videos were published on a web page to run the studies remotely and thus access a larger number of participants (this was strongly influenced by the impact of the Covid-19 pandemic). The site, first gathered demographic data such as gender, age, experience with computers and experience with video games, then provided instructions on how to run the experiment, and finally asked participants to agree to a consent form before starting with the experiment. The web page also showed the sequence of all videos in a random order (balanced Latin squares) to avoid undesirable learning or fatigue factors affecting our results. For each video, questions regarding the perception of realism of the overall crowd simulation, the trajectories and the animations were asked. The specific questions appear in Table 2.

---

[1] https://www.cs.upc.edu/~npelechano/videos/CGI2021perceptionAnimCrowds.
mp4.

Fig. 1. Images from the videos: (BL) Bots with just locomotion. (BA) Bots with animation variety (walking, chatting, sitting down, and talking on the phone). (HL) Humanoids with just locomotion. (HA) Humanoids with animation variety.

Each participant could see the videos only once and answered the three questions using a Likert scale from 0 to 7, where 0 means *strongly disagree* and 7 means *strongly agree*. We wanted to study the differences across all the possible combinations of type of avatar and animation variety.

Table 2. Questionnaire

Q1	Do you consider this video to be a realistic representation of a crowd? (Does it display the behaviors expected of a real crowd?)
Q2	Do you think this video could represent recorded trajectories from the real world?
Q3	Do you consider that the animations shown appear realistic?

3.2 Participants

Since the study was available through a public web page, we could reach a larger variety of profiles. Therefore, we tried to reach for university students, and also participants without computer science background. We gathered a total of 81 responses from anonymous participants (38 females, 43 males) aged from 14 to 62 ($\mu = 32$, $\sigma = 14$). Half of them had very high experience with computers (6 or above in a 7 points Likert scale), and high (4 or above) with video games (see details in Fig. 4 in the appendix).

3.3   Hypothesis

Our set of hypothesis was the following:

$H1$: The overall crowd simulation will be perceived as being more realistic when having animation variety with humanoid figures (for condition HA).
$H2$: Trajectories will be perceived as being more realistic when having animation variety.
$H3$: Animation variety will increase the perceived realism of the crowd animation for both bots and humanoids.

3.4   Statistical Analysis

Our goal is to understand whether having animation variety and using realistic humanoid figures, can affect the perceived realism of a crowd simulation. To do so, we analyze the differences across our 4 conditions (HA, HL, BA and BL). For all dependent variables, we establish a significance level to $\alpha = 0.05$. Normality of the data in each factor level, was tested with a Ryan-Joiner test, and the homogeneity of variances for each factor level was tested using the Levene's test (see results from both tests in appendix, Tables 3 and 4) .

Since the data follows a normal distribution and all variances are equal among the factor levels, we can apply a one-way analysis of variance (ANOVA) for the three hypothesis. Pos-hoc was then performed using a Tukey Pairwaise comparison with Bonferroni correction to analyze any significant effects between conditions.

4   Results

4.1   Realism of Simulated Crowds (H1)

We first studied the overall perceived realism achieved for each crowd simulation condition (BA, BNA, HA, and HNA). A one way ANOVA with significance level $\alpha = 0.05$ showed that there was a main effect ($F_{(3,320)} = 10.27, p = 0.000$). This validates our first hypothesis $H1$ because it proves that not all the means of the realism scores are equal, and thus we can further study which condition is significantly different from others. Pos-hoc was then performed using a Tukey Pairwaise comparison with Bonferroni correction. It was found that the perceived realism of HA ($\mu_{HA} = 5.38$) was significantly higher that all other three conditions ($\mu_{BA} = 4.5, \mu_{HL} = 4.18$, and $\mu_{BL} = 4.18$).

There was no significant difference among any other combination of conditions. Therefore animation variety offered a higher realism only when human avatars were used, but it did not have an impact when using bots. Similarly, when using only locomotion, the perceived realism was the same regardless of the avatar appearance being a robot or a humanoid.

Our statistical analysis showed an interaction effect between the animation type and appearance, but no main effect on only one of the variables.

4.2   Realism of Trajectories (H2)

Our second hypothesis was that animation variety and human appearance would affect the perceived realism of the avatars trajectories. We thus asked participants to determine whether the avatars' trajectories appeared to be real pedestrians' trajectories. A one way ANOVA with significance level $\alpha = 0.05$ showed that there was a main effect ($F_{(3,320)} = 11, p = 0.000$). This also validates hypothesis H2. Pos-hoc was then performed using a Tukey Pairwaise comparison with Bonferroni correction. It was found that the trajectories realism of HA ($\mu_{HA} = 5.43$) was significantly higher that all other three conditions ($\mu_{BA} = 4.75, \mu_{HL} = 4.02$, and $\mu_{BL} = 4.38$). Therefore having humanoids with animation variety achieves higher levels of perceived realism on the trajectories. Trajectories realism for BA was also significantly higher than for condition HL, which means that animation variety with bots can make users perceived the trajectories as being more realistic than having humanoids that only perform locomotion. This shows that animation variety in a simulated crowd can have a very large impact on the plausibility of the trajectories. An interesting observation from our results was that if only locomotion was used, then trajectories had a higher level of realism when rendering bots ($\mu_{BL} = 4.38$) as opposed to humanoids ($\mu_{HL} = 4.02$). However this difference is only an observed trend, as it was not statistically significant. As in the previous case, our statistical analysis showed an interaction effect between the animation type and appearance, but no main effect on only one of the variables.

4.3   Realism of Animation (H3)

Finally we studied the overall perceived realism of the animations for each crowd simulation condition (BA, BL, HA, and HL). A one way ANOVA with significance level $\alpha = 0.05$ showed that there was a main effect ($F_{(3,320)} = 10.71, p = 0.000$). This validates our third hypothesis H3. Pos-hoc using a Tukey Pairwaise comparison with Bonferroni correction, found that the perceived realism of HA ($\mu_{HA} = 5.16$) was significantly higher than all other three conditions ($\mu_{BA} = 4.3, \mu_{HL} = 4.02$, and $\mu_{BL} = 3.67$). There was no significant difference among any other combination of conditions. Once again, our statistical analysis showed an interaction effect between the animation type and appearance, but no main effect on only one of the variables. Therefore animation variety offered a higher realism only when human avatars were used, but it did not have an impact when using bots. When using the same animation variety for both humanoids and bots, participants perceived that the humanoid render made the animation look significantly more realistic than when rendering bots (Fig. 2).

5   Discussion

Having human-like avatars performing a variety of animations beyond walking, can significantly enhance the overall perceived realism of a simulated crowd, only

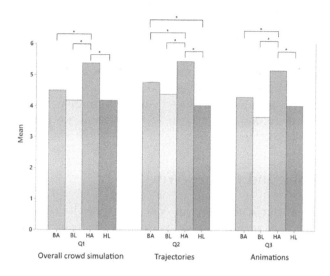

Fig. 2. Results

if we use humanoids. If we use bot avatars, we can say that there is a trend to perceive them as more realistic when including animation variety, however this difference is not statistically significant. So, it appears that animations play a more important role than appearance, in terms of enhancing the perceived realism or a simulated crowd. Another very interesting outcome of our study is that if we can only display locomotion animations, then improving the appearance of the avatars will not increase the overall realism of our simulated crowd. This finding is consistent with a previous study that we performed in an immersive VR emergency experiment, where they studied the differences in realism and presence when improving the appearance of the virtual characters [17].

Trajectories were perceived as better resembling real humans when having animation variety. For the case of having human avatars, this difference was significantly higher. It was also higher when using bots, although we can only refer to as a trend, since the difference was not statistically significant. It is interesting though, that including animation variety over a crowd of bots made the trajectories realism significantly higher that a human like crowd that only perform locomotion. We also observed that when using only locomotion, the bot appearance rated higher in trajectory realism than the human appearance. This finding was also a trend as it was not significantly higher, however it could be explained by the Uncanny Valley effect. Therefore, if we were interested in perceptually validating the output trajectories of a crowd simulation model, it maybe counterproductive to render highly realistic avatars if they are simply walking.

The results on perceived animation variety were very similar to those for overall realism of the crowd. Humanoids with animation variety was perceived as showing more realistic animation than any of the other 3 conditions. An interesting outcome of our study is that, even though we had the exact same animations for both bots (BA) and humanoids (HA), the second one (HA) was perceived as showing significantly more realistic animations that the first condition (BA). Therefore, appearance can affect the way we perceive animation quality.

6   Conclusions and Future Work

From the results of our study, we can conclude that the combination of having human like avatars with animation variety can increase the overall realism of a crowd simulation, trajectories and animation. And not only that, but if we ask users to evaluate the trajectories of a crowd simulation that only performs locomotion, the realism may be rated as higher if we render bots instead of humanoids. Although this difference was not statistically significant in our experiment, we would like to further study this issue, because it could have a very important impact when it comes to validating and comparing crowd simulation models through perceptual studies.

In all our results, animation variety combined with humanoid figures achieved the highest levels of perceived realism. Our experiments, showed the strong impact that animation variety can have on the perceptual evaluation of a crowd, to the extend that all three factors (overall simulation, trajectories and animations) where rated as significantly more realistic when having animation variety. This was also observed for bots, although not with a statistically significant difference. This shows that if we want to further achieve believable and plausible crowd simulation model for computer graphics applications, we need to dedicate more resources to improve animation variety, and not only to develop better local movement methods.

In future work we would like to evaluate whether this conclusions are also observed in immersive VR, were virtual humanoids have the same size as the participant and animation artifacts or unnatural local movement can have a stronger negative effect on the plausibility of the crowd. In such setup, we would like to also evaluate presence, to understand the impact that good quality animations can have on the participant perception.

Appendix

Fig. 3. Images showing the city scene from different points of view.

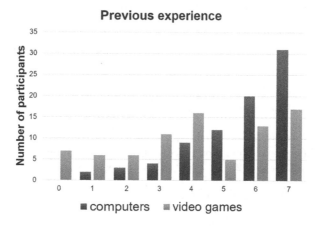

Fig. 4. Participants' previous experience.

Table 3. Ryan-Joiner correlation coefficients and p-values.

Cond.	Crowd realism	Trajectories	Animations
BNA	RJ = 0.997	RJ = 0.996	RJ = 0.997
	$p > 0.1$	$p > 0.1$	$p > 0.1$
BA	RJ = 0.990	RJ = 0.992	RJ = 0.985
	$p > 0.1$	$p > 0.1$	$p = 0.055$
HNA	RJ = 0.999	RJ = 0.996	RJ = 0.997
	$p > 0.1$	$p > 0.1$	$p > 0.1$
HA	RJ = 0.989	RJ = 0.989	RJ = 0.992
	$p > 0.1$	$p > 0.1$	$p > 0.1$

Table 4. Levene's values and their corresponding p-values for each factor level

Realism of crowd	Trajectories	Realism of animations
Value = 0.53	Value = 1.45	Value = 0.18
p-value = 0.665	p-value = 0.229	p-value = 0.912

References

1. Bailenson, J.N., Yee, N., Merget, D., Schroeder, R.: The effect of behavioral realism and form realism of real-time avatar faces on verbal disclosure, nonverbal disclosure, emotion recognition, and copresence in dyadic interaction. Pres. Teleoper. Virt. Environ. **15**(4), 359–372 (2006)
2. van den Berg, J., Lin, M., Manocha, D.: Reciprocal velocity obstacles for real-time multi-agent navigation. In: ICRA, pp. 1928–1935 (2008). https://doi.org/10.1109/ROBOT.2008.4543489
3. Berton, F., et al.: Crowd navigation in vr: exploring haptic rendering of collisions. IEEE Trans. Vis. Comput. Graph., 1 (2020). https://doi.org/10.1109/TVCG.2020.3041341.
4. Bruneau, J., Olivier, A.H., Pettre, J.: Going through, going around: a study on individual avoidance of groups. IEEE Trans. Vis. Comput. Graph. **21**(4), 520–528 (2015)
5. Dickinson, P., Gerling, K., Hicks, K., Murray, J., Shearer, J., Greenwood, J.: Virtual reality crowd simulation: effects of agent density on user experience and behaviour. Virt. Reality **23**(1), 19–32 (2018). https://doi.org/10.1007/s10055-018-0365-0
6. Durupinar, F., Allbeck, J., Pelechano, N., Badler, N.: Creating crowd variation with the ocean personality model. In: Proceedings of the 7th International Joint Conference on Autonomous Agents and Multiagent Systems, AAMAS '08, vol. 3, pp. 1217–1220. International Foundation for Autonomous Agents and Multiagent Systems, Richland (2008)
7. Gamage, V., Ennis, C.: Examining the effects of a virtual character on learning and engagement in serious games. In: Proceedings of the 11th Annual International Conference on Motion, Interaction, and Games (MIG'18), pp. 1–9. ACM (2018). https://doi.org/10.1145/3274247.3274499
8. Gonzalez-Franco, M., et al.: The rocketbox library and the utility of freely available rigged avatars for procedural animation of virtual humans and embodiment. Front. Virt. Reality **1**, 20 (2020)

9. Guy, S.J., Kim, S., Lin, M.C., Manocha, D.: Simulating heterogeneous crowd behaviors using personality trait theory. In: Proceedings of the 2011 ACM SIGGRAPH/Eurographics symposium on computer animation, pp. 43–52. ACM (2011)

10. Knob, P., Balotin, M., Musse, S.R.: Simulating crowds with ocean personality traits. In: Proceedings of the 18th International Conference on Intelligent Virtual Agents, pp. 233–238. ACM (2018)

11. Kyriakou, M., Pan, X., Chrysanthou, Y.: Interaction with virtual crowd in immersive and semi-immersive virtual reality systems. Comput. Anim. Virt. Worlds 28(5), e1729 (2017)

12. Liu, Z., Liu, T., Ma, M., Hsu, H.H., Ni, Z., Chai, Y.: A perception-based emotion contagion model in crowd emergent evacuation simulation. Comput. Anim. Virt. Worlds 29(3–4), e1817 (2018)

13. López, A., Chaumette, F., Marchand, E., Pettré, J.: Character navigation in dynamic environments based on optical flow. In: Computer Graphics Forum, vol. 38, pp. 181–192. Wiley Online Library (2019)

14. Lynch, S.D., Kulpa, R., Meerhoff, L.A., Pettre, J., Cretual, A., Olivier, A.H.: Collision avoidance behavior between walkers: global and local motion cues. IEEE Trans. Vis. Comput. Graph. 24(7), 2078–2088 (2017)

15. McDonnell, R., Breidt, M., Bülthoff, H.H.: Render me real? investigating the effect of render style on the perception of animated virtual humans. ACM Trans. Graph. 31(4) (2012). https://doi.org/10.1145/2185520.2185587

16. Mixamo (2018). https://www.mixamo.com/

17. Molina, E., Ríos, A., Pelechano, N.: Avatars rendering and its effect on perceived realism in virtual reality. In: 2020 IEEE International Conference on Artificial Intelligence and Virtual Reality (AIVR), pp. 222–225. IEEE (2020)

18. Mori, M.: The uncanny valley. Energy 7(4), 33–35 (1970)

19. Narang, S., Best, A., Randhavane, T., Shapiro, A., Manocha, D.: Pcdvr: simulating gaze-based interactions between a real user and virtual crowds. In: Proceedings of the 22nd ACM Conference on Virtual Reality Software and Technology, pp. 91–100. ACM (2016)

20. Pelechano, N., Allbeck, J., Badler, N.: Controlling individual agents in high-density crowd simulation. In: Proceedings Symposium Computer Animation 2007, pp. 99–108 (2007). https://doi.org/10.1145/1272690.1272705

21. Pelechano, N., Stocker, C., Allbeck, J., Badler, N.: Being a part of the crowd: towards validating vr crowds using presence. In: Proceedings of the 7th International Joint Conference on Autonomous Agents and Multiagent Systems, vol. 1, pp. 136–142 (2008)

22. Randhavane, T., Bera, A., Kapsaskis, K., Sheth, R., Gray, K., Manocha, D.: Eva: generating emotional behavior of virtual agents using expressive features of gait and gaze. In: ACM Symposium on Applied Perception 2019, pp. 1–10 (2019)

23. Ronchi, E.: Developing and validating evacuation models for fire safety engineering. Fire Saf. J. 120, 103020 (2020)

24. Şahin, C., Rokne, J., Alhajj, R.: Human behavior modeling for simulating evacuation of buildings during emergencies. Physica A Stat. Mech. Appl. 528, 121432 (2019)

25. Volonte, M., et al.: Effects of virtual human appearance fidelity on emotion contagion in affective inter-personal simulations. IEEE Trans. Vis. Comput. Graph. 22, 1–1 (2016). https://doi.org/10.1109/TVCG.2016.2518158

26. Volonte, M., Duchowski, A.T., Babu, S.V.: Effects of a virtual human appearance fidelity continuum on visual attention in virtual reality. In: Proceedings of the 19th ACM International Conference on Intelligent Virtual Agents, pp. 141–147 (2019)

27. Wiggins, J.S.: The Five-Factor Model of Personality: Theoretical Perspectives. Guilford Press, New York (1996)

28. Wisessing, P., Zibrek, K., Cunningham, D.W., Dingliana, J., McDonnell, R.: Enlighten me: importance of brightness and shadow for character emotion and appeal. ACM Trans. Graph. (TOG) **39**(3), 1–12 (2020)

29. Zell, E., et al.: To stylize or not to stylize? the effect of shape and material stylization on the perception of computer-generated faces. ACM Trans. Graph. **34**(6) (2015). https://doi.org/10.1145/2816795.2818126

30. Zhao, H., et al.: Assessing crowd management strategies for the 2010 love parade disaster using computer simulations and virtual reality. J. Roy. Soc. Interf. **17**(167), 20200116 (2020)

31. Zhou, R., Ou, Y., Tang, W., Wang, Q., Yu, B.: An emergency evacuation behavior simulation method combines personality traits and emotion contagion. IEEE Access **8**, 66693–66706 (2020)

32. Zibrek, K., Martin, S., McDonnell, R.: Is photorealism important for perception of expressive virtual humans in virtual reality? ACM Trans. Appl. Percept. **16**(3) (2019). https://doi.org/10.1145/3349609

Computer Vision

Virtual Haptic System for Shape Recognition Based on Local Curvatures

Guillem Garrofé[1], Carlota Parés[1], Anna Gutiérrez[1], Conrado Ruiz Jr[1,2],
Gerard Serra[1], and David Miralles[1(✉)]

[1] Grup de Recerca en Tecnologies Media, La Salle - Universitat Ramon Llull,
Barcelona, Catalonia, Spain
david.miralles@salle.url.edu
[2] De La Salle University, Manila, Philippines

Abstract. Haptic object recognition is widely used in various robotic
manipulation tasks. Using the shape features obtained at either a local
or global scale, robotic systems can identify objects solely by touch. Most
of the existing work on haptic systems either utilizes a robotic arm with
end-effectors to identify the shape of an object based on contact points,
or uses a surface capable of recording pressure patterns. In this work, we
introduce a novel haptic capture system based on the local curvature of
an object. We present a haptic sensor system comprising of three aligned
and equally spaced fingers that move towards the surface of an object
at the same speed. When an object is touched, our system records the
relative times between each contact sensor. Simulating our approach in
a virtual environment, we show that this new local and low-dimensional
geometrical feature can be effectively used for shape recognition. Even
with 10 samples, our system achieves an accuracy of over 90% without
using any sampling strategy or any associated spatial information.

Keywords: Shape recognition · Haptic perception · Robotic
simulation · Tactile recognition · Haptic capture

1 Introduction

The robot's ability to recognize objects has been extensively studied over the
past years. Whereas object recognition using computer vision has progressed
substantially with the abundance of visual data and powerful machine-learning
algorithms [9], haptic approaches have received relatively little attention [11].
Unlike vision and audition, haptic exploration involves direct interaction with
the object being explored, which presents significant challenges in both control
and sensing. Despite the recent advancements and availability of tactile sensors,
unimodal haptic object recognition is still limited in part by the time-consuming
task of acquiring the abundance of training data required by most modern algorithms.

Object shapes can be haptically assessed at two scales: local and global [10].
At a local scale, the shape can be revealed by a single touch, which is analogous

© Springer Nature Switzerland AG 2021
N. Magnenat-Thalmann et al. (Eds.): CGI 2021, LNCS 13002, pp. 41–53, 2021.
https://doi.org/10.1007/978-3-030-89029-2_3

Fig. 1. Simulation of robotic exploration of a stimulus. The robotic system is provided with a three-finger gripper, with a contact sensor at the end of each finger. The red arrows point out the trajectory followed by the contact sensors when extracting their time differences. (Color Figure online)

to the human cutaneous sense of touch localized in the skin. At a global scale, kinesthetic cues associated with the position and movement of the end-effectors in space may be integrated with local features to recognize the objects. Evidently, the combination of both approaches may improve haptic perception. Local and global methods have been extensively studied, but no single perfect approach exists as haptic sensors differ substantially according to the task that has to be performed. For instance, global shapes have the ability to generalize an entire object with a single vector, which facilitates classification with the appropriate machine learning algorithms. On the other hand, local shapes may be harder to classify but they are more robust to occlusion and clutter.

The growing demand for dexterous robotic manipulations with robots that have a strong haptic sensing has fostered the use of virtual sensors for the identification of promising sensors and algorithms [16]. Moreover, virtual haptic systems reduce the effort and time required to collect haptic data. Because of this, in this work, we take advantage of virtual environments to develop a novel haptic sensor that can extract object geometric properties at a local level. We present a haptic data capture system that has an end-effector with three equally spaced fingers, which include a contact sensor (CS) at the end for detecting contact with objects (see Fig. 1). For each touch, we obtain a three-component vector, where each value corresponds to the time difference between the first contact with the object and the subsequent contact. From the collection of these simple samples and without any type of spatial information, we show the potential that this new haptic capture system can have.

The main contributions of this paper are as follows:

- A novel haptic data capture system based on local features with very low dimensionality.

– From the captured local features, we build a new global shape descriptor
  called CTD (Curvature from Temporal Differences in haptic touch) that
  depicts in a single distribution the local geometrical shapes of an object.

2   Related Work

Haptic shape recognition is of paramount importance in robotics to perform
multiple tasks such as grasping and in-hand manipulation [19]. Accordingly,
over the past years, several promising approaches based on tactile data have
been developed [1,13,17]. These methods can be divided into at least three
categories according to their inputs [11]: 1) the distribution of contact points; 2)
the pressure patterns in tactile arrays; 3) the combination of contact points and
pressure patterns.

Methods based on contact points use the spatial coordinates of the robot's
end-effectors when they contact the object to constrain its geometry and globally identify its shape [1,23]. These approaches, despite being successful in constrained scenarios where objects tend to be fixed and stationary, can be time-
consuming when excessive contacts are required for recognizing the global object
shape. Moreover, the precision of such contact points is strongly related to the
chaining of transformations involving the locations of contact points and hand
pose configurations, which tends to be error-prone [7].

With the development of high-resolution tactile arrays, multiple methods
based on tactile patterns have also been proposed. Tactile sensors that can
retrieve pressure patterns can be based on the measure of contact forces or
the deformation of a soft elastomer skin. The latter allows tactile patterns to
be handled as images, which can be processed and treated as computer vision
descriptors. For instance, the use of an optical tactile sensor like GelSight [22]
with high-resolution and limited geometry has successfully assisted many challenging robotic tasks [3]. However, despite its successes, this type of tactile sensor faces several challenges, like the costly computation algorithms required for
manipulating its high dimensional raw output [14]. Moreover, mapping data into
a lower dimensionality feature space deprives of the physical meaning of the data.

Given the two previously presented methods it becomes clear that fusing
both tactile sensing modalities would be beneficial for object recognition tasks.
If the information of tactile patterns and contact points is combined, more robust
methods can be developed [12,20]. However, all the previously mentioned methods are susceptive to real-world limitations as most modern machine learning
algorithms require large datasets for model training and the task of collecting
such an amount of data is time-consuming [21]. Therefore, to save time and
resources, robotic simulators can be employed so that only a limited number of
real experiments are required to finally deploy the model in the real scenario
[6]. To this end, most commercial robots include a digital version that can be
integrated into a robot simulator like Gazebo [4].

In this article, we take advantage of the benefits of virtual environments
and present a novel tactile sensor that can capture the local geometry of an

object without any information regarding its location. Unlike tactile patterns, our method is very low dimensional with only 3 numerical values, which can, in turn, be transformed into a single value while keeping part of its geometrical information. Besides, our local geometric features can be aggregated to create a distribution that globally describes the geometry of an object (CTD).

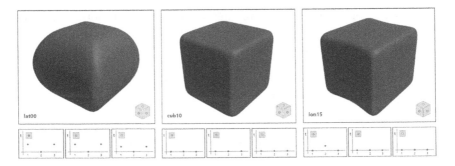

Fig. 2. Sample 3-feature vectors (graphically illustrated). (lat00), Sample features for a stimulus with mostly concave surfaces. (cub10), Sample features for a stimulus with mostly flat surfaces. (lon15), Sample features for a stimulus with 2 convex surfaces.

3   Data Capture

3.1   Stimuli

The stimuli used in this experiment were generated by a parametric shape model [5]. This model allowed us to create a parameter space of novel, three-dimensional, similar cubic objects. In the present study, the "base object" in the family is a cube with rounded edges and the rest of members were created by varying one parameter (n_2) of the model (see Fig. 3b). The resulting 9 stimuli in the parameter space are shown in Fig. 3a.

3.2   Data Collection

Unlike visual sensing, tactile sensors can perceive several physical properties (e.g., shape, size, weight, temperature, hardness) of an object directly. In this work, we have implemented a virtual environment with the capability of generating sensor data from rendered 3D objects. Specifically, we have developed a virtual tactile sensor that can easily capture the local shape features of an object.

Inspired by human haptic curvature discrimination using the time differences between the moments at which middle, index, and ring fingers contact a stimulus [15], our haptic sensor consists of three aligned and equally spaced contact sensors that move towards the surface of an object at the same speed. When an object is touched, our system extracts the relative times between each contact sensor, i.e., it measures the time difference between the first contact with the object and the subsequent contacts. Hence, we capture a three-value feature $(\Delta t_1, \Delta t_2, \Delta t_3)$, where Δt_i is the time elapsed from the first sensor contact and the contact of sensor i. If the first contact corresponds to contact sensor i, then $\Delta t_i = 0$. In Fig. 2, we can observe a three-value feature for every face of three stimuli. Given the symmetry of our stimuli, a representative sample for each of the three different faces of a stimulus is shown.

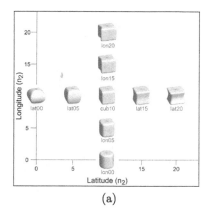

(a)

$$r(\varphi) = \left[\left| \frac{cos(m\varphi/4)}{a} \right|^{n_2} + \left| \frac{sin(m\varphi/4)}{b} \right|^{n_3} \right]^{-\frac{1}{n_1}}$$

(b)

Fig. 3. (a) Parameter space showing the 9 objects used in this study at the location defined by their parameter values. Only parameter n_2 of the proposed model has been varied. (b) Superformula. Equations for creating the three-dimensional objects [5].

In our virtual environment created with Unity (version 2019.4.11f1), both digital 3D objects and contact sensors are provided with colliders that allow the detection of the interception between the object and the sensors. Specifically, the contact sensors are provided with sphere colliders and the object with a mesh collider. The collision detection is continuous and sweep-based, i.e., it uses a Time Of Impact (TOI) algorithm to compute potential collisions for the contact sensors by sweeping its forward trajectory using its velocity in that moment. If there is a contact along the sensor's direction, the algorithm computes the time of impact and moves the contact sensor until that time. For the ease of implementation of this novel haptic sensor, we have depicted each contact sensor as a sphere with a 0.3 cm radius. Moreover, we have set a 1.5 cm distance between each sensor. These sizes are determined based on the size of the stimuli, approximately 7 cm on each side in our case. For each touch, the virtual sensor is randomly placed in a plane orthogonal to one of the object's coordinate axes (see Fig. 4). Bounding boxes are used to ensure contact sensors can traverse the object collider.

Fig. 4. The touching process followed during the explorations of an object. (1) The contact sensors (red dots) are aligned and placed according to a random-oriented vector (green line) contained by a plane perpendicular to one of the object's axes. (2) The contact sensors move synchronously towards the object. (3) The time differences are recorded when the contact sensors traverse the collider of the object. (Color figure online)

The recorded time differences conform to a discrete function that provides the system with local shape information regarding the object being explored (see Fig. 2). For each stimulus of this study, 20,000 random touches over the surface have been captured, leading to a dataset with a total of 180,000 samples for the nine objects. In the following sections, we show how this data can be fed into a classifier to recognize an object given a set of features.

4   Classifiers

In this section, we present two classification schemes, which aim to identify the objects of this study from the haptic data digitally acquired. We employ a method based on Probability Distribution Functions (PDFs) and a machine learning classifier that combines eXtreme Gradient Boosting (XGBoost) with Naïve Bayes (NB).

4.1   Probability Density Function Based

From the information provided by the relative times of the contact sensors, we can measure the curvature located at each contact of the manipulated object. This curvature can be obtained by computing the second derivative of the former mentioned times. The concavity and convexity of the object will be reflected in the values of the second derivative. Thus, the different curvatures forming the global surface can be extracted and used as a descriptor (see Fig. 5a).

The global descriptor of a shape (CTD) consists of the Probability Distribution Function of the second derivatives from its surface. Those feature values associated to the differential parts of an object will allow us to create PDFs that can be differentiated with a sufficient number of samples (see Fig. 5b). Kernel Density Estimation has been used to generate the PDFs for each figure [18].

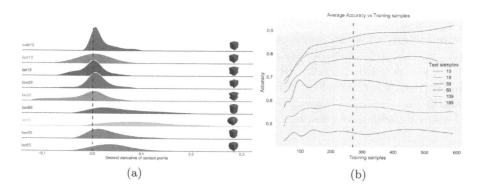

(a)   (b)

Fig. 5. (a) Reference PDF descriptors based on the second derivative of the surface of each object. 270 samples have been used to generate the reference PDFs. (b) PDF-based classifier accuracy according to the number of samples used to generate the reference distributions. For different number of test samples, the accuracy evolution is shown. The dashed line indicates the number of samples (270 samples) that provides great accuracies for few test samples. (Color figure online)

The Kullback-Leibler divergence [8] measures how different is one probability distribution from another probability distribution used as a reference. Therefore, the PDFs resulting from a test manipulation can be compared to the reference PDFs through the Kullback-Leibler divergence. In order to predict the object associated to the test samples, the algorithm measures the divergence between the test PDF and the 9 train PDFs. The predicted object is the one whose divergence is minimum, i.e.,

$$\widehat{y} = \underset{y \in [1,9]}{argmin}[D_{KL}(P||Q_y)]$$

where P is the probability distribution of the curvatures obtained from the test subset and Q_y is the training PDF corresponding to object y.

When comparing PDFs, a crucial parameter is the number of samples taken to generate the corresponding distributions. If the reference distribution is retrieved from a large group of samples and the test one contains only a small number of samples, their divergence may still be considerable even if they correspond to the same object. Thus, computing divergences between objects' PDFs of a different number of samples can lead to a higher confusion among objects.

As it can be seen in Fig. 5b, to achieve high accuracies with few samples, a similar amount of samples have to be used when training the model. In this case, 270 training samples provide the best balance between the achieved accuracy and the number of test samples needed to reach this value.

4.2   Bayesian XGBoost

XGBoost [2] is an advanced implementation of a gradient boosting machine that builds an ensemble of models sequentially, typically decision trees, with each new model attempting to correct the deficiencies of the previous model. Given a feature vector, individual decisions from each weak learner are added together, obtaining the probability of that sample belonging to each of the classes (see Fig. 6 for a detailed diagram). Specifically, our XGBoost model contains 100 weak learners, where each learner is a Decision Tree with a maximum depth of 6 levels. We have set a 0.3 learning rate, and we have chosen *gbtree* as our booster, and *multi:softprob* as our learning objective.

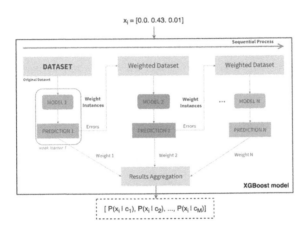

Fig. 6. XGBoost classifier diagram. x_i, test feature vector; $P(x_i|C_j)$, probability of x_i belonging to class C_j. In our case, each model is a decision tree of at most 6 levels, the number of weak learners is $N = 100$, and the learning rate is 0.3.

Given that our feature space consists of a three-value vector, as described in Sect. 3, a classification architecture that builds a decision based upon a set of features is needed. Considering that each of our vector values is a sample of a random variable that represents the physical properties of an object, we built a naïve Bayes model that assumes strong independence between feature vectors and uses the resulting probabilities of the XGBoost model as the likelihood of a feature belonging to a class. With this method, we combine individual feature estimations and select the class that maximizes $P(c|X, O)$, where X is a set of features, c is a class label, and O denotes the prior information that all the elements in the set belong to the same class.

Specifically, $P(c|X, O)$ can be formulated as:

$$P(c|X, O) = \prod_{i=1}^{r} P(x_i|c)$$

where r is the total number of feature vectors in the X set and $P(x_i|c)$ is the probability of feature vector x_i belonging to class c, which has been obtained from the XGBoost model.

5   Results

For each of the previously presented classifiers, a 10-fold cross-validation procedure was applied to assess their efficiency and avoid overfitting. Specifically, we tested the accuracy of the classifiers for every possible number of samples, generating 10 groups of 200 samples for each fold, leading to a total of 100 tests for value per figure. To have a precise representation of the accuracy evolution, we tested the classifier for 30 different feature-set sizes distributed in a logarithmic scale ranging from 10 to 200.

5.1   Probability Density Function Based

Figure 7a depicts the accuracy evolution of the PDF-based classifier as the number of samples per distribution increases and, therefore, a more accurate descriptor is achieved. It can be seen that it needs 50 samples to reach an accuracy of 75.66%($\pm$5.93) and with 200 samples it achieves an accuracy of 88.44%($\pm$5.35). Given this multi-class classification task, it is also important to observe the accuracies of each individual class and the similarities between them. In Fig. 7b, the confusion matrix that corresponds to 88% (200 samples per test) of accuracy is shown.

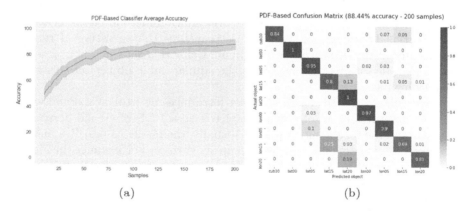

(a)   (b)

Fig. 7. (a) PDF-based classifier accuracy evolution according to the number of samples taken to generate the test PDFs. The system's reference distributions contain 270 samples per object (see dashed line in Fig. 5b). (b) PDF-based classifier's confusion matrix with 200 samples test distributions (88.44% accuracy).

5.2   Bayesian XGBoost

In Fig. 8a, we can find the accuracy evolution of the Bayesian XGBoost classifier as the number of samples per vector-set increases. It can be seen that with only 10 samples the classifier achieves a 90%($\pm$3.32) average accuracy. In Fig. 8b, we include the confusion matrix that corresponds to the 90% prediction accuracy. It can be observed that some classes (lon15, lat15) get more confused than others (cub10, lat00).

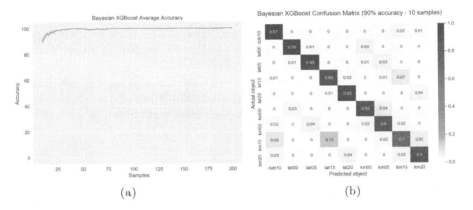

(a)   (b)

Fig. 8. (a) Bayesian XGBoost performance. Global accuracy with 95% confidence interval depicted in light green. (b) Bayesian XGBoost classifier's confusion matrix at 10 samples (90% accuracy). (Color figure online)

6   Discussion

This work introduces a shape-based object recognition method based on a novel robotic virtual haptic sensor. Our dataset captures the curvature of random points located at the surface of the 3D stimuli. Using this data, we have presented two different algorithms that recognize the similar cubic objects of this study with very high accuracies.

In particular, the PDF-based classifier introduces an explicit method where the local curvatures of an object are depicted as a PDF of second derivatives extracted from the three contact points. Visually, the reader can easily identify if the object contains any flat, concave or convex surface. For instance, in Fig. 5a, it can be seen that the cube with rounded edges (1st row – blue line) is essentially flat (0-centered PDF), whereas the 3D surface of lat00 (7th row – pink line) is mostly concave (wide range of positive second derivative values). Beyond accuracy, the PDF classifier has been used for the high geometric content of its descriptors (CTD).

Another interesting aspect of the PDF-based classifier is its reduced number of training samples. Given that it needs to commensurate the number of training samples with the number of test samples, we can train the model with fewer samples than most deep learning techniques.

Regarding the Bayesian XGBoost classifier, we cannot interpret the grounds of its decisions as readily as with the PDF-based classifier. However, this model's performance highly surpasses the one with PDFs, given that a 90% accuracy is achieved with only 10 samples instead of 200. This significant improvement reveals that the proposed novel haptic sensor may prove to be very competitive if implemented in a real setting.

Another important point to analyze regarding the presented results is the perceived similarities between the stimuli. From Figs. 7b and 8b, we can observe that every stimulus is mostly confused with another stimulus, e.g., lat05 is mainly confused with lon05. It is particularly interesting to highlight the symmetry of the confusion matrices, as objects that share similar curvatures are considerably perceived as similar (see Fig. 3a), leading to the premise that shape curvature underpins classification decisions.

Concerning the confusion matrix of the PDF-based classifier (see Fig. 7b), the reader may notice that the object with lower accuracy (lon15) is also the less recognizable object of the Bayesian XGBoost classifier. Moreover, the symmetry acknowledged in Fig. 8b, can also be slightly observed in the PDF-based confusion matrix. It should be pointed out that with the presented methods, the perceived similarity between a pair of objects comes from two different processes and this can lead to a non-symmetrical confusion matrix. Such commonality between the two confusion matrices may be interesting for understanding and comparing the results of different classifiers that are fed with the same data.

7   Conclusions and Future Work

In this paper, we have presented a new haptic capture system based on a local geometric feature related to the curvature of the contact area. This feature is extracted from a simple three-component vector generated by the temporal differences between the interactions of the contact sensors and the object. Unlike other approaches that work with high-resolution data, like images extracted from tactile patterns, we work with very low dimensional data. This fact allows us to run simple machine learning algorithms. In addition, with the ensemble of samples generated for an object we can directly generate a global shape descriptor that includes information about the geometry of an object, which, in turn, we can use to recognize such object. The feature collected by our capture method has allowed our classifiers to discriminate even between very similar stimuli. With our proposal, we achieve accuracies of more than 90% with only 10 samples. The low misclassification rate of the classifiers leads us to believe that this method can be extended to heterogeneous stimuli.

Some avenues we want to pursue in future work include: 1) Test our capture method with a state-of-the-art benchmark. 2) Extend our results to object classification instead of recognition. 3) Study the robustness of the system by introducing errors in the captured data. 4) Develop haptic exploration strategies to decrease the number of samples needed to recognize/classify objects.

References

1. Allen, P.K., Roberts, K.S.: Haptic object recognition using a multi-fingered dextrous hand. Columbia University, Technical report (1988)
2. Chen, T., Guestrin, C.: Xgboost: a scalable tree boosting system. In: Proceedings of the 22nd ACM Sigkdd International Conference on Knowledge Discovery and Data Mining, pp. 785–794 . ACM, New York (2016) (2016)
3. Dong, S., Yuan, W., Adelson, E.H.: Improved gelsight tactile sensor for measuring geometry and slip. In: 2017 IEEE/RSJ International Conference on Intelligent Robots and Systems (IROS), pp. 137–144. IEEE (2017)
4. Gazebo (2021). http://gazebosim.org/
5. Gielis, J.: A generic geometric transformation that unifies a wide range of natural and abstract shapes. Am. J. Botany **90**(3), 333–338 (2003)
6. Gomes, D.F., Paoletti, P., Luo, S.: Generation of gelsight tactile images for sim2real learning. arXiv preprint arXiv:2101.07169 (2021)
7. Gorges, N., Navarro, S.E., Wörn, H.: Haptic object recognition using statistical point cloud features. In: 2011 15th International Conference on Advanced Robotics (ICAR), pp. 15–20. IEEE (2011)
8. Kullback, S., Leibler, R.: On information and sufficiency. Ann. Math. Stat. **22**, 79–86 (2006)
9. LeCun, Y., Bengio, Y., Hinton, G.: Deep learning. Nature **521**(7553), 436 (2015). https://doi.org/10.1038/nature14539
10. Lederman, S.J., Klatzky, R.L.: Haptic perception: a tutorial. Attent. Percept. Psychophys **71**(7), 1439–1459 (2009)
11. Luo, S., Bimbo, J., Dahiya, R., Liu, H.: Robotic tactile perception of object properties: a review. Mechatronics **48**, 54–67 (2017)
12. Luo, S., Mou, W., Althoefer, K., Liu, H.: Iterative closest labeled point for tactile object shape recognition. In: 2016 IEEE/RSJ International Conference on Intelligent Robots and Systems (IROS), pp. 3137–3142. IEEE (2016)
13. Navarro, S.E., Gorges, N., Wörn, H., Schill, J., Asfour, T., Dillmann, R.: Haptic object recognition for multi-fingered robot hands. In: 2012 IEEE Haptics Symposium (HAPTICS), pp. 497–502. IEEE (2012)
14. Polic, M., Krajacic, I., Lepora, N., Orsag, M.: Convolutional autoencoder for feature extraction in tactile sensing. IEEE Rob. Autom. Lett. **4**(4), 3671–3678 (2019)
15. Pont, S.C., Kappers, A.M., Koenderink, J.J.: Similar mechanisms underlie curvature comparison by static and dynamic touch. Percept. Psychophys. **61**(5), 874–894 (1999)
16. Rouhafzay, G., Cretu, A.M.: A virtual tactile sensor with adjustable precision and size for object recognition. In: 2018 IEEE International Conference on Computational Intelligence and Virtual Environments for Measurement Systems and Applications (CIVEMSA), pp. 1–6. IEEE (2018)
17. Schneider, A., Sturm, J., Stachniss, C., Reisert, M., Burkhardt, H., Burgard, W.: Object identification with tactile sensors using bag-of-features. In: 2009 IEEE/RSJ International Conference on Intelligent Robots and Systems, pp. 243–248. IEEE (2009)
18. Scott, D.W.: Multivariate density estimation and visualization. In: Gentle, J., Hardle, W., Mori, Y. (eds.) Handbook of Computational Statistics, pp. 549–569. Springer, Heidelberg (2012). https://doi.org/10.1007/978-3-642-21551-3_19
19. Soh, H., Demiris, Y.: Incrementally learning objects by touch: online discriminative and generative models for tactile-based recognition. IEEE Trans. Haptics **7**(4), 512–525 (2014)

20. Spiers, A.J., Liarokapis, M.V., Calli, B., Dollar, A.M.: Single-grasp object classification and feature extraction with simple robot hands and tactile sensors. IEEE Trans. Haptics **9**(2), 207–220 (2016)
21. Wang, Y., Huang, W., Fang, B., Sun, F.: Elastic interaction of particles for robotic tactile simulation. arXiv preprint arXiv:2011.11528 (2020)
22. Yuan, W., Dong, S., Adelson, E.H.: Gelsight: high-resolution robot tactile sensors for estimating geometry and force. Sensors **17**(12), 2762 (2017)
23. Zhang, M.M., Kennedy, M.D., Hsieh, M.A., Daniilidis, K.: A triangle histogram for object classification by tactile sensing. In: 2016 IEEE/RSJ International Conference on Intelligent Robots and Systems (IROS), pp. 4931–4938. IEEE (2016)

Stable Depth Estimation Within Consecutive Video Frames

Fei Luo, Lin Wei, and Chunxia Xiao$^{(\boxtimes)}$

School of Computer Science, Wuhan University, Wuhan, Hubei, China
{luofei,2019282110158,cxxiao}@whu.edu.cn

Abstract. Deep learning based depth estimation methods have been proven effective and promising, especially learning depth from monocular video. Depth-from-video is the real sense of unsupervised depth estimation, as it doesn't need depth ground truth or stereo image pairs as supervision. However, most of existing depth-from-video methods did not think of frame-to-frame depth estimation stability. We found depths within temporally consecutive frames exist instability although single image depth can be estimated well by recent works. Thus, this work aims to solve this problem. Specifically, we define a temporal smoothness term for the depth map and propose a temporal stability loss to constrain depths of the same objects within consecutive frames to keep their stability. We also propose an inconsistency check processing according to the differences between synthetic view frames and their original RGB frame. Based on the inconsistency check, we propose a self-discovered mask to handle the moving and occluded objects. Experiments show that the proposed method is effective and can estimate stable depth results within temporally consecutive frames. Meanwhile, it achieves competitive performance on the KITTI dataset.

Keywords: Depth estimation · Monocular video · Depth stability

1 Introduction

Depth estimation is a fundamental task in computer vision. It can be used in many fields, such as autonomous driving, 3D reconstruction, robotics and VR/AR. There are several ways for depth acquisition, for example, by time-of-flight(ToF) sensor used in smart phone or LIDAR sensor used in autonomous driving vehicles. Using depth sensors to detect distance usually is an expensive way and suffers from noise and structural artifacts, especially in presence of reflective, transparent, or dark surface. Differently, learning depth from RGB images or monocular video sequences is an attractive way.

Depth-from-image methods can be divided into two categories, one is the traditional way. Besides the binocular stereo vision, it can use SFM or MVS [1,2]. The other is the learning based way. Although the traditional methods are effective in many cases, its reliance on feature correspondence has problems in regions

© Springer Nature Switzerland AG 2021
N. Magnenat-Thalmann et al. (Eds.): CGI 2021, LNCS 13002, pp. 54–66, 2021.
https://doi.org/10.1007/978-3-030-89029-2_4

of low texture, occlusions. Additionally, the SFM based methods only generate a sparse or semi-dense depth. On the contrary, the learning based methods can estimate a dense depth. It also can be further divided into two categories, the supervised and the unsupervised (self-supervised). In general, the learning based methods rely on large data sets to learn the relationship between features in the image and the distance in the depth map. However, collecting high quality depth ground truth to supervise learning is a costly work. Recently, self-supervised methods have been proposed, without needing the depth ground truth. They use stereo image pairs [3–5] or monocular video sequences [6–10]. Comparing the self-supervised methods, depth from monocular video sequences is more convenient than the stereo image pairs, because monocular video is much more easier to acquire. Zhou et al. [10] has proven that training networks using monocular video is feasible. The model consists of two parts. One is the single-view depth estimation network and the other is the camera pose estimation network. Using the estimated depth and camera pose, it can warp the image from one viewpoint to other viewpoints, and then employ the image reconstruction loss as supervision to train the model. It has its own challenges. For instance, the performance limitation arises due to the moving objects that violate the underlying static scene assumption. Subsequently, more depth-from-video methods [11,12] have been proposed.

Most existing methods did not think of frame-to-frame depth stability. Our work aims to estimate stable depth within consecutive frames to solve this problem. The main contributions in this work can be summarized as follows:

First, we define a temporal smoothness term, which is the median of the estimated depth. Based on this term, we propose a temporal stability loss to constrain depth stability within consecutive frames.

Second, we propose a self-discovered mask for moving objects and occlusions by checking the inconsistency between synthesized views' images and raw RGB images. Different from other methods, our method does not require additional optical flow or semantic segmentation which makes the framework simpler.

Third, our method can estimate stable depth for the identical objects within consecutive frames. Our method achieves competitive performance on KITTI [13].

2   Related Work

Traditional Methods. When estimating the depth from the video, mostly used theory is the Structure-from-Motion. It starts with feature extraction and matching. During the reconstruction process, bundle adjustment is iteratively applied to optimize the target loss function. Over the past years, a variety of traditional methods have been proposed. There are mature tools like Colmap [14], which is widely used to obtain initial coarse depth or camera pose parameters. However, its reliance on feature correspondence has problems in regions of low texture, occlusions, thin structure, and etc. These limitations commonly exist in practice. Thus, deep learning based methods have been proposed to address them.

Supervised Methods. Accurately estimating depth from a single image is ill-posed, because the same input image can project to multiple plausible depths. Learning based methods have shown their superiority in solving this problem. Many enhancement techniques have been proposed, including combining local predictions [15], non-parametric scene sampling [16] and so on. With the development of deep learning, CNN-based monocular depth estimation methods came up. By utilizing two networks, Eigen et al. [17] showed that depth can be estimated from a single image using Convolution Neural Network. They designed a coarse-to-fine network to estimate the single-view depth and used the ground truth acquired by range sensor as the supervision to train the network. Although these supervised methods show their better performance, it is still an expensive way to collect enough depth ground truth in various conditions.

Unsupervised/Self-supervised Methods. For alleviating the reliance on ground truth, unsupervised methods have been proposed. The main supervision signal comes from the novel view synthesis procedure. Specifically, with known depth and camera pose, it can reconstruct nearby views from a given image, and optimize the photometric reprojection loss to supervise the training.

One form of unsupervised/self-supervised learning comes from stereo image pairs. Garg et al. [3] proposed to use a calibrated stereo camera pair setup, where depth was produced as an intermediate output and supervision came from reconstruction of one image in a stereo pair from the input of the other. Since the binocular stereo vision has fixed parallel cameras, it doesn't need to record the cameras' trajectory. Godard et al. [4] developed an approach to learn single-view depth using rectified stereo input during training and proposed a left-right disparity consistency loss term to improve the performance.

The other form of unsupervised/self-supervised learning is to use monocular video sequences to train the networks. Besides the depth estimation network, the model also needs a network to estimate camera poses for consecutive frames. Zhou et al. [10] proposed one fully unsupervised framework based on monocular videos. They introduce an additional ego-motion network to estimate the camera poses within consecutive frames. With the estimated depth and camera pose, image reconstruction as in [3] is applied and photometric loss is used as supervision signal to train the networks. But the performance is limited by moving objects that violate the underlying static scene assumption. To handle moving objects, Geonet [9] introduced an additional optical flow network, and treated monocular depth, optical flow and ego-motion estimation from videos as a jointly unsupervised learning framework. They declare that the 3D scene is composed of static background and moving objects, which is defined as rigid flow and non-rigid flow. Thus, the approach should contain two stages, including the rigid structure reasoning stage to reconstruct the rigid scene and the non-rigid motion refinement stage to localize non-rigid motion. Although it can improve performance, it also brings more computation cost. Mahjourian et al. [7] presented a differentiable 3D loss function which can establish the geometry consistency between consecutive frames and thereby improved depth and ego-motion estimation. Monodepth2 [6] is commonly thought to be one of the state of the art methods. It shows that a simple model just with a minimum reprojection loss, a full-resolution multi-scale sampling method and auto masking also can make estimation well. But Monodepth2 fails to estimate the proper depth for the far distant parts like the sky, and does not work well for the stable depth estimation.

3   Method

Our method learns depth from monocular video without needing ground truth supervision, and aims to produce stable depth within temporally consecutive frames. In this section, we first introduce the fundamental idea behind the training in monocular unsupervised depth estimation, and then describe our proposed loss functions and the network (Fig. 1).

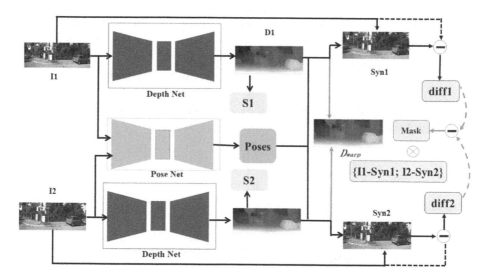

Fig. 1. Overview of our method. It contains a depth estimation network and a pose estimation network. Given two temporally consecutive video frames I_1 and I_2, the DepthNet can estimate their depth maps D_1 and D_2, PoseNet can estimate the camera poses from I_1 to I_2 and I_2 to I_1. Then we compute the temporal smoothness term S_1 and S_2 and the temporal smoothness loss L_{ts}. By warping D_1 using the camera pose, we obtain the warped depth map D_{warp} in the image plane of I_2. Then we compute the geometric consistency loss L_{dgc} according to D_{warp} and D_2. With estimated depths, camera poses and pre-computed camera intrinsics matrix K, we reconstruct $syn1$ in the image plane of I_1 from I_2 and reconstruct $syn2$ in the image plane of I_2 from I_1 in the same way. Then we compute the photometry difference $diff1$ between $syn1$ and I_1 and compute $diff2$ between $syn2$ and I_2. Finally we conduct photometry inconsistency check to get a weight mask $Mask$ using $diff1$ and $diff2$.

As the photometric loss is not applicable in low-texture nor homogeneous region of the scene, some works [4,18] employ a smoothness term to regularize the estimated depth map. In our work, we also treat the depth estimation task as minimizing the photometric loss. With the estimated depth map D_t and the camera pose $T_{t \to s}$, we synthesize $I_{s \to t}$ by warping the source view image I_s, where differentiable bilinear interpolation is used as in [10]. With the synthesized $I_{s \to t}$ and the reference view image I_t, we can formulate the photometric reprojection error as follows:

$$L_p = \sum_s \|pe\,(I_t - I_{s \to t})\|_1 \tag{1}$$

where

$$I_{s \to t} = I_s K T_{t \to s} D_t K^{-1} \tag{2}$$

Here we choose $L1$ loss because of its robustness to compute the difference between reference view and synthesized view. pe denotes the reconstruction error, e.g. the $L1$ distance in pixel space; K denote the pre-computed camera intrinsic matrix. We use the differentiable bilinear sampling to sample the source images. To handle illumination changes in real-world scenes, we also add an image dissimilarity loss SSIM [19]. Finally formulate photometric loss function as follows:

$$L_p = \sum_s (\alpha \|I_t - I_{s \to t}\|_1 + \beta\,(1 - SSIM\,(I_t, I_{s \to t}))) \tag{3}$$

where $\alpha = 0.15$ and $\beta = 0.85$ in our model. we also adopt the edge-aware smoothness loss used in [18].

$$L_s = \sum_p \left(e^{-\Delta I_t(p)} \cdot \Delta D_t\,(p)\right)^2 \tag{4}$$

where Δ is the first derivative along spatial directions. p stands for the points in target image.

3.1 Temporal Stability Loss

With the consecutive estimated depths D_a and D_b, we compute the temporal smoothness term S_a for D_a and S_b for D_b. We then simply formulate the temporal stability loss as follows:

$$L_{ts} = |S_a - S_b| \tag{5}$$

where

$$S = median\,(D) \tag{6}$$

median denotes the operation of computing the median of the given depth map. Current learning based methods works always output scale-inconsistent results. Such inconsistency would lead to the flutter phenomenon when continuously viewing these depth results. Eventually, scales of depths in a sequence should all agree with each other. To address it, we constrain the global scale of the depths within consecutive frames to acquire stable depth results with a temporal stability loss. The optimization not only encourages the global scale consistency between neighbouring frames but also transfers this consistency to the entire sequence in a chain mode.

3.2 Inconsistency Check and Self-discovered Mask

Another issue for depth-from-video methods is to deal with the moving and occluded objects. As the principle of monocular unsupervised depth estimation assumes that only camera could change position and the other objects in the scene keep static. When these assumptions are broken down, for example existing some walking people or running cars in the scene, depth estimation within these regions would get poor performance. Recent works usually introduce additional optical flow network [9,18,20] or semantic segmentation network [11] to solve it. However, it makes the model become complex and brings extra computation cost during training. Here, we introduce 1) a photometry inconsistency check processing on the differences between original RGB image and its synthesized view images and 2) a self-discovered mask to locate these moving or occluded objects regions (Fig. 2).

We use the original RGB image and its synthesized view images to generate a mask. Specifically, with the estimated depths D_a, D_b and camera pose $T_{a \to b}$, $T_{b \to a}$, we can reconstruct I_a' from I_b using D_a, $T_{b \to a}$ and pre-computed camera intrinsics K. Then we compute the photometric differences $P_{daa'}$ between I_a and I_a'. Similarly, We can reconstruct I_b' from I_a and compute $P_{dbb'}$. Then we can conduct the photometry inconsistency check by computing the differences between $P_{daa'}$ and $P_{dbb'}$. The main idea is that if the estimated depth and camera pose are accurate enough, then the synthesised view images would be very similar to the original RGB images. Thus the difference between $P_{daa'}$ and $P_{dbb'}$ should be at a low level. But the regions which contain the moving objects violate the prior assumption, therefore the difference in these regions might be at a high level. We can assign different weights for static regions and non-static regions while computing loss. Monodepth2 had a similar auto-masking technique which applied a per-pixel mask to the loss. It describes that the auto-masking can filter out pixels that do not change appearance from one frame to the next in the sequence and make the network ignore objects which move at the same velocity with the camera. However, Monodepth2's estimated depths in the far distant places had improper results with this auto-masking. E.g: the sky. The reason is that comparing to nearby objects, far distant sky is always thought to be relatively static within consecutive frames, so the auto-masking will filter out pixels in these regions. It would make depths in the far distant regions come from their nearby objects' depths. On the contrary, our method does not have such problem.

$$P_d^{dif} = |P_{daa'} - P_{dbb'}| \tag{7}$$

Here, $P_{daa'}$ and $P_{dbb'}$ are the matrices with the same size as the input images and the result P_d^{dif} is also a matrix.

Fig. 2. Illustration of depth estimation in the far distant regions. Top to bottom: consecutive input RGB images, Monodepth2 [6] depth results and our depth results. Our method has proper depths for the far distant sky, and Monodepth2 gets the depths from the nearby objects.

We make P_d^{dif} between 0 and 1 and propose a weight mask M based on the photometry inconsistency check as follows:

$$M = 1 - P_d^{dif} \tag{8}$$

The mask can assign low/high weights for inconsistent/consistent pixels and can be used to weight the original photometric loss L_p. We have a modified photometric loss as:

$$L_p^m = M \cdot L_p \tag{9}$$

By using such modified mask, it alleviates the negative impact from the moving objects and occlusion during training.

3.3   De-scaled Geometry Consistency Loss

To enforce the geometry consistency on the estimated depth results, the work [21] proposed a geometry consistency loss. Based on this loss term, we put forward an improved de-scaled geometry consistency loss. We also require that the target view depth D_t and the source view depth D_s conform with the same 3D scene structure, and minimize their difference. The improvement is that before computing the difference between D_t and D_s, we calculate the de-scaled depth map $\bar{D}$ using the temporal smoothness term mentioned above.

$$\bar{D} = D/S \tag{10}$$

Then we compute the de-scaled depth inconsistency map $\bar{D}_{dif}$ defined as follows:

$$\bar{D}_{dif} = \sum_p \frac{\left| \bar{D}_{t \to s}(p) - \bar{D}_s'(p) \right|}{\bar{D}_{t \to s}(p) + \bar{D}_s'(p)} \tag{11}$$

where $\bar{D}_{t \to s}$ is the computed de-scaled source view depth map of I_s by warping the de-scaled target view depth $\bar{D}_t$ using $T_{t \to s}$, and $\bar{D}_s'$ is the interpolated depth map from the computed de-scaled depth map $\bar{D}_s$(the same as the photometric warping, $\bar{D}_s$ can not be directly used, because the warping flow may not lie on the pixel grid). We normalize their difference by dividing their sum. It is more intuitive than the absolute distance, for it treats points at different absolute depths equally in optimization. Further, the function is symmetric and outputs from 0 to 1, which could contribute to numerical stability in training. With the de-scaled depth inconsistency map, we can simply define the proposed de-scaled geometry consistency loss as:

$$L_{dgc} = \bar{D}_{dif} \tag{12}$$

It minimizes the geometric distance of estimated depth between consecutive frames and enforces their stability.

Finally, the overall objective function for training can be formulated as follows:

$$L = \alpha L_p^m + \beta L_s + \gamma L_{ts} + \delta L_{dgc} \tag{13}$$

3.4 Network Architecture

Our model mainly contains the depth estimation network and the camera pose estimation network. For the depth estimation network, we use DispResNet [18], which takes a single RGB image as input and outputs a depth map. For the camera pose network, we use PoseResNet [21], which estimates a 6D camera pose from a concatenated RGB image pair. Following [10], we also use a snippet of three sequential video frames as a training sample, where we set the second image as the reference frame to compute loss with other two frames and then inverse their roles to compute loss again for maximizing the data usage. The data is also augmented with randomly horizontal flipping,cropping and scaling during training.

4 Experiments

In this section, we evaluate our method's performance, and compare it with other representative ones. We train and test on KITTI raw dataset [13] using Eigen [17] splite that is the same with related works [6,7,9]. We firstly introduce the training details, and then present qualitative and quantitative comparison results

4.1 Training Details

We implement our method using Pytorch. For all experiments, we set photometric loss weight α as 0.3 and depth smoothness loss weight β as 0.1, temporal smoothness loss weight γ as 0.1, de-scale geometry consistency loss weight δ as 0.5. During training, we use Adam optimizer with B1 = 0.9, B2 = 0.999, learning rate of 0.0004 and mini-batch size of 4. We train the network in 150 epochs with 1000 randomly sampled batches in one epoch, and validate the model per epoch. We use the data split of Eigen [17]. We also follow Zhou et al.'s [10] pre-processing to remove static frames before training and use the same camera intrinsics for all images. We resize the images to 832×256 during training.

Table 1. Monocular depth estimation results on KITTI 2015. Depth denotes using depth ground truth while training, Pose denotes using binocular/stereo pairs(pose supervision) while training, Mono denotes using monocular video sequences while training.

Method	Supervision	Abs Rel	Sq Rel	RMSE	RMSE log	$\delta < 1.25$	$\delta < 1.25^2$	$\delta < 1.25^3$
Eigen et al. [17]	Depth	0.203	1.548	6.307	0.282	0.702	0.890	0.958
Liu et al. [22]	Depth	0.202	1.614	6.523	0.275	0.678	0.895	0.965
Garg et al. [3]	Pose	0.152	1.226	5.849	0.246	0.784	0.921	0.967
Godard et al. [4]	Pose	0.124	1.388	6.125	0.217	0.841	0.936	0.975
Kuznietsov et al. [23]	Pose+Depth	0.113	0.741	4.621	0.189	0.862	0.960	0.986
Yang et al. [24]	Pose+Depth	0.097	0.734	4.442	0.187	0.888	0.958	0.980
Zhou et al. [10]	Mono	0.208	1.768	6.856	0.283	0.678	0.885	0.957
Yang et al. [25]	Mono	0.182	1.481	6.501	0.267	0.725	0.906	0.963
Mahjourian et al. [7]	Mono	0.163	1.240	6.220	0.250	0.762	0.916	0.968
GeoNet [9]	Mono	0.149	1.060	5.567	0.226	0.796	0.935	0.975
Wang et al. [8]	Mono	0.151	1.257	5.583	0.228	0.810	0.936	0.974
Df-net [20]	Mono	0.150	1.124	5.507	0.223	0.806	0.933	0.973
Bian et al. [21]	Mono	0.137	1.089	5.439	0.217	0.830	0.942	0.975
Casser et al. [26]	Mono	0.141	1.026	5.291	0.215	0.816	0.945	0.979
Ranjan et al. [18]	Mono	0.148	1.149	5.464	0.226	0.815	0.935	0.973
Klingner et al. [27]	Mono	0.117	0.907	4.844	0.196	0.875	0.958	0.980
MonoDepth2 [6]	Mono	0.115	0.903	4.863	0.193	0.877	0.959	0.981
Johnston et al. [28]	Mono	0.106	0.861	4.699	0.185	0.889	0.962	0.982
Guizilini et al. [29]	Mono	0.111	0.785	4.601	0.189	0.878	0.960	0.982
Zhao et al. [30]	Mono	0.113	0.704	4.581	0.184	0.871	0.961	0.984
Ours	Mono	0.115	0.817	4.707	0.190	0.879	0.961	0.982

Table 2. Ablation study on our model on KITTI dataset using Eigen split.

Variant	Abs Rel	Sq Rel	RMSE	RMSE log	$\delta < 1.25$	$\delta < 1.25^2$	$\delta < 1.25^3$
baseline	0.135	1.212	5.136	0.212	0.841	0.945	971
baseline+L_{ts}	0.120	0.976	4.907	0.202	0.856	0.956	0.979
baseline+$Mask$	0.118	1.032	4.875	0.196	0.849	953	0.969
Ours(full)	0.115	0.817	4.707	0.190	0.879	0.961	0.982
baseline w/o pt	0.146	1.508	5.302	0.243	0.828	0.932	0.969
Ours w/o pt	0.127	1.070	4.897	0.210	0.868	0.947	0.977
Ours(resnet18)	0.118	0.871	4.908	0.195	0.865	0.957	0.981
Ours(resnet50)	0.115	0.817	4.707	0.190	0.879	0.961	0.982

4.2   Comparisons and Ablation Study

We evaluate our monocular depth estimation method on Eigen's test set which contains 697 images. As shown in Table 1, our method achieves competitive performance, comparing with the state-of-the-art methods on monocular video sequences. More important, our unsupervised method can estimate high quality stable depths within consecutive frames. For example, the car depth and the landmark depth as shown in Fig. 3. The other methods estimated unstable depth in these regions. To validate the proposed loss terms and other contributions'

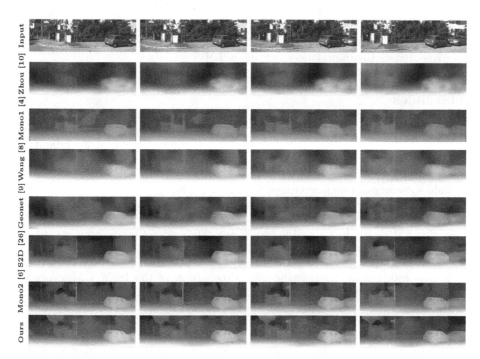

Fig. 3. Comparison of monocular depth estimation on temporally consecutive frames among zhou *et al.* [10], Godard *et al.* [4], Wang *et al.* [8], Geonet [9], Struct2depth [26], Monodepth2 [6] and ours. Our method estimates stable and high quality depth results.

effectiveness, we perform ablation study by changing various components in our method. In Table 2, we first validate the proposed temporal stability loss and the photometry inconsistency check. Considering that different number of network layers influences the model, we also carry out experiments with different layers of network. We follow previous works in initializing our encoders with weights pretrained on ImageNet [31]. So we also compare the results of our proposed model with or without ImageNet pretrained weights while training.

5   Conclusions and Future Work

We have proposed a new unsupervised/self-supervised monocular depth estimation method, which can estimate stable depth results within temporally consecutive frames. Meanwhile, our depth estimation method achieves competitive performance, comparing with the state-of-the-art methods on the KITTI dataset. As the perfect implementation of depth estimation from the video needs both accurate estimation of depth and camera pose, we would focus on improving camera pose estimation and dealing with more complex motions in future.

Acknowledgments. This work is partially supported by the Key Technological Innovation Projects of Hubei Province (2018AAA062), NSFC (No. 61972298), Wuhan University-Huawei GeoInformatices Innovation Lab.

References

1. Yang, L., Yan, Q., Fu, Y., Xiao, C.: Surface reconstruction via fusing sparse-sequence of depth images. IEEE Trans. Vis. Comput. Graph. **24**(2), 1190–1203 (2017)
2. Liao, J., Fu, Y., Yan, Q., Luo, F., Xiao, C.: Adaptive depth estimation for pyramid multi-view stereo. Comput. Graph. **97**, 268–278 (2021)
3. Garg, R., B.G., V.K., Carneiro, G., Reid, I.: Unsupervised CNN for single view depth estimation: geometry to the rescue. In: Leibe, B., Matas, J., Sebe, N., Welling, M. (eds.) ECCV 2016. LNCS, vol. 9912, pp. 740–756. Springer, Cham (2016). https://doi.org/10.1007/978-3-319-46484-8_45
4. Godard, C., Mac Aodha, O., Brostow, G.J.: Unsupervised monocular depth estimation with left-right consistency. In: Proceedings of the IEEE Conference on Computer Vision and Pattern Recognition, pp. 270–279 (2017)
5. Tonioni, A., Tosi, F., Poggi, M., Mattoccia, S., Stefano, L.D.: Real-time self-adaptive deep stereo. In: Proceedings of the IEEE/CVF Conference on Computer Vision and Pattern Recognition, pp. 195–204 (2019)
6. Godard, C., Mac Aodha, O., Firman, M., Brostow, G.J.: Digging into self-supervised monocular depth estimation. In: Proceedings of the IEEE/CVF International Conference on Computer Vision, pp. 3828–3838 (2019)
7. Mahjourian, R., Wicke, M., Angelova, A.: Unsupervised learning of depth and ego-motion from monocular video using 3d geometric constraints. In: Proceedings of the IEEE Conference on Computer Vision and Pattern Recognition, pp. 5667–5675 (2018)
8. Wang, C., Buenaposada, J.M., Zhu, R., Lucey, S.: Learning depth from monocular videos using direct methods. In: Proceedings of the IEEE Conference on Computer Vision and Pattern Recognition, pp. 2022–2030 (2018)
9. Yin, Z., Shi, J.: Geonet: unsupervised learning of dense depth, optical flow and camera pose. In: Proceedings of the IEEE Conference on Computer Vision and Pattern Recognition, pp. 1983–1992 (2018)
10. Zhou, T., Brown, M., Snavely, N., Lowe, D.G.: Unsupervised learning of depth and ego-motion from video. In: Proceedings of the IEEE Conference on Computer Vision and Pattern Recognition, pp. 1851–1858 (2017)
11. Chen, W., Qian, S., Deng, J.: Learning single-image depth from videos using quality assessment networks. In: Proceedings of the IEEE/CVF Conference on Computer Vision and Pattern Recognition, pp. 5604–5613 (2019)
12. Zhou, J., Wang, Y., Qin, K., Zeng, W.: Moving indoor: unsupervised video depth learning in challenging environments. In: Proceedings of the IEEE/CVF International Conference on Computer Vision, pp. 8618–8627 (2019)
13. Geiger, A., Lenz, P., Urtasun, R.: Are we ready for autonomous driving? the kitti vision benchmark suite. In: 2012 IEEE Conference on Computer Vision and Pattern Recognition, pp. 3354–3361. IEEE (2012)

14. Schonberger, J.L., Frahm, J.M.: Structure-from-motion revisited. In: Proceedings of the IEEE Conference on Computer Vision and Pattern Recognition, pp. 4104–4113 (2016)
15. Saxena, A., Sun, M., Ng, A.Y.: Make3d: learning 3d scene structure from a single still image. IEEE Trans. Pattern Anal. Mach. Intell. **31**(5), 824–840 (2008)
16. Karsch, K., Liu, C., Kang, S.B.: Depth transfer: depth extraction from video using non-parametric sampling. IEEE Trans. Pattern Anal. Mach. Intell. **36**(11), 2144–2158 (2014)
17. Eigen, D., Puhrsch, C., Fergus, R.: Depth map prediction from a single image using a multi-scale deep network. In: 28th Annual Conference on Neural Information Processing Systems 2014, NIPS 2014, pp. 2366–2374. Neural information processing systems foundation (2014)
18. Ranjan, A., et al.: Competitive collaboration: Joint unsupervised learning of depth, camera motion, optical flow and motion segmentation. In: Proceedings of the IEEE/CVF Conference on Computer Vision and Pattern Recognition, pp. 12240–12249 (2019)
19. Wang, Z., Bovik, A.C., Sheikh, H.R., Simoncelli, E.P.: Image quality assessment: from error visibility to structural similarity. IEEE Trans. Image Process. **13**(4), 600–612 (2004)
20. Zou, Y., Luo, Z., Huang, J.B.: Df-net: unsupervised joint learning of depth and flow using cross-task consistency. In: Proceedings of the European Conference on Computer Vision (ECCV), pp. 36–53 (2018)
21. Bian, J., et al.: Unsupervised scale-consistent depth and ego-motion learning from monocular video. In: Advances in Neural Information Processing Systems, vol. 32, pp. 35–45 (2019)
22. Liu, F., Shen, C., Lin, G., Reid, I.: Learning depth from single monocular images using deep convolutional neural fields. IEEE Trans. Pattern Anal. Mach. Intell. **38**(10), 2024–2039 (2015)
23. Kuznietsov, Y., Stuckler, J., Leibe, B.: Semi-supervised deep learning for monocular depth map prediction. In: Proceedings of the IEEE Conference on Computer Vision and Pattern Recognition, pp. 6647–6655 (2017)
24. Yang, N., Wang, R., Stuckler, J., Cremers, D.: Deep virtual stereo odometry: leveraging deep depth prediction for monocular direct sparse odometry. In: Proceedings of the European Conference on Computer Vision (ECCV), pp. 817–833 (2018)
25. Yang, Z., Wang, P., Xu, W., Zhao, L., Nevatia, R.: Unsupervised learning of geometry with edge-aware depth-normal consistency. arXiv preprint arXiv:1711.03665 (2017)
26. Casser, V., Pirk, S., Mahjourian, R., Angelova, A.: Depth prediction without the sensors: Leveraging structure for unsupervised learning from monocular videos. In: Proceedings of the AAAI Conference on Artificial Intelligence, vol. 33, no. 01, pp. 8001–8008 (2019)
27. Klingner, M., Termöhlen, J.A., Mikolajczyk, J., Fingscheidt, T.: Self-supervised monocular depth estimation: solving the dynamic object problem by semantic guidance, pp. 582–600 (2020)
28. Johnston, A., Carneiro, G.: Self-supervised monocular trained depth estimation using self-attention and discrete disparity volume. In: Proceedings of the IEEE/CVF Conference on Computer Vision and Pattern Recognition, pp. 4756–4765 (2020)

29. Guizilini, V., Ambrus, R., Pillai, S., Raventos, A., Gaidon, A.: 3d packing for self-supervised monocular depth estimation. In: Proceedings of the IEEE/CVF Conference on Computer Vision and Pattern Recognition, pp. 2485–2494 (2020)
30. Zhao, W., Liu, S., Shu, Y., Liu, Y.J.: Towards better generalization: joint depth-pose learning without posenet. In: Proceedings of the IEEE/CVF Conference on Computer Vision and Pattern Recognition, pp. 9151–9161 (2020)
31. Russakovsky, O., et al.: Imagenet large scale visual recognition challenge. Int. J. Comput. Vis. **115**(3), 211–252 (2015)

Progressive Multi-scale Reconstruction for Guided Depth Map Super-Resolution via Deep Residual Gate Fusion Network

Yang Wen[1], Jihong Wang[2(✉)], Zhen Li[2], Bin Sheng[1], Ping Li[3], Xiaoyu Chi[4], and Lijuan Mao[2(✉)]

[1] Department of Computer Science and Engineering, Shanghai Jiao Tong University, Shanghai, China
{wenyang,shengbin}@sjtu.edu.cn
[2] Shanghai University of Sport, Shanghai, China
{wjh,lizhen,maolijuan}@sus.edu.cn
[3] The Hong Kong Polytechnic University, Kowloon, Hong Kong
p.li@polyu.edu.hk
[4] Qingdao Research Institute of Beihang University, Qingdao, China
terry.chi@goertek.com

Abstract. Depth maps obtained by consumer depth sensors are often accompanied by two challenging problems: low spatial resolution and insufficient quality, which greatly limit the potential applications of depth images. To overcome these shortcomings, some depth map super-resolution (DSR) methods tend to extrapolate a high-resolution depth map from a low-resolution depth map with the additional guidance of the corresponding high-resolution intensity image. However, these methods are still prone to texture copying and boundary discontinuities due to improper guidance. In this paper, we propose a deep residual gate fusion network (DRGFN) for guided depth map super-resolution with progressive multi-scale reconstruction. To alleviate the misalignment between color images and depth maps, DRGFN applies a color-guided gate fusion module to acquire content-adaptive attention for better fusing the color and depth features. To focus on restoring details such as boundaries, DRGFN applies a residual attention module to highlight the different importance of different channels. Furthermore, DRGFN applies a multi-scale fusion reconstruction module to make use of multi-scale information for better image reconstruction. Quantitative and qualitative experiments on several benchmarks fully show that DRGFN obtains the state-of-the-art performance for depth map super-resolution.

Keywords: Depth map super-resolution · Gate fusion network · Color image guidance · Attention mechanism · Multi-scale

1 Introduction

Depth information is necessary for many applications, such as 3D reconstruction. However, the low spatial resolution and insufficient quality problems of

N. Magnenat-Thalmann et al. (Eds.): CGI 2021, LNCS 13002, pp. 67–79, 2021.
https://doi.org/10.1007/978-3-030-89029-2_5

the depth map acquired by low-cost depth cameras are inevitable. To meet application requirements, efficient depth map super-resolution techniques to recover the potential high-resolution (HR) depth maps from their low-resolution (LR) version are particularly urgent. At present, the existing depth map super-resolution methods can be roughly divided into filtering-based methods [1,2], energy minimization-based methods [3,4] and the learning-based methods [5,6]. Even these methods have greatly improved the performance of DSR, there are still some key problems to be solved, such as the discontinuity of the depth boundary and inherent ambiguity in the reconstruction content.

From SRCNN [7], deep network-based image super-resolution methods have become mainstream. However, the improvement of single image super-resolution performance has hit a bottleneck, because it is hard to generate the image details from a single LR image. One breakthrough is to use relevant reference images to provide additional information. Yang et al. [8] propose an adaptive color-guided autoregressive for depth map recovery. Yang et al. [9] has shown that LR image super-resolution can acquire useful information from a reference image. These methods raise the question of how to make full use of the information of the reference image. It is because that improper guidance will cause texture copying and boundary discontinuities. In this paper, a color-guided gate fusion module is proposed. In addition, attention mechanisms including spatial attention and channel attention have been explored in recent deep network based methods [10,11]. Attention mechanisms have shown strong feature expression ability and can effectively improve the performance of related computer vision tasks. In contrast to these mentioned methods, this paper focus on both spatial attention and channel attention as well as color feature attention. Furthermore, multi-scale technology has been applied in recent deep network based image super-resolution methods [12]. These works show that making use of multi-scale information is important for depth map super-resolution based on deep networks. Different from [12] fusing features at different scales to obtain more informative features, this paper proposes to reconstruct high-resolution depth maps from features at different scales by guiding with color features.

Based on the above analysis, this paper proposes a novel color-guided deep residual gate fusion network (DRGFN) with progressive multi-scale reconstruction for DSR. DRGFN applies a color image, which acquires from the same scene of the depth map, to progressively guide the depth map reconstruction process. In contrast to the existing works, DRGFN guides the reconstruction by using a color guided gate fusion module, which not only considers each pixel's importance of the reference color image but also alleviates the misalignment between color images and depth maps. In addition, the attention module of DRGFN focuses on the importance of both depth maps and color images, while the attention module of the existing works mainly focuses on the different pixel's importance of the LR depth map. Furthermore, DRGFN guides the reconstruction at multi-scale and generates the reconstruction at multiple scales.

In conclusion, our contributions are as follows:

– We propose a novel deep residual gate fusion network (DRGFN) for depth map super-resolution. DRGFN makes use of the information of a reference color image, the attention mechanism, and the multi-scale technology.
– We introduce a color guided gate fusion module to fuse the depth features and the reference color features. This module generates content-adaptive attention that makes DRGFN not only consider each pixel's importance of both the LR depth maps and the reference color images but also alleviate the misalignment between color images and depth maps.
– We present to guide the reconstruction at multi-scale and generate the reconstruction at multi-scale simultaneously. Experimental results show DRGFN can achieve state-of-the-art performance.

2   Related Work

Depth Map Super-Resolution: Recently, many depth map super-resolution methods have been proposed and color image guided depth map super-resolution becomes mainstream. In [6], Hui et al. applied an HR color image to guide the super-resolution process of LR depth map by concatenating the color image features and the depth map features at different scales. In [13], Gu et al. introduced task-driven learning to obtain the optimized guidance tailored to specific depth map enhancement tasks. In [14], Ye et al. proposed to learn a binary map of depth edge location from LR depth map and corresponding color image, and then applied the acquired edges to guide the depth filling process. In [15], Wen et al. applied a coarse-to-fine strategy to progressively recover the high-frequency details of the depth map. In [16], Lutio et al. applied a multi-layer perception to do the pixel-to-pixel mapping from the guided images to the depth maps. In [17], Ye et al. proposed a multi-branch aggregation network to progressively recover the depth map.

Attention Based Deep Network: Attention-based deep networks have shown impressive success in many fields. In [18], Wang et al. proposed a residual attention network for image classification, in which the stacked attention modules generate attention-aware features to improve the classification performance. Hu et al. [10] and Dai et al. [11] successfully applied the attention-based deep network for single image super-resolution. In [19], Zhang et al. proposed a gate module to fuse the deblurring features and the super-resolution features for joint image deblurring and super-resolution. Differently, we try to fuse the reference color image features and the depth map features to guide the depth map super-resolution with attention and multi-scale guidance.

Multi-Scale Based Deep Network: Multi-scale technology is widely used in the traditional image restoration and enhancement fields [20]. Recently, many deep network-based methods also show the importance of multi-scale information. In [12], Shi et al. proposed a dilated convolution based inception module to fuse different scale features. In [21], Fu et al. integrated the pyramid modules into the deep network for monocular depth estimation. Zhang et al. [8] and Yang et al. [9] transferred the reference image information to the super-resolution image at multiple scales.

3   Proposed Method

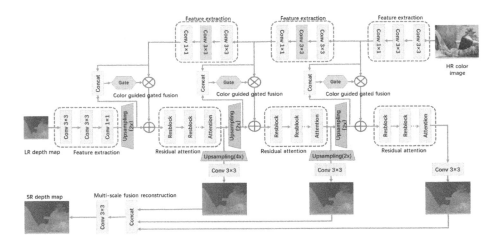

Fig. 1. The framework of our proposed DRGFN. It mainly includes residual attention module, color guided gate fusion module and multi-scale fusion module three components. The color feature is obtained by the feature extraction module from the input HR color image. The depth feature is learned by a series of attention-based residual blocks. After the mutual fusion of the color feature and the depth feature, effective color-guided information for the depth map is adaptively obtained through the gate module. In addition, we use the multi-scale fusion module to effectively optimize the results in a coarse-to-fine manner.

3.1   Overview

The framework of our proposed DRGFN is shown in Fig. 1. It contains a color information extraction branch and a depth map super-resolution branch. The former extracts different scale information from a high-resolution color image for guiding the depth map super-resolution process. The latter contains a feature extraction module, several residual attention modules, a color guided gate fusion module, and a multi-scale fusion reconstruction module. The color guided gate fusion module effectively fuses the color information and the depth information, and the multi-scale fusion reconstruction module is utilized to effectively optimize the results in a coarse-to-fine manner.

3.2   Color Information Extraction Branch

As shown in Fig. 1, the color information extraction branch contains two kinds of feature extraction modules. The first one cascades three convolution layers, in which the kernel sizes of the first to the third layers are 3×3, 3×3, and 1×1, respectively. The stride of the convolution operation is 1 and the padding operation is used, which preserves the resolution of the extracted feature. The second one also cascades three convolutions layers and the kernel sizes of the first to the third layers are also 3×3, 3×3, and 1×1, respectively. However, the stride of the second convolution layer is 2 in the second kind of feature extraction module, which results in extracting different scale information. By cascading multiple feature extraction modules, the color information extraction branch provides multi-scale guidance information for the depth map SR branch.

3.3   Depth Map Super-Resolution Branch

As shown in Fig. 1, the input of the depth map super-resolution branch is a single low-resolution depth map. After a feature extraction module, the depth map super-resolution branch alternately iterates a color guided gate fusion module and a residual attention module to progressively generate the depth map with different scales. Finally, the depth map super-resolution branch uses a multi-scale fusion reconstruction module to obtain the final high-resolution depth map. The feature extraction module is the same as the first feature extraction module of the color information extraction branch, so next, we only introduce the residual attention module, the color guided gate fusion module, and the multi-scale fusion reconstruction module, respectively.

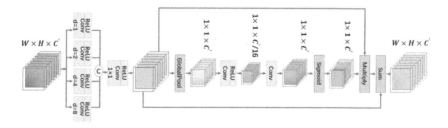

Fig. 2. The architecture of the attention module with ASPP and channel attention.

Residual Attention Module. Inspired by reference [22], we proposed to use a residual attention module for depth image super-resolution based on channel attention. In contrast to the existing methods, we applied the channel attention module (Refer to Fig. 2) in the residual convolution block to highlight the high-frequency details and enhance the feature representation of different filters to alleviate the problem of the loss of high-frequency information in the DSR task.

The channel attention model we use is shown in Fig. 2. Firstly, for the feature T with a tensor size of $(H \times W \times C')$ obtained from the previous residual block, we first apply an ASPP block [23] to further capture the multi-scale features of T and enlarge the receptive field. The dilated rates are set to $1, 2, 4$ and 8. The tensor T' is obtained by 1×1 convolution layer which is operated on the fused feature that concatenates the output from four parallel atrous convolution layers. With the help of ASPP block, the multi-scale context information obtained is helpful to handle the problem of misalignment between HR color guidance image and LR depth image. To further take advantage of the diversity and difference of expression ability among different feature channels, we use the channel attention mechanism [24] to improve the expression ability of the network. In our channel attention block, one global pooling is performed on the tensor output from ASPP block to aggregate the multi-scale features across spatial dimensions and obtain the statistic information of each feature map in T'. Then, after the Conv/ReLU/Conv combination, a sigmoid gating unit is used to learn the nonlinear mapping between different channels. According to the weight value activated by Sigmoid, the weighted multi-scale features are intelligently updated by dot product operation and the original feature T' is added to obtain the final concern feature. This process is formulated as:

$$T' = (Relu(Conv_1(ASPP(T)))) \tag{1}$$

$$T_W = \sigma(Conv_3(Relu(Conv_2(Pool(T'))))) \tag{2}$$

$$T_A = T' + T' \times T_W \tag{3}$$

where $ASPP(T)$ is the ASPP block, T' represents the feature map throughout the ASPP block. The tensor is converted from size $1 \times 1 \times C$ to size $1 \times 1 \times C/16$ after $Conv_2$ and then back to the $1 \times 1 \times C$ after $Conv_3$. $\sigma(\cdot)$ denotes the sigmoid gateway. T_A is a channel attention weighted feature map that will be used as input to the next layer.

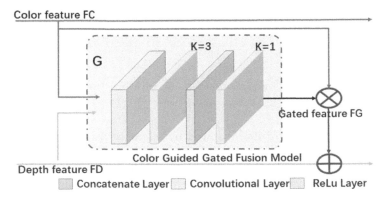

Fig. 3. The architecture of color guided gate fusion module.

In order to enhance the expression ability of the network and capture more high-frequency information that is beneficial to DSR, every two residual blocks are followed by the ASPP-attention block to form the residual attention module.

Color Guided Gate Fusion Module. Although HR color maps can provide similar structural information for depth map super resolution, studies have shown that improper use of color maps can cause texture copying and depth bleeding artifacts due to color and depth discontinuity. Given this, we have introduced a color guided gate module that adaptively selects the appropriate color information for the depth map rather than simply combining the two directly. In this manner, we can fully exploit the correlation between the features from depth image and color image. The proposed color guided gate fusion module is shown in Fig. 3. As shown, the color branch feature F_C and the corresponding depth feature F_D are fused by a network G and then fed into the depth map super-resolution branch. This module can be formulated as:

$$F_G = G\left(F_C, F_D; \theta\right) \otimes F_C + F_D \tag{4}$$

where F_G is the fused output, θ is the network parameter of G, $\otimes$ is the element-wise multiplication. The network G contains a concatenation layer, a convolution layer with kernel 3×3 followed by a ReLu activation layer, and a convolution layer with kernel 1×1.

Multi-scale Fusion Reconstruction Module. To make use of multi-scale information, this module first reconstructs a depth map at each scale, and then fuses the results of all scales to get the final HR result. We use a deconvolution layer with a kernel size of 3×3 to enlarge the feature resolution. After the feature is enlarged to the desired resolution by using a deconvolution layer, a convolution layer with a kernel size of 3×3 is used to generate an HR depth map at each scale. To get the final result, we concatenate the results of all scales and fuse them by using a convolution layer with a kernel size of 3×3. This process can be formulated as:

$$O = Conv\left(Concat\left(O^1, \cdots, O^k, \cdots, O^n\right)\right) \tag{5}$$

where O is the final HR depth map, O^k is the HR depth map generated from the kth scale, n is the scale number, and the kernel size of this convolution layer is 3×3.

3.4 Loss Function

We wanted each super-resolution result to be as close as possible to the true high-resolution depth map, so we constrained the results at each scale. The Mean Square Error (MSE) is the loss function for the reconstructed result at the kth scale, which is formulated as:

$$L_k = \|O^k - D^{HR}\| \tag{6}$$

Since people pay different attention to each scale and tend to focus on the higher scale, especially the result of the last layer, we weighted the fusion of all output layers, specifically set as:

$$L_m = \sum_{k=1}^{K} \frac{k}{N} L_k \tag{7}$$

where $N = K(K + 1)/2$. The whole Loss in our paper is defined as:

$$L = L_m + \|O - D^{HR}\| + \alpha TV(O) \tag{8}$$

where TV is the total variation [25] loss to encourage spatial smoothness in the generated HR depth map. α is set 0.05 in this paper.

4   Experimental Results

4.1   Implementation Details

Dataset and Parameter Setting: During the training process, we select 36 RGB-D images from Middlebury 2001 (6 images), Middlebury 2006 (21 images) and Middlebury 2014 datasets (9 images). For evaluation, we test on Middlebury 2003 datasets (including 4 scenes) [26]. The LR depth images are produced from the selected high-resolution depth images by nearest-neighbor downsampling. Throughout our experiments, the ADAM solver for training with parameters $\beta_1 = 0.9$ and $\beta_2 = 0.999$. The batch-size is set to 2 for all the methods limited by the memory. The initial learning rate is fixed to 0.0001 for the first 20 epochs and then decay to one-tenth every 20 epochs. We implement our method on the NVIDIA 1080Ti GPU with the PyTorch framework.

Baseline Methods: For qualitative and quantitative analysis of the performance of the proposed method, the classical algorithms we compare mainly include: (1) methods based on traditional methods: bicubic interpolation method, Joint Geodesic Filtering (JGF) [2], Cross-based Local Multipoint Filtering (CLMF) [27], Coupled Dictionary Learning with Local Constraints (CDLLC) [28], Joint Super Resolution and Denoising (JSRD) [29], Xie *et al.* [30], Patch Based method (PB) [31], Huang *et al.* [32]. (2) methods based on convolutional neural network: SRCNN [7], MSG-Net [6], Wang *et al.* [33]. ATGV-Net [34], Song [5], GSRPT [16], DEIN [13] and CCFN [15]. All comparison algorithms use the same environment configuration and training data. The experimental results are based on the code provided by the author and the relevant indicators.

4.2   Quantitative Evaluation

In order to quantitatively evaluate our proposed DRGFN, factors 2, 4 and 8 are used to evaluate our results and other state-of-the-art methods in Middlebury 2003 database, respectively. First, we obtain the LR depth image by smoothing and down-sampling the real image, and then use average absolute difference

(MAD) as evaluation index. For MAD, the smaller the better. Table 1 shows the quantitative DSR results on the Middlebury dataset 2003 in MAD with three upsampling factors. MAD in Table 1 focuses on measuring the absolute error between the reconstructed HR and the ground truth map. The results in the tables show that our method is superior to almost all other state-of-the-art methods, including conventional methods and convolutional neural network-based methods.

Table 1. Quantitative DSR results on the Middlebury dataset 2003 (Noiseless Case) in MAD with three upsampling factors.

	Tsukuba			Venus			Teddy			Cones		
	2×	4×	8×	2×	4×	8×	2×	4×	8×	2×	4×	8×
KSVD [35]	2.48	4.30	6.78	0.59	1.22	3.15	2.97	5.17	8.93	3.97	6.45	12.51
SRCNN [7]	2.99	5.52	8.64	0.71	1.30	3.23	3.98	6.92	14.12	4.99	8.64	16.18
CDLLC [28]	2.41	4.15	6.59	0.71	1.18	3.08	2.99	4.72	9.13	3.68	5.79	11.23
Huang *et al.* [32]	3.53	6.20	9.32	0.67	1.45	3.61	3.88	7.37	15.24	4.52	8.44	15.38
PB [31]	1.57	2.52	3.69	0.39	0.66	1.83	4.13	8.03	17.90	4.35	9.73	17.69
JSRD [29]	1.40	2.37	3.52	0.38	0.59	1.69	1.71	3.13	6.23	1.96	3.23	6.53
Xie [30]	1.27	2.36	3.50	0.37	0.54	1.62	1.61	3.11	6.18	1.72	3.09	6.27
ATGV-Net [34]	1.52	2.41	3.59	0.40	0.63	1.76	5.35	5.37	7.62	4.63	5.74	7.36
Song [5]	1.25	2.23	3.49	0.39	0.53	1.60	1.63	3.10	4.52	1.71	3.05	4.37
Wang [33]	3.12	3.24	5.68	0.68	1.21	2.87	3.92	4.27	5.67	4.83	8.72	9.35
MSG-Net [6]	1.22	2.21	3.44	0.35	0.51	1.58	1.59	3.07	3.69	1.68	2.98	3.73
GSRPT [16]	1.53	2.14	3.27	0.34	0.60	1.46	1.62	3.02	3.78	1.66	2.78	3.62
DEIN [13]	1.19	1.98	2.24	0.29	0.42	1.11	1.72	2.55	2.48	1.44	2.17	3.40
CCFN [15]	1.16	2.18	3.42	0.33	0.51	1.56	1.58	2.98	3.58	1.64	2.89	3.70
Our	1.15	1.96	2.21	0.29	0.39	1.23	1.51	2.51	2.45	1.41	2.15	3.37

4.3   Qualitative Evaluation

Figure 4 is the visual comparison of DSR on Middlebury database with upsampling scale 8. In order to facilitate visual comparison, super-resolution error pixels are marked in red and compared with other state-of-the-art super-resolution methods. The red dots represent error points, the fewer the better. It shows that our reconstructed super-resolution depth images yield more attractive results than previous approaches, especially at the boundary of the depth maps.

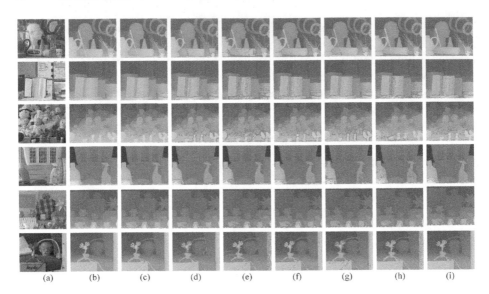

(a)   (b)   (c)   (d)   (e)   (f)   (g)   (h)   (i)

Fig. 4. Visual comparison of DSR on Middlebury database (upsampling scale 8), the reconstructed error pixel is marked with red. (a) Color image. (b) Ground truth. (c) Our results. (d) CLMF [27]. (e) JBF [1]. (f) JGF [2]. (g) ATGV-Net [34]. (h) Song [5]. (i) CCFN [15]. (Color figure online)

5   Conclusion

This paper has proposed an effective deep residual gate fusion network (DRGFN) network for depth map super-resolution. DRGFN makes use of the information of a reference color image, the attention mechanism, and the multi-scale technology. The introduced color guided gate fusion module can effectively generate content-adaptive attention, which makes DRGFN consider each pixel's importance of both the LR depth maps and the reference color images and alleviate the misalignment problem between color images and depth maps. The multi-scale guidance and multi-scale generation fusion further enhance DRGFN's performance. The residual attention module with ASPP and channel attention can make full use of context information to strengthen the feature expression ability of the network, so as to obtain effective high-frequency information and promote the DSR performance. Experimental results have shown the proposed DRGFN achieves state-of-the-art performance. Our future work will explore the application of the proposed color guided gate fusion module to other image restoration and enhancement tasks.

Acknowledgement. This work was supported in part by the National Natural Science Foundation of China under Grants 62077037 and 61872241, in part by Shanghai Municipal Science and Technology Major Project under Grant 2021SHZDZX0102, in part by the Science and Technology Commission of Shanghai Municipality under Grants 18410750700 and 17411952600, in part by Shanghai Lin-Gang Area Smart

Manufacturing Special Project under Grant ZN2018020202-3, and in part by Project of Shanghai Municipal Health Commission(2018ZHYL0230).

References

1. Yang, Q., Yang, R., Davis, J., Nistér, D.: Spatial-depth super resolution for range images. In: IEEE Conference on Computer Vision and Pattern Recognition, pp. 1–8 (2007)
2. Liu, M.-Y., Tuzel, O., Taguchi, Y.: Joint geodesic upsampling of depth images. In: IEEE Conference on Computer Vision and Pattern Recognition, pp. 169–176 (2013)
3. Ferstl, D., Reinbacher, C., Ranftl, R., Rüther, M., Bischof, H.: Image guided depth upsampling using anisotropic total generalized variation. In: IEEE International Conference on Computer Vision, pp. 993–1000 (2013)
4. Jiang, Z., Hou, Y., Yue, H., Yang, J., Hou, C.: Depth super-resolution from rgb-d pairs with transform and spatial domain regularization. IEEE Trans. Image Process. **27**(5), 2587–2602 (2018)
5. Song, X., Dai, Y., Qin, X.: Deep depth super-resolution: learning depth super-resolution using deep convolutional neural network. In: Lai, S.-H., Lepetit, V., Nishino, K., Sato, Y. (eds.) ACCV 2016. LNCS, vol. 10114, pp. 360–376. Springer, Cham (2017). https://doi.org/10.1007/978-3-319-54190-7_22
6. Hui, T.-W., Loy, C.C., Tang, X.: Depth map super-resolution by deep multi-scale guidance. In: Leibe, B., Matas, J., Sebe, N., Welling, M. (eds.) ECCV 2016. LNCS, vol. 9907, pp. 353–369. Springer, Cham (2016). https://doi.org/10.1007/978-3-319-46487-9_22
7. Dong, C., Loy, C.C., He, K., Tang, X.: Image super-resolution using deep convolutional networks. IEEE Trans. Pattern Anal. Mach. Intell. **38**(2), 295–307 (2015)
8. Zhang, Z., Wang, Z., Lin, Z., Qi, H.: Image super-resolution by neural texture transfer. In: Proceedings of the IEEE Conference on Computer Vision and Pattern Recognition, pp. 7982–7991 (2019)
9. Yang, F., Yang, H., Fu, J., Lu, H., Guo, B.: Learning texture transformer network for image super-resolution. In: Proceedings of the IEEE/CVF Conference on Computer Vision and Pattern Recognition, pp. 5791–5800 (2020)
10. Hu, Y., Li, J., Huang, Y., Gao, X.: Channel-wise and spatial feature modulation network for single image super-resolution. IEEE Trans. Circ. Syst. Video Technol. **30**, 3911–3927 (2019)
11. Dai, T., Cai, J., Zhang, Y., Xia, S.-T., Zhang, L.: Second-order attention network for single image super-resolution. In: Proceedings of the IEEE Conference on Computer Vision and Pattern Recognition, pp. 11 065–11 074 (2019)
12. Shi, W., Jiang, F., Zhao, D.: Single image super-resolution with dilated convolution based multi-scale information learning inception module. In: 2017 IEEE International Conference on Image Processing (ICIP), pp. 977–981. IEEE (2017)
13. Gu, S., Zuo, W., Guo, S., Chen, Y., Chen, C., Zhang, L.: Learning dynamic guidance for depth image enhancement. In: IEEE Conference on Computer Vision and Pattern Recognition (CVPR) 2017, pp. 712–721 (2017)
14. Ye, X., Duan, X., Li, H.: Depth super-resolution with deep edge-inference network and edge-guided depth filling. In: 2018 IEEE International Conference on Acoustics, Speech and Signal Processing (ICASSP), pp. 1398–1402. IEEE (2018)

15. Wen, Y., Sheng, B., Li, P., Lin, W., Feng, D.D.: Deep color guided coarse-to-fine convolutional network cascade for depth image super-resolution. IEEE Trans. Image Process. **28**(2), 994–1006 (2019)
16. Lutio, R.D., D'aronco, S., Wegner, J.D., Schindler, K.: Guided super-resolution as pixel-to-pixel transformation. In: Proceedings of the IEEE International Conference on Computer Vision, pp. 8829–8837 (2019)
17. Ye, X., Sun, B., Wang, Z., Yang, J., Xu, R., Li, H., Li, B.: PMBANet: progressive multi-branch aggregation network for scene depth super-resolution. IEEE Trans. Image Process. **29**, 7427–7442 (2020)
18. Wang, F., et al.: Residual attention network for image classification. In: Proceedings of the IEEE Conference on Computer Vision and Pattern Recognition, pp. 3156–3164 (2017)
19. Zhang, X., Dong, H., Hu, Z., Lai, W.-S., Wang, F., Yang, M.-H.: Gated fusion network for joint image deblurring and super-resolution. In: BMVC (2018)
20. Glasner, D., Bagon, S., Irani, M.: Super-resolution from a single image. In: 2009 IEEE 12th International Conference on Computer Vision, pp. 349–356. IEEE (2009)
21. Fu, H., Gong, M., Wang, C., Batmanghelich, K., Tao, D.: Deep ordinal regression network for monocular depth estimation. In: Proceedings of the IEEE Conference on Computer Vision and Pattern Recognition, pp. 2002–2011 (2018)
22. Guo, J., Ma, S., Guo, S.: MAANet: multi-view aware attention networks for image super-resolution. CoRR, vol. abs/1904.06252 (2019)
23. Chen, L.-C., Papandreou, G., Kokkinos, I., Murphy, K., Yuille, A.L.: Deeplab: semantic image segmentation with deep convolutional nets, atrous convolution, and fully connected crfs. IEEE Trans. Pattern Anal. Mach. Intell. **40**(4), 834–848 (2017)
24. Zhang, Y., Li, K., Li, K., Wang, L., Zhong, B., Fu, Y.: Image super-resolution using very deep residual channel attention networks. CoRR, vol. abs/1807.02758 (2018)
25. Johnson, J., Alahi, A., Fei-Fei, L.: Perceptual losses for real-time style transfer and super-resolution. In: Leibe, B., Matas, J., Sebe, N., Welling, M. (eds.) ECCV 2016. LNCS, vol. 9906, pp. 694–711. Springer, Cham (2016). https://doi.org/10.1007/978-3-319-46475-6_43
26. Scharstein, D., Szeliski, R.: High-accuracy stereo depth maps using structured light. In: IEEE Conference on Computer Vision and Pattern Recognition, vol. 1, pp. 195–202 (2003)
27. Lu, J., Shi, K., Min, D., Lin, L., Do, M.N.: Cross-based local multipoint filtering. In: IEEE Conference on Computer Vision and Pattern Recognition, pp. 430–437 (2012)
28. Xie, J., Chou, C.-C., Feris, R., Sun, M.-T.: Single depth image super resolution and denoising via coupled dictionary learning with local constraints and shock filtering. In: IEEE International Conference on Multimedia and Expo, pp. 1–6 (2014)
29. Xie, J., Feris, R.S., Yu, S.-S., Sun, M.-T.: Joint super resolution and denoising from a single depth image. IEEE Trans. Multimedia **17**(9), 1525–1537 (2015)
30. Xie, J., Feris, R.S., Sun, M.-T.: Edge-guided single depth image super resolution. IEEE Trans. Image Process. **25**(1), 428–438 (2016)
31. Mac Aodha, O., Campbell, N.D.F., Nair, A., Brostow, G.J.: Patch based synthesis for single depth image super-resolution. In: Fitzgibbon, A., Lazebnik, S., Perona, P., Sato, Y., Schmid, C. (eds.) ECCV 2012. LNCS, vol. 7574, pp. 71–84. Springer, Heidelberg (2012). https://doi.org/10.1007/978-3-642-33712-3_6

32. Huang, J.-B., Singh, A., Ahuja, N.: Single image super-resolution from transformed self-exemplars. In: IEEE Conference on Computer Vision and Pattern Recognition, pp. 5197–5206 (2015)
33. Wang, Z., Liu, D., Yang, J., Han, W., Huang, T.: Deep networks for image super-resolution with sparse prior. In: IEEE International Conference on Computer Vision, pp. 370–378 (2015)
34. Riegler, G., Rüther, M., Bischof, H.: ATGV-Net: accurate depth super-resolution. In: Leibe, B., Matas, J., Sebe, N., Welling, M. (eds.) ECCV 2016. LNCS, vol. 9907, pp. 268–284. Springer, Cham (2016). https://doi.org/10.1007/978-3-319-46487-9_17
35. Zeyde, R., Elad, M., Protter, M.: On single image scale-up using sparse-representations. In: International Conference on Curves and Surfaces, pp. 711–730 (2012)

SE_EDNet: A Robust Manipulated Faces Detection Algorithm

Chaoyang Peng, Lihong Yao, Tanfeng Sun$^{(\boxtimes)}$, Xinghao Jiang, and Zhongjie Mi

School of Electronic Information and Electrical Engineering,
Shanghai Jiao Tong University, Shanghai, China
{cypeng,yaolh,tfsun,xhjiang,jimmymi_95}@sjtu.edu.cn

Abstract. Face manipulation techniques have raised concern over potential threats, which demand effective images forensic methods. Various approaches have been proposed, but when detecting higher-quality manipulated faces, the performance of previous method is not good enough. To prevent the abuse of these techniques and improve the detection ability, this paper proposes a new algorithm named Squeeze-Excitation Euclidean Distance Network (SE_EDNet) to detect manipulated faces, which is suitable for Deepfakes and GANs detection. SE_EDNet use Euclidean distance to describe similaity of vectors, which gives higher weights to important areas than traditional self-attention mechanism. Further, we take frequency into account and extract residuals information, which are obtained by a second-order filter. Then residuals are combined with original images as the input features for the network. Comparison experiment shows SE_EDNet performs better than existing algorithms. Extensive robustness experiments on Celeb-DF and DFFD demonstrate that proposed algorithm is robust against attacking on AUC scores and Recalls.

Keywords: Manipulated faces · Image forensics · Image residuals · SE_EDNet

1 Introduction

With the progress of face manipulation techniques, AI-synthesized faces are spreading on the Internet in the form of pictures or videos. Based on forged areas, manipulated images can be classified into two categories. The first method only tampers with some specific area, such as expressions, attributes or identities. The second one can generate entire synthesized face, and recent works mainly concentrate on various GANs [1,2]. Original face and four types of manipulated faces are shown in Fig. 1.

To counter image manipulation, numerous detection algorithms have been proposed. For Deepfakes detection, early methods use visual artifacts to detect manipulated images [3,4]. For example, Li et al. [4] use CNN to detect the boundary of source and target face. For GANs detection, because images generated by

© Springer Nature Switzerland AG 2021
N. Magnenat-Thalmann et al. (Eds.): CGI 2021, LNCS 13002, pp. 80–88, 2021.
https://doi.org/10.1007/978-3-030-89029-2_6

GANs are smoother than shot by camera, some researchers use texture as feature to deal with this task. Nataraj et al. [5] calculate the co-occurrence matrices of original channel and Li et al. [6] do similar work in first-order differential residual domain. Recent detection methods are based on deep models, especially CNN [7–9]. Afchar et al. [7] use inception module to detect manipulation.

| (a) Original | (b) Expression replace | (c) Attribute replace | (d) Identity replace | (e) Generate entire face |

Fig. 1. Original face and four types of manipulated faces

From a larger perspective, manipulated faces detection can be regarded as a classification task to discern fake and real images. But Second-generation manipulated faces have high visual quality, which is difficult to distinguish by visual artifacts. CNN is the most popular method to deal with classification tasks, but it performs poorly in capturing global information and directly repeating convolution layers is computationally inefficient [10].

To capture global information, we propose an algorithm named SE_EDNet that gives the region of interest (ROI) higher weights than previous self-attention [10] mechanism. AUC of SE_EDNet achieves to 99.71% on Celeb-DF [11]. Besides, a series of experiments are conducted, indicating that SE_EDNet is robust to attacks, especially under noise conditions.

2   Detection Algorithms

2.1   Framework

The framework of the proposed method is shown in Fig. 2. (1) Data Preprocessing: Frames are sampled from videos and faces are extracted. (2) Input Fusion: Image residuals in YCrCb color spaces are obtained by a second-order residuals filter, then image residuals are merged into original RGB channel to get a six-channel input. (3) Classification Network: SENet is selected as the backbone, then Att module and ED module are used to replace the last block of each layer in SENet. Through the classification network, whether a face has been manipulated can be detected.

2.2   Network Structure

SE_AttNet and SE_EDNet are proposed. The structures of them are as below. Different from previous works, correlations of positions and channels are both considered in this paper.

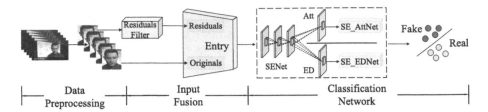

Fig. 2. Overall framework of proposed method

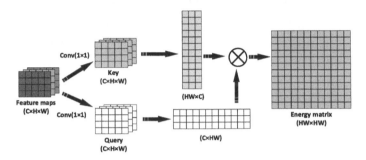

Fig. 3. Calculation process of matrix Energy. ⊗ denotes matrix multiplication.

SE_AttNet. Attention mechanism has been widely used under various scenes [10,12] because capturing long-range dependency is significant to recognition. In attention mechanism, transposition of Key (K) is multiplied by Query (Q), then the Energy matrix (E) contains the correlation of each pair of pixels. The calculation process of E in attention is shown in Fig. 3. In essence, matrix multiplication computes the inner product of some vectors. The dimension of E is HW×HW, and each element represents the correlation of two positions. To compare with proposed algorithm, the reason why inner product can reflect similarity is explained below.

If there is a strong correlation between two positions, their corresponding vectors will be similar, so the inner product will be large. For $\vec{a}$ and $\vec{b}$, the inner product can be represented by Eq. 1.

$$\vec{a} \bullet \vec{b} = \left\| \vec{a} \right\| \left\| \vec{b} \right\| \cos \theta \tag{1}$$

As is shown in Fig. 4(a), projection of $\vec{b}$ on $\vec{a}$ multiplied by the length of $\vec{a}$ equals inner product and the angle between $\vec{a}$ and $\vec{b}$ is θ. When θ is an acute angle, the inner product will be positive.

In essence, SENet [13] does attention operations on the channel dimension. Theoretically, considering the weights of both positions and channels will be helpful. So SE_AttNet is obtained by replacing the last SE block of every layers with attention (Att) module.

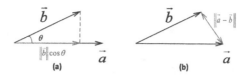

Fig. 4. (a): Inner product; (b): Euclidean distance

SE_EDNet. Apart from inner product, Euclidean distance can also be used to calculate similarity. Contrary to inner product, the more similar two vectors are, the smaller Euclidean distance between them is. That is, the similarity of vectors and Euclidean distance show negative correlation. So when Euclidean distance is selected to describe similarity, minus will be introduced. Therefore, ($\lambda - Euclidean\ distance$) is used to represent the similarity, where λ is the threshold.

To calculate attention map, a matrix ($M_{i,j}$) is obtained by Eq. 2, whose range is 0–1. The negative value of E will be mapped to a small value in M, which means a small weight.

$$M_{i,j} = softmax(E_{i,j}) \qquad (0 \leq i, j \leq HW) \tag{2}$$

Different from inner product, distance shown in Fig. 4(b) is calculated, then λ is adjusted to make ($\lambda - \left\|\overrightarrow{a} - \overrightarrow{b}\right\|$) negative when θ is not small enough. This operation means more elements in M will be close to 0. Therefore, proposed algorithm can neglect unimportant areas and give more weights to positions with higher correlation. The new Energy matrix (E) is defined as:

$$E_{i,j} = \lambda - \sqrt{\sum_{k=1}^{C} d_k^2} \qquad (0 \leq i, j \leq HW) \tag{3}$$

$$d_k = f(K)_{i,k} - f(Q)_{j,k} \qquad (0 \leq i, j \leq HW) \tag{4}$$

In fact, as softmax is translation invariant, λ can be removed. But for a more generic expression, λ is retained in this paper, because there are other activation functions can be selected. Function f transforms the dimension of K and Q from C×H×W to HW×C. C denotes the number of feature maps and i, j and k represent indices of matrix.

The above process of calculating similarity is coined as ED module. Similar to SE_AttNet, SE_EDNet is obtained by replacing several blocks of SENet with ED module.

2.3   Image Residuals in YCrCb Color Space

Manipulated images are usually generated in RGB space, so they pay less attention to the information in other color spaces. By computing correlations between

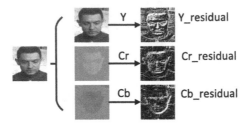

Fig. 5. Image residuals in YCrCb Color Space

adjacent pixels in some color spaces, Li et al. [6] found that chrominance components are more discernible than other channels between real and GANs images. Furthermore, compared with visible spatial inconsistencies, the divergence is larger in the residual domain. Therefore, a second-order differential [14] filter is applied to obtain image residuals, namely,

$$R_{j,k}^c = I_{j,k+1}^c + I_{j+1,k}^c - 2I_{j,k}^c \tag{5}$$

I represents original image, R represents image residuals, and c is the channel index that belongs to {Y, Cr, Cb}. Because manipulated images are generally perform poorly in detail, the high-frequency components of images are good features to detect them. Image residuals achieve this goal, which can extract high-frequency information of images. Image residuals in YCrCb Color Space are shown in Fig. 5. On the other hand, to make use of low-frequency information as well, image residuals are combined with original RGB channel to get a six-channel input for the networks (input fusion in Fig. 2).

3   Experiment Analysis

3.1   Setup

Network. In the experiments, SE_ResNet50 is used as the backbone and ImageNet-pretrained model is loaded. Then the last block of each layer is replaced by Att module and ED module. The learning rate is set to 5e−5 of Adam optimizer. After 50 epochs, the best model is selected as the final result based on validation loss.

Dataset. The proposed method is evaluated on two challenging datasets. The first one is Celeb-DF [11], in which images are manipulated by DeepFakes. The other dataset contains various GANs images from DFFD [15].

Celeb-DF: It is the second-generation Deepfakes dataset, containing 5639 high-quality Deepfakes videos, 590 real videos and 300 YouTube videos. Due to data imbalance, different frame rates are set for fake and real videos. 60 and 8 are set for fake and real videos respectively. As a result, 41366 positive frames

Table 1. AUC Scores Comparison (* denotes the method trained on other datasets.)

Method	AUC Score (%)
Multi-task* [16]	54.30
HeadPose* [17]	54.60
Meso-4* [7]	54.80
FWA* [4]	56.90
Capsule* [8]	57.50
DSP-FWA* [18]	64.60
RCN [19]	74.87
Triplet [9]	99.20
SENet (baseline)	99.53
SE_EDNet	99.71
SE_AttNet	**99.77**

and 40992 negative frames are obtained as train set. To extract faces, MTCNN is used as the detector, in which margin is 50 and size is 224×224.

DFFD: Because Celeb-DF does not contain GANs images, part of DFFD is used as the second dataset. StyleGAN_CelebA, StyleGAN_FFHQ, PGGAN_V1, PGGAN_V2, StarGAN are used as fake images and FFHQ, CelebA are used as real images in the experiments.

3.2 Comparison Experiment

The AUC scores of proposed method are compared with other methods' mentioned in Celeb-DF dataset that made a benchmark. However, the above methods are trained on other datasets but tested on Celeb-DF, which is unfair. Recently, Triplet [9] is proposed, which is trained and tested on Celeb-DF. The experimental results are listed in Table 1. In the experiments, six-channel input is sent to SENet, SE_AttNet and SE_EDNet respectively.

Table 1 shows that methods trained and tested on different dataset perform worse. A reasonable explanation is the weak generalization ability of these models. For the sake of fairness, our results are compared with recent works that have the same datasets. RCN [19] uses CNN and LSTM to capture image and temporal information, but it does not perform well. Triplet [9] uses a triplet network architecture to detect Deepfakes, which improves the AUC greatly. Compared with these methods, the AUC of proposed algorithm performs better. When using six-channel as input, AUC score can even achieve 99.53% on pure SENet, which outperforms Triplet [9]. After replacing the last block of SENet with self-attention mechanism, SE_EDNet gets 99.71% and SE_AttNet gets 99.77%, which further improve the AUC performance.

Experimental results indicate proposed algorithm can obtain better results due to combining attention mechanism and Squeeze-Excitation module.

Table 2. Attack operation

Operations	Parameters
Original	Original images without any operation
MF3	Median filter, window size $= 3 \times 3$
MF5	Median filter, window size $= 5 \times 5$
JPEG95	Jpeg compression, quality factor $= 95$
JPEG90	Jpeg compression, quality factor $= 90$
JPEG85	Jpeg compression, quality factor $= 85$
Noise1	Gaussian noise, $\mu = 0$, $\sigma^2 = 10$
Noise2	Gaussian noise, $\mu = 0$, $\sigma^2 = 50$
Noise3	Gaussian noise, $\mu = 0$, $\sigma^2 = 100$

Table 3. Performance against attacking on Celeb-DF (* denotes baseline)

Process	AUC (%)				Recall			
	Triplet [9]	SENet*	SE_AttNet	SE_EDNet	Triplet [9]	SENet*	SE_AttNet	SE_EDNet
Original	99.2	99.53	**99.77**	99.71	0.9307	0.9488	0.9590	**0.9703**
MF3	99.13	99.41	**99.65**	99.60	0.9214	0.9597	0.9691	**0.9770**
MF5	98.37	99.42	**99.62**	99.59	0.9123	0.9586	0.9708	**0.9768**
JPEG95	99.10	99.37	**99.65**	99.61	0.9204	0.9651	0.9691	**0.9814**
JPEG90	98.83	99.35	**99.62**	99.58	0.9176	0.9660	0.9695	**0.9816**
JPEG85	98.26	99.31	**99.59**	99.29	0.9078	0.9653	**0.9692**	0.9434
Noise1	99.01	99.23	99.57	**99.64**	0.9135	0.9427	0.9536	**0.9672**
Noise2	98.03	98.66	99.08	**99.23**	0.8657	0.8749	0.9118	**0.9183**
Noise3	96.53	97.90	98.43	**98.70**	0.8012	0.8220	0.8867	**0.9030**

3.3   Robustness Performance Analysis

To prove SE_EDNet shows stronger robustness, some common image processing operations are used to post-process the test set, such as JPEG compression,
median filters and Gaussian noise. Original means no postprocessing of the test
set. MF3 and MF5 use median filters with window size of 3 and 5 respectively.
JPEG85 $\sim$ JPEG95 indicate JPEG compression using different quality factor.
Noise1 $\sim$ Noise3 represent Gaussian noise. μ is the mean of the normal distribution, and σ^2 is variance. The details are listed in Table 2.

Table 3 shows AUC scores and Recalls of Celeb-DF. For AUC scores,
SE_AttNet and SE_EDNet perform better than SENet and Triplet under original experimental condition. When adding some disturbances, SE_AttNet and
SE_EDNet still perform better, which means combining attention mechanism
with SENet is helpful. Furthermore, compared with SE_EDNet, AUC Scores
of other methods drop rapidly under noise conditions, which means they are
more susceptible to noise attack. Compared with previous methods, results of
SE_EDNet are above 99.2% except for Noise3, because the noise intensity is too
high. For Recalls, SE_EDNet performs best under almost all conditions except

Table 4. Performance against attacking on DFFD (* denotes baseline)

Process	AUC (%)				Recall			
	Triplet [9]	SENet*	SE_AttNet	SE_EDNet	Triplet [9]	SENet*	SE_AttNet	SE_EDNet
Original	98.23	99.47	**99.71**	99.69	0.9415	0.9565	0.9860	**0.9990**
MF3	98.09	**98.89**	98.08	98.34	0.9357	0.9705	0.9550	**0.9945**
MF5	97.47	98.09	98.11	**98.23**	0.9315	0.9700	0.9560	**0.9945**
JPEG95	98.17	98.96	**99.49**	99.07	0.8705	0.8970	**0.9630**	0.9500
JPEG90	97.45	98.76	**99.24**	99.20	0.8669	0.8890	0.9460	**0.9620**
JPEG85	96.86	98.65	98.46	**99.07**	0.8285	0.8690	**0.9700**	0.9500
Noise1	96.87	98.38	99.07	**99.14**	0.9004	0.9235	0.9530	**0.9905**
Noise2	95.23	96.49	97.19	**97.49**	0.8365	0.8670	0.8900	**0.9500**
Noise3	93.02	95.47	95.93	**96.11**	0.7965	0.8290	0.8751	**0.9030**

for JPEG85. Experimental results show that our algorithm is more robust than others under the conditions in Table 2.

To prove proposed method is not only effective in Deepfakes, but also can detect GANs, similar experiments are conducted on DFFD. Table 4 shows that SE_EDNet performs better than others on average. In particular, SE_EDNet outperforms the other three methods when under noise conditions.

A possible reason why SE_EDNet performs not well on JPEG is that the 8×8 block is infered from the previous one, which enhances the relevance of two adjacent blocks. Thus, difference between important and unimportant areas is reduced, that is to say, the function of ED module is weakened.

4   Conclusion

In this paper, a manipulated faces detection algorithm is proposed, which outperforms existing methods and is more robust under noise conditions. Because SE_EDNet can filter out more interferences from useless information, it gives more weights on decisive positions than traditional attention mechanism. In the future, we will do some experiments across different datasets and improve generalizability.

Acknowledgement. The work is suppoted by the BAIDU supports Ministry of Education's Education Cooperation Program(No. 2012115PCK00690).

References

1. Cao, J., Hu, Y., Yu, B., He, R., Sun, Z.: 3d aided duet gans for multi-view face image synthesis. IEEE Trans. Inf. Forensics Secur. **14**, 2028–2042 (2019)
2. Choi, Y., Uh, Y., Yoo, J., Ha, J.W.: Stargan v2: diverse image synthesis for multiple domains. In: Proceedings of the IEEE/CVF Conference on Computer Vision and Pattern Recognition, pp. 8188–8197 (2020)

3. Fernandes, S., et al.: Predicting heart rate variations of deepfake videos using neural ode. In: 2019 IEEE/CVF International Conference on Computer Vision Workshop (ICCVW), pp. 1721–1729 (2019)

4. Li, Y., Lyu, S.: Exposing deepfake videos by detecting face warping artifacts. In: Proceedings of the IEEE Conference on Computer Vision and Pattern Recognition Workshops, pp. 46–52 (2019)

5. Nataraj, L., Mohammed, T.M., Chandrasekaran, S., Flenner, A., Bappy, J.H., Roy-Chowdhury, A.K., Manjunath, B.S.: Detecting gan generated fake images using co-occurrence matrices. Electron. Imaging **5**, 1–7 (2019)

6. Li, H., Li, B., Tan, S., Huang, J.: Identification of deep network generated images using disparities in color components. Signal Process. **174**, 107616 (2020)

7. Afchar, D., Nozick, V., Yamagishi, J., Echizen, I.: Mesonet: a compact facial video forgery detection network. In: 2018 IEEE International Workshop on Information Forensics and Security (WIFS), pp. 1–7 (2018)

8. Nguyen, H., Yamagishi, J., Echizen, I.: Capsule-forensics: Using capsule networks to detect forged images and videos. In: 2019 IEEE International Conference on Acoustics, Speech and Signal Processing (ICASSP), pp. 2307–2311 (2019)

9. Kumar, A., Bhavsar, A., Verma, R.: Detecting deepfakes with metric learning. In: 2020 8th International Workshop on Biometrics and Forensics (IWBF), pp. 1–6 (2020)

10. Wang, X., Girshick, R., Gupta, A., He, K.: Non-local neural networks. In: Proceedings of the IEEE Conference on Computer Vision and Pattern Recognition, pp. 7794–7803 (2018)

11. Li, Y., Yang, X., Sun, P., Qi, H., Lyu, S.: Celeb-df: a large-scale challenging dataset for deepfake forensics. In: Proceedings of the IEEE/CVF Conference on Computer Vision and Pattern Recognition, pp. 3207–3216 (2020)

12. Zhang, H., et al.: Context encoding for semantic segmentation. In: Proceedings of the IEEE Conference on Computer Vision and Pattern Recognition, pp. 7151–7160 (2018)

13. Hu, J., Shen, L., Sun, G.: Squeeze-and-excitation networks. In: Proceedings of the IEEE Conference on Computer Vision and Pattern Recognition, pp. 7132–7141 (2018)

14. Fridrich, J., Kodovsky, J.: Rich models for steganalysis of digital images. IEEE Trans. Inf. Forensics Secur. **7**, 868–882 (2012)

15. Dang, H., Liu, F., Stehouwer, J., Liu, X., Jain, A.K.: On the detection of digital face manipulation. In: Proceedings of the IEEE/CVF Conference on Computer Vision and Pattern Recognition, pp. 5781–5790 (2020)

16. Nguyen, H.H., Fang, F., Yamagishi, J., Echizen, I.: Multi-task learning for detecting and segmenting manipulated facial images and videos. In: IEEE International Conference on Biometrics: Theory, Applications and Systems (BTAS), pp. 1–8 (2019)

17. Yang, X., Li, Y., Lyu, S.: Exposing deep fakes using inconsistent head poses. In: ICASSP 2019–2019 IEEE International Conference on Acoustics, Speech and Signal Processing (ICASSP), pp. 8261–8265 (2019)

18. Dsp-fwa. https://github.com/yuezunli/DSP-FWA. Accessed 7 Oct 2020

19. Güera, D., Delp, E.J.: Deepfake video detection using recurrent neural networks. In: 2018 15th IEEE International Conference on Advanced Video and Signal Based Surveillance (AVSS), pp. 1–6 (2018)

PointCNN-Based Individual Tree Detection Using LiDAR Point Clouds

Wenyuan Ying, Tianyang Dong[✉], Zhanfeng Ding, and Xinpeng Zhang

Zhejiang University of Technology, Hangzhou, China
dty@zjut.edu.cn

Abstract. Due to the rapid development of deep learning technology in recent years, many scholars have applied deep learning technology to the field of remote sensing imagery. But few have directly applied LiDAR point clouds to 3D neural networks for tree detection. And the existing methods usually have better detection results in a specific single scene, but in some complex scenes, such as containing diverse types of trees, urban forests and high forest density, the detection results are not satisfactory. Therefore, this paper presents a PointCNN-based method of 3D tree detection using LiDAR point clouds, which aims to improve the detection accuracy of trees in complex scenes and versatility. This method first builds a canopy height model (CHM) using raw LiDAR point clouds and obtains rough seed points on CHM. Then it extracts the detection samples consisting of single tree's point cloud data based on the rough seed points. Next, the 3D-CNN classifier based on PointCNN is adopted to classify detection samples, and the classification results are used for filtering seed points. Finally, our method performs the tree stagger analysis on those close seed points. This study selected twelve experimental plots from study areas in Bend, Central Oregon, USA. Based on the results of our experiments, the highest matching score and average score reached 91.0 and 88.3. Experimental results show that our method can effectively extract tree information in complex scenes.

Keywords: LiDAR · Single tree detection · CHM · PointCNN · Tree stagger

1 Introduction

Forest is important renewable resource on earth and the material basis for the survival and development of forestry. Forestry involves the management of natural resources in forests and urban areas, which include monitor, forecast and analyze tree conditions [1]. And using remote sensing to collect forest resource information has become an effective and reliable alternative to traditional field sampling methods [2]. With the rapid increase of sensor resolution and computing power, as well as the reduction in acquisition cost, automated single tree extraction is becoming increasingly feasible. In particular, the application of LiDAR point clouds in forestry has brought new ideas to forestry investigation [3]. At present, LiDAR point clouds have become an important means for reflecting 3D forest structures and are widely used for tree height calculation [4], tree volume extraction and biomass estimation [5–7].

© Springer Nature Switzerland AG 2021
N. Magnenat-Thalmann et al. (Eds.): CGI 2021, LNCS 13002, pp. 89–100, 2021.
https://doi.org/10.1007/978-3-030-89029-2_7

Currently, researchers have proposed many different methods for extracting tree information from point clouds. These methods are mainly divided into three categories: the raster-based method, point cloud-based method and methods combining raster and point method [8].

The Raster-based Method. The raster-based method converts the original point cloud data into a rasterized image, thereby transforming the processing of the point cloud data into the processing of the image. Most traditional tree detection algorithms, such as local maximum, region growing, and watershed segmentation [9–12], can be applied to rasterized images. Rasterized images for tree crown delineation mainly are digital surface model (DSM) and CHM. The raster-based method usually looks for a local maximum in the CHM to detect trees and considers this seed point as the top of tree. Although there are some methods can be directly applied to the CHM, these methods have high commission rate in most cases. Therefore, the existing ITCD method based on the CHM tends to improve the existing tree extraction algorithms for specific application scenarios. Zhen et al. [13] proposed an agent-based region growing algorithm that considers the growth process of trees to solve the competition problem caused by crown adhesion. Khosravipour et al. [14] developed a new algorithm that generates a pit-free CHM raster by using subsets of the lidar points to close pits. Xu et al. [15] proposed a novel tree detection approach based on crown morphology information. Although the raster-based method is relatively mature and faster, when performs tree segmentation, it is susceptible to be disturbed by non-tree objects such as buildings, which lead to reduction in detection accuracy. And the raster-based method cannot make good use of the 3D properties of LiDAR point clouds.

The Point Cloud-based Method. To make better use of the 3D properties of LiDAR point clouds, researchers have proposed tree detection methods that directly use point cloud data. There are two main types of tree detection methods based on point cloud data: the clustering method and voxel-based single tree segmentation. The tree crown extraction method based on K-means clustering is a commonly used iterative partitioning approach that uses seed points and distance criteria to partition point cloud data. Morsdorf et al. [16] firstly used the local maximum to extract seed points and the cluster analysis of point cloud data to extract individual trees. Kandare et al. [17] proposed a method for detecting overstory trees and lower shrubs using Airborne Laser Scanning (ALS) point cloud data's two-dimensional and three-dimensional K-means clustering techniques. Voxel is another way to conduct ITCD research in recent years. It is also a basic 3D element for exploring canopy structures. Dai et al. [18] used multi spectral ALS data to delineate the individual tree and isolated tree crown by the mean shift segmentation method. Jaskierniak et al. [19] proposed a novel bottom-up ITCD algorithm uses kernel densities to stratify the vegetation profile and differentiate understorey from the rest of the vegetation. Although the point cloud-based method has better segmentation results, this method has high requirements for LiDAR point density. And this kind of method is generally not suitable for multiple tree species scenarios.

The Method Combining the Raster and Point Cloud. In recent years, the method combining the raster and point methods had been proposed by researchers for ITCD research [20]. This type of method generally uses priori information to improve the accuracy of canopy detection. For example, Heinzel et al. [21] proposed a watershed segmentation method based on prior knowledge. Duncanson et al. [22] combined image and point cloud methods to analyze tree characteristics and proposed a multi-layer tree crown extraction method based on the watershed segmentation method, which can solve the problem of detecting understory trees to some extent. The method of combining grid and point method is also usually aimed at scenes with a single tree species, it does not have good versatility on tree detection.

Therefore, this paper presents a PointCNN-based method of 3D tree detection using LiDAR point clouds. This method first filters the massive data of the detection scene by combining with traditional tree detection methods, so that the input data can meet the requirements of the PointCNN classifier. Then this method conducts a more in-depth analysis of tree stagger on the results produced by the classifier, which further improves the detection accuracy. Experimental results show that we have successfully applied PointCNN to tree detection, and our method is more versatile while maintaining high detection accuracy.

2 Method

2.1 Overview

The overall flowchart of tree detection is described in the following sections, as shown in Fig. 1. First, the proposed method needs to preprocess point cloud data to generate CHM of the corresponding region. Then the method generates the sample to be tested by obtaining the maximum value of the local height on the CHM as the seed point. Then method used the extracted detection samples to train the classifier which can be used to filter rough seed points as the first screening. Finally, the stagger analysis of seed points was performed to determine whether two close seed points belong to a same tree as the second screening. The seed points remaining after two filter were taken as the locations of the detected trees.

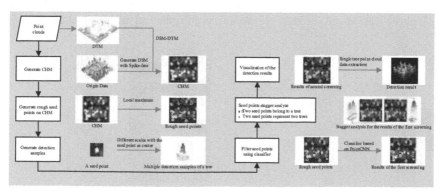

Fig. 1. Flowchart of tree detection.

2.2 Build CHM

In this study, the spike-free algorithm [23] was used to generate the DSM. The spike-free algorithm considers all relevant LiDAR returns and systematically prevents the formation of spikes during the TIN construction. The resulting spike-free TIN can be rasterized onto a grid to obtain a pit-free DSM raster. Compared to using the first-return DSM, spike-free algorithm can improve the accuracy of seed point location. Then subtract the DTM from the DSM by the LAStools [24] tool to obtain CHM.

2.3 Generate Detection Sample

The approach finds those local maxima on the rasterized CHM, and regards these maxima as seed points. The approach goes through the following steps:

(1)A low-pass filter is applied to the rasterized CHM for smoothing the surface and reducing the number of local maxima.
(2)Local maxima are located by using a circular moving window. According to the experiment, the window size is set to seven, because it can not only extract sufficient local maximum but also ensure that the seed points have practical significance as treetops.
(3)The Pixel of the CHM is labelled as local maxima if its value is greater than all other values in the window, provided that it is greater than some minimum height above ground.

The detailed method is described below. The point cloud data is vertically projected to the horizontal plane, and the method regard the generated seed points as the center of squares, extract all the point cloud data in square regions of different scales as detection samples. It was found through experiments that when the basic interval scale was 0.5 m, the extracted sample could make the final detection effect better. Figure 2 shows the detection samples of different scales, it can be seen from the figure that when the interval scale is small, the sample is mainly the trunk part of the tree, when the interval scale is expanded to a suitable size, a complete tree can be obtained, when the interval scale is too large, the sample often contains disturbance data such as building and other trees. Therefore, it is necessary to filter out samples which are too large and too small through sample classification and keep samples which could reflect an independent and complete tree.

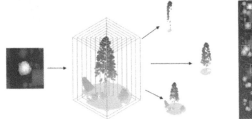
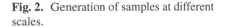

Fig. 2. Generation of samples at different scales.

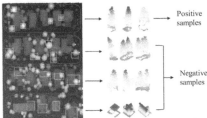

Fig. 3. Positive and negative samples.

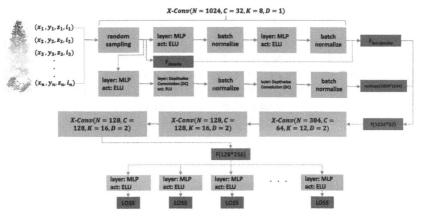

Fig. 4. 3D-CNN architecture for classification, the blue blocks represent layers of the network and the red blocks show the changing shape of the data as it moves through the network, and x, y, z are the coordinates of points, i is the intensity of points, N and C denote the output representative point number and feature dimensionality, K is the neighboring point number for each representative point, and D is the X-$Conv$ dilation rate (Color figure online).

2.4 Sample Classifier

As shown in Fig. 3, detection samples are marked as positive samples and negative samples. The positive sample consists of a complete tree. And the negative samples are divided into three types, which are incomplete single tree, interlaced multiple trees, single tree intertwined with other things. In order to train the 3D-CNN classifier fully, 1200 positive samples and 1800 negative samples were manually labeled, 600 for each negative sample type. These samples are taken randomly from six training plots.

The architecture of classifier is based on PointCNN [25], which is a 3D-CNN designed for classifying LiDAR scans of objects. The structure of network model is shown in Fig. 4. The classifier accepts a set of 4D point cloud data as input, gradually transforms the input points into fewer representative points through four X-$Conv$ layers, these representative points are more feature-rich. The last X-$Conv$ layer outputs 128 representative points. The size of the receptive field is shown in Formula (1) [25]. This receptive field helps to main the depth of the network, while keeping its growth rate, such that the deeper representative points could "see" increasingly larger portions of the entire shape. Lastly, the fully connected layers are added to the last X-$Conv$ layer output, followed by a loss, for training the network.

$$S_{receptivefield} = K \times D \tag{1}$$

Where $S_{receptivefield}$ is the size of receptive field, K is the neighboring point number for each representative point, and D is the X-$Conv$ dilation rate.

In this method, dropout was applied before the last fully connected layer to reduce over-fitting. We used ADAM optimizer [26] with an initial learning rate 0.01 for the training of the model and considered samples with a class score greater than 0.9 as positive samples which composed by complete trees.

2.5 Tree Stagger Analysis

As shown in Fig. 5, when the branches of two trees are staggered with each other, it is difficult to detect the trees staggered. Two situations are described below to explain how staggered trees affect detection. (1) The two trees actually existing were mistakenly identified as one tree. (2) There are multiple local maxima in the CHM, which leads to the single tree being incorrectly identified as multiple trees.

The specific tree stagger analysis method is as follows. In the aerial view of seed point, the method randomly selects a seed point as the starting point, then find the nearest seed point iteratively, all seed points are arranged as $S_i(i = 1, 2, \ldots, n)$, n is the total number of seed points. As shown in Fig. 6, the method is used to determine whether two adjacent seed points S_i and S_{i+1} belong to the same tree. The positions of the seed point S_i and S_{i+1} in the aerial view are (x_i, y_i) and (x_{i+1}, y_{i+1}), r_i and r_{i+1} are the minimum tree radius obtained by the classifier. The method draws circles with the positions of the seed points S_i and S_{i+1} as center, r_i and r_{i+1} as radius in the aerial view, calculate the degree of overlap of S_i and S_{i+1} according to Formula 2.

$$OD = \frac{S_{S_i \cap S_{i+1}}}{S_{S_i \cup S_{i+1}}} \tag{2}$$

OD represents the degree of stagger between two trees, $S_{S_i \cap S_{i+1}}$ is the total area where two trees intersect, $S_{S_i \cap S_{i+1}}$ is the sum of the area of two trees. The specific calculation process is shown in the following formula.

$$S_{S_i \cap S_{i+1}} = \theta_i \times r_i{}^2 + \theta_{i+1} \times r_{i+1}{}^2 - r_i \times d \times \sin\theta_i \tag{3}$$

$$S_{S_i \cup S_{i+1}} = \pi \times \left(r_i{}^2 + r_{i+1}{}^2\right) - S_{S_i \cap S_{i+1}} \tag{4}$$

$$\theta_i = \cos^{-1}((r_i{}^2 + d^2 - r_{i+1}{}^2)/(2 \times r_i \times d)) \tag{5}$$

$$\theta_{i+1} = \cos^{-1}((r_{i+1}{}^2 + d^2 - r_i{}^2)/(2 \times r_{i+1} \times d)) \tag{6}$$

$$d = \sqrt{(x_i - x_{i+1})^2 + (y_i - y_{i+1})^2} \tag{7}$$

We set the tree stagger threshold OD to 0.1. When $OD < 0.1$, the two seed points are considered to represent two trees. When $OD \geq 0.1$, the two seed points are considered to belong to the same tree, and the corresponding seed point with a smaller radius is deleted.

3 Results

3.1 Detection Result

This experiment used a large study area to verify the final tree detection effect, and the study area is located in Bend, Central Oregon, USA [27]. The study area contains

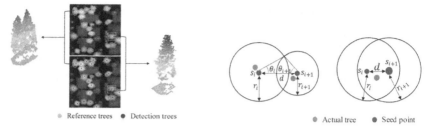

Fig. 5. Tree stagger.   **Fig. 6.** Filter staggered seed points.

buildings and trees, the tree species include oak, Quercus dentata, American elm, Oregon pine and hickory. The point cloud data was collected in May 2014 by the RieglVQ-480 laser measurement system. We extracted twelve sets of small-scale experimental areas from the study area, of which six plots were used for training the classifier, and other six plots were used for test. The characteristics of point cloud data in the study area are shown as follows. Flying altitude AGL: 300M; Scan angle range: ±30; Laser beam divergence: 0.3 m rad; Laser pulse length: 1550 nm; Total coverage area: 8 km^2; Point density: 18 pts/m^2.

Twelve experimental plots were selected from the study area, of which six experimental plots were used to train the classifier. In the other six experimental plots, there were 158 reference trees. The six experimental plots did not overlap each other and each plot was a square with a side length of 60 m. In the experiment, the pixel size was 0.3 m, the sliding window size was 7, DSM was constructed with a freezing distance of 0.9 m, the tree stagger threshold was 0.1, the maximum threshold of sample radius was 7 m, the sample interval scale was 0.5 m and the positive sample category score was 0.9.

The experimental results are compared by the following parameters [28]. N_{test}: Number of trees actually detected in the experimental plot. N_{ref}: Number of reference trees manually calibrated in the experimental plot. N_{match}: Number of detected trees in the experimental plot that can be matched to reference trees. H: The height of the most closely matched tree from extracted tree. H_{ref}: The height of the corresponding reference trees. CW: The crown width of the most closely matched tree from extracted trees. CW_{ref}: The crown width of the corresponding reference tree. R_{extr}: Detection rate; R_{mat}: Matching rate. $Rcom$: Commission rate. R_{om}: Omission rate); E_H: Average height difference. E_{CW}: Average crown width difference. MAE_H: Absolute average height difference. MAE_{CW}: Absolute average crown width difference. $RMSE_H$: Root-mean-squared-error of height. $RMSE_{CW}$: Root-mean-squared-error of crown width). M (Matching score): $M = 100 \times R_{mat} / (R_{mat} + R_{com} + R_{om})$.

Figure 7 shows the results of two seed point screenings in six plots, the points in the red box are invalid seed points which filtered out. It can be seen from the figure that the classifier based on PointCNN filters out a large number of seed points which representing the building, but cannot filter out those seed points which are close to each other, and then successfully filters out invalid staggered seed points through seed point stagger analysis.

Figure 8 shows a top view and a side view of the tree detection results in the original point cloud data. The data contained in the yellow box represents the detected trees. Figure 9 shows the tree detection results on CHM in six experimental plots. From the evaluation of experimental results, the tree extraction method for complex scenes proposed in this study can extract trees in the study aera well. The statistical data of the tree extraction results are shown in Table 1.

Plot	P1	P2	P3	P4	P5	P6
Rough seed points						
Seed points filtered by PointCNN-based classifier						
Seed points filtered by stagger analysis						

‾ Filtered seed points   ● Seed points

Fig. 7. The process of seed point filtering

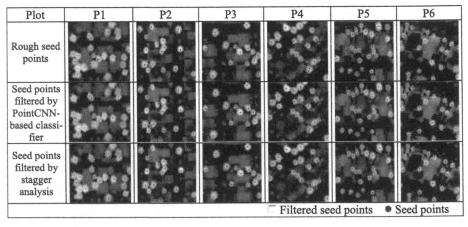

Plot	P1	P2	P3	P4	P5	P6
Top view						
Side view						

Fig. 8. Detection results on point cloud data in six plots (Color figure online)

Table 1 shows the tree extraction results in the different experimental plots. Among the six experimental plots, P3 and P5 had the highest matching score, with a score of 91.0, and the lowest matching score occurred at P4, with a score of 84.2. The average matching rate of trees in six plots was 98% which indicates that the method can detect most of trees. The average commission rate and omission rate were 12% and 2% respectively. The average of average height difference and average crown width difference were 0.38 m and 0.50 m respectively. The average of absolute average height difference and absolute

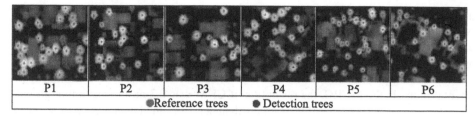

P1	P2	P3	P4	P5	P6
●Reference trees		● Detection trees			

Fig. 9. Detection results on CHM in six plots

average crown width difference were 0.46 m and 0.70 m respectively. The average of Root-mean-squared-error of height and Root-mean-squared-error of crown width were 0.64 m and 0.99 m respectively. The analysis of above data shows that the method of this study can extract trees well.

Table 1. Experimental results

Plot	P1	P2	P3	P4	P5	P6
N_{test}	35	24	21	28	36	31
N_{ref}	35	21	19	25	32	26
N_{match}	33	21	19	24	32	26
R_{extr}	100%	114%	111%	112%	113%	119%
R_{mat}	94%	100%	100%	96%	100%	100%
R_{com}	6%	13%	10%	14%	11%	16%
R_{om}	6%	0%	0%	4%	0%	0%
E_H	0.31	0.46	0.35	0.44	0.33	0.41
E_{CW}	0.58	0.24	0.47	0.81	0.52	0.36
MAE_H	0.39	0.5	0.43	0.49	0.39	0.57
MAE_{CW}	0.77	0.52	0.64	0.94	0.69	0.63
$RMSE_H$	0.63	0.47	0.52	1.01	0.71	0.5
$RMSE_{CW}$	1.03	0.98	1.13	0.93	0.89	0.96
M	88.7	88.5	91	84.2	91	86.2

3.2 Comparison with Related Research

To verify the performance of the proposed method, the results of the proposed method were compared with the experimental results of the marker-controlled region growing method (MCRG) [13], which used the position of the treetop detected by the local maxima with variable window sizes. The maker-controlled watershed segmentation method (MCWS) [29], which the treetops were detected by searching local maxima in canopy maxima model with variable window sizes. The itcLiDAR delineation algorithm [30], which directly processed the input point cloud data for tree detection. In addition, we used a multiscale morphological algorithm (MMA) [31] to construct the CHM, and applied the itcIMG delineation algorithm [32] to CHM for single tree extraction.

Table 2 shows the tree extraction results with five different methods in the six experimental plots. In the MCRG, the resolution of CHM was 0.3 m, the maximum growth range was 5 pixels (1.5 m) and the farthest distance from the canopy edge to the seed point was 10 pixels (3 m). In the MMA method, 5 m was selected as the threshold according to the experimental data, and in the itcIMG method, the window size value was adaptively adjusted. It can be seen from the experimental results that the accuracy rates of MCRG and MCWS are relatively close and the accuracy rates of itcLiDAR and MMA-itcIMG are better. The average matching scores of MCRG, MCWS, itcLiDAR and MMA-itcIMG are 64.9, 58.5, 73.6 and 84.3 respectively. The matching score of our method is 88.3. Therefore, our method has better tree detection results in complex scenes.

Table 2. Comparison of tree extraction results

Plot		P1	P2	P3	P4	P5	P6
MCRG [13]	R_{com}	49%	57%	67%	40%	46%	43%
	R_{om}	9%	5%	0%	0%	3%	0%
	M	61.3	60.8	60	71.2	66.5	69.7
MCWS [29]	R_{com}	61%	62%	75%	52%	54%	57%
	R_{om}	9%	10%	0%	4%	3%	12%
	M	56.8	55.9	57.1	63.2	63	56.5
itcLiDAR [30]	R_{com}	23%	30%	40%	27%	19%	32%
	R_{om}	11%	0%	5%	4%	9%	4%
	M	72	76.9	67.7	76.2	76.2	72.8
MMA-itcIMG [31, 32]	R_{com}	13%	17%	9%	21%	12%	12%
	R_{om}	5%	2%	3%	1%	1%	7%
	M	83.4	82.9	88.1	81.6	87.5	82.4
Proposed-M	R_{com}	6%	13%	10%	14%	11%	16%
	R_{om}	6%	0%	0%	4%	0%	0%
	M	88.7	88.5	91	84.2	91	86.2

4   Conclusion

Most of the existing tree detection methods are usually used in a certain scene, but it does not have good versatility for those complex scenes with many species of trees and more non-tree interference factors. Therefore, we proposed a hybrid single tree detection method based on LiDAR point clouds for tree detection. This method innovatively used 3D-CNN for classifying samples, which solved the limitation of traditional methods for multi-tree species detection. In addition, a method was proposed to analyze the stagger of trees to further improve the detection accuracy. In order to evaluate the effectiveness of our method, twelve experimental plots were selected from the study area, of which six experimental plots were used for training the classifier, and the remaining six experimental plots were used for testing. In addition, four methods were added for comparison. The experimental results show that the proposed method has lower commission and omission when detecting trees and has better versatility for complex tree scenes.

Trees detection in tall dense forest remains an open challenge, because of increasing occlusion levels towards the ground. Although our method improves the detection accuracy in multi-tree species scenes, our method may fail to detect the understory trees due to the occlusion of the overstory trees when there are a large number of understory trees in high dense forest. In the future work, we will solve the problem of occlusion by overstory trees.

Acknowledgement. This research was supported by the National Natural Science Foundation of China under Grant No. 62072405 and Zhejiang Provincial Natural Science Foundation of China under Grant No. LGF20F020017.

References

1. Maltamo, M., Næsset, E., Vauhkonen, J. (eds.): Forestry Applications of Airborne Laser Scanning. Concepts and Case Studies. Managing Forest Ecosystem, vol. 27, p. 460, Springer, Netherlands (2014). https://doi.org/10.1007/978-94-017-8663-8
2. Hyyppä, J., Hyyppä, H., Inkinen, M., Engdahl, M., Linko, S., Zhu, Y.-H.: Accuracy comparison of various remote sensing data sources in the retrieval of forest stand attributes. Forest Ecol. Manag. **128**, 109–120 (2000)
3. Wulder, M.A., et al.: Lidar sampling for large-area forest characterization: a review. Remote Sens. Environ. **121**, 196–209 (2012)
4. Unger, D.R., Hung, I.K., Brooks, R., Williams, H.: Estimating number of trees, tree height and crown width using LiDAR data. GISci. Remote Sens. **51**, 227–238 (2014)
5. Kwak, D.-A., et al.: Estimating stem volume and biomass of Pinus koraiensis using LiDAR data. J. Plant Res. **123**, 421–432 (2010)
6. Zhou, T., Popescu, C.S., Lawing, M.A., Eriksson, M., Strimbu, M.B., Bürkner, C.P.: Bayesian and classical machine learning methods: a comparison for tree species classification with LiDAR waveform signatures. Remote Sens.-Basel **10**, 39 (2017)
7. García, M., Riaño, D., Chuvieco, E., Danson, F.M.: Estimating biomass carbon stocks for a Mediterranean forest in central Spain using LiDAR height and intensity data. Remote Sens. Environ. **114**, 816–830 (2010)
8. Zhen, Z., Quackenbush, J.L., Zhang, L.: Trends in automatic individual tree crown detection and delineation—evolution of LiDAR data. Remote Sens.-Basel **8**, 333 (2016)
9. Wulder, M., Niemann, K.O., Goodenough, D.G.: Local maximum filtering for the extraction of tree locations and basal area from high spatial resolution imagery. Remote Sens. Environ. **73**, 103–114 (2000)
10. Monnet, J.-M., Mermin, E., Chanussot, J., Berger, F.: Tree top detection using local maxima filtering: a parameter sensitivity analysis. In: 10th International Conference on LiDAR Applications for Assessing Forest Ecosystems (Silvilaser 2010), p. 9 (2010)

11. Hirschmugl, M., Ofner, M., Raggam, J., Schardt, M.: Single tree detection in very high resolution remote sensing data. Remote Sens. Environ. **110**, 533–544 (2007)
12. Bottai, L., Arcidiaco, L., Chiesi, M., Maselli, F.: Application of a single-tree identification algorithm to LiDAR data for the simulation of stem volume current annual increment. J. Appl. Remote Sens. **7**, 073699 (2013)
13. Zhen, Z., Quackenbush, L.J., Stehman, S.V., Zhang, L.: Agent-based region growing for individual tree crown delineation from airborne laser scanning (ALS) data. Int. J. Remote. Sens. **36**, 1965–1993 (2015)
14. Khosravipour, A., Skidmore, A.K., Isenburg, M., Wang, T., Hussin, Y.A.: Generating Pit-free canopy height models from airborne LiDAR. Photogramm Eng. Rem. S. **80**, 863–872 (2014)
15. Xu, W., Deng, S., Liang, D., Cheng, X.: A crown morphology-based approach to individual tree detection in subtropical mixed broadleaf urban forests using UAV LiDAR data. Remote Sens. **13**, 1278 (2021)
16. Morsdorf, F., Meier, E., Kötz, B., Itten, K.I., Dobbertin, M., Allgöwer, B.: LIDAR-based geometric reconstruction of boreal type forest stands at single tree level for forest and wildland fire management. Remote Sens. Environ. **92**, 353–362 (2004)
17. Kandare, K., Dalponte, M., Gianelle, D., Chan, J.C.: A new procedure for identifying single trees in understory layer using discrete LiDAR data. In: 2014 IEEE Geoscience and Remote Sensing Symposium. IEEE, pp. 1357–1360 (2014)
18. Dai, W., Yang, B., Dong, Z., Shaker, A.: A new method for 3D individual tree extraction using multispectral airborne LiDAR point clouds. ISPRS J. Photogramm. **144**, 400–411 (2018)
19. Jaskierniak, D., et al.: Individual tree detection and crown delineation from Unmanned Aircraft System (UAS) LiDAR in structurally complex mixed species eucalypt forests. ISPRS J. Photogramm. Remote Sens. **171**, 171–187 (2021)
20. Reitberger, J., Schnörr, C., Krzystek, P., Stilla, U.: 3D segmentation of single trees exploiting full waveform LIDAR data. ISPRS J. Photogramm. **64**, 561–574 (2009)
21. Heinzel, J.N., Weinacker, H., Koch, B.: Prior-knowledge-based single-tree extraction. Int. J. Remote Sens. **32**, 4999–5020 (2011)
22. Duncanson, L.I., Cook, B.D., Hurtt, G.C., Dubayah, R.O.: An efficient, multi-layered crown delineation algorithm for mapping individual tree structure across multiple ecosystems. Remote Sens. Environ. **154**, 378–386 (2014)
23. Khosravipour, A., Skidmore, A.K., Isenburg, M.: Generating spike-free digital surface models using LiDAR raw point clouds: a new approach for forestry applications. Int. J. Appl. Earth Obs. **52**, 104–114 (2016)
24. LAStools. https://rapidlasso.com/lastools/
25. Li, Y., Bu, R., Sun, M., Wu, W., Di, X., Chen, B.: PointCNN: convolution on X-transformed points. Adv. Neural Inf. Process. Syst. 820–830 (2018)
26. Kingma, D.P., Adam, J.B.: A method for stochastic optimization. ICLR (2014)
27. Cook, D.B., et al.: NASA Goddard's LiDAR, hyperspectral and thermal (G-LiHT) airborne imager. Remote Sens.-Basel **5**, 4045–4066 (2013)
28. Eysn, L., et al.: A benchmark of LiDAR-based single tree detection methods using heterogeneous forest data from the alpine space. Forests **6**, 1721–1747 (2015)
29. Chen, Q., Baldocchi, D., Gong, P., Kelly, M.: Isolating individual trees in a savanna woodland using small footprint Lidar data. Photogramm. Eng. Rem. S. **72**, 923–932 (2006)
30. Dalponte, M., Coomes, D.A.: Tree-centric mapping of forest carbon density from airborne laser scanning and hyperspectral data. Methods Ecol. Evol. **7**, 1236–1245 (2016)
31. Liu, L., Lim, S., Shen, X., Yebra, M.: A multiscale morphological algorithm for improvements to canopy height models. Comput. Geosci.-UK **130**, 20–31 (2019)
32. Dalponte, M., Reyes, F., Kandare, K., Gianelle, D.: Delineation of individual tree crowns from ALS and hyperspectral data: a comparison among four methods. Eur. J. Remote Sens. **48**, 365–382 (2015)

Variance Weight Distribution Network Based Noise Sample Learning for Robust Person Re-identification

Xiaoyi Long[1], Ruimin Hu[1(✉)], and Xin Xu[2]

[1] School of Computer Science, Wuhan University, Wuhan, China
[2] School of Computer Science and Technology,
Wuhan University of Science and Technology, Wuhan, China

Abstract. Person re-identification (re-ID) usually requires a large amount of well-labeled training data to learn generalized discriminative person feature representations. Most of current deep learning models assume that all training data are correctly labeled. However, noisy data commonly exists due to incorrect labeling and person detector errors or occlusions in large scale practical applications. Both types of noisy data can influence model training, while they are ignored by most re-ID models so far. In this paper, we propose a robust deep re-ID model, called variance weight distribution network (VWD-Net), to address this problem. Different from the traditional representations of each person image as a feature vector, the variance weight distribution network focuses on the following three aspects. 1) An improved Gaussian distribution and its variance are used to represent the uncertainty of person features. 2) A well-designed loss in the variance weight distribution network is used to delegate the distribution uncertainty with respect to the training data. 3) The noisy labels are rectified for further optimization on the model training performance. The large scale variance/uncertainty has been assigned to noisy samples and then rectifies their labels, in order to mitigate their negative impact on the training process. Extensive experiments on two benchmarks demonstrate the robustness and effectiveness of VWD-Net.

Keywords: Person re-identification · Noise sample learning · Feature distribution

1 Introduction

Person re-identification (re-ID) [26] is a cross-camera special person retrieval task, which is an important problem in intelligent surveillance scenarios. Given a query person image, it aims to retrieve images of the same identity from gallery acquired by different cameras. Re-ID has attracted attention in academia and industry. However, noisy data commonly exists due to false labeling, person detector errors, or occlusions in real world, as illustrated in Fig. 1(a). In addition,

© Springer Nature Switzerland AG 2021
N. Magnenat-Thalmann et al. (Eds.): CGI 2021, LNCS 13002, pp. 101–112, 2021.
https://doi.org/10.1007/978-3-030-89029-2_8

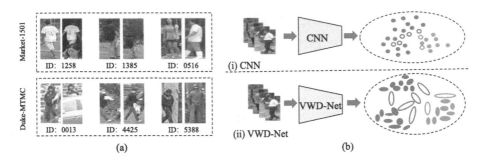

Fig. 1. (a) Illustration of noisy samples on Market-1501 and Duke-MTMC, including outlying samples and label noise samples. The former is caused by person detector errors or occlusions, and the latter is due to human annotation errors. Each pair of images have the same identity, with the inner on the left and the outlier on the right. (b) The feature embeddings extracted by (i) conventional CNN and (ii) our VWD-Net in the presence of noisy samples. Among them, circles/ellipses mean noisy samples and solid shapes denote clean samples.

less noisy data usually requires a large amount of labor for labeling, meanwhile, with the state-of-the-art approaches saturating the public benchmark performance, as well as real open-world scenarios often require a large amount of training data. Therefore, the existing manually cropped dataset is no longer sufficient to satisfy the practical requirements, and the person images of the recent benchmark for person re-ID are acquired by the existing person detectors. Yet, in the open world scenario, the performance of the existing re-ID method degrades dramatically due to the presence of noisy data. In this paper, we study the robust re-ID problem with noisy data, *i.e.*, person detector errors or occlusions and person images are incorrectly annotated as other wrong identities.

Currently, Several works [3,9] have been made to study noisy data in person re-ID, which provides some insights to solve labeling errors and outlier samples. For noisy data, there are typically two types of noisy data that can be considered. The first type is label noise, *i.e.*, person images are assigned wrong IDs and the second type of noisy data comes from outlier. Different from the first type of noise, this type of samples has the correct identity and is prevalent on the existing benchmark data sets, due to person detector errors or occlusion caused outliers, as shown in the first and second columns of Fig. 1(a). Both types of noise can have a negative impact on the re-ID model when it is trained. In the feature space, noisy data are often far from the inliers of the same class. Normally, in order to pull the distance between the noisy samples and the center of the class, such a re-ID model will sacrifice the differentiation of the class, and this will result in degradation of the model performance.

In this paper, we propose a variance weight distribution network (VWD-Net) to solve these two types of noisy data. With VWD-Net, each person image is represented by a feature distribution instead of a feature vector as in traditional deep learning. In particular, each image is represented by a Gaussian distribution. The mean of the distribution represents the normal feature vector for re-ID matching, while the variance measures the uncertainty of the features. That is, given a noisy training sample, rather than forcing it to be closer to other inliers in the same class, VWD-Net computes a large variance, indicating that it is unsure what feature values should be assigned to that sample or not. Training samples with larger variance have less impact on the learned feature embedding space. Thus, this extra dimension allows the model to focus more on clean inliers rather than overfitting noisy samples, resulting in better classification differentiability, as shown in Fig. 1(b), and better generalization of the test data.

Our contributions are as follows: (1) The problem of learning re-ID models that are robust to both labeled noise and outlier samples is identified for the first time, and a unified solution is given. (2) A new deep re-ID model called variance weighted distribution network (VWD-Net) is proposed, which treats each learned deep feature as a distribution to account for feature uncertainty and to mitigate the effect of noisy samples. (3) Rectifying Label Learning is designed so that noisy labels can be rectified for training in model optimization. An extensive comparative evaluation shows that the proposed model outperforms the existing model on 2 benchmarks, including Market-1501 [29], and Duke-MTMC [30]. We show that VWD-Net is particularly effective under a large amount of label noise or the more challenging open-world re-ID setting.

2   Related Work

2.1   Deep Person Re-ID Models

Existing re-ID models are designed for learning more discriminative and robust person features, and can be broadly classified into two categories, namely representation learning and metric learning. The representation learning is devoted to learning invariant person feature representations, while the metric learning is concerned with learning discriminative distance metrics. In recent years, many deep learning-based re-ID models [10] have been designed to solve various problems with the help of the powerful ability of deep learning to extract features. Combining global features and local features, learned person re-ID models have achieved human-level performance on commonly used person Re-ID datasets [13]. However, most of them rely heavily on large-scale, well-annotated training data, which will lead the performance to degrade significantly. All these efforts have the potential to handle some outlier samples due to partial human detection as shown in Fig. 1(a). However, almost none of the existing deep re-ID models can provide a principled solution to identify different outliers in order to reduce their impact. Moreover, to the best of our knowledge, the label noise problem has never been solved.

2.2   Person Re-ID with Sample Noise

There has been some preliminary work [25] done on sample noise. Current studies are divided into two categories: image-based person re-ID and video-based person re-ID. The first one corresponds to image noise [8] and the second one tackles with outlier frames in video [24]. To deal with the background noise at the edges of each image [28], a deep attention model is used to reduce the background noise in the person images [8]. In [18], the authors also try mask guided contrastive attention model to reduce the background influence. There is also some work from pose estimation techniques to handle localized noise regions [17]. For more accurate label estimation, a novel top-k counts label prediction was proposed to eliminate false labeling in [25]. All of these methods mentioned above try to tackle the sample noise caused by incomplete person detectors or trackers. The difference is that we try to study person re-ID model learning with both label noise and outlier samples, which is more challenging.

2.3   Robust Deep Learning with Label Noise

Although the label noise has rarely been studied in person re-ID, it is widely studied in the field of machine learning [2]. More specifically, robust deep learning in image classification tasks [6] has been studied, where clean label data mining is a popular approach to address label noise problem. For example, in the case of relatively few clean labels, label noise is handled with a label cleaning network [22] and a joint optimization framework [20]. Existing deep learning methods can be categorized into two groups depending on whether human supervision or assumptions are required. The first group requires additional noise labeling or sample separation assumptions to verify which samples contain noise. Some of these methods are represented by [11] using knowledge graphs for noise labeling to propose a unified distillation framework. The second group does not require additional noise annotation or pattern estimation. These methods perform iterative label correction by bootstrapping [16] or loss correlation [14] to reduce label noise. In addition, smoothing [19] or entropy regularization [15] is widely used to address the label overfitting problem. In this paper, we will take a second group approach to conduct an experimental study in person re-ID and improve outlier samples and noisy labels to boost performance.

2.4   Feature Distribution Modelling

As we know, traditional CNNs are directly mapping a image to a fixed dimensional feature vector in the feature space. But for some other types of data, such as video data, it is possible to map them to predefined distributions. The most typical is [21], where the paper proposes to map a video consisting of multiple key frames as a Gaussian distribution, with the corresponding mean and covariance being the statistical values of these frames, and each frame corresponding to a vector. Based on modeling a class as a Gaussian Mixture distribution, [23] proposed a common formulation of cross-entropy loss reformulation. Another alternative idea is to use a generative model to deal with this problem, in [7], using a variational auto-encoder to assist in unconditional image generation. This idea has been widely used in metric learning, mainly for solving the variance and invariance within the disentanglement class [12]. Unlike [12,21,23], we aim to resolve the noisy samples by rectify labels and thus enhance the robust-ness.

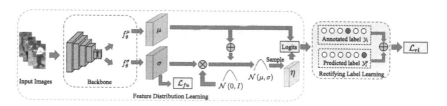

Fig. 2. The pipeline for learning robust person re-ID models with noisy datas. It mainly consists of two parts: (1) Feature Distribution Learning, which is used to weaken the negative impact of outlier samples on the model training; (2) Rectifying Label Learning, which is used to correct noisy labels, so that mislabeled data are rectified and used for training to optimize model performance.

3   Methodology

In this paper, we address two types of noise problems with VWD-Net in person re-ID task, including label and outlier. As shown in Fig. 2, the method consists of two main branches: 1) one branch generates the mean vector, which constructs the intra-class center, and 2) the other branch generates the covariance matrix, can be somewhat viewed as a disentangle process. In the next section, we will explain the two branches, mean vector and covariance matrix in detail.

3.1   Conventional Baseline Model

Given the training set $I = \{I_1, I_2, \ldots, I_N\}$ of N images with M classes $i.e.$, , M person identities. Note that each training person image I_i is mapped by $\mathcal{X}_i$ with label $\mathcal{Y}_i$. To map person images in the embedding space, we employ a feature embedding model $f_\theta(\cdot)$, where θ is the parameters of CNN. The predicted score of $\mathcal{X}_i$ belonging to class j is s_i^j. The predicted probability of $\mathcal{X}_i$ belonging to class j is calculated by the softmax function, which is represented as:

$$p_{(\mathcal{Y}_j|\mathcal{X}_i)} = \frac{\exp\left(s_i^j\right)}{\sum_{k=1}^{M} \exp\left(s_i^j\right)}, j = 1, \cdots, M \tag{1}$$

Then the loss function can be obtained by calculating the cross entropy between the predicted probability score $p_{(\mathcal{Y}_j|\mathcal{X}_i)}$ and its label $\mathcal{Y}_i$. That is to say, the overall loss function for all training samples can be formulated as follows:

$$\mathcal{L}_{ce} = -\frac{1}{N}\sum_{i=1}^{N} \log\left(p_{(\mathcal{Y}_i|\mathcal{X}_i)}\right) \tag{2}$$

where $\mathcal{Y}_i$ is the label of sample $\mathcal{X}_i$, and $p_{(\mathcal{Y}_i|\mathcal{X}_i)}$ represents the probability that sample $\mathcal{X}_i$ is predicted to be of class $\mathcal{Y}_i$. Note that $\mathcal{Y}_i$ contains label noise, which can limit the discriminative power of the re-ID model.

3.2   Feature Uncertainty Distribution Learning

Different from the traditional baseline, which represents person images as feature vectors, our method estimates the variance of feature vectors produced by the embedding network, *i.e.*, feature uncertainty. In other word, the outputs of our VWD-Net are transformed into Gaussian distribution by the mean μ and variance σ over the original feature vector. Furthermore, we convert the original feature vector into a feature distribution, *i.e.*, a random feature variable. Specifically, with our neural network, we parametrically convert the feature vectors of image $f_\theta(I)$ into Gaussian distribution by means μ and variances σ.

As shown in Fig. 2, we split the penultimate layer of the backbone into two parts, which are used to calculate the mean μ and variance σ, respectively. The specific implementation is such that we delete the penultimate layer and then add two new layers after the penultimate layer, which are $f_\theta^\mu \left(f_\theta^{(l-1)}(I) \right) \rightarrow \mu$ and $f_\theta^\sigma \left(f_\theta^{(l-1)}(I) \right) \rightarrow \sigma$, where l indicates the number of backbone network layers. The role of $f_\theta^\mu(\cdot)$ is essentially the same as that of $f_\theta^{(l)}$, which is to produce the feature mean estimation μ. And $f_\theta^\sigma(\cdot)$ is to represent the uncertainty of the above feature mean estimation. The computation of the covariance matrix is very sophisticated and it is enough to have its diagonal while satisfying our objective. Therefore, the output vector of $f_\theta^\mu(\cdot)$ has the same dimensions as $f_\theta^\sigma(\cdot)$.

By above procedures, we can get the mean vector μ and the variance σ. With the purpose of avoiding the variance collapses to zero during the training process in order to increase the uncertainty level of the overall samples, we introduce a feature uncertainty loss function to ensure a good uncertainty of the entire model training. Inspired by cross entropy, we use entropy to measure the uncertainty of individual training samples with required variance σ. Thus, the entropy of an arbitrary Gaussian distribution $\mathcal{D} \sim \mathcal{N}(\mu, \sigma)$ can be formulated as follows:

$$S = \frac{1}{2} \log(\det(2\pi e \sigma)) \tag{3}$$

As we have previously mentioned, only the diagonal of the covariance matrix is required to satisfy our requirement and the diagonal is satisfying the Gaussian distribution. Then the entropy for the i-th image is:

$$S^{(i)} = \frac{k}{2}(\log 2\pi + 1) + \frac{1}{2} \sum_j^k \log \left(\text{diag} \left(\sigma^{(i)} \right)_j \right) \tag{4}$$

where k is the dimension of the feature, $diag(\cdot)$ means the diagonal of the covariance matrix, and j denotes the index of dimension. In this case, the Feature Uncertainty Loss is calculated as follows:

$$\mathcal{L}_{fu} = \max \left(0, \alpha - \sum_{i=1}^{N} S^{(i)} \right) \tag{5}$$

where N is the total number of images, i is the index of images, and α is the constraint boundary of all uncertainties. It is also important to know that clean samples have small variance and noisy samples have relatively large variance. Furthermore, instead of directly making the sample obey the distribution $\mathcal{D} \sim \mathcal{N}(\mu, \sigma)$, we conduct two steps: 1) convert to a standard Gaussian distribution $\mathcal{D}_u \sim \mathcal{N}(0, 1)$ with mean 0 and variance 1; 2) obtain the final Gaussian distribution $\mathcal{D} \sim \mathcal{N}(\mu, \sigma)$ by computing $\mu + \mathcal{D}_u * \sigma$. Finally, it is possible to separate the training part, which facilitates the pass of gradient.

3.3   Rectifying Label Learning

To minimize the negative impact of noisy labels to the model, we introduce the Rectifying Label Learning framework (shown in Fig. 2) after the feature uncertainty distribution to rectify the noisy labels and optimize the network parameters. As mentioned above, clean data with correct labels facilitates the process of training a better performing re-ID model. Therefore, the model trained with clean data can assist to predict the labels of the input images and thereby serve to rectify the noisy labels. Hence, we propose Rectifying Label Learning, which can take into account both labeled and predicted labels, and it is defined as follows:

$$\mathcal{L}_{rl} = -\frac{1}{N} \sum_{i=1}^{N} \log \left(p_{(\hat{y}_i | x_i)} \right) \tag{6}$$

$$\hat{y}_i = \arg\max_{y_i} \left\{ p_{(y_1 | x_i)}, p_{(y_2 | x_i)}, \cdots, p_{(y_M | x_i)} \right\} \tag{7}$$

where $\hat{y}_i$ corresponds to the label of the input sample x_i being predicted during the training process. This process can help in the rectification of wrong labels.

3.4   Overall Classification Loss

Feature Distribution Uncertainty Loss. Similar to Eq. 2, the loss function of the above branch in Fig. 2 for μ is calculated as follows:

$$\mathcal{L}_{ce}^{\mu} = -\frac{1}{N} \sum_{i=1}^{N} \log \left(p_{(y_i | \mu_i)} \right) \tag{8}$$

Analogously, the calculation of the loss function of the branch below in Fig. 2 for η can be expressed as follows.

$$\mathcal{L}_{ce}^{\eta} = -\frac{1}{N} \sum_{j=1}^{N} \log \left(p_{(y_j | \eta_j)} \right) \tag{9}$$

where $\eta \sim \mathcal{N}(\mu, \sigma)$. Then the first half of the above and below two branches in Fig. 2 are used to map the sample as a feature distribution, $i.e.,$, $\mathcal{D} \sim \mathcal{N}(\mu, \sigma)$, and finally the loss function of these two parts, called Feature Distribution Loss, is calculated as follows.

$$\mathcal{L}_{fd} = \mathcal{L}_{ce}^{\mu} + \beta * \mathcal{L}_{ce}^{\eta} \tag{10}$$

where β is the weight of $\mathcal{L}_{ce}^{\eta}$ and is set to 0.1 in this paper. It is worth noting that the classifier gradually reduces the variance σ during training stage, thus bringing VWD-Net back to the traditional model. So on this basis, we add the feature uncertainty constraint to ensure that our variance remains stable, which ultimately constitutes our Feature Distribution Uncertainty Loss, $i.e.,$, $\mathcal{L}_{fdu} = \mathcal{L}_{fd} + \frac{1}{\sigma} * \mathcal{L}_{fu} + \sigma$, as follows:

$$\mathcal{L}_{fdu} = \mathcal{L}_{ce}^{\mu} + \beta * \mathcal{L}_{ce}^{\eta} + \frac{1}{\sigma} * \mathcal{L}_{fu} + \sigma \tag{11}$$

Overall Classification Loss. The overall total loss function is a weighted combination of the Feature Uncertainty Distribution Learning and Rectifying Label Learning. Overall Classification Loss is defined as follows:

$$\mathcal{L}_{overall} = \mathcal{L}_{fdu} + \gamma(t) * \mathcal{L}_{rl} \tag{12}$$

More details are as follows:

$$\mathcal{L}_{overall} = \mathcal{L}_{ce}^{\mu} + \beta * \mathcal{L}_{ce}^{\eta} + \frac{1}{\sigma} * \mathcal{L}_{fu} + \sigma + \gamma(t) * \mathcal{L}_{rl} \tag{13}$$

where $\gamma(t) = \exp\left(-2.0 * \left(1 - \frac{t}{t_m}\right)^2\right)$, denotes a monotonically increasing function about the training epoch, controlling the contribution of the rectified labels and annotated labels. t_m means the total number of training epochs. In practice, we default an assumption that the number of wrong labels in the dataset is very small. In other words, the model can predict the correct labels of the wrongly annotated samples, so that the rectification of the wrong labels can be achieved and the negative impact of the wrongly annotated samples on the model can be reduced to improve the effectiveness of model training.

4   Experiments

4.1   Datasets and Settings

(1) Datasets. In this paper, we use two commonly used large scale person re-ID datasets, Market-1501 [29] and Duke-MTMC [30], respectively. The details of the two datasets are described as follows:

The **Market-1501** [29] is a large-scale person re-ID dataset with 1501 identities, captured by 6 different cameras in Tsinghua University. This dataset contains [1] 32,668 bounding boxes captured by the DPM detector. It contains

12,936 images of 751 identities for training. In the testing set, it contains 3,368 query images of other 750 identities and 19,732 pedestrian images as gallery.

The **Duke-MTMC** [30] is another widely used large-scale person re-ID dataset, which was captured by 8 different cameras in Duke University. This dataset was originally designed for multi-person, multi-camera tracking. It contains 1404 annotated identities with 36411 hand-drawn bounding boxes. The training set contains 16,522 images of 702 identities. The test set contains another 702 identities, including 2,228 query images and 17,661 images as gallery.

(2) Label noise simulation. Normally, the number of data outliers in benchmark is generally large, while label noise is relatively rare. In order to explore the influences of label noise on model training, we increase the percentage of label noise in this experiment to show its robustness. Two types of noise are considered, random noise and patterned noise. For random noise, a random percentage of training images were selected and their identity labels were randomly assigned to the wrong images. For patterned noise, we use a model trained with clean data to obtain the features of each training sample and search for the visually most similar samples using Euclidean distance. Then, for the randomly selected training samples, their identity labels are assigned to the most similar samples with different identities. For each noise type, three percentages are considered: 10%, 20% and 50%. For each noise percentage, five runs are performed in sample selection and label assignment due to randomness, and the overall reported result is the average of the five runs.

(3) Evaluation Metrics. We use cumulative matching characteristics (CMC) [4] at rank$-k$ and mean average precision (mAP) [29] as evaluation metrics according to the standard evaluation protocol.

4.2   Implementation Details

In this paper, we use ResNet50 [5] as the backbone to extract features. In total, we compared VWD-Net with five methods [5,9,16,16,27]. For a fair comparison, all methods use ResNet50 as the backbone and the training settings are kept the same as our VWD-Net. To keep the comparison fair, in our experiments, 10% of the training set is used as the clean reference set and the clean network is trained using the code provided by the authors. At the end of training, the most likely 20% of the noise was removed from the entire training set, and then the rest was trained to obtain the re-ID model. This is also different from all other models that do not require the removal of explicit noise samples. The biggest difference is that we added the Rectifying Label Learning module to enable the model to correct the labels of label noise data.

In total, we divide the experimental training procedure into two steps: (1) based on the pre-trained model ResNet50 on ImageNet, set the batch size to 32 and the number of steps to 60,000 on the re-ID dataset, where the optimizer uses Adam [7], the learning rate is 3.5×10^{-3}, and the default momentum terms are: $\delta_1 = 0.9$ and $\delta_2 = 0.999$; (2) using the trained network parameters from step (1), continue training μ and σ with the same batch size, 20,000 steps, and a learning rate of 5×10^{-4}. The proposed method VWD-Net was implemented on Tensorflow and trained with NVIDIA RTX 2080Ti GPU.

4.3 Comparison with the State-of-the-Arts

The comparison results of random noise and patterned noise are shown in Table 1. We can observe the following results: (1) Our VWD-Net has the best performance in all compared methods. (2) VWD-Net achieves good performance in feature modeling compared to ResNet50, and brings good results in error label correction compared to DistributionNet, which leads to further performance improvement. (3) Patterned noise has a greater impact on the performance of the model compared to random noise, which also indicates that pedestrians wearing similar clothes are more difficult to recognize. (4) 50% noise has the greatest impact on the performance of the model, but of course this is a particularly extreme simulation setting, in reality, it should be about 10%-20%. (5) VWD-Net has a performance improvement compared to DistributionNet improved, which indicates a significant correction result for our Rectifying Label Learning.

Table 1. Results on Market-1501 and Duke-MTMC with random noise and patterned noise. Methods: B: ResNet50-Baseline [5], H: Bootstrap hard [16], S: Bootstrap soft [16], C: CleanNet [9], D: DistributionNet [27], V: VWD-Net.

Noise	Method	Random noise				Patterned noise			
		Market-1501		Duke-MTMC		Market-1501		Duke-MTMC	
		Rank-1	mAP	Rank-1	mAP	Rank-1	mAP	Rank-1	mAP
10%	B	55.50	79.39	42.60	63.78	25.87	51.46	18.26	36.10
	H	57.28	80.79	92.20	64.54	25.76	51.08	18.74	36.57
	S	55.37	79.77	41.84	62.79	25.50	50.47	18.01	35.68
	C	59.14	81.41	47.88	68.09	26.64	52.47	18.80	36.28
	D	61.47	82.31	47.99	68.61	27.04	52.40	20.74	37.69
	V	63.23	83.21	48.32	69.32	28.35	53.25	22.34	38.36
20%	B	45.36	71.68	34.94	56.73	23.49	48.44	16.96	33.71
	H	46.03	72.71	34.23	55.66	23.40	48.25	16.93	33.76
	S	45.49	71.46	34.13	55.52	24.08	49.51	16.83	33.13
	C	44.22	71.40	33.98	55.07	24.28	49.54	17.03	33.79
	D	53.40	77.03	40.87	62.39	24.41	49.25	18.49	34.48
	V	56.32	78.83	42.16	64.01	25.27	50.71	20.47	35.16
50%	B	28.01	55.14	18.83	37.47	20.74	44.04	14.17	29.59
	H	28.22	54.87	19.88	38.87	19.87	42.87	14.32	30.00
	S	27.78	55.17	19.27	37.70	20.72	43.86	13.65	28.35
	C	26.08	52.73	19.01	38.96	19.90	43.01	13.70	28.46
	D	35.14	61.08	25.82	45.98	21.42	44.84	15.95	30.75
	V	36.32	63.32	27.05	46.94	23.48	45.72	17.65	32.25

5 Conclusion

In this paper, to effectively solve the two problems of noisy labels and outlying samples in person re-ID, we model the feature distribution and propose the Rectifying Label Learning module to correct the incorrect labels. Specifically, each feature space is modeled as a Gaussian distribution to estimate the uncertainty of the features. On the one hand, we reduce the negative impact on the network by assigning larger variances to outlying samples. On the other hand, the training data is optimized by correcting the incorrect labels to improve the network performance. The effectiveness and robustness of our method is verified by extensive experiments.

References

1. Felzenszwalb, P.F., Girshick, R.B., McAllester, D., Ramanan, D.: Object detection with discriminatively trained part-based models. IEEE Trans. Pattern Analysis Mach. Intell. **32**(9), 1627–1645 (2009)
2. Frénay, B., Verleysen, M.: Classification in the presence of label noise: a survey. IEEE Trans. Neural Networks Learn. Syst. **25**(5), 845–869 (2013)
3. Goldberger, J., Ben-Reuven, E.: Training deep neural-networks using a noise adaptation layer, pp. 1–9 (2017)
4. Gray, D., Brennan, S., Tao, H.: Evaluating appearance models for recognition, reacquisition, and tracking. In: Proceedings of the IEEE International Workshop on Performance Evaluation of Tracking and Surveillance, pp. 1–7 (2007)
5. He, K., Zhang, X., Ren, S., Sun, J.: Deep residual learning for image recognition. In: Proceedings of the IEEE Conference on Computer Vision and Pattern Recognition, pp. 770–778 (2016)
6. Jiang, L., Zhou, Z., Leung, T., Li, L.-J., Fei-Fei, L.: Mentornet: Learning data-driven curriculum for very deep neural networks on corrupted labels. In; International Conference on Machine Learning, pp. 2304–2313. PMLR (2018)
7. Kingma, D.P., Ba, J.: Adam: a method for stochastic optimization. arXiv preprint arXiv:1412.6980 (2014)
8. Lan, X., Wang, H., Gong, S., Zhu, X.: Deep reinforcement learning attention selection for person re-identification. In: British Machine Vision Conference, pp. 1–16 (2017)
9. Lee, K.-H., He, X., Zhang, L., Yang, L.: Cleannet: transfer learning for scalable image classifier training with label noise. In: Proceedings of the IEEE Conference on Computer Vision and Pattern Recognition, pp. 5447–5456 (2018)
10. Li, W., Zhu, X., Gong, S.: Harmonious attention network for person re-identification. In: Proceedings of the IEEE Conference on Computer Vision and Pattern Recognition, pp. 2285–2294 (2018)
11. Li, Y., Yang, J., Song, Y., Cao, L., Luo, J., Li, L.-J.: Learning from noisy labels with distillation. In: Proceedings of the IEEE International Conference on Computer Vision, pp. 1910–1918 (2017)
12. Lin, X., Duan, Y., Dong, Q., Lu, J., Zhou, J.: Deep variational metric learning. In: Proceedings of the European Conference on Computer Vision, pp. 689–704 (2018)
13. Luo, H., Jiang, W., Zhang, X., Fan, X., Qian, J., Zhang, C.: Alignedreid++: dynamically matching local information for person re-identification. Pattern Recogn. **94**, 53–61 (2019)

14. Patrini, G., Rozza, A., Menon, A.K., Nock, R., Qu, L.: Making deep neural networks robust to label noise: a loss correction approach. In: Proceedings of the IEEE Conference on Computer Vision and Pattern Recognition, pp. 1944–1952 (2017)
15. Pereyra, G., Tucker, G., Chorowski, J., Kaiser, Ł., Hinton, G.: Regularizing neural networks by penalizing confident output distributions. arXiv preprint arXiv:1701.06548 (2017)
16. Reed, S., Lee, H., Anguelov, D., Szegedy, C., Erhan, D., Rabinovich, A.: Training deep neural networks on noisy labels with bootstrapping. arXiv preprint arXiv:1412.6596 (2014)
17. Saquib Sarfraz, M., Schumann, A., Eberle, A., Stiefelhagen, R.: A pose-sensitive embedding for person re-identification with expanded cross neighborhood re-ranking. In: Proceedings of the IEEE Conference on Computer Vision and Pattern Recognition, pp. 420–429 (2018)
18. Song, C., Huang, Y., Ouyang, W., Wang, L.: Mask-guided contrastive attention model for person re-identification. In: Proceedings of the IEEE Conference on Computer Vision and Pattern Recognition, pp. 1179–1188 (2018)
19. Szegedy, C., Vanhoucke, V., Ioffe, S., Shlens, J., Wojna, Z.: Rethinking the inception architecture for computer vision. In: Proceedings of the IEEE conference on computer vision and pattern recognition, pp. 2818–2826 (2016)
20. Tanaka, D., Ikami, D., Yamasaki, T., Aizawa, K.: Joint optimization framework for learning with noisy labels. In: Proceedings of the IEEE Conference on Computer Vision and Pattern Recognition, pp. 5552–5560 (2018)
21. Tzelepis, C., Mezaris, V., Patras, I.: Linear maximum margin classifier for learning from uncertain data. IEEE Trans. Pattern Anal. Mach. Intell. **40**(12), 2948–2962 (2017)
22. Veit, A., Alldrin, N., Chechik, G., Krasin, I., Gupta, A., Belongie, S.: Learning from noisy large-scale datasets with minimal supervision. In: Proceedings of the IEEE Conference on Computer Vision and Pattern Recognition, pp. 839–847 (2017)
23. Wan, W., Zhong, Y., Li, T., Chen, J.: Rethinking feature distribution for loss functions in image classification. In: Proceedings of the IEEE Conference on Computer Vision and Pattern Recognition, pp. 9117–9126 (2018)
24. Ancong, W., Zheng, W.-S., Lai, J.-H.: Robust depth-based person re-identification. IEEE Trans. Image Process. **26**(6), 2588–2603 (2017)
25. Ye, M., Lan, X., Yuen, P.C.: Robust anchor embedding for unsupervised video person re-identification in the wild. In: Proceedings of the European Conference on Computer Vision, pp. 170–186 (2018)
26. Ye, M., Shen, J., Lin, G., Xiang, T., Shao, L., Hoi, S.C.H.: Deep learning for person re-identification: a survey and outlook. In: IEEE Transactions on Pattern Analysis and Machine Intelligence (2021)
27. Yu, T., Li, D., Yang, Y., Hospedales, T.M., Xiang, T.: Robust person re-identification by modelling feature uncertainty. In: Proceedings of the IEEE International Conference on Computer Vision, pp. 552–561 (2019)
28. Zhao, R., Ouyang, W., Wang, X.: Unsupervised salience learning for person re-identification. In: Proceedings of the IEEE Conference on Computer Vision and Pattern Recognition, pp. 3586–3593 (2013)
29. Zheng, L., Shen, L., Tian, L., Wang, S., Wang, J., Tian, Q.: Scalable person re-identification: a benchmark. In: Proceedings of the IEEE International Conference on Computer Vision, pp. 1116–1124 (2015)
30. Zheng, Z., Zheng, L., Yang, Y.: Unlabeled samples generated by gan improve the person re-identification baseline in vitro. In: Proceedings of the IEEE International Conference on Computer Vision, pp. 754–3762 (2017)

Monocular Dense SLAM with Consistent Deep Depth Prediction

Feihu Yan[1], Jiawei Wen[1], Zhaoxin Li[2], and Zhong Zhou[1(✉)]

[1] State Key Laboratory of Virtual Reality Technology and Systems,
Beihang University, Beijing 100191, China
zz@buaa.edu.cn
[2] Institute of Computing Technology, Chinese Academy of Sciences,
Beijing 100190, China

Abstract. Monocular simultaneous localization and mapping (SLAM) that using a single moving camera for motion tracking and 3D scene structure reconstruction, is an essential task for many applications, such as vision-based robotic navigation and augmented reality (AR). However, most existing methods can only recover sparse or semi-dense point clouds, which are not adequate for many high-level tasks like obstacle avoidance. Meanwhile, the state-of-the-art methods use multi-view stereo to recover the depth, which is sensitive to the low-textured and non-Lambertian surface. In this work, we propose a novel dense mapping method for monocular SLAM by integrating deep depth prediction. More specifically, a classic feature-based SLAM framework is first used to track camera poses in real-time. Then an unsupervised deep neural network for monocular depth prediction is introduced to estimate dense depth maps for selected keyframes. By incorporating a joint optimization method, predicted depth maps are refined and used to generate local dense submaps. Finally, contiguous submaps are fused with the ego-motion constraint to construct the globally consistent dense map. Extensive experiments on the KITTI dataset demonstrate that the proposed method can remarkably improve the completeness of dense reconstruction in near real-time.

Keywords: Dense mapping · Visual SLAM · Monocular depth prediction

1 Introduction

Taking advantage of the universality and simplicity of camera sensors, monocular SLAM [2,24], which typically performs localization while building a 3D map of the surrounding environment simultaneously by using only a single camera, has

Supported by the National Key Research and Development Program of China under Grant 2018YFB2100601, and National Natural Science Foundation of China under Grant (61872023, 61702482).

N. Magnenat-Thalmann et al. (Eds.): CGI 2021, LNCS 13002, pp. 113–124, 2021.
https://doi.org/10.1007/978-3-030-89029-2_9

been extensively studied in the past two decades and has been deployed in various applications, including online 3D modeling [16], AR [11,12], and autonomous navigation [4].

SLAM methods can be basically classified into feature-based [14] and direct approaches [5,6]. Feature-based methods normally extract a set of point features from images, which are used to steadily track camera poses and reconstruct sparse 3D point clouds. Direct method utilize images directly without any abstraction and can generate semi-dense maps [5,6], but the sensitivity to luminosity changes makes them not as robust as feature-based methods in many application scenarios. However, neither sparse nor semi-dense 3D maps are adequate for tasks like obstacle avoidance or interaction of virtual and physical objects.

Unlike RGB-D SLAM systems [9,15] that can directly obtain dense depth information from depth sensors for dense reconstruction, it is challenging for monocular SLAM methods to estimate a consistent dense map. One of the main reasons is that the commonly used multi-view stereo method is sensitive to the low-textured and non-Lambertian surface, which leads to incomplete depth estimation. Based on the plane assumption, some works utilize superpixels [3,19] or depth interpolation [20] to generate dense maps, which improve the 3D reconstruction completeness for planar environments. Nonetheless, these works are limited to non-planar scenes and tend to over-smooth the surface details.

More recently, with the rapid development of deep learning techniques, deep neural networks [8] did dramatically boost the performance of depth prediction from monocular images (depth-from-mono). Subsequently, some works try to combine traditional SLAM systems with deep depth prediction networks [10,18,21]. However, most of these works focus on small indoor scenes and are not generalized to large-scale outdoor environments. Moreover, most methods use the depth prediction as the prior fed into the SLAM system, or directly use it in the RGB-D SLAM framework, without considering the introduced additional uncertainty introduced, which makes the reconstruction heavily dependent on the accuracy of the depth estimation.

In this paper, we propose a novel dense mapping method for monocular SLAM with consistent deep depth prediction. Our method utilizes the classic feature-based SLAM framework, ORB-SLAM2 [14], to track camera poses in real-time. When one new keyframe is created, it is fed into an unsupervised deep neural network [8] to predict the corresponding depth map, which will be refined and used in the subsequent process to generate the local 3D submap. Finally, contiguous submaps will be fused with the ego-motion constraint to construct a globally consistent dense map. The main contributions of this work are summarized as follows: 1) We present a novel dense mapping method for monocular visual SLAM, which integrates the deep depth prediction with the feature-based SLAM framework. 2) We propose a joint optimization method from 2D and 3D aspects to deal with the uncertainty introduced by the predicted depth, and generate a globally consistent dense map with the ego-motion constraint.

2 Related Work

2.1 Monocular Visual SLAM

In the past two decades, monocular SLAM has been extensively investigated and a large variety of advanced algorithms have been proposed. There are two main categories, feature-based and direct methods. The feature-based methods need to extract feature points first, which ensures robustness but also leads to extremely sparse reconstruction. Typically, ORB-SLAM2 [14] is one of the most widely used feature-based SLAM frameworks, which contains full capabilities including loop closing for a complete SLAM system. Directly using the raw pixels without any abstraction, direct methods have the ability to provide more expressive semi-dense maps, however, they have to spend extra efforts to deal with photometric changes [5].

In general, compared to direct methods, feature-based SLAM systems are not sensitive to photometric changes and perform better when the camera is moving forward, which makes them more suitable for many outdoor scenarios. Considering robustness, practicability, and scalability, we choose the widely used ORB-SLAM2 [14] as the basic framework to track poses of the moving camera, meanwhile, its loop closing thread can correct the accumulated drift and provide help for the construction of a globally consistent map.

2.2 Dense Mapping

Most dense SLAM systems typically build dense maps with available depth information using RGB-D cameras, such as [9,15]. However, since the depth camera can only provide reliable measurements in a limited range, the applicable working scenarios of these methods are limited, usually indoor scenes.

Some researchers have investigated how to obtain dense maps using a single monocular camera and proposed many charming works. Newcombe et al. [16] presented a dense SLAM system that generates smooth depth estimates by a non-convex optimization process. This system needs GPU to optimize the variational model, and the high computational cost limits its availability in large-scale environments. Concha et al. [3] proposed a dense mapping approach, which combines semi-dense maps [6] with superpixels. This work performs well in indoor scenes where low-texture regions are usually flat. Teixeira et al. [19] proposed a dense reconstruction method for small unmanned aerial vehicles (UAVs), which combines ORB-SLAM [13] with superpixels to provide a local semi-dense reconstruction in real-time.

Inspired by [3], Xue et al. [22] proposed a real-time monocular dense mapping method, which replaces the superpixel method with another efficient homogeneous region detector. Wang et al. [20] proposed a monocular dense mapping method for UAV navigation, which uses the quadtree-based pixel selection to accelerate the mapping.

Although these works have achieved amazing experiments, building denser maps is still a challenging task for large-scale outdoor scenes, partly due to the widespread existence of low-textured and non-planar areas.

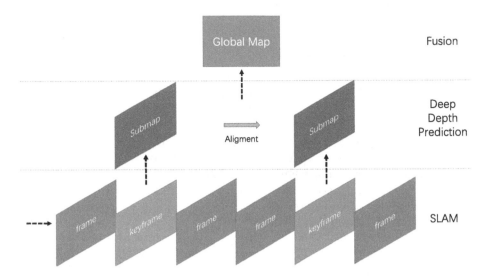

Fig. 1. System Overview. Camera poses are estimated by the SLAM system. Then submaps are generated from selected keyframs with refined deep depth prediction. Finally, optimized submaps are fused into a globally consistent dense map.

2.3   SLAM with Deep Depth Prediction

In recent years, with the rapid development of deep learning technology, convolutional neural networks (CNNs) have been widely used in monocular depth estimation. Some researchers have tried to fuse deep depth prediction with traditional SLAM systems. As the efficiency and accuracy of depth prediction have been significantly improved, this fusion has become a trend.

Tateno et al. [18] proposed a breakthrough work, which combines CNN-based depth prediction with LSD-SLAM [6] to obtain dense maps. They also proposed an extension that fuses semantic labels with the dense map. Ji et al. [10] presented a depth fusion framework, which exploits the sparse depth estimation from ORB-SLAM [13] and the CNN-inferred depth to generate a dense reconstruction. These two methods use the direct method and the feature point method as the SLAM framework, and the application scenarios are mostly indoor scenes. Wang et al. [21] proposed a surfel-based dense mapping method, which can fuse dense maps for large-scale outdoor scenes. When using a monocular camera, ORB-SLAM2 [14] in RGB-D mode is used to track camera poses with the deep depth prediction. In order to gain the run-time efficiency, surfels are used to represent the map, but also reduce the density of the point cloud.

3   System Overview

The pipeline of our work is illustrated in Fig. 1. We first use the state-of-the-art visual SLAM system, ORB-SLAM2 [14], to estimate the camera poses and extract keyframes. Then an unsupervised deep neural network [8] is introduced to predict a dense depth map for each keyframe. Refined depth maps are used to generate submaps from keyframes. Finally, contiguous submaps are fused to obtain a globally consistent dense map.

More specifically, when one new frame F_i comes, it is firstly tracked with respect to the reference keyframe K_r. If it is too far from the reference keyframe or the visual change conditions are met [14], F_i is chosen to generate a new keyframe. Every new keyframe is simultaneously fed into the deep neural network to estimate a dense depth map D_i.

Given the camera pose R, t and the dense depth estimation D_i of each keyframe, we aim to automatically generate a consistent dense map in near real-time. To achieve this, we first refine the depth map D_i using a joint optimization method. The local 3D submap S_i for each keyframe K_i can be obtained using the refined depth map $\hat{D}_i$. Then a classical point cloud registration method is used to estimate the spatial relationship between contiguous local submaps. Finally, 3D point clouds are fused with the camera ego-motion constraint to obtain a consistent dense map. An example of dense mapping is shown in Fig. 2.

4   Local Mapping with Depth Refinement

Given the depth maps predicted by the deep neural network [8], we can easily construct local 3D submaps with intrinsic camera parameters. However, the depth value predicted by the network contains more noise than the depth measurement obtained by the depth sensor. To refine the depth prediction, we mainly consider dealing with the 2D image areas that are likely to cause uncertainty in the depth prediction; in addition, we also need to filter out outliers in the 3D submaps.

4.1   2D Image Analysis

Intuitively, there are three types of image areas that mainly cause uncertainty in the depth prediction, including image boundaries, object contours, and pixels far away from the optical center of the camera.

Image Boundary. In the process of depth prediction, the deep neural network [8] learns to predict the pixel-level depth by incorporating an inbuilt left-right consistency check. Given the baseline d, the camera focal length f, and the predicted image disparity d for per pixel, the depth z can be obtained as follows,

$$z = bf/d \tag{1}$$

Intuitively, due to the lack of left-right consistency in the areas located at the image boundary, the depth estimation is more likely to produce high-uncertainty predictions.

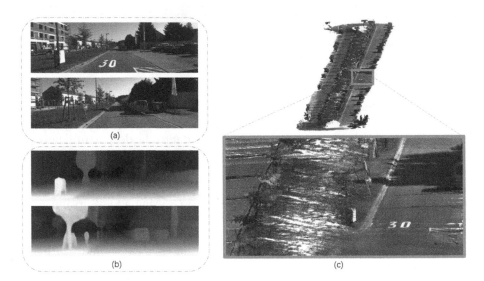

Fig. 2. The proposed method achieves dense mapping for monocular SLAM by fusing the deep depth prediction to recover a consistent 3D dense map. (a) shows two example keyframes extracted from KITTI sequence 06. (b) illustrates the corresponding depth map predicted by the unsupervised deep neural network [8]. (c) shows the global dense map (top) and details of the region labeled at blue wireframes (bottom). (Color figure online)

To ensure efficient depth estimation, we first crop the depth image according to the visual overlap area. In other words, the depth estimation near the image boundary will be discarded, which also reduces the computing consumption. As illustrated in Fig. 2(c), the final dense map discards the boundary parts while keeping the middle regions.

Object Contour. We observe that, as shown in Fig. 2(b), the depth near the contour of the object is typically over-smoothed, such as the contours of trees and cars in the figure. Therefore, we regard the image area near the contour of the object as another factor that easily leads to uncertainty for depth estimation.

We use a filter-based method to optimize the depth information. More specifically, we use a Gaussian weight function, which calculates the corresponding weight to refine the predicted depth. In order to ensure the distinguishability of the boundaries of different objects, we combine the information of color and depth difference within a small neighborhood $S_{p_i} = \{p_j\}$ around a pixel p_i into a multilateral filtering process. The refined depth can be obtained as follows,

$$\hat{D}_{p_i} = \frac{1}{W_{p_i}} \sum_{p_j \in S_{p_i}} G_{\sigma_s}(\|p_i - p_j\|) G_{\sigma_c} \left(\|I_{p_i} - I_{p_j}\|\right) G_{\sigma_d} \left(\|D_{p_i} - D_{p_j}\|\right) D_{p_i} \quad (2)$$

where i and j are pixel indexes, I_p is the color, and D_p is the corresponding depth in the predicted depth map D. G denotes the Gaussian filter kernel, while the parameters σ_e, σ_c, and σ_d are used to adjust the spatial similarity, the color similarity, and the depth similarity, respectively. W_{p_i} is used for normalization.

According to Eq. 2, areas with sharp color or depth changes in the depth map will be enhanced, while the other areas will be smoothed.

Far Points. In stereo vision, if a 3D point is farther from the camera, the uncertainty of its depth estimation will typically be greater. Similarly, since the depth estimation network relies on the parallax information from the left-right image pairs, which could cause high uncertainty for far points. Thus, we need to detect the pixels corresponding to the far point in the image.

As suggested in ORB-SLAM2 [14], keypoints will be classified as close or far when using stereo cameras. More specifically, a stereo keypoint will be classified as the close point when its depth is less than 40 times the stereo baseline, otherwise, it is classified as a far point. In this work, we follow the strategy to detect far points and discard them when building local submaps.

4.2 3D Outlier Detection

Due to the occlusion, etc., it is difficult to avoid outliers in the predicted depth [8], which may introduce additional errors for the global mapping process. Thus, an outlier detection process is required to refine the generated submaps.

In this work, LOF (Local Outlier Factor) [1] is used to detect outliers in 3D submaps. More specifically, we calculate the LOF score for each 3D point P_i as follows,

$$LOF(P_i) = \frac{\sum_{P_j \in N_k(P_i)} \frac{lrd_k(P_j)}{lrd_k(P_i)}}{|N_k(P_i)|} \tag{3}$$

where $N_k(\cdot)$ is the k-nearest neighborhood of one 3D point and $|N_k(\cdot)|$ its size, and $lrd_k(\cdot)$ is the reciprocal of the average distance from one point to all its neighbors.

When $LOF(P_i) > 1$, it means that the local point set around P_i is sparser than its neighbor points, and P_i can be regarded as a candidate outlier.

5   Global Dense Mapping with Egomotion Constraints

It is worth noting that the unsupervised deep neural network [8] uses pairs of rectified stereo images that have the known camera baseline for training. Thus, the predicted depth contains implied scale constraint from the camera baseline, which encourages us to use the Iterative Closest Point (ICP) algorithm to align adjacent submaps and generate the global dense map.

To guarantee a consistent global map, we refine contiguous submaps according to the ego-motion estimation of corresponding keyframes from the SLAM system. On the one hand, the ego-motion obtained by SLAM is continuously optimized, and the deep prediction network will only produce the result once.

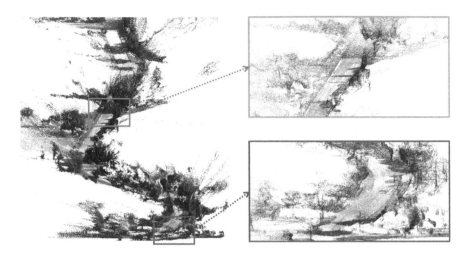

Fig. 3. Qualitative result of the dense mapping on the KITTI sequence 13. The details of the regions labeled at green and blue wireframes are also shown in the zoom-in patches (right). (Color figure online)

On the other hand, the loop closing thread of the SLAM system can help to address the scale drift.

Inspired by [23], we propose a simple scale factor $f = t_{slam}/t_{icp}$ to guarantee a consistent scale, which is the ratio between the translational motion of the SLAM system t_{slam} and ICP t_{icp}. In contrast to [23] which refines the ego-motion and the depth map alternately, the continuously optimized camera poses of the SLAM system rather than the constant depth prediction from the deep neural network are trusted in our work. Another benefit is that, when local optimization or loop closure occurs, submaps corresponding to adjusted keyframes can be updated just simply by multiplying the updated matrix calculated from the SLAM system.

Thus, we use the scale factor to refine the depth estimation. More specifically, the scale factor is used to update the initial ICP transformation matrix T_s^{s+1} estimated between two adjacent submaps:

$$\hat{\mathbf{T}}_s^{s+1} = \begin{pmatrix} \mathbf{R}_s^{s+1} & f\mathbf{t}_s^{s+1} \\ \mathbf{0} & 1 \end{pmatrix} \qquad (4)$$

Then $\hat{\mathbf{T}}_s^{s+1}$ can be used to refine the depth maps. Please refer to [23] for more technical details.

6   Evaluation

In this section, we conduct experiments to verify the effectiveness of our method on the KITTI dataset [7]. The proposed method is based on the monocular mode of ORB-SLAM2 [14], which is used to track camera poses, detect keyframes, and

Fig. 4. Qualitative comparisons on dense mapping results of the KITTI sequence 00 using (a) Surfel-Mapping [21] (b) GEM [17] and (c) our method.

close loops. We use an unsupervised deep neural network [8] to obtain dense depth maps. Since the network performs amazingly on the KITTI dataset, it is only fine-tuned on the KITTI training set. All the experiments are carried out on a standard desktop PC with Intel Xeon CPU at 3.5 GHz, 32 GB of RAM, and NVIDIA GeForce GTX 1080 GPU.

6.1   Qualitative Results

Here we discuss the completeness of the final 3D map. Figure 2(c) shows the recovered dense map on the KITTI sequence 06 datasets using our method. The global map shown on the top is quite dense, and the zoom-in patches on the bottom perform well in fine details while keeping consistent scene structure, such as the traffic sign and the road surface. Please note that as explained in Sect. 4.1, the depth predictions near the image boundaries have been discarded, thus areas on both sides of the road are mostly incomplete.

Similarly, Fig. 3 demonstrates the recovered dense point cloud of the KITTI sequence 13 using our method, where the zoomed-in areas verify the density and consistency of the global map.

Qualitative comparisons are demonstrated in Fig. 4, where reconstructed dense maps are built by Surfel-Mapping [21] using stereo cameras, GEM [17] using LiDAR, and our work using a monocular camera, respectively. Our method shows significant superiority for dense mapping over previous work. Moreover, the top row shows the details of a loop closure region and our method can generate smoother local maps.

Our method also has some shortcomings. Figure 5 shows the dense mapping result generated on the KITTI sequence 16 by our method. The details of the region labeled at green wireframes show the performance of our work when dealing with static scenes, i.e., the sign on the road could be clearly identified. However, when dealing with dynamic objects, submaps may not be aligned well in these regions. For example, in the failure case marked by red wireframes, the moving white car could not be registration successfully, which leads to 3D ghosting in the global map. In future work, we will try to introduce semantic information or object detection to deal with this problem.

Fig. 5. Qualitative results on the KITTI sequence 16, including successful and failed cases. The global dense map generated from our work is shown on the top, while the details together with two corresponding example frames of the regions labeled at green and red wireframes are also shown in the zoom-in patches (bottom). (Color figure online)

6.2   Quantitative Results

Table 1 shows the quantitative results on the KITTI sequence 00. Since the ground-truth point cloud is not available, we mainly report the density, completeness, and running time in this section. Note that the number of points is calculated from the final global map, while the completeness is the average ratio of pixels with valid depth estimation (the discarded ones will not be counted) for all keyframes. It demonstrates that the proposed method can generate denser maps.

Table 2 displays the average computational cost for each step. Specifically, the submap optimization takes the majority of the time, i.e. almost 3 s per keyframe, while the other processes could perform in real-time. Since one new keyframe will be generated when more than 20 frames have passed in the SLAM system, our work could run in near real-time (6–7 fps). Moreover, we can further reduce the number of selected keyframes to improve the efficiency of the dense mapping thread.

Table 1. Number of Points (K) and Average Keyframe Completeness (%).

Methods	ORB-SLAM2 [14]	Surfel-Mapping [21]	Ours
Points	50.6	1422.968	18563
Completeness	0.05	2.2	19.85

Table 2. Average computational cost of each step for per keyframe (ms)

SLAM	Depth	Submap	Global
Tracking	Prediction	Optimization	Fusion
23	30	3000	35

7 Conclusion

In this paper, we present a novel dense mapping approach for monocular SLAM that fuses both the monocular depth prediction and the camera ego-motion estimation, bridging the classic feature-based SLAM system and the deep neural network. Submaps are generated according to the refined depth prediction of keyframes, and the fusion is realized simply by aligning contiguous submaps with ego-motion constraints. Experiments on the KITTI dataset demonstrate that our method could obtain dense maps on large-scale outdoor scenes in near real-time. In the future, we plan to further refine the global point clouds and focus on dealing with dynamic objects using more semantic information.

References

1. Breunig, M.M., Kriegel, H.P., Ng, R.T., Sander, J.: Lof: identifying density-based local outliers. SIGMOD Rec. **29**(2), 93–104 (2000)
2. Cadena, C., Carlone, L., Carrillo, H., Latif, Y., Scaramuzza, D., Neira, J., Reid, I., Leonard, J.J.: Past, present, and future of simultaneous localization and mapping: toward the robust-perception age. IEEE Trans. Rob. **32**(6), 1309–1332 (2016)
3. Concha, A., Civera, J.: Dense piecewise planar tracking and mapping from a monocular sequence. In: Proceedings of the International Conference on Intelligent Robots and Systems (IROS) (2015)
4. Deng, X., Zhang, Z., Sintov, A., Huang, J., Bretl, T.: Feature-constrained active visual slam for mobile robot navigation. In: 2018 IEEE International Conference on Robotics and Automation (ICRA), pp. 7233–7238 (2018)
5. Engel, J., Koltun, V., Cremers, D.: Direct sparse odometry. IEEE Trans. Pattern Anal. Mach. Intell. **40**(3), 611–625 (2018)
6. Engel, J., Schöps, T., Cremers, D.: LSD-SLAM: large-scale direct monocular SLAM. In: European Conference on Computer Vision (ECCV) (2014)
7. Geiger, A., Lenz, P., Urtasun, R.: Are we ready for autonomous driving? the kitti vision benchmark suite. In: Conference on Computer Vision and Pattern Recognition (CVPR) (2012)

8. Godard, C., Aodha, O.M., Brostow, G.J.: Unsupervised monocular depth estimation with left-right consistency. In: 2017 IEEE Conference on Computer Vision and Pattern Recognition (CVPR), pp. 6602–6611 (2017)
9. Hermans, A., Floros, G., Leibe, B.: Dense 3d semantic mapping of indoor scenes from rgb-d images. In: 2014 IEEE International Conference on Robotics and Automation (ICRA), pp. 2631–2638 (2014)
10. Ji, X., Ye, X., Xu, H., Li, H.: Dense reconstruction from monocular slam with fusion of sparse map-points and cnn-inferred depth. In: 2018 IEEE International Conference on Multimedia and Expo (ICME), pp. 1–6 (2018)
11. Klein, G., Murray, D.: Parallel tracking and mapping for small ar workspaces. In: 2007 6th IEEE and ACM International Symposium on Mixed and Augmented Reality, pp. 225–234 (2007)
12. Liu, H., Zhang, G., Bao, H.: Robust keyframe-based monocular slam for augmented reality. In: 2016 IEEE International Symposium on Mixed and Augmented Reality (ISMAR), pp. 1–10 (2016)
13. Mur-Artal, R., Montiel, J.M.M., Tardós, J.D.: Orb-slam: a versatile and accurate monocular slam system. IEEE Trans. Rob. **31**(5), 1147–1163 (2015)
14. Mur-Artal, R., Tardós, J.D.: Orb-slam2: an open-source slam system for monocular, stereo, and rgb-d cameras. IEEE Trans. Rob. **33**(5), 1255–1262 (2017)
15. Newcombe, R.A., et al.: Kinectfusion: real-time dense surface mapping and tracking. In: 2011 10th IEEE International Symposium on Mixed and Augmented Reality, pp. 127–136 (2011)
16. Newcombe, R.A., Lovegrove, S.J., Davison, A.J.: Dtam: dense tracking and mapping in real-time. In: 2011 International Conference on Computer Vision, pp. 2320–2327 (2011)
17. Pan, Y., Xu, X., Ding, X., Huang, S., Wang, Y., Xiong, R.: Gem: online globally consistent dense elevation mapping for unstructured terrain. IEEE Trans. Instrum. Meas. **70**, 1–13 (2021)
18. Tateno, K., Tombari, F., Laina, I., Navab, N.: Cnn-slam: real-time dense monocular slam with learned depth prediction. In: IEEE Computer Society Conference on Computer Vision and Pattern Recognition (CVPR) (2017)
19. Teixeira, L., Chli, M.: Real-time local 3d reconstruction for aerial inspection using superpixel expansion. In: 2017 IEEE International Conference on Robotics and Automation (ICRA), pp. 4560–4567 (2017)
20. Wang, K., Ding, W., Shen, S.: Quadtree-accelerated real-time monocular dense mapping. In: 2018 IEEE/RSJ International Conference on Intelligent Robots and Systems (IROS), pp. 1–9 (2018)
21. Wang, K., Gao, F., Shen, S.: Real-time scalable dense surfel mapping. In: 2019 International Conference on Robotics and Automation (ICRA), pp. 6919–6925 (2019)
22. Xue, T., Luo, H., Cheng, D., Yuan, Z., Yang, X.: Real-time monocular dense mapping for augmented reality. In: Proceedings of the 25th ACM International Conference on Multimedia, MM 2017, pp. 510–518. Association for Computing Machinery, New York (2017)
23. Yin, X., Wang, X., Du, X., Chen, Q.: Scale recovery for monocular visual odometry using depth estimated with deep convolutional neural fields. In: 2017 IEEE International Conference on Computer Vision (ICCV), pp. 5871–5879 (2017)
24. Younes, G., Asmar, D.C., Shammas, E.A.: A survey on non-filter-based monocular visual SLAM systems. CoRR abs/1607.00470 (2016)

3D Shape-Adapted Garment Generation with Sketches

Yijing Chen[1], Chuhua Xian[1(✉)], Shuo Jin[2], and Guiqing Li[1]

[1] School of Computer Science and Engineering, South China University of Technology, Guangzhou 510006, China
chhxian@scut.edu.cn
[2] BlueFire AI, Hong Kong, China

Abstract. Garment generation or reconstruction is becoming extremely demanding for many digital applications, and the traditional process is time-consuming. In recent years, garment reconstruction from sketch leveraging deep learning and principal component analysis (PCA) has made great progress. In this paper, we present a data-driven approach wherein 3D garments are directly generated from sketches combining given body shape parameters. Our framework is an encoder-decoder architecture. In our network, sketch features extracted by DenseNet and body shape parameters were encoded to latent code respectively. Then, the new latent code obtained by adding two latent codes of the sketch and human body shape is decoded by a fully convolutional mesh decoder. Our network enables the body shape adapted detailed 3D garment generation by leveraging garment sketch and body shape parameters. With the fully convolutional mesh decoder, the network can show the effect of body shape and sketch on the generated garment. Experimental results show that the fully convolutional mesh decoder we used to reconstruct the garment performs higher accuracy and maintains lots of detail compared with the PCA-based method.

Keywords: 3D Garment Reconstruction · Sketch-based modeling · Body shape adapted · Mesh decoder

1 Introduction

Designing garments that adapting to the shape of the body is an age-old problem in the fashion industry. In the traditional flowcharts, designing real or virtual garments is a complex and time-consuming process with iterative steps. Firstly, experienced designers carry out design ideas based on the shape of a person, and then draw the sketch of the garment. Then, the pattern maker makes the garment patterns and sews them into a whole garment. This process can be summarized into two steps: the 2D sketches for the initial design, and the 3D garment construction according to the body shape. Mapping the 2D garment sketch design to a 3D body requires a good understanding of the 3D space of the human body to adapt to the shape, and it is not an intuitive process. For

© Springer Nature Switzerland AG 2021
N. Magnenat-Thalmann et al. (Eds.): CGI 2021, LNCS 13002, pp. 125–136, 2021.
https://doi.org/10.1007/978-3-030-89029-2_10

a garment designer, changes often take place for a new style garment to adapt various body shapes. If the corresponding 3D garment is generated through complicated steps for each modification, the design cycle of the garment will become longer and labor-intensive, especially for designers who do not have much design experience.

To reduce the design cost and shorten the design cycle, a straightforward way is that a garment can be generated automatically by some images or sketches. In this paper, we propose a sketch-based shape adapted garments generation method. Given a human body shape as a reference, users can draw a garment sketch in the white plane. Then using the sketch and the human body shape as input, our method can generate the shape adapted 3D garment. We use a sketch encoder and a body shape encoder to extract the features respectively. Then the sketch feature and the body shape parameters are added together to form the latent code. With this latent code as input, the mesh decoder is applied to reconstruct the 3D garment in the mesh.

Our method is an end-to-end network. To train such a network requires gaining sufficient garment data. However, there is no publicly available garment dataset that both provides the 3D garments and corresponding human body shapes. Thus, we construct a large dataset with garments adapted to various human body shapes.

In summary, the main contributions of our paper are as follows:

- A large 3D garment dataset is constructed. This dataset consists of 3070 sets of 2D garment sketches, 3D garment meshes, and the corresponding human body shape parameters, which can be used to train an end-to-end network for garment generation applications.
- Using the 2D garment sketch as input, combined with human body shape parameters, an end-to-end neural network is proposed to generate a 3D garment mesh that fits a specific human body shape.
- A fully convolutional mesh decoder is integrated into the proposed network to improve the computational performance, precision, and accuracy compared to the PCA-based methods.

2   Related Work

Garment Modeling. Taking a single image as input, Zhou et al. [31] estimate the pose and body shape of the mannequin, and interpret the garment outline to generate an initial 3D garment model. Similar to Zhou et al., Jeong et al. [13] extracted silhouette edges from the input image and lifted them to 3D garments. Danundefinedřek et al. [7] take an image as input and obtain the target garment by learning the deformation of the reference garment. Taking RGBD data as input, the system proposed by Chen et al. [5] detects and classifies garments components, and then stitchs the templates to model garments. Wang et al. [28] model the garment by learning a shared shape space. Tiwari et al. [26] estimate and visualize the dressing effect of a garment in various sizes.

Garment Capture. Pritchard *et al.* [22] use a stereo image pair to reconstruct a garment. Color-coded patterns are used by Scholz *et al.* [25] and White *et al.* [29] to reconstruct a garment from a multi-view setup. Bradley *et al.* [4] present a multi-view capture system for garments but eliminating the need for a color-coded pattern. Popa *et al.* [21] add details to the coarse meshes captured from the multi-view video, and Wang *et al.* [27] solve a similar problem using a data-driven approach. Pons-Moll *et al.* [20] capture the body and garment shape from the 3D sequence. Kamel *et al.* [3] propose a comparison algorithm between two skeletons motions based on the quantified metrics, which is helpful for garment capture.

Garment Re-targeting. Guan *et al.* [9] propose a parameterized model of the human body shape and pose parameters. Neophytou *et al.* [18] retarget a garment by replacing deformation with residual transformations between a naked mesh and the dressed mesh. Pons-Moll *et al.* [20] estimate the displacement of clothing after computing the minimally clothed shape and a multi-cloth alignment. Wang *et al.* [28] retarget a garment through learning a shared shape space. Gundogdu *et al.* [10] utilize deep networks to fuse garment features at varying levels of details with body features. Santesteban *et al.* [24] used a recurrent neural network to separates global garment from local garment wrinkles. Patel *et al.* [19] decompose the deformation into a high frequency and a low frequency to retarget a garment. Xu *et al.* [30] predict dressing fit for ready-made garments on different individuals. Tiwari *et al.* [26] completed the retargeting through deep learning.

Sketch-based Modeling. Robson *et al.* [23] analyze the factors that influenced the silhouettes depicted in the sketches and predict the garment. Jung *et al.* [14] proposed a sketch-based modeling method for developable surfaces. To model freeform shapes with complex curvature patterns, Li *et al.* [16] use a sketch-based modeling method utilizing the bending strokes. The method presented by Wang *et al.* [28] take as input a sketch to predict the garment fitting the specific body.

Due to the irregular sampling and connections in the mesh data, it is hard to use a deep learning method such as convolutional neural networks (CNN) to process mesh directly. Thus many methods [7,18,19,28] introduced Principal Component Analysis (PCA) to obtain a low-frequency vector to represent a garment mesh. However, the information loss due to performing PCA leads to accuracy loss of the mesh. Recently, Zhou *et al.* [32] proposed a fully convolutional mesh autoencoder that can process arbitrary registered mesh data directly, which inspires our work.

3   The Proposed Method

3.1   Overview of the Network Architecture

As illustrated in Fig. 1, our garment generation network is an end-to-end architecture. The proposed network mainly consists of three modules: the sketch encoder the human body shape encoder and the mesh decoder based on a fully convolutional mesh decoder. Firstly, the input sketch image is fed into the DenseNet for features extraction and generates a sketch descriptor **S**. Then the sketch descriptor is encoded by the sketch encoder. Meanwhile, the human body shape parameter **P**, which is a 10-dimensional vector provided by *SMPL* [17] to describe the body shape variation, is encoded by the body shape encoder. Then, two latent code are added up to obtain the latent code **C**. Finally, the fully convolutional mesh decoder takes the latent code **C** as the input and reconstructs the 3D garment which is detailed and adapted to specific human body shape. In our network, the 3D garment is reprensted by the triangular mesh data structure. We will give more details as follows.

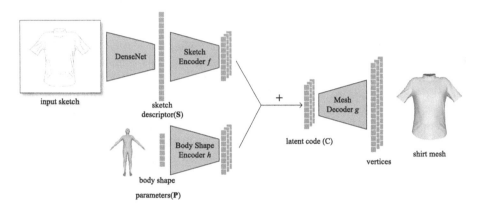

Fig. 1. Overview of the proposed garment generation network based on fully convolutional mesh decoder. It mainly consists of three modules: the sketch encoder module, the body shape encoder module, and the convolutional mesh decoder module.

3.2   Sketch Encoder and Body Shape Encoder

Sketch Encoder. The garment sketch is essentially a grey image which is drawed by users or generated by other tools, and it will be transformed into RGB image as the input of the sketch encoder network. To extract features from the input sketch image, we utilize the DenseNet [11] (the DenseNet-161 architecture provided in the TorchVision library [2]) to generate a 2208-dimensional sketch descriptor **S**. Then the sketch encoder takes the sketch descriptor **S** as input and generate the latent code. The detail parameters of this the sketch encoder is described in Fig. 2. Fully connected blocks are fully connected layers followed by Rectifying Linear Unit (RELU) activations and batch normalization. The 2208-dimensional descriptor **S** is converted to a 100-dimensional vector through series of fully connected blocks. The last max-pooling layer yields a latent code with size 22 and 9 channels.

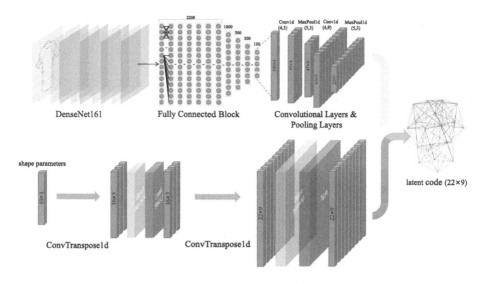

Fig. 2. The Sketch Encoder consists of DenseNet, 10 fully connected layers, 2 convolutional layers, and 2 pooling layers. Each fully connected layer is followed by RELU activation and batch normalization. The Body Shape Encoder is consists of 2 one-dimensional transposed convolution and corresponding batch normalization and activations. The 2 activations are Leak ReLU and Tanh respectively.

Body Shape Encoder. The body shape parameter $\mathbf{P}$ is a 10-dimensional vector provided by *SMPL* to describe the human body shape. To obtain the latent code with the size of 22 and the channel of 9, we compose the body shape encoder with 2 transposed 1D convolution layers which followed by batch normalization and different activations respectively. The detailed architecture of the body shape encoder is illustrated in Fig. 2.

3.3 Fully Convolutional Mesh Decoder

Although the PCA-based methods are able to produce descriptive latent spaces and useful for capturing details of garment meshes, the reduction of dimensionality will result in a loss of accuracy. Inspired by the work in [32], we introduce a fully convolution mesh decoder to conduct the operations in this step.

The Variant Convolution and TransConv. Suppose the output graph $\mathcal{Y}$ which has vertices y_i is sampled from the input graph $\mathcal{X}$ which has vertices x_i. In graph $\mathcal{X}$, let $\mathcal{N}(i)$ is a local region of y_i, and it has E_i vertices $x_{i,j}$, $j = 1, .., E_i$. Given the Weight Basis $B = \{\mathbf{B}_k\}_{k=1}^{M}$ ($\mathbf{B}_k \in \mathbb{R}^{I \times O}$) and locally variant coefficients(vc) $A_{i,j} = \{\alpha_{i,j,k}\}_{k=1}^{M}, \alpha \in \mathbb{R}$, then the weights of $x_{i,j}$ is computed as:

$$\mathbf{W}_{i,j} = \sum_{k=1}^{M} \alpha_{i,j,k} \mathbf{B}_k, \tag{1}$$

and convolution can be represented as:

$$\mathbf{y}_i = \sum_{x_{i,j} \in \mathcal{N}(i)} \mathbf{W}_{i,j}^T \mathbf{x}_{i,j} + \mathbf{b} \tag{2}$$

here $\mathbf{b}$ is the learned bias, $A_{i,j}$ are different for each vertex $x_{i,j}$, and B is shared and learned globally.

The vdPool, vdUnpool, vdUpRes and vdDownRes. Within the pooling kernel radius, because the vertices in arbitrary graph are distributed unevenly, the max or average pooling will induce poor performance. To overcome this problem, Zhou *et al.* [32] introduce the variant density(vd) coefficients which are learnable parameters into the network.

The aggregation functions in vdPool and vdUpPooling layers are:

$$M\mathbf{y}_i = \sum_{j \in \mathcal{N}(i)} \rho' x_{i,j}, \qquad \rho' = \frac{|\rho_{i,j}|}{\sum_{j=1}^{E_i} |\rho_{i,j}|}, \tag{3}$$

where M is the average size of a neighborhood $\mathcal{N}(i)$ of $x_{i,j}$, $\rho_{i,j} \in \mathbb{R}$ is the training parameter and $\rho'_{i,j}$ is the density value. Then, the residual layer is defined as:

$$\mathbf{y}_i = \sum_{x_{i,j} \in \mathcal{N}(i)} \rho' \mathbf{C} \mathbf{x}_{i,j} \tag{4}$$

here C is an identity matrix when the input and output feature dimensions are the same, or is a learned matrix when the input and output feature dimensions are different.

Details of the Decoder Network. We downsampled the mesh firstly. After multiple downsampling of the mesh, multiple connectivities with different topologies and numbers of vertices are obtained. As shown in Fig. 3, the latent code

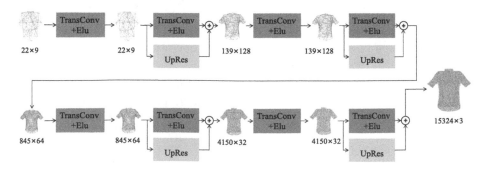

Fig. 3. The structure of the convolutional mesh decoder. It mainly consists of 8 TransConv blocks and 4 UpRes blocks.

is decoded to vertices data of the 3D garment mesh by 8 transposed convolutional (TransConv) blocks and 4 up-residual (UpRes) blocks. In each TransConv block, following each TransConv layer is an exponential linear unit (ELU) [6] activations.

3.4   Loss Function

Our loss function for training consists of two items. One is the $L1$ laplacian loss(L_{lap}), and the other is $L1$ geometric loss(L_{geo}):

$$L = \lambda_1 L_{lap} + \lambda_2 L_{geo} \tag{5}$$

The $L1$ laplacian loss is used to smooth the vertices:

$$L_{lap} = \frac{1}{m} \sum_{i=1}^{m} |lap'_i - lap_i|,$$

$$lap_i = \frac{1}{E_i} \sum_{j=1}^{E_i} (y_i - y_j), \qquad lap'_i = \frac{1}{E_i} \sum_{j=1}^{E_i} (y'_i - y'_j) \tag{6}$$

where E_i is the number of vertices in neighborhood $\mathcal{N}(i)$ of y_i or y'_i. The $L1$ geometric loss is defined as:

$$L_{geo} = \frac{1}{m} \sum_{i=1}^{m} |y'_i - y_i| \tag{7}$$

In our implementation, we set $\lambda_1 = \lambda_2 = 1$ in Eq. (5).

4   Experiments

4.1   Dataset Construction

We construction a dataset with 3730 sets of data. Figure 4 shows an example in our dataset. Each set of data contains a 3D garment mesh, a corresponding flattened mesh, a sketch image, a 3D male body mesh, and its body shape parameter. To construct the dataset, we firstly sample 746 male bodies with the same A-pose from the FashionPose [15] dataset. We simulated garments over body samples using the cloth simulator in CLO3D [1], and then obtained the draped garments and the flattened meshes of each garment. To ensure the consistency of the mesh topology, we use one of the simulated garments as the standard template. Each flattened mesh corresponding to each garment is aligned with the template flattened mesh via the $ARAP$ [12] deformation. Then we locate the vertices of template flattened mesh in the associated triangle of each flattened garment mesh via the barycentric coordinates. Finally, the vertices of the template 3D garment mesh are mapped to each 3D garment mesh. Then, the 3730 3D garment meshes with the same topology and different shapes are generated using these mentioned steps. With these 3D garment meshes, we generate their corresponding sketches using the Suggestive Contours method [8].

Fig. 4. The dataset includes 5 types of 3D shirt garments. Each set has a male human model with the body shape parameter named "betas.txt", a topology unified mesh, a flattened mesh, and the corresponding 2D sketch.

4.2 Results

We split the dataset into training (80%), evaluating (10%), and testing sets (10%). The network is trained with batch size = 32, learning rate = 0.0001, learning rate decay = 0.9 every epoch, using Geforce RTX 3090,Cuda 11.1 and PyTorch 1.8.0. As listed in Table 1, with 500 epochs of training, the mean test errors of training, evaluating, and testing data are 3.581, 3.717, 3.714 mm respectively. Table 1 also show the parameter count of both methods. Our method takes an average of 0.033 s to generate a 3D garment from the input 2D sketch. We also replaced the decoder with a fully connected neural network and represented the mesh with PCA, and the mean test errors of training, evaluating, and testing data are 13.020, 13.595, 13.294 mm respectively. It can be seen that our method is significantly better than the PCA-based method.

Table 1. The average per vertex error (mm) on our dataset and the parameter count of both methods. The results of our method are better than the results of PCA-based method.

Dataset	Geometric error of ours (mm)	Geometric error of PCA (mm)
Train	3.581	13.020
Evaluate	3.717	13.595
Test	3.714	13.294
Param	39,417,570	32,360,658

The result of 3D garments generated from the testing dataset is visualized in Fig. 5. The red color indicates a large error while the blue color indicates a minor error. Obviously, the errors mainly appear in the hem and sleeve part of the garment. Although there are some errors, the generated garments are closed to ground truth garments from the perspective of the shape and the detail. Figure 5 also shows the comparison of the results of using PCA and our method, and our method is better than PCA.

We also compared other clothing modeling methods. As shown in Table 2, we have adopted the same measurement standards as the original paper, and ours results are better.

Table 2. Comparison with other methods. Average per vertex error (mm) and the normalized L^2 distance percentage (%).

	Sizer [26]	Tailornet [19]	Garnet [10]	Wang's [28]	Ours
Error (mm)	15.54	10.2	–	–	**3.714**
Error (%)	–	–	1.15	3.01	**1.12**

We also test the proposed method using the same input sketch with various body shapes. Figure 6 shows four examples of the results. In this figure, it can be seen that the same garment can be well adapted to different body shapes, and keeps the same style.

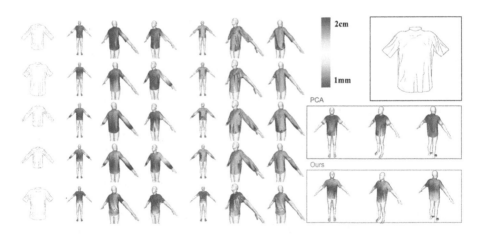

Fig. 5. Error visualization of 5 examples of the generated results. The errors mainly appear in the hem and sleeve part. The ground truth garments are represented by a gray mesh. Compared with the results of using PCA, ours has a better effect. (Color figure online)

In this work, we implement a user interface based on the network (Fig. 7), which allows the user to edit the sketch or body and the 3D draped garment is updated at interactive rates. The 2D sketch can be imported from an image file and edit on the painting board. Different body shapes can be specified by editing the parameters. With different body shapes and sketches, the 3D garments fitting the body is updated in real-time at interactive rates.

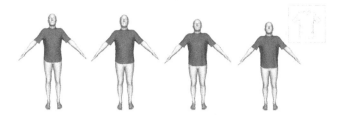

Fig. 6. Four examples of the same 2D garment with different human body shapes. The results show that the same garment can be well adapted to different human body shapes.

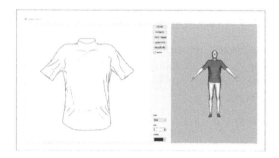

Fig. 7. The user interface allows the user to edit the sketch or body and the 3D draped garment is updated in real-time at interactive rates.

5   Conclusion

In this paper, we propose a sketch-based 3D garment generation method. Taking the 2D garment sketch and the parameters of the human body shape as input, our method can generate a 3D garment mesh based on a fully convolutional mesh decoder network. We construct a garment dataset with 3730 sets for the training network. The results of testing show that the proposed method performs well when reconstructing 3D garments. Moreover, the user interface we implemented allows users to edit the sketch or body and 3D draped garment is updated at interactive rates, and the generated 3D garment can be adapted to different human body shapes.

Acknowledgments. This paper is supported by Natural Science Foundation of Guangdong Province (No. 2021A1515011849, No. 2019A1515011793) and the Fundamental Research Funds for the Central Universities (No. 2020ZYGXZR042).

References

1. Clo - 3d fashion design software (2021). https://www.clo3d.com/
2. torchvision.models - torchvision master documentation (2021). https://pytorch. org/vision/stable/models.html

3. Aouaidjia, K., Sheng, B., Li, P., Kim, J., Feng, D.D.: Efficient body motion quantification and similarity evaluation using 3-d joints skeleton coordinates. IEEE Trans. Syst. Man Cybern. Syst. **51**(5), 2774–2788 (2021). https://doi.org/10.1109/TSMC.2019.2916896
4. Bradley, D., Popa, T., Sheffer, A., Heidrich, W., Boubekeur, T.: Markerless garment capture. In: ACM SIGGRAPH 2008 Papers, pp. 1–9 (2008)
5. Chen, X., Zhou, B., Lu, F.X., Wang, L., Bi, L., Tan, P.: Garment modeling with a depth camera. ACM Trans. Graph. **34**(6), 203–1 (2015)
6. Clevert, D.A., Unterthiner, T., Hochreiter, S.: Fast and accurate deep network learning by exponential linear units (elus). arXiv preprint arXiv:1511.07289 (2015)
7. Danundefinedřek, R., Dibra, E., Öztireli, C., Ziegler, R., Gross, M.: Deepgarment: 3d garment shape estimation from a single image. Comput. Graph. Forum **36**(2), 269–280 (2017). https://doi.org/10.1111/cgf.13125
8. DeCarlo, D., Finkelstein, A., Rusinkiewicz, S., Santella, A.: Suggestive contours for conveying shape. In: ACM SIGGRAPH 2003 Papers, pp. 848–855 (2003)
9. Guan, P., Reiss, L., Hirshberg, D.A., Weiss, A., Black, M.J.: Drape: dressing any person. ACM Trans. Graph. (TOG) **31**(4), 1–10 (2012)
10. Gundogdu, E., Constantin, V., Seifoddini, A., Dang, M., Salzmann, M., Fua, P.: Garnet: a two-stream network for fast and accurate 3d cloth draping. In: Proceedings of the IEEE/CVF International Conference on Computer Vision, pp. 8739–8748 (2019)
11. Huang, G., Liu, Z., Van Der Maaten, L., Weinberger, K.Q.: Densely connected convolutional networks. In: Proceedings of the IEEE Conference on Computer Vision and Pattern Recognition, pp. 4700–4708 (2017)
12. Igarashi, T., Moscovich, T., Hughes, J.F.: As-rigid-as-possible shape manipulation. ACM Trans. Graph. (TOG) **24**(3), 1134–1141 (2005)
13. Jeong, M.H., Han, D.H., Ko, H.: Garment capture from a photograph. Comput. Animation Virtual Worlds **26**, 291–300 (2015)
14. Jung, A., Hahmann, S., Rohmer, D., Begault, A., Boissieux, L., Cani, M.P.: Sketching folds: developable surfaces from non-planar silhouettes. ACM Trans. Graph. **34**(5), November 2015. https://doi.org/10.1145/2749458
15. Lassner, C., Romero, J., Kiefel, M., Bogo, F., Black, M.J., Gehler, P.V.: Unite the people: Closing the loop between 3d and 2d human representations. In: Proceedings of the IEEE Conference on Computer Vision and Pattern Recognition, pp. 6050–6059 (2017)
16. Li, C., Pan, H., Liu, Y., Tong, X., Sheffer, A., Wang, W.: Bendsketch: Modeling freeform surfaces through 2d sketching. ACM Trans. Graph. **36**(4), July 2017. https://doi.org/10.1145/3072959.3073632
17. Loper, M., Mahmood, N., Romero, J., Pons-Moll, G., Black, M.J.: Smpl: a skinned multi-person linear model. ACM Trans. Graph. (TOG) **34**(6), 1–16 (2015)
18. Neophytou, A., Hilton, A.: A layered model of human body and garment deformation. In: 2014 2nd International Conference on 3D Vision, vol. 1, pp. 171–178. IEEE (2014)
19. Patel, C., Liao, Z., Pons-Moll, G.: Tailornet: Predicting clothing in 3d as a function of human pose, shape and garment style. In: Proceedings of the IEEE/CVF Conference on Computer Vision and Pattern Recognition, pp. 7365–7375 (2020)
20. Pons-Moll, G., Pujades, S., Hu, S., Black, M.J.: Clothcap: seamless 4d clothing capture and retargeting. ACM Trans. Graph. (TOG) **36**(4), 1–15 (2017)
21. Popa, T., et al.: Wrinkling captured garments using space-time data-driven deformation. In: Computer Graphics Forum, vol. 28, pp. 427–435. Wiley Online Library (2009)

22. Pritchard, D., Heidrich, W.: Cloth motion capture. In: Computer Graphics Forum, vol. 22, pp. 263–271. Wiley Online Library (2003)
23. Robson, C., Maharik, R., Sheffer, A., Carr, N.: Context-aware garment modeling from sketches. Comput. Graph. **35**(3), 604–613 (2011)
24. Santesteban, I., Otaduy, M.A., Casas, D.: Learning-based animation of clothing for virtual try-on. In: Computer Graphics Forum, vol. 38, pp. 355–366. Wiley Online Library (2019)
25. Scholz, V., Stich, T., Magnor, M., Keckeisen, M., Wacker, M.: Garment motion capture using color-coded patterns. In: ACM SIGGRAPH 2005 Sketches, pp. 38-es (2005)
26. Tiwari, G., Bhatnagar, B.L., Tung, T., Pons-Moll, G.: Sizer: a dataset and model for parsing 3d clothing and learning size sensitive 3d clothing. arXiv preprint arXiv:2007.11610 (2020)
27. Wang, H., Hecht, F., Ramamoorthi, R., O'Brien, J.F.: Example-based wrinkle synthesis for clothing animation. In: ACM SIGGRAPH 2010 Papers, pp. 1–8 (2010)
28. Wang, T.Y., Ceylan, D., Popovic, J., Mitra, N.J.: Learning a shared shape space for multimodal garment design (2018)
29. White, R., Crane, K., Forsyth, D.A.: Capturing and animating occluded cloth. ACM Trans. Graph. (TOG) b(3), 34-es (2007)
30. Xu, H., Li, J., Lu, G., Zhang, D., Long, J.: Predicting ready-made garment dressing fit for individuals based on highly reliable examples. Comput. Graph. **90**, 135–144 (2020). https://doi.org/10.1016/j.cag.2020.06.002. https://www.sciencedirect.com/science/article/pii/S0097849320300911
31. Zhou, B., Chen, X., Fu, Q., Guo, K., Tan, P.: Garment modeling from a single image. In: Computer Graphics Forum, vol. 32, pp. 85–91. Wiley Online Library (2013)
32. Zhou, Y., Wu, C., Li, Z., Cao, C., Ye, Y., Saragih, J., Li, H., Sheikh, Y.: Fully convolutional mesh autoencoder using efficient spatially varying kernels. arXiv preprint arXiv:2006.04325 (2020)

Geometric Computing

Light-Weight Multi-view Topology Consistent Facial Geometry and Reflectance Capture

Penglei Ji, Hanchao Li, Luyan Jiang, and Xinguo Liu$^{(\boxtimes)}$

State Key Lab of CAD & CG, Zhejiang University, Hangzhou 310000, China
{jpl,hanson_li,jly21821048}@zju.edu.cn, xgliu@cad.zju.edu.cn

Abstract. We present a light-weight multi-view capture system with different lighting conditions to generate a topology consistent facial geometry and high-resolution reflectance texture maps. Firstly, we construct the base mesh from multi-view images using the stereo reconstruction algorithms. Then we leverage the mesh deformation technique to register a template mesh to the reconstructed geometry for topology consistency. The facial and ear landmarks are also utilized to guide the deformation. We adopt the photometric stereo and BRDF fitting methods to recover the facial reflectance field. The specular normal which contains high-frequency information is finally utilized to refine the coarse geometry for sub-millimeter details. The captured topology consistent finer geometry and high-quality reflectance information can be used to produce a lifelike personalized digital avatar.

1 Introduction

Photo-realistic human face modeling is a challenge in computer graphics and computer vision fields. Traditional capturing pipeline has been widely used in film or game industry. However, it is very time-consuming, and needs plenty of expensive artist inputs to refine the coarse geometry and reflectance maps manually.

A variety of methods have been proposed to reconstruct high-quality facial geometry and high-resolution reflectance [18,32]. Debevec *et al.* [9] designed a light stage to capture face from a set of viewpoints under a dense sampling of the incident illumination. However, this method can only obtain the specific reflectance from fixed view directions and can not recover the geometry from the measurement data. Ghosh *et al.* [14] used the polarized spherical gradient illumination to acquire the detailed facial geometry with diffuse and specular photometric information from multiple viewpoints. Fyffe *et al.* [11] presented a near-instant facial geometry and reflectance capture system using several cameras and external flashes based on the photometric stereo techniques. They trimmed away the redundant faces manually and obtained a geometry with inconsistent topology. Fyffe *et al.* [12] optimized the photo-consistency constraints between

© Springer Nature Switzerland AG 2021
N. Magnenat-Thalmann et al. (Eds.): CGI 2021, LNCS 13002, pp. 139–150, 2021.
https://doi.org/10.1007/978-3-030-89029-2_11

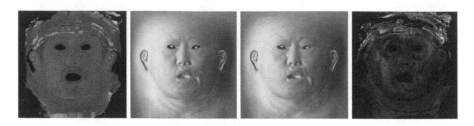

Fig. 1. From left to right: diffuse albedo, diffuse normal, specular normal and specular roughness. The resolution of the recovered reflectance maps is 4000 × 4000.

different views to construct a consistent face topology based on a shared template mesh. The mesh optimization procedure is based on the optical flow and the Laplacian mesh and volumetric deformation. However, the facial details recovered are based on the assumption that the darker is deeper, and miss some realistic details compared to the photometric stereo based methods.

In this paper, we propose a light-weight high-quality face geometry and reflectance capture system. Our method is able to capture a full head geometry with extract ear shape compared to the similar capture system [11]. It allows for a capture system simpler and cheaper than a light stage, *e.g.* no polarizers and less light sources. The basic idea of the reflectance capture is simulating different lighting and view directions as a simplified light stage, and then using the dense measurement data to fit the physical based microfacet BRDF model, rather than the simple empirical Blinn-Phong model. Figure 1 shows the recovered reflectance maps.

Fig. 2. Synthetic images rendered using the captured geometry and reflectance maps.

Figure 2 shows some synthetic photo-realistic images using the captured facial geometry and reflectance. The main contributions of our work are summarized as follows:

– We design a light-weight facial capture system to capture multi-view facial images under different lighting directions.
– We adopt a non-rigid mesh deformation technique, which leverages the facial and ear landmarks, to align the shared template mesh with the reconstructed mesh for a topology consistent geometry.

– We demonstrate the effectiveness of our recovered texture maps by rendering under several fixed point light sources and image-based illuminations.

2   Related Work

2.1   High-Quality Facial Geometry

To acquire high-quality facial geometry, the laser scanner is widely used to produce geometry with sub-millimeter details [3,4]. However, it still has a lot of drawbacks, including the demand for special expensive hardwares and the requirement of staying still for a quite long time.

Passive multi-view face reconstruction systems [2,5,6,17,19] have been proposed to obtain a high-quality facial geometry under uniform illumination conditions. They exploit the mesoscopic features or edge strain [17] to refine the base geometry for more details. However, they can only reconstruct a diffuse albedo map from multi-view images and do not take the specular components into consideration, which is pretty important in realistic rendering. Ghosh et al. [14] constructed the geometry using the stereo reconstruction methods which compute a depth map for each viewpoint image, and then merged multiple depth maps into a single mesh. They represented the facial geometry using a cylinder as a base mesh and a displacement map. For micro-surface details, Ma et al. [20] proposed the gradient illumination to recover high-resolution detail to refine the coarse geometry. The coarse geometry is obtained using stereo pairs of cameras with a video projector placed between them. This procedure requires five seconds to capture data, including eight gradient patterns and five structured light images. Graham et al. [16] captured the skin micro-geometry using a 12-light capture dome similar to polarized gradient illumination.

2.2   Facial Appearance Capture

Facial appearance capture has achieved significant progress in recent years [18]. Existing measurement-based facial appearance capture and modeling can be divided into two categories: image-based and model-based. The image-based methods capture the total reflectance field from a fixed viewpoint. Debevec et al. [9] designed a light stage to capture the 4D reflectance field for image-based relighting.

The model-based methods need a 3D geometry and then capture the surface reflectance. Weyrich et al. [26] modeled the measured data to fit a spatially-varying analytic BRDF, a diffuse albedo map, and diffuse subsurface scattering. They also design a measurement device using an image-based version of a fiber optic spectrometer with a linear array of optical fiber detectors. Zickler et al. [31] exploited the spatial coherence to estimate the reflectance function from a set of images of the known geometry by formulating the SBRDF estimation as a scattered-data interpolation problem. Some researchers [7,10,23] explored the intrinsic image decomposition to recover the albedo and shading.

Physical based skin models are based on a microfacet distribution model. Ghosh *et al.* [15] fit a microfacet BRDF model for high-resolution surface orientation. Ghosh *et al.* [13] estimated the spatially varying specular roughness and tangent vector of per point from polarized second-order spherical gradient illumination.

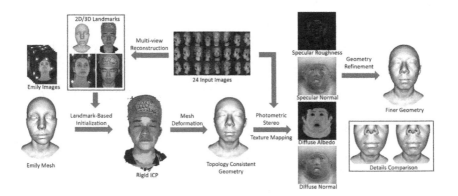

Fig. 3. The pipeline of our facial capture system. The input is the 24 input images captured under different lighting conditions in about 100 ms. The Digital Emily project is used as the shared template. (1) We generate a coarse mesh using the software Photo-Scan. (2) We adopt the face and ear landmarks to initialize the rigid transformation. (3) We utilize the non-rigid mesh deformation technique to register the template mesh with our facial geometry. (4) Based on the diffuse and specular separation, we leverage the photometric stereo and BRDF fitting to calculate the diffuse albedo, diffuse normal, specular roughness and specular normal. (5) High-frequency details from the specular normal map are finally integrated into the coarse mesh for finer geometry.

3   System Overview

Our system consists of two components: geometry recovery based on the stereo reconstruction and reflectance capture based on the photometric stereo, as illustrated in Fig. 3. We build the facial measurement system using 24 Canon 800D cameras and 8 MK-14EXT flashlights based on work [11]. Figure 4 shows the photographs of our capture system. The 24 cameras are divided into 8 groups, and each group shares the same lighting condition. The trigger signals of the cameras and the flashlights are generated using an arduino micro-controller. We capture images at ISO 100 to avoid the noise as much as possible. All lenses are employed 55 mm to capture the face details. The f-stop is set to 16 to obtain a high depth-of-field. The exposure time is set to 1/100 s. The subjects sit in the chair with a headrest to keep head being still in the about 100 ms capture procedure. The flashlights are modeled as point light source, and their positions and poses can be estimated from the camera parameters exported from PhotoScan.

4   Proposed Method

4.1   Landmarks Based Initialization

We use the publicly available "Digital Emily" [1] mesh, texture coordinates, seven associated photographs and camera parameters as the shared template. We leverage the facial landmark detector to detect the 276 facial landmarks in the template photographs and our captured images.The 3D landmarks in the template mesh and our coarse mesh are then calculated based on the multi-view geometry given the camera parameters.

Fig. 4. The facial measurement system consists of 24 cameras and 8 flashlights. The red circles mark the flashes. (Color figure online)

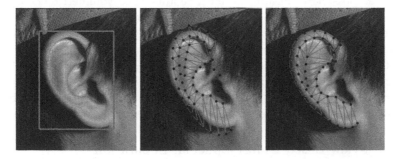

Fig. 5. From left to right: the detected ear bounding box, the initial shape for the active appearance method, the detected ear landmarks.

We also implement an ear landmarks detector for better non-rigid registration. We adopt the faster-rcnn [22] which is widely used in object detection as our network architecture, and pre-train it on the COCO-dataset. We then fine-tune the detection networks on the ear datasets [29] and some ear images labeled by ourselves. We finally apply the patch-based active appearance model [8] to localize the 55 ear landmarks. The detected ear landmarks are shown in Fig. 5.

Based on the 2D landmarks, we back-project them into 3D space for 3D landmarks. After obtaining the 3D landmarks of the template mesh and our coarse mesh, we firstly scale the template mesh based on the mean distance between landmarks, and then align the scaled template mesh with the coarse mesh rigidly based on the corresponding landmark pairs.

4.2   Mesh Deformation

Due to the existence of noise and incompleteness, we cooperate the as-rigid-as-possible mesh deformation technique [25] with the volumetric laplacian deformation [28] to obtain a topology consistent facial geometry. The goal is to deform the template mesh X to our reconstructed coarse mesh Y. We parameterize the mapping function as a 3×3 rotation matrix R_i for each template vertex X_i.

We formulate the total energy function as a weighted sum of the four energy terms, including the landmark matching term, the matching term, the as-rigid-as-possible term and the volumetric term.

$$E(Z, R_i|_{i=1}^n) = w_1 E_{landmark} + w_2 E_{match} + w_3 E_{arap} + w_4 E_{volumetric} \qquad (1)$$

The unknown variable Z indicates the vertex coordinates of the template after deformation, and is organized in $n \times 3$ matrix with n is the number of the template mesh vertices.

The landmark matching energy involves the face and ear landmarks of two meshes to guide the registration. The matching energy measures how close the deformed template mesh to the target Y. The as-rigid-as-possible energy term is adopted to keep that the transformations of the neighboring points should be similar as possible to ensure the local rigidity. The volumetric energy term is used to avoid the intersection of the triangles, and is similar to as-rigid-as-possible energy term using tetrahedral mesh. The tetrahedral mesh is generated using the open-source software TetGen [24].

The total energy function is optimized iteratively by starting with $Z = X$. Firstly, given the initial guess Z, the local rotations R_i are estimated. Then, the new positions are obtained by fixing R_i. The further optimization is performed by repeating the above two steps until the convergence.

4.3   Multi-view Based Diffuse-Specular Separation

Our face skin consists of a diffuse component which models the subsurface scattering in the skin and a specular component which measures the reflectance on the oily layer. We follow the method [30] to extract the component without specular reflectance. Assuming the specular color is the same as the light color $\vec{s} = (1, 1, 1)$, we rotate the RGB color (p_i^r, p_i^g, p_i^b) of the 3D point p in the visible view i into the SUV so-called color space (p_i^s, p_i^u, p_i^v) to make the s component aligned to the light color $\vec{s}$. Then the two components u and v perpendicular to the s component contain no specular component. We define the chroma intensity as $p_i^c = \sqrt{p_i^{u2} + p_i^{v2}}$. We then calculate the chroma normal $\vec{n}_c$ using the Lambertian photometric stereo method from the chroma intensity.

Due to the soft and smooth property of the chroma normal, the chroma normal is not suitable for constructing detailed facial geometry. The finer geometry can be derivated from the specular normal. However, the specular component is not equal to the p_i^s value. We leverage the multi-view information to calculate the diffuse and the specular component. We calculate the weighted blend RGB color as

$$(\bar{p}^r, \bar{p}^g, \bar{p}^b) = \frac{\sum_{i=0}^k w_i \ (p_i^r, p_i^g, p_i^b)}{\sum_{i=0}^k w_i} \tag{2}$$

where $w_i = (1 - (\vec{n}_c \cdot \vec{h}_i)^{10})^2$, $\vec{h}_i$ is the half-way vector between the light direction and view direction, and k is the number of visible views. For the region with high specular, the w_i is set small to suppress the specular component. The blend RGB color is then used to separate the diffuse and the specular components, which are then used to extract the diffuse albedo, specular normal and specular roughness. Figure 6 shows an example of the diffuse and specular separation results.

Fig. 6. From left to right: original image, diffuse component, specular component.

4.4   Surface Normal and BRDF Estimation

Let us employ the traditional Lambertian photometric stereo [27] to calculate the chrome normal from the chroma intensities. The lighting equation is $\rho_d(\vec{n}_d \cdot \vec{L}) = P_d$, where the power of point light source is assumed to be 1, $\vec{n}_d$ is the unknown normal, ρ_d is the albedo, $\vec{L} = [\vec{l_1} \ \vec{l_2} \ \cdots \ \vec{l_k}]^T$ is the normalized light direction, $P_d = [p_1 \ p_2 \ \cdots \ p_k]^T$ is the pixel intensity with $p_i = 0$ pixels are omitted. Let $\vec{\beta} = \rho_d \vec{n}_d$, the solution via pseudo-inverse is:

$$\vec{\beta} = (L^T L)^{-1} L^T P \tag{3}$$

$$\rho_d = ||\vec{\beta}||, \ \vec{n}_d = \vec{\beta}/||\vec{\beta}|| \tag{4}$$

For the specular photometric stereo, we model it using Blinn-Phong model. The lighting equation is $\rho_s \frac{\alpha+2}{2\pi}(\vec{n}_s \cdot \vec{H})^\alpha = P_s$, where ρ_s is the unknown specular intensity, $\vec{n}_s$ is the unknown specular normal, α is the unknown exponent parameter and $\vec{H} = [\vec{h_1} \ \vec{h_2} \ \cdots \ \vec{h_k}]^T$ is the normalized half-way vector. Let

$\vec{\gamma} = \rho_s{}^{1/\alpha}\vec{n}_s$, the solution is similar to the lambertian photometric stereo. We assume the α measured in [26].

$$(\frac{\alpha + 2}{2\pi})^{1/\alpha}(\vec{\gamma} \cdot \vec{H}) = P_s^{1/\alpha} \tag{5}$$

After obtaining the specular normal n_s, we use a simple iterative inverse rendering method to solve the unknown roughness parameter $m \in [0, 1]$. We calculate the geometry function G, Beckmann distribution function D and Schlick fresnel term F. We relight the point under the known lighting conditions using the specular normal n_s and roughness m and retain the best m that produces the maximum photo-consistency to the captured images.

4.5   Finer Geometry Optimization

The coarse geometry is obtained from the multi-view reconstruction, and the detailed normal information can be estimated from the photometric stereo. Finally, we adopt the extracted high frequency specular normal map to enhance the topology consistent coarse mesh using the method [21]. It reduces the optimization problem to solving a linear system, which can be solved very effectively for large meshes. The optimization procedure consists of two steps. We firstly use the measured point positions to correct the normal fields, and then use the linear constraints and a sparse solver to optimize the final positions. Figure 7 shows the comparison of the coarse geometry and the detailed face mesh.

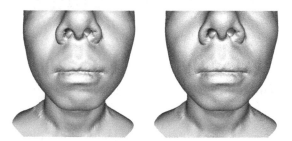

Fig. 7. Left: coarse topology consistent mesh. Right: more details are enhanced into the coarse geometry with mesh optimization.

5   Results

We run the experiments on a PC with Intel Core i7-4790K CPU, the initial multi-view reconstruction takes about 20 min, the landmark-based initialization and the mesh deformation takes about 5 min, the photometric stereo based BRDF estimation takes about 12 min. The final mesh optimization procedure takes about 5 min.

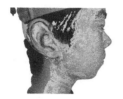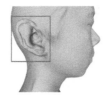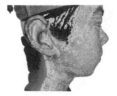

Fig. 8. Left: mesh deformation without ear landmark constraints. Right: mesh deformation with the guidance of the ear landmarks. It is obvious that the ear landmarks improves the 3D registration performance.

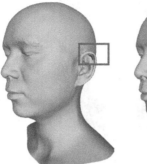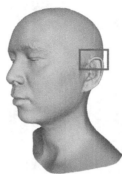

Fig. 9. The intuitive comparison of the volumetric as-rigid-as-possible energy term. The mesh optimized with the volumetric energy term (right) performs better than that optimized without the volumetric term (left).

We show the effect of the ear landmarks in the mesh deformation procedure in Fig. 8. The alignment error is a bit larger without the assistance of the ear landmarks, compared to the optimization result which considers the ear landmarks. Due to the incomplete ear landmarks, the inner geometry of the ear is not aligned very well. Figure 9 validates the effectiveness of the volumetric energy term. In the ear region, the volumetric term prevents the intersection of the triangles.

The recovered reflectance maps are shown in Fig. 1, including the diffuse albedo, diffuse normal, specular normal and roughness. The texture coordinates of the full head are generated with the subdivision procedure. The synthetic results are shown in Fig. 10. From left to right: facial geometry, two synthetic views and zoom-in facial details. Compared to the previous method [11] which only considers the face region, our system can produce the full head model with consistent topology.

Figure 11 shows some synthetic renderings under novel high dynamic image-based lighting. The captured facial geometry and reflectance are used to produce photo-realistic synthetic images.

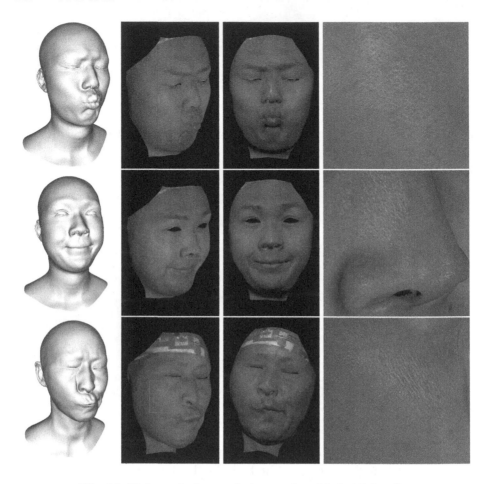

Fig. 10. High resolution rendering results with facial details.

Fig. 11. Synthetic images rendered using the captured geometry and reflectance maps under different image-based illuminations.

6   Conclusion

In this paper, we present a practical facial geometry and reflectance capture system, which utilizes the multi-view reconstruction and photometric stereo techniques. Compared to previous facial geometry and reflectance capture system, our method produces more complete and topology consistent head models. For better mesh deformation, we also leverage the facial and ear landmarks to assist the alignment procedure. Also, the fitted physical-based Cook-Torrance model can synthesize photo-realistic images, compared to the empirical Blinn-Phong model. The consistent facial topology is pretty important for dynamic facial capture. The full head model is also beneficial for adding some other important facial elements, including the eyes, teeth and hairs.

Acknowledgments. The authors would like to thank the anonymous reviewers for their valuable comments and helpful suggestions. This work was supported by the National Natural Science Foundation of China under Grants Nos. 61872317.

References

1. Alexander, O., Rogers, M., Lambeth, W., Chiang, M., Debevec, P.: The digital emily project: photoreal facial modeling and animation. In: ACM SIGGRAPH Course (2009)
2. Beeler, T., Bickel, B., Beardsley, P., Sumner, B., Gross, M.: High-quality single-shot capture of facial geometry. ACM Trans. Graph. **29**(4), 1–9 (2010)
3. Blanz, V., Scherbaum, K., Vetter, T., Seidel, H.: Exchanging faces in images. Comput. Graph. Forum **23**(3), 669–676 (2004)
4. Blanz, V., Vetter, T.: A morphable model for the synthesis of 3D faces. In: Proceedings of the 26th Annual Conference on Computer Graphics and Interactive Techniques (1999)
5. Bradley, D., Heidrich, W., Popa, T., Sheffer, A.: High resolution passive facial performance capture. ACM Trans. Graph. **29**(4), 1–10 (2010)
6. Cao, C., Bradley, D., Zhou, K., Beeler, T.: Real-time high-fidelity facial performance capture. ACM Trans. Graph. **34**(4), 46:1–46:9 (2015)
7. Chen, Z., Gao, T., Sheng, B., Li, P., Chen, C.L.P.: Outdoor shadow estimating using multiclass geometric decomposition based on BLS. IEEE Trans. Cybern. **50**(5), 2152–2165 (2020)
8. Cootes, T.F., Edwards, G.J., Taylor, C.J.: Active appearance models. IEEE Trans. Pattern Anal. Mach. Intell. **23**(6), 681–685 (2001)
9. Debevec, P.E., Hawkins, T., Tchou, C., Duiker, H.P., Sarokin, W., Sagar, M.: Acquiring the reflectance field of a human face. In: Proceedings of the 27th Annual Conference on Computer Graphics and Interactive Techniques (2000)
10. Ding, S., Sheng, B., Hou, X., Xie, Z., Ma, L.: Intrinsic image decomposition using multi-scale measurements and sparsity: intrinsic image decomposition. Comput. Graph. Forum **36**(6), 251–261 (2017)
11. Fyffe, G., Graham, P., Tunwattanapong, B., Ghosh, A., Debevec, P.: Near instant capture of high resolution facial geometry and reflectance. Comput. Graph. Forum **35**(2), 353–363 (2016)
12. Fyffe, G., et al.: Multi-view stereo on consistent face topology. Comput. Graph. Forum **36**(2), 295–309 (2017)

13. Ghosh, A., Chen, T., Peers, P., Wilson, C.A., Debevec, P.: Estimating specular roughness and anisotropy from second order spherical gradient illumination. Comput. Graph. Forum **28**(4), 1161–1170
14. Ghosh, A., Fyffe, G., Tunwattanapong, B., Busch, J., Yu, X., Debevec, P.: Multiview face capture using polarized spherical gradient illumination. ACM Trans. Graph. **30**(6), 1–10 (2011)
15. Ghosh, A., Hawkins, T., Peers, P., Frederiksen, S., Debevec, P.: Practical modeling and acquisition of layered facial reflectance. ACM Trans. Graph. **27**(5), 1–10 (2008)
16. Graham, P., et al.: Measurement-based synthesis of facial microgeometry. Comput. Graph. Forum **32**, 335–344 (2013)
17. Ichim, A., Bouaziz, S., Pauly, M.: Dynamic 3D avatar creation from hand-held video input. ACM Trans. Graph. **34**(4), 1–14 (2015)
18. Klehm, O., et al.: Recent advances in facial appearance capture. Comput. Graph. Forum **34**(2), 709–733 (2015)
19. Li, T., Bolkart, T., Black, M.J., Li, H., Romero, J.: Learning a model of facial shape and expression from 4D scans. ACM Trans. Graph. **36**(6), 194:1–194:17 (2017)
20. Ma, W.C., Hawkins, T., Peers, P., Chabert, C.F., Debevec, P.E.: Rapid acquisition of specular and diffuse normal maps from polarized spherical gradient illumination. In: Eurographics Conference on Rendering Techniques (2007)
21. Nehab, D., Rusinkiewicz, S., Davis, J., Ramamoorthi, R.: Efficiently combining positions and normals for precise 3D geometry. ACM Trans. Graph. **24**(3), 536–543 (2005)
22. Ren, S., He, K., Girshick, R., Sun, J.: Faster R-CNN: towards real-time object detection with region proposal networks. IEEE Trans. Pattern Anal. Mach. Intell. **39**(6), 1137–1149 (2017)
23. Sheng, B., Li, P., Jin, Y., Tan, P., Lee, T.Y.: Intrinsic image decomposition with step and drift shading separation. IEEE Trans. Vis. Comput. Graph. **26**(2), 1332–1346 (2020)
24. Si, H.: Tetgen, a delaunay-based quality tetrahedral mesh generator. ACM Trans. Math. Softw. **41**(2), 1–36
25. Sorkine, O., Alexa, M.: As-rigid-as-possible surface modeling. In: Eurographics Symposium on Geometry Processing, pp. 109–116 (2007)
26. Weyrich, T., Matusik, W., Pfister, H., Bickel, B., Gross, M.: Analysis of human faces using a measurement-based skin reflectance model. ACM Trans. Graph. **25**(3), 1013 (2006)
27. Woodham, R.J.: Photometric stereo: a reflectance map technique for determining surface orientation from intensity. Proc. SPIE **155**, 136–143 (1979)
28. Zhou, K., Huang, J., Snyder, J., Liu, X., Bao, H., Guo, B., Shum, H.: Large mesh deformation using the volumetric graph Laplacian. ACM Trans. Graph. **24**(3), 496–503 (2005)
29. Zhou, Y., Zaferiou, S.: Deformable models of ears in-the-wild for alignment and recognition. In: IEEE International Conference on Automatic Face and Gesture Recognition, pp. 626–633. IEEE (2017)
30. Zickler, T., Mallick, S.P., Kriegman, D.J., Belhumeur, P.N.: Color subspaces as photometric invariants. Int. J. Comput. Vis. **79**(1), 13–30 (2008)
31. Zickler, T., Ramamoorthi, R., Enrique, S., Belhumeur, P.N.: Reflectance sharing: predicting appearance from a sparse set of images of a known shape. IEEE Trans. Pattern Anal. Mach. Intell. **28**(8), 1287–1302 (2006)
32. Zollhofer, M., et al.: State of the art on monocular 3D face reconstruction, tracking, and applications. Comput. Graph. Forum **37**(2), 523–550 (2018)

Real-Time Fluid Simulation with Atmospheric Pressure Using Weak Air Particles

Tian Sang, Wentao Chen, Yitian Ma, Hui Wang, and Xubo Yang[✉]

Digital ART Laboratory, Shanghai Jiao Tong University, Shanghai, China
{sangtian0820,yangxubo}@sjtu.edu.cn

Abstract. Atmospheric pressure is important yet often ignored in fluid simulation, resulting in many phenomena being overlooked. This paper presents a particle-based approach to simulate versatile liquid effects under atmospheric pressure in real time. We introduce weak air particles as a sparse sampling of air. The weak air particles can be used to efficiently track liquid surfaces under atmospheric pressure, and are weakly coupled with the liquid. We allow the large-mass liquid particles to contribute to the density estimation of small-mass air particles and neglect the air's influence on liquid density, leaving only the surface forces of air on the liquid to guarantee the stability of the two-phase flow with a large density ratio. The proposed surface force model is composed of density-related atmospheric pressure force and surface tension force. By correlating the pressure and the density, we ensure that the atmospheric pressure increases as the air is compressed in a confined space. Experimental results demonstrate the efficiency and effectiveness of our methods in simulating the interplay between air and liquid in real time.

Keywords: Fluid simulation · Real-time simulation · Position based fluids · Atmospheric pressure · Surface tension · Air-liquid interaction

1 Introduction

Atmospheric pressure can create visually interesting phenomena when interacting with liquids. One of the most typical examples is Torricelli's experiment. When a mercury-filled glass tube is held upside down in a basin of mercury, the liquid inside the tube will fall down and eventually stabilize at a height of about 760 mm above the level in the basin. The mercury column's height is independent of the depth, internal diameter and tilt angle of the tube as a result of atmospheric pressure acting on the surface of the mercury in the basin.

However, it is common in computer graphics to ignore atmospheric pressure and assume a free-surface boundary condition at the interface when simulating fluids, since air has little contribution to the liquid motion. In order to capture liquid behaviors attributable to atmospheric pressure, we propose a particle-based

© Springer Nature Switzerland AG 2021
N. Magnenat-Thalmann et al. (Eds.): CGI 2021, LNCS 13002, pp. 151–164, 2021.
https://doi.org/10.1007/978-3-030-89029-2_12

Fig. 1. The mercury column is supported by the atmospheric pressure (a) and its height is independent of the tilt angle of the tube (b). When the tube is broken (c), the column will drop to the level of the mercury in the basin, resulting from exposure of the column's upper surface to atmospheric pressure. Tubes of different shapes holding mercury columns of the same height are shown on the right (d–e).

method to handle the interplay between air and liquid and provide various interactive scenes, including the simulation of Torricelli's experiment (Fig. 1(a–c)).

Calculating and applying the atmospheric pressure force is the most critical and challenging part of our simulation. Previous particle-based methods investigated how atmospheric pressure affects the liquid and focused on the visual details on liquid surfaces. Ghost SPH [30] sampled a narrow layer of ghost particles near the liquid surface to improve the boundary treatment. He et al. [10] proposed a novel surface force model to simulate the sparsely sampled thin features in free surface flows. However, it is difficult to simulate the liquid phenomena under atmospheric pressure with these methods. Take Torricelli's experiment as an example, the mercury in the basin is under atmospheric pressure, while the mercury column inside the tube is not (see Fig. 2). It is the pressure difference that supports the mercury column. Surfaces under atmospheric pressure are hard to track without simulating air particles. As a result, the surface forces cannot be applied properly. Simulating air and liquid as a two-phase flow can track the interface and capture the interactive effects at the same time. Solenthaler and Pajarola [31] recalculated the fluid density by a measure of particle densities to handle the discontinuities at interfaces between multiple fluids with high density contrasts. Chen et al. [5] proposed a corrected density re-initialization to obtain smooth pressure fields on fluid interfaces. Owing to the large density ratio, simulating air and liquid with strong two-way coupling either suffers from severe instabilities or requires high resolution and huge computational cost.

In this work, we introduce weak air particles as a sparse sampling of air to model the atmospheric pressure. Weak air particles are weakly coupled with the liquid particles. Liquid contributes to the density estimation of air, and air exerts surface forces on the liquid. In this way, we can simulate the two-phase flow with a large density ratio stably, and locate surfaces under atmospheric pressure efficiently. Our method uses a two-scale approach and set the radii of air particles larger than fluid particles to reduce the performance overhead. With the real-time tracking of the air-liquid interface, we can then apply surface forces on the located boundary. The surface forces consist of atmospheric pressure force and surface tension force. The atmospheric pressure force is improved based on He et al. [10] by taking the dynamic density of air and solid boundary particles into consideration. The density-related scheme ensures that the pressure increases as the air is compressed in a confined space. Moreover, we apply the surface tension model proposed by Akinci et al. [2] to smoothen the liquid surface. Finally, the scene of Torricelli's experiment is simulated. Users can observe how the height of the mercury column is affected by changing tube shapes, tilt angles and liquid densities. The interactive scenes tackle the challenges of carrying out Torricelli's experiment in practice, as the experiment demands hazardous materials such as mercury and long glass tubes which is difficult to acquire. With our virtual scenes, users can perform experiments in a risk-free environment without hazards or high costs. In other scenes like the simplified U tube manometer and underwater bubbles, users can also observe the interplay between air and liquid. Experiments demonstrate that our model can simulate versatile liquid behaviors under atmospheric pressure effectively.

The main contributions of our work can be summarized as:

- A particle-based method which uses weak air particles as a sparse sampling of air to track surfaces under atmospheric pressure stably and efficiently. Our weak air-liquid coupling ensures the stability of two-phase flow with a large density ratio.
- A surface force model consists of atmospheric pressure and surface tension to simulate visually plausible atmospheric pressure effects. Our atmospheric pressure force correlates air density and pressure, and makes sure that the pressure increases as the air is compressed.
- An interactive application where users can perform Torricelli's experiment and observe the interplay between air and liquid in real time.

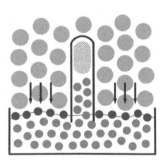 

Fig. 2. (Left) An illustration of Torricelli's experiment. The orange ones represent weak air particles. The blue ones represent liquid particles and the dark blue ones are the air-liquid boundary particles. The liquid surface in the basin is under atmospheric pressure, while the surface inside the tube is not. Above the liquid column is a vacuum (shaded area). (Right) Air-liquid interface particles tracked by weak air particles are marked in red. Note that there are no interface particles inside the tube. (Color figure online)

2 Related Work

2.1 Particle-Based Fluid Simulation

Particle-based fluid simulation has been an active research topic in computer graphics for many years, particularly for its computational efficiency and numerical stability. One of the most popular methods is Smooth Particle Hydrodynamics (SPH) [7,20], which was adopted by Müller et al. [25] to simulate fluids with free surfaces. Many follow-up SPH-based approaches were dedicated to enforcing incompressibility [3,12,21,32]. Among these methods, Position Based Fluids (PBF) [21] is favored by many interactive applications for its efficiency and stability. PBF models incompressible fluids using density constraints in the context of the Position Based Dynamics (PBD) framework [26].

2.2 Fluid Simulation with Atmospheric Pressure

Atmospheric pressure is caused by the gravitational attraction of the planet to the air. The interplay between air and liquid can produce visually interesting phenomena. Air is a fluid with a very small density, and its coupling with liquid can be simulated as a two-phase flow. There are methods like volume-of-fluid (VOF) [17], regional level-sets [14], Fluid Implicit Particle (FLIP) [4] and Material-Point Method (MPM) [6,36] that can track the interface and handle multi-fluid simulation. Li et al. [18] offered a general multiphase flow solver based on kinetic models to simulate air-water flows. Moreover, many SPH-based multiphase flows researches have been conducted in both computational physics [5,24] and computer graphics [28,33,34]. Macklin et al. [22] simulated immiscible two-phase liquid with low density ratio based on PBF. Solenthaler and Pajarola [31] handled density discontinuities between multiphase flows with large density differences up to 100, but cannot deal with complex interfaces. Some methods focus specifically on air-water mixtures and bubble animations [11,15,19], but the simulation of atmospheric pressure is ignored. The density ratio of water and air is about 1000 : 1 in reality, and simulating strong coupling two-phase flow with large density difference either incurs high computational costs or suffers from severe instabilities.

In addition to multiphase flow simulation, Goldade et al. [8] took a different approach and proposed a constraint-based bubbles model, allowing distinct liquid bodies to physically interact across completely unsimulated air. However, their FLIP-based liquid simulator cannot meet the need for real-time performance and high interactivity. Schechter et al. [30] created a narrow layer of ghost particles in the surrounding air and solid, using a ghost treatment to improve the quality of basic SPH fluid simulation. He et al. [10] developed an efficient way to calculate the air pressure force for free surface flows and simulate sparsely sampled thin features robustly without using air particles. Previous particle-based methods focused on handling the detailed boundary conditions of scenes like bubbles and thin features of free surface flows, but are not suitable for dealing with the contribution of atmospheric pressure on bulk fluids.

3   Background

Although our method can be integrated into any particle-based methods like SPH, our primary focus is on PBF mainly because the position-based approach is stable, controllable, and well-suited for interactive environments. Position Based Fluids rely on the PBD framework. In general, PBD uses a set of non-linear constraint functions that works on position $\mathbf{x}$ and mass m. To enforce the incompressibility of fluid, PBF solves the density constraint by:

$$C_i(\mathbf{x}) = \frac{\rho_i}{\rho_0} - 1 \leq 0, \tag{1}$$

with ρ_0 being the rest density of fluid and ρ_i the current density of particle i. This inequality constraint is inserted for every particle in the simulation, which results in an evaluation of ρ_i. Following SPH, any scalar quantities ϕ of particle i can be interpolated by a weighted sum of contributions from all particles nearby with index j:

$$\phi_i = \sum_j m_j \frac{\phi_j}{\rho_j} W(\mathbf{x}_i - \mathbf{x}_j, h), \tag{2}$$

where W is the kernel function with support radius h. Therefore, the density of particle i can be estimated as:

$$\rho_i = \sum_j m_j W(\mathbf{x}_i - \mathbf{x}_j, h). \tag{3}$$

To find the $\Delta \mathbf{x}_i$ that satisfies the position-correction configuration of PBD, we need to solve the constraints of the form:

$$C_i(\mathbf{x} + \Delta \mathbf{x}) \approx C_i(\mathbf{x}) + \nabla C_i(\mathbf{x}) \Delta \mathbf{x} = 0, \tag{4}$$

where C_i refers to the i-th constraint, $\mathbf{x} = [\mathbf{x}_1, \mathbf{x}_2, ..., \mathbf{x}_n]^T$ represents the vector of particle positions. The estimation of $\Delta \mathbf{x}$ is given by:

$$\Delta \mathbf{x} = \lambda_i \nabla C_i(\mathbf{x}), \tag{5}$$

with λ_i being a scaling factor along the gradient. Combining Eq. 4 and Eq. 5, λ_i is given by:

$$\lambda_i = -\frac{C_i(\mathbf{x})}{\sum_j |\nabla C_i(\mathbf{x})|^2 + \epsilon}, \tag{6}$$

where ϵ is a soften coefficient which is added to avoid singularities. Using λ_i, positions updated after each constraint can be processed by:

$$\Delta \mathbf{x}_i = \frac{1}{\rho_0} \sum_j (\lambda_i + \lambda_j) \nabla W(\mathbf{x}_i - \mathbf{x}_j, h). \tag{7}$$

Thus the equation includes corrections from neighbor particles density constraint.

4   Weak Air Particles

The air has weight, and it presses against everything it touches. In Torricelli's experiment, the mercury column is supported by the atmospheric pressure difference between the liquid surface in the basin and the liquid surface in the tube. As a result, finding surfaces under atmospheric pressure is critical. Traditional particle-based boundary detection methods using SPH-based kernel interpolation [25,27] or visibility operator Hidden Point Removal [13,29] can classify surface particles. However, the liquid-air interface cannot be distinguished with these methods. Simulating air and liquid as a two-phase flow can locate the liquid particles in contact with air, but the large density ratio of air and liquid can cause severe instability when coupling. Therefore, we introduce weak air particles to track the air-liquid boundary and deal with the instability problem caused by large density differences.

As for the air-liquid interface, we allow weak air particles to be weakly coupled with the liquid. More specifically, liquid affects the density calculation of air, and air exert surface forces on the liquid. In addition, we make the radii of weak air particles larger than the radii of liquid particles to reduce the computational overhead. Referring to Adams et al. [1], a particle p_j is considered the neighbor of particle p_i if $||\mathbf{x}_i - \mathbf{x}_j|| \leq max(h_i, h_j)$, where h represents the SPH support radius calculated by $h = 2r$. Throughout our work, we use Ω_a, Ω_l and Ω_s to denote the set of air particles, liquid particles and solid particles respectively. Given that the mass of air particles is much smaller than that of liquid particles and based on the PBF position correction formula Eq. 7, we calculate the position update of the weak air particles $\Delta\mathbf{x}_i$ by:

$$\Delta\mathbf{x}_i = \frac{1}{\rho_{a,0}}(\sum_{j\in\Omega_a}(\lambda_i + \lambda_j)\nabla W(\mathbf{x}_i - \mathbf{x}_j, h_i)$$
$$+ k_l \sum_{j\in\Omega_l}(\lambda_i + \lambda_j)\nabla W(\mathbf{x}_i - \mathbf{x}_j, h_i) \qquad (8)$$
$$+ k_s \sum_{j\in\Omega_s}\lambda_i\nabla W(\mathbf{x}_i - \mathbf{x}_j, h_i)),$$

where $\rho_{a,0}$ represents the rest density of the air, and the parameter k_l and k_s denote small positive constants to ensure the stability of the small-mass air particles when colliding with the large-mass liquid and solid particles.

Correspondingly, the position update of the liquid particles is calculated by:

$$\Delta\mathbf{x}_i = \frac{1}{\rho_{l,0}}(\sum_{j\in\Omega_l}(\lambda_i + \lambda_j)\nabla W(\mathbf{x}_i - \mathbf{x}_j, h_i)$$
$$+ \sum_{j\in\Omega_s}\lambda_i\nabla W(\mathbf{x}_i - \mathbf{x}_j, h_i)), \qquad (9)$$

where $\rho_{a,0}$ is the rest density of the liquid. The contribution of the air particles is neglected compared to Eq. 8.

By introducing weak air particles, our method can handle the two-phase flow with 1 : 1000 density contrast and get visually plausible results. In addition, the air-liquid boundary particles can be marked efficiently in the process of neighbor searching. We create a dam break example and compare our method with the PBF two-way coupling method [23] in Fig. 3. This example indicates that strong coupling of two-phase flow with a large density ratio can cause severe particle penetration and instability, and simulating weak air particles can reliably avoid this problem.

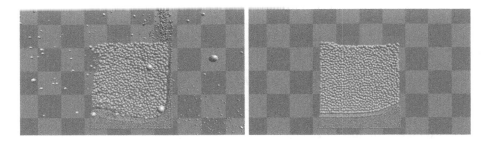

Fig. 3. Dam break. Compared with the classical PBF two-phase flow method (left), our method can ensure the stability of the coupling (right).

5 Surface Force Model

Once the weak air particles are simulated, the air-liquid interface can be accurately tracked by neighbor searching, and then the surface forces can be applied on the located boundary. Our surface force model consists of two forces, including atmospheric pressure force and surface tension force.

5.1 Density-Related Atmospheric Pressure Force

Following the method proposed by He et al. [10], the air pressure force at the liquid particle i can be calculated as:

$$\mathbf{F}_i^{atm} = -V_i p_0 \sum_{j \in \Omega_a} V_j \nabla W(\mathbf{x}_i - \mathbf{x}_j, h_i), \qquad (10)$$

where V represents the volume of the particle, p_0 is a constant accounting for the air pressure at each air particle j. By assuming that air particles and liquid particles are smoothly and uniformly distributed, $\mathbf{F}^{atm}$ can be formulated as the sum of attraction forces:

$$\mathbf{F}_i^{atm} = V_i p_0 \sum_{j \in \Omega_l} V_j \nabla W(\mathbf{x}_i - \mathbf{x}_j, h_i), \qquad (11)$$

According to the combined ideal gas law $\frac{PV}{T} = k$, the pressure of the gas will increase when compressed in an enclosed space at an unchanged temperature.

Under such circumstances, we provide an explicit solution to correlate the pressure and the density by introducing a factor $A_i = \frac{\rho_i}{\rho_{a,0}}$ for each weak air particle. Substituting A_i into Eq. 2 gives:

$$A_i = \sum_{j \in \Omega_a} \frac{m_a}{\rho'_{a,0}} W(\mathbf{x}_i - \mathbf{x}_j, h_i). \tag{12}$$

Note that $\rho'_{a,0}$ is the rest density of the air approximated only by the air particles at the interface. Intuitively, A_i represents the relative density of the air phase compared with the rest status and will increase during the compression.

In addition, to cope with the liquid particle jittering issues near the boundary, we take solid boundary particles into consideration, and the improved atmospheric pressure force can be written as:

$$\mathbf{F}_i^{atm} = A_i V_i p_0 \left(\sum_{j \in \Omega_l} V_j \nabla W(\mathbf{x}_i - \mathbf{x}_j, h_i) + \sum_{j \in \Omega_s} V_j \nabla W(\mathbf{x}_i - \mathbf{x}_j, h_i) \right). \tag{13}$$

5.2   Surface Tension Force

We observe that the surface normal field computation in Eq. 13 can lead to particle clustering, and slight disturbances could cause instability, especially on a large flat liquid surface. Therefore, we apply the surface tension force proposed by Akinci et al. [2] to improve our force model:

$$\mathbf{F}_i^{st} = \sum_{j \in \Omega_l} K_{ij} \left(-\gamma m_i m_j C(|\mathbf{x}_i - \mathbf{x}_j|) \frac{\mathbf{x}_i - \mathbf{x}_j}{|\mathbf{x}_i - \mathbf{x}_j|} - \gamma m_i (\mathbf{n}_i - \mathbf{n}_j) \right)$$
$$\mathbf{n}_i = h_i \sum_{j \in \Omega_l} \frac{m_j}{\rho_j} \nabla W(\mathbf{x}_i - \mathbf{x}_j, h_i), \tag{14}$$

where i and j are neighboring fluid particles, $K_{ij} = \frac{2\rho_{l,0}}{\rho_i + \rho_j}$ is a symmetrized correction factor, γ is the surface tension coefficient ranging from 0 to 1, C is a spline function and $\mathbf{n}_i$ represents the normal information reformed from the gradient of the smoothed color field [25]. The first term of Eq. 14 calculates the cohesion force which makes the neighboring liquid particles attract each other, and the second term is an additional force counteracting surface curvature to minimize the surface area. Figure 4 compares our method with and without the surface tension, and demonstrates that applying this force can smoothen the liquid surface and improve visual quality.

As described above, the atmospheric pressure force is calculated based on atmospheric pressure and surface normal field pointing to the liquid, and the surface tension force is given by cohesion term and surface area minimization term. We combine these two forces and finally compute the surface force as $\mathbf{F}_i^s = \mathbf{F}_i^{atm} + \mathbf{F}_i^{st}$.

Experiments in Sect. 7 demonstrate the versatility of our method in different simulation scenarios where atmospheric pressure plays a pivotal role in liquid behaviors.

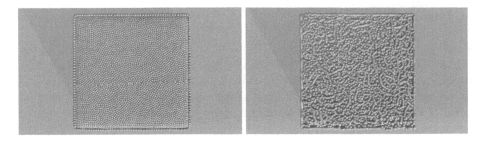

Fig. 4. Liquid surfaces under atmospheric pressure with (left) and without (right) surface tension.

6 Implementation

Implemented with compute shaders, our fluid solver is executed on GPU in parallel. For real-time liquid rendering, we follow the method of Yu and Turk [35] to compute particle anisotropy, and adopt screen-space filtering [16] to reconstruct the fluid surface.

The simulation loop of weak air particles is outlined in Algorithm 1. We follow the hash implementation by Green [9] for neighbor searches (steps 4–6). When handling the air-liquid interface (steps 8–12), an weak coupling approach is used to handle the high density ratio of air and liquid, as described in Sect. 4. Note that for liquid particles, we calculate and exert the surface forces after step 16. To reduce the performance overhead caused by introducing weak air particles, we set the radii of air particles to twice the size of liquid particles without affecting our simulation result.

Algorithm 1. Simulation Loop for Weak Air Particles

1: **for all** weak air particles i **do**
2:     predict position $\mathbf{x}_i^* \Leftarrow \mathbf{x}_i + \Delta t \mathbf{v}_i + \Delta t^2 \mathbf{f}_{ext}(\mathbf{x}_i)$
3: **end for**
4: **for all** weak air particles i **do**
5:     find neighboring particles $N_i(\mathbf{x}_i^*)$
6: **end for**
7: **while** $iter < solverIterations$ **do**
8:     **for all** weak air particles i **do**
9:         perform liquid-air detection, solid-air detection and response
10:        solve all density constraints for $\Delta \mathbf{x}_i$
11:        update $\mathbf{x}_i^* \Leftarrow \mathbf{x}_i^* + \Delta \mathbf{x}_i$
12:    **end for**
13: **end while**
14: **for all** weak air particles i **do**
15:     update velocity $\mathbf{v}_i \Leftarrow \frac{1}{\Delta t_s}(\mathbf{x}_i^* - \mathbf{x}_i)$
16:     update position $\mathbf{x}_i \Leftarrow \mathbf{x}_i^*$
17: **end for**

---

7   Results

We integrate our methods into the PBF solver and run all examples on a laptop with an 8-core Intel i7-10875H CPU (2.3 GHz), an NVIDIA GeForce RTX 2070 graphics card, and 32 GB of RAM. Table 1 shows the performance data and related parameters for all example scenes, including Torricelli's experiment, simplified U tube manometer, droplet and underwater bubbles. As for the related parameters, p_0 is a constant representing the air pressure used to calculate the atmospheric pressure force, and γ is the surface tension coefficient defined in [2]. For all example scenes, we choose the collision stability coefficients $k_l = k_s = 0.01$ and use 2 iterations. Compared with the basic PBF solver, the average computational time overhead of weak air particles is 17.2%.

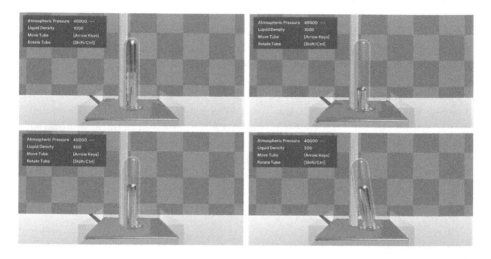

Fig. 5. The interactive scene of Torricelli's experiment. Top-left is the initial state of the experiment. After the slide is removed, the mercury column falls down and stabilizes (top-right). Users can observe how the height of the mercury column is affected by changing liquid density, atmospheric pressure (bottom-left) and tilt angle of the tube (bottom-right).

In Fig. 5, we recreate the interactive scene of Torricelli's experiment. With our weak air particles, the surface forces can be applied on the liquid-air interface particles in the basin accurately, and the mercury column can be supported by the atmospheric pressure difference between the liquid surface in the basin and the liquid surface in the tube. Apparently, these two surfaces can hardly be distinguished by methods of not simulating air particles [10] or only simulating a narrow layer of air particles [30], and thus the mercury column cannot be held up. Figure 1(b) demonstrates that our surface force model can ensure the height of the mercury columns to be the same in all tubes. We simulate air particles to exert atmospheric pressure force on the liquid surface, and according to the formula for calculating pressure $P = \rho g h$, the vertical height h is only related to the liquid density ρ and atmospheric pressure P, and is independent of the shape of the tube. Figure 6 shows a simplified U tube manometer. By correlating atmospheric pressure and air density, when the air at the left side is squeezed by the piston, its volume decreases, pressure increases, and the liquid levels are no longer equal due to the pressure difference. Figure 7 shows how our density-related atmospheric pressure model can be used to simulate underwater air bubbles. Applying surface forces on the liquid-air boundary particles around the bubble can make the air particles gather together, and the bubbles rise due to the density difference.

Table 1. Performance data and parameter values for demo scenes.

	Torricelli (Fig. 5)	Different tubes (Fig. 1)	U tube (Fig. 6)	Bubbles (Fig. 7)
# Fluid particles	27646	49102	9292	36100
# Solid particles	17496	26249	14799	10124
# Weak air particles	17556	18000	836	3636
Atmospheric pressure p_0	4×10^4	6×10^4	2×10^4	3×10^4
Surface tension coefficient γ	0.4	0.5	1	0.4
Solve fluid (ms)	3.622	5.791	1.688	4.597
Solve air (ms)	1.012	1.391	0.733	1.118
Rendering (ms)	1.489	3.355	0.908	0.761
Total (ms)	6.123	10.537	3.329	6.476

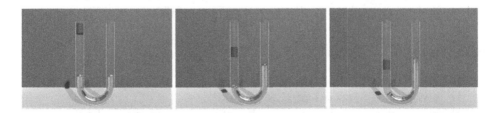

Fig. 6. A simplified U tube manometer. Our method can simulate the interaction between compressed air and liquid.

Fig. 7. A bubble in the water body. As the bubble rises, its pressure decreases and its volume increases.

8   Conclusion and Future Work

We have presented a comprehensive solution for real-time fluid simulation with atmospheric pressure. We introduce weak air particles to weakly couple with the liquid and track the liquid surface under atmospheric pressure, avoiding the defect that strong two-way coupling methods cannot simulate multiphase flow with large density ratios in real time. In addition, a novel surface force model composed of density-related atmospheric pressure force and surface tension force is proposed based on the existing force model. Dynamic air density is taken into consideration to handle situations where the air is compressed.

One of the main limitations, which is also an interesting direction for our future work, is that the coupling force between air and liquid is not symmetric. The current weak coupling method neglects the contribution of air to liquid, thus can not enforce the incompressibility of air. Improving the coupling method can further lead to a more stable system to simulate more atmospheric-related fluid phenomena, such as small-scale bubbles and air-driven flows. Moreover, the performance overhead can be further reduced by introducing adaptive mechanisms. The weak air particles can be split and merged as needed, or the simulation time-steps can be modified adaptively.

Acknowledgments. We thank all the reviewers for their insightful comments. We thank Qian Chen and Yue Wang for their valuable feedback. This work was supported by the National Key Research and Development Program of China (2018YFB1004902) and the National Natural Science Foundation of China (61772329, 61373085).

References

1. Adams, B., Pauly, M., Keiser, R., Guibas, L.J.: Adaptively sampled particle fluids. ACM Trans. Graph. (TOG) **26**(3), 48-es (2007)
2. Akinci, N., Akinci, G., Teschner, M.: Versatile surface tension and adhesion for SPH fluids. ACM Trans. Graph. (TOG) **32**(6), 1–8 (2013)
3. Becker, M., Teschner, M.: Weakly compressible SPH for free surface flows. In: Proceedings of the 2007 ACM SIGGRAPH/Eurographics Symposium on Computer Animation, pp. 209–217 (2007)
4. Boyd, L., Bridson, R.: Multiflip for energetic two-phase fluid simulation. ACM Trans. Graph. (TOG) **31**(2), 1–12 (2012)
5. Chen, Z., Zong, Z., Liu, M., Zou, L., Li, H., Shu, C.: An SPH model for multiphase flows with complex interfaces and large density differences. J. Comput. Phys. **283**, 169–188 (2015)
6. Gao, M., et al.: Animating fluid sediment mixture in particle-laden flows. ACM Trans. Graph. (TOG) **37**(4), 1–11 (2018)
7. Gingold, R.A., Monaghan, J.J.: Smoothed particle hydrodynamics: theory and application to non-spherical stars. Mon. Not. R. Astron. Soc. **181**(3), 375–389 (1977)
8. Goldade, R., Aanjaneya, M., Batty, C.: Constraint bubbles and affine regions: reduced fluid models for efficient immersed bubbles and flexible spatial coarsening. ACM Transactions on Graphics (TOG) **39**(4), 43:1–15 (2020)

9. Green, S.: Particle simulation using CUDA. NVIDIA Whitepaper **6**, 121–128 (2010)
10. He, X., Wang, H., Zhang, F., Wang, H., Wang, G., Zhou, K.: Robust simulation of sparsely sampled thin features in SPH-based free surface flows. ACM Trans. Graph. (TOG) **34**(1), 1–9 (2014)
11. Ihmsen, M., Akinci, N., Akinci, G., Teschner, M.: Unified spray, foam and air bubbles for particle-based fluids. Vis. Comput. **28**(6), 669–677 (2012)
12. Ihmsen, M., Cornelis, J., Solenthaler, B., Horvath, C., Teschner, M.: Implicit incompressible SPH. IEEE Trans. Visual Comput. Graph. **20**(3), 426–435 (2013)
13. Katz, S., Tal, A., Basri, R.: Direct visibility of point sets. ACM Trans. Graph. (TOG) **26**(3), 24-es (2007)
14. Kim, B.: Multi-phase fluid simulations using regional level sets. ACM Trans. Graph. (TOG) **29**(6), 1–8 (2010)
15. Kim, J.-H., Kim, W., Lee, J.: Physics-inspired approach to realistic and stable water spray with narrowband air particles. Vis. Comput. **34**(4), 461–471 (2017). https://doi.org/10.1007/s00371-017-1353-1
16. van der Laan, W.J., Green, S., Sainz, M.: Screen space fluid rendering with curvature flow. In: Proceedings of the 2009 Symposium on Interactive 3D Graphics and Games, pp. 91–98 (2009)
17. Langlois, T.R., Zheng, C., James, D.L.: Toward animating water with complex acoustic bubbles. ACM Trans. Graph. (TOG) **35**(4), 1–13 (2016)
18. Li, W., Liu, D., Desbrun, M., Huang, J., Liu, X.: Kinetic-based multiphase flow simulation. IEEE Trans. Vis. Comput. Graph. **27**(7), 3318–3334 (2020)
19. Liu, S., Wang, B., Ban, X.: Multiple-scale simulation method for liquid with trapped air under particle-based framework. In: 2020 IEEE Conference on Virtual Reality and 3D User Interfaces (VR), pp. 842–850. IEEE (2020)
20. Lucy, L.B.: A numerical approach to the testing of the fission hypothesis. Astron. J. **82**, 1013–1024 (1977)
21. Macklin, M., Müller, M.: Position based fluids. ACM Trans. Graph. (TOG) **32**(4), 1–12 (2013)
22. Macklin, M., Müller, M., Chentanez, N., Kim, T.Y.: Unified particle physics for real-time applications. ACM Trans. Graph. (TOG) **33**(4), 1–12 (2014)
23. Macklin, M., et al.: Small steps in physics simulation. In: Proceedings of the 18th annual ACM SIGGRAPH/Eurographics Symposium on Computer Animation, pp. 1–7 (2019)
24. Monaghan, J.J., Rafiee, A.: A simple SPH algorithm for multi-fluid flow with high density ratios. Int. J. Numer. Meth. Fluids **71**(5), 537–561 (2013)
25. Müller, M., Charypar, D., Gross, M.H.: Particle-based fluid simulation for interactive applications. In: Symposium on Computer Animation, pp. 154–159 (2003)
26. Müller, M., Heidelberger, B., Hennix, M., Ratcliff, J.: Position based dynamics. J. Vis. Commun. Image Represent. **18**(2), 109–118 (2007)
27. Orthmann, J., Hochstetter, H., Bader, J., Bayraktar, S., Kolb, A.: Consistent surface model for SPH-based fluid transport. In: Proceedings of the 12th ACM SIGGRAPH/Eurographics Symposium on Computer Animation, pp. 95–103 (2013)
28. Ren, B., Li, C., Yan, X., Lin, M.C., Bonet, J., Hu, S.M.: Multiple-fluid SPH simulation using a mixture model. ACM Trans. Graph. (TOG) **33**(5), 1–11 (2014)
29. Sandim, M., Cedrim, D., Nonato, L.G., Pagliosa, P., Paiva, A.: Boundary detection in particle-based fluids. In: Computer Graphics Forum, pp. 215–224. Wiley Online Library (2016)
30. Schechter, H., Bridson, R.: Ghost SPH for animating water. ACM Trans. Graph. (TOG) **31**(4), 1–8 (2012)

31. Solenthaler, B., Pajarola, R.: Density contrast SPH interfaces. In: Proceedings of the 2008 ACM SIGGRAPH/Eurographics Symposium on Computer Animation, pp. 211–218 (2008)
32. Solenthaler, B., Pajarola, R.: Predictive-corrective incompressible SPH. ACM Trans. Graph. (TOG) **28**(3), 1–6 (2009)
33. Yan, X., Jiang, Y.T., Li, C.F., Martin, R.R., Hu, S.M.: Multiphase SPH simulation for interactive fluids and solids. ACM Trans. Graph. (TOG) **35**(4), 1–11 (2016)
34. Yang, T., Chang, J., Lin, M.C., Martin, R.R., Zhang, J.J., Hu, S.M.: A unified particle system framework for multi-phase, multi-material visual simulations. ACM Trans. Graph. (TOG) **36**(6), 1–13 (2017)
35. Yu, J., Turk, G.: Reconstructing surfaces of particle-based fluids using anisotropic kernels. ACM Trans. Graph. (TOG) **32**(1), 1–12 (2013)
36. Zhang, F., Zhang, X., Sze, K.Y., Lian, Y., Liu, Y.: Incompressible material point method for free surface flow. J. Comput. Phys. **330**, 92–110 (2017)

Human Poses and Gestures

Reinforcement Learning for Quadruped Locomotion

Kangqiao Zhao[1,2], Feng Lin[1,2(✉)] 🆔, and Hock Soon Seah[2] 🆔

[1] China-Singapore International Joint Research Institute, Singapore, Singapore
{kangqiao001,asflin}@ntu.edu.sg
[2] School of Computer Science and Engineering, Nanyang Technological University, Singapore, Singapore
ahsseah@ntu.edu.sg

Abstract. In adversarial games like VR hunting which involves predators and preys, locomotive behaviour of the non-player character (NPC) is crucial. For effective and realistic quadruped locomotion, major technical contributions of this paper are made to inverse kinematics embedded motion control, quadruped locomotion behaviour adaptation and dynamic environment informed reinforcement learning (RL) of the NPC agent. Behaviour of each NPC can be improved from the top-level decision making such as pursuit and escape down to the actual skeletal motion of bones and joints. The new concepts and techniques are illustrated by a specific use case of predator and prey interaction, in which the objective is to create an intelligent locomotive predator to reach its autonomous steering locomotive prey as fast as possible in all the circumstances. Experiments and comparisons are conducted against the Vanilla dynamic target training; and the RL agent of the quadruped displays more realistic limb movements and produces faster locomotion towards the autonomous steering target.

Keywords: Adversarial game · Locomotive behaviour · Reinforcement learning

1 Introduction

1.1 Objectives

In adversarial games like virtual reality (VR) hunting [1, 2] which involves predators and preys, locomotive behaviour of the in-application non-player character (NPC) is a key issue. It will largely affect the overall quality of the game. Specifically, motion control, behaviour adaptation and machine learning of the NPC should be studied for a quality VR game user experience.

Aimed at effective and realistic quadruped locomotion, major technical contributions of this paper are made to inverse kinematics embedded motion control, quadruped locomotion behaviour adaptation and dynamic environment informed reinforcement learning of the NPC agent. Instead of designing specific dynamics algorithms, the NPC agent can be trained with reinforcement learning (RL) in the entire behaviour system by configuring the desired game environment and a set of hyperparameters. Behaviour of each NPC

© Springer Nature Switzerland AG 2021
N. Magnenat-Thalmann et al. (Eds.): CGI 2021, LNCS 13002, pp. 167–177, 2021.
https://doi.org/10.1007/978-3-030-89029-2_13

can be improved from the top-level decision making such as pursuit and escape down to the actual skeletal motion of bones and joints. The new concepts and techniques will be illustrated by a specific use case of in-game predator and prey interaction, in which the objective is to create an intelligent locomotive predator to reach its autonomous steering locomotive prey as fast as possible in all the circumstances.

1.2   Analytic Reviews on Previous Work

Strategies for Navigation and Pathfinding. Navigation and pathfinding have long been researched in computer graphics and robotics. The goal is to find the most suitable algorithm for the character of study to generate an optimal path between its current location and the destination location while steering the character along that trajectory [3].

One of the popular approaches to path planning is based on environment modelling [4]. The pre-processing step of modelling the environment is required before an optimal route can be found for the agent. During this process, the walkable area of the terrain is represented in navigation meshes and visibility graphs. In the earlier days, E. W. Dijkstra [5] introduces the first leading graph traversal algorithm that finds the shortest path between two nodes on the graph. Based on that, Hart introduces the widely used A* pathfinding algorithm for further improvement [6]. Nowadays, frequently used algorithms that apply this kind of graph traversal approach are based on these two algorithms and their variants [7]. Nevertheless, the downsides of this approach include slow execution time, unable to deal with dynamic obstacles, and requirement for pre-processing of a mesh graph representing the paths.

Similar to A* and Dijkstra that directly searches for the entire optimal path before steering, the RRT (Rapidly-exploring Random Trees) algorithm that is first introduced by Steven LaValle takes a different approach by not relying on environment modelling [8]. Pathfinding and terrain constructing are processed simultaneously by expanding a tree from the starting position based on randomly sampled data of the space until the distance between the current position and the target position reaches the threshold. RRT based approaches in general have a short execution time and are efficient in finding the optimal solution. However, this algorithm is unable to quickly react on an unreachable target, thus falls into deadlock in real applications.

Reynold [9] introduces the concept of steering force on autonomous vehicles to achieve a set of various behaviours. The agents are simplified into point masses and their movement is dependent on the steering force exerted on them. The advantage of this rule-based approach is that it is efficient and easy to implement, and it does not require any pre-processing steps such as environment modelling and agent training, therefore it is suitable for real-time simulation. However, since the agent is assimilated as a particle with mass to incorporate with force-driven displacement, autonomous steering behaviours only provide solution toward the navigation and steering layer of an integrated behaviour system, with the locomotion layer leaved unsolved. Moreover, point mass cannot embody the rotating inertia of real rigid bodies and the movement and heading direction of the agent may produce unrealistic locomotion.

Reinforcement Learning in Pathfinding. Self-adaptive approaches that orient toward autonomous and intelligent agents have been introduced. The concept of RL comes from "Q-learning" which is a value-based, off-policy algorithm [10]. "Q-learning" is extended to other RL algorithms with neural networks, resulting in deep "Q-learning" [11]. However, there are problems when it deals with a large number of states, such as intractability, unguaranteed value function, continuous rather than discrete states, and the requirement of long-term rather short-term reward. Policy gradient methods [12] optimize a parameterized policy using gradient descent with long-term cumulative rewards rather than optimizing values. When the agent receives a positive reward by performing an action, the probability of repeating this kind of actions will be increased in the future, and vice-versa.

2   Methodology

2.1   Modelling Quadruped Locomotion

Locomotive behaviour adaption by RL algorithms is based on modelling of the in-application NPC. Refer to Fig. 1, a quadruped is modelled by its position $p = [Px, Py, Pz]$, velocity v, acceleration a, each denoted by a 3-basis vectors with respect to a local dynamic coordinate system; and its x-axis always pointing toward the current heading direction.

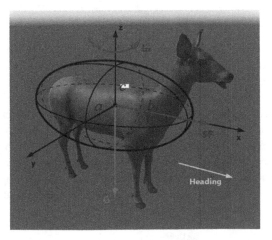

Fig. 1. Quadruped locomotion model

According to the rules of kinematics [13–15], if an external force is exerted on a rigid body, it will generate a corresponding acceleration, velocity and finally an update on its position. This process is similar for external torque and rotational displacement. Supposing that during our training process, the update interval is Δt. If a new force and torque is generated and exerted on the target at the start of each iteration, its position p_t

and heading direction h_t thus can be constantly updated. Algorithm 1 describes an entire steering iteration.

Algorithm 1. Autonomous Steering: The position and heading direction of the NPC are updated by respectively updating navigation force SF, acceleration a, velocity v and torque ST, angular acceleration α and angular velocity ω. The mass and moment of inertia of the target are denoted as m and I, and the update interval is denoted as Δt.

$t = 0$;
while simulation is running **do** {
    for each target **do** {
        Update navigation force SF ($SF < F_{max}$);
        Update torque ST ($ST < T_{max}$);
        $a_t = \frac{SF}{m}$;
        $\alpha_t = \frac{ST}{I}$;
        $v_t = v_0 + a_t \Delta t$ ($v_t < v_{max}$);
        $\omega_t = \omega_0 + \alpha_t \Delta t$ ($\omega_t < \omega_{max}$);
        $p_t = p_0 + \frac{v_0 + v_t}{2} \Delta t$;

$$h_t = \begin{bmatrix} \cos(\frac{\omega_0 + \omega_t}{2} \Delta t) & -\sin(\frac{\omega_0 + \omega_t}{2} \Delta t) & 0 \\ \sin(\frac{\omega_0 + \omega_t}{2} \Delta t) & \cos(\frac{\omega_0 + \omega_t}{2} \Delta t) & 0 \\ 0 & 0 & 1 \end{bmatrix} h_0;$$

    } **end for**
    $t = t + \Delta t$;
} **end while**

At the decision-making layer, locomotion behaviour is dependent on how the external forces and torques are computed. The definition of *expected velocity* v_e is the ideal velocity that the quadruped is willing to accomplish at its current state. For example, when a prey is to flee away from its predator, the magnitude of the expected velocity is the maximum speed it can reach v_{max}, one of the parameters which can be tuned for different quadrupeds. The direction of the expected velocity is heading from the predator to the prey. If this expected velocity is multiplied by the mass of the prey, we get the corresponding expected momentum p_e. According to the impulse-momentum theorem: For an object to generate a change in momentum, force must be applied to the object for equivalent impulse. When this steering force SF given is a constant force during the current time interval Δt, it can be expressed as:

$$J_F = \int_t^{t+\Delta t} SF dt = mv_e - mv_o$$

To illustrate the updates of the steering force, Algorithm 2 describes a basic strategy for calculating the steering force during the fleeing process. (The same can be done for the steering torque ST.)

Algorithm 2. Fleeing: Compute a fleeing force for prey based on the position of the pursuer. The current velocity of the animal is denoted as v and the current velocity of the target is denoted as v_t. Their respective positions are p_i and p_t. In addition, T represents the predicted interval and v_{max} represents the maximum velocity of the NPC.

---

for each NPC i in flee **do**
    //Compute Interval
    $T = \frac{\|p_t - p_i\|}{v_{max} + v_t}$
    $v_e = (p_i - (p_t + v_t * T)).\,normalized * v_{max}$
    $\Delta v = v_e - v$
    $F = \frac{m}{\Delta t} * \Delta v$
end for

At the skeletal movement layer, inverse kinematics is applied as illustrated in Fig. 2(a). A general spherical joint has three degrees of freedom in terms of rotational motion: roll (rotation around x axis), pitch (rotation around y axis) and yaw (rotation around z axis). A ball-and-joints has all three degrees of freedom; on the other hand, a hinge joint only has one (pitch). Each leg consists of two hinge joints (knee) and two ball-and-socket joints (elbow and ankle). An entire iteration of a waking gait cycle can be divided into two phases for each of the four legs: the "swing" and "stance" phases [1]. In the "swing" phase, the foot joint swings in the air and the sub-root joint follows the motion of the root joint. In the "stance" phase, the position of the foot joint is fixed and the sub-root joint follows the motion of the root joint. During the entire simulation process the distance between the root joint and the four sub-root joints, the mutual distance between the four sub-root joints remains constant. Some visual demonstrations of the two phases are shown in Fig. 2(b).

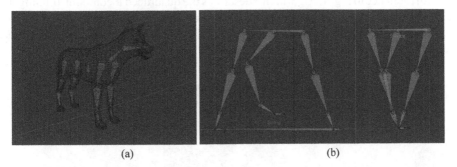

(a)   (b)

Fig. 2. (a) Quadruped locomotion model with inverse kinematics (b) swing and stance phases

2.2 Reinforcement Learning

The inverse kinematics (IK) embedded quadruped agent consists of a total number of 13 meshes and 12 configurable joints (3 joints on each leg) as shown in Fig. 3(a). The mass of each mesh and angular motion constraints of each joint is set to imitate the body structure of a quadruped to the largest extent.

The agent observations include the position and velocity vectors; it also takes its limb movements. The limbs should properly take turns in performing the swing and stance phases for different behaviours. Refer to Fig. 3(b), when the agent observes walking (right-lower), the limbs of one side is under swing phase (in the air), the limbs of other side must be under stance phase (on the ground). It is similar for running (upper-left), when the front limbs are under swing phase, the hind limbs are required to stay on the ground and vice versa. These IK constraints are implemented by adding collision detection between the foot mesh and the ground into agent observation and punishment for misconduct into the reward function.

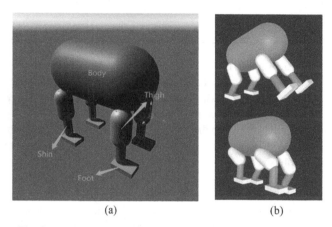

(a)   (b)

Fig. 3. (a) Quadruped agent and (b) IK-embedded locomotion

With reference to Fig. 4, Algorithm 3 describes the quadruped locomotion training. In the RL procedure, the key to training the agent toward desired movements and behaviours is a properly defined reward function, not only on the navigation but also the locomotion of each limb that generate realistic movements.

(a) Hovering   (b) Obstacle-Avoiding   (c) Fleeing and Pursuing

Fig. 4. RL Behaviour types of the agents during RL training (The pursuit agent tracked in blue, and the target agent tracked in red) (Color figure online)

Algorithm 3 Simulation of Quadruped Training: PPO-based cliped surrogate training. Discount factor for future rewards is denoted as γ. Generalized Advantage Estimate parameter for variance-bias configuration is denoted as λ. Divergence threshold betweem new and old policy is denoted as ϵ.

1: **while** training simulation is running **do**
2:     //Initialize policy θ parameters
3:     **for** iteration i **do**
4:         **for** each quadruped agent n in pursuing **do**
5:             //Run policy in the enviroment in T timesteps and update data into initial vectors
6:             //Generalized Advantage Estimator (GAE)
7:
$$A_t^{GAE} = \sum_{i=0}^{\infty} (\gamma\lambda)^l \delta_{t+l}^V$$

8:         **end for**
9:         //Surrogate Objective (cliped)
10:         $L(\theta) = E[min(clip(r_t(\theta), 1 - \epsilon, 1 + \epsilon)A_t, r_t(\theta)A_t)]$
11:         Update Policy θ with gradient of objective $\widehat{g}$
12:     **end for**
13: **end while**

To configure the target movement, the autonomous steering is introduced in this study. The target agent is driven by a combination of steering behaviours including *Flee*, *Hover* and *CollisionAvoidance* [2], as illustrated in Fig. 4. At the beginning of a new episode, the target agent first chooses a random position on the terrain to respawn. After spawning, instead of staying on that position and wait for the pursuit agent to reach it, it will first perform a collision detection against a pursuit agent within its detection radius. If the pursuit agent is not detected, it proceeds to execute the *Hover* behaviour; otherwise, to execute the *Flee* behaviour. In both *Hover* and *Flee*, the target agent will always be constrained by the *CollisionAvoidance* force to keep itself from getting cornered.

The training configurations are summarized below:

- **Objective**: Pursuit agent needs to catch up with the target agent as fast as possible while keeping its balance and correct limb movements;
- **Observations**: Velocity vectors of the quadruped model (both pursuit and target's body mesh), collision detections between the body mesh and the ground, body mesh of the pursuit and target, four foot meshes and the ground;
- **Action:** A total number of 39 continuous action corresponding to the rotation and strength of each joint.
- **Reward:**

    (i)   The product of how body velocity matches with the goal velocity and how body direction matches with the *predicted* pursuit direction toward the target. (a value between 0 and 1)
    (ii) *Body* mesh collides between the pursuit and target: +1 (current episode ends)
    (iii) *Body* mesh collides with the ground: −1 (current episode ends)
    (iv) *Foot* mesh misconduct: −1 (current episode ends)

- **Target:** Autonomous steering combination: *Hover*, *Flee* and *CollisionAvoidance*.

3   Experiment and Comparative Evaluation

A screenshot of the experiment with the quadruped locomotion is shown in Fig. 5. The training environment consists of nine identical terrains and quadruped agent training simultaneously to speed up training. The entire neural network takes 243 floats as input and output 39 floats as continuous action for rotation and strength of each joint. The main policy network consists of 3 hidden layers and 512 hidden units.

Fig. 5.   Screenshot on quadruped locomotion: pursuit agent of a wolf chasing its target agent of a deer

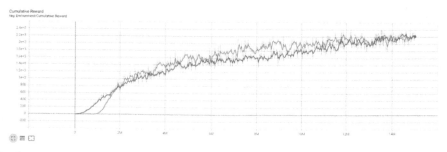

Fig. 6.   Cumulative reward through 15,000,000 steps of PPO (curve in orange color) and SAC (curve in blue color). Training using autonomous steering target, reaching around 2200 which surpasses the benchmark reward of 2000 with the existing vanilla dynamic target training. (Color online figure)

For comparison with the existing methods, as shown in Fig. 6, after 15,000,000 steps of training with PPO and Soft Actor Critic (SAC), cumulative reward of both algorithms with an autonomous steering target reached around 2200 which surpassed the benchmark reward of 2000 training with vanilla dynamic target.

In this experiment, two timers recording the episode length for both agents are set. Results are generated based on a total number of 100 episodes. Mean episode length for the Vanilla wolf agent is 8.1658(s); and that of the quadruped locomotion agent is 6.1141(s), which outperforms the Vanilla agent by approximately 25% faster in an arbitrary environment (randomly set by the autonomous steering deer agent).

4 Discussion and Conclusion

We have studied the main model-free machine learning approaches [16–18] including Deep Q Network (DQN), Deep Deterministic Policy Gradient (DDPG), Trust Region Policy Optimization (TRPO), Deep Deterministic Policy Gradient (DDPG), Proximal Policy Optimization (PPO) and Soft Actor-Critic (SAC). And based on these, we have presented our theoretic analyses with the important technical features.

First, inspired by traditional Q-learning, DQN is the beginning of a successful combination of convolutional neural networks (CNN) and RL. Although DQN can now successfully handle tasks with high observation spaces, it is still not suitable for environment with continuous action spaces. DDPG which is based on Deterministic Policy Gradient (DPG) extends DQN through an actor-critics approach. Compared with DQN, DDPG is able to operate in continuous action spaces using a deterministic policy. Similar to DDPG, TRPO also uses two NN instances for both actor and critics. Therefore, we have exploited the major advantages of this algorithm that the update size during training is constrained by a "trust region" to avoid new policy diverging too much relative to the existing policy. This technical contribution makes the training process easier.

Next, built upon TRPO, PPO introduced by OpenAI in 2017 is a new approach towards policy gradient algorithms, in particular, a novel objective function is used and is updated during the training procedure in multiple epochs of mini-batches per data sample. TRPO is also meant to determine an appropriate step size, but implementation of PPO is simpler and easier to solve. By applying these strategies, we have deviced a new algorithm to avoid network parameters from updating too far out of range, in contrast to those using the Vanilla Policy Gradient algorithm. Instead of adding new constraint parameters, we directly involve these constraints into the objective function itself to achieve better efficiency.

In conclusion, locomotive behaviours of the NPC will largely affect the overall quality of the adversarial games. Motion control, behaviour adaptation and RL of the NPC show significant improvement on user experience. Major technical contributions of this study are made to inverse kinematics embedded motion control, quadruped locomotion behaviour adaptation and dynamic environment informed reinforcement learning of the NPC agent. Instead of designing specific dynamics algorithms, the NPC agent can be trained with RL in the entire behaviour system.

The proposed concepts and techniques have been illustrated by a specific use case of in-game predator and prey interaction. Aimed at an intelligent locomotive predator to reach its autonomous steering locomotive prey as fast as possible in all the circumstances, the PPO learning scheme is combined with the autonomous steering target for a more challenging training environment. The quadruped target is also an intelligent agent that is capable of hovering, fleeing and obstacle avoiding. Such an autonomous steering target enables a variety of different behaviours. In fact, the same approach can also be used to train intelligent fleeing agent and much more.

Acknowledgement. This work is partially supported by the MOE AcRF RG93/20 grant by the Ministry of Education, Singapore, as well as the 206-A021006 grant by China-Singapore International Joint Research Institute.

References

1. Zhao, K., Lin, F., Seah, H.S.: Steering autonomous animals in VR hunting. In: SPIE Proceedings of International Workshop on Advanced Image Technology (IWAIT'21), Japan, pp. 5–6 Jan 2021
2. Zhao, K., Lin, F., Seah, H.S.: Collective intelligence of autonomous animals in VR hunting. In: IEEE VR 2021 Workshop on 3D Content Creation for Simulated Training in Extended Reality (IEEE VR21 TrainingXR), Portugal, 27 Mar–3 Apr 2021
3. Omar, S., Benatitallah, R., Duvivier, D., Artiba, A.H., Belanger, N., Feyzeau, P.: Path planning: a 2013 survey. In: IEEE International Conference on Industrial Engineering and Systems Management (IEEE IESM 2013) (2013)
4. De, J., Zhang, X., Lin, F., Cheng, L.: Transduction on directed graphs via absorbing random walks. IEEE Trans. Pattern Anal. Mach. Intell. **40**(7), 1770–1784 (2018)
5. Dijkstra, E.W.: A note on two problems in connexion with graphs. Numer. Math. **1**(1), 269–271 (1959)
6. Hart, P.E., Nilsson, N.J., Raphael, B.: A formal basis for the heuristic determination of minimum cost paths. IEEE Trans. Syst. Sci. Cybern. **4**(2), 100–107 (1968)
7. Cui, X., Shi, H.: A*-based pathfinding in modern computer games. Int. J. Comput. Sci. Netw. Secur. **11**(1), 125–130 (2011)
8. LaValle, S.M.: Rapidly-exploring random trees: a new tool for path planning, CiteSeer, pp. 98–11 (1998)
9. Reynolds, C.W.: Steering behaviors for autonomous characters. Game Dev. Conf. **1999**, 763–782 (1999)
10. Watkins, C.J.C.H., Dayan, P.: Q-learning. Mach. Learn. **8**(3–4), 279–292 (1992)
11. Fan, J., Wang, Z., Xie, Y., Yang, Z.: A theoretical analysis of deep Q-learning. In: Learning for Dynamics and Control, PMLR, pp. 486–489 (2020)
12. Kai, K., Deisenroth, M.P., Brundage, M., Bharath, A.A.: Deep reinforcement learning: a brief survey. IEEE Signal Process. Mag. **34**(6), 26–38 (2017)
13. Lou, C., et al.: Dynamic balance measurement and quantitative assessment using wearable plantar-pressure insoles in a pose-sensed virtual environment. Sensors **18**(12), 4193 (2018)
14. Zhongke, W., Lin, F., Seah, H.S., Yun, C.K.: Evaluation of difference bounds for computing rational Bézier curves and surfaces. Comput. Graph. **28**(4), 551–558 (2004)
15. Cai, J., Lin, F., Seah, H.S.: Graphical Simulation of Deformable Models. Springer, Cham (2016). https://doi.org/10.1007/978-3-319-51031-6
16. Leong, M.C., Prasad, D.K., Lee, Y.T., Lin, F.: Semi-CNN architecture for effective spatio-temporal learning in action recognition. Appl. Sci. **10**(2), 557 (2020)

17. Stepanova, S., Lin, F., Lin, V.C.-L.: A hopfield neural classifier and its FPGA implementation for identification of symmetrically structured DNA motifs. J. VLSI Signal Process. Syst. Signal Image Video Technol. **48**(3), 239–254 (2007)

18. Ma, J., Lin, F., Wesarg, S., Erdt, M.: A novel Bayesian model incorporating deep neural network and statistical shape model for pancreas segmentation. In: Frangi, A.F., Schnabel, J.A., Davatzikos, C., Alberola-López, C., Fichtinger, G. (eds.) MICCAI 2018. LNCS, vol. 11073, pp. 480–487. Springer, Cham (2018). https://doi.org/10.1007/978-3-030-00937-3_55

Partially Occluded Skeleton Action Recognition Based on Multi-stream Fusion Graph Convolutional Networks

Dan Li and Wuzhen Shi[✉]

Shenzhen University, No. 3688, Nanhai Avenue, Nanshan District, Shenzhen, China
1910433059@email.szu.edu.cn, wzhshi@szu.edu.cn

Abstract. Skeleton-based action recognition methods have been widely developed in recent years. However, the occlusion problem is still a difficult problem at present. Existing skeleton action recognition methods are usually based on complete skeleton data, and their performance is greatly reduced in occluded skeleton action recognition tasks. In order to improve the recognition accuracy on occluded skeleton data, a multi-stream fusion graph convolutional network (MSFGCN) is proposed. The proposed multi-stream fusion network consists of multiple streams, and different streams can handle different occlusion cases. In addition, joint coordinates, relative coordinates, small-scale temporal differences and large-scale temporal differences are extracted simultaneously to construct more discriminative multimodal features. In particular, to the best of our knowledge, we are the first to propose the simultaneous extraction of temporal difference features at different scales, which can more effectively distinguish between actions with different motion amplitude. Experimental results show that the proposed MSFGCN obtains state-of-the-art performance on occluded skeleton datasets.

Keywords: Occluded skeleton action recognition · Graph convolutional network · Multi-stream fusion network · Multimodal features

1 Introduction

Human action recognition plays an important role in video understanding. It has become one of the most significant and challenging task in the field of computer vision, and it is widely used in video surveillance, human-computer interaction, sports analysis, virtual reality and so on. Video actions can be represented as RGB videos, depth maps, infrared images and skeleton sequences. The purpose of action recognition is to identify the category of the action from these forms of video action.

Traditional action recognition methods are usually based on RGB sequence. Recent RGB-based methods use convolutional neural networks to extract the features of each frame, and then use recurrent neural networks or methods derived

© Springer Nature Switzerland AG 2021
N. Magnenat-Thalmann et al. (Eds.): CGI 2021, LNCS 13002, pp. 178–189, 2021.
https://doi.org/10.1007/978-3-030-89029-2_14

from recurrent neural networks to extract temporal information [9]. A classic approach is to extract temporal information through optical flow information [13]. Some scholars also proposed to use a 3D convolutional neural network to directly extract feature information from video [17]. These methods have achieved good results on specific datasets, but they all have common disadvantages. As RGB videos often have complex backgrounds, they are also affected by illumination, view and other conditions, which will lead to performance degradation in practical applications. In addition, these methods often come with expensive computing power.

In recent years, with the continuous progress and development of low-cost 3D data acquisition equipment, such as the Kinect sensor and the continuous evolution of human pose estimation algorithm, the human action recognition algorithm based on skeleton data has gradually come into the field of view of scholars, and has been widely studied. Compared with RGB data, skeleton data is not affected by view, illumination, background and other conditions, and is robust to the environment. At the same time, the requirement of computing power for action recognition method based on skeleton data is greatly reduced. The action recognition methods based on human skeleton can be divided into manual feature methods and deep learning methods. The manual feature methods capture joint motion information by designing hand-made features. Deep learning-based action recognition networks mainly include recurrent neural networks (RNN) [2,14,23], convolutional neural networks (CNN) [1] and graph convolutional networks (GCN) [21].

Occlusion is a difficult task in action recognition. However, the existing skeleton action recognition methods are usually based on the complete skeleton data, without considering the problem of occlusion in the real scene. Many occlusion cases will reduce the action recognition performance, such as the occlusion of objects in the scene, the occlusion of characters themselves in the process of movement, and the occlusion of characters to characters in multi-person action recognition. To deal with the occlusion problem, we propose a multi-stream fusion network, in which different streams focus on different occlusion conditions, so that the fusion network can deal with multiple occlusion problems simultaneously. In addition, the recent RGB-based method [13] shows that optical flow is a useful information in action recognition task. Inspired by this, MS-AAGCN [11] applied similar motion information to the skeleton action recognition task. However, only the differences between adjacent frames were considered in previous works. For some actions with a small motion amplitude, such as arm swing when walking, the motion features were not obvious between adjacent frames. Therefore, we considered extracting motion features in a larger scale.

The main contributions of this paper are as follows:

- In order to deal with the problem of low recognition accuracy caused by various occlusion, we build a multi-stream fusion network, in which different streams handle occlusion under different conditions.
- In this paper, joints and relative coordinates, small scale and large scale temporal difference are simultaneously used to construct more discrimina-

tive multi-modal features. In particular, we propose for the first time the simultaneous extraction of motion features at different scales to distinguish motions with different motion amplitudes.
– We construct the occluded datasets by occluding the joints of two large-scale skeleton action recognition datasets. On these occluded datasets, we demonstrate the effectiveness of the proposed method through experiments.

2   Related Work

2.1   Manual Feature Extraction Method

A simple and effective action descriptor is obtained by using hierarchical covariance matrix according to coordinate information, and the correlation and coordination among joints in the action are extracted by using the characteristics of covariance matrix [3]. Zanfir et al. [22] use means the action of motion vector sequence, manual extraction can also include the characteristics of a joint relative coordinates [19], the rotation and translation between body parts [18], etc. However, most of these methods rely on manual parts or rules to analyze spatial patterns, which can only perform well on some specific datasets [20], making it difficult for action recognition algorithms to be promoted to a wider range of applications.

2.2   RNN/CNN-Based Method

RNN-based approaches typically model skeleton data as a series of coordinate vectors along spatial and temporal dimensions, with each vector representing a human joint. Du et al. [2] proposed an end-to-end layered bidirectional RNN, which divides the human skeleton into five parts according to the physical structure of the human body and sends them into five subnetworks respectively to capture the rich dependent relationships between different parts of the human body. In order to further improve the learning of the temporal context of skeleton sequences, there are also some methods based on the improved RNN for skeleton action recognition tasks. Song et al. [14] proposed an end-to-end spatio-temporal attention model, which selectively pays attention to discriminative joints in every frame input from the network, and gives different attention to different frames. The skeleton data is modeled as pseudo images in the CNN-based method according to the manually designed conversion rules. Different coding methods are proposed to encode five spatial skeleton features into the images [1]. Li et al. [5] proposed a shape motion representation method based on geometric algebra, which makes full use of the information provided by skeleton sequences.

2.3   GCN-Based Method

Yan et al. [21] constructed a general graph-based dynamic skeleton modeling formula, and for the first time applied graph-based neural network to the skeleton action recognition task. Shi et al. [10] proposed using two-stream network (2s-AGCN) to improve the recognition performance. 2s-AGCN takes the temporal difference of the two joints as the vector representation of the skeleton at that point as the motion information according to the physical connection of the body joints. The motion information contains not only the length information of the bone, but also the direction information. AS-GCN [4] adopts multi-task learning, which can not only identify human actions, but also use multi-task learning strategies to predict the posture of the human body at the next moment. The introduction of action prediction module helps to capture more detailed features, so as to improve recognition performance. The commonly used methods for skeleton action recognition are to firstly extract spatial information of skeleton sequence by graph convolution, and then to extract temporal information by temporal convolution. This method has limitations in obtaining complex spatial-temporal dependencies. Liu et al. [7] proposed a unified spatial-temporal graph convolution operator G3D to model spatial-temporal dependencies directly from skeleton sequences. Si. et al. [12] proposed the combination of graph convolution and recurrent neural network, and proposed the attention enhanced graph convolution LSTM network (AGC-LSTM), which can not only capture the discriminant features of spatial structure and temporal dynamics, but also explore the co-occurrence relationship between spatial and temporal domains.

3   Proposed Method

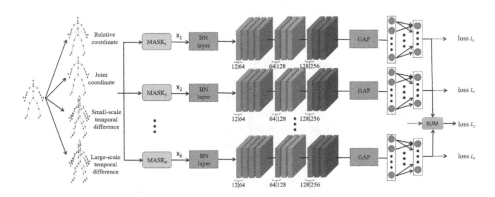

Fig. 1. The pipeline of MSFGCN consists of six streams. x_i is preprocessed skeleton data for different streams. GAP is global average pooling.

The overall structure of the partially occluded multi-stream fusion graph convolutional network proposed by us is shown in Fig. 1, in which the multimodal features are first extracted and then fused and optimized by a spatial-temporal graph convolutional network. In addition, the proposed MSFGCN has multiple streams to deal with different occlusion cases. For the input skeleton data, the multimodal features are firstly extracted. The relative coordinates, small scale temporal difference and large scale temporal difference of the skeleton data were calculated respectively, and then the multimodal features were obtained by combining the original joint coordinate data in the channel dimension. The multimodal features are then fed into different streams, where multimodal features need to be multiplied by a corresponding mask to obtain skeleton data for different occlusion conditions. A full connection layer is added after each stream. The output of each full connection layer is added to get the final output. We use the cross entropy loss function to optimize the model.

3.1   Multimodal Feature Extraction

Some actions are very similar in spatial features, such as standing up and sitting down. To distinguish the two actions, temporal features should be taken into account. In the skeleton action recognition task based on RGB videos, the optical flow information can be used to model the temporal features. Inspired by optical flow, MS-AAGCN [11] applied motion features to skeleton action recognition tasks. The work [16] argues that relative coordinates can provide more information than absolute coordinates and Song et al. [15] input the relative coordinates into the graph convolutional network as input features. Inspired by previous work, we construct multi-modal information as the input feature of the network. The multimodal information is composed of original joint coordinates, small scale temporal difference, large scale temporal difference and relative coordinates. The size of the original joint coordinate data X is $C_{in} \times T \times V$. The size of the multimodal feature obtained by combining the four features on the channel dimension is $4C_{in} \times T \times V$. The small scale temporal difference is expressed as X_s. $x_s = x_{t+1} - x_t$, where x_s represents the small-scale temporal difference of time s in X_s. The large-scale temporal difference X_l. $x_l = x_{t+\tau} - x_t$, where x_l represents the large-scale temporal difference of time l in X_l and τ is the number of frames spaced. The relative coordinate X_r is the difference between the joint and the center joint. Small-scale temporal difference are used to capture features with large motion amplitude, while large-scale temporal difference are used to capture features with small motion amplitude. Adding relative coordinates can make the input data more robust to position changes.

3.2   Spatial-Temporal Graph Convolutional Network

Skeleton sequences are often represented as 2D or 3D coordinates of joints that are naturally connected within each frame according to the physical structure of the human body. According to the definition method of graph in ST-GCN, we use spatial-temporal graph to form the hierarchical representation of skeleton sequence. For a skeleton sequence containing T frame, we express the skeleton graph as G = (V,E), where V represents all joints of skeleton sequence and E represents the edges connecting these joints.   The spatial-temporal graph convolution network consists of ten spatial-temporal graph convolution layers. Figure 2 shows the structure of a spatial-temporal graph convolution layer. The

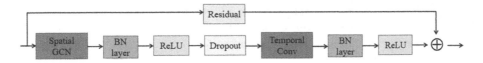

Fig. 2. The structure of a ST-GCN layer.

spatial-temporal graph convolution layer consists of graph convolution layer and temporal convolution layer. The setting of the output channel in the spatial-temporal graph convolutional network is the same as that in ST-GCN. The first four layers have 64 channels for output. The follow three layers have 128 channels and the last three layers have 256 channels.

Graph Convolution Layer. Yan et al. [21] defined the convolution on topology graph according to the traditional convolution. In space, the convolution of the joint v_i on the graph was expressed as the following formula

$$f_{out}(v_i) = \sum_{v_j \in B_i} \frac{1}{Z_{ij}} f_{in}(v_j) w(l_i(v_j)) \tag{1}$$

Where B_i represents adjacent joints, $f(v)$ represents the feature of joint v, and w represents the weight. In 2D convolution, each pixel has fixed adjacency points, so these pixels can be indexed in a fixed order. However, there is no fixed index relation in the topology graph, and the number of adjacency points of each joint may be different. To solve this problem, the index order of adjacent joint points is obtained by dividing the adjacency points into different subsets. Each subset shares a weight, $l(v)$ is the subset label of the corresponding vertex, Z_{ij} is equal to the cardinality of the corresponding subset, It is used to balance the contribution of each set. In ST-GCN, the author uses three partitioning strategies to segment subsets. In this paper, we segment subsets according to distance. In the skeleton action recognition task, the form of the input skeleton sequence is [C,T,V], where C is the number of channels, T is the number of frames of the sequence, and V is the number of joints within a frame. Equation 1 can be converted to

$$f_{out} = \sum_{k}^{K_v} W_k (f_{in} A_k) \odot M_k \tag{2}$$

While K_v represents the size of the convolution kernel on the spatial dimension, namely, the adjacency point is divided into K_v subsets, the adjacency matrix A_k is the kth part of the adjacency matrix. M_k is a learnable mask that represents the strength of the connection between joints.

Temporal Convolution Layer. The above graph convolution layer only fuses joint features in the spatial dimension, while the temporal convolution layer fuses joint features in the temporal dimension. There is a connection between the same joints between adjacent frames. The temporal convolution is a $K_t \times 1$ convolution where K_t is the kernel size in the temporal dimension. As shown in Fig. 2, we also use batch normalization and residual connections for the temporal convolution layers.

3.3 Occlusion Sensitive Multi-stream Fusion Networks

In reality, there may be occlusion of objects or inaccurate prediction of human pose estimation algorithm, which will lead to incomplete input skeleton sequence and thus affect the accuracy of action recognition. In order to reduce this influence, we construct a multi-stream fusion network, which contains multiple streams, each stream is a spatial-temporal graph convolutional network. The multi-stream fusion network is composed of six streams. The first stream is a complete feature extraction network, which is used to extract the complete features and ensure that the network can accurately identify the action category of the input data when the complete skeleton data is input. The human body is divided into five parts: the left arm, the right arm, the left leg, the right leg and the trunk. For each of the remaining streams, we occlude each of these five parts of the input skeleton data to simulate occluding different parts of the human body. We multiplied the original input data with different masks, i.e., $x_i = x \odot \text{mask}_i$. mask_1 - mask_6 represent masks for non-occluding, occluding left arm, occluding right arm, occluding left leg, occluding right leg, and occluding trunk, respectively. Figure 3(a) shows the results of different joint coordinate data with different masks, and Fig. 3(b) shows the results of different modal data with the same mask. Each stream of our MSFGCN strives to obtain discriminative features from different masked results for action recognition, which makes our MSFGCN can deal with the problem of occluded target recognition more robustly.

In previous multi-stream networks, each stream is trained and optimized separately. Finally, the Softmax results of each stream are added together to obtain a merged score as a prediction label. Different from previous methods, we combine multiple streams for training. The output results of the full connection layer of each stream are added up, and then the final result $\hat{y}$ is obtained through the classification of Softmax classifier. The output of each stream is $\hat{y}_i$. In order to force each stream to try its best to extract discriminative features from different occlusion conditions, we apply cross entropy constraint on each stream. The loss function of each stream is

$$Loss_i = -y \log \hat{y}_i \qquad (3)$$

The output $\hat{y}$ of the model is the sum of the output of each stream.

$$\hat{y} = \sum_{i=1}^{S} \hat{y}_i \qquad (4)$$

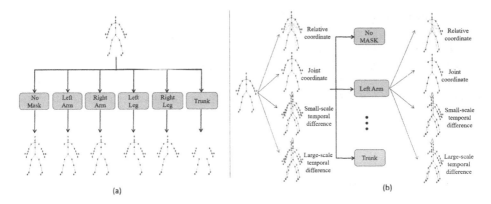

Fig. 3. The input data for different streams. (a) the input data for the six streams (only show the joint). (b) the input data for the second stream (occluded left arm).

For the final fusion result, the loss function is

$$L = -y \log \hat{y} + \sum_{i=1}^{S} Loss_i \tag{5}$$

Where S is the number of streams.

4 Experiments

4.1 Datasets

The NTU-RGBD dataset is the most popular and authoritative indoor action recognition dataset. It contains four types of data, including RGB, depth, 3D skeleton and infrared data. NTU-RGB+D 60 [8] consists of 56,000 action clips of 60 types of action, which were shot by 40 volunteers in an indoor environment. Each action was shot by three cameras at the same height and different angles. The dataset contains the 3D coordinates of the joints of each frame detected by the Kinect V2 depth sensor. Each frame is composed of 25 joints and there are no more than 2 subjects in each video. The author recommends two benchmark tests, namely Cross-Subject (CS) and Cross-View (CV). The Cross-Subject divides the dataset into a training set (40,320 videos) and a verification set (16,560 videos). The participants in these two subsets are different. The training set in the cross-view contains 37,920 videos captured by the second and third cameras, and the verification set contains 18,960 videos captured by the first camera. NTU RGB+D 120 [6] extends NTU RGB+D 60 by adding 57,367 skeleton sequences in 60 additional action classes, for a total of 113,945 samples in 120 classes. The authors suggested two test benchmarks, one for Cross-Setting (CSet) and the other for Cross-Subject. Cross-Settings 54,468 samples were collected from half of the camera settings for training and the remaining 59,477 samples for testing. The Cross-Subject selects 63,026 samples from the subjects for training and the remaining 50,919 samples for testing.

In order to verify the robustness of our approach to occluded skeletons, we constructed a synthetic occluded dataset based on the CS benchmark of NTU-RGBD 60 dataset and the CSet benchmark of NTU-RGBD 120 dataset according to the method proposed in RAGCN [15]. We preprocesses the skeleton data before it is input into the network model, and sets the corresponding eigenvalue of the key joint to 0. For training, we set up a total of five occlusion joints, including occlusion of the left arm, right arm, hands, legs and trunk.

4.2   Implementation Details

All experiments are conducted on the PyTorch deep learning framework. Our model is trained with stochastic gradient desent with momentum of 0.9. The size of spatial convolution kernel is 2, and the size of temporal convolution kernel is 5. The learning rate is set as 0.1 and is divided by 10 at the 20th epoch and 40th epoch. The training process is ended at the 50th epoch. We randomly dropout the features at 0.5 probability after each ST-GCN unit to avoid overfitting.

4.3   Experimental Results

Experimental Results on Standard Datasets. We compare the performance of our proposed method with previous methods on two datasets, NTU-RGBD 60 and NTU-RGBD 120. The experimental results are shown in Table 1. Although our model could not achieve the results of state-of-the-art, there was a significant performance gain compared to the baseline (ST-GCN). And the performance of our method is improved on partially occluded data sets, which will be discussed in the next section.

Table 1. Comparison of the SOTA methods on the two benchmarks of NTU 60 and NTU 120 in accuracy (%)

Model	Year	Data	CS	CV	CSub	CSet
ST-GCN [21]	2018	Skeleton	81.5	88.3	70.7	73.2
AS-GCN [4]	2019	Skeleton	86.8	**94.2**	77.7	78.9
RA-GCN [15]	2020	Skeleton	87.3	93.6	81.1	**82.7**
MSFGCN	2021	Skeleton	**88.1**	92.6	**81.9**	81.4

Experimental Results on Partially Occluded Datasets. We test the effectiveness of the proposed module in the partially occluded skeleton dataset. The tests were performed using CS benchmarks on the NTU-RGBD 60 dataset and CSet benchmarks on the NTU-RGBD 120 dataset. In Table 2, the numbers 1 to 5 means left arm, right arm, two hands, two legs, and trunk are marked respectively. As shown in Table 2, there is a huge difference between MSFGCN and other methods.

Table 2. Experimental results (%) with partly occlusion on the CS benchmark of NTU 60 (TOP) and the CSet benchmark of NTU 120 (BOTTOM)

Model	None	1	2	3	4	5
ST-GCN [21]	80.7	71.4	60.5	62.6	77.4	50.2
RAGCN [15]	87.3	75.9	62.1	69.2	83.3	72.8
MSFGCN	**88.1**	**77.8**	**64.7**	**77.9**	**85.1**	**77.6**
ST-GCN [21]	73.2	59.7	47.3	52.5	68.5	48.5
RAGCN [15]	**82.7**	68.5	54.9	**57.5**	**79.0**	69.9
MSFGCN	81.4	**69.1**	**55.8**	52.6	78.3	**70.2**

Ablation Studies. The importance of relative coordinates and small scale motion features has been confirmed by RA-GCN, and we tested the importance of multi-stream fusion network and large-scale temporal difference using CS benchmarks on the NTU-RGBD 60 dataset. The experimental results are shown in Table 3, in which the numbers 1 to 5 means left arm, right arm, two hands, two legs, and trunk are marked respectively. Compared with the single-stream network, the multi-stream fusion network achieves excellent performance on both the complete dataset and the partially occluded dataset. The multi-stream network here does not add large-scale temporal difference. The performance of MSFGCN reached the best when the temporal difference was added. The recognition performance was improved by 0.2% on the complete dataset and by 1.5%, 2.3% and 0.1% on the data set covering the right arm, hands and legs, respectively.

Table 3. Experimental results (%) with partly occlusion on the CS benchmark of NTU 60

Model	None	1	2	3	4	5
Single-stream	85.0	72.2	58.9	55.4	79.6	66.4
Multi-stream	87.9	**77.8**	63.2	75.6	85.0	**78.0**
MSFGCN	**88.1**	**77.8**	**64.7**	**77.9**	**85.1**	77.6

5   Conclusion

In this paper, in order to solve the problem of poor performance in occluded action recognition tasks and the difficulty in identifying some similar actions, we proposed a multi-stream fusion graph convolutional network. Different streams can process different types of occlusion data so as to improve the recognition accuracy on occlusion datasets. In addition, to the best of our knowledge, this is the first time that multi-scale temporal differences have been used to model skeletal action, allowing the model to extract more discriminative motion information.

Acknowledgements. This work was supported in part by the National Science Foundation of China under Grant 62101346, in part by the Guangdong Basic and Applied Basic Research Foundation under Grant 2021A1515011702 and in part by the Stable Support Plan for Shenzhen Higher Education Institutions under Grant 20200812104316001.

References

1. Ding, Z., Wang, P., Ogunbona, P.O., Li, W.: Investigation of different skeleton features for CNN-based 3D action recognition. In: 2017 IEEE International Conference on Multimedia and Expo Workshops (ICMEW), pp. 617–622. IEEE (2017)
2. Du, Y., Wang, W., Wang, L.: Hierarchical recurrent neural network for skeleton based action recognition. In: Proceedings of the IEEE Conference on Computer Vision and Pattern Recognition, pp. 1110–1118 (2015)
3. Hussein, M.E., Torki, M., Gowayyed, M.A., El-Saban, M.: Human action recognition using a temporal hierarchy of covariance descriptors on 3D joint locations. In: Twenty-Third International Joint Conference on Artificial Intelligence (2013)
4. Li, M., Chen, S., Chen, X., Zhang, Y., Wang, Y., Tian, Q.: Actional-structural graph convolutional networks for skeleton-based action recognition. In: Proceedings of the IEEE/CVF Conference on Computer Vision and Pattern Recognition, pp. 3595–3603 (2019)
5. Li, Y., Xia, R., Liu, X., Huang, Q.: Learning shape-motion representations from geometric algebra spatio-temporal model for skeleton-based action recognition. In: 2019 IEEE International Conference on Multimedia and Expo (ICME), pp. 1066–1071. IEEE (2019)
6. Liu, J., Shahroudy, A., Perez, M., Wang, G., Duan, L.Y., Kot, A.C.: NTU RGB+ D 120: a large-scale benchmark for 3d human activity understanding. IEEE Trans. Pattern Anal. Mach. Intell. **42**(10), 2684–2701 (2019)
7. Liu, Z., Zhang, H., Chen, Z., Wang, Z., Ouyang, W.: Disentangling and unifying graph convolutions for skeleton-based action recognition. In: Proceedings of the IEEE/CVF Conference on Computer Vision and Pattern Recognition, pp. 143–152 (2020)
8. Shahroudy, A., Liu, J., Ng, T.T., Wang, G.: NTU RGB+ D: a large scale dataset for 3D human activity analysis. In: Proceedings of the IEEE Conference on Computer Vision and Pattern Recognition, pp. 1010–1019 (2016)
9. Sharma, S., Kiros, R., Salakhutdinov, R.: Action recognition using visual attention. In: Neural Information Processing Systems (NIPS) Time Series Workshop (2015)
10. Shi, L., Zhang, Y., Cheng, J., Lu, H.: Two-stream adaptive graph convolutional networks for skeleton-based action recognition. In: Proceedings of the IEEE/CVF Conference on Computer Vision and Pattern Recognition, pp. 12026–12035 (2019)
11. Shi, L., Zhang, Y., Cheng, J., Lu, H.: Skeleton-based action recognition with multi-stream adaptive graph convolutional networks. IEEE Trans. Image Process. **29**, 9532–9545 (2020)

12. Si, C., Chen, W., Wang, W., Wang, L., Tan, T.: An attention enhanced graph convolutional LSTM network for skeleton-based action recognition. In: Proceedings of the IEEE/CVF Conference on Computer Vision and Pattern Recognition, pp. 1227–1236 (2019)
13. Simonyan, K., Zisserman, A.: Two-stream convolutional networks for action recognition in videos. arXiv preprint arXiv:1406.2199 (2014)
14. Song, S., Lan, C., Xing, J., Zeng, W., Liu, J.: An end-to-end spatio-temporal attention model for human action recognition from skeleton data. In: Proceedings of the AAAI Conference on Artificial Intelligence, vol. 31 (2017)
15. Song, Y.F., Zhang, Z., Shan, C., Wang, L.: Richly activated graph convolutional network for robust skeleton-based action recognition. IEEE Transactions on Circuits and Systems for Video Technology (2020)
16. Thakkar, K., Narayanan, P.: Part-based graph convolutional network for action recognition. arXiv preprint arXiv:1809.04983 (2018)
17. Tran, D., Bourdev, L., Fergus, R., Torresani, L., Paluri, M.: Learning spatiotemporal features with 3D convolutional networks. In: Proceedings of the IEEE international Conference on Computer Vision, pp. 4489–4497 (2015)
18. Vemulapalli, R., Arrate, F., Chellappa, R.: Human action recognition by representing 3D skeletons as points in a lie group. In: Proceedings of the IEEE Conference on Computer Vision and Pattern Recognition, pp. 588–595 (2014)
19. Wang, J., Liu, Z., Wu, Y., Yuan, J.: Mining actionlet ensemble for action recognition with depth cameras. In: 2012 IEEE Conference on Computer Vision and Pattern Recognition, pp. 1290–1297. IEEE (2012)
20. Wang, L., Huynh, D.Q., Koniusz, P.: A comparative review of recent Kinect-based action recognition algorithms. IEEE Trans. Image Process. **29**, 15–28 (2019)
21. Yan, S., Xiong, Y., Lin, D.: Spatial temporal graph convolutional networks for skeleton-based action recognition. In: Proceedings of the AAAI Conference on Artificial Intelligence, vol. 32 (2018)
22. Zanfir, M., Leordeanu, M., Sminchisescu, C.: The moving pose: an efficient 3D kinematics descriptor for low-latency action recognition and detection. In: Proceedings of the IEEE International Conference on Computer Vision, pp. 2752–2759 (2013)
23. Zhang, P., Lan, C., Xing, J., Zeng, W., Xue, J., Zheng, N.: View adaptive recurrent neural networks for high performance human action recognition from skeleton data. In: Proceedings of the IEEE International Conference on Computer Vision, pp. 2117–2126 (2017)

Social-Scene-Aware Generative Adversarial Networks for Pedestrian Trajectory Prediction

Binhao Huang[1], Zhenwei Ma[1], Lianggangxu Chen[2], and Gaoqi He[1,2(✉)]

[1] East China University of Science and Technology, 130 Meilong Road, Shanghai, China
gqhe@cs.ecnu.edu.cn
[2] East China Normal University, 3663 Zhongshan North Road, Shanghai, China

Abstract. Pedestrian trajectory prediction is crucial across a wide range of applications like self-driving vehicles and social robots. Such prediction is challenging because crowd behavior is inherently determined by various factors, such as obstacles, stationary crowd groups and destinations which were difficult to effectively represent. Especially pedestrians tend to be greatly affected by the pedestrians in front of them more than those behind them, which were often ignored in literature. In this paper, we propose a novel framework of Social-Scene-Aware Generative Adversarial Networks (SSA-GAN), which includes three modules, to predict the future trajectory of pedestrians in dynamic scene. Specifically, in the Scene module, we model the original scene image into a scene energy map by combining various scene factors and calculating the probability of pedestrians passing at each location. And the modeling formula is inspired by the distance relationship between pedestrians and scene factors. Moreover, the Social module is used to aggregate neighbors' interactions on the basis of the correlation between the motion history of pedestrians. This correlation is captured by the self-attention pooling module and limited by the field of view. And then the Generative Adversarial module with variety loss can solve the multimodal problem of pedestrian trajectory. Extensive experiments on publicly available datasets validate the effectiveness of our method for crowd behavior understanding and trajectory prediction.

Keywords: Pedestrian trajectory prediction · Energy map · Self-attention · Social interaction · Crowd behavior

1 Introduction

With the increase of population and diversity of human activities, crowd behavior understanding and trajectory prediction are of major importance for various domains, such as visual surveillance [1, 2] and robotics community [3, 4]. And pedestrian trajectory prediction helps self-driving vehicles and social robots better plan their own path forward [1, 3]. Humans in dynamic scenes have the will to exert causal forces to change their motion and constantly adjust their paths as they bypass obstacles to reach their destinations [5]. This complicated planning process is partially internal, which makes predicting pedestrians' trajectories from observations challenging. Hence, in addition to past movement

© Springer Nature Switzerland AG 2021
N. Magnenat-Thalmann et al. (Eds.): CGI 2021, LNCS 13002, pp. 190–201, 2021.
https://doi.org/10.1007/978-3-030-89029-2_15

history, a multitude of aspects should be taken into account, for instance latent predetermined destinations, other moving pedestrians, and stationary crowd groups [6, 7, 14]. Stationary crowd groups tend to stay in place for a long time, which cause pedestrians who are going to their destinations to avoid such groups in advance and change their trajectory in a large range, as shown in Fig. 1.

Fig. 1. Illustration of a scenario where the target pedestrian tends to make large turns and by-pass stationary groups to reach his destination. The orange circle represents the stationary groups, and the red and green line represent the fake and real trajectories, respectively. (Color figure online)

Traditional methods like social forces [8] capture human-human interaction through hand-crafted functions [9] which normally fail to build crowd interactions in crowded spaces. In the past few years, deep learning methods have shined in various fields [21, 26, 27]. And there are some works [7, 12] on groups show that the influence of groups on pedestrians cannot be ignored, which is difficult to be well represented in deep learning modeling. However, existing predictors still have two problems: (1) Stationary crowd groups and destinations would greatly affect the direction of pedestrians but was often ignored in deep learning modeling. (2) Pedestrian's future trajectory is often influenced by pedestrians in front, and it's inappropriate to treat all pedestrians in the social pooling equally.

In this paper, we propose a novel framework of Social-Scene-Aware Generative Adversarial Networks (SSA-GAN) to sequentially predict the coordinate displace-ment between two frames for each pedestrian. We model the original scene image into a scene energy map, and it helps the model to obtain a more refined surrounding environment. Especially in the social pooling, multi-scale energy map information is used to make pedestrians get local and global information. At the same time, the self-attention module which is based on the pedestrians' field of view (FoV) make the interaction between pedestrians more in line with real social situations. The contribu-tions of our paper are summarized as follows:

(1) A scene energy map method is proposed, which can jointly model scene factors such as obstacles, destinations, and stationary crowd groups that affect the process of pedestrians moving forward.
(2) A social self-attention pooling module based on FoV is proposed to handle trajectory interaction between pedestrians, which can better simulate the forward intention of pedestrians in real scenes.

(3) Experimental results on 5 public datasets prove the effectiveness of the method. And extensive ablation studies were performed on Central Station dataset to better understand each proposed component.

2 Related Work

2.1 Crowd Interaction

The traditional model for crowd Interaction was proposed by Helbing and Robicquet [8]. Their Social Force model used attractive forces to guide pedestrians toward their destinations, and repulsive forces to avoid collisions. Growd interaction can be divided into human-group interaction and human-human interaction. Human-group interaction mainly includes group detection and stationary time estimation for crowd group analysis [2, 7, 12]. Recently, there are many deep learning-based models been proposed. For example, Shuai proposed Behaviour-CNN which uses CNN to model crowd interactions [2]. Social-LSTM encoded the human-human interactions into a social descriptor [1]. Xu used a softmax way to assign different weights to other pedestrians based on spatial affinity [10]. In the past two years, the RNN-based models have achieved great success [1, 10, 11], and all these methods use different ways to share the hidden states of RNNs to model interactions between pedestrians in crowded scenes. And Huang etc. introduce graph neural networks in trajectory prediction [16], which believes that the position of pedestrians in the scene can be regarded as the nodes in the graph.

2.2 Multimodal Trajectory Prediction

Some work has proposed the importance of the inherent multimodal nature of human paths [13]. This shift of emphasis to planning for multiple future paths has led many recent works to incorporate multi-modality in their trajectory prediction models. Gup-ta propose a Generative Adversarial Network (GAN) [17] based framework with a novel social pooling mechanism to generate multiple future trajectories in accordance to social norms [13]. Sadeghian also propose a GAN-based framework named SoPhie, which utilizes path history of all the agents and the scene context information [15]. SoPhie employs a social attention mechanism with physical attention, which helps in learning social information across the agent interactions. However, these socially-aware approaches do not take into account the pedestrians' ultimate destinations, which play a key role in shaping their movement in the scene. A few works also ap-proach trajectory prediction via an inverse reinforcement learning (IRL) setup [18, 20].

3 Method

In this section, we will introduce the framework of Social-Scene-Aware Generative Adversarial Networks, which includes three modules: Scene module, Social module, and GAN module. The Scene module can capture information such as obstacles, stationary crowds and exits in the scene. The Social module will focus on the interaction between pedestrians, including the pedestrian's attention weight and scope of vision. The GAN module can help deal with the multimodality of pedestrian trajectories, and select the one closest to the ground truth among possible future trajectories (Fig. 2).

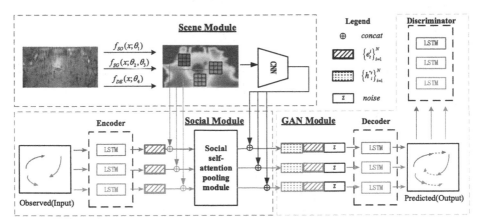

Fig. 2. Overview of model. Our model contains three key components: the Scene energy graph module, the Social self-attention pooling module, and the Generative adversarial module.

3.1 The Formulation for Pedestrian Trajectory Prediction

Assuming that there are N pedestrians p_1, p_2, ..., p_N, and t is the current time stamp (frame). The spatial location (coordinate) of the ith pedestrian $p_i (i \in [1, N])$ at time t is denoted as $S_t^i = [x_t^i, y_t^i]$. Given the spatial coordinates $S_{1:t_{obs}}$ of each pedestrian from start time to observed time t_{obs}, trajectory prediction aims at predicting the coordinates in the future time period from $t_{obs} + 1$ to $t_{obs} + T$, i.e., $S_{t_{obs}+1:t_{obs}+T}$. Different from the previous work [2] which predicts all the coordinates in all these frames simultaneously, we sequentially predict the coordinates in each future frame.

3.2 Scene Module

The scene module has three major components, Scene Obstacles, Stationary Groups and Destination. Human walking path selection is similar to water flow [7], which means that a pedestrian usually selects the most convenient and efficient path for reaching the destination. Based on this objective phenomenon, a general scene energy map M is proposed to model the traveling difficulty of every location of the scene. Different factors may have particular effects on pedestrian decision making. In our model, the energy map M is modeled with three channels, which are represented by f_{SO}, f_{SG} and f_{DE}. $M(x)$ is pixel-wise modeled by combining the channels:

$$M(x; \Theta) = f_{SO}(x; \theta_1) \times f_{SG}(x; \theta_2, \theta_3) \times f_{DE}(x; \theta_4) \tag{1}$$

where $\Theta = [\theta_1, \theta_2, \theta_3, \theta_4]^T$ are weighting parameters for different terms.

Moreover, people tend to keep a distance from these obstacles and moving pedestrians and are not likely to walk very close to them. It is more difficult to walk through denser stationary crowds. Therefore, these channels can be modeled as following:

$$f_{SO}(x; \theta_1) = exp(-\frac{\theta_1}{d_1(x, SO)}) \tag{2}$$

$$f_{SG}(x; \theta_2, \theta_3) = exp(-\sum_{j=1}^{n} \frac{\theta_2}{d_2(x, SG_j) + \theta_3 d_3(SG_j)}) \tag{3}$$

$$f_{DE}(x; \theta_4) = exp(-\theta_4 d_4(x, DE)) \tag{4}$$

where SO is a set of locations occupied by scene obstacles, and $d_1(x,SO) = min_{y_1 \in SO} \|x - y_1\|_2^2$ measures the distance from the current location x to its nearest scene obstacle location y_1. $SG_j (j \in [1, n])$ is the jth stationary crowd group region, $d_2(x,SG_j) = min_{y_2 \in SG_j} \|x - y_2\|_2^2$ measures the distance from the current location x to the nearest stationary crowd group region y_2, and $d_3(SG_i) \in (0, +\infty)$ is calculated as the average distance among group members. Larger d_3 represents lower crowd density. And DE is a set of positions of fixed exits in the scene, and $d_4(x,DE) = min_{y_3 \in DE} \|x - y_3\|_2^2$ measures the distance from the current location x to the nearest exit y_3.

And then we normalize the energy map $M(x; \Theta)^t$ at time t and use a Convolutional Neural Network (CNN) to extract the global scene features V_{Sce}^t. It can help pedestrians better understand the global scene information.

$$V_{Sce}^t = CNN(m(x; \Theta)^t; W_{cnn}) \tag{5}$$

where $CNN(\cdot)$ is VGGnet-19 which is initialized by pre-training on ImageNet, and W_{cnn} is the embedding weight.

3.3 Social Module

The social module proposed in SGAN ignores the surrounding scene information, and the scene energy map can just make up for this information. The scene energy map information in the neighborhood around the target pedestrian represents the social activity value for the pedestrian's next step and it is coded by multilayer perceptron together with the position information of pedestrians. As a common knowledge, pedestrians' future trajectories are always influenced by people in front. As demonstrated in Fig. 3, future trajectories of target A are influenced by targets B and C who are in A's field of view (FoV). Target D does not interfere A's trajectory decision even when he runs to A. We approximately take pedestrians' moving directions at the last step as their head orientations. And then we can get the function of FoV:

$$f_{FoV}(b_{ij}) = \begin{cases} 1, & if \ cos(b_{ij}) \geq \beta \\ 0, & otherwise \end{cases} \tag{6}$$

where β is set as an empirically threshold -0.2 and b_{ij} represents the angle of agent j from agent i.

When dealing with social pooling, we consider the neighboring environment information of each pedestrian. At the same time, in order to better express the weight of each pedestrian's mutual influence, we have introduced a self-attention mechanism, which can obtain the mutual weight of each hidden state separately, without calculating the position difference of each pedestrian like SGAN. Firstly, we extract the current i^{th} pedestrian's

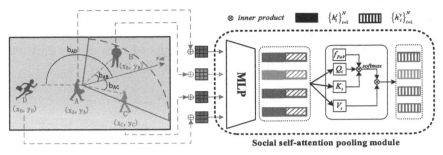

Fig. 3. Overview of the social self-attention pooling module. Target pedestrian's position information and neighborhood map information are jointly encoded, and then the updated embeddings are obtained through the self-attention layer combined with the FOV information.

neighboring environment information a_t^i from the energy map and pedestrian trajectory embedding e_t^i from history:

$$a_t^i = CNN(H_{r \times s}^i(m(x; \Theta)^t); W_a) \tag{7}$$

$$e_t^i = LSTM_{enc}(S_{1:t_{obs}}^i; W_e) \tag{8}$$

$$h_t^i = MLP(a_t^i, e_t^i; W_h) \tag{9}$$

where $H_{r \times s}^i(\cdot)$ represents the $r \times s$ neighboring environment information around the ith pedestrian intercepted from the energy map. Secondly, for each pedestrian's trajectory and neighborhood information embeddings $\{h_t^1, h_t^2, \cdots, h_t^N\}$, we combine the self-attention mechanism and the field of view information to obtain an updated embeddings $\{h_t'^1, h_t'^2, \cdots, h_t'^N\}$.

The structure of the self-attention block is given by Fig. 3. The self-attention block first learns the query matrices Q, key matrix K and the value matrix V given the inputs. And at time t, we have

$$Q_t = f_Q\left(\{h_t^i\}_{i=1}^N\right); \quad K_t = f_K\left(\{h_t^i\}_{i=1}^N\right); \quad V_t = f_V\left(\{h_t^i\}_{i=1}^N\right) \tag{10}$$

where f_Q, f_K and f_V are the corresponding query, key and value functions shared at time $t = t_{obs} + 1, \cdots, t_{obs} + T$.

3.4 Generative Adversarial Networks Module

In this section, we use Generative Adversarial Networks (GAN) module that takes the social and global-scene context vectors for each pedestrian i.

Our generator is a decoder LSTM, $LSTM_{dec}(\cdot)$. We simply concatenate the noise vector z and these context vectors as the input $h_t''^i = (e_t^i, h_t'^i)$. Thus, the generated t^{th} future state's sample for each pedestrian is attained by:

$$\hat{S}_t^i = LSTM_{dec}(V_{Sce}^t, e_t^i, h_t'^i, z; W_{dec}) \tag{11}$$

Where W_{dec} is the training weight of the LSTM decoder.

The discriminator in our case is another LSTM, $LSTM_{dis}(\cdot)$, which its input is a randomly chosen trajectory sample from the either ground truth or predicted future paths for each pedestrian up to t^{th} future time frame, i.e. $T^i_{1:t} \sim p(\hat{S}^i_{1:t}, S^i_{1:t})$

$$\hat{L}^i_t = LSTM_{dis}(T^i_{1:t}; W_{dis}) \tag{12}$$

where $\hat{L}^i_t$ is the predicted label from the discriminator for the chosen trajectory sample to be a ground truth (real) $\hat{S}^i_{1:t}$ or predicted (fake) $S^i_{1:t}$ with the truth label $L^i_t = 1$ and $L^i_t = 0$, respectively. To train SSA-GAN, we use the following losses which consists of two parts: adversarial and variety. The adversarial loss is as follows:

$$\mathcal{L}_{GAN}(\hat{L}^i_t, L^i_t) = \min_G \max_D \mathbb{E}_{T^i_{1:t} \sim p(S^i_{1:t})}[L^i_t log \hat{L}^i_t] + \mathbb{E}_{T^i_{1:t} \sim p(\hat{S}^i_{1:t})}[(1 - L^i_t)log(1 - \hat{L}^i_t)] \tag{13}$$

The variety loss is used to fit the best-predicted trajectory in L2 loss while maintaining multimodal outputs. We follow its definition proposed in SGAN and the variety loss is defined as follows:

$$\mathcal{L}_{variety} = \min_k \left\| S^i - \hat{S}^i(k) \right\|_2 \tag{14}$$

where S^i and $\hat{S}^i(k)$ are ground-truth and the kth predicted trajectories, respectively. k is a hyper-parameter and is set to 20 according to SGAN.

4 Experiments

In this section, we first evaluate our method on the commonly used datasets such as ETH [24] and UCY [25] to prove the universality of our model, and then on a recent and larger dataset, i.e. Central Station dataset [7] to prove the influence of scene factors such as stationary groups and destinations. We also compare its performance against the various baselines on these datasets. Next, we present a qualitative analysis of our model on the effectiveness of the energy map and social self-attention block. Finally, we finish the section by demonstrating some qualitative results on how our GAN based approach provides a good indication of path traversability for pedestrians.

4.1 Evaluation Metrics and Baselines

Similar to SGAN, we use two error metrics: (1).Average Displacement Error (ADE): Average L2 distance between the ground truth trajectory and the predicted trajectory over all predicted time steps. (2). Final Displacement Error (FDE): The Euclidean distance between the true final destination and the predicted final destination at the last step of prediction. We take 8 frames (3.2 s) as a sequence and 12 frames (4.8 s) as the target sequence for prediction to have a fair comparison with all the existing works.

We compare SSA-GAN with a wide range of baselines, including: (1) Linear: A simple temporal linear regressor; (2) V-LSTM: a vanilla temporal LSTM; (3) S-LSTM:

each pedestrian is modeled with an LSTM, and the hidden state is pooled with neighbors at each time-step; (4) CIDNN: a modularized approach for spatio-temporal crowd trajectory prediction with LSTMs; (5) SGAN: a stochastic trajectory predictor with GANs; (6) SoPhie: one of the SOTA stochastic trajectory predictors with LSTMs; (7) SR-LSTM: the SOTA trajectory predictor with motion gate and pair-wise attention to refine the hidden state encoded by LSTM to obtain social interactions.

4.2 Quantitative Evaluations

ETH and UCY: We compare our model to various baselines in Table 1 which are expressed in the form of "ADE/FDE", reporting the average displacement error (ADE) in meter space, as well as the final displacement error (FDE).

Table 1. Comparison results with state-of-the-art methods in the ETH and UCY datasets. We report the "ADE/FDE" for T = 12 in meters. (low is preferred and is labeled with bold fonts).

Dataset Method	ETH	HOTEL	UNIV	ZARA1	ZARA2	AVG
Linear [1] (2016)	1.33/2.94	0.39/0.72	0.82/1.59	0.62/1.21	0.77/1.48	0.79/1.59
S-LSTM [1] (2016)	0.77/1.60	0.38/0.80	0.58/1.28	0.51/1.19	0.39/0.89	0.53/1.15
CIDNN [10] (2018)	1.25/2.32	1.31/1.86	0.51/1.07	0.90/1.28	0.50/1.04	0.89/1.73
SGAN [13] (2018)	0.81/1.52	0.72/1.61	0.60/1.26	0.34/0.69	0.42/0.84	0.58/1.18
SoPhie [15] (2019)	0.70/1.43	0.76/1.67	0.54/1.24	0.30/0.63	0.38/0.78	0.54/1.15
SR-LSTM [11] (2019)	**0.63/1.25**	0.37/0.74	0.51/1.10	0.41/0.90	0.32/0.70	0.45/0.94
SSA-GAN (Ours)	0.66/**1.25**	**0.35/0.69**	**0.40/0.94**	**0.23/0.38**	**0.26/0.53**	**0.38/0.76**

As expected, we see that in general the linear model performs the worst, as it is unable to model the complex social interactions between different humans and the interactions between humans and their scene factors. We also notice that S-LSTM provides an improvement over the linear baseline, due to its use of social pooling, and that SGAN provides an improvement to this LSTM baseline, by approaching the problem from a generative standpoint. SoPhie uses physical attention on image that brings more environmental information, while SR-LSTM pays more attention to the alignment of states. Our final SSA-GAN model, consisting of energy map and self-attention pooling module outperformed the previous models, suggesting that reasonable use of scene information and social information allows for robust model predictions.

Central Station Dataset: We next verify the effectiveness of our method on the Central Station Dataset and compare it to various baselines in Table 2, reporting the ADE and FDE in pixel space.

Much like the previous datasets, with CSD we see that the linear baseline performs the worst, with S-LSTM and SGAN providing an improvement in accuracy. In the ablation experiment, V-GAN is a GAN that does not consider any interaction, the S_1A-GAN

Table 2. Comparison results with state-of-the-art methods in the Central Station Dataset. We report the "ADE/FDE" for T = 12 in meters. (low is preferred and is labeled with bold fonts).

Classic method	CSD	Our method	CSD
Linear	0.91/0.99	V-GAN	0.75/1.56
S-LSTM	0.76/1.60	S_1A-GAN	0.55/1.17
CIDNN	0.70/1.55	S_2A-GAN	0.50/1.06
SGAN	0.61/1.30	SSA-GAN	**0.42/0.81**

(Social-aware GAN) considers the social self-attention pooling layer and the S_2A-GAN (Scene-aware GAN) considers the scene energy graph. It can be seen that the self-attention module of SSA-GAN based on the pedestrian's field of view in the real scene provides a significant improvement in accuracy. The scene energy map further improves the accuracy because it fully considers various factors in the scene and performs joint modeling, such as stationary crowds, obstacles and exits in the scene. In addition, S_2A-GAN performs better than S_1A-GAN potentially suggesting that understanding scene context is slightly more helpful in a prediction task.

4.3 Qualitative Evaluations

In order to make our model more intuitive and effective, we apply our model to the real scenarios of ETH, UCY and CSD respectively to prove the effectiveness of the model through a visual way. Figure 4 shows that in a real scene, the use of different modules will produce different trajectory distributions.

The trajectories generated by SGAN are more blurred and scattered, while S_1A-GAN, which only uses the self-attention pooling layer, has been significantly improved and the goal is clearer. And S_2A-GAN, which only uses the scene energy map, is more sensitive to scenes, more yearning for open scenes, and somewhat repulsive to obstacles (such as corners). Finally, SSA-GAN, which combines social and scene information, has a clearer distribution of pedestrian trajectories, that is, it will not only respond to the state of the surrounding pedestrians, but also consider the scene information.

Figure 5 shows that in the CSD scenario, pedestrians face the situation where there are many stationary groups and exits. In Fig. 5, (a1) and (b1) represent the situation of stationary groups and exits respectively, (a2) and (b2) represent the prediction results of different models respectively. Among them, black represents the observed trajectory, blue represents the label, yellow is the result of SGAN, and green is the result of SSA-GAN. It can be seen intuitively from the figure that the application of our model can better understand these scene factors, and then make better judgments on the direction of pedestrians.

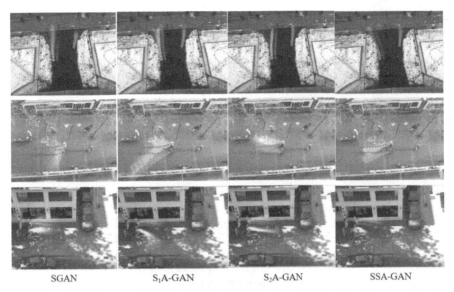

SGAN   S₁A-GAN   S₂A-GAN   SSA-GAN

Fig. 4. Example of the potential distribution of different models in the real scene. The more perfect the model, the more accurately it can guide the direction of pedestrians.

Fig. 5. The stationary groups and exits in the Central Station Dataset have a significant impact on pedestrian trajectories.

5 Conclusion

In this paper, we design a Social-Scene-aware GAN (SSA-GAN) for pedestrian trajectory prediction. Our model models different scene factors in the scene into a scene energy map, which contains more information than a single scene segmentation network. In addition, we propose a FoV-based social self-attention pooling module to process the trajectory interaction between pedestrians, which is closer to the real scene. To summarize, our model can capture rich social and scene information and extensive experiments on publicly available datasets validate the effectiveness of our method for trajectory prediction.

Acknowledgement. This work was supported by the Natural Science Foundation of Shanghai (Grant 19ZR1415800), Shanghai Science and Technology Commission (Grant 21511100700), the Research Project of Shanghai Science and Technology Commission (Grant 20dz2260300), the Fundamental Research Funds for the Central Universities.

References

1. Alahi, A., Goel, K., Ramanathan, V., et al.: Social LSTM: human trajectory prediction in crowded spaces. In: Proceedings of the IEEE Conference on Computer Vision and Pattern Recognition, pp. 961–971 (2016)
2. Radenović, F., Tolias, G., Chum, O.: CNN image retrieval learns from BoW: unsupervised fine-tuning with hard examples. In: Leibe, B., Matas, J., Sebe, N., Welling, M. (eds.) ECCV 2016. LNCS, vol. 9905, pp. 3–20. Springer, Cham (2016). https://doi.org/10.1007/978-3-319-46448-0_1
3. Chandra, R., Bhattacharya, U., Bera, A., et al.: Traphic: trajectory prediction in dense and heterogeneous traffic using weighted interactions. In: Proceedings of the IEEE/CVF Conference on Computer Vision and Pattern Recognition, pp. 8483–8492 (2019)
4. Tang, Y.C., Salakhutdinov, R.: Multiple futures prediction. arXiv preprint arXiv:1911.00997 (2019)
5. Ziebart, B.D., Ratliff, N., Gallagher, G., et al.: Planning-based prediction for pedestrians. In: IEEE/RSJ International Conference on Intelligent Robots and Systems, pp. 3931–3936 (2009)
6. Shao, J., Change, L.C., Wang, X.: Scene-independent group profiling in crowd. In: Proceedings of the IEEE Conference on Computer Vision and Pattern Recognition, pp. 2219–2226 (2014)
7. Yi, S., Li, H., Wang, X.: Understanding pedestrian behaviors from stationary crowd groups. In: Proceedings of the IEEE Conference on Computer Vision and Pattern Recognition, pp. 3488–3496 (2015)
8. Helbing, D., Molnar, P.: Social force model for pedestrian dynamics. Phys. Rev. E **51**(5), 4282 (1995)
9. Mehran, R., Oyama, A., Shah, M.: Abnormal crowd behavior detection using social force model. In: IEEE Conference on Computer Vision and Pattern Recognition, pp. 935–942 (2009)
10. Xu, Y., Piao, Z., Gao, S.: Encoding crowd interaction with deep neural network for pedestrian trajectory prediction. In: Proceedings of the IEEE Conference on Computer Vision and Pattern Recognition, pp. 5275–5284 (2018)
11. Zhang, P., Ouyang, W., Zhang, P., et al.: SR-LSTM: State refinement for LSTM towards pedestrian trajectory prediction. In: Proceedings of the IEEE/CVF Conference on Computer Vision and Pattern Recognition, pp. 12085–12094 (2019)
12. Yi, S., Wang, X., Lu, C., et al.: L0 regularized stationary time estimation for crowd group analysis. In: Proceedings of the IEEE Conference on Computer Vision and Pattern Recognition, pp. 2211–2218 (2014)
13. Gupta, A., Johnson, J., Fei-Fei, L., et al.: Social gan: Socially acceptable trajectories with generative adversarial networks. In: Proceedings of the IEEE Conference on Computer Vision and Pattern Recognition, pp. 2255–2264 (2018)
14. Vaswani, A., Shazeer, N., Parmar, N., et al.: Attention is all you need. arXiv preprint arXiv:1706.03762 (2017)

15. Sadeghian, A., Kosaraju, V., Sadeghian, A., et al.: Sophie: an attentive gan for predicting paths compliant to social and physical constraints. In: Proceedings of the IEEE/CVF Conference on Computer Vision and Pattern Recognition, pp. 1349–1358 (2019)
16. Huang, Y., Bi, H., Li, Z., et al.: STGAT: modeling spatial-temporal interactions for human trajectory prediction. In: Proceedings of the IEEE/CVF International Conference on Computer Vision, pp. 6272–6281 (2019)
17. Goodfellow, I.J., Pouget-Abadie, J., Mirza, M., et al.: Generative Adversarial Nets. MIT Press (2014)
18. Ho, J., Ermon, S.: Generative adversarial imitation learning. arXiv preprint arXiv:1606.03476 (2016)
19. Tao, C., Jiang, Q., Duan, L., et al.: Dynamic and static context-aware LSTM for multi-agent motion prediction. arXiv preprint arXiv:2008.00777 (2020)
20. Zou, H., Su, H., Song, S., et al.: Understanding human behaviors in crowds by imitating the decision-making process. In: Proceedings of the AAAI Conference on Artificial Intelligence, vol. 32(1) (2018)
21. Yang, W., Sheng, B., et al.: Deep color guided coarse-to-fine convolutional network cascade for depth image super-resolution. IEEE Trans. Image Process. Public. IEEE Signal Process. Soc. (2018)
22. Da, K.: A method for stochastic optimization. arXiv preprint arXiv:1412.6980 (2014)
23. Pellegrini, S., Ess, A., Van Gool, L.: Improving data association by joint modeling of pedestrian trajectories and groupings. In: Daniilidis, K., Maragos, P., Paragios, N. (eds.) ECCV 2010. LNCS, vol. 6311, pp. 452–465. Springer, Heidelberg (2010). https://doi.org/10.1007/978-3-642-15549-9_33
24. Lerner, A., Chrysanthou, Y., Lischinski, D.: Crowds by example. In: Computer Graphics Forum. Blackwell Publishing Ltd, Oxford, UK, vol. 26(3), pp. 655–664 (2007)
25. He, K., Zhang, X., Ren, S., et al.: Deep residual learning for image recognition. In: Proceedings of the IEEE conference on computer vision and pattern recognition, pp. 770–778 (2016)
26. Chen, Z., Hu, Z., Sheng, B., et al.: Simplified non-locally dense network for single-image dehazing. Visual Comput. 36(9), 2189–2200 (2020)
27. Zhang, B., Sheng, B., Li, P., et al.: Depth of field rendering using multilayer-neighborhood optimization. In: IEEE Transactions on Visualization and Computer Graphics, p. 1 (2019)

Image Processing

Cecid Fly Defect Detection in Mangoes Using Object Detection Frameworks

Maria Jeseca C. Baculo$^{1,2(\boxtimes)}$ iD, Conrado Ruiz Jr$^{2(\boxtimes)}$ iD, and Oya Aran$^{2(\boxtimes)}$ iD

^{1} Don Mariano Marcos Memorial State University, 2504 Agoo, La Union, Philippines
mjbaculo@dmmmsu.edu.ph
^{2} De La Salle University, Manila, Philippines
cons.ruizjr@delasalle.ph, aran.oya@dlsu.edu.ph

Abstract. Mango export has experienced rapid growth in global trade over the past few years, however, they are susceptible to surface defects that can affect their market value. This paper investigates the automated detection of a mango defect caused by cecid flies, which can affect a significant portion of the production yield. Object detection frameworks using CNN were used to localize and detect multiple defects present in a single mango image. This paper also proposes modified versions of R-CNN and FR-CNN replacing its region search algorithms with segmentation-based region extraction. A dataset consisting of 1329 cecid fly surface blemishes was used to train the object detection models. The results of the experiments show comparable performance between the modified and existing state-of-the-art object detection frameworks. Results show that Faster R-CNN achieved the highest average precision of 0.901 at aP_{50} while the Modified FR-CNN has the highest average precision of 0.723 at aP_{75}.

Keywords: Defect detection · Image processing · Region-based CNN · Convolutional neural networks

1 Introduction

The Carabao mango is a highly exported variety of mangoes known for its aroma and exotic taste. Recently, however, its production has experienced a decline in yield due to the heavy infestation of cecid flies. The cecid fly defect produces a circular blemish on the mango surface that affects its quality, quantity, and market value. The first major infestation was recorded in 2013, which affected up to 90% of mango production [10]. At present, many plantations succumb to these attacks as there are no insecticides are yet proven to eliminate the cecid flies. Therefore, experts can only advise farmers to practice appropriate field sanitation, bagging, pruning, and many other pest management practices to control the infestation. These practices are being done on large mango plantations. Meanwhile, for small-scale local farmers, fogging and chemical spraying is a customary practice. An automated defect detection system may help farmers, small and large-scale alike, identify damages, and apply the appropriate and timely prevention technique to increase their yield.

© Springer Nature Switzerland AG 2021
N. Magnenat-Thalmann et al. (Eds.): CGI 2021, LNCS 13002, pp. 205–216, 2021.
https://doi.org/10.1007/978-3-030-89029-2_16

At present, small and large-scale farms still employ manual approaches to monitor, harvest, and classify Carabao mangoes. During pre-harvest, farmers outsource workers to perform chemical sprays and would practice fruit bagging before maturation to prevent a major infestation. Since the fruits are bagged, the detection of defects for fruits are being done after harvest, where certified mango sorters are hired to classify the mangoes according to marketability and identify the defects that affect the selling price of the produce. Mango sorters unwrap and classify the mangoes individually. The fruit evaluation alone takes about 7–10 s on average and still depends on the proficiency of the mango sorters. It is also important to note that some defects have similar appearances. For instance, a non-expert may have difficulty distinguishing cecid fly defects with some cases of scab and anthracnose diseases that may be misclassified as stem-end rot defects.

Deep Neural Networks has revolutionized the analysis of visual imagery and is used in several leaf disease detection models [13,17]. In contrast to other thriving research on plant diseases, there are only a few related works that focus on CNN-based approaches for fruit defect detection. In [5], KNN, SVM, MLP, and CNN were used to classify healthy and defective Carabao mangoes. The authors aim to identify which learning algorithms will generalize accurate classification given the dataset. Results show that CNN was able to outperform the other machine learning algorithms used. However, the model developed does not localize or classify the specific defect that damages the mangoes.

This paper proposes a CNN-based framework to detect the occurrence of cecid fly defects in mango images. Currently, no other study has considered cecid fly defects, specifically where the images in the dataset can contain mangoes with multiple blemishes. While some of these blemishes are due to cecid fly defects, others are caused by other factors. As an approach to this problem, the authors experimented on using object detector frameworks to localize and classify mangoes with multiple blemishes. Modified versions of Region-based CNNs and Fast region-based CNNs were proposed, in which the region search algorithm was replaced with blemish segmentation. A comparison of the performance of several CNN-based object detection models on our mango dataset to detect cecid fly defects was also presented along the discussion of results.

The related works are presented in the next section. Section 3 presents the data gathering procedures and proposed methodology to detect cecid fly damage in mangoes. Section 4 includes the discussion of the results of the detection framework. Lastly, Sect. 5 presents the conclusions derived from the results as well as future activities relevant to this study.

2   Towards Automatic Defect Detection in Agricultural Produce

Most of the recent works in plant and fruit disease detection have implemented object classification frameworks [1,9,19]. [6] was the sole study that investigated the use of region-based object detection frameworks to localize and identify the types of defects found in leaves. The authors compared the performance of three detectors, which consisted of the Faster Region-based Convolutional Neural Network (Faster R-CNN), Region-based Fully Convolutional Network (R-FCN), and Single Shot Multibox Detector (SSD) trained with VGG net and ResNet. Their dataset is composed of 5000 leaf images with 43,398 annotated samples after augmentation. It is also noted that the number of instances per class is different. The class with the lowest bounding boxes was of the Powdery Mildew which accounts for 338 while the labels for leaf molds peaked with 11,922 boxes. Their results manifest that plain networks perform better than deeper networks, such as the case of Faster R-CNN with VGG-16 with a mean AP of 83%, compared to the same meta-architecture with ResNet-50. They also discussed the role of data augmentation, which boosted the mAP from 55% to 83%.

While region-based CNNs have been proven to perform well in leaves, they have not been used in the field of fruit defect detection. [15] presented a multi-class classification model for identifying strawberry defects using CNN. They combined images of infected fruits and leaves acquired from specialized chambers that cultivated the fungus that caused the defects. The structure of the network was made of 5 convolution layers, 5 pooling layers, and 2 fully connected layers. They used a rectified nonlinear activation function (ReLU) after every convolution. Their model was able to achieve up to 92% accuracy in training 1788 healthy, and 2316 powdery mildew infections, and 3277 gray mold rot infected strawberry images. Similar to the input images in plant disease detection, the input images used in this study include one defect per instance.

Several studies have also focused on the integration of technology with the operations of mango farming. Various machine learning algorithms were utilized in mango fruit grading, yield approximation, and defect detection. A recent paper utilized five machine learning algorithms which include the K-Nearest Neighbor (KNN), Support Vector Machine (SVM), Multilayer Perceptron (MLP), and Convolutional Neural Network (CNN) to train a binary mango classifier using a dataset with 1296 instances. They also proposed a mango segmentation technique using k-means clustering combined with color channel segmentation and range filtering techniques. Their paper discussed the comparison of the performance of classifiers trained using segmented and not segmented mango images. The CNN-based classifier was able to outperform the other machine learning classifiers in both segmented and non-segmented images. The use of CNN with its segmentation technique was able to increase the performance of the classifier by 8.33%. It is also important to note that in previous works, the Support Vector Machine algorithm has been one of the prominent approaches in mango grading and defect classification [4,11,12,14] and only a few CNN-based architectures.

Mango classification and defect detection make use of parameters that can be extracted from a fruit's image which focuses on its size, shape, color, and surface blemishes. To represent these parameters, previous studies utilized different feature extraction methods [2,16,20]. A comparative study of feature extraction methods in defect classification was conducted by [3]. Their experiments used 1766 mango images acquired under natural light with a white background in a specialized image acquisition set-up. Their approach involved image cropping, rescaling, background extraction using morphological operators, and feature extraction. The features extracted from the mango images were the intensity features, local binary patterns (LBP), Discrete Fourier Transforms (DFT), and Discrete Cosine Transform (DCT), Hu with intensity, and Gabor filters. These features were used as attributes to train the Neural Network (NN) classifier which used three different activation functions (i.e., linear, logistic, and softmax). The highest accuracy rate was equivalent to 90.26% in both logistic and softmax activation function.

In [21], two mango pathogens were detected using the enhanced Wavelet-PCA based statistical feature extraction and Modified Rotation Kernel Transformation (MRKT). In their paper, 500 instances of powdery mildew-infected flowers and anthracnose-infected leaves and fruits were acquired. The surface blemishes in various mango parts are segmented using Adaptive K-Means Clustering and edge detection. The MRKT directional feature vector and 20 statistical measures were computed and combined to make up the 32 nodes of the input layer of the trained Artificial Neural Network. The ANN was composed of four hidden layers with four nodes each. Their experiments generated a training accuracy of 98.50% for flowers, 98.75% for fruits, and 98.70% for leaves.

It can be seen from these studies that each of the instances used to train the classifiers to contain one, exclusive defect without localization. Our study aims to localize and identify a specific surface blemish, where multiple blemishes exist, and associate each of these blemishes with a distinct class via the use of object detection frameworks.

3   Methodology

3.1   Image Acquisition

Our dataset is composed of 1329 instances of surface blemishes extracted from 318 Carabao mango images. The defects were annotated by the expert mango sorters during the harvest season in May 2018. The images were acquired in NEF format with a 6000 × 4000 image size using a Nikon d3400 DSLR camera. A whiteboard was used as the background and the images were taken in both natural and artificial lighting and each image has exactly one mango object. Figure 1 shows sample images that were included in the dataset.

3.2   Data Preparation

Given the variation caused by the non-uniform sources of light, the images were preprocessed to perform color correction and enhance the features of the input images. Automatic white balance, gamma correction and image sharpening were applied to these images. The blemishes were annotated with the assistance of an expert who identified the defects based on human recognition after harvest. Their annotations were transformed digitally using the Matlab Image Labeler

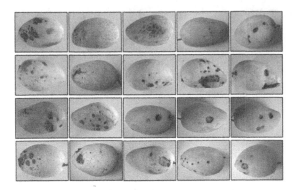

Fig. 1. Sample images in the mango dataset.

application. The resulting dataset includes the RGB images of defective mangoes along with the bounding box ground truth and label. 1329 cecid fly defect instances were extracted from 318 mango images. A percentage split was used to divide the dataset to train and test set. 10% (31 images) of the dataset containing 199 blemishes were used for testing. The test images were re-scaled to 1500 × 2000 to use computational resources efficiently during test time. The models' smallest image dimension parameter was tuned to cater to these smaller images.

3.3   Object Detection Frameworks

Five object detection frameworks were compared to identify the defects found in the Carabao mangoes. Three of these frameworks are state-of-the-art methods: Region-based CNNs [8], Fast Region-based CNNs [7], and Faster region-based CNNs [18]. In addition to these frameworks, two other frameworks are proposed: modified versions of Region-based and Fast Region-based CNNs. The modified versions use a different region proposal extraction, which includes a selective search algorithm with the proposed segmentation technique. These frameworks employ the two-way detection technique which involves separate methods for region proposal extraction and classification.

The specifications of the convolutional layers used to extract the feature vectors for the different frameworks are given in Table 1. In the experiments, the frameworks presented were trained using three different depths of CNN which includes 3-layered, 5-layered convolutional layers and a pre-trained VGG-16. The 3 and 5-layered architectures were trained from scratch while the predefined weights in VGG-16 was used. These network structures were selected to test whether the models trained were able to generalize the correct labels and bounding box predictions. The base learning rate used was 0.002 and the maximum number of epochs was set to 100. Also, the training was performed without augmentation. The device used for training utilizes a GeForce GTX 1050 graphics card with 8 GB RAM. The models were trained using the Matlab Deep Learning, Image Processing, and Parallel Processing Toolboxes.

Table 1. 3 and 5 layered CNN specifications

ConvNet layers		Size	Filters	Stride
Input image		128 × 128		
1	Convolution	11 × 11	32	1
	Max pool	2 × 2		2
2	Convolution	5 × 5	32	1
	Max pool	2 × 2		2
3*	Convolution	3 × 3	64	1
	Max pool	2 × 2		2
4	Convolution	3 × 3	64	1
	Max pool	2 × 2		2
5*	Convolution	3 × 3	64	1
	Max pool	2 × 2		2
Fully connected layer				
Softmax activation function				

Region-Based Convolutional Neural Networks (R-CNN)
R-CNNs implement object proposal algorithms to detect multiple objects within a single image [8]. The RCNN uses the selective search algorithm to extract the bounding boxes. Once the proposals are created, the R-CNN transforms the region into the standard size of the input layer. The final layer of the architecture also adds an SVM classifier to generate the predicted labels.

Modified Region-Based Convolutional Neural Networks (MR-CNN)
A modified version of R-CNN is proposed, the proposed approach replaces the selective search algorithm with a segmentation technique to extract the region proposals. In addition, a Softmax classifier at the final layer was used instead of the SVM classifier and the bounding box regressor in the original RCNN.

The proposed region proposal extraction uses adaptive binarization and thresholding for H and V channels to extract the binary masks. The RGB image was initially converted to grayscale then adaptive binarization was used to compute a threshold for each pixel using a local mean intensity around the neighborhood of the pixel. The main idea of this technique is to set every pixel to black if the brightness is 50% lower than the average brightness of the neighboring pixel in the window. In addition to the application of adaptive binarization, a threshold for the H and V channel was applied to ensure that blemishes with lighter shades were included in the binary mask.

The resulting masks were aggregated and cleaned using morphological operators. The aggregated mask may contain multiple blemishes of varying sizes. The size of these blemishes needs to be large enough to find relevant patterns so all blemishes whose size is less than 128 × 128 were removed. Each of the blemishes are isolated by computing the crop parameters used in [4]. These parameters are also used as the values needed for the bounding box of these blemishes. The RGB image of the blemishes and the bounding box values will serve as the region proposals to be classified by CNN with a softmax classifier. Combined instances of soft and hard negatives served as the negative regions for this framework. The soft negatives were manually annotated while the hard negatives were extracted from either misclassified blemishes or those with IoU lower than 0.3. Figure 2 shows the proposed modified R-CNN framework.

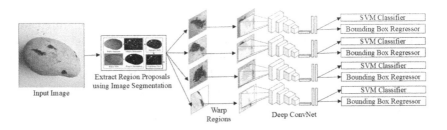

Fig. 2. Modified region-based convolutional neural network (MR-CNN)

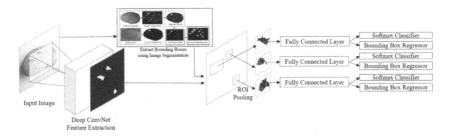

Fig. 3. Modified fast region-based convolutional neural network (MFR-CNN)

Fast R-CNN has been proposed as a way to reduce the computational expense of R-CNN across the 2,000 regions [7]. Instead of using three different models, the Fast RCNN makes use of a single ConvNet model which returns the regions of interests accordingly. The Region of Interest (RoI) pooling is also added to reshape the regions to the standard input size. These regions are passed to the fully connected layer for classification and prediction of the bounding boxes.

Modified Fast Region-Based Convolutional Neural Networks (MFR-CNN)
The region searching algorithm used in Fast R-CNNs with the selective search algorithm was replaced with segmentation technique. This is similar to the modification performed for R-CNNs presented in Sect. 3.3.

The default implementation of Fast R-CNN in Matlab made use of the Edge Boxes algorithm for extracting the region proposals, which generates 1000 region proposals to be classified. Similar to the Modified R-CNN, the Edge Boxes region proposal extraction for Fast R-CNN is replaced with our custom segmentation technique, which proposes all the blemishes found in the mango object as the regions. The flowchart of the Modified Fast R-CNN can be found in Fig. 3.

Faster Region-Based Convolutional Neural Networks (Faster R-CNN)
The Faster R-CNN introduced the Region Proposal Network (RPN) which replaced the slow performance of the selective search object proposal algorithm [18]. The intuition of Faster R-CNN was that the object proposals can be derived from the features of the image which are already available during the forward pass of the CNN.

The RPN uses the sliding window over the feature maps generated by the CNN. In each of these windows, anchor boxes of varying shapes and sizes are generated. The RPN is also responsible for predicting the probability of the presence of an object in an anchor box. To better fit the anchor boxes to the objects, an anchor box regressor is also implemented. The boxes are then passed to the RoI pooling layer to be reshaped. Aside from these, there are a plethora of object detection models which can be used to recognize multiple objects from a single image. To achieve a high recognition rate, these models need to be provided with an ample amount of labels and bounding boxes as ground truth.

4   Experimental Results

The average precision of the models was computed to compare the performance of the object detectors. The average Precision, (aP), is the average of the ratio of true positive instances to all positive instances of objects in the detector, based on the ground truth. In classification, *precision* can be computed by dividing the number of correctly predicted labels to the total number of 'positive' labels generated by the model. The 'positive' labels pertain to all predictions made by the model belonging to cecid fly defect including the false positive predictions. In region-based CNNs, correct predictions need to satisfy an overlap threshold between the predicted bounding boxes and the ground truth bounding boxes. The threshold pertains to the Intersection over Union (IoU) values of these boxes. The IoU of the boxes is defined as:

$$IoU = \frac{Area of Overlap}{Area of Intersection}$$

For the following experiments, two different IoU thresholds were used:.50 and .75. The .50 threshold was set since this is considered the standard threshold for object detection. A higher IoU threshold of .75 is set to better evaluate the accuracy of the predicted bounding box localization. aP_{50} pertains to the average precision of cecid fly defects given a .50 IoU threshold while aP_{75} pertains to the average precision of defects with .75 threshold.

Table 2. Performance of Cecid fly detection models

Architecture		aP_{50}	aP_{75}	Average detection time
R-CNN	3 ConvLayers	0.185	0.055	5.06 s
	5 ConvLayers	0.351	0.162	8.12 s
	VGG-16	0.424	0.200	12.38 s
MR-CNN	3 ConvLayers	0.543	0.305	5.18 s
	5 ConvLayers	0.648	0.502	7.04 s
	VGG-16	0.692	0.489	10.17 s
Fast R-CNN	3 ConvLayers	0.529	0.287	3.21 s
	5 ConvLayers	0.615	0.365	4.53 s
	VGG-16	0.703	0.471	8.26 s
MFR-CNN	3 ConvLayers	0.538	0.321	3.05 s
	5 ConvLayers	0.663	0.514	3.56 s
	VGG-16	0.872	**0.723**	7.04 s
Faster	3 ConvLayers	0.471	0.307	1.6 s
R-CNN	5 ConvLayers	0.701	0.433	2.01 s
	VGG-16	**0.901**	0.599	5.57 s

The results presented in Table 2 show that the proposed models, MR-CNN and MFR-CNN achieve higher aP values for both thresholds than their counterparts, R-CNN and FR-CNN, respectively. The proposed models also have lower average detection times. Among all five models, Faster R-CNN achieved the highest average precision of 0.901 at aP_{50} while the Modified FR-CNN has the highest average precision of 0.723 at aP_{75}. Although the aP of the MR-CNN, FR-CNN, and MFR-CNN is comparable to the performance of Faster R-CNN, the latter was able to perform the detection faster. This result is intuitive since region searching in the latter is being done in the features of the image which are already available during the forward pass of the CNN. However, MFR-CNN outperformed all the other frameworks when the IoU is set to a higher threshold. This is also evident in the confusion matrices presented in Fig. 4.

It can also be observed that the two models have the highest aPs given the two IoU thresholds. The IoU computes how accurate the predicted bounding boxes are localized in correspondence to the ground truth boxes. A predicted bounding box that strongly overlaps the ground truth indicates a high IoU. In this study, two IoU thresholds were set for correctly detected defects to assess which of these models were able to localize the blemishes better. The results show that in comparison with the other frameworks, the models trained with MFR-CNN has the least decrease in performance as the IoU threshold got higher. This implies that the MFR-CNN has better localization than Faster R-CNN and also indicates that the region search via segmentation was able to boost the

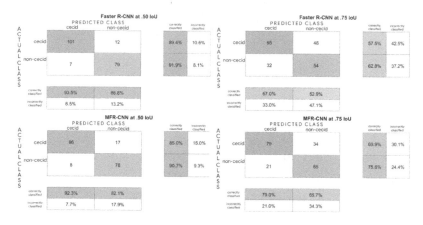

Fig. 4. Confusion matrices of MFR-CNN and faster R-CNN at different IoU thresholds

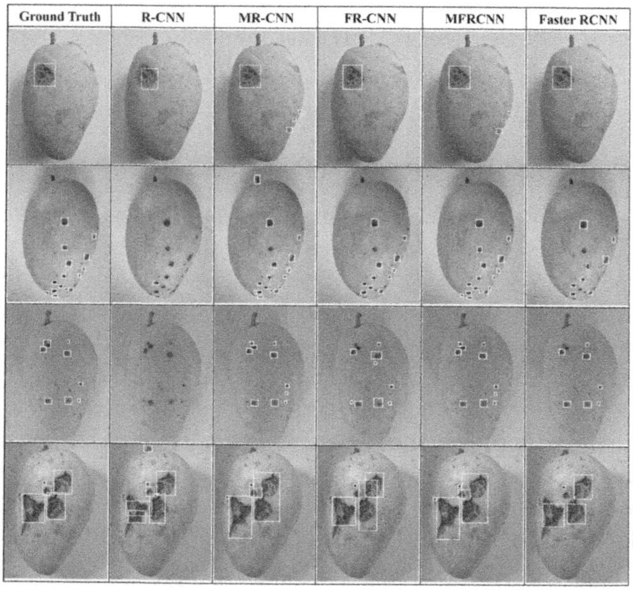

Fig. 5. Result of object detection frameworks on sample test images

performance as it was specially designed to cater to the color properties of these blemishes.

Figure 5 shows sample detections generated by the defect detection models trained with 1130 region proposals belonging to cecid fly defects. Results on the test images show that it was able to generalize well with mango images with scattered, disconnected blemishes with a single label. On the other hand, the model had difficulty in detecting defects that are occluded with shadows due to non-uniformity in lighting, multiple defects that are close in proximity with varying sizes and connected blemishes that may belong to different classes.

5   Conclusion and Future Works

The result of the experiments in this paper demonstrates the potential of object detection frameworks to localize and classify fine-grained blemishes present in mango fruits. The performance of the models was further improved by replacing the predefined region search algorithms of well-known frameworks with a segmentation-based region searching. For the lower IoU threshold, Faster R-CNN was able to outperform the rest of the models in terms of speed and precision. On the other hand, the proposed MFR-CNN outperformed the other models in accuracy when a higher IoU threshold is used. MFR-CNN was able to locate and classify smaller blemishes that the rest of the models were not able to detect. The difficulty in detection may be attributed to different illumination conditions, size variations, and blemish proximity and connectivity.

In future works, the authors aim to collect and annotate more images belonging to multiple defect classes and train a multi-class defect detection model. Further tuning of the FR-CNN and Faster R-CNN may also be performed and the improvement on feature extraction using deeper CNN architectures may also be investigated.

The development of a real-time and accurate defect detection model may be used as part of an automated framework to aid the manual classification performed by farmers. In this automated system, a video of conveyed mangoes can be acquired in a shooting chamber equipped with a camera and rollers to automatically rotate the objects. The video input will be sent to a computer where image processing and defect detection will be implemented. Image processing can be used to extract specific frames from the video and resulting images can be subjected to pre-processing. Eventually, the defect detection models may be used to identify specific mango defects for crop surveillance and defect management.

References

1. Amara, J., Bouaziz, B., Algergawy, A., et al.: A deep learning-based approach for banana leaf diseases classification. In: BTW (Workshops), pp. 79–88 (2017)
2. Anurekha, D., Sankaran, R.A.: Efficient classification and grading of MANGOES with GANFIS for improved performance. Multimedia Tools Appl. **79**(5), 4169–4184 (2019). https://doi.org/10.1007/s11042-019-07784-x
3. Ashok, V., Vinod, D.: A comparative study of feature extraction methods in defect classification of mangoes using neural network. In: 2016 Second International Conference on Cognitive Computing and Information Processing (CCIP), pp. 1–6. IEEE (2016)
4. Baculo, M.J.C., Marcos, N.: Automatic mango detection using image processing and HOG-SVM. In: Proceedings of the 2018 VII International Conference on Network, Communication and Computing, pp. 211–215. ACM (2018)

5. Baculo, M.J.C., Ruiz, C.: Image-based classification and segmentation of healthy and defective mangoes. In: Eleventh International Conference on Machine Vision (ICMV 2018), vol. 11041, p. 1104117. International Society for Optics and Photonics (2019)

6. Fuentes, A., Yoon, S., Kim, S., Park, D.: A robust deep-learning-based detector for real-time tomato plant diseases and pests recognition. Sensors **17**(9), 2022 (2017)

7. Girshick, R.: Fast R-CNN. In: Proceedings of the IEEE International Conference on Computer Vision, pp. 1440–1448 (2015)

8. Girshick, R.B., Donahue, J., Darrell, T., Malik, J.: Rich feature hierarchies for accurate object detection and semantic segmentation. CoRR abs/1311.2524 (2013). http://arxiv.org/abs/1311.2524

9. Hanson, A., Joel, M., Joy, A., Francis, J.: Plant leaf disease detection using deep learning and convolutional neural network. Int. J. Eng. Sci. **5324** (2017)

10. Inquirer, P.D.: Harvest drop expected as mango growers battle cecid flies (2018). https://newsinfo.inquirer.net/970431/harvest-drop-expected-as-mango-growers-battle-cecid-flies

11. Khan, M.S., Uandai, S.B., Srinivasan, H.: Anthracnose disease diagnosis by image processing, support vector machine and correlation with pigments. J. Plant Pathol. **101**(3), 749–751 (2019). https://doi.org/10.1007/s42161-019-00268-9

12. Khoje, S., Bodhe, S.: Comparative performance evaluation of size metrics and classifiers in computer vision based automatic mango grading. Int. J. Comput. Appl. **61**(9) (2013)

13. Mohanty, S.P., Hughes, D.P., Salathé, M.: Using deep learning for image-based plant disease detection. Front. Plant Sci. **7**, 1419 (2016)

14. Naik, S.: Non-destructive mango (mangifera indica l., cv. kesar) grading using convolutional neural network and support vector machine. Available at SSRN 3354473 (2019)

15. Park, H., JeeSook, E., Kim, S.H.: Crops disease diagnosing using image-based deep learning mechanism. In: 2018 International Conference on Computing and Network Communications (CoCoNet), pp. 23–26. IEEE (2018)

16. Patel, K.K., Kar, A., Khan, M.A.: Common external defect detection of mangoes using color computer vision. J. Instit. Eng. (India): Series A **100**(4), 559–568 (2019). https://doi.org/10.1007/s40030-019-00396-6

17. Ramcharan, A., Baranowski, K., McCloskey, P., Ahmed, B., Legg, J., Hughes, D.P.: Deep learning for image-based cassava disease detection. Front. Plant Sci. **8**, 1852 (2017)

18. Ren, S., He, K., Girshick, R., Sun, J.: Faster R-CNN: towards real-time object detection with region proposal networks. In: Advances in Neural Information Processing Systems, pp. 91–99 (2015)

19. Sladojevic, S., Arsenovic, M., Anderla, A., Culibrk, D., Stefanovic, D.: Deep neural networks based recognition of plant diseases by leaf image classification. Comput. Intell. Neurosci. **2016** (2016)

20. Thong, N.D., Thinh, N.T., Cong, H.T.: Mango classification system uses image processing technology and artificial intelligence. In: 2019 International Conference on System Science and Engineering (ICSSE), pp. 45–52. IEEE (2019)

21. Ullagaddi, S., Raju, S.V.: An enhanced feature extraction technique for diagnosis of pathological problems in mango crop. Int. J. Image, Graph. Sign. Process. **9**(9), 28 (2017)

Twin-Channel Gan: Repair Shape with Twin-Channel Generative Adversarial Network and Structural Constraints

Zhenjiang Du[1], Ning Xie[1(✉)], Zhitao Liu[1], Xiaohua Zhang[2], and Yang Yang[1]

[1] University of Electronic Science and Technology of China, Chengdu, China
[2] Hiroshima Institute of Technology, Hiroshima, Japan
zhxh@cc.it-hiroshima.ac.jp

Abstract. The establishment of 3D content with deep learning has been a focus of research in computer graphics during past years. Recently, researchers analyze 3D shapes through the dividing-and-conquer strategy with the geometry information and the structure information. Although many works perform well, there are still several problems. For example, the geometry information missing and not plausible in structure. In this work, we propose the Twin-channel GAN for the 3D shape completion. In this framework, the structure information is well studied via the structural constraints for optimizing the details of 3D shapes. The experimental results also demonstrated that our method achieves better performance.

Keywords: Geometric analysis · Deep learning · Twin-channel GAN · Shape repair · Structural constraint

1 Introduction

Deep learning such as CNN is approved as the powerful tool to learn the geometric representation for 3D modeling in recent years [1,2]. However, it is hard to ensure the rationality of the component-based structure of the 3D shape. Nowadays, structure-aware modeling is well studied, because it is proved that provides a higher-level understanding of the shape [3–5] by considering geometry information and structure information together. The shape produced by these methods has better quality in geometric and structural details. However, the generated results of these methods will still have some defeats such as geometry information missing and not plausible in structure. So, We propose a method which based on geometry information and structure information to repair the structure-aware method's results to improve the visual quality.

For the geometry aspect, the previous methods may encounter information missing to affect the quality of the generated. Nowadays, there are a lot of works to infer the missing regions. It is commonly used to recover the missing regions via the geometric smoothing such as Poisson Surface reconstruction [6] and Laplacian hole filling [7]. However, this geometric operator can only maintain the high level information but not deal well with details. To solve this,

© Springer Nature Switzerland AG 2021
N. Magnenat-Thalmann et al. (Eds.): CGI 2021, LNCS 13002, pp. 217–228, 2021.
https://doi.org/10.1007/978-3-030-89029-2_17

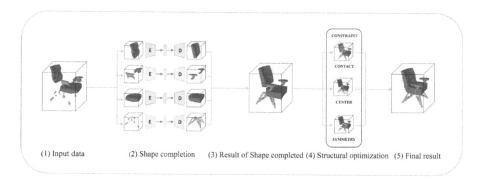

(1) Input data   (2) Shape completion   (3) Result of Shape completed (4) Structural optimization (5) Final result

Fig. 1. The pipeline of our method. (1) **Input data**. The input data is the generation of structure-aware network, which may have some defects. (2) **Shape completion**. We send the data into completed network to complete the geometry information. (3) **Result of shape completed**. The results of shape completed may have some problems in structure. And we hope that the final generated result is more physically reasonable.(4) **Structure optimization**. We set some constraints and use quadratic programming to solve these structural problems. (5) **Final result**. In the end, we will get a repaired 3D shape.

data-driven method is proposed by deep learning such as using 3D-Encoder-Predictor [8], which infer the missing information in the corrupted dataset. However, the other training dataset is necessary with the complete shape information. Following the spirit of introVAE [9], we propose a method called Twin-channel GAN that do not need corrupted dataset to infer the missing information. We combine GANs [10] and VAEs [11], and use VAEs as the generator of GANs. We replace the discriminator with the encoder of VAEs, which reduces the network's structure to improve the stability during training. Besides, to enhance the feature representation, we construct GANs with encoder and decoder of VAEs. We call the whole network Twin-channel GAN. After training, the encoder encodes the incomplete data into the latent space, and the decoder can infer the missing information based on the existing information and distribution.

On the other hand, the results of structure-aware networks may meet structural problems and we show the main structural problems in Fig. 1. The picture of input data show the problems. We consider the reason for these problems is that parts do not satisfy some relationships. We summarize three main relationships based on these problems, including: 1) Supporting Relationship. 2) Center point Relationship. 3) Symmetry Relationship. For supporting relationship, such as the chair's seat support the chair's back, we hope that the back will be slightly inserted into the seat. For center point relationship, we consider that the center points of the main parts of shapes are in a straight line. For symmetry relationship, such as the armrest of chair, they might be asymmetric. The generated results meet this condition in usual but sometimes not. Inspired by [12] and [3], we hope to add some constraints based on the relationship and use quadratic programming to optimize the structure information.

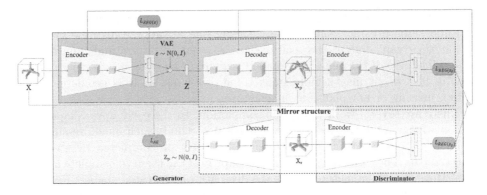

Fig. 2. This is the detail of our network. Our network only uses encoder and decoder. We combine encoder and decoder to form a generator and then replace discriminator with encoder. To enhance the features, we made a mirror enhancement, sampling z_p from Gaussian distribution as input, then go through the decoder and encoder to get an output. The result of the judgment will eventually affect the changes of the parameters of the entire network.

Figure 1 also shows the pipeline of our method. Inputting a data which have some problems in geometry and structure, and after the method we propose to optimize, we can get a visually better result. For details, please refer to the Sect. 3. And our contribution can be summarized as follows:

- Our work proposes a method to repair shape from geometry information and structure information based on structure-aware network.
- We propose Twin-channel GAN for the completion of geometry information.
- We set some new constraints and use quadratic programming to optimize the structure information to make results plausible in structure.

2   Related Work

Deep learning has been a research hot field in decades, and there are a lot of great works for generating such as generative adversarial network(GANs) [10] and variational autoencoder(VAEs) [11]. Because of the large datasets for 3D CAD models have been published [1]. 3D convolutional networks have been proposed for 3D deep learning. Wu et al. [2] proposed the use of 3D-CNNs generative tasks in the 3D field. They use a volumetric representation in their network. But this method will be limited by the resolution. Based on this work, Wang et al. [13] have proposed the octree method for improving the results of 3D deep learning for 3D shape. And structure information is also considered. Wang et al. [14] provides ways to reconstruct shapes by recovering 3D shape structures as cuboids from partially reconstructed objects. Averkiou et al. [12] propose a method to analyze the structural relationship of different parts to build 3D

shapes. Recently, a lot of works have considered analyzing geometry information and structure information jointly [3–5]. The advantage of these methods
is that they can analyze the relationship between the parts and improve the
fine-grainedness of the generated shape by dividing the shape into parts. As we
described above, it may usually suffer some problems, such as geometry information missing or not plausible in structure.

There are several works for shape completion. In the early days, shape completion was generally solved by mathematical methods such as addressing this
problem as a continuous energy minimization [15] or completed by structure
detected [16]. They detect symmetries of shape and use them to complete missing
data. However, these methods limit the diversity of generated shapes. Recently,
deep learning methods have been proposed. Sharma et al. [17] introduced a
method which can estimate voxel occupancy grids from noisy data by a fully
convolutional autoencoder. It is almost the first work for shape completion in
3D deep learning. Dai et al. [8] proposed a method called 3D-ED-GAN for 3D
shape completion, and it add LSTM(Long Short-Term Memory) to improve the
resolution of shape. Son et al. [18] introduced a method to synthesize the 3D
scenes and proposed an algorithm for 3D scene completion. These works are usually based on voxel grids and there are also some methods' data representation
is point cloud such as [19,20], and the characteristics of point cloud can reduce
computational overhead. Neither point clouds nor voxel, they just complete the
geometry information of the shape from the geometric features, but our method
combines the current structure-aware to complete the geometry information and
optimize structure information.

3   Method

3.1   Geometry Information Completion

As we described above, GANs has the ability to infer missing information. So we
choose to use the structure of GANs for the completion of geometry information.
It is usually difficult to train for GANs. To solve this, we follow the structure of
introVAE [9], a network that has a great performance in image generation. We
also combine GANs and VAEs to improve the stability. After that, we apply this
network for 3D shape completed and we call this network Twin-channel GAN.
The entire network training does not require corrupted data, and it also has the
ability of shape completion. The overall network structure is shown in Fig. 2.
The loss of the network is as follows:

$$\ell_E = \ell_{KL}(z) + \alpha \sum_{s=r,p} [m - \ell_{KL}(z_h)]^+ + \beta \sum_{s=r,p} \ell_{AE}(x, x_s), \qquad (1)$$

$$\ell_G = \alpha \sum_{s=r,p} \ell_{KL}(Enc(x_s)) + \beta \sum_{s=r,p} \ell_{AE}(x, x_s). \qquad (2)$$

For Eq. 1, $\ell_{KL}(z)$ is a Kullback-Leibler(KL) divergence of the encoder's result
of the input data. $[\cdot]^+ = max(0, \cdot)$ and m is a positive margin. ℓ_{AE} is the reconstruction loss of the input data and the generated data. For Eq. 2, $Enc()$ is the

result of the encoder. α and β are the hyper-parameters to control the balance of the network. The encoder consists of five volumetric fully convolutional layers with a kernel size of $4 \times 4 \times 4$ and a stride of 2. Batch normalization and ReLU layers are inserted between convolutional layers. The decoder reverses the encoder, except that a tanh nonlinearity is used in the last layer.

We leverage the network to learn the data distribution. After training, we combine encoder and decoder to get a VAEs. And this network has the ability to complement. Because of the fitting ability of this network, we can input an incomplete data into this network to get a complete data.

3.2 Structure Information Optimization

As we described in previous sections, generating shapes with structure information will cause some structural problems. In Sect. 1, we define three kinds of relationships in structure. In order to make the generated shapes satisfy these relationships, we set three constraints, including contact constraint, center point constraint, and symmetry constraint, and we use quadratic programming to calculate the results. After optimization, these shapes can satisfy the above relationships to reduce problems in structure. Specifically, we define c_i and p_i to respectively represent the ith part's center position and it's size (half of the length, width and height). We set the objective function as:

$$\min \sum_i \left\| c_i' - c_i \right\|^2 + \eta \left\| p_i' - p_i \right\|^2.$$

Contact Constraint. When two parts have a supporting relationship, we use this constraint to optimize. if j^{th} part supports i^{th} part, we believe that the bottom of the ith part should be embedded in the jth part. Besides, there may be connections in different directions, we set t as the direction. The parameter, $t = 0, 1, 2$ respectively represents x, y and z direction. We define the contact constraint as: $c_j[t] + p_j[t] - \sigma_1 p_j[t] \leq c_i[t] - p_i[t] \leq c_j[t] + p_j[t] - \sigma_2 p_j[t]$. In the formula given, we use σ to control the embedding depth of the two parts connections.

Center Point Constraint. Most man-made shapes are axis-symmetrical structures, and the center points of the main parts of these shapes are in a straight line, such as the center point of the chair's leg and center point of the chair's seat. Based on this, we propose a center point constraint. If i^{th} part's center point and j^{th} part's center point are in the same straight line. So, we define the center point constraint as: $c_i[t] = c_j[t]$. Where t represents the direction of the x, y, and z axis.

Symmetry Constraint. If the generated i^{th} part and j^{th} part have reflective symmetry with respect to a given plane. The size of two symmetrical parts should be equal. In addition, the two parts need to be parallel to each other. The symmetry constraint as: $s_i - s_j = 0$, $((c_i + c_j)/2 - o_1) \cdot n = 0$, $((c_i - c_j)) \cdot (d - o_2) = 0$, $((c_i - c_j)) \cdot (d - o_3) = 0$. Where n and o_1 are the normal vector to the symmetry plane and a point on the symmetry plane, respectively. d represent the intersection of the line between the center points of the two parts that are symmetric about the plane and the plane of symmetry. o_2 and o_3 represent another two different points on the symmetry plane.

3.3   Fine-Tune

Due to the resolution of the data and processing nature of the decoder, the generated object may have some float voxels. For each voxel, we compute the distance between the voxel and the neighbors. We summarize the equation as: $\ell(v) = \sum_v D(v)$. Where v denotes each voxel of the 3D object. $D(v)$ denotes the distance between the voxel and its neighbors. We use $L1$ to compute the distance. When $\ell(v)$ is less than a threshold, we discard this voxel. Besides, for different types of shapes, such as chairs, etc., they have symmetrical parts. These parts may have different results due to different missing geometry information. For the symmetrical parts, we chose one and replace the original symmetrical part's geometry information with this part's to ensure consistency.

4   Experiments and Evaluation

4.1   Implementation Details

Training dataset are taken from ModelNet [1], a big dataset for geometry deep learning. All 3D shapes are split into parts and each part has been consistently aligned and scaled. Each category also has a fixed number of semantic parts. The geometry of each part is provided as a voxel map and the structure is provided as the bounding boxes. The dataset we used include chairs (1200), airplanes (1600), and guitar (779). We use ADAM for the network optimization with an initial learning rate of 0.0001. Batch size is set to 64. We set the latent space's dimension as 256. We set α as 0.25 and β as 0.5. As described above, we use quadratic programming to repair the structure information. For ease of implementation, we follow [21] to implement our code.

4.2   Shape Repair

In order to show the improvement result of our method on the structure-aware method, we train the network of our method as we described. And then, we use these network to build a standard VAEs for each part of the shape after training. After that, we fed the results which generated by sructure-aware methods into the special VAEs to get complete results. Note that due to the difference in the amount of missing information in the shape, we need to iterate this process multiple times until getting a good 3D shape in visual based on geometry information. As described above, the results may also meet the structural problems. We use the methods mentioned in Sect. 3.2 to optimize the structure information. Specifically, we set the constraints based on prior knowledge, and each shape needs to meet the corresponding constraints to ensure the rationality of the structure. We use the methods of quadratic programming to calculate the results. In the next, we use the methods we mentioned above to fine-tune the results to make it better in visual.

Table 1. MMD and COV score results (Without structure information)

Dataset	Chair		Airplane		Guitar	
Evalution	MMD	COV	MMD	COV	MMD	COV
SAGNet(without ST)	13.41	0.32	7.63	0.28	9.72	0.44
TCG(without ST)	**10.80**	0.28	**7.00**	0.28	**8.65**	0.39

4.3   Results and Discussion

To evaluate the quality of the results, we use the methods of MMD(Minimum Matching Distance) and COV(Coverage) [19] to measure the results. These two metrics are used to evaluate the fidelity and diversity of a generative model, respectively. Note that, since one generated sample can be affected by parts from different training shapes, we evaluate MMD and COV with parts and calculate the average. To compute the COV score, we list all the generated parts, and match to the closest parts in the training data. Then we pick shapes which these matched parts belong to and calculate the fraction of the picked shapes to the shapes in training data as the COV score. And for COV, the higher the better. To evaluate the fidelity, we enumerate all parts within one training shape and match each part to the corresponding generated one with the minimum distance. Then we compute the mean distance of these parts as the matching score of one shape. Finally we average the matching scores of all shapes as the MMD score. For MMD, the lower the better.

We compare our results with SAGNet [4]. To perform a fair comparison, we run the code provided by SAGNet on our machine. And then, we optimize the results by our method. The final results are shown in Fig. 3. SC means shape completed results. SC+CON means shape completed within contact constraint. SC+CEN means shape completed within center point constraint. SC+SYM means shape completed within symmetry constraint. Our results use all methods we described above. After that, we generate point clouds based on the results. For each part, we sample a fixed number of points to calculate. Firstly, we compare our results with those of SAGNet without the structure information to measure the ability of completion. To do this, we do not use bounding-box, that is, we do not put structural information into our calculation results, and only compare the completed results of our network. For all the length of the border of the bounding-box, we set it to 1 to eliminate the difference of structure. Table 1 shows the calculation results. In the next, we combine the structure information to compare the results of the entire shape. And the results are show in Table 2.

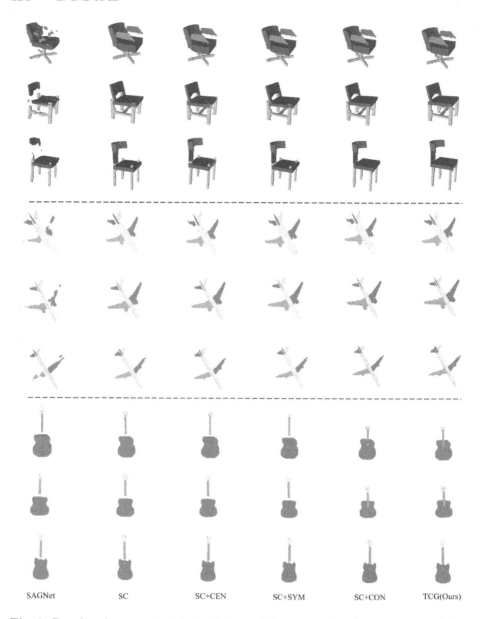

SAGNet   SC   SC+CEN   SC+SYM   SC+CON   TCG(Ours)

Fig. 3. Results of our method. Note that we did not optimize the symmetry relationship for the guitar. For typesetting, we take the optimized results of the center point relationship.

Table 2. MMD and COV score results (With structure information)

Dataset	Chair		Airplane		Guitar	
Evalution	MMD	COV	MMD	COV	MMD	COV
SAGNet	0.0025	0.37	0.00049	0.36	0.00043	0.55
SC	0.0024	0.37	0.00039	0.36	0.00043	0.57
SC+CON	0.0023	0.36	0.00040	0.38	0.00042	0.57
SC+CEN	0.0023	0.37	0.00039	0.36	0.00043	0.58
SC+SYM	0.0023	0.37	0.00040	0.36	–	–
TCG(Ours)	**0.0023**	**0.37**	**0.00036**	**0.41**	**0.00042**	**0.58**

Table 3. Contact score

Dataset	Chair	Airplane	Guitar
SAGNet	0.89	0.69	0.62
SC	0.89	0.69	0.62
SC+CEN	0.89	0.70	0.62
SC+CON	0.99	0.89	0.99
SC+SYM	0.89	0.76	–
TCG(Ours)	**0.99**	**0.90**	**0.99**

To measure the connection relationship, we set up a method to judge. We call it contact score. Specifically, if i^{th} part supports j^{th} part, we think that j^{th} part needs to slightly embedded in i^{th} part. It means $c_j[d] - s_j[d] <= c_i[d] + s_i[d]$, where d is the direction. If the two parts satisfy the above relationship, they are connected, and we rely on prior knowledge to calculate the connection of shapes. In our experiment, we generate 1000 shapes for each class and calculate the results of the contact rate as we described above. At last, we get the contact rate for each category of shape. We call it contact score. It measures the connection of shapes. The results show in Table 3. For this score, the higher the value, the better the results.

We use the symmetry score to measure the center point relationship and symmetry relationship of the shape. For the symmetry score, we set a fixed symmetry plane for all of shapes. Because the symmetry of the bounding-box about the plane greatly affects the matching of voxel, we firstly only use voxel for comparison. We do an asymmetric transformation for each part and calculate the matching rate of voxel between the original part and the symmetrically transformed part. Table 4 shows our calculation results. Note that fus means fusage, and emp means empennage. For the entire shape, we add bounding-box to compute each voxel's coordinate, after that we compare whether the voxel of 3D shape and its symmetry object's voxel matched. It may cause some deviations because of the symmetric transformation. So we set a threshold, and

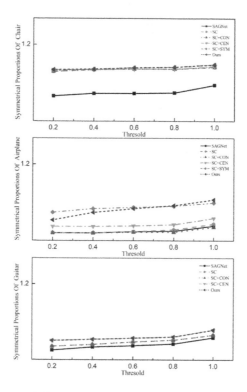

Fig. 4. Symmetry score of the whole shape. For the threshold, we chose the size of a voxel as the initial threshold. We set 0.2, 0.6, 0.4, 0.8 as the ratio, and multiply these ratios by the initial threshold as the new threshold.

Table 4. Symmetry score of part.

Dataset	Chair					Airplane						Guitar		
Part	back	seat	arm_r	arm_l	leg	fus	$wing_r$	$wing_l$	emp_u	emp_r	emp_l	head	strings	body
SAGNet	0.67	0.89	0.63	0.56	0.78	0.91	0.59	0.61	0.80	0.75	0.62	0.79	0.85	0.88
TCG(Ours)	**0.81**	**0.98**	**0.99**	**0.99**	**0.96**	0.91	**0.99**	**0.99**	**0.86**	**0.99**	**0.99**	**0.84**	**0.88**	0.88

for two different voxels, if the error within the threshold range, we still think they are matched. Figure 4 shows the results of symmetry score within different threshold for the whole shape. For this score, the higher the value, the better the symmetry of the shape.

5   Limitation and Future Work

The experimental results show that our method can achieve good results. But there are still some limitations here. First of all, our network learns parts of the shape. For some parts, they need to be fed into the standard VAEs which we built multiple times before getting the repaired result. Secondly, our method can not complete the part which has a lot of missing information. Under this circumstances, our network deals with the voxels as float voxel and remove them and we will get a completely missing part. Thirdly, the parts whose features are not obvious, such as the main body of the guitar, the fuselage of the airplane, etc., may not be good after completing. We consider this may caused by the dataset. Because the dataset we used is has few samples and it is a little small for deep learning. In the next, we will make a larger dataset that satisfies our training requirements.

6 Conclusion

In this paper, we proposed a method to optimize the structure-aware network' results by geometry information and structure information respectively. We build a VAEs trained by Twin-channel GAN to complete the missing geometry information. Besides, we set some constraints to optimize structural problems. With these two methods, we ensure the rationality of the generated results.

Acknowledgments. This work is part of the research supported by the Fundamental Research Funds for the Central Universities No. Y03019023601008011, the interactive Technology Research Fund of the Research Center for Interactive Technology Industry, School of Economics and Management, Tsinghua University (No. RCITI2021T006) and sponsored by TiMi L1 Studio of Tencent corporation.

References

1. Zhirong Wu, Shuran Song, Aditya Khosla, Fisher Yu, Linguang Zhang, Xiaoou Tang, Jianxiong Xiao: 3d shapenets: A deep representation for vol-umetric shapes. In: Proceedings of the IEEE conferenceon computer vision and pattern recognition, pp. 1912–1920 (2015)
2. Jiajun Wu, Chengkai Zhang, Tianfan Xue, Bill Freeman, Josh Tenenbaum: Learning a probabilistic latent space of object shapesvia 3d generative-adversarial modeling. In: Advances inneural information processing systems, pp. 82–90 (2016)
3. Gao, L., Yang, J., Tong, W., Yuan, Y.-J., Hongbo, F., Lai, Y.-K., Zhang, H.: Sdm-net: deep generative network for structured deformable mesh. ACM Trans. Graph. **38**(6), 1–15 (2019)
4. Wu, Z., Wang, X., Lin, D., Lischinski, D., Cohen-Or, D., Huang, H.: SAGNet: structure-aware generative network for 3D-shape modeling. ACM Trans. Graph. (Proceedings of SIGGRAPH 2019) **38**(4), 91:1–91:14 (2019)
5. Mo, K., Guerrero, P., Yi, L., Su, H., Wonka, P., Mitra, N.J., Guibas, L.J.L: Structe-dit: learning structural shape variations. In: 2020 IEEE/CVF Conference on Computer Vision and Pattern Recognition, CVPR 2020, 13–19 June 2020, pp. 8856–8865. IEEE (2020)
6. Kazhdan, M., Bolitho, M., Hoppe, H.: Poisson surface reconstruction. In: Proceedings of the Fourth Eurographics Symposium on Geometry Processing, vol. 7 (2006)
7. Nealen, A., Igarashi, T., Sorkine, O., Alexa, M.: Laplacian mesh optimization. In: Proceedings of the 4th International Conference on Computer Graphics and Interactive Techniques in Australasia and Southeast Asia, pp. 381–389 (2006)

8. Dai, A., Ruizhongtai Qi, C., Nießner, M.: Shape completion using 3d-encoder-predictor cnns and shape synthesis. In: Proceedings of the IEEE international conference on computer vision, pp. 6545–6554 (2017)
9. Huang, H., Li, Z., He, R., Sun, Z., Tan, T.: Introvae: introspective variational autoencoders for photographic image synthesis. In: Advances in Neural Information Processing Systems, pp. 52–63 (2018)
10. Goodfellow, I.J., et al.: Generative adversarial networks. Adv. Neural Inf. Process. Syst. **3**, 2672–2680 (2014)
11. Kingma, D.P., Welling, M.: Auto-encoding variational bayes. In: 2nd International Conference on Learning Representations (2014)
12. Averkiou, M., Kim, V.G., Zheng, Y., Mitra, N.J.: ShapeSynth: parameterizing model collections for coupled shape exploration and synthesis. In: Computer Graphics Forum, vol. 33, pp. 125–134. Wiley Online Library (2014)
13. Wang, P.-S., Liu, Y., Guo, Y.-X., Sun, C.-Y., Tong, X.: O-CNN: octree-based convolutional neural networks for 3D shape analysis. ACM Trans. Graph. **36**(4), 72 (2017)
14. Wang, J., Fang, Z.: GSIR: generalizable 3D shape interpretation and reconstruction. In: Vedaldi, A., Bischof, H., Brox, T., Frahm, J.-M. (eds.) ECCV 2020. LNCS, vol. 12358, pp. 498–514. Springer, Cham (2020). https://doi.org/10.1007/978-3-030-58601-0_30
15. Sorkine, O., Cohen-Or, D.: Least-squares meshes. In: Proceedings of the IEEE Shape Modeling Applications, pp. 191–199 (2004)
16. Mitra, N.J., Guibas, L.J., Pauly, M.: Partial and approximate symmetry detection for 3D geometry. ACM Trans. Graph. **25**(3), 560–568 (2006)
17. Sharma, A., Grau, O., Fritz, M.: VConv-DAE: deep volumetric shape learning without object labels. In: Hua, G., Jégou, H. (eds.) ECCV 2016. LNCS, vol. 9915, pp. 236–250. Springer, Cham (2016). https://doi.org/10.1007/978-3-319-49409-8_20
18. Song, S., Yu, F., Zeng, A., Chang, A.X., Savva, M., Funkhouser, T.: semantic scene completion from a single depth image. In: Proceedings of the IEEE International Conference on Computer Vision, pp. 1746–1754 (2017)
19. Achlioptas, P., Diamanti, O., Mitliagkas, I., Guibas, L.: Learning representations and generative models for 3D point clouds. In: International Conference on Machine Learning, pp. 40–49 (2018)
20. Richard, A., Cherabier, I., Oswald, M.R., Pollefeys, M., Schindler, K.: KAPLAN: a 3D point descriptor for shape completion. In: International Conference on 3D Vision, 3DV 2020, Virtual Event, Japan, 25–28 November 2020, pp. 101–110. IEEE (2020)
21. Diamond, S., Boyd, S.P.: CVXPY: a python-embedded modeling language for convex optimization. J. Mach. Learn. Res. **17**(83), 1–5 (2016)

CoPaint: Guiding Sketch Painting with Consistent Color and Coherent Generative Adversarial Networks

Shiqi Jiang, Chenhui Li$^{(\boxtimes)}$, and Changbo Wang

East China Normal University, Shanghai 200062, China
chli@cs.ecnu.edu.cn

Abstract. Art design plays an important role in attracting users. Through art design, some sketches are more in line with aesthetics. Traditionally, we need to artificially color many series of black-and-white sketches using the same color, which is time-consuming and difficult for art designers. In addition, coherent sketch painting is challenging to automate. We propose a GAN-based approach CoPaint for sketch colorization. Our neural network takes as its input two black-and-white sketches with different rotation angles and produces a series of high-quality colored images of consistent color. We present an approach to generate a coherent sketch painting dataset. We also propose a paired generator network with shared weights that consists of convolutional layers and batch-normal layers. In addition, we propose a similarity loss that makes the images produced by the generator more similar. The provided experiments demonstrate the effectiveness of our approach.

Keywords: Generative adversarial networks · Image processing · Image to image

1 Introduction

In the art designs of games and manga, the existing methods color sketches well but cannot guarantee color consistency, which means that inconsistent colors appear in the same place at different angles when rotating in space. When designing game items, designers usually draw a series of sketches first and then add consistent colors to this series of sketches. Generally, when designers are designing, they do not consider the effect of other factors on color, such as lighting, but consider only the color of the object itself. In the process of coloring, when coloring the first sketch of this series, designers need to choose the right color for each part of the image. After that, considering the next sketch of that series is time-consuming and difficult.

Electronic supplementary material The online version of this chapter (https://doi.org/10.1007/978-3-030-89029-2_18) contains supplementary material, which is available to authorized users.

The existing coloring methods usually focus only on the results of individual image coloring and have useful effects. In the automatic image coloring method of Cheng et al. [4], the grayscale image can be colored very well, but this method is not the best for sketch colorization. In image coloring based on user interaction, color-based coloring [29], reference-based coloring [27] and tag-based coloring [12] use a variety of interactive methods to make the colors of a picture more realistic. However, to obtain a series of similar images to achieve similar colors, many complicated interactions are required, which is inconvenient. For paired inputs, it seems that we can use a matching method such as the scale-invariant feature transform (SIFT) [17] to solve the problem. However, the inputs of our method are black-and-white sketches. The feature point matching method can match only the feature points, but the coloring problem requires consideration of the area color; thus, this method is not suitable for sketch coloring. The existing region-based matching methods are computationally intensive and have poor robustness. Thus, this method is not suitable for our problem.

(a) Example1: anime avatar

(b) Example2: cartoon character

Fig. 1. Examples of coherent sketch paintings. (Color figure online)

Our problem is how to consistently colorize sketches of an object from different angles. Hence, to obtain coherent sketch painting, we propose a colorization method based on conditional generative adversarial networks (cGANs) [11]. To realize the network structure, we build a dataset by Unity, which can be applied to different scenes. To measure the color difference between generated images, we introduce image similarity as a new loss function. As shown in Fig. 1, the input of the generator network is monochrome sketches from different angles, and the results are coherent colored images.

In summary, our contributions are as follows:

Coherent Colorization Network. We propose an adversarial coherent sketch painting network, which is based on the cGAN and siamese network.

Similarity Loss. Besides adversarial loss, we add similarity loss to our network. This method shifts the focus from generating a real image to generating a similar image.

A Dataset for the Network Training. We make a dataset for training our network. The dataset consists of images with different angles and the corresponding sketches.

2 Related Work

2.1 Generative Adversarial Networks (GANs)

Traditional methods use convolutional neural networks (CNNs) to generate goal images, which are not satisfactory owing to their low resolution. Generative adversarial networks (GANs) [7] and improved methods based on them [13] have achieved high-quality results. Based on the GAN model, an improved unsupervised method [3] can be used to generate reasonable samples. However, due to the limited research on visualizing GANs, Radford proposed deep convolutional GANs (DCGANs) [21], in which there are a set of stable constraints and visualize filters that can learn to draw specific objects. The cGAN [18] is an extension to the original GAN. Both the generator and the discriminator of the cGAN add additional information as the condition. Based on existing works, a "U-Net"-based architecture [22] has achieved impressive results. Pix2Pix [11] is based on the cGAN and guarantees that the generated image and the input image match. Pix2Pix relies on U-Net instead of the encoder-decoder model, which reduces information from the input layers. In this paper, we utilize this method to design our network because it is suitable for learning feature codings.

2.2 Colorization

Colorization using optimization [14] is a method in which grayscale images are colored via optimized methods. An important assumption here is that for two adjacent pixels, if their brightnesses are similar, their colors should also be similar. Specifically, a deep network needs to learn only the color tendency of samples [23] and uses edge detection. Therefore, this method is time-saving and inexpensive. Two methods for coloring images are scribble-based colorization [23] and example-based colorization [10]. Scribble-based colorization with an edge detection algorithm is an effective method that can avoid coloring out of bounds. Example-based colorization uses example colors to color target grayscale images.

Traditional methods use texture information to color sketches. Sykora [25] proposed a simple and flexible method that does not rely on style-specific features. Zhang [30] provided a color palette to guide user towards color selections at any location. The automatic color selection method [29] and the automatic painting method [15] can generate a colorful image that satisfies a user's requirements.

In general, the current automation methods cannot meet our needs that we color series of sketches with consistent colors, and interaction-based methods [19] or low complexity algorithm [6] require interactions and cannot deal with the area of complex sketch well. Therefore, we propose an automated method to achieve consistent coloring.

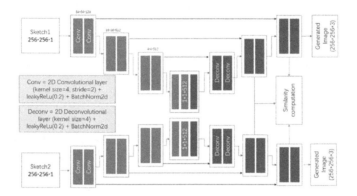

Fig. 2. The structure of the generator network. The number in parentheses indicates the tensor dimensions (width × height × channel).

3   Methods

3.1   Overview

Our problem is how to achieve a coherent sketch colorization. To solve this problem, we propose a network to synchronously extract features from two input sketches. In training, two generators are utilized with shared parameters and structures. In testing, only one generator is used.

3.2   Dataset

Colored Image Generation. As shown in Fig. 3, it is challenging to look for pictures of rotation relationships. To obtain our dataset, we use a 3D render engine to build it. To produce colored pictures, we prepare a large number of models. Then, we rotate the models or control the camera to obtain colored images from different angles. We control the lighting to ensure that the lighting will not affect the results. In addition to the images generated by 3D render engine, we collect anime images with different angles from Pixiv [1].

Sketch Extraction. After obtaining the colored images, we need to extract sketches as the input of the generator. Due to the inefficiency and low accuracy of the traditional algorithm, as shown in Fig. 4, we use sketchKeras [16] to obtain low-noise sketches with real-style edges. In actual practice, we also use other algorithms to generate sketches to avoid overfitting to one style of sketch input. For some images with complex patterns that usually have too much noise, we smooth out these images.

The resolution of our all images is 256 × 256. We make an input sequence to control the order of samples that enter training each time.

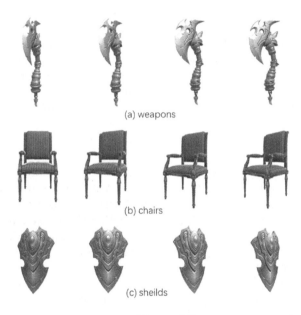

(a) weapons

(b) chairs

(c) sheilds

Fig. 3. Images photographed by Unity. We use different categories of models to obtain the images. Each model performs rotations over certain angles.

3.3   Network Structure

We adapt two generators and one discriminator in our method. In the generators, as shown in Fig. 2, we use two branches that share the same architecture and parameters [5]. When we finally generate the image, we also obtain the feature code of the image and calculate the similarity of the image. In detail, we use batch-normalized convolutional structure [9] followed by ReLU. For the encoding process, the input is downsampled to obtain and analyze the low-level local pixel values of a sketch to extract local features. In the decoder network, we use deconvolutional layers. In particular, in the last layer, we use a combination of bilinear interpolation and a convolution layer instead of the deconvolution layer to avoid noise in the generated results. The same information can be shared between the sketch and corresponding colored images in sketch painting, such as the edges. Thus, to the generators, we add a skip connection [22] to share information. In the discriminator, we take the generated images and labels as input. We use convolutional layers (kernel size = 4, stride = 2, padding = 1), batchnorm layers and LeakyReLU to produce 32×32 feature maps.

3.4 Loss Function

Our method is based on the GAN, so we use the GAN loss to generate high-quality images. $\mathcal{L}_{GAN}$ can be expressed as:

$$\mathcal{L}_{GAN}(G, D) = E_{x \sim p_{data}(x)} \left[logD\left(x|y\right) \right] + E_{z \sim p_z(z)} \left[log\left(1 - D\left(G\left(z\right)\right)\right) \right] \quad (1)$$

where G tries to minimize the loss, while D tries to maximize it. x means the generated images and y means the label. z is the sketch

The use of only the GAN loss function and L1 loss cannot guarantee color consistency. Therefore, we propose a similarity loss function (SLF) that uses feature codings to make colors coherent, which can be expressed as:

$$\mathcal{L}_{cos}(g) = 1 - \frac{g(x_1)g(x_2)}{\|g(x_1)\|\|g(x_2)\|} \quad (2)$$

where we obtain feature codings from two images $g(x_1)$ and $g(x_2)$. In the calculation process, we transform the feature map into a one-dimensional tensor (a high-dime- nsional vector). $\|g(x_1)\|$ and $\|g(x_2)\|$ denote the lengths of the feature coding vectors. The value of the function is between 0 and 1. If the calculated result is closer to 1, the pictures are more similar. When calculating gradients of x_1, we truncate x_2. Therefore, the network only needs to calculate the parameters related to x_1.

The total-variation loss [2] can keep the color changing slowly and generate spatially smooth images, which can be expressed as:

$$\mathcal{L}_{tv} = \frac{1}{H \times W \times C} \|\nabla_x(G(z)) + \nabla_y(G(z))\| \quad (3)$$

where we calculate the gradients in two directions (∇_x and ∇_y) for each pixel of the generated image $G(z)$.

We calculate the similarity loss in different layers of the deconvolution to ensure the color consistency of the results. The feature maps of the lower layer contains more information, so the weights of SLF in different layers are different. We use SLF in the last four layers. So total SLF can be expressed as:

$$\mathcal{L}_{slf}(g) = \lambda_1 * \mathcal{L}_{cos}(g_5) + \lambda_2 * \mathcal{L}_{cos}(g_6) + \lambda_3 * \mathcal{L}_{cos}(g_7) + \lambda_4 * \mathcal{L}_{cos}(g_8) \quad (4)$$

where g_n means different layers and $\lambda_1, \lambda_2, \lambda_3, \lambda_4$ are hyperparameters.

Our final loss function is

$$\mathcal{L}^* = arg \min_G \max_D \mathcal{L}_{cGAN}(G, D) + \mathcal{L}_{slf}(g) + \lambda E_{x,y,z}[\|y - G(x, z)\|_1] + \mathcal{L}_{tv} \quad (5)$$

4   Experiments

4.1   Training Strategy

During training, two generators are trained jointly with shared parameters and structure. At every step, two sketches are used as the input to the generator. For images taken from the same model, we use a series of those images that are rotated approximately 40° as images that can be input simultaneously. If this angle is set too large, the similarity of the sketch itself will be very low, which will lead to large errors in the network training. This series of images with a rotation angle of 40° consists of pictures for every 10°.

As shown in Fig. 4, although the input is obtained through the extraction tool, it is quite different from the sketch used in the actual application, as the actual sketch does not have as much noise as the generated sketch. Thus, after completing the main training, we use the real sketch to train over several epochs.

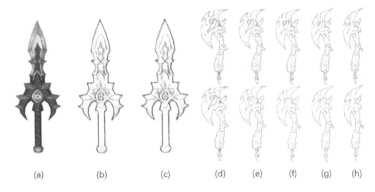

(a)   (b)   (c)   (d)   (e)   (f)   (g)   (h)

Fig. 4. Comparison of sketches. On the left, (a): Training label photographed by using Unity. (b): Sketch extracted by using sketchKeras (c): Smoothed sketch. On the right, Top: Sketch obtained by the sketch extraction tool; Bottom: Actual application of the sketch.

4.2   Dataset Generation

Our method of constructing the dataset is to generate colored images first and then extract the sketch. To easily generate colored images, we use a rendering engine to create the dataset. We use several models from the Unity asset store. Then, we put only one item in the scene at a time. We set the background color of the scene to white, which is usually the color of the sketch background, and place an item in the middle of the scene by adjusting the position of the camera. At each angle of rotation in space, the item can be photographed by the camera. In total, we use approximately four hundred models and generate a picture at every 10°. However, as shown in Fig. 3, weapons can be rotated once, but shields can be rotated only in the front range class. We generated approximately ten thousand images and make training sequence.

Besides, we manually adjust the position of the camera randomly to obtain images with different angles. We also collect images with different angles from Pixiv. There are about 120k images in total. Eighty percent of images are for training and the rest for testing.

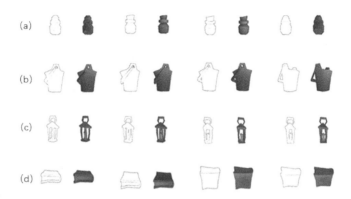

Fig. 5. Results of colorization with different angles. The pictures in each row are generated by the same object. (Color figure online)

4.3   Analysis on Angles

Figure 5 shows four sets of images with different rotation angles. The images in each row are the results of coloring the lines at different angles. When focusing on the coloring effect of each row of pictures, we can find that such results are consistent. Although we do not deliberately study the effect of lighting on the coloring results, the results generated by our network also have the colorization of lighting effects. This set of pictures can be used to explain how our method can color images of different angles coherently and naturally.

Due to the automatic coloring method, we use the same input to compare our colorization results to those of other neural-network-based methods without interacting with the user. As shown in Fig. 6, the first row presents the results of PaintsChainer [20], with inconsistent colors and some noise. The second row shows the results of Style2paints [29] for different colors. In contrast, as the last row shows, our method yields good results in terms of color consistency. By comparison, we believe that our method has higher quality on a single image.

5   Evaluation

5.1   Quality Analysis

What we are carrying out here, in actuality, is a type of sketch painting. The difference between ours and others is that our approach can keep the colors

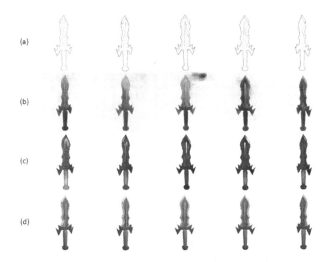

Fig. 6. Comparison with PaintsChainer and Style2paint. (a) Sketches to be colored. (b) Images produced by PaintsChainer. (c) Images produced by Style2paints. (d) Ours. (Color figure online)

coherent. Thus, we compare our method to Style2paint and PaintsChainer. We also compare the results for two angles: 10° and 20°. The images we generate can be seen as two parts: the sketch and the colored areas. It is difficult to calculate the similarity in the color area, so we estimate the color similarity by calculating the overall image similarity and the sketch similarity. The formula can be expressed as:

$$S_c = S_i + (1 - S_s) \tag{6}$$

where S_c means color similarity and S_i means image similarity and S_s means sketch similarity. We use traditional SSIM [26] to calculate sketch similarity. Image similarity is more difficult to define and calculate than sketch similarity.

We use three methods to evaluate image similarity. First, we use the improved SSIM to calculate the similarity between two images. We compare images on each channel, and then calculate the average of the differences for each channel. We calculate the score of SSIM according to Eq. 6. Besides, we consider color histogram (CH) [24]. In color painting, we do not need to consider the spatial location information of a pixel. What we should compare is the image color distribution. Therefore, the color histogram can be the standard of evaluation. This evaluation method can show that the results obtained by our method have higher consistency in terms of the color distribution. Finally, we use the peak signal-to-noise ratio (PSNR) [8]. For an RGB three-channel image, we need to calculate the mean square error of each channel of the two images first and then subtract the value of sketch similarity. Finally, we obtain the value of the PSNR. The larger the value is, the higher the quality of the image. The closer the values of the PSNR are, the more similar the two pictures are.

Table 1. Color similarity evaluation. We use three common similarity comparison methods to evaluate our method. We also compare our methods with other automatic coloring methods.

	PaintsChainer	Style2paints	Ours
SSIM(10)	0.91	0.94	**0.95**
SSIM(20)	0.88	0.92	**0.93**
CH(10)	55.48%	69.01%	**74.74%**
CH(20)	56.79%	66.78%	**72.62%**
PSNR(10)	19.67dB	21.45dB	**25.66dB**
PSNR(20)	18.03dB	19.24dB	**21.72dB**

As shown in Table 1, our experimental results achieve high scores in all three of the above evaluations. Based on similar structures, our method guarantees color consistency; hence, the scores of the SSIM and CH are higher. For the PSNR scores, there are some slight differences in the sketch itself; thus, in the evaluation, the scores are not the same but are very similar. We find that the result at 20° is worse than the result at 10°. When the rotation angle becomes larger, although the color is consistent, the similarity of the sketch is reduced, which leads to a decline in the score. In addition to color similarity, Table 1 can also show that our method also obtains high scores in single image evaluation compared to other methods.

5.2   Color Consistency Analysis

Besides image quality evaluation methods, we use manual methods to compare color consistency in detail. We manually select parts and calculate their color similarity as shown in Fig. 7. For the complex part, such as the yellow circle, we

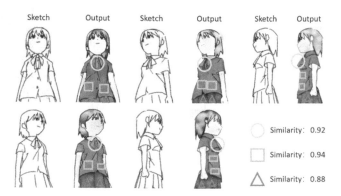

Fig. 7. We make manually selections. The marking parts are examples of calculating the similarity of areas. (Color figure online)

use multiple very small kernels to select the area and then calculate the average color similarity of this part.

5.3   Ablation Studies

We use SSIM to calculate the similarity of images. Table 2 shows that using SLF can bring a significant improvement in color consistency. In detail, Table 3 shows the effect of SLF on the results at different levels. For example, when calculating the similarity loss of feature maps in the 7th layer, we also calculate that in the 8th layer. We find that using SLF at the low layer has little effect, because color features are low-level features. Therefore, we use SLF in the last four layers.

Table 2. Color consistency comparison between different loss function.

	GAN+L1	GAN+L1+SLF
SSIM	0.72	0.88

We consider whether SLF will change the shape of the original sketches. We use our model to test sketches when the label is the input sketch. As shown in Table 4, using SLF will not have a significant impact on the original sketches. Therefore, When we evaluate the two pictures, we can ignore the structural changes and focus on the differences in color.

Table 3. Difference in color consistency between different number of SLF.

	SLF(8)	SLF(7)	SLF(6)	SLF(5)	SLF(4)
SSIM	0.81	0.86	0.87	0.88	0.88

Table 4. We compare the difference between the output sketches after using SLF and the original sketches.

	SLF(8)	SLF(7)	SLF(6)	SLF(5)	SLF(4)
L1 distance	0	0.01	0.01	0.02	0.02

6   Conclusions and Limitations

In this paper, we present a GAN-based sketch painting method (CoPaint) to produce coherent colored images. To train our network, we build a dataset and our dataset can be extended to other application, such as cartoon design. We propose a similarity loss function (SLF) for coherent color. Comparisons with other methods and ablation experiments show that our method performs well.

However, our approach has several limitations. Our method does not guarantee color consistency well when the angle is large. In this case, we believe that our method may treat this picture as a new picture. Moreover, in our experiments, we consider only the color of an object and ignore the effects of other factors on the color (such as lighting).

Going forward, we will study how to ensure the color consistency of an image at a large angle of rotation by adding a reference [28]. Besides, we will look for additional detailed constraints to make the pictures cleaner [29].

References

1. Pixiv. http://www.pixiv.net
2. Aly, H.A., Dubois, E.: Image up-sampling using total-variation regularization with a new observation model. IEEE Trans. Image Process. **14**(10), 1647–1659 (2005)
3. Bousmalis, K., Silberman, N., Dohan, D., Erhan, D., Krishnan, D.: Unsupervised pixel-level domain adaptation with generative adversarial networks. In: The IEEE Conference on CVPR, vol. 1, p. 7 (2017)
4. Cheng, Z., Yang, Q., Sheng, B.: Deep colorization. CoRR abs/1605.00075 (2016)
5. Chopra, S., Hadsell, R., LeCun, Y., et al.: Learning a similarity metric discriminatively, with application to face verification. In: CVPR, vol. 1, pp. 539–546 (2005)
6. Fourey, S., Tschumperlé, D., Revoy, D.: A fast and efficient semi-guided algorithm for flat coloring line-arts. Eurographics Association (2018)
7. Goodfellow, I., et al.: Generative adversarial nets. In: Advances in Neural Information Processing Systems, vol. 27, pp. 2672–2680. Curran Associates, Inc. (2014)
8. Hore, A., Ziou, D.: Image quality metrics: PSNR vs. SSIM. In: 2010 20th International Conference on Pattern Recognition, pp. 2366–2369. IEEE (2010)
9. Ioffe, S., Szegedy, C.: Batch normalization: Accelerating deep network training by reducing internal covariate shift. arXiv preprint arXiv:1502.03167 (2015)
10. Ironi, R., Cohen-Or, D., Lischinski, D.: Colorization by example. In: Rendering Techniques, pp. 201–210. Citeseer (2005)
11. Isola, P., Zhu, J.Y., Zhou, T., Efros, A.A.: Image-to-image translation with conditional adversarial networks. In: 2017 IEEE Conference on CVPR, pp. 5967–5976. IEEE (2017)
12. Kim, H., Jhoo, H.Y., Park, E., Yoo, S.: Tag2pix: Line art colorization using text tag with secat and changing loss. arXiv preprint arXiv:1908.05840 (2019)
13. Lesort, T., Stoian, A., Goudou, J.-F., Filliat, D.: Training discriminative models to evaluate generative ones. In: Tetko, I.V., Kůrková, V., Karpov, P., Theis, F. (eds.) ICANN 2019. LNCS, vol. 11729, pp. 604–619. Springer, Cham (2019). https://doi.org/10.1007/978-3-030-30508-6_48
14. Levin, A., Lischinski, D., Weiss, Y.: Colorization using optimization. In: ACM TOG, vol. 23, pp. 689–694. ACM (2004)
15. Liu, Y., Qin, Z., Wan, T., Luo, Z.: Auto-painter: cartoon image generation from sketch by using conditional wasserstein generative adversarial networks. Neurocomputing **311**, 78–87 (2018)
16. lllyasviel: sketchkeras. https://github.com/lllyasviel/sketchKeras
17. Lowe, D.G.: Distinctive image features from scale-invariant keypoints. Int. J. Comput. Vision **60**(2), 91–110 (2004)

18. Mirza, M., Osindero, S.: Conditional generative adversarial nets. CoRR abs/1411.1784 (2014), http://arxiv.org/abs/1411.1784
19. Parakkat, A.D., Madipally, P., Gowtham, H.H., Cani, M.: Interactive flat coloring of minimalist neat sketches. Eurographics Association (2020)
20. pfnet: Paintschainer. https://paintschainer.preferred.tech/index_zh.html
21. Radford, A., Metz, L., Chintala, S.: Unsupervised representation learning with deep convolutional generative adversarial networks (2015)
22. Ronneberger, O., Fischer, P., Brox, T.: U-net: convolutional networks for biomedical image segmentation. In: Navab, N., Hornegger, J., Wells, W.M., Frangi, A.F. (eds.) MICCAI 2015. LNCS, vol. 9351, pp. 234–241. Springer, Cham (2015). https://doi.org/10.1007/978-3-319-24574-4_28
23. Sangkloy, P., Lu, J., Fang, C., Yu, F., Hays, J.: Scribbler: Controlling deep image synthesis with sketch and color. In: IEEE Conference on CVPR, vol. 2 (2017)
24. Swain, M.J., Ballard, D.H.: Color indexing. Int. J. Comput. Vision **7**(1), 11–32 (1991)
25. Sýkora, D., Dingliana, J., Collins, S.: Lazybrush: Flexible painting tool for hand-drawn cartoons. In: Computer Graphics Forum, vol. 28, pp. 599–608. Wiley Online Library (2009)
26. Wang, Z., Bovik, A.C., Sheikh, H.R., Simoncelli, E.P., et al.: Image quality assessment: from error visibility to structural similarity. IEEE Trans. Image Process. **13**(4), 600–612 (2004)
27. Xian, W., et al.: Texturegan: Controlling deep image synthesis with texture patches. In: Proceedings of the IEEE Conference on CVPR, pp. 8456–8465 (2018)
28. Yin, W., Fu, Y., Sigal, L., Xue, X.: Semi-latent GAN: learning to generate and modify facial images from attributes. CoRR abs/1704.02166 (2017)
29. Zhang, L., Li, C., Wong, T.T., Ji, Y., Liu, C.: Two-stage sketch colorization. In: SIGGRAPH Asia 2018 Technical Papers, p. 261. ACM (2018)
30. Zhang, R., et al.: Real-time user-guided image with learned deep priors. arXiv:1705.02999 (2017)

Multi-Stream Fusion Network for Multi-Distortion Image Super-Resolution

Yang Wen[1], Yupeng Xu[2], Bin Sheng[1(✉)], Ping Li[3], Lei Bi[4], Jinman Kim[4], Xiangui He[2], and Xun Xu[2(✉)]

[1] Department of Computer Science and Engineering, Shanghai Jiao Tong University, Shanghai, China
{wenyang,shengbin}@sjtu.edu.cn
[2] Department of Ophthalmology, Shanghai General Hospital, Shanghai, China
kevinxyp@live.com, drxuxun@sjtu.edu.cn
[3] Department of Computing, The Hong Kong Polytechnic University, Kowloon, Hong Kong
p.li@polyu.edu.hk
[4] School of Information Technologies, The University of Sydney, Sydney, Australia
{lei.bi,jinman.kim}@sydney.edu.au

Abstract. Deblurring, denoising and super-resolution (SR) are important image recovery tasks that are committed to improving image quality. Despite the rapid development of deep learning and vast studies on improving image quality have been proposed, the most existing recovery solutions simply deal with quality degradation caused by a single distortion factor, such as SR focusing on improving spatial resolution. Since very little work has been done to analyze the interaction and characteristics of the deblurring, denoising and SR mixing problems, this paper considers the multi-distortion image recovery problem from a holistic perspective and introduces an end-to-end multi-stream fusion network (MSFN) to restore a multi-distortion image (low-resolution image with noise and blur) into a clear high-resolution (HR) image. Firstly, MSFN adopts multiple reconstruction branches to extract deblurring, denoise and SR features with respect to different degradations. Then, MSFN gradually fuses these multi-stream recovery features in a determined order and obtains an enhanced restoration feature by using two fusion modules. In addition, MSFN uses fusion modules and residual attention modules to facilitate the fusion of different recovery features from the denoising branch and the deblurring branch for the trunk SR branch. Experiments on several benchmarks fully demonstrate the superiority of our MSFN in solving the multi-distortion image recovery problem.

Keywords: Multi-distortion · Multi-stream · Super-resolution

© Springer Nature Switzerland AG 2021
N. Magnenat-Thalmann et al. (Eds.): CGI 2021, LNCS 13002, pp. 242–251, 2021.
https://doi.org/10.1007/978-3-030-89029-2_19

1   Introduction

In computer vision, capturing high-quality HR images has attracted great attention from academia and the industry community. However, in limited hardware conditions (small prime lenses, consumer sensors, especially mobile devices), there are practical difficulties in obtaining such high-quality HR images [1,2]. The limitations mainly arise in three aspects. First, the image acquired directly by the image sensor is usually noisy. In particular, the larger the pixel density of the sensor, the more obvious the noise. Secondly, most of the lenses used in mobile devices are fixed lenses with short focal length, which not only brings difficulties to remote object imaging but also limits the resolution of the image. Third, the captured image is inevitably blurry due to camera shake or relative motion between the object and the camera.

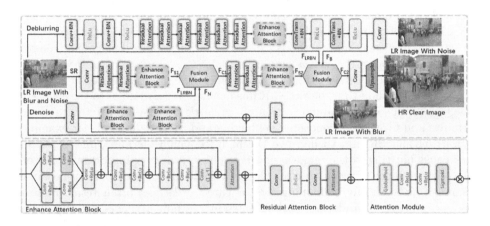

Fig. 1. The framework of proposed MSFN. MSFN mainly contains three branches: deblurring branch, trunk SR branch and denoising branch. MSFN takes the LR image with blur and noise as input and produces clear high-resolution reconstructed image. The deblurring branch and the denoising branch produce the LR image with noise and the LR image with blur, respectively. The denoising feature F_N obtained by the denoising branch and the deblurring feature F_B obtained by the deblurring branch are gradually fused to the SR branch through fusion modules, respectively.

For previous image recovery studies, such as denoising, deblurring and super-resolution (SR) tasks, are all processed separately to break through the above hardware limitations. (1) Super-resolution aims to recovery a high-resolution image from a low-resolution (LR) one. Convolutional neural network (CNN) based SR methods have shown incomparable superior performance compared with the traditional methods. SRCNN [3] pioneered the application of convolutional neural network to image super-resolution. Then, FSRCNN [4], VDSR [5], LapSRN [6], EDSR [7] and other classical deep-learning based single image SR methods show incomparable performance. In [8], a local implicit image function (LIIF) is introduced for continuous image representation. In [9], Gu *et al.*

propose a local attribution map (LAM) to visualize and understand the super-resolution networks. However, when the input LR image is polluted by noise and blur simultaneously, the enhancement of the texture and detail of the image using SR algorithm will cause the blur and artifacts amplification. Even if the input image contains slight noise or blurring, minor problems will be magnified. (2) Deblurring is to solve the effect of blurring on image quality. In [10], Xu *et al.* propose an end-to-end CNN model which includes two sub-networks to recover the latent sharp image. In [11], Hradiš *et al.* propose a 15 layers deeper network to implement the text image deblurring task. Then, DeblurGAN [12], SRN-GAN [13], CycleGAN [14] and others generative adversarial network (GAN) are widely used in blind image motion deblurring. However, these methods can only roughly remove the blur in the image, but cannot simultaneously remove the noise and improve the spatial resolution of the image. (3) Denoising is the process of reducing noise in a digital image. Classical denoising methods such as BM3D [15] and WNNM [16] are based on priori knowledge of non-local self-similarity. Recently, CNN-based denoising methods [17–21] have shown a relatively satisfactory performance. However, these methods can only deal with noise but cannot remove the blur and enlarge the spatial resolution.

To overcome the existing limitations and meet the practical needs, it is urgent to propose a method to restore the LR image with blur and noise to the clear HR image simultaneously. The motivation of our work is two-fold. Firstly, since the formulas and targets for denoising, deblurring and SR are different, for example, deblurring and SR aim to improve the high-frequency details while denoising may cause blurring in the removal of image noise, it is very important to determine the sequence of reconstruction tasks for multi-distortion recovery network. Secondly, since simply combining two or three tasks can often result in serious performance degradation, such as introducing new artifacts and obscuring [22,23], a direct and effective multi-distortion image recovery method is very important. In conclusion, our contributions include: First, we verify the effects of different reconstruction sequences on the multi-distortion restoration task and adopt a progressive multi-stream fusion model for multi-distortion image SR. Second, we gradually fuse relevant recovery information from the denoise and deblurring branches into the SR network by the proposed fusion module. In addition, we use residual attention module to effectively extract additional reconstruction information from the auxiliary branches.

2   Method

The framework of our proposed MSFN is shown in Fig. 1. The MSFN includes deblurring branch, denoising branch and the trunk SR recovery branch. The input of MSFN is the LR image contaminated by both noise and motion blur. The deblurring branch is to recovery the potential LR deblurred image and integrate the deblurring features F_B directly into the SR recovery branch. Similarly, the denoising branch removes the noise and fuses the denoising features F_N into the SR recovery branch. The trunk SR recovery branch gradually integrates the

F_N from denoising branch and F_B from deblurring branch into the SR recovery process according to the multiple reconstruction execution order (firstly denoising and then deblurring), so as to not only amplify the spatial resolution, but also handle the motion blur and noise simultaneously. Besides, we use fusion module to enhance the fusion of effective contextual information and promote the restoration of multi-distortion images.

SR Recovery Branch: The trunk SR recovery branch aims to achieve multi-distortion image SR recovery. It contains two basic feature extraction modules which contains two residual attention blocks followed by one enhancement attention block to extract the basic SR features. It also contains two multi-stream fusion modules to gradually fuse the feature F_N of denoising branch and the feature F_B of deblurring branch, so as to further enhance the ability of structure and detail preservation in the SR reconstruction image. Finally, one upsampling layer is followed by one convolution layer at the tail of SR branch. Details are shown in Fig. 1.

Denoising Branch: To eliminate the noise in the multi-distortion image, we refer to the image denoising method RIDNet [24] and use an auxiliary denoising branch to extract the denoising feature F_N. Then, the feature F_N is fused into the trunk SR recovery branch. The denoising branch mainly consists of two convolution layers followed by two enhance attention blocks based on dilation convolution and attention mechanism. Denoising structure is shown in Fig. 1.

Deblurring Branch: To effectively remove motion blur for the multi-distortion images, we use an auxiliary deblurring branch to extract deblurring features F_B and gradually fuse F_B into the trunk SR recovery branch according to restoration order. The deblurring branch firstly includes two couples of convolution layers with batch normalization layer and ReLU, then 6 residual attention blocks followed by one enhance attention block. Finally, two transposed convolution layers with batch normalization layer and ReLU are set at the tail of the deblurring branch. The details are shown in Fig. 1.

2.1 Multi-Stream Fusion

Since the input image is polluted by many distortion factors and various distortion reconstruction tasks interact with each other, we theoretically analyze and experimentally verify the effect of different reconstruction task sequences on the overall performance to determine the optimal sequence of multi-stream fusion. Firstly, we tend to minimize the impact of noise by denoising before doing other tasks. If the denoising operation is followed by SR or deblurring, the noise will further affect the processing of SR and deblurring tasks, and produce serious artifacts. Second, previous joint deblurring and SR research [22,23] have shown that the fusion of deblurring information into the SR reconstruction network is more effective than the implementation of each task separately. This takes full advantage of the relationship between deblurring and SR to avoid error accumulation and reduce complexity.

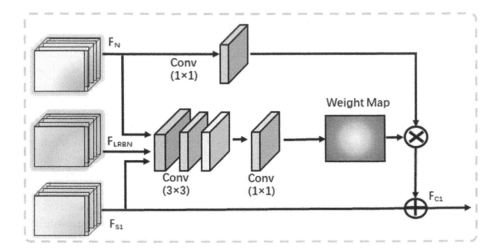

Fig. 2. The framework of the fusion module. I_{LRBN} denotes the input LR image with noise and motion blur. The input feature I_{LRBN}, the SR feature F_{S1} and the denoising feature F_N are first concatenated and then go through a series of convolution to get the weight map. F_{C1} is the weighted fusion feature obtained by fusion module and used as the partial input of the SR recovery branch.

2.2   Fusion Module

Our MSFN aims to recovery the HR clear image from the LR image contaminated by both noise and motion blur. To better extract SR features from the images with complex degradation, we use the fusion modules to merge the SR recovered features and the deblurring/denoising features. This fusion mechanism has been proved to be powerful in discovering the importance of features in multi-mode fusion [22]. Figure 2 shows the fusion process of SR and denoising features. First, the input image feature I_{LRBN}, SR feature F_{S1}, denoising feature F_N are concatenated by concatenation layer and then fused through two convolution layers with kernel 3×3 and 1×1. Second, the weight map and the denoising feature F_N convoluted with kernel 1×1 are dot multiplied to obtain the weighted feature, which is then added to the SR feature F_{S1} to obtain the weighted feature F_{C1}. The specific process is shown in Eq. 1 to Eq. 3.

$$F_{Cat} = Concat(F_{S1}, F_{LRBN}, F_N) \tag{1}$$

$$F_M = Conv_2(Relu(Conv_1(F_{Cat})) \tag{2}$$

$$F_{C1} = Conv_2(F_N) \otimes F_M + F_{S1} \tag{3}$$

where $Concat$ denotes the concatenation operation. $Conv_1(\cdot)$ and $Conv_2(\cdot)$ denote the convolution layer with kernel 3×3 and kernel 1×1, respectively. $\otimes$ denotes the matrix multiplication. For fusing the deblurring feature F_B with the SR recovery feature, the steps are similar to those of denoising feature.

2.3   Deep Supervision

The whole loss function of MSFN to implement constraints between the input and output fields is defined as:

$$Loss = \min L_{sr}(\widehat{I}_{HR}, I_{HR}) + \alpha L_{db}(\widehat{I}_{LRN}, I_{LRN}) \\ + \beta L_{dn}(\widehat{I}_{LRB}, I_{LRB})) \tag{4}$$

$$L_{sr} = \min \left\| \widehat{I}_{HR} - I_{HR} \right\|_2^2 \tag{5}$$

$$L_{db} = \min \left\| \widehat{I}_{LRN} - I_{LRN} \right\|_2^2 \tag{6}$$

$$L_{dn} = \min \left\| \widehat{I}_{LRB} - I_{LRB} \right\|_1 \tag{7}$$

Where L_{sr}, L_{db} and L_{dn} are the loss functions for the SR recovery branch, the denoising branch and the deblurring branch, respectively. α and β are the weighted parameters to balance the different loss functions. $\widehat{I}_{HR}$ is the recovered HR image from trunk SR branch. I_{HR} is the original sharp HR image. $\widehat{I}_{LRN}$ is the recovered noisy LR image without blur from the deblurring branch. I_{LRN} is original noisy LR image without blur. $\widehat{I}_{LRB}$ is the recovered blurry LR image without noise from the denoising branch. I_{LRB} is original blurry LR image without noise.

3   Experimental Results

3.1   Data Preprocessing and Network Training

To verify the recovery performance of MSFN on the multi-distortion images (LR images with blur and noise), we use the classical GoPro dateset [25] which contains total 200 pairs of HR blurry and sharp images for training and testing. In our experiments, we firstly do data augmentation by resizing each HR image pair with three random scales (within the scale of 0.5 and 1.0) and cropping each data pair into 256×256 blocks with the step of 128. We then obtain the pairs of LR blurry patches (I_{LRB}) and LR sharp patches (I_{LR}) by downsampling the responding HR pairs images. To constrain the denoising branch and deblurring branch to further promote the acquisition of high quality HR reconstructed images, we finally generate the LR noisy image (I_{LRN}) and the LR degraded image with blur and noise (I_{LRBN}) by adding gaussian noise to I_{LR} and I_{LRB}, respectively. Totally, we get 107,584 stacks ($I_{LRB}, I_{LRN}, I_{LRBN}, I_{LR}, I_{HR}$) for training and testing. Wherein, I_{LRB} and I_{LRN} used as constraint labels for the denoising and deblurring branches, respectively. The paired I_{LRBN} and I_{HR} are respectively used as the input and output of the main recovery branch.

We implement our MSFN model with Pytorch and the NVIDIA GTX 2080Ti GPU for all the training and evaluation. We optimize our network by the ADAM solver with $\beta 1 = 0.9$ and $\beta 2 = 0.999$. During training, 1×10^6 iterations are required. The trade-off weight parameter α and β in Eq. (4) are set to 0.05 and 0.05. The learning rate is set to 1×10^{-4}. Limited by the memory, the batch size is set to 8.

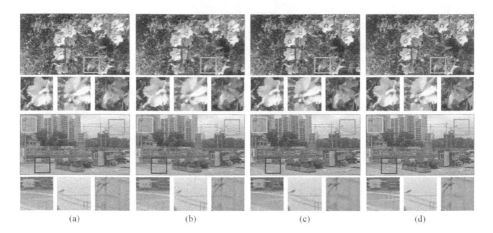

| (a) | (b) | (c) | (d) |

Fig. 3. Visual comparison of the multi-distortion image SR using different methods. (a) The input multi-distortion image. (b) RIDNet [24] + DeblurGAN [12] + EDSR [7]. (c) End-to-end method. (d) Our result.

3.2   Model Analysis

We study the influence of different pipeline sequences on the performance of the multi-distortion image recovery task to provide an experimental basis for our subsequent multi-stream fusion. Based on the existing models, we implement different processing pipes and test with SR factor of 4 and noise level of 25 on our generated training dataset. For example, DN [24] → DB [12] → SR [7] represents the deblurring operation followed by the denoising operation, and finally the SR is realized. The quantitative comparison results in Table 1 shows that executing DN [24] first or DB [12] first yields nearly the same performance. Although SR performes firstly can achieve a relatively ideal reconstruction effect, the amplified features will increase the resource consumption of subsequent tasks. If the denoising is not performed firstly, the performance of subsequent tasks will decline sharply due to the artifacts and error accumulation. Thus, we chooses to first fuse the denoising features and then fuse the deblurring features in the trunk SR recovery branch.

3.3   Results Analysis

To prove the effectiveness of our method for handling the problem of multi-distortion image recovery, we have done vast qualitative and quantitative experiments with several competing methods. Table 2 shows the comparative results of quantitative indicators. The end-to-end recovery method contains the same reconstruction network module as our method, which directly rebuilds the input LR blurry and noisy image into the HR sharp image. Different from our method, it does not adopt the multi-branch fusion. In the experiment, we use the same training data to retrain the end-to-end recovery method to ensure the fairness of

Table 1. Quantitative comparison of different pipelines on the denoising, deblurring and SR mixture distoration problem.

Model/Noise Level = 25	PSNR	SSIM
DB [12]→DN [24]→SR [7]	21.6361	0.5913
DB [12]→SR [7]→DN [24]	21.7009	0.5949
SR [7]→DB [12]→DN [24]	16.0332	0.1530
SR [7]→DN [24]→DB [12]	15.9984	0.1522
DN [24]→DB [12]→SR [7]	21.6164	0.5854
DN [24]→SR [7] ,DB [12]	21.6854	0.5857

Table 2. Quantitative comparison of our MSFN with other competitive methods. The best results are highlighted in bold.

Method	Noise level	PSNR	SSIM
DN [24]→DB [12]→SR [7]	10	23.040	0.595
End-to-End		24.122	0.811
Our		**25.311**	**0.842**
DN [24]→DB [12]→SR [7]	25	21.616	0.585
End-to-End		22.367	0.628
Our		**23.594**	**0.702**

the comparative experiment. From Table 2, we can see that our PSNR and SSIM are respectively ahead of other optimal methods. Obviously, our method shows superior performance both compared to end-to-end recovery method and the cascading recovery method. This is mainly because our method can asymptotically integrate denoising and deblurring features to reduce error accumulation and strengthen recovery constraints. In addition, the fusion module further promotes the fusion of effective recovery information. Figure 3 shows the qualitative comparison of several classical recovery methods with our MSFN. It clearly shows that our method achieves the more sharp HR recovery image with rich detail and structure, especially in the colored border area.

4   Conclusion

In this paper, we propose a multi-stream fusion network to achieve multi-distortion image super-resolution. The proposed MSFN not only verifies the influence of different degradation causes on the multi-distortion recovery task, but also determines the optimal recovery sequence. Meanwhile, the ability of the network to extract various recovery features is gradually enhanced by the constraints of the denoising branch and the deblurring branch. Additionally, our proposed fusion module further facilitates the fusion of various reconstructed features into the recovery network. Vast quantitative and qualitative experiments show that our MSFN can achieve LR blurry and noisy image recovery more effectively than most advanced methods. Furthermore, we will focus on optimizing the multi-distortion recovery model and solving the restoration problem of multi-distortion images in real scenes. It is expected to obtain better multi-distortion recovery effect and apply it to the actual scene.

Acknowledgement. This work was supported in part by the National Natural Science Foundation of China under Grants 62077037 and 61872241, in part by Shanghai Municipal Science and Technology Major Project under Grant 2021SHZDZX0102, in part by the Science and Technology Commission of Shanghai Municipality under Grants 18410750700 and 17411952600, in part by Shanghai Lin-Gang Area Smart Manufacturing Special Project under Grant ZN2018020202-3, and in part by Project of Shanghai Municipal Health Commission(2018ZHYL0230).

References

1. Zhang, B., Sheng, B., Li, P., Lee, T.: Depth of field rendering using multilayer-neighborhood optimization. IEEE Trans. Vis. Comput. Graph. **26**(8), 2546–2559 (2020)
2. Nazir, A., et al.: OFF-eNET: an optimally fused fully end-to-end network for automatic dense volumetric 3d intracranial blood vessels segmentation. IEEE Trans. Image Process. **29**, 7192–7202 (2020)
3. Dong, C., Loy, C.C., He, K., Tang, X.: Learning a deep convolutional network for image super-resolution. In: European Conference on Computer Vision, pp. 184–199 (2014)
4. Dong, C., Loy, C.C., Tang, X.: Accelerating the super-resolution convolutional neural network. In: Leibe, B., Matas, J., Sebe, N., Welling, M. (eds.) ECCV 2016. LNCS, vol. 9906, pp. 391–407. Springer, Cham (2016). https://doi.org/10.1007/978-3-319-46475-6_25
5. Kim, J., Lee, J.K., Lee, K.M.: Accurate image super-resolution using very deep convolutional networks. In: 2016 IEEE Conference on Computer Vision and Pattern Recognition (CVPR) (2016)
6. Lai, W., Huang, J., Ahuja, N., Yang, M.: Deep laplacian pyramid networks for fast and accurate super-resolution. In: IEEE Conference on Computer Vision and Pattern Recognition (CVPR), vol. 2017, pp. 5835–5843 (2017)
7. Lim, B., Son, S., Kim, H., Nah, S., Lee, K.M.: Enhanced deep residual networks for single image super-resolution. In: 2017 IEEE Conference on Computer Vision and Pattern Recognition Workshops (CVPRW) (2017)
8. Chen, Y., Liu, S., Wang, X.: Learning continuous image representation with local implicit image function, CoRR, vol. abs/2012.09161 (2020)
9. Gu, J., Dong, C.: Interpreting super-resolution networks with local attribution maps, CoRR, vol. abs/2011.11036 (2020)
10. Xu, L., Ren, J.S., Liu, C., Jia, J.: Deep convolutional neural network for image deconvolution. In: Ghahramani, Z., Welling, M., Cortes, C., Lawrence, N.D., Weinberger, K.Q. (eds.) Advances in Neural Information Processing Systems 27, Curran Associates Inc, pp. 1790–1798 (2014). http://papers.nips.cc/paper/5485-deep-convolutional-neural-network-for-image-deconvolution.pdf
11. Hradiš, M.: Convolutional neural networks for direct text deblurring. In: British Machine Vision Conference 2015 (2015)

12. Matas, J.: Deblurgan: blind motion deblurring using conditional adversarial networks. In: 2018 IEEE/CVF Conference on Computer Vision and Pattern Recognition (CVPR) (2018)
13. Xin, T., Gao, H., Shen, X., Wang, J., Jia, J.: Scale-recurrent network for deep image deblurring. In: 2018 IEEE/CVF Conference on Computer Vision and Pattern Recognition (CVPR) (2018)
14. Madam, N.T., Kumar, S., Rajagopalan, A.N.: Unsupervised class-specific deblurring. In: 15th European Conference, Munich, Germany, 8–14 September 2018, proceedings, part x (2018)
15. Dabov, K., Foi, A., Katkovnik, V., Egiazarian, K.: Color image denoising via sparse 3d collaborative filtering with grouping constraint in luminance-chrominance space. In: 2007 IEEE International Conference on Image Processing. IEEE (September 2007)
16. Gu, S., Zhang, L., Zuo, W., Feng, X.: Weighted nuclear norm minimization with application to image denoising, pp. 2862–2869 (2014)
17. Lefkimmiatis, S.: Non-local color image denoising with convolutional neural networks, pp. 5882–5891 (2017)
18. Zhang, K., Zuo, W., Chen, Y., Meng, D., Zhang, L.: Beyond a gaussian denoiser: Residual learning of deep cnn for image denoising. IEEE Trans. Image Process. **26**(7), 3142–3155 (2017)
19. Zhang, K., Zuo, W., Zhang, L.: Ffdnet: toward a fast and flexible solution for CNN-based image denoising. IEEE Trans. Image Process. **27**(9), 4608–4622 (2018)
20. Tai, Y., Yang, J., Liu, X., Xu, C.: Memnet: a persistent memory network for image restoration, pp. 4549–4557 (2017)
21. Guo, S., Yan, Z., Zhang, K., Zuo, W., Zhang, L.: Toward convolutional blind denoising of real photographs, pp. 1712–1722 (2019)
22. Zhang, X., Dong, H., Hu, Z., Lai, W.-S., Wang, F., Yang, M.-H.: Gated fusion network for joint image deblurring and super-resolution, CoRR, vol. abs/1807.10806 (2018)
23. Liang, Z., Zhang, D., Shao, J.: Jointly solving deblurring and super-resolution problems with dual supervised network. In: IEEE International Conference on Multimedia and Expo (ICME), vol. 2019, pp. 790–795 (2019)
24. Anwar, S., Barnes, N.: Real image denoising with feature attention. In: IEEE International Conference on Computer Vision, pp. 3155–3164 (2019)
25. Nah, S., Kim, T.H., Lee, K.M.: Deep multi-scale convolutional neural network for dynamic scene deblurring, pp. 257–265 (2017)

Generative Face Parsing Map Guided 3D Face Reconstruction Under Occluded Scenes

Dapeng Zhao[1] and Yue Qi[1,2,3(✉)]

[1] State Key Laboratory of Virtual Reality Technology and Systems,
School of Computer Science and Engineering at Beihang University, Beijing, China
qy@buaa.edu.cn
[2] Peng Cheng Laboratory, Shenzhen, China
[3] Qingdao Research Institute of Beihang University, Qingdao, China

Abstract. Over the past few years, single-view 3D face reconstruction methods can produce beautiful 3D models. Nevertheless, the input of these works is unobstructed faces. We describe a system designed to reconstruct convincing face texture in the case of occlusion. Motivated by parsing facial features, we propose a complete face parsing map generation method guided by landmarks. We estimate the 2D face structure of the reasonable position of the occlusion area, which is used for the construction of 3D texture. An excellent anti-occlusion face reconstruction method should ensure the authenticity of the output, including the topological structure between the eyes, nose, and mouth. We extensively tested our method and its components, qualitatively demonstrating the rationality of our estimated facial structure. We conduct extensive experiments on general 3D face reconstruction tasks as concrete examples to demonstrate the method's superior regulation ability over existing methods often break down. We further provide numerous quantitative examples showing that our method advances both the quality and the robustness of 3D face reconstruction under occlusion scenes.

Keywords: 3D face reconstruction · Face parsing · Occluded scenes

1 Introduction

3D face reconstruction refers to synthesizing a 3D face model given one input face photo. It has a wide range of applications, such as face recognition and digital entertainment [25]. Existing methods mainly concentrate on unobstructed faces, thus limiting the scenarios of their actual applications. Reconstructing a 3D face model from a single photo is a classical and fundamental problem in computer vision. The reconstruction task is challenging as human face structure partial invisibility when considering occluded scenes. Over the past five years, the related problem of face inpainting in images has gradually developed to the rationality of face photo generation in the most extreme scenes [15].

© Springer Nature Switzerland AG 2021
N. Magnenat-Thalmann et al. (Eds.): CGI 2021, LNCS 13002, pp. 252–263, 2021.
https://doi.org/10.1007/978-3-030-89029-2_20

We cannot use artificial intelligence to robustly predict the 3D texture of the occluded area of the face. On the other hand, when faces are partially occluded, existing methods often indiscriminately reconstruct the occluded area. With the assistance of face parsing map, we find a way to identify the occluded area and reconstruct the input image to a reasonable 3D face model. The main contributions are summarized as follows:

- We propose a novel algorithm that combines feature points and face parsing map to generate face with complete facial features.
- To address the problem of invisible face area under occluded scenes, we propose synthesizing input face photo based on Generative Adversarial Network rather than reconstructing 3D face directly.
- We have improved the loss function of our 3D reconstruction framework for occluded scenes. Our method obtains state-of-the-art qualitative performance in real-world images.

2 Related Works

2.1 Generic Face Reconstruction

The classic methods use reference 3D face models to fit the input face photo. Some recent techniques use Convolution Neural Networks (CNNs) to regress landmark locations with the raw face image. Some recent techniques firstly used CNNs to predict the 3DMM parameters with input face image.

2.2 Face Image Synthesis

Deep pixel-level face generating has been studied for a few years. Many methods achieve remarkable results. EdgeConnect [12] shows impressive proceeds which disentangling generation into two stages: edge generator and image completion network. Contextual Attention [22] takes a similar two-step approach. First, it produces a base estimate of the invisible region. Next, the refinement block sharpens the photo by background patch sets. The typical limitations of current face image generate schemes are the necessity of manipulation, the complexity of fundamental architectures, the degradation in accuracy, and the inability of restricting modification to local region.

3 Our Approach

3.1 Landmark Prediction Task

Figure 1 shows the entire process of our work. In the landmark prediction task, we found that generating accurate 68 feature points $\mathbf{Z_{lmk}} \in \mathbb{R}^{2 \times 68}$ was a crucial part under occlusion scenes. The architecture $\mathcal{N}_{lmk}$ aims to generate landmarks from a corrupted face photo $I_{cor} : \mathbf{Z_{lmk}} = \mathcal{N}_{lmk}(I_{cor}; \theta_{lmk})$, where θ_{lmk} denotes the trainable parameters. Since we want to focus more on efficiency and follow

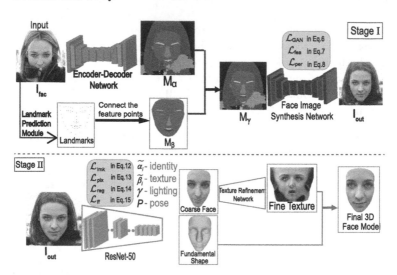

Fig. 1. Overall our pipeline. We first remove the occluded area and reconstruct the face with complete facial features. Then we utilize ResNet-50 and texture refinement network to reconstruct the final 3D model.

face parsing map generation task, we built a sufficiently effective $\mathcal{N}_{\text{lmk}}$ upon the MobileNet-V3 [6]. $\mathcal{N}_{\text{lmk}}$ is focused on feature extraction, unlike traditional landmark detectors. The final module is realized by fully connecting the fused feature maps. We set the loss function $\mathcal{L}_{lmk}$ as follows:

$$\mathcal{L}_{lmk} = \left\| \mathbf{Z}_{\text{lmk}}^{(i)} - \hat{\mathbf{Z}}_{\text{gt}}^{(i)} \right\|_2^2 \tag{1}$$

where $\hat{\mathbf{Z}}_{\text{gt}}^{(i)}$ denotes the ith ground truth face landmarks.

3.2   Face Parsing Map Generation

Pixel-level recognition of occlusion and face skin areas is a prerequisite for our framework to ensure accuracy. To benefit from the annotated face dataset CelebAMask-HQ [10], we used an encoder-decoder architecture $\mathcal{N}_\alpha$ based on U-Net [17] to estimate pixel-level label classes. Given a squarely resized face image $\mathbf{I_{fac}} \in \mathbb{R}^{H \times W \times 3}$, we applied the trained face parsing model $\mathcal{N}_\alpha$ to obtain the parsing map $\mathbf{M}_\alpha \in \mathbb{R}^{H \times W \times 1}$. On the other hand, given the landmarks $\mathbf{Z_{lmk}} \in \mathbb{R}^{2 \times 68}$, we connected the feature points to form a region. Then these regions can form a parsing map $\mathbf{M}_\beta \in \mathbb{R}^{H \times W \times 1}$ including facial features. Please notice that, in our work, we assumed that facial features only include only five parts, including facial skin, eyebrows, eyes, nose and lips. The final map $\mathbf{M}_\gamma \in \mathbb{R}^{H \times W \times 1}$ (see Fig. 2) without occluded objects needs $\mathbf{M}_\alpha$ plus $\mathbf{M}_\beta$. In order to generate $\mathbf{M}_\gamma$ including the complete facial features, we designed Algorithm 1.

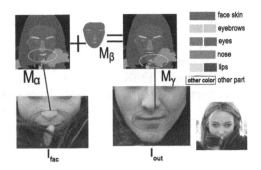

Fig. 2. Our face parsing map generation module, which follows Algorithm 1. The results shown in the figure show that our method finally successfully removed the occlusion of fingers and hair

---

Algorithm 1. Face Parsing Map Plus Algorithm, our proposed algorithm. All experiments in the papers Map **A** and Map **B** have the same width and height.

Input: A_i, pixels point on the face parsing map **A**. B_i, pixels point on the face parsing map **B**. $V(z)$, the function of getting the grayscale value of point z. $X(i)$, the horizontal coordinate value of i in the map. $Y(i)$, the vertical coordinate value of i in the map. W, the width of the map. H, the height of the map. S, the gray value range of the facial features area (only include four parts:eyebrows, eyes, nose, lips). O, gray value range of the facial skin area.

Input: Face parsing map **A** and **B**

Output: C_i, pixels point on the new face parsing map **C**

1: **while** $Y(i) <=$ H **do**   ▷ Start to generate complete face skin
2:          **while** $X(i) <=$ W **do**
3:                  **if** $A_i \in$ O **then**
4:                          $C_i \leftarrow A_i, X(i) + 1 \leftarrow X(i)$
5:                  **else if** A_i **NOT** $\in$ O **AND** $B_i \in$ O **then**
6:                          $C_i \leftarrow B_i, X(i) + 1 \leftarrow X(i)$
7:                  **else** $C_i \leftarrow A_i, X(i) + 1 \leftarrow X(i)$
8:          **end while**
9:      $Y(i) + 1 \leftarrow Y(i)$
10: **end while**
11:
12: **while** $Y(i) <=$ H **do**   ▷ Start to generate complete facial features
13:          **while** $X(i) <=$ W **do**
14:                  **if** $A_i \in$ S **then**
15:                          $C_i \leftarrow A_i, X(i) + 1 \leftarrow X(i)$
16:                  **else if** A_i **NOT** $\in$ S **AND** $B_i \in$ S **then**
17:                          $C_i \leftarrow B_i, X(i) + 1 \leftarrow X(i)$
18:                  **else** $C_i \leftarrow A_i, X(i) + 1 \leftarrow X(i)$
19:          **end while**
20:      $Y(i) + 1 \leftarrow Y(i)$
21: **end while**

3.3 Face Image Synthesis with GAN

Face Image Synthesis Network. To benefit from the Pix2Pix architecture, we proposed a Face Image Synthesis Network (FISN) $\mathcal{N}_{et}$, which was based on Pix2PixHD [26] as a backbone. FISN receives $\mathbf{I_{fac}} \in \mathbb{R}^{H \times W \times 3}$ and $\mathbf{M}_\alpha$ as inputs. The detailed architecture is shown in Fig. 1. To fuse $\mathbf{I_{fac}}$ and $\mathbf{M}_\alpha$, we used Spatial Feature Transform (SFT) layer [14] learned a mapping function $\mathcal{M}$ that outputs a parameter pair (γ, β) based on the prior condition Ψ from the features $\mathbf{M}_\alpha$. A pair of affine transformation parameters (γ, β) model the prior Ψ . Here, the mapping equation can be expressed as $(\gamma, \beta) = M(\Psi)$. After obtaining (γ, β) , the transformation is carried out by the SFT layer:

$$SFT(\mathbf{F_{map}}|\gamma, \beta) = \gamma \odot F + \beta \tag{2}$$

where $\mathbf{F_{map}}$ denotes the feature maps from $\mathbf{I_{fac}}$, $\odot$ denotes Hadamard product. Therefore, we conditioned spatial information $\mathbf{M}_\alpha$ on style data $\mathbf{I_{fac}}$ and generated affine parameters (x_i, y_i) followed $(x_i, y_i) = \mathcal{N}_{et}(I_{fac}, M_\alpha)$. Related research [14] showed that ordinary normalization layers would "wash away" semantic information. To transfer (x_i, y_i) to new mask input $\mathbf{M}_\gamma$, we utilized semantic region-adaptive normalization (SEAN) [29] on residual blocks z_i in the FISN. Let H, W and C be the height, width and the number of channels in the activation map of the deep convolutional network for a batch of N samples. The modulated activation value at the site was defined as:

$$SEAN(z_i, x_i, y_i) = x_i \frac{z_i - \mu(z_i)}{\sigma(z_i)} + y_i \tag{3}$$

where $\mu(z_i)$ and $\sigma(z_i)$ are the mean and standard deviation of the activation ($n \in N, c \in C, y \in H, x \in W$) in channel c :

$$\mu(z_i) = \frac{1}{NHW} \sum_{n,y,x} h_{n,c,y,x} \tag{4}$$

$$\sigma(z_i) = \sqrt{\frac{1}{NHW} \sum_{n,y,x} \left((h_{n,c,y,x})^2 - \mu(z_i)^2 \right)} \tag{5}$$

FISN is a generator that learns the style mapping between $\mathbf{I_{fac}}$ and $\mathbf{M}_\gamma$ according to the spatial information provided by $\mathbf{M}_\alpha$. Therefore, face features (*e.g.* eyes style) in $\mathbf{I_{fac}}$ are shifted to the corresponding position on $\mathbf{M}_\gamma$ so that FISN can synthesis image $\mathbf{I_{out}}$ which removed occlusion.

Loss Function. The design of our loss function for FISN is inspired by Pix2PixHD [26], MaskGAN [10] and SEAN [29], which contains three components:

(1) *Adversarial loss.* Let D_1 and D_2 be two discriminators at different scales, $\mathcal{L}_{GAN}$ is the conditional adversarial loss defined by

$$\mathcal{L}_{GAN} = \mathbb{E}\left[\log\left(D_{1,2}\left(\mathbf{I_{fac}}, \mathbf{M}_\alpha\right)\right)\right] + \mathbb{E}\left[1 - \log\left(D_{1,2}\left(\mathbf{I_{out}}, \mathbf{M}_\alpha\right)\right)\right] \tag{6}$$

(2) *Feature matching loss* [26]. Let T be the total number of layers in discriminator D .$\mathcal{L}_{fea}$ is the feature matching loss which computed the L_1 distance between the real and generated face image defined by

$$\mathcal{L}_{\mathbf{fea}}=\mathbb{E}\sum_{i=1}^{T}\left\|D_{1,2}^{(i)}\left(\mathbf{I_{fac}},\mathbf{M}_{\alpha}\right)-D_{1,2}^{(i)}\left(\mathbf{I_{out}},\mathbf{M}_{\alpha}\right)\right\|_{1} \tag{7}$$

(3) *Perceptual loss* [8]. Let N be the total number of layers used to calculate the perceptual loss, $F^{(i)}$ be the output feature maps of the ith layer of the VGG network [21].$\mathcal{L}_{per}$ is the perceptual loss which computes the L_1 distance between the real and generated face image defined by

$$\mathcal{L}_{\mathbf{per}}=\mathbb{E}\sum_{i=1}^{N}\frac{1}{M_i}[\left\|F^{(i)}\left(\mathbf{I_{fac}}\right)-F^{(i)}\left(\mathbf{I_{out}}\right)\right\|_{1}] \tag{8}$$

The final loss function of FISN used in our experiment is made up of the above-mentioned three loss terms as:

$$\mathcal{L}_{FISN}=\mathcal{L}_{GAN}+\lambda_1\mathcal{L}_{\mathbf{fea}}+\lambda_2\mathcal{L}_{\mathbf{per}} \tag{9}$$

where we set $\lambda_1=\lambda_2=10$ respectively in our experiments.

3.4   Camera and Illumination Model

Given an face image, we adopt the Basel Face Model (BFM) [16]. After the 3D face is reconstructed, it can be projected onto the image plane with the perspective projection:

$$V_{2d}\left(\mathbf{P}\right) = f * \mathbf{P_r} * \mathbf{R} * \mathbf{S_{mod}} + \mathbf{t_{2d}} \tag{10}$$

where $V_{2d}\left(\mathbf{P}\right)$ denotes the projection function that turned the 3D model into 2D face positions, f denotes the scale factor, $\mathbf{P_r}$ denotes the projection matrix, $\mathbf{R} \in SO(3)$ denotes the rotation matrix, $\mathbf{S_{mod}}$ denotes the shape of the face and $\mathbf{t_{2d}} \in \mathbb{R}^3$ denotes the translation vector.

We approximated the scene illumination with Spherical Harmonics (SH) [3] for face. Thus, we can compute the face as Lambertian surface and skin texture follows:

$$\mathbf{C}\left(\mathbf{r_i}, \mathbf{n_i}, \boldsymbol{\gamma}\right) = \mathbf{r_i} \odot \sum_{b=1}^{B^2}\boldsymbol{\gamma_b}\varPhi_b\left(\mathbf{n_i}\right) \tag{11}$$

where $\mathbf{r_i}$ denotes skin reflectance, $\mathbf{n_i}$ denotes surface normal, $\odot$ denotes the Hadamard product, $\boldsymbol{\gamma} \in \mathbb{R}^9$ under monochromatic lights condition, $\varPhi_b : \mathbb{R}^3 \to \mathbb{R}$ denotes SH basis function, B denotes the number of spherical harmonics bands and $\boldsymbol{\gamma_b} \in \mathbb{R}^3$ (here we set $B = 3$) denotes the corresponding SH coefficients.

Therefore, parameters to be learned can be denoted by a vector $\boldsymbol{y} = (\widetilde{\alpha_i}, \widetilde{\beta_i}, \boldsymbol{\gamma}, \boldsymbol{p}) \in \mathbb{R}^{175}$, where $\mathbf{p} \in \mathbb{R}^6 = \{\boldsymbol{pitch, yaw, roll, f, t_{2D}}\}$ denotes face poses. In this work, we used a fixed ResNet-50 [5] network to regress these coefficients. The loss function of ResNet-50 follows Eq. 16. We then got the fundamental shape $\mathbf{S_{base}}$ (coordinate, e.g. x, y, z) and the coarse texture $\mathbf{T_{coa}}$ (albedo, e.g. r, g, b). We used a coarse-to-fine network based on graph convolutional networks of Lin *et al.* [11] for producing the fine texture $\mathbf{T_{fin}}$.

3.5   Loss Function of 3D Reconstruction

Given a generated image $\mathbf{I_{out}}$,we used the ResNet to regress the corresponding coefficient y. The design of loss function for ResNet contained four components:

(1) Landmark Loss. As facial landmarks convey the structural information of the human face, we used landmark loss to measure how close projected shape landmark vertices to the corresponding landmarks in the image $\mathbf{I_{out}}$. We ran the landmark prediction module $\mathcal{N}_{lmk}$ to detect 68 landmarks $\left\{z_{lmk}^{(n)}\right\}$ from the training images. We obtained landmarks $\left\{l_{y}^{(n)}\right\}$ from rendering facial images. Then, we computed the loss as:

$$\mathcal{L}_{lmk}\left(y\right) = \frac{1}{N} \sum_{n=1}^{N} \left\| z_{\mathrm{lmk}}^{(n)} - l_{y}^{(n)} \right\|_{2}^{2} \tag{12}$$

where $\|\cdot\|_{2}$ denotes the L_2 norm.

(2) Accurate Pixel-wise Loss. The rendering layer renders back an image $\mathbf{I_y}^{(i)}$ to compare with the image $\mathbf{I_{out}^{(i)}}$. The pixel-wise loss is formulated as:

$$\mathcal{L}_{\mathrm{pix}}\left(y\right) = \frac{\sum_{i \in \mathcal{M}} P_i \cdot \left\| \mathbf{I_{out}^{(i)}} - \mathbf{I_y^{(i)}} \right\|_2}{\sum_{i \in \mathcal{M}} P_i} \tag{13}$$

where i denotes pixel index, $\mathcal{M}$ is the reprojected face region which obtained with landmarks [13], $\|\cdot\|_{2}$ denotes the L_2 norm and P_i is occlusion attention coefficient which is described as follows. To gain robustness to accurate texture, we set $P_i = \begin{cases} 1 & \text{if } i \in \text{facial features of } M_\alpha \\ 0.1 & \text{otherwise} \end{cases}$ for each pixel i.

(3) Regularization Loss. To prevent shape deformation and texture degeneration, we introduce the prior distribution to the parameters of the face model. We add the regularization loss as:

$$\mathcal{L}_{\mathrm{reg}} = \omega_\alpha \left\| \widetilde{\boldsymbol{\alpha_i}} \right\|^2 + \omega_\beta \left\| \widetilde{\boldsymbol{\beta_i}} \right\|^2 \tag{14}$$

here, we set $\omega_\alpha = 1.0$, $\omega_\beta = 1.75\text{e-}3$ respectively.

(4) Face Features Level Loss. To reduce the difference between 3D face with 2D image, we define the loss at face recognition level. The loss computes

the feature difference between the input image $\mathbf{I_{out}}$ and rendered image $\mathbf{I_y}$. We define the loss as a cosine distance:

$$\mathcal{L}_{ff}=1-\frac{<G(\mathbf{I_{out}}),G(\mathbf{I_y})>}{\|G(\mathbf{I_{out}})\|\cdot\|G(\mathbf{I_y})\|} \tag{15}$$

where $G(\cdot)$ denotes the feature extraction function by FaceNet [19], $<\cdot,\cdot>$ denotes the inner product.

In summary, the final loss function of 3D face reconstruction used in our experiment is made up of the above-mentioned four loss terms as:

$$\mathcal{L}_{3D}=\lambda_3\mathcal{L}_{lmk}+\lambda_4\mathcal{L}_{pix}+\lambda_5\mathcal{L}_{reg}+\lambda_6\mathcal{L}_{ff} \tag{16}$$

where we set $\lambda_3=1.6e-3, \lambda_4=1.4, \lambda_5=3.7e\text{-}4, \lambda_6=0.2$ respectively in all our experiments.

4   Implementation Details

Considering the question of landmark predictor, the 300-W dataset [18] has labeled ground truth landmarks, while the CelebA-HQ dataset [9] does not. We generated the ground truth of CelebA-HQ by the Faceboxes predictor [28] as the reference. In experiments shown in this work, we use the 256×256 images for training the landmark predictor $\mathcal{N}_{lmk}$ and the batch size $= 16$. The learning rate of $\mathcal{N}_{lmk}$ is $10e-4$. We use the trained face parsing model $\mathcal{N}_\alpha$ [10] to generate $\mathbf{M}_\alpha$. We obtain $\mathbf{M}_\gamma$ according to Algorithm 1. FISN follows the design of Pix2PixHD [26] with four residual blocks. To train the FISN, we used the CelebAMask-HQ dataset which has 30000 semantic labels with a size of 512×512. Each label clearly marked the facial features of the face.

FISN does not use any ordinary normalization layers (*e.g.* Instance Normalization) which will wash away style information. Before training the ResNet, we take the weights from pre-trained of R-Net [3] as initialization. We set the input image size to 224×224 and the number of vertices to 35709. We design our texture refinement network based on the Graph Convolutional Network method of Lin *et al.* [11]. We do not adopt any fully-connected layers or convolutional layers in the refinement network refer to related research [11]. This will reduce the performance of the module.

5   Experimental Results

5.1   Qualitative Comparisons with Recent Works

Figure 3 shows our results compared with the other work. The last two columns show our results.The remaining columns demonstrate the results of 3DDFA [4], DF^{2}Net [27] and Chen *et al.* [2]. Qualitative results show that our method surpasses other methods. Figure 3 shows that our method can reconstruct a complete face model under occlusion scenes such as glasses, jewelry, palms, and hair. Other methods focused on generating high-resolution face textures. These frameworks cannot effectively deal with occluded scenes.

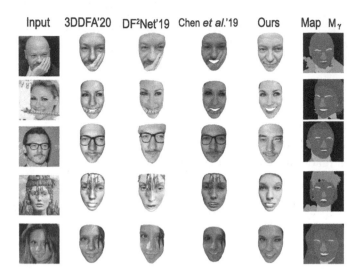

Fig. 3. Comparison of qualitative results. Baseline methods from left to right: 3DDFA, DF²Net, Chen *et al.* and our method.

5.2   Quantitative Comparison

Fig. 4. Comparison of error heat maps on the MICC Florence datasets. Digits denote 90% error (mm).

Comparison Result on the MICC Florence Datasets. MICC Florence dataset [1] is a 3D face dataset that contains 53 faces with their ground truth models. We artificially added some occluders as input. We calculated the average 90% largest error between the generative model and the ground truth model. Figure 4 shows that our method can effectively handle occlusion.

Occlusion Invariance of the Foundation Shape. Our choice of using the ResNet-50 to regress the shape coefficients is motivated by the unique robustness to extreme viewing conditions in the paper of Deng *et al.* [3]. To fully support the application of our method to occluded face images, we test our system on the Labeled Faces in the Wild datasets (LFW) [7]. We used the same face test system from Anh *et al.* [24], and we refer to that paper for more details.

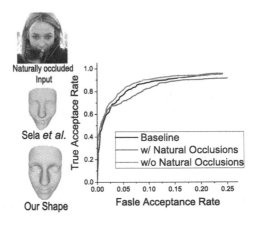

Fig. 5. Reconstructions with occlusions. Left: Qualitative results of Sela *et al.* [20] and our shape. Right: LFW verification ROC for the shapes, with and without occlusions.

Figure 5 (left) shows the sensitivity of the method of Sela et al. [20]. Their result clearly shows the outline of a finger. Their failure may be due to more focus on local details, which weakly regularizes the global shape. However, our method recognizes and regenerates the occluded area. Our method much robust provides a natural face shape under common occlusion scenes. Though 3DMM also limits the details of shape, we use it only as a foundation and add refined texture separately.

Table 1. Quantitative evaluations on LFW.

Method	100%-EER	Accuracy	nAUC
Tran *et al.* [23]	89.40 ± 1.52	89.36 ± 1.25	95.90 ± 0.95
Ours (w/ Occ)	85.75 ± 1.12	86.49 ± 0.97	93.89 ± 1.31
Ours (w/o Occ)	90.57 ± 1.43	89.87 ± 0.71	96.59 ± 0.37

We further quantitatively verify the robustness of our method to occlusions. Table 1 (top) reports verification results on the LFW benchmark with and without occlusions (see also ROC in Fig. 5 (right)). Though occlusions clearly impact recognition, this drop of the curve is limited, demonstrating the robustness of our method.

6   Conclusions

In this work, we present a novel single-image 3D face reconstruction method under occluded scenes with high fidelity textures. Comprehensive experiments have shown that our method outperforms previous methods by a large margin in terms of both accuracy and robustness. Future work includes combining our method with Transformer architecture to further improve accuracy.

Acknowledgment. This paper is supported by National Natural Science Foundation of China (No. 62072020), National Key Research and Development Program of China (No. 2017YFB1002602), Key-Area Research and Development Program of Guangdong Province (No. 2019B010150001) and the Leading Talents in Innovation and Entrepreneurship of Qingdao (19-3-2-21-zhc).

References

1. Bagdanov, A.D., Del Bimbo, A., Masi, I.: The florence 2d/3d hybrid face dataset. In: Proceedings of the 2011 Joint ACM Workshop on Human Gesture and Behavior Understanding, pp. 79–80 (2011)
2. Chen, A., Chen, Z., Zhang, G., Mitchell, K., Yu, J.: Photo-realistic facial details synthesis from single image. In: Proceedings of the IEEE International Conference on Computer Vision, pp. 9429–9439 (2019)
3. Deng, Y., Yang, J., Xu, S., Chen, D., Jia, Y., Tong, X.: Accurate 3d face reconstruction with weakly-supervised learning: From single image to image set. In: Proceedings of the IEEE Conference on Computer Vision and Pattern Recognition Workshops (2019)
4. Guo, J., Zhu, X., Yang, Y., Yang, F., Lei, Z., Li, S.Z.: Towards fast, accurate and stable 3d dense face alignment. arXiv preprint arXiv:2009.09960 (2020)
5. He, K., Zhang, X., Ren, S., Sun, J.: Deep residual learning for image recognition. In: Proceedings of the IEEE Conference on Computer Vision and Pattern Recognition, pp. 770–778 (2016)
6. Howard, A., et al.: Searching for mobilenetv3. In: Proceedings of the IEEE/CVF International Conference on Computer Vision, pp. 1314–1324 (2019)
7. Huang, G.B., Mattar, M., Berg, T., Learned-Miller, E.: Labeled faces in the wild: A database forstudying face recognition in unconstrained environments. In: Workshop on Faces in 'Real-Life' Images: Detection, Alignment, and Recognition (2008)
8. Johnson, J., Alahi, A., Fei-Fei, L.: Perceptual losses for real-time style transfer and super-resolution. In: Leibe, B., Matas, J., Sebe, N., Welling, M. (eds.) ECCV 2016. LNCS, vol. 9906, pp. 694–711. Springer, Cham (2016). https://doi.org/10.1007/978-3-319-46475-6_43
9. Karras, T., Aila, T., Laine, S., Lehtinen, J.: Progressive growing of gans for improved quality, stability, and variation. arXiv preprint arXiv:1710.10196 (2017)
10. Lee, C.H., Liu, Z., Wu, L., Luo, P.: Maskgan: towards diverse and interactive facial image manipulation. In: Proceedings of the IEEE/CVF Conference on Computer Vision and Pattern Recognition, pp. 5549–5558 (2020)
11. Lin, J., Yuan, Y., Shao, T., Zhou, K.: Towards high-fidelity 3d face reconstruction from in-the-wild images using graph convolutional networks. arXiv preprint arXiv:2003.05653 (2020)
12. Nazeri, K., Ng, E., Joseph, T., Qureshi, F.Z., Ebrahimi, M.: Edgeconnect: Generative image inpainting with adversarial edge learning. arXiv preprint arXiv:1901.00212 (2019)
13. Nirkin, Y., Masi, I., Tuan, A.T., Hassner, T., Medioni, G.: On face segmentation, face swapping, and face perception. In: 2018 13th IEEE International Conference on Automatic Face & Gesture Recognition (FG 2018), pp. 98–105. IEEE (2018)

14. Park, T., Liu, M.Y., Wang, T.C., Zhu, J.Y.: Semantic image synthesis with spatially-adaptive normalization. In: Proceedings of the IEEE Conference on Computer Vision and Pattern Recognition, pp. 2337–2346 (2019)
15. Parkhi, O.M., Vedaldi, A., Zisserman, A.: Deep face recognition (2015)
16. Paysan, P., Knothe, R., Amberg, B., Romdhani, S., Vetter, T.: A 3d face model for pose and illumination invariant face recognition. In: 2009 Sixth IEEE International Conference on Advanced Video and Signal Based Surveillance, pp. 296–301. IEEE (2009)
17. Ronneberger, O., Fischer, P., Brox, T.: U-net: convolutional networks for biomedical image segmentation. In: Navab, N., Hornegger, J., Wells, W.M., Frangi, A.F. (eds.) MICCAI 2015. LNCS, vol. 9351, pp. 234–241. Springer, Cham (2015). https://doi.org/10.1007/978-3-319-24574-4_28
18. Sagonas, C., Tzimiropoulos, G., Zafeiriou, S., Pantic, M.: 300 faces in-the-wild challenge: the first facial landmark localization challenge. In: Proceedings of the IEEE International Conference on Computer Vision Workshops, pp. 397–403 (2013)
19. Schroff, F., Kalenichenko, D., Philbin, J.: Facenet: a unified embedding for face recognition and clustering. In: Proceedings of the IEEE Conference on Computer Vision and Pattern Recognition, pp. 815–823 (2015)
20. Sela, M., Richardson, E., Kimmel, R.: Unrestricted facial geometry reconstruction using image-to-image translation. In: Proceedings of the IEEE International Conference on Computer Vision, pp. 1576–1585 (2017)
21. Simonyan, K., Zisserman, A.: Very deep convolutional networks for large-scale image recognition. arXiv preprint arXiv:1409.1556 (2014)
22. Song, Y., et al.: Contextual-based image inpainting: Infer, match, and translate. In: Proceedings of the European Conference on Computer Vision (ECCV), pp. 3–19 (2018)
23. Tuan Tran, A., Hassner, T., Masi, I., Medioni, G.: Regressing robust and discriminative 3d morphable models with a very deep neural network. In: Proceedings of the IEEE Conference on Computer Vision and Pattern Recognition, pp. 5163–5172 (2017)
24. Tun Trn, A., Hassner, T., Masi, I., Paz, E., Nirkin, Y., Medioni, G.: Extreme 3d face reconstruction: Seeing through occlusions. In: Proceedings of the IEEE Conference on Computer Vision and Pattern Recognition, pp. 3935–3944 (2018)
25. Wang, S., Cheng, Z., Deng, X., Chang, L., Duan, F., Lu, K.: Leveraging 3d blendshape for facial expression recognition using CNN. Sci. China Inf. Sci **63**(120114), 1–120114 (2020)
26. Wang, T.C., Liu, M.Y., Zhu, J.Y., Tao, A., Kautz, J., Catanzaro, B.: High-resolution image synthesis and semantic manipulation with conditional gans. In: Proceedings of the IEEE Conference on Computer Vision and Pattern Recognition, pp. 8798–8807 (2018)
27. Zeng, X., Peng, X., Qiao, Y.: Df2net: a dense-fine-finer network for detailed 3d face reconstruction. In: Proceedings of the IEEE International Conference on Computer Vision, pp. 2315–2324 (2019)
28. Zhang, S., Zhu, X., Lei, Z., Shi, H., Wang, X., Li, S.Z.: Faceboxes: a cpu real-time face detector with high accuracy. In: 2017 IEEE International Joint Conference on Biometrics (IJCB), pp. 1–9. IEEE (2017)
29. Zhu, P., Abdal, R., Qin, Y., Wonka, P.: Sean: image synthesis with semantic region-adaptive normalization. In: Proceedings of the IEEE/CVF Conference on Computer Vision and Pattern Recognition, pp. 5104–5113 (2020)

Compact Double Attention Module Embedded CNN for Palmprint Recognition

Yongmin Zheng[1], Lunke Fei[1(✉)] [iD], Wei Jia[2], Jie Wen[3], Shaohua Teng[1], and Imad Rida[4]

[1] School of Computers, Guangdong University of Technology, Guangzhou, China
[2] School of Computer and Information, Hefei University of Technology, Hefei, China
[3] Laboratory Shenzhen Medical Biometrics Perception and Analysis Engineering, Harbin Institute of Technology, Shenzhen, China
[4] Laboratory Biomechanics and Bioengineering, University of Technology of Compiegne, Compiegne, France

Abstract. Palmprint-based biometric recognition has received tremendous attention due to its several advantages such as high security, non-invasive and good hygiene propensities. Recent deep convolutional neural network (CNN) has been successfully applied for palmprint recognition and achieved promising performance due to its breakthroughs in image classification, which however usually requires a massive amount of labeled samples to finetune the network. In this paper, we propose a compact CNN with limited layers for palmprint recognition by embedding double attention mechanisms into the convolutional layers. Specifically, we first design a channel attention module to learn and select the discriminative channel maps by adaptively optimizing the attention weights among all channels. Then, we engineer a location attention module to learn the position-specific features of the palmprints. Both the channel and location attention modules are subsequently embedded into each convolutional layer, such that more discriminative features can be efficiently exploited during feature learning. Lastly, we train a fully convolutional network as the classifier for feature identification. Extensive experimental results on three widely used databases demonstrate the effectiveness of the proposed method in comparison with the state-of-the-arts.

Keywords: Pattern recognition · Biometric recognition · Palmprint recognition · Attention mechanism · Convolutional neural network

1 Introduction

With the rapid development of electronic payment and information safety, biometric authentication using physiological or behavioral traits, such as faces, fingerprints, iris and gait to identify individuals has received tremendous attention

© Springer Nature Switzerland AG 2021
N. Magnenat-Thalmann et al. (Eds.): CGI 2021, LNCS 13002, pp. 264–275, 2021.
https://doi.org/10.1007/978-3-030-89029-2_21

[1]. As two of the most widely used biometrics technologies, face and fingerprint recognitions have been successfully deployed in many practical applications [2,3]. However, during the outbreak of COVID-19, people wear masks and avoid contacting surfaces, making the conventional face and fingerprint recognition systems unavailable. As a relatively new biometric trait, palmprint contains rich characteristics such as principle lines, wrinkles and textures, which are treated to be unique to an individual. In addition, scanning a palmprint is not only fast due to its easy self-positioning but also highly acceptable due to its contactless and non-invasive properties. Therefore, palmprint recognition is a promising biometric technology and has drawn wide research attention.

In recent years, there have been a large number of methods proposed for palmprint recognition, which can be roughly classified into two categories: hand-crafted feature representation and learning-based feature representation. Hand-crafted feature representation methods usually directly extract the intrinsic features from palmprint images such as line features and direction features for palmprint recognition. For example, Xu et al. [4] proposed a discriminative and robust competitive code (DRCC) to extract more accurate direction features. Qiu et al. [5] extracted multiple direction features with large neighboring direction response differences for palmprint recognition. Zhao et al. [6] proposed a salient and discriminative descriptor (SDD) by jointly learning noise and salient information from the palmprint images. Zhao et al. [7] extracted the complete and salient local direction patterns to form the complete and discriminative direction feature for palmprint recognition. More hand-crafted feature representation methods can be found in a survey for palmprint feature extraction and recognition [8].

By contrast, the learning-based feature representation methods usually convert the original palmprint images into another subspace of features and then select the discriminative features for palmprint recognition, and the representative methods include the subspace learning, sparse representation and deep-learning methods. For example, Imad et al. [9] proposed a 2DLDA-based method for palmprint recognition. Liang et al. [10] proposed an orientation space code and designed a novel multi-feature sparse representation of two-phase for palmprint matching. Li et al. [11] proposed joint discriminative sparse coding for handbased multimodal recognition. Recently, there have been a trend to use deep learning method for palmprint recognition due to its promising effectiveness on image classification. For instance, Minaee et al. [12] designed a scattering network based on the wavelet transforms for palmprint feature extraction. Shao et al. [13] proposed a deep distillation hashing algorithm to convert palmprint images to binary codes for palmprint recognition. In general, the deep-learning method designs a complex deep architecture containing many layers such as multiple convolutional layers, pooling layers and classifier layers, which usually require plenty of labeled samples to finetune the network. However, palmprint images are usually limited because it is difficult to collect a large number of samples.

In this paper, we propose a compact double attention module embedded CNN (CDAM-Net) with few layers for palmprint feature extraction and recognition. We first extract the latent discriminative information based on convolution operations. Inspired by the fact that different convolution operation maps and positions of palmprint data have different discriminative powers for the final feature representations, we subsequently embed channel-attention and location-attention mechanisms into each convolutional layer. By doing these, the discriminative features of palmprint can be more efficiently exploited. Then, unlike the common fully connected network, we adopt a fully convolutional network (FCN) as the feature classifier for palmprint recognition. To the best of our knowledge, this is the first work with attempt to extend the attention mechanisms for palmprint recognition tasks. Finally, we conduct comparative experiments on three benchmark databases to demonstrate the effectiveness of the proposed method.

The rest of the paper is organized as follows. Section 2 reviews the related work. Section 3 elaborates our proposed CDAM-Net method. Section 4 presents the experimental results, and Sect. 5 offers the conclusion of the paper.

2   Related Work

In this section, we first briefly review CNN-based methods for palmprint recognition. Then, we introduce the basic idea of the attention mechanism that has been widely used for discriminative feature learning.

2.1   CNN-Based Palmprint Recognition Methods

Convolutional neural network (CNN) has achieved encouraging breakthroughs in pattern recognition and computer vision tasks. Inspired by these, there have also been many CNN-based approaches proposed for palmprint recognition [14]. For instance, Dian et al. [15] employed the AlexNet [16] to extract features for palmprint recognition. Tarawneh et al. [17] first extracted palmprint features by pretrained deep neural networks such as VGG-16 [18] and then used SVM for feature classification. In addition, Genovese et al. [19] proposed a CNN-based PalmNet based on the winner-take-all Gabor filtering responses and PCA principles. It is seen that most existing CNN-based palmprint recognition methods are usually pretrained on general image classification databases and then optimized on a large scale of labeled palmprint samples.

2.2   Attention Mechanism

Attention mechanism aims to bias the allocation of available computational resources towards the most informative features. Recently, many efforts have been devoted to embed attention mechanisms into network for discriminative feature learning. Unlike common model that treats input information without any distinction, attention module embedded network (AM-Net) focus on important information and suppress unnecessary ones during feature learning, so that the discriminative features can be effectively exploited. For example, Hu et al. [20] proposed squeeze-and-excitation (SE-block) that learned the channel-wise attention weights between channels to adaptively recalibrate feature responses for performance improvement. Woo et al. [21] presented a convolutional block attention module (CBAM) to learn the attention weights from both spatial and channel dimensions. In addition, Li et al. [22] proposed a selective kernel networks (SKNet) to dynamically generate convolutional kernel weights for scalable image classification. In this paper, we propose a compact DAM-Net by embedding double attention modules into limited convolutional layers for palmprint recognition.

3 The Proposed Method

In this section, we first present the overall framework of the proposed CDAM-Net. Then, we illustrate the mechanisms of the double attention modules.

3.1 The Framework of CDAM-Net

It is seen that deep CNN with powerful learning abilities has achieved impressive success for image classification tasks. In this paper we propose a compact CNN with five convolution layers for palmprint recognition. Figure 1 shows the overall pipeline of our proposed network. Specifically, our proposed CDAM-Net contains two sub-networks, i.e., feature extraction sub-network and feature recognition sub-network. The feature extraction sub-network consists of three convolutional layers, each of which has the size of 3 × 3, and the stride of 1 pixel, and is followed by the BN, ReLU and MaxPool layers. To better extract the discriminative features of the palmprint images from both channel and location levels, we subsequently embed double attention modules into each convolutional layer. After that, two convolutional layers, 512 and C convolutional kernels with the size of $w \times w$ and 1×1 are equipped to the classifier for palmprint feature recognition, where C is the number of classes in the database and w is the size of the final output from the feature extraction sub-network. Finally, a C-way softmax produces the classification results for palmprint recognition. It is worth noting that the flat operation is removed from our CDAM-Net, so that the spatial properties of the features can be well preserved during feature learning.

3.2 Double Attention Module (DAM)

Most existing studies have shown that different channels of the convolutional layers play different important roles for the final discriminative features. In addition, different palmprint regions have different structural information and it is desirable to extract position-specific features for discriminative feature representation. Motivated by these, in this paper, we design a DAM to respectively learn the attention weights from both the channel and location levels. Figure 2 shows the main idea of the proposed DAM. Given an intermediate feature map X, DAM first learns channel-wise attention weights among channels to extract a channel-specific feature map $F1$ and then learns the location-wise attention weights for final discriminative feature map $F2$ extraction. The overall process of the DAM can be summarized as:

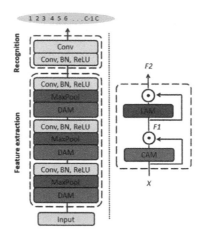

Fig. 1. (Left) The overall pipeline of our CDAM-Net method. First, we use three layers of convolution embedded with double attention modules (details shown in right) to extract discriminative features of the palmprints. Then, we engineer two convolutional layers for palmprint feature classification.

$$F1 = CAM(X) \odot X, \ and \ F2 = LAM(F1) \odot F1, \tag{1}$$

where $\odot$ denotes element-wise multiplication. $CAM(X)$ and $LAM(F1)$ respectively represent the learned channel-wise attention weights and location-wise attention weights. We first use the channel attention module (CAM) to convert the original image map into a channel-specific feature map, and then use the location attention module (LAM) to further learn the position-specific feature map. In the following, we present the detailed engineering of the CAM and LAM.

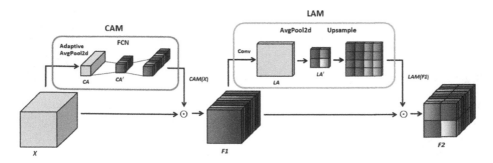

Fig. 2. The basic idea of the proposed DAM containing a channel attention module (CAM) and a location attention module (LAM), where the CAM aims to learn the channel-specific feature maps and the LAM exploits the position-specific features from palmprint images.

Channel Attention Module. Channel attention performs discriminative feature selections by amplifying the valuable feature channels and meanwhile suppressing the useless ones, which has been widely used in CNN for discriminative feature learning. Inspired by these, we design a channel attention module (CAM) to learn different attention weights for different convolutional channels. Previous studies [20] have shown that the average pooling of spatial statistics can effectively represent the local information of samples. Due to these, given an intermediate feature map $X \in \mathbb{R}^{W \times H \times C}$, we use adaptive average pooling to aggregate information from each input channel to obtain a spatial context descriptor, i.e., $CA \in \mathbb{R}^{1 \times 1 \times C}$. To preserve spatial structure information, we then forward the CA to two 1×1 convolutional layers for channel-wise attention weights learning. Finally, we adopt a sigmoid function to normalize the output channel-wise attention weights, i.e., $CAM(X)$. The calculation of the channel-wise attention weights can be represented as follows:

$$\begin{aligned} CAM(X) &= \sigma(FCN(AdaptiveAvgPool2d(X))) \\ &= \sigma(W_2(W_1(CA))), \end{aligned} \tag{2}$$

where σ denotes the sigmoid function for weight calibration, $W_1 \in \mathbb{R}^{1 \times C \times \frac{C}{R}}$ and $W_2 \in \mathbb{R}^{1 \times \frac{C}{R} \times C}$ represent the parameters of the two convolutional layers in the FCN respectively. In this paper, R is empirically set to 8 for efficient calculation.

Location Attention Module. In general, as shown in Fig. 3, different regions of a palmprint usually have different characteristics such as different line and wrinkle distributions, which generally have different discriminative information. Therefore, different receptive fields should be applied different attention weights during the feature learning. To this end, we engineer a location attention module (LAM) to adaptively learn the position-specific discriminative features from palmprint images. Specifically, for the output feature map with channel attention, i.e., $F1 \in \mathbb{R}^{W \times H \times C}$, we first feed it into a convolutional layer to learn a new attention feature descriptor, i.e., $LA \in \mathbb{R}^{W \times H \times 1}$, for 2-D spatial information representation. Then, we compute the average values to represent the local information weights, e.g., $LA' \in \mathbb{R}^{\frac{W}{T} \times \frac{H}{T} \times 1}$, by using a similar average pooling operation, where T decides the squeeze scale factor between the regions. In this paper, we empirically set T to 2. Moreover, we use a simple up-sample scheme to recover the same size with the $F1$ to broadcast the learned location-wise attention weights LA' to each position. Finally, it is normalized as the output location-wise attention weights, referred to as $LAM(F1)$, by using the sigmoid function. The location-wise attention weights calculation can be described as follows:

$$LAM(F1) = \sigma(Upsample(AvgPool2d(Conv(1, F1)))), \tag{3}$$

where $Conv(1,F1)$ represents a convolution calculation with the filter size of the 1×1 on the input $F1$.

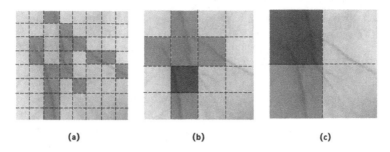

Fig. 3. Different regions of palmprint images usually have different line and texture characteristics. For example, (a) the yellow regions of palmprint have more line features than the other regions, and (b)(c) the red regions of palmprint contains more line features than the others. (Color figure online)

4   Experiments

In this section, we first conduct comparative experiments to evaluate the proposed method on three widely used palmprint databases. Then, we implement different variants of the AM embedded network and offer some visual results to evaluate the effectiveness of the DAM. Finally, we analyse different parameter settings of the DAM.

4.1   Databases

The CASIA palmprint database contains 5501 palmprint images from 310 individuals for both the left and right hands [23]. Each hand provided 8 to 10 palmprint images. In this experiment, we treat the left and right palms of an individual as two different classes, so there are from 620 different classes of samples in the CASIA database.

TongJi University (TJU) palmprint database contains 12,000 grayscale palmprint images collected from 600 different palms of 300 volunteers, including 192 men and 108 women [24]. Each palm provided 20 samples in two separated sessions. To improve the computational efficiency and without loss of generality, we form a subset by randomly selecting 10 palmprint images per palm to conduct experiments.

HeFei University of Technology (HFUT) palmprint database includes 16,000 palmprint images from 400 subjects of 800 hands, each of which provided 20 samples [25]. In our experiment, we form a dataset by randomly selecting 10 samples per palm so that 8000 samples of 800 classes are used.

4.2   Palmprint Identification Results

Palmprint identification is a "one-to-many" comparison procedure to identify the class of a query sample. In this section, we conducted palmprint identification experiments and compared the proposed method with most state-of-the-art methods to evaluate its effectiveness. Specifically, for each database, we randomly selected n palmprint images per palm to form the training set and used the remaining images as the query samples to evaluate performance, where n was set to 3 to 5 respectively. The recently published palmprint recognition methods such as DRCC, DoN [26], Ordinal code [23], neighboring direction indicator (NDI) [27], LDDC [5] and the representative VGG-16 were implemented. The VGG-16 network was first pretrained on the ImageNet database, and then fine tuned on the given palmprint databases. In addition, we implemented a variant of our proposed method by replacing the DAM with CBAM, referred to as CBAM-Net. All CNN-based methods were trained with the batch size 16 and the learning rate 1e-2 in 500 epochs. For a fair comparison, all the methods were performed for 10 times, and the average rank-one identification accuracy rates were reported. Table 1 tabulates the identification results of different methods on the CASIA, TJU and HFUT databases.

It can be seen from Table 1 that the proposed method consistently outperforms the other seven compared methods in term of identification accuracy rates. First, the proposed method achieves much better recognition performance than the conventional local palmprint feature descriptors such as DRCC, DoN, Ordinal code, NDI and LDDC. This is because these feature descriptors are handcrafted, which usually extract limited features and cannot robust represent contactless palmprint images captured under different environments. Second, our proposed CDAM-Net obviously improves the recognition performance over the VGG-16. The possible reason is that our proposed method embeds both channel and location attention mechanisms into the CNN, which can learn more channel-specific and position-specific discriminative features from palmprint images, so that better identification accuracy rates can be obtained. In addition, compared with CBAM-Net, our method also produces a better performance, demonstrating the promising effectiveness of the DAM for special palmprint recognition tasks.

Table 1. The average identification accuracy rates of different methods on the CASIA, TJU and HFUT databases.

Database	n	DRCC	DoN	Ordinal	NDI	LDDC	CBAM-Net	VGG-16	CDAM-Net
CASIA	3	73.83	60.21	58.40	62.35	95.29	97.31	94.65	**97.34**
	4	76.33	59.84	63.22	67.05	95.89	98.27	97.31	**98.37**
	5	77.26	65.55	66.45	69.33	96.18	98.63	97.88	**98.83**
TJU	3	99.05	98.35	98.49	99.10	99.80	99.60	96.29	**99.81**
	4	99.31	98.81	99.25	99.32	99.93	99.94	98.56	**99.97**
	5	99.58	99.25	99.41	99.68	99.94	**100.00**	99.47	**100.00**
HFUT	3	97.30	96.85	97.59	98.34	**99.82**	97.86	94.64	**99.82**
	4	98.07	98.35	97.84	98.73	99.93	98.69	97.35	**99.96**
	5	99.39	98.68	98.81	99.45	99.97	99.38	98.45	**100.00**

4.3   Effectiveness of the DAM

To evaluate the effectiveness of the DAM, we formed different AM embedded networks (AM-Net) and compared them with the CDAM-Net method. Specifically, we first referred the original five layers CNN without embedding both the CAM and LAM as the plain CNN. Then, we formed two networks by respectively embedding CAM and LAM into the plain CNN, which were referred to as CAM-Net and LAM-Net. Further, we also compared two different orders of channel and location attention modules arranging networks, including the first-channel-then-location AM network (referred to as CDAM-CL) and first-location-then-channel AM network (referred to as CDAM-LC). In this experiment, we implemented palmprint identification on the three palmprint databases to compare them, more experimental protocols refer to Subsect. 4.2. Figure 4 reports the average identification accuracy rates obtained based on different networks. It can be seen that in most instances, both the CAM and LAM can improve the recognition performance over the plain network, validating theirs effectiveness on discriminative palmprint feature learning. In addition, CDAM-CL performs better than the CDAM-LC. This because the channel maps usually contain the complete palmprint information that is suitable for the subsequent location-specific feature learning and selection.

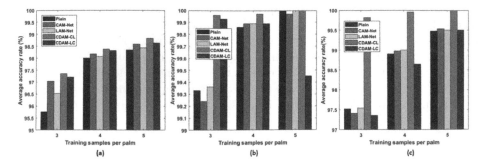

Fig. 4. The average identification accuracy rates of different AM embedded networks versus different number of training samples on the (a) CASIA, (b) TJU and (c) HFUT databases.

To better show the feature learning procedures of the DAM, we visualized the output maps of the two sub-modules. Figure 5 shows the feature maps learned by the CAM and LAM layers for the first convolutional layer. From which, we can see that the brightness of 32 different output channels obviously variant during the CAM feature learning. This is because the CAM adaptively enhances the importance of the discriminative feature channels. After that, the LAM learns detailed position-features and the discriminative positions such as line features are usually highlighted.

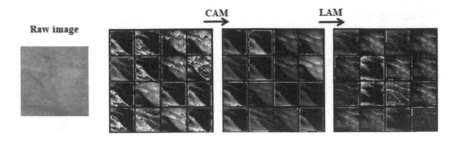

Fig. 5. The visualized feature maps obtained by DAM from the first convolution layer.

4.4   Parameter Analysis

CAM and LAM aim to obtain specific attention weights of palmprint features in two different levels, which actually have different parameter settings, such as the pooling mode, the size of convolutional kernel and the sub-network structure in the CAM. In this section, we set both sub-network structure as fully connected network (FC) and fully convolutional network (FCN) respectively, and set the pooling mode as adaptive MaxPool, AvgPool operations respectively in the CAM. In addition, for the LAM, we set both convolutional kernel size and pooling mode as 1×1 (Conv1), 3×3 (Conv3) and MaxPool, AvgPool operations respectively. We compared average identification accuracy rates of the two AMs versus different setting schemes on the CASIA database when 5 samples per palm are provided, as shown in Fig. 6. We can see that the CAM-Net method consistently achieves the best accuracy rates when it is equipped with FCN and adaptive AvgPool. The LAM-Net method can achieve promising recognition performance with the convolutional kernel size of 1×1 and AvgPool. Therefore, our proposed CDAM-Net has a suitable network structure for combining the CAM and LAM.

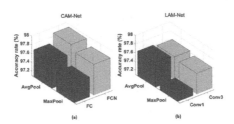

Fig. 6. The average identification accuracy rates of the (a) CAM-Net and (b) LAM-Net with different parameter settings on the CASIA database.

5   Conclusion

In this paper, we propose a compact CNN by embedding double attention mechanisms into limited convolutional layers for palmprint recognition. We respectively design channel and location attention modules to obtain the attention weights for both channel and position aspects, such that the discriminative features of palmprint images can be efficiently extracted. In particular, our proposed CDAM-Net contains only five convolutional layers, highly efficiently performing network training and palmprint recognition. Extensive experimental results on three widely used palmprint databases clearly demonstrate the promising effectiveness and efficiency of the proposed method. For future work, it could be interesting to extend our proposed CDAM-Net to other pattern recognition tasks such as texture image classification to further demonstrate its effectiveness.

Acknowledgments. This work was supported in part by the Guangzhou Science and technology plan project under Grant 202002030110, in part by the Natural Science Foundation of Guangdong Province under Grant 2019A1515011811, and in part by the National Natural Science Foundation of China under Grants 62076086 and 61972102.

References

1. Fei, L., Zhang, B., Tian, C., Teng, S., Wen, J.: Jointly learning multi-instance hand-based biometric descriptor. Inf. Sci. **562**, 1–12 (2021)
2. Hu, G., Yang, Y., Dong, Y., Kittler, J., Hospedales, T.: When face recognition meets with deep learning: an evaluation of convolutional neural networks for face recognition. In: IEEE International Conference on Computer Vision Workshop, pp. 384–392 (2015)
3. Wang, R., Han, C., Wu, Y., Guo, T.: Fingerprint classification based on depth neural network. Comput. Sci. **137**(25), 640–641 (2014)
4. Xu, Y., Fei, L., Wen, J., Zhang, D.: Discriminative and robust competitive code for palmprint recognition. IEEE Trans. Syst. Man Cybern. Syst. **48**(2), 232–241 (2018)
5. Qiu, Z., Fei, L., Teng, S., Zhang, W., Jia, W.: Local discriminative direction extraction for palmprint recognition. In: Chinese Conference on Biometrics Recognition, pp. 3–11 (2019)
6. Zhao, S., Zhang, B.: Learning salient and discriminative descriptor for palmprint feature extraction and identification. IEEE Trans. Neural Netw. Learn. Syst. **31**(12), 5219–5230 (2020)
7. Zhao, S., Zhang, B.: Learning complete and discriminative direction pattern for robust palmprint recognition. IEEE Trans. Image Process. **30**, 1001–1014 (2021)
8. Fei, L., Lu, G., Jia, W., Teng, S., Zhang, D.: Feature extraction methods for palmprint recognition: a survey and evaluation. IEEE Trans. Syst. Man Cybern. Syst. **49**(2), 346–363 (2019)
9. Rida, I., Al-Maadeed, S., Mahmood, A., Bouridane, A., Bakshi, S.: Palmprint identification using an ensemble of sparse representations. IEEE Access **6**, 3241–3248 (2018)
10. Liang, L., Chen, T., Fei, L.: Orientation space code and multi-feature two-phase sparse representation for palmprint recognition. Int. J. Mach. Learn. Cybern. **11**(7), 1453–1461 (2019). https://doi.org/10.1007/s13042-019-01049-7

11. Li, S., Zhang, B.: Joint discriminative sparse coding for robust hand-based multimodal recognition. IEEE Trans. Inf. Forensics Secur. **16**, 3186–3198 (2021)
12. Minaee, S., Wang, Y.: Palmprint recognition using deep scattering network. In: IEEE International Symposium on Circuits and Systems, pp. 1–4 (2017)
13. Shao, H., Zhong, D., Du, X.: Deep distillation hashing for unconstrained palmprint recognition. IEEE Trans. Instrum. Meas. **70**, 1–13 (2021)
14. Jia, W., Gao, J., Xia, W., Zhao, Y., Min, H., Lu, J.T.: A performance evaluation of classic convolutional neural networks for 2d and 3d palmprint and palm vein recognition. Int. J. Autom. Comput. **18**(1), 18–44 (2021)
15. Dian, L., Dongmei, S.: Contactless palmprint recognition based on convolutional neural network. In: International Conference on Signal Processing, pp. 1363–1367 (2016)
16. Krizhevsky, A., Sutskever, I., Hinton, G.: Imagenet classification with deep convolutional neural networks. In: Annual Conference on Neural Information Processing Systems, pp. 1106–1114 (2012)
17. Tarawneh, A.S., Chetverikov, D., Hassanat, A.B.: Pilot comparative study of different deep features for palmprint identification in low-quality images. In: Hungarian Conference on Computer Graphics and Geometry (2018)
18. Simonyan, K., Zisserman, A.: Very deep convolutional networks for large-scale image recognition. In: International Conference on Learning Representations (2015)
19. Genovese, A., Piuri, V., Plataniotis, K.N., Scotti, F.: Palmnet: Gabor-PCA convolutional networks for touchless palmprint recognition. IEEE Trans. Inf. Forensics Secur. **14**(12), 3160–3174 (2019)
20. Hu, J., Shen, L., Albanie, S., Sun, G., Wu, E.: Squeeze-and-excitation networks. IEEE Trans. Pattern Anal. Mach. Intell. **42**(8), 2011–2023 (2020)
21. Woo, S., Park, J., Lee, J.Y., Kweon, I.S.: CBAM: convolutional block attention module. In: European Conference on Computer Vision (2018)
22. Li, X., Wang, W., Hu, X., Yang, J.: Selective kernel networks. In: IEEE Conference on Computer Vision and Pattern Recognition, pp. 510–519 (2019)
23. Sun, Z., Tan, T., Wang, Y., Li, S.: Ordinal palmprint represention for personal identification. In: IEEE Computer Society Conference on Computer Vision and Pattern Recognition, pp. 279–284 (2005)
24. Zhang, L., Li, L., Yang, A., Shen, Y., Yang, M.: Towards contactless palmprint recognition: a novel device, a new benchmark, and a collaborative representation based identification approach. Pattern Recogn. **69**(1), 199–212 (2017)
25. Jia, W., et al.: Palmprint recognition based on complete direction representation. IEEE Trans. Image Process. **26**(9), 4483–4498 (2017)
26. Zheng, Q., Kumar, A., Pan, G.: A 3d feature descriptor recovered from a single 2d palmprint image. IEEE Trans. Pattern Anal. Mach. Intell. **38**(6), 1272–1279 (2016)
27. Fei, L., Zhang, B., Xu, Y., Yan, L.: Palmprint recognition using neighboring direction indicator. IEEE Trans. Hum. Mach. Syst. **46**(6), 298–787 (2016)

M2M: Learning to Enhance Low-Light Image from Model to Mobile FPGA

Ying Chen[1], Wei Wang[1,2(✉)], Wei Hu[1,2], and Xin Xu[1,2]

[1] School of Computer Science and Technology, Wuhan University of Science and Technology, Wuhan, Hubei, People's Republic of China
[2] Hubei Province Key Laboratory of Intelligent Information Processing and Real-time Industrial System, Wuhan University of Science and Technology, Wuhan, Hubei, People's Republic of China
wangwei8@wust.edu.cn

Abstract. With the development of convolutional neural networks, the effectiveness of low-light image enhancement techniques have been greatly advanced. However, the calculate-intensive and memory-intensive characteristics of convolutional neural networks make them difficult to be implemented in mobile platform with low power and limited bandwidth. This paper proposes a complete solution for low-light image enhancement from CNN model to mobile (M2M) FPGA. The proposed solution utilizes a pseudo-symmetry quantization method to compress the low-light image enhancement model, and an accelerator to permit the processing ability of the system significantly. We implemented the whole system on a customized FPGA SOC platform (a low-cost chip, Xilinx Inc. ZYNQ^{TM} XC7Z035). Extensive experiments show that our method achieved competitive results with the other three platforms, *i.e.* achieved better speed compare to ARM and CPU; and achieved better power efficiency compared to ARM, CPU, and GPU.

Keywords: Low light image enhancement · Model to mobile FPGA · Model quantization

1 Introduction

From the past to the foreseeable future, high quality image acquisition is always an important computer vision task and serve as a basis for the following image detection, recognition, and understanding tasks. Meanwhile, poor visibility environment pose great challenges to clarity and integrity visual information of image, such as low-light condition [1–3]. In order to solve this problem, Convolutional Neural Networks (CNN) flourished with breakthrough results [4,5]. However, CNN-based methods are computationally intensive, highly storage demanding, and energy consuming. Meanwhile, many real-time industrial applications in

This work was supported by the Natural Science Foundation of China (U1803262, 61602349, and 61440016).

scientific exploration and civilian fields cannot meet the hardware requirements for these deep learning approaches, such as aerial vehicles [6], ground vehicles [7], and underwater vehicles [8] since their platform have limited computational resources. Therefore, hardware-based low light image enhancement research is in great demand.

Deep learning-based low-light image enhancement methods have attracted attention in this decade and are mainly classified into two types of methods, CNN-based and GAN-based. To reference the existing photo-shopping software that uses the 'curve' function to automatically adjust the brightness, Guo et al. [9] designed a CNN to fit the curve. Wei et al. [10–13] designed CNN for deep hybrid models by Retinex theory. Cai et al. [14] considered the low-light image enhancement technique as an exposure conversion task and designed a set of exposure factors for multi-exposure fusion to enhance the image. Xu et al. [15–17] enhances low-light images while suppressing noise by unsharpening detail information such as color and brightness. There are also various approaches using Retinex theory [18], which generally breaks down the images into reflectance and illumination. On this basis, Li et al. [19,20] proposed different types of different approaches by modifying and extending the Retinex model. GAN network-based approaches have been proposed [21–23], while work [23] combines the advantages of CNN and GAN to enhance the image in two stages. However, due to the nature of CNN and GANs, they are both resource-intensive and difficult to deploy on embedded mobile FPGA platforms. Recently, Xu et al. [24] implemented an FPGA-based low-light image enhancement by Adaptive Histogram Equalization (AHE) method. The speed can be accelerated without CNN, but also without significant performance improvement. Consequently, implementing CNN-based algorithms directly on mobile terminals for low-light environments still need to be addressed. **Unfortunately**, no work has been seen so far to implement deep-learning-based low-light image enhancement on mobile FPGA-embedded platforms.

There are some works on CNN model compression in related vision task. In the software approach of model quantizied compression, some researches have shown that the inference of CNN can be accelerated using approximate value computation [25–28]. Both the precision and operands of CNN can be reduced without seriously affecting the inference performance. The throughput rate and energy efficiency of the computation are improved by a minimum number of weights precision to reduce the total amount of bandwidth required to relieve bandwidth pressure. In the hardware approach, there are accelerations designed of by buffer management [29,30], bandwidth optimization [31,32], and other methods have been proposed. This direction targets to accelerate the system computation by fully utilization of resources on FPGA. Due to the limited resources of FPGA devices and the large number of operations designed in the deep topology, state-of-the-art implementations promote limited parallelism by mapping a limited number of processing units on FPGA [33]. Both works achieved a reasonable accuracy and a comparable speed, but still cannot overcome the fact that the system almost loses its detection capability under the low-light conditions.

To the best of our knowledge, we are the first deep learning based solution for low-light image enhancement from model to mobile (M2M) FPGA. We follow the general scheme o.f deep learning tasks deploy on FPGA: a quantized model to reduce storage and computing requirements while minimizing the impact on results. After that, we layout the overall algorithm onto the FPGA and add an acceleration to CNN. Finally, we input the image after grid and compare the results. Moreover, we propose a dynamic way to make the images smooth after gird. Specifically, this paper makes contributions as following:

1. We propose the first CNN-based low-light image enhancement on FPGA. We show that the enhancement on a low-cost FPGA chip is comparable to existing stat-of-art works on GPU.
2. We analyze the distribution of model weights and propose a solution to the difficulty of quantized compression of low-light image enhancement model weights.
3. We propose an accelerator for CNN-based low-light image enhancement, which eases the on-chip conflicts between limited computational power and increased cost.

2   Approach

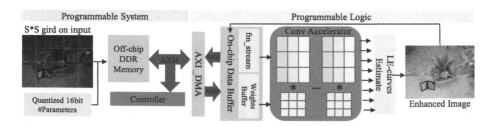

Fig. 1. Overall system framework.

The proposed system framework is shown in Fig. 1. The framework design mainly consists of off-chip memory, off-chip interconnect, on-chip buffer, on-chip interconnect, acceleration processing unit, and LEC processing unit. First, we store all the data to be processed in the off-chip memory DDR. Due to on-chip resource and bandwidth constraints, the data is first cached in on-chip buffers before being provided to the acceleration and communicated through the AXI bus. We design a double buffer for weights and feature maps data to cover the computation time and data transfer time. PE is the basic computation unit within the convolutional acceleration. The on-chip interconnect is dedicated to the data communication between PE and the on-chip buffer. Finally, we splice all the enhanced pixel data in the cache as the final image result and return the output. In this section, we will introduce our quantification method on the software side in Sect. 2.1 and our optimization method on the hardware side in Sect. 2.2.

2.1 Quantization

Model quantization is an optimization technique that can effectively reduce the model size and accelerate deep learning inference. Quantization can reduce memory bandwidth and storage space, and deep learning models mainly record weights and biases for each layer. In the FP32 model, each weight value originally requires 32-bit storage space, but after quantization, only fewer bits are needed. This means that the low-precision inference process will significantly reduce the memory access bandwidth requirement and improve the cache hit rate, especially for memory-bound element-wise operators such as batch-norm, relu, element-wise sum, and so on.

Quantification increases system throughput and reduces system latency. For a Direct Memory Access (DMA) with a dedicated register width of 32 bits, one instruction can process only one values at a time when the data type is FP32, but when we use a lower precision representation of the data, one instruction can process more pairs of values at a time. In this case, the theoretical computational speed peak of the chip can be increased several times. Quantification is the process of mapping values from $\mathcal{W}$ whose domain is usually continuous to countable $\mathcal{Y}$, whose domain contains much less data values [34]. For low-precision CNN, the full-precision matrix $\mathcal{W} \in \mathbb{R}$ for each layer is defined in $\mathcal{W}$ domain and maps with a quantization function $\mathcal{F}$, then results in a weight matrix $Q_{i,j} \in \mathbb{Q}$:

$$Q_{i,j} = \mathcal{F}(\mathcal{W})_{i,j}. \tag{1}$$

Specifically for each tensor, we use w_f to denote the original floating-point tensor, $\mathcal{Y}_i$ to denote the quantized tensor result of the function $\mathcal{F}$, q_w to denote the quantization ratio, i.e., the scaling ratio, and n to denote the number of bytes of the quantized value. Then the asymmetric quantization formula algorithm is as follows:

$$\begin{aligned} \mathcal{Y}_{ps} &= round\left((w_f - min_{w_f}) \frac{2^n - 1}{max_{w_f} - min_{w_f}}\right) \\ &= round(q_w w_f - min_{w_f} q_w) \\ &= round(q_w w_f - z_w). \end{aligned} \tag{2}$$

The zero point is usually an integer:

$$q_w = fix\left(q_w min(w_f)\right). \tag{3}$$

Therefore, the 0 value in a floating-point number corresponds to exactly this integer after quantization. This also means that the zeropoint can quantize the data 0 in the floating-point number without error. This reduces the extra error in quantization from zero-padding operations (such as padding zero in the convolution). However, from the above equation, we can find that the result of q_w

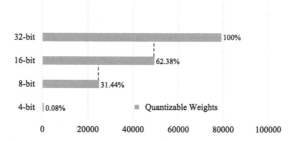

Fig. 2. Distribution of the validity of the weights after quantification at different scales.

can only be a non-negative number, which also means that it cannot reasonably handle signed integer quantization.

We show the distribution of the weights of the model for this image enhancement task in Fig. 2. Through the analysis we found that the precision of the weights of this particular model is unequally distributed, some of the weights have high precision and the positive and negative signs of the model weights have a decisive impact on the results. Therefore, neither symmetric nor asymmetric quantization can solve the practical difficulties. In this regard, we propose the pseudo-symmetric quantization formula:

$$
\mathcal{Y}_i = \left\{ \begin{array}{ll} round\left(\dfrac{2^{n-1}-1}{max_{w_f}}\right), & s.t.\ w_f > 0 \\[3mm] round\left(-\dfrac{2^{n-1}-1}{min_{w_f}}\right), & s.t.\ w_f \leq 0 \end{array} \right\}. \tag{4}
$$

We control the overflow of data by fixed points. Given a number α and a target fixed point target $<IL, FL>$, we define α as the largest integer multiple of $\beta = 2^{-FL}$ less than or equal to α. The quantized weights in fix-point α_{fixed} is as fellow:

$$
fix(\alpha, <IL, FL>) = \left\{ \begin{array}{ll} \lfloor \alpha \rfloor, & s.t.\ w_f > 0 \\[2mm] \lfloor \alpha \rfloor + \beta, & s.t.\ w_f \leq 0 \end{array} \right\}. \tag{5}
$$

Here, we bring the quantized tensor $\mathcal{Y}_i$ into α, the final quantization result is obtained.

2.2   Hardware Optimizations

Convolutional computation is the most important component of CNN, which involves three-dimensional multiplication and accumulation operations where most of the computational resources are used. CNN is difficult to deploy on FPGA mobile platforms, A complete convolution computation requires six dimensional loops, which are the channel of the output feature maps, the channel of the input feature maps, the height of the feature maps, the width of the

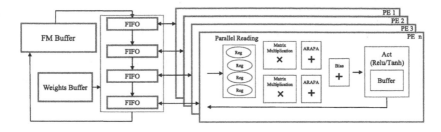

Fig. 3. Acceleration processing unit architecture design.

feature maps, the height of the convolution kernels and the width of the convolution kernels. It mainly reflects the computational intensities and memory intensities of the convolutional computation process centrally. In order to make convolutional computation run efficiently on FPGA mobile platforms, we need to design a convolutional accelerator to speed it up.

First, the load imbalance of the weights after quantization will reduce the hardware efficiency. Different factors will be consumed by multiple PEs, so the operations of all PEs must be synchronized. However, the different scale quantization makes hardware computations on different data more complex and irregular, shifting is necessary for different layers and thus requires a well-designed controller. The hardware design should support input vector sharing for multi-channel systems, to perform multiple networks with vectors at the same time.

We derive a legitimate design variant of the equivalent convolutional computational implementation through loop scheduling and allocation management, the structure of which is shown in Fig. 3. The target of computational optimization is to achieve efficient loop unrolling/pipelining while making the best possible utilization of all computational resources provided by the FPGA hardware platform.

As shown in Fig. 3, we first extract several process functions from the main convolutional computing operation. Then, we use FIFOs to connect them with blocking read and non-blocking write All process functions run concurrently, and the execution of each function is triggered by the arrival of data, thus reaching instruction-level parallelism [35]. For a given array, the data sharing relationships between different loop iterations of a loop dimension can be classified into three types: (1) Independent data sharing relationships, which generate direct connections between buffers and computation engines. (2) Unrelated data sharing relationships, which generate broadcast connections. (3) Dependent data sharing relationships, which generate complex topological interconnections. We choose the appropriate solution to six loops of convolutional data sharing by concerning [36]. The loop dimension is also chosen to be unrolled to avoid the complex connection topology of all arrays. Output channels and input channels are arranged to the innermost loop level.

Loop unrolling can improve the utilization of large computational resources in FPGA devices. Unfolding along different loop dimensions will result in different implementation variables [37]. The extent to which data is shared with two instances of the implementation whether or not it is unrolled will affect the complexity of the generated hardware, and ultimately affect the number of unrolled copies and the frequency of hardware operations. On entry to PE, we map part of the length of data directly to the registers in one clock cycle, reducing the extremely time-consuming read operations. This can lead to critical clock disorder, and we stabilize the clock by skipping the compute and write operations in that cycle with a small amount of wait.

3   Experimental Results

Table 1. FPGA resource utilization.

Module	LUTs	FFs	BRAMs	DSP48Es
CNN	78685	48433	437	640
	(45%)	(14%)	(43%)	(71%)
LEC	45310	18257	355	100
	(32%)	(5%)	(36%)	(11%)
Total	132995	66690	792	740
	(77%)	(19%)	(79%)	(82%)

We followed the work of [9] for the network structure design and training. A set of pixel-level curve parameter maps is input for the corresponding higher-order curves. Seven symmetrically spliced convolutional layers were used to form the CNN, each layer containing 32 convolutional kernels of size 3×3 with a stride of 1, followed by a ReLU or Tanh activation function. No down-sampling and batch normalization layers are used, which would break the connection between adjacent pixels. The last convolutional layer is used to prepare a parametric mapping of 24 channels for the next eight iterations through the Tanh activation function, of which three channels are used for each iteration. To fully leverage the power of wide dynamic range adjustment, we include both low-light and over-light images into our training set. For this purpose, we use multi-exposure sequences from Part 1 of the SICE dataset [14] to train the network. We randomly split the images of Part 1 with different exposure levels into two parts, most of which are used for training and the rest for validation. We use the PyTorch framework to train on an NVIDIA Titan Xp GPU, and store the trained model in integer format on the DDR3 memory of the FPGA board after quantization.

We implemented our system design on a Xillinx Inc. custom development board with a dual-core ARM Cortex-A9, a ZYNQ XC7Z035-2FFG676-2 FPGA, and 1 GB of DDR3 SDRAM storage. The FPGA resources are 171, 900 LUTs, 343, 800 FFs, 1,000 18 Kb BRAMs, and 900 DSP48Es, making it a low-cost development board with few resources. We use Xilinx Inc. Vivado 2018.3 synthesized and deployed with a clocking constraint of 100 Mhz. Our implementation uses

132,995 LUTs, 66,690 FFs, 792 18 Kb BRAMs, and 740 DSP48Es for the example of 16-bit quantization of weights and biases with fixed-point storage. Table 1 shows the details of the resource utilization. There are two main time-consuming parts in our implementation, the CNN module executes the stored deep learning model and the LEC module accomplishes the LE-curve estimation, which provides the final output image.

3.1 Visual Comparisons

| Input | AHE | Ours |

Fig. 4. Visual comparison with FPGA-based AHE method [24].

Compare with Another FPGA-Based Method. We give a visual comparison of another state-of-the-art FPGA-based AHE methods [24] with the results of our 16-bit quantization scheme in Fig. 4. In the left-up and left-down corners, there are dark regions in the FPGA-based AHE [24] results while our results reveal the underlying sky and river color. Moreover, FPGA-based AHE method [24] eliminates the over-exposure spotlight in the middle of this image while our approach trustfully preserve the spotlight and brighten the neighboring dark regions. By implementing our CNN-based methods, we achieved better effects in brightness, color reproduction and realism.

Compare with Other GPU-Based Methods. We give a visual comparison of other state-of-the-art GPU-based methods with the results of our 16-bit quantization scheme in Fig. 5. We compared with EnlightenGan [22], Kind [13], RetinexNet [10] and ZERO-DCE [9]. There are some over-exposure regions exist in the result of Kind [13]and RetinexNet [10], since the color saturation decreases in their first, fourth and fifth images. On the contrary, our FPGA-based result enhances the visual perception intuitively, strengthening the dark areas and preserving the original image colors without significant noise and chromatic aberration.

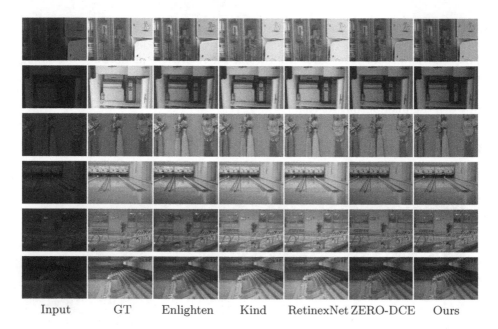

Input   GT   Enlighten   Kind   RetinexNet ZERO-DCE   Ours

Fig. 5. Visual comparison of other state-of-the-art GPU-based methods with the results of our 16-bit quantization scheme

3.2   Comparison with Other Platforms

We compared our approach on FPGA with other platforms. We resize the images to 200×133 and chose the NVidia Titan-Xp GPU, Intel i7-8700 CPU, and Cortex-A9 embedded ARM for comparison. We tested the power consumption. The power consumption of GPU and CPU is taken from the user manual. To test the latency, we set the batch size to one, the frames per second (FPS) of our system is 7.37. In Table 2 we show the comparison between the FPGA platform and other platforms. Compared to ARM Cortex-A9, we are 41 times faster and 99 times power efficient. Compared to the CPU, we are 38 times faster and 40 times power efficient. And compared to GPU, we are 1.2 times more power-efficient. Consequently, our approach is suited for low-light image enhancement on embedded platforms.

Table 2. Comparison with other platforms with our low-light image enhancement.

Platform	GPU	CPU	Embedded ARM	FPGA
Device	Titan Xp	i7-8700	Cortex-A9	XC7Z035
Technique (nm)	16	16	14	28
Clock Freq	1.5 GHz	3.20 GHz	833 MHz	100 MHz
Memory	12 GB GDDR5X	64 GB DDR4	500 MB DDR3	17.5 MB BRAM
Power (W)	250	85	3.8	3.9
Performance	389.90	1.67	0.18	7.37
Energy efficiency (FPS/W)	1.56	0.019	0.047	1.89

4   Conclusion

In this paper, we present the first method for deep learning-based low-light image enhancement on FPGA. To reduce the storage and computational requirements, we propose a pseudo-symmetric quantization method. For the compression ratio of different quantization scales and the impact on the results, we choose an optimal quantization scheme to compress the model to reduce the impact on the results. After that, we deploy the overall algorithm to a low-cost Xillinx Inc. custom FPGA development board and accelerate the CNN by our proposed acceleration design scheme. Therefore, our method is suitable for low-light image enhancement on embedded FPGA.

References

1. Xu, X., Liu, L., Zhang, X., Guan, W., Hu, R.: Rethinking data collection for person re-identification: active redundancy reduction. Pattern Recogn. **113**(4), 107827 (2021)
2. Xu, X., Wang, S., Wang, Z., Zhang, X., Hu, R.: Exploring image enhancement for salient object detection in low light images. ACM Trans. Multimedia Comput. Commun. Appl. **17**(8), 1–19 (2020)
3. Xie, P., Xu, X., Wang, Z., Yamasaki, T.: Unsupervised video person re-identification via noise and hard frame aware clustering, pp. 1–6 (2021)
4. Mu, N., Xu, X., Zhang, X., Lin, X.: Discrete stationary wavelet transform based saliency information fusion from frequency and spatial domain in low contrast images. Pattern Recogn. Lett. **115**, 84–91 (2018)
5. Mu, N., Xu, X., Zhang, X.: Salient object detection in low contrast images via global convolution and boundary refinement. In: 2019 IEEE/CVF Conference on Computer Vision and Pattern Recognition Workshops (CVPRW), pp. 743–751 (2019)
6. Hu, J., Zhang, H., Song, L., Han, Z., Poor, H.V.: Reinforcement learning for a cellular internet of UAVs: protocol design, trajectory control, and resource management. IEEE Wirel. Commun. **27**(1), 116–123 (2020)
7. Yu, W., Shaobo, W., Xinting, H.: Cooperative path planning of UAVs & UGVs for a persistent surveillance task in urban environments. IEEE Internet Things J. **8**, 4906–4919 (2020)

8. Wang, Y., Ma, X., Wang, J., Wang, H.: Pseudo-3d vision-inertia based underwater self-localization for AUVs. IEEE Trans. Veh. Technol. **69**(7), 7895–7907 (2020)
9. Guo, C., et al.: Zero-reference deep curve estimation for low-light image enhancement. In: Proceedings of the IEEE/CVF Conference on Computer Vision and Pattern Recognition, pp. 1780–1789 (2020)
10. Wei, C., Wang, W., Yang, W., Liu, J.: Deep retinex decomposition for low-light enhancement. In: BMVC, p. 155 (2018)
11. Wang, R., Zhang, Q., Fu, C.-W., Shen, X., Zheng, W.-S., Jia, J.: Underexposed photo enhancement using deep illumination estimation. In: Proceedings of the IEEE/CVF Conference on Computer Vision and Pattern Recognition, pp. 6849–6857 (2019)
12. Ren, W., et al.: Low-light image enhancement via a deep hybrid network. IEEE Trans. Image Process. **28**(9), 4364–4375 (2019)
13. Zhang, Y., Zhang, J., Guo, X.: Kindling the darkness: a practical low-light image enhancer. In: Proceedings of the 27th ACM International Conference on Multimedia, pp. 1632–1640 (2019)
14. Cai, J., Shuhang, G., Zhang, L.: Learning a deep single image contrast enhancer from multi-exposure images. IEEE Trans. Image Process. **27**(4), 2049–2062 (2018)
15. Zhu, M., Pan, P., Chen, W., Yang, Y.: EEMEFN: low-light image enhancement via edge-enhanced multi-exposure fusion network. Proc. AAAI Conf. Artif. Intell. **34**, 13106–13113 (2020)
16. Yang, K.-F., Zhang, X.-S., Li, Y.-J.: A biological vision inspired framework for image enhancement in poor visibility conditions. IEEE Trans. Image Process. **29**, 1493–1506 (2019)
17. Xu, K., Yang, X., Yin, B., Lau, R.W.H.: Learning to restore low-light images via decomposition-and-enhancement. In: Proceedings of the IEEE/CVF Conference on Computer Vision and Pattern Recognition, pp. 2281–2290 (2020)
18. Land, E.H.: The retinex theory of color vision. Sci. Am. **237**(6), 108–129 (1977)
19. Guo, X., Li, Y., Ling, H.: LIME: low-light image enhancement via illumination map estimation. IEEE Trans. Image Process. **26**(2), 982–993 (2016)
20. Li, M., Liu, J., Yang, W., Sun, X., Guo, Z.: Structure-revealing low-light image enhancement via robust retinex model. IEEE Trans. Image Process. **27**(6), 2828–2841 (2018)
21. Kim, G., Kwon, D., Kwon, J.: Low-lightgan: low-light enhancement via advanced generative adversarial network with task-driven training. In: 2019 IEEE International Conference on Image Processing (ICIP), pp. 2811–2815. IEEE (2019)
22. Jiang, Y., et al.: EnlightenGAN: deep light enhancement without paired supervision. IEEE Trans. Image Process. **30**, 2340–2349 (2021)
23. Yang, W., Wang, S., Fang, Y., Wang, Y., Liu, J.: From fidelity to perceptual quality: a semi-supervised approach for low-light image enhancement. In: Proceedings of the IEEE/CVF Conference on Computer Vision and Pattern Recognition, pp. 3063–3072 (2020)
24. Canran, X., Peng, Z., Xuanzhen, H., Zhang, W., Chen, L., An, F.: FPGA-based low-visibility enhancement accelerator for video sequence by adaptive histogram equalization with dynamic clip-threshold. IEEE Trans. Circuits Syst. I Regul. Pap. **67**(11), 3954–3964 (2020)
25. Zhu, C., Han, S., Mao, H., Dally, W.J.:L Trained ternary quantization. arXiv preprint arXiv:1612.01064 (2016)
26. Choi, J., Wang, Z., Venkataramani, S., Chuang, P.I.-J., Srinivasan, V., Gopalakrishnan, K.: PACT: parameterized clipping activation for quantized neural networks. arXiv preprint arXiv:1805.06085 (2018)

27. Dong, Z., Yao, Z., Arfeen, D., Gholami, A., Mahoney, M.W., Keutzer, K.: HAWQ-V2: Hessian aware trace-weighted quantization of neural networks. In: Advances in Neural Information Processing Systems, pp. 18518–18529 (2020)
28. Shen, S., et al.: Q-BERT: Hessian based ultra low precision quantization of BERT. Proc. AAAI Conf. Artif. Intell. **34**, 8815–8821 (2020)
29. Hegde, K., Yu, J., Agrawal, R., Yan, M., Pellauer, M., Fletcher, C.: UCNN: exploiting computational reuse in deep neural networks via weight repetition. In: 2018 ACM/IEEE 45th Annual International Symposium on Computer Architecture (ISCA), pp. 674–687. IEEE (2018)
30. Albericio, J., et al.: Bit-pragmatic deep neural network computing. In: Proceedings of the 50th Annual IEEE/ACM International Symposium on Microarchitecture, pp. 382–394 (2017)
31. Kwon, H., Samajdar, A., Krishna, T.: MERI: enabling flexible dataflow mapping over DNN accelerators via reconfigurable interconnects. ACM SIGPLAN Not. **53**(2), 461–475 (2018)
32. Lu, H., Wei, X., Lin, N., Yan, G., Li, X.: Tetris: re-architecting convolutional neural network computation for machine learning accelerators. In: 2018 IEEE/ACM International Conference on Computer-Aided Design (ICCAD), pp. 1–8. IEEE (2018)
33. Zhang, J., Chen, X., Song, M., Li, T.: Eager pruning: algorithm and architecture support for fast training of deep neural networks. In: 2019 ACM/IEEE 46th Annual International Symposium on Computer Architecture (ISCA), pp. 292–303. IEEE (2019)
34. Faraone, J., Fraser, N., Blott, M., Leong, P.H.W.: SYQ: learning symmetric quantization for efficient deep neural networks. In: Proceedings of the IEEE Conference on Computer Vision and Pattern Recognition, pp. 4300–4309 (2018)
35. Han, S., et al.: EIE: efficient inference engine on compressed deep neural network. ACM SIGARCH Comput. Archit. News **44**(3), 243–254 (2016)
36. Zhang, C., Li, P., Sun, G., Guan, Y., Xiao, B., Cong, J.: Optimizing FGPA-based accelerator design for deep convolutional neural networks. In: Proceedings of the 2015 ACM/SIGDA International Symposium on Field-Programmable Gate Arrays, pp. 161–170 (2015)
37. Chen, Y.-H., Krishna, T., Emer, J.S., Sze, V.: Eyeriss: an energy-efficient reconfigurable accelerator for deep convolutional neural networks. IEEE J. Solid-State Circ. **52**(1), 127–138 (2016)

Character Flow Detection and Rectification for Scene Text Spotting

Beiji Zou[1,2], Wenjun Yang[1,2], Kaiwen Li[1,2], Enquan Huang[1,2], and Shu Liu[1,2(✉)]

[1] School of Computer Science and Engineering, Central South University, Changsha 410083, China
sliu35@csu.edu.cn
[2] Hunan Engineering Research Center of Machine Vision and Intelligent Medicine, Changsha 410083, China

Abstract. Text can be widely found in natural scenes. However, it is considerably difficult to detect and recognize the scene text due to its variations and distortions. In this paper, we propose a three-stage bottom-up scene text spotter, including text segmentation, text rectification and text recognition. The text segmentation part adopts a feature pyramid network (FPN) to extract character instances by combining local and global information, then a joint network of FPN and bidirectional long short-term memory is developed to explore the affinity among the isolated characters, which are grouped into character flows. The text rectification part utilizes a spatial transformer network to deal with the complex deformation of the character flows, thus enhancing their readability. Finally, the rectified text is recognized through an attention-based sequence recognition network. Extensive experiments are conducted on several benchmarks, showing that our approach achieves the state-of-the-art performance.

Keywords: Text spotting · Scene text · Text segmentation · Character flow · Text rectification

1 Introduction

Text is used to record, communicate and inherit culture. As one of the most influential inventions in human history, text plays an important role in daily life. With the development of the internet and mobile phones, a large number of multi-oriented scene images and videos are generated. Since text helps people understand the contents of the object intuitively and rapidly, the effective scene text detection and recognition is of great necessity for multimedia applications based on content understanding, such as image retrieval, intelligent inspection, industrial automation, robot navigation, and instant translation.

The topic of text spotting in natural scene has been studied for a long time, it includes text detection and text recognition. Many excellent text detection

© Springer Nature Switzerland AG 2021
N. Magnenat-Thalmann et al. (Eds.): CGI 2021, LNCS 13002, pp. 288–299, 2021.
https://doi.org/10.1007/978-3-030-89029-2_23

and recognition algorithms have emerged and achieved notable success [1–6]. Nevertheless, most current recognition models are troubled with handle irregular text from the environment, these troubles includes text of various shapes, arbitrary-oriented text, and multi-language text. In order to solve these problems. Jaderberg et al. [7] read the entire image into the convolutional neural network (CNN), and it effectively extracted text features. At the same time, the text recognition process is directly completed. However, the complexity of multi-shape and multi-language text is not considered. With the popularity of recurrent neural networks (RNNs) for scene text recognition, CNN-based methods are combined with RNNs for better learning of text context information. Shi et al. [8] proposed a CRNN text recognition descriptor, which is an end-to-end trainable network with both CNNs and RNNs, and the model is based on connectionist temporal classification. CRNN effectively solves the recognition problem of indefinite length text sequence. However, recognizing multi-oriented text in natural scene is still a problem. He et al. [9] proposed an end-to-end textspotter network, which includes text detection and recognition. They adopt text alignment layer and character attention mechanism to handle multi-oriented text region. Some small text and heavily slanted text can be recognized well. Additionally, Liu et al. [10] introduced the region of interest rotation (RoIRotate) operation to associate the feature region corresponding to the text with the recognition, which realize multi-oriented text detection and recognition with only a small amount of calculation through weight sharing, but shows limitations when handling curved and arbitrary-shaped text. Yin et al. [11] adopt multi-scale sliding window to solve the recognition problem of changing character shape. However, It contains a large number of non-text candidates and consumes a lot of computing resources when extracting text using the proposed method. Liao et al. [12] proposed a mask textspotter based on MaskRCNN [13]. Mask textspotter is a model that recognizes curved and arbitrary-shaped text using a segmentation approach, but shows limitations when handling multi-language text. To recognize multi-oriented and multi-language text, Liu et al. [4] proposed a character-aware neural network based on character segmentation, which detects and rectifies individual characters in the scene text. It has strengths in handling different types of distortion text. Another character segmentation based method is character region attention for text spotting proposed by Baek et al. [1].

In this paper, we propose a novel scene text spotting framework. As illustrated in Fig. 1, it consists of three parts: text segmentation, text rectification and text recognition. Firstly, we apply feature pyramid network (FPN) [14] to segment the multi-oriented and multi-scale character instances, which facilitates the correction of text. The affinity among isolated characters is obtained by a joint network of FPN and bidirectional long short-term memory (BLSTM) [15]. We then construct the character flows by combining character instances and their affinity. Secondly, we rectify the irregular text by a spatial transformer network (STN) [16]. Finally, we recognize the text by an attention-based sequence recognition network (ASRN) [17]. Our main contributions are summarized as follows.

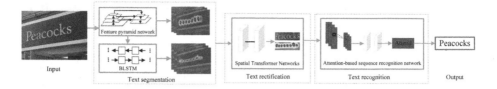

Fig. 1. The overview of our three-stage framework for scene text spotting.

- We propose a three-stage text spotter to solve the problems of multi-oriented and multi-language scene text detection and recognition.
- The character segmentation and construction of text flows lay the foundation for text recognition.
- The spatial character transformer network is introduced to rectify the irregular text, which improves the accuracy of text recognition.

2   Proposed Method

2.1   Text Segmentation

Text segmentation refers to the separation of text pixels from the background. The method of word segmentation may lead to the mis-classification of text instances [18], for example, mis-taking multiple adjacent word instances for the same one. Instead, the character segmentation can address such problems.

In this paper, we adopt FPN [14] with ResNet-50 to obtain character proposals, and then integrate FPN and BLSTM to predict affinity between adjacent characters by exploring their sequential context. The network structure of FPN in Fig. 2(a). It is a top-down architecture that combines global features and local features. The network takes $h \times w \times 3$ fixed size inputs, and the features convolutional layer stage1–stage5 is applies infrastructure of residual network. Each stage has an up-sampling operation via bilinear interpolation and a skip connection to obtain fused feature maps, then adding feature maps bit by bit. Each fused map are fed into Kernel (3×3)-BN-ReLU layers and is reduced to 256 channels. Then it passes through n Kernel (1×1)-Up-Sigmoid layers and the text character region proposals are extracted from each fused maps. And then a BLSTM network is applied subsequently to predict the affinity between adjacent character region proposals. The network structure of BLSTM in Fig. 2(b). Finally, we group the sequence of isolated characters into a character flow. Our original detector loss can be written as

$$L_{total} = \sum_p (\lambda L_{class} + L_{connect}) \tag{1}$$

Where λ is the weight to balance the two losses, and is set to 2.

According to PixelLink [19], L_{class} is the matrix of instance-balanced cross-entropy loss on character and non-character prediction. In Eq. 2, S is area of

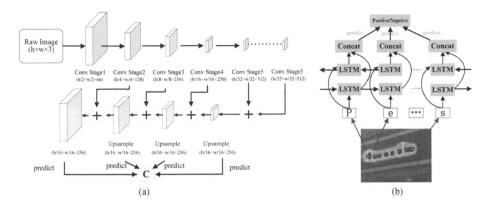

Fig. 2. Text segmentation process. (a) The structure of FPN, where "→", ⊕, and ⓒ represent the convolution operation, bitwise addition, and fusion map for prediction result, respectively. (b) The structure of BLSTM.

character instance and W is weight matrix according to [19], N is sum of pixels for a images, p is pixel, $y_p \in (0, 1)$ is label of pixel, P_p is probability of predicting a positive pixel.

$$L_{class} = \frac{W}{4NS} \sum_p -(y_p \cdot log(P_p) + (1 - y_p) \cdot log(1 - P_p)) \tag{2}$$

$L_{connect}$ is computed as Eq. 3, where S_p^* is the confidence map of the ground truth defined as Eq. 4, and S_p is the predicted region score. The parameters c, $R(c)$, and p denote the ground truth of character, the annotated region of character affinity box, and the pixel in $R(c)$, respectively.

$$L_{connect} = -||S_p^* - S_p||_2^2 \tag{3}$$

$$S_p^* = \begin{cases} 1 & if \quad p \in R(c) \\ 0 & otherwise \end{cases} \tag{4}$$

2.2 Text Rectification

Unlike ordinary objects in natural scene images, text often appear in arbitrary scales and orientations, as well as various fonts and languages, these irregular texts are often difficult to recognize. The recognition of irregular text has been previously studied for scene text images [20]. However, traditional recognition methods are inefficient for non-horizontal and multi-language text recognition [5, 17]. Therefore, this paper uses STN [16] to correct the detected text lines, so that vertical, oblique or deformed text is corrected to a horizontal arrangement and formal, as shown in Fig. 3. The segmented text image is sent to the STN to predict its compensation map. The compensation value is the displacement required for each text pixel distance, thereby moving the character pixels in the initial image to achieve text correction. This process aims to improve the readability and recognition accuracy of scene text.

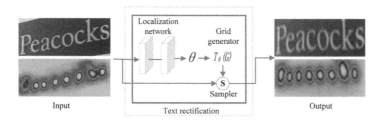

Fig. 3. Text rectification process, including text localization, grid generation and image sampling.

Localization Network. The localization network is used to localize the region of characters, the CNN in the localization network used by us is the well known ResNet by He et al. [21]. It is takes the input feature map with character instances $I \in R^{C \times H \times W}$, where I means feature map, R means real number field, C means channels, H and W means height and weight of the feature map, and outputs the parameters θ of the transformation that shall be applied. In Eq. 5 θ means affine transformation coefficient, and A_θ^n means affine transformation coefficient matrices, where $n \in \{0, \cdots, N-1\}$, N is the number of characters for I.

$$A_\theta^n = \begin{bmatrix} \theta_{11}^n \theta_{12}^n \theta_{13}^n \\ \theta_{21}^n \theta_{22}^n \theta_{23}^n \end{bmatrix} \tag{5}$$

Grid Generator. The grid generator is used to generate a pixel matrix for the grid of current character regions. It takes the input the grid coordinates x_{W_0} and y_{H_0} of character regions for input feature map I with H_0 height and width W_0, and outputs the grid coordinates x_{W_i} and y_{H_i} of rectificated character regions. The transformation formula is Eq. 6. During inference we can extract the N resulting grids which contain the bounding boxes of the text regions found by the localization network.

$$\begin{pmatrix} x_{W_i} \\ y_{H_i} \\ 1 \end{pmatrix} = A_\theta^n \begin{pmatrix} x_{W_0} \\ y_{H_0} \\ 1 \end{pmatrix} = \begin{bmatrix} \theta_{11}^n \theta_{12}^n \theta_{13}^n \\ \theta_{21}^n \theta_{22}^n \theta_{23}^n \end{bmatrix} \begin{pmatrix} x_{W_0} \\ y_{H_0} \\ 1 \end{pmatrix} \tag{6}$$

Image Sampling. A downsampling operation is used to allow back propagation loss. If the weight is a decimal, the value obtained must also be a decimal, this makes it impossible for us to use gradient descent to return the gradient [16]. To solve the problem of output coordinates as decimals, Jaderberg et al. [16] use bilinear interpolation to sampling. In this paper, we also use bilinear sampling to extract the value at a given coordinate by bilinear interpolating the values of the nearest neighbors. The formulas are as shown in Eq. 7 and Eq. 8.

$$O_{i,j}^n = \sum_w^{W_0} \sum_h^{H_0} I_{hw} U_{max} V_{max} \tag{7}$$

$$\begin{cases} U_{max} = max(0, 1 - |u_i^n - w|) \\ V_{max} = max(0, 1 - |v_j^n - h|) \end{cases} \tag{8}$$

Where $O_{i,j}^n$ is output feature maps, width w and height h for feature map I, (i, j) is location coordinate and $i \in W_0$, $j \in H_0$. u_i^n and v_j^n are the grid coordinates for each $n \in N$.

2.3 Text Recognition

The text recognition process is to predict a character sequence directly from the rectified image. Commonly-used text recognition algorithms generally include three steps: preprocessing, feature extraction, and classifier recognition. The preprocessing is to denoise, enhance, zoom and other operations on the image to minimize noise and background interference, and highlight the text area. Feature extraction it is to extract features such as text edges, strokes, structure, etc., for the classifier to learn. The text is finally recognized through the trained classifier.

Recent works [5,17] have demonstrated the effectiveness of text recognition network based on attention. The ASRN model, that adopts the attention mechanism and recurrent neural network, is therefore used in this paper. As shown in Fig. 4, the rectified text image is used as input, and the text area is gathered through the attention mechanism. The CNN is used to extract the text features and output the feature sequence. It is sent to the BLSTM and combined with the context information to generate the target prediction sequence. Finally, the prediction of each frame is converted into a label sequence through the conversion layer to obtain the text recognition result. Our objective function loss in text recognition module can be written as

$$L_{reg} = -\sum_i logp(Y_i|X_i) \tag{9}$$

Where L_{reg} is the objective function loss. $p(Y_i|X_i)$ means the generation probability of the character sequence, Y_i from the cropped feature representation, X_i means the i-th word box.

3 Experiments and Discussions

3.1 Datasets and Implementation Details

ICDAR2013 dataset [22] contains 462 real scene images. Among them, 229 images are selected for training and the remaining 233 images for testing. It is the benchmark in the 2013 Robust Reading Competition, which focuses on

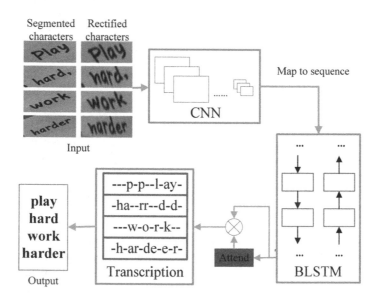

Fig. 4. Text recognition process, including feature extraction, context learning, attention and transcription modules.

the horizontal text detection in the wild. ICDAR2015 dataset [23] contains 1500 real scene images. Among them, 1,000 images are selected for training and the remaining 500 images for testing. It is the benchmark in the 2015 Robust Reading Competition, which focuses on the arbitrary-oriented text detection in the wild. All text lines in these two datasets are annotated with bounding boxes and transcripts, and the text regions are annotated by 4 vertices of a quadrangle.

The pre-training data consists of 850,000 synthetic images released by Gupta et al. [24] and 800,000 synthetic images released by Jaderberg et al. [25]. We initialize the network with a pre-trained model and then fine-tune it on two ICDAR benchmarks. During fine-tuning, synthetic images are mixed with the ratio of 1:5. We take 36 characters to cover alphabets and numbers, and take about 4,000 characters for the multi-language dataset. All experiments are conducted under the framework of PyTorch, CUDA 8.0, so our models are GPU-accelerated.

3.2 Text Detection and Rectification Results

Text detection is an important prerequisite for scene text spotting in this paper. We detect text through a character segmentation network, which is pre-trained on the SynthText dataset and then fine-tuned on ICDAR2013 and ICDAR2015 respectively. Examples of text detection results are shown in Fig. 5.

Text rectification is expected to advance the text recognition performance. The effect of the rectification module is investigated by removing STN from our framework. As can be seen in Table 1, it indeed improves the accuracy of text recognition. Examples of text rectification results are given in Fig. 6.

Fig. 5. Character segmentation results.

Table 1. The effect of text rectification on the text recognition accuracy.

Methods	ICDAR2013	ICDAR2015
With rectification	**93.2%**	**73.6%**
Without rectification	88.4%	68.2%

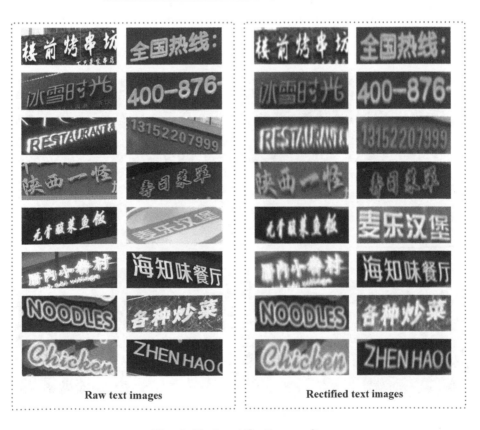

Raw text images

Rectified text images

Fig. 6. Text rectification results.

3.3   Comparison with the State of the Art

We compare our text recognition accuracy against several recent works, shown in Table 2. It can be observed that our approach achieves the state-of-the-art performance. This is probably because we have obtained the excellent detection and rectification results, making the final recognition process simpler and easier. Examples of text recognition results are visualized in Fig. 7.

Table 2. Comparison of different text recognition methods.

Methods	ICDAR2013	ICDAR2015
Yin et al. [11]	81.4%	–
Shi et al. [20]	88.6%	–
Shi et al. [8]	89.6%	–
Cheng et al. [26]	89.4%	66.2%
Jaderberg et al. [7]	90.8%	–
Cheng et al. [27]	–	68.2%
Luo et al. [17]	92.4%	68.8%
Xie et al. [28]	–	68.9%
Li et al. [29]	91.0%	69.2%
Qi et al. [6]	92.8%	72.9%
Ours	**93.2%**	**73.6%**

(a)

(b)

Fig. 7. Examples of text recognition results on (a) ICDAR2013 and (b) ICDAR2015.

4 Conclusions

In this paper, we present a novel text spotter, which is a bottom-up structure consisting of three modules, text segmentation, text rectification and text recognition. First, a character segmentation model is adopted to solve the problem of text mis-segmentation. FPN and BLSTM is strong enough to combine local and global contextual information, which is conducive to dealing with various text fonts and sizes. Second, STN is flexible enough to rectify the irregular text. Finally, the ASRN obtains more context information to accurately recognize all types of text (such as English, number and Chinese). Extensive experiments are conducted on ICDAR2013 and ICDAR2015 datasets to demonstrate the outstanding performance of our approach.

Acknowledgements. This work was supported in part by the National Natural Science Foundation of China under Grant 61902435, in part by Hunan Provincial Natural Science Foundation of China under Grant 2019JJ50808, and in part by the 111 Project under Grant B18059.

References

1. Baek, Y., et al.: Character region attention for text spotting. In: Vedaldi, A., Bischof, H., Brox, T., Frahm, J.-M. (eds.) ECCV 2020. LNCS, vol. 12374, pp. 504–521. Springer, Cham (2020). https://doi.org/10.1007/978-3-030-58526-6_30
2. Wang, T., et al.: Decoupled attention network for text recognition. In: Proceedings of the AAAI Conference on Artificial Intelligence, vol. 34, pp. 12216–12224 (2020)
3. Wan, Z., He, M., Chen, H., Bai, X., Yao, C.: TextScanner: reading characters in order for robust scene text recognition. Proc. AAAI Conf. Artif. Intell. **34**, 12120–12127 (2020)
4. Liu, W., Chen, C., Wong, K.Y.: Char-Net: a character-aware neural network for distorted scene text recognition. In: Proceedings of the AAAI Conference on Artificial Intelligence, pp. 7154–7161 (2018)
5. Shi, B., Yang, M., Wang, X., Lyu, P., Yao, C., Bai, X.: ASTER: an attentional scene text recognizer with flexible rectification. IEEE Trans. Pattern Anal. Mach. Intell. **41**(9), 2035–2048 (2018)
6. Qi, X., Chen, Y., Xiao, R., Li, C.-G., Zou, Q., Cui, S.: A novel joint character categorization and localization approach for character-level scene text recognition. In: Proceedings of the IEEE International Conference on Document Analysis and Recognition Workshops, pp. 83–90 (2019)
7. Jaderberg, M., Simonyan, K., Vedaldi, A., Zisserman, A.: Reading text in the wild with convolutional neural networks. Proc. Int. J. Comput. Vis. **116**, 1–20 (2016)
8. Shi, B., Bai, X., Yao, C.: An end-to-end trainable neural network for image-based sequence recognition and its application to scene text recognition. J. IEEE Trans. Pattern Anal. Mach. Intell. **39**(11), 2298–2304 (2016)
9. He, T., Tian, Z., Huang, W., Shen, C., Qiao, Y., Sun, C.: An end-to-end textspotter with explicit alignment and attention. In: Proceedings of the IEEE/CVF Conference on Computer Vision and Pattern Recognition, pp. 5020–5029 (2018)

10. Liu, X., Liang, D., Yan, S., Chen, D., Qiao, Y., Yan, J.: FOTS: fast oriented text spotting with a unified network. In: Proceedings of the IEEE Conference on Computer Vision and Pattern Recognition, pp. 5676–5685 (2018)
11. Yin, F., Wu, Y., Zhang, X., Liu, C.: Scene text recognition with sliding convolutional character models. arXiv preprint arXiv:1709.01727 (2017)
12. Liao, M., Lyu, P., He, M., Yao, C., Wenhao, W., Bai, X.: Mask text spotter: an end-to-end trainable neural network for spotting text with arbitrary shapes. IEEE Trans. Image Process. **43**(2), 532–548 (2021)
13. He, K.-M., Gkioxari, G., Dollar, P., Girshick, R.: Mask R-CNN. In: Proceedings of the IEEE Conference on Computer Vision and Pattern Recognition, pp. 2961–2969 (2017)
14. Lin, T.-Y., Dollár, P., Girshick, R., He, K., Hariharan, B., Belongie, S.: Feature pyramid networks for object detection. In: Proceedings of the IEEE Conference on Computer Vision and Pattern Recognition, pp. 936–944 (2017)
15. Graves, A., Schmidhuber, J.: Framewise phoneme classification with bidirectional LSTM and other neural network architectures. J. Neural Netw. **18**(5–6), 602–610 (2005)
16. Jaderberg, M., Simonyan, K., Zisserman, A., kavukcuoglu, K.: Spatial transformer networks. In: Proceedings of the Advances in Neural Information Processing Systems, pp. 2017–2025 (2015)
17. Luo, C., Jin, L., Sun, Z.: MORAN: a multi-object rectified attention network for scene text recognition. Pattern Recogn. **90**, 109–118 (2019)
18. Li, X., Wang, W., Hou, W., Liu, R.-Z., Lu, T., Yang, J.: Shape robust text detection with progressive scale expansion network. In: Proceedings of the IEEE Conference on Computer Vision and Pattern Recognition, pp. 9336–9345 (2019)
19. Deng, D., Liu, H., Li, X., Cai, D.: PixelLink: detecting scene text via instance segmentation. In: Proceedings of the AAAI Conference on Artificial Intelligence, pp. 6773–6780 (2018)
20. Shi, B., Wang, X., Lyu, P., Yao, C., Bai, X.: Robust scene text recognition with automatic rectification. In: Proceedings of the IEEE Conference on Computer Vision and Pattern Recognition, pp. 4168–4176 (2016)
21. He, K., Zhang, X., Ren, S., Sun, J.: Deep residual learning for image recognition. In: Proceedings of the IEEE Conference on Computer Vision and Pattern Recognition, pp. 770–778. IEEE (2016)
22. Karatzas, D.: ICDAR 2013 robust reading competition. In: Proceedings of International Conference on Document Analysis and Recognition, pp. 1484–1493 (2013)
23. Karatzas, D., et al.: ICDAR 2015 competition on robust reading. In: Proceedings of International Conference on Document Analysis and Recognition, pp. 1156–1160 (2015)
24. Gupta, A., Vedaldi, A., Zisserman, A.: Synthetic data for text localisation in natural images. In: Proceedings of the IEEE Conference on Computer Vision and Pattern Recognition, pp. 2315–2324 (2016)
25. Jaderberg, M., Simonyan, K., Vedaldi, A., Zisserman, A.: Synthetic data and artificial neural networks for natural scene text recognition. arXiv preprint arXiv:1406.2227v4 (2014)
26. Cheng, Z., Bai, F., Xu, Y., Zheng, G., Pu, S., Zhou, S.: Focusing attention: towards accurate text recognition in natural images. In: Proceedings of the IEEE International Conference on Computer Vision, pp. 5086–5094 (2017)

27. Cheng, Z., Xu, Y., Bai, F., Niu, Y., Pu, S., Zhou, S.: AON: towards arbitrarily-oriented text recognition. In: Proceedings of the IEEE/CVF Conference on Computer Vision and Pattern Recognition, pp. 5571–5579 (2018)
28. Xie, H., Fang, S., Zha, Z., Yang, Y., Li, Y., Zhang, Y.: Convolutional attention networks for scene text recognition. ACM Trans. Multimedia Comput. Commun. Appl. (TOMM) **15**(1s), 3:1–3:17 (2019)
29. Li, H., Wang, P., Shen, C., Zhang, G.: Show, attend and read: a simple and strong baseline for irregular text recognition. Proc. AAAI Conf. Artif. Intell. **33**, 8610–8617 (2019)

A Deep Learning Method for 2D Image Stippling

Zhongmin Xue[1], Beibei Wang[1(✉)], and Lei Ma[2(✉)]

[1] Nanjing University of Science and Technology, Nanjing, China
{xuezhongmin,beibei.wang}@njust.edu.cn
[2] Peking University, Beijing, China
lei.ma@pku.edu.cn

Abstract. Stippling is a fascinating art form, which is widely used in printing industry. In computer graphics, digital color stippling produces colored points with a certain distribution (e.g. blue noise distribution) from an input color image. However, it is challenging as each color channel should be evenly distributed with respect to each other channel. Deep learning approaches have shown great advantage on many image stylization applications and have not been utilized for stippling yet. The main reason is that stippling has strict constrains, which requires an even and random distribution of the points. In this paper, we propose the first deep learning approach for stippling, which is able to produce point distribution visually similar to stippling. We regard the stippling results as a 3D point cloud structure where the third channel represents for colors. Then we propose a deep network to transform images to points distribution, consisting of a feature extracting encoder to extract features from the input image and a point generating decoder to translate the features into stippling form. We exploit a spectrum loss to achieve the even distribution. As a result, our method can produce color stippling with reasonable cost. Experiments show that our method can produce stippling with a reasonable balance between the quality of the results and the computational efficiency.

Keywords: Color stippling · Point-based models · Point distribution

1 Introduction

Image stylization has been an interesting and popular topic recently, which transforms an input image into specific art styles, like oil painting, cartoon, etc. [2,7]. They have broad applications, e.g. movies, video games, and animation. Stippling is one of the interesting art formats. It is composed of a large number of random points, where these points meet a certain distribution (see Fig. 1). By controlling the color and size of each point, the visual effect of these points is similar to the original image at a certain distance. As one of the popular image stylization techniques, stippling is an attractive research topic.

© Springer Nature Switzerland AG 2021
N. Magnenat-Thalmann et al. (Eds.): CGI 2021, LNCS 13002, pp. 300–311, 2021.
https://doi.org/10.1007/978-3-030-89029-2_24

Deep learning based approaches have been widely exploited in image stylization. They have shown promising results in capturing and synthesizing many stylistic forms of depiction, like, in cartoon style [2] and portrait style [14]. However, it has not been applied on stippling, due to its difficulties in maintaining details in results and the lack of training data. Current stippling works are all non-learning based methods. Dart throwing [3] and Lloyd process [16] are two classic sampling algorithms to produce blue noise distribution. There are some stippling algorithms based on them [5,24], however, they can only get black and white dots. Wei [25] extended the traditional single-class Poisson disk sampling to multi-class sampling, which can be used in color stippling perfectly. This method produces pretty good results especially in perspective of spectrum, but the cost is still expensive. Ma et al. [17] proposed a fast digital stippling algorithm, achieving generating stippling in real time. The algorithm is based on a pre-computed blue noise point set constructed by an incremental Voronoi set (IVS) and a real-time parallel rejection strategy. It is able to produce high-quality stippling at real-time performance, although some artifacts might be noticeable.

In this paper, we propose the first deep learning based method for color stippling. Our method takes a set of images and corresponding stippling for training. We use a ResNet50 [8] to extract features from an input image, and then pass them to a decoder similar to Lim et al. [15]. In addition, we use a spectrum loss function to enforce an even and random distribution. Finally, we design an effective algorithm to remove overlapped points, yielding a more decent appearance.

To summarize, the main contributions of this paper are:

- a deep architecture that transforms images to stippling,
- a spectrum loss function to control the distribution of points,
- and a point removal algorithm to refine the stippling results.

Fig. 1. An example of stippling produced by [18].

We first introduce some related work in Sect. 2. We introduce our method in Sect. 3 and the experiment details in Sect. 4. Then we show some results in Sect. 5 and conclude in Sect. 6.

2 Related Work

We briefly review the related works on image stylization, stippling and point cloud.

2.1 Image Stylization

In recent years, deep learning method has been widely used in image styliza-tion (or neural style transfer). Among them, the work of Gatys et al. [7] can be regarded as a pioneering work. They used image representations derived from convolutional neural networks (CNN) optimized for target recognition. These image representations make high-level image information more clear. Gram matrix was introduced to separate and recombine the image content and style of natural images, to produce new images with high perceptual quality. Li et al. [13] proposed a new Markov random field (MRF) loss to replace Gram loss to better preserve the local structure in the image.

The above methods are based on online image optimization [10], thus they are pretty slow. Fast neural methods based on offline model optimization are another branch of neural style transfer. Johnson et al. [11] trained a forward CNN to define and optimize the perceptual loss function to generate high-quality images. Zhang et al. [27] introduced a CoMatch layer and is able to support multiple styles in a model.

Huang et al. [9] proposed Adaptive Instance Normalization (AdaIN), with the style and content features extracted by VGG as input. AdaIN can directly normalize the content in the image into different styles, by training on large-scale style and content maps.

These methods can't be used in stippling directly, since points are generated in stippling rather than images.

2.2 Stippling

We refer the reader to the survey of Martin et al. [19] for a more complete overview about stippling. We group the stippling approaches into two categories: Poisson disk sampling based and Voronoi diagram based.

Poisson disk sampling [3] is one of the traditional sampling methods to obtain samples with blue noise property. Wei [25] extended the traditional single-class Poisson disk sampling to multi-class sampling, which is suitable for color stip-pling. It is the first work used for high-quality color stippling, but it is time consuming. Qin et al. [22] proposed to use Wasserstein center of gravity with multiple density distribution constraints and introduced a regularization term, which controls the spatial regularity of blue noise sampling, and reduces conflicts between the required centroids of Voronoi cells for multiple sampling, resulting in more efficient color stippling.

The other group is Voronoi diagram based methods. Deussen [5] proposed to create a stipple by generating an initial point set, and then processed it through a relaxation on the Voronoi diagram. The generated point pattern is an approximation of the Poisson disk distribution. This method can produce efficient interactive stipple, however, it blurs the image. Secord [23] proposed to use the weighted centroid Voronoi diagram to generate stipples from gray-scale images, with two ways: an iterative way to generate high-quality stippling images, and a real-time way with pre-calculated point distributions to quickly stipple images. Balzer et al. [1] proposed a stippling method for constructing the centroid of the Voronoi region. The resulting distribution has high-quality blue noise characteristics and accurately adapts to the given density function. This method is similar to the commonly used Lloyd method, but avoids its disadvantages. Xu et al. [26] used point triangulation to constrain the generated topology to produce high-quality results. Ma et al. [17] proposed an instant stippling method, using a pre-computed blue noise point set constructed by an IVS, which can achieve a reasonable balance between the quality of the results and the computational efficiency. Later, it's extended to color stippling [18], which is able to achieve high-quality results with real-time.

2.3   Deep Point Generation/Processing

In color stippling, the dots are considered as points, thus we also review the related works on points generation or processing with deep learning based approaches. Charles et al. [20] proposed PointNet, which takes a point cloud as input and is able to be used in many applications, ranging from object classification and segmentation to scene semantic analysis. PointNet is further improved in PointNet++ [21], by introducing a hierarchical neural network that recursively applies PointNet to the nested division of input point sets. Fan et al. [6] proposed a 3D reconstruction approach, generating point cloud from a single image, in which earth moving distance and chamfer distance were used as the distance measurement between point clouds.

3   Our Method

We propose an encoder-decoder framework for 2D image stippling, which takes an image as input and produces a 3D point set, where two channels represent the coordinates on the image, and the third channel represents the point color. We use a 3D point set as our output rather than a 2D image, since a point set is more precise and flexible to represent stippling. The architecture (Sect. 3.1) of our network contains an encoding component which encodes the input image into a latent feature vector and a decoding component which decodes the latent vector to a point set. To optimize the distribution of the points, we propose a spectrum loss (see Sect. 3.2). In the end, we remove the overlapped points as a post-process to get visually pleasing results (Sect. 3.3).

3.1   Network Architecture

We propose a network with an encoder-decoder framework, which takes an image as an input and outputs a set of points. Figure 2 shows the network architecture.

We first use a ResNet50 [8] as an encoder to extract the feature of the input image into a latent vector $z \in R^{1024}$. The fully connected layer of ResNet50 is slightly customized, by changing the output channel to 1024.

Then we employ AdaIN Decoder [15] to transform the latent vector to points. The decoder consists of three components: a Multi-layer Perceptron (MLP), a grid decoder and a generator. The MLP has one layer only and is used for resizing the vector. The grid decoder decodes the input latent vector to another latent vector represented as a $32 \times 32 \times 32$ grid. We can simply consider that the grid features divide the output space into cells, and each cell is a latent vector containing the information(location and color) of points in it. The latent vector z from the encoder is transformed by a MLP before fed to grid decoder.

The generator transforms the latent vector to points. More specificity, the generator includes two MLPs (a point density MLP and a point location MLP) to generate point density and point coordinate from the latent vector respectively. The density estimator MLP predicts whether a cell is empty and point density in a cell. These information are fed to the location MLP to produce the number of points and their coordinates in each cell according to the input dot count.

In the end, we obtain the final stippling results by switching the third dimension to points color using the same rule as in the dataset. Then we project the dots onto 2D images. We scale first two channels to adjust the dot size. The radius of each dot is set considering the output image size. In practice, we use 1.4 for a 256×256 image.

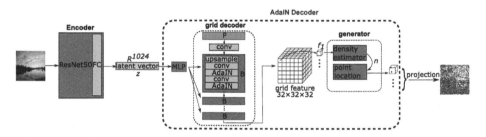

Fig. 2. Our network includes an encoder which is a ResNet50 and a decoder which is similar to AdaIN Decoder [15]. FC means the fully connected layer. In the encoder, the number of output channel of FC layer in ResNet50 is set to 1024 to get the latent vector $z \in R^{1024}$. The decoder includes an MLP, a grid decoder and a generator. The latent vector generated from the encoder is passed to the MLP in decoder first, and then fed to the grid decoder, which outputs grid features. The grid features divide the output space into cells, and each cell is a latent vector containing the information (location and color) of points in it. f_i represents the latent vector in the i_{th} cell. The vector in each cell is fed to the generator to produce a point set. The generator consists of a density MLP and a point location MLP: the density estimator MLP predicts the number of points m in a single cell and the point location MLP thereby generates m points' coordinates. In the end, a projection is performed to transform the 3D output into 2D points with colors.

3.2   Loss Function

The loss of our network consists of two components: (1) the content loss $L_c(X, Y)$, which drives the network to generate results accurate in content, and (2) the spectrum loss $L_s(X, Y)$, which constraints the distribution of points. Low content loss ensures results accurate in content. In stippling, accurate content means that point colors are accurate so the result looks close to input image at a certain distance. $Y \in R^{m \times 3}$ is the output of network, and $X \in R^{n \times 3}$ is the stippling reference, where m and n are the numbers of points respectively. Our loss function is defined as:

$$L_{\text{total}} = L_c(X, Y) + \omega L_s(X, Y), \tag{1}$$

where ω is the weight to balance the two components. In our experiments, we set $\omega = 0.1$ to get a smooth training process and a satisfying convergence.

We employ the loss function of AdaIN Decoder [15] as our content loss, including a Chamfer loss and a loss restrain points with a large error, a loss which penalizing any generated points that are too far away from their cell centers, a loss that measures density accuracy and a loss that measures empty probability accuracy. Please refer to [15] for more details.

Since stippling usually has the blue noise property, and spectrum is usually used to measure this property, we propose a spectrum loss to drive the distribution of the points. In practice, we found it hard to train using the intuitive 2D spectrum. Hence, we use the 1D form-radial spectrum instead.

$$L_s = ||RS(X) - RS(Y)||_1, \tag{2}$$

where $RS(X)$ means the radial spectrum on point set X.

Similar to [12], the spectrum loss L_s is defined as the L1 loss between of the output stippling and a blue noise point set generated with [4].

We use the spectrum of a blue noise point set to compute the loss, rather than the spectrum of the stippling reference, for two reasons: first, the spectrum of reference is not an exact blue noise spectrum, which exists undesired peak at low-frequency interval; second, it's more costly to use the spectrum of reference, as each input image requires a spectrum. Thus, we use a standard blue noise as reference.

3.3   Point Removal

It's difficult for network to produce a perfectly even point set, while the overlapped points in stippling influence the visual perception significantly. Therefore, we design a point removal algorithm as a post-process, to further improve the quality of stippling result. First, we double the output number of points in reference to eliminate blank area in results. Then we remove the overlapped points. We divide the output space into a 32×32 grid. Then we put points of original stippling results into the grid one by one and check overlapping situation in it and its neighbor cells, and remove the overlapped points. The overlapped points are dropped with equal probability.

4   Experiment and Training

We implement our model with PyTorch. All experiments were performed on a 2.20 GHz 8 cores Intel Xeon CPU and an NVIDIA RTX2080Ti GPU.

4.1   Dataset

It's difficult to get large amount of stippling results created by artists, we thus prepare our dataset with Ma et al. [18], considering both quality and performance. Wei [25] is able to produce higher quality, but it's too expensive to obtain a dataset with it.

The dataset contains input photos, their corresponding stippling and a radial spectrum table. Regarding the input image, we use photos downloaded from https://www.kaggle.com/datasets and additional 4000 photos collected from the Internet, where most of them are landscape scenes. Thus, we have 8000 pairs in our dataset, while 95% used for training and 5% used for validation. The photos as input are pre-processed into the same form that ResNet requires, including resizing and normalizing.

Then we use Ma et al. [18] to generate the stippling. Wei [25] and Ma et al. [18] are two typical color stippling algorithms. Generally, Wei [25] can achieve the best distribution quality, but it requires considerable amount of points, which is time consuming and not suitable for deep learning. Although Ma et al. [18] can introduce some patterns, it produce quite nice results with much less points effectively. In our case, using Ma et al. [18] to generate the stippling references is more appropriate. Each stippling is in the form of $n \times 3$ where n means the count of points in each stippling and 3 means each point's coordinate: x, y, and color c. In our experiments, we set n as 2500. The network depends on the input points count, thus different counts of dots require different dataset generation and training. Regarding the color type, it could be arbitrary color space. We tried the color space RGBCMYK. The network trained for RGBCMYK can also be used for other color space. Please see the result in Fig. 5.

4.2   Network Details

The structure of the grid decoder is P-C512-U-C512-C256-U-C256-C128-U-C128-C64-U-C64-C62. P is the learnable constant parameter block with size $512 \times 2 \times 2 \times 2$. C_x represents 3D convolution layers without bias, with x output channel, $3 \times 3 \times 3$ kernel size, stride of 1, and zero-padding of 1. U refers to upsample layer. Dropout with a probability of 0.2 is applied after P and every C. AdaIN is applied after every dropout layer and P with the scaling and translation parameters provided by transformed z. ELU is applied after every AdaIN except for the last one.

The density estimator MLP is constructed as FC16-FC8-FC4-FC2. There are a batchnorm and an ELU except for the last one after every fully connected layer. The location MLP is constructed as FC64-FC64-FC32-FC32-FC16-FC16-FC8-FC3. There is a ELU after every FC layer except for the last one.

4.3   Training

Our network was trained using AMSGrad with $\beta_1 = 0.9$ and $\beta_2 = 0.999$. The learning rate is set to be 0.0005, and the batch size is set as 8. Other hyperparameters are set the same as [15]. We start the training without spectrum loss to accelerate the model converge and then include the spectrum loss after about 300 epochs. The loss gets converged after about 600 epochs and the entire training costs about 30 h.

4.4   Other Details

In the point removal step, the point radius used for overlap judgment is the same in stippling reference, which is 1.4 for a 256×256 image. Our final stippling is saved in a *.svg* format.

5   Result

In Sect. 5.1, we show our results and compare them with state-of-the-art stippling algorithms. In Sect. 5.2, we present an ablation experiment to analyze the effect of each component in the model.

5.1   Comparison with Previous Works

We compare our method with other stippling algorithms (Ma et al. [18], Wei [25]) in Fig. 3. Overall, our result has correct color, comparing the thumbnails with the input image. Also, the distribution of points in our result is relatively even, although it cannot reach the blue noise distribution. In our experiments, to get 5000 points, our method costs 0.22 s to generate these points and 0.66 s for removal, while Wei [25] costs more than 5 s depending on the source image.

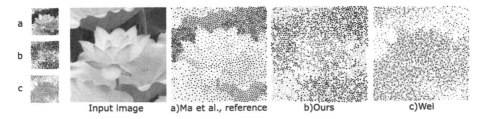

Fig. 3. Comparison of our method, Ma et al. [18] and Wei [25]. The dot count is set as 2500 in all of these methods. The left most three images are thumbnails of results for the three methods. (Color figure online)

We also show the stippling result for an uniform input image in Fig. 4. Our method is able to produce an even and random distribution, similar to Ma et al. [18].

The output color space is set to be RGBCMYK, but we can change it without retraining the model. For example, cyan is a combination of blue and green. So, a cyan point can be replaced by a blue or green one with an equal possibility. Figure 5 shows an example.

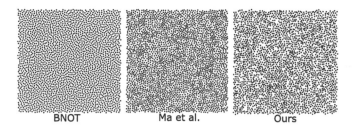

Fig. 4. Comparison of our method, BNOT [4] and Ma et al. [18] for an uniform input image. Our method produces a good visual effect, although our method can't achieve a blue noise appearance.

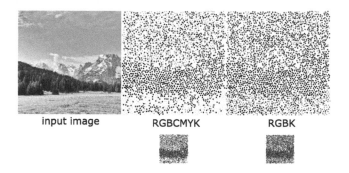

Fig. 5. Our network is able to support different input color types: RGBCMYK for the middle image and RGBK for the right image. (Color figure online)

5.2 Ablation Experiment

We perform the ablation experiment to study each component of our method in Fig. 6: the spectrum loss and the point removal.

Without spectrum loss, the stippling results look more randomly distributed. Figure 7 shows a close-up of this comparison. The spacing is more even with spectrum especially at where the colors are smooth.

Without removal, there are many overlapped points and the tone seems darker. After performing removal on them, the results are much closer to the reference visually.

5.3 Limitations

Our methods have several limitations. First, our method cannot guarantee the blue noise property even for an input image with uniform color. Second, our network depends on the dot counts in the stippling, which leads to dataset regeneration and retraining when changing the dot count. In Fig. 8, we use a trained model for other point number, resulting in unpleasant stippling results.

Fig. 6. Ablation experiments on the spectrum loss and points removal.

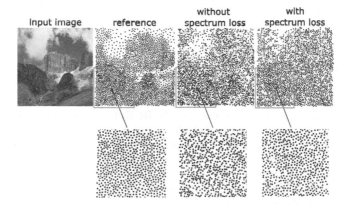

Fig. 7. Close-up view of the first image in Fig. 6. The spectrum loss improves the distribution of the dots.

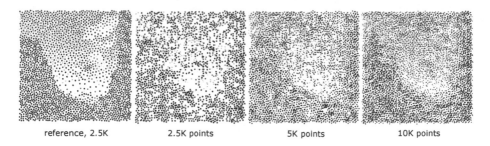

| reference, 2.5K | 2.5K points | 5K points | 10K points |

Fig. 8. Different output point number of our results. We didn't perform removal to keep the point number.

6 Conclusion and Future Work

In this paper, we propose a deep learning based approach for color stippling, which transforms an input image to stippling. To our best knowledge, this is the first deep learning method for stippling. We proposed an encoder-decoder framework, further with a spectrum loss function to obtain an even and random point distribution. In the end, our method is able to produce visually pleasing stippling results.

Our result can't guarantee the blue noise spectrum currently. In future work, we think a better network architecture could be helpful to this problem. We also plan to extend our method to 3D stippling.

References

1. Balzer, M., Schlömer, T., Deussen, O.: Capacity-constrained point distributions: a variant of Lloyd's method. ACM Trans. Graph. (TOG) **28**(3), 1–8 (2009)
2. Chen, Y., Lai, Y.K., Liu, Y.J.: CartoonGAN: generative adversarial networks for photo cartoonization. In: Proceedings of the IEEE Conference on Computer Vision and Pattern Recognition, pp. 9465–9474 (2018)
3. Cook, R.L.: Stochastic sampling in computer graphics. ACM Trans. Graph. (TOG) **5**(1), 51–72 (1986)
4. De Goes, F., Breeden, K., Ostromoukhov, V., Desbrun, M.: Blue noise through optimal transport. ACM Trans. Graph. (TOG) **31**(6), 1–11 (2012)
5. Deussen, O., Hiller, S., Van Overveld, C., Strothotte, T.: Floating points: a method for computing stipple drawings. Comput. Graph. Forum **19**, 41–50 (2000)
6. Fan, H., Su, H., Guibas, L.J.: A point set generation network for 3d object reconstruction from a single image. In: Proceedings of the IEEE Conference on Computer Vision and Pattern Recognition, pp. 605–613 (2017)
7. Gatys, L.A., Ecker, A.S., Bethge, M.: Image style transfer using convolutional neural networks. In: Proceedings of the IEEE Conference on Computer Vision and Pattern Recognition, pp. 2414–2423 (2016)
8. He, K., Zhang, X., Ren, S., Sun, J.: Deep residual learning for image recognition. In: Proceedings of the IEEE Conference on Computer Vision and Pattern Recognition, pp. 770–778 (2016)

9. Huang, X., Belongie, S.: Arbitrary style transfer in real-time with adaptive instance normalization. In: Proceedings of the IEEE International Conference on Computer Vision, pp. 1501–1510 (2017)
10. Jing, Y., Yang, Y., Feng, Z., Ye, J., Yu, Y., Song, M.: Neural style transfer: a review. IEEE Trans. Vis. Comput. Graph. **26**(11), 3365–3385 (2019)
11. Johnson, J., Alahi, A., Fei-Fei, L.: Perceptual losses for real-time style transfer and super-resolution. In: Leibe, B., Matas, J., Sebe, N., Welling, M. (eds.) ECCV 2016. LNCS, vol. 9906, pp. 694–711. Springer, Cham (2016). https://doi.org/10.1007/978-3-319-46475-6_43
12. Leimkühler, T., Singh, G., Myszkowski, K., Seidel, H.P., Ritschel, T.: Deep point correlation design. ACM Tran. Graph. (TOG) **38**(6), 1–17 (2019)
13. Li, C., Wand, M.: Combining Markov random fields and convolutional neural networks for image synthesis. In: Proceedings of the IEEE Conference on Computer Vision and Pattern Recognition, pp. 2479–2486 (2016)
14. Li, X., Zhang, W., Shen, T., Mei, T.: Everyone is a cartoonist: selfie cartoonization with attentive adversarial networks. In: 2019 IEEE International Conference on Multimedia and Expo (ICME), pp. 652–657. IEEE (2019)
15. Lim, I., Ibing, M., Kobbelt, L.: A convolutional decoder for point clouds using adaptive instance normalization. Comput. Graph. Forum **38**, 99–108 (2019)
16. Lloyd, S.: Least squares quantization in PCM. IEEE Trans. Inf. Theor. **28**(2), 129–137 (1982)
17. Ma, L., Chen, Y., Qian, Y., Sun, H.: Incremental Voronoi sets for instant stippling. Vis. Comput. **34**(6–8), 863–873 (2018)
18. Ma, L., Deng, H., Wang, B., Chen, Y., Boubekeur, T.: Real-time structure aware color stippling. In: ACM SIGGRAPH 2019 Posters, pp. 1–2 (2019)
19. Martín, D., Arroyo, G., Rodríguez, A., Isenberg, T.: A survey of digital stippling. Comput. Graph. **67**, 24–44 (2017)
20. Qi, C.R., Su, H., Mo, K., Guibas, L.J.: PointNet: deep learning on point sets for 3D classification and segmentation. In: Proceedings of the IEEE Conference on Computer Vision and Pattern Recognition, pp. 652–660 (2017)
21. Qi, C.R., Yi, L., Su, H., Guibas, L.J.: PointNet++: deep hierarchical feature learning on point sets in a metric space. Adv. Neural. Inf. Process. Syst. **30**, 5099–5108 (2017)
22. Qin, H., Chen, Y., He, J., Chen, B.: Wasserstein blue noise sampling. ACM Trans. Graph. (TOG) **36**(5), 1–13 (2017)
23. Secord, A.: Weighted Voronoi stippling. In: Proceedings of the 2nd International Symposium on Non-photorealistic Animation and Rendering, pp. 37–43 (2002)
24. Vanderhaeghe, D., Barla, P., Thollot, J., Sillion, F.X.: Dynamic point distribution for stroke-based rendering. In: Eurogaphics Symposium on Rendering, pp. 139–146. Eurographics Association (2007)
25. Wei, L.: Multi-class blue noise sampling. ACM Trans. Graph. (TOG) **29**(4), 1–8 (2010)
26. Xu, Y., Liu, L., Gotsman, C., Gortler, S.J.: Capacity-constrained delaunay triangulation for point distributions. Comput. Graph. **35**(3), 510–516 (2011)
27. Zhang, H., Dana, K.: Multi-style generative network for real-time transfer. In: Leal-Taixé, L., Roth, S. (eds.) ECCV 2018. LNCS, vol. 11132, pp. 349–365. Springer, Cham (2019). https://doi.org/10.1007/978-3-030-11018-5_32

Medical Imaging

In Silico Heart Versatile Graphical Interface with Systole and Diastole Phases Customizable for Diversified Arrhythmias Simulations

C. M. G. Godoy, M. C. Selusniacki, V. S. dos Santos, C. C. Godoy,
G. M. dos Santos, and R. C. Coelho[✉]

Science and Technology Institute, Federal University of São Paulo, São José dos
Campos, São Paulo, SP, Brazil
rccoelho@unifesp.br
https://www.unifesp.br/campus/sjc/

Abstract. Heart computational models in graphical interfaces provide realistic cardiac beating simulation and suitable user interactivity. This work presents an interface for heart simulation specially devised to control the cardiac systole and diastole phases for arrhythmia simulations while simultaneously interacting with the heart model. The simulation consists of rigging the mesh of a 3D heart model to generate keyframes for morphing. The interface provides cardiac beating motion simulation at a regular rate and arrhythmias adjustable by the user. It also provides, in real-time, information and control of the cardiac phase durations. Furthermore, the user can manipulate and interact with the heart model using a naked-eye hologram interface. The interface is applicable in cardiology education and training and can upgrade for exploring new medical applications in In-Silico cardiology. The present work's main contribution and technical novelty concern devising a heart beating simulator customizable to the patient cardiac rhythm.

Keywords: Educational simulation · Graphical environment · Medical simulation · Graphical interface · Animation

1 Introduction

The term *In Silico* Heart allusions to the heart's computational modeling and simulation in the cardiology area [1]. In this context, the interactive visualization of animated three-dimensional (3D) heart models in virtual environments is a handy computational resource for medical simulation, education, or training [2,3]. It can occur, for example, in cases where simulation demands either preoperative planning or virtual intraoperative manipulation or medical training [3], or even for interaction with patients in cardiologic healthcare [4]. In many cases, it demands accurate data of heart movements (displacements, times, or

© Springer Nature Switzerland AG 2021
N. Magnenat-Thalmann et al. (Eds.): CGI 2021, LNCS 13002, pp. 315–326, 2021.
https://doi.org/10.1007/978-3-030-89029-2_25

deformations) and highly elaborated computer graphics techniques [6,7]. All such resources rely on the virtual environments' suitability and the realistic three-dimensionality of heart models for the simulation [8,9]. Thus, various heart models aim to supply realistic simulation of the beating heart and suitable user interactivity [10,11].

Virtual laboratories, which employ heart models and virtual environments, have proved useful to cut costs, improve the teaching/learning process in academic settings, or help medical simulations before actual cardiac surgical procedures [11]. For example, Ong and colleagues [13] used Virtual Reality for planning a surgery, which is applicable in infants or adults with congenital heart disease, and demonstrated, in real-time, internal and external views of the heart. Similarly, Plasencia and colleagues [14], by performing virtual interactive visualization of the heart model, helped confirm a pediatric heart transplant's compatibility using comparisons in the real heart's physical characteristics. The virtual heart models' visualization frequently occurs in monitors, that is, in a 2D display. In the literature, it is possible to find several forms of three-dimensional visualization, as Virtual Reality, Augmented Reality, and Holography. Virtual Reality applies conveniently to health areas, mainly research and investments in medical treatments and procedures [6,13]. Albeit important, it often requires the use of head-mounted displays (HMD), which can cause motion sickness and other side effects due to overuse, or greatly constraints the total users able to interact.

Augmented Reality applied to the health field intends to improve user interaction in simulations. For example, Xie *et al.* [15] developed a prototype that aims to scan the human body and, using Augmented Reality, project virtual organs of a person on his/her own body. In this case, it is necessary to use Augmented Reality glasses, like Microsoft HoloLens, to undergo the technique. An alternative approach to avoid using HMD or glasses is to apply computer-generated hologram techniques to create 3D images in a naked-eye hologram interface proposed by Dennis Gabor [16]. Fortunately, a not expensive approach, the so-called Pepper hologram pyramid technique, allows naked-eye 3D (pseudo) visualization and interaction with scenes or medical anatomy [17,18].

Concerning the importance of improving the heart simulation *per se*, it would be interesting to evolve it to allow the user to control the cardiac beating motion (systole and diastole) for patient customizable arrhythmia simulations while simultaneously interacting with the heart model in a convenient 3D visualization platform (including holographic visualization). Thus, this work presents a versatile computational interface specially devised and developed to meet such demands.

2   Heart Simulation Review

The literature is plenty of works about heart simulators, including the electrical activity of the heart. For example, Quarteroni *et al.* [9] proposed coupling multiscale and multiphysics models to simulate the cardiac electrophysiology system with activation-contraction mechanisms and the hemodynamics inside the heart chambers. The work developed by Coelho and colleagues [19] presents, in an applicative to mobile devices, a simplified 3D virtual heart model (only external surface) which simulates the cardiac beat according to electrocardiogram parameters. In a more sophisticated cardiac model, Mauriello *et al.* [20] developed software to visualize the heart's internal and external parts. The heart model came from a reconstruction based on the computed tomography scan. The software allows the heart's dissections to visualize the inner part and shows the ventricles' animations to demonstrate their relaxation and contraction movements.

As for hemodynamics specifically, Doost *et al.* [21] presented a review of heart blood flow simulators. This review included studies of physiological and various pathological conditions of the left ventricle. They concluded that the simulators are the right track for developing a useful clinical tool to aid the physician with the heart function analysis.

The theoretical bases of the tools above have the appropriate means of implementation well established in the literature [6–8]. There are also laboratories specifically dedicated to heart simulation at universities abroad. For example, the Johns Hopkins University addresses simulations of virtual hearts customized to patients in the context of the so-called custom cardiology [22]. At the same time, the University of Minnesota offers "The Visible Heart Laboratory" for high-level educational purposes in heart anatomy and function [23].

Finally, some modern and sophisticated computational simulators of the heart allow realistic simulation of the beating heart, mainly regarding its anatomy, functionalities [24], and simulations of the heart's physiology and biophysics [25]. Such modern heart models usually require a high-capacity computer for image processing, which may difficult their implementation.

3   Methods

The virtual heart model used in the present work is available for free use in http://free3d.com/3d-model/human-heart-2-79840.html (accessed on 11/06/2017). It is a human heart model divided into three parts, as shown in Fig. 1.

The graphical interface performs the heartbeat simulation, which is essentially an animation process. It consists of using the 3D software Autodesk Maya for rigging the mesh of the 3D heart model, which, in turn, generated key-frames for morphing.

Initially, the animation procedure occurred by applying a skeletal tree and using keyframe animation to create a fluid movement. The skeletal tree consisted of four main bones that branch out from the root bone. Each main bone places around each quadrant's central area (right and left atria; left and right ventricles) of the heart (Fig. 2 (a)). One additional extension bone comes out from each main bone of the ventricles. Three auxiliary bones branch out from each of the four following bones: two atrium main bones and two ventricle extension bones to cover more surface area. Each one has its influence field, as illustrated in Fig. 2 (b).

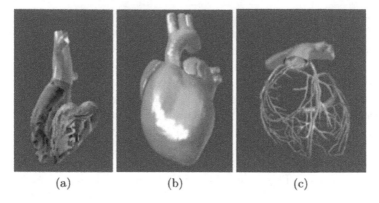

(a)   (b)   (c)

Fig. 1. Parts that compose the heart model used in this work. (a) Vena cava and the inner part of the atria and ventricles; (b) external part of atria and ventricles, with the aorta artery; (c) pulmonary trunk and coronary arteries.

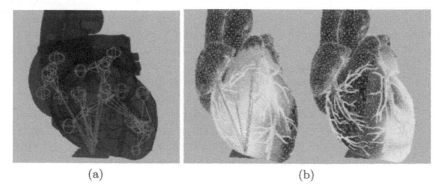

(a)   (b)

Fig. 2. Examples of bones and influence fields. (a) Bones for the animation of the heart and its influence areas. View of the bones positioned over the mesh. The influence hierarchy occurs according to the following colors: orange (root bone), yellow (main quadrant bones), lime (auxiliary atrium bones or extended ventricle bones), green (auxiliary ventricle bones). (b) Darker and colder colors mean lower influence, whereas brighter and hotter colors mean elevated influence. Only illustrations of the external part. (Color figure online)

A specialist helped to match the atria and ventricles movements to echocardiogram images. That was fundamental to compose a realistic animation, including the thickening of ventricle walls as systole occurs. By using the keyframe animation technique, every step of the heart movement composed each quadrant individually. According to the actual heartbeat cycle, the heart movement occurred through distorting, inflating, and deflating the 3D heart mesh. This process repeated itself for every atrium and ventricle for all steps of the cardiac cycle. It yielded different static models of the same heart, each on a different phase of the cycle. That enables the use of each heart model as a realistic keyframe

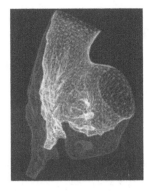

Fig. 3. Example of wireframe morphing applied to the left ventricle internal wall. The relaxed ventricle is in light gray and fully contracted in white.

to animate models through morphing. Thus, the initial wireframe's vertices are deformed in time intervals until the object gets the shape of a distorted mesh (Fig. 3).

The graphical interface has two windows: one to manipulate the image and the other to prompt images of the heart model for holographic projection. The window to holographic projection divides into four parts (by diagonal) to implement holographic projection in the Pepper pyramid, as shown in Fig. 4. Each part of the window presents a side of the heart model. The fixed model projects from the bottom of the window. In the next part of the window, the model rotates 90° in the Y and Z-axes, and so on. All the interactions made by the user in the graphic interface affect all four models.

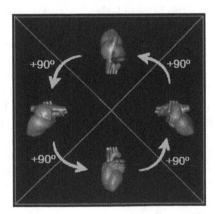

Fig. 4. Illustration of the graphical window used in the holographic projection shows the heart model's rotation to obtain the four heart images.

The graphical environment - developed in C programming language and using API OpenGL [26] and GLUI and GLUT libraries - presents the virtual human heart's animation according to the cardiac beating. The heart simulations and interactions obtained with the interface represent the practical results of the present work.

The morphing technique's choice regards the realistic movement and simple implementation, requiring less computer image processing capacity. The program applies that technique considering the current phase and the next phase of the animation cycle. Each phase of the cycle takes a certain amount of time to occur. The default time values obtention occurred by analyzing an electrocardiogram signal and extracting (by a specialist) the time of each cycle phase manually. A text file stores these time values read by the animation program. Then they are converted into the number of frames that each phase of the cycle takes to occur. The beating heart's adjustable values implemented in simulation defined maximum, minimum or typical values of every cardiac phase duration (atrial contraction, ventricular contraction/atrial relaxation, ventricular relaxation, resting) and cardiac normal or arrhythmias (bradycardia, tachycardia, or atria-ventricular block). The setup used for this adjustment and definition of those parameters was a computer Core I7, RAM 16 GB, equipped with a graphic card GeForce GTX 1060, 6 GB.

4 Results

The interface (Fig. 5) aimed to supply a versatile graphical interaction between the user and the heartbeat simulator. The user can also interact simultaneously with the heart model performing manipulation (rotation, exploded view, transparency, cut, clip, and erase in Manipulation and Cutting Planes buttons). The left side of Fig. 5 (a) shows the Manipulation button expanded, where it is possible to control the rotation (running the ball button), transparency (as shown in this figure), and zoom using sliders. The heart's transparency allows the user to see the ventricles and atria's internal and external parts. Clipping and Erasing perform by the mouse.

The Reset button allows resuming the heart to its initial state after performing any model manipulation. The interface also stores a history of commands. Therefore, using the Undo button, it is possible to undo the last command from history.

A specialist advised the heart model's fragmentation to allow the separation of the main components of the heart in the left and right atrium and left and right ventricle. The fragmentation excluded valves and coronary arteries (leaving only the pulmonary aorta, artery and vein, and the vena cava), as the present work focused on representing the cardiac chambers' realistic movements. The Explode button allows the user to detach the heart in parts for an "exploded view" during the cardiac cycle (Fig. 5 (b)). In this case, separated parts keep moving as if they were attached to the heart. By customizing cardiac cycle durations or merely letting the heartbeat occur at a regular rate, it is possible to see each detachable

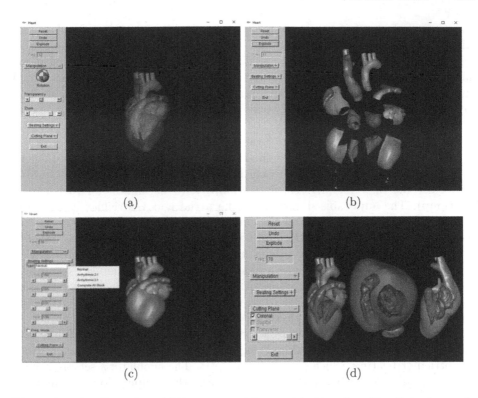

Fig. 5. Graphical Interface. (a) Resources of the graphical interface (details in the text); (b) Exploded view of the heart model. Its movements are observable as the cardiac cycle occurs; (c) Phases of heart motion (atrial contraction, atrial relaxation/ventricular contraction, ventricular relaxation, and rest); (d) cuts of the heart using typical orthogonal anatomical planes of echocardiographic images: Transversal (x-axis), Sagittal (y-axis), and Longitudinal planes (z-axis).

part of the heart's movement in more detail. The reset button reassembles the heart.

The simulator provides, in real-time, information and control of phases of the heartbeat rate simulated. Like the work of Coelho and colleagues [19], the phases are 1) atrial contraction and atrial relaxation/ventricular contraction (both comprise the systole), and 2) ventricular relaxation and resting (both comprise the diastole). The heart rate obtains by determining the time elapsed between starting the first phase of the cardiac cycle (atrial contraction at the systole start) until it completes the last phase (heart resting at the diastole end). That elapsed time converts into the cardiac rate (frequency) and shows in the graphical interface as beats per minute (bpm) (Freq box).

By expanding the Beating Settings button (Fig. 5 (c)), it is possible to see options to control the duration of the cardiac cycle phases (the first four sliders), a slider to adjust the heartbeat rate simulation as normal rhythm, bradycardia, or tachycardia (the last slider), and choose different types of AV (Atrio Ventricular) blocks. By pressing the options menu in Type, the user can simulate and adjust AV blocks of either first, second, third-degree, or total AV blocks.

Figure 5 (d) shows the button Cutting Plane expanded. Each cutting plane has its slider. It is possible to make cuts in the heart in the typical orthogonal anatomical planes of the echocardiographic images - transversal (X-axis), sagittal (Y-axis), and longitudinal planes (Z-axis) - and, thus, visualize the internal parts of it during the cardiac beating.

Table 1 summarizes the range of values of the adjustable parameters in the simulator. The typical values are those considered clinically normal. In contrast, the minimum and maximum cardiac rate values correspond to the lowest adjustable value for bradycardia (40 bmp) and the highest for tachycardia (150 bmp). The adjustable durations of the atrial and ventricular contraction and relaxation (AC; VC/AR and VR) and cardiac resting interval (Rest) allow setting intermediary values of the cardiac rates (regular, bradycardia, and tachycardia). The durations setting occurs in steps of 1 ms (using slider). Cardiac rate adjusts in steps of 1 bpm (using slider). The resting duration (Rest) adjusts according to the previously set values of AC, VR/AR, and VR. Atrioventricular block (AVB) sets in three recurrent cardiac abnormal situations: total AVB, 3:1 block and 2:1 block. In this arrhythmia simulation, the user can still adjust all cardiac phase durations as the cardiac beating occurs. This process's differential relies on simulating the arrhythmogenic effect of blocking atrial beating from a ventricular beating, which provokes the AVB. The simulator's setting ranges occur according to the bench test performed with the computational setup used.

Table 1. Adjustable cardiac parameters.

Parameter	Symbol	Minimum	Typical	Maximum	Unity
Atrial contraction	AC	60	100	140	ms
Ventricular contraction/atrium relaxation	VC/AR	60	150	180	ms
Ventricular relaxation	VR	60	150	180	ms
Resting	Rest	220	350	1000	ms
Cardiac rate	Freq	40	80	150	bpm
Atrial ventricular block	Block	2:1	3:1	Total	–

The graphical interface also generates images for the holographic interface. The heart model beats in slow motion for the holography creation regarding the convenient user naked-eye visualization and manipulation. Figure 6 shows 3D images of the heart in a naked-eye hologram interface created using the so-called Pepper hologram pyramid technique. Such a technique allows the observation and interaction with scenes of medical anatomy [17,18]. The heart hologram visualizes inside the pyramid positioned on a projection screen where the interface prompts four heart images for the hologram creation. Such a resource concedes a freely moving naked-eye 3D visualization for the cardiac model while the user interacts with it.

Fig. 6. Visualization of the heart model inside of the holographic pyramid. Below are the prompts of four heart images for the hologram creation.

5   Discussion

Virtual models of the heart in graphical interfaces allow anatomical and physiological exploration of that organ in ways impossible in the real world. Accordingly, this work presents a heart simulation interface specially devised to allow the user to control the cardiac beating motion while simultaneously interacts with the heart model in a diversified manner. In the most modern and sophisticated approaches, precise heartbeat simulation occurs with accurate and anatomically detailed heart models [2,6]. It suggests that the present work simulation interface would improve significantly by upgrading the heart model to a more detailed one.

By using a less refined heart model (only external parts), Coelho and colleagues [19] developed an interesting and simplified graphical environment for mobile devices where a 3D virtual heart model simulates the beating heart's external parts according to electrocardiogram parameters, pre-setting cardiac rates, or phases of the cardiac cycle [19]. The present work simulation evolves much further and distinguishes significantly from it, as the user can adapt systole and diastole duration to heartbeat interval settings according to expected physiological variations. Additionally, it grants simulation of internal and external parts of the heart, which, beyond allowing a heartbeat anatomically more realistic, with a variety of cardiac rate and arrhythmias, allows emulating the physiological thickening of the ventricle's walls at the systole. Most importantly, it allows concomitantly to all of that, the heart-beating motion timing modifications (systole and diastole) or cardiac rhythm adjustments for arrhythmias simulations in real-time.

The present work simulation also differs from many other authors who intended interactive visualization of 3D beating heart models in virtual environments [2,8,10]. More specifically, Mauriello and colleagues [20] developed exciting software to visualize the heart's internal and external parts and show the ventricles' animations to demonstrate their relaxation and contraction movements. However, again, distinctly from the present work interface, that work and the others do not provide concomitant resources for heart manipulations or arrhythmias simulations in real-time.

The simulator customizable beating parameters (see Table 1) comply with the heartbeat's clinical values in regular rates or arrhythmias. The simulable arrhythmias in the platform – bradycardia, which includes AV blocks, or tachycardia, which comprises sinus tachycardia - represent prevalent and crucial cardiac rhythm alterations [27,28]. That implies that the presented interface complies with a relevant and straightforward improvement of versatile computational tool developments aiming at heart simulation in normal or abnormal situations. That is feasible as systole or diastole phases are adjustable quickly and precisely.

As for the possibility of holographic visualization implemented in the developed interface, it is essential to mention existing several other forms of three-dimensional visualization, such as Virtual or Augmented Reality [30]. However, holography can improve planning for complex surgeries, further improving medical interaction by allowing naked-eye 3D visualization for natural depth perception [18].

Diversified simulations and visualization techniques - such as *in silico* hearts for drug tests, Extended Reality, and Holograms - evolved to have applications in cardiology teaching or training [10,17]. Accordingly, the present work's approach may contribute naturally to the heart simulation and visualization, including personalized *in silico* cardiology, by reproducing a beating heart with cardiac arrhythmias of clinical relevance for medical training.

As a whole, the present work presented a graphical environment where the heart beating simulation can customize to the patient cardiac rhythm. The graphical interface essentially supports the customizable heartbeat simulation. The blood flow or other aspects of the heart function were not the objects of study, neither providing a realistic rendering of the heart model. The simulator differential, advantage, and focus concern the possibility of adjusting each phase of the cardiac cycle individually to simulate normal and abnormal (arrhythmias) heartbeat rhythms. Another essential differential concerns the fact that atrial and ventricles movements were based on echocardiogram and ECG data and matched to the heart model by specialists. Thus, the simulator can emulate the beating heart to data of diversified patients. Such differential was fundamental to compose patient customized and realistic animation, including the thickening of ventricle walls as systole occurs.

6   Conclusion

The graphical interface developed is a versatile tool for diversified cardiac simulations and visualizations as it allows controlling the cardiac beating motion, creating regular rates or arrhythmias, while the user simultaneously interacts with the heart model. Those features are naturally in the educational context as they derive from clinically relevant data for the training of medical students or health professionals. Additionally, such an interface is a kind of tool already proved helpful in cut costs and improving the teaching/learning process in academic settings.

Thus, the interface has feasible usages, at least, for primary education and training in cardiology. Additionally, it exhibits versatility and potentiality for future upgrades to explore new medical training and benefit state-of-the-art surgical planning.

Acknowledgment. The authors are grateful to FAPESP (Fundação de Amparo à Pesquisa do Estado de São Paulo, Brazil; grant: 2017/22949-3) for the financial support.

References

1. Acero, J.C., et al.: The 'Digital Twin' to enable the vision of precision cardiology. Eur. Heart J. **41**(48), 4556–4564 (2020)
2. Kariya, T., et al.: Personalized perioperative multi-scale, multi-physics heart simulation of double outlet right ventricle. Ann. Biomed. Eng. **48**(6), 1740–1750 (2020). https://doi.org/10.1007/s10439-020-02488-y
3. Silva, N.A., Southworth, M., Raptis, C., Silva, J.: Emerging applications of virtual reality in cardiovascular medicine. JACC: Basic Transl. Sci. **3**(3), 420–430 (2018)
4. Tuli, S., et al.: HealthFog: an ensemble deep learning based smart healthcare system for automatic diagnosis of heart diseases in integrated IoT and fog computing environments. Futur. Gener. Comput. Syst. **104**, 187–200 (2020)
5. Lamata, P., et al.: An automatic service for the personalization of ventricular cardiac meshes. J. R. Soc. Interface **11**(91), 20131023 (2013)
6. Pantelidis P., et al.: Virtual and augmented reality in medical education, medical and surgical education - past, present and future. In: IntechOpen (2017). https://www.intechopen.com/books/medical-and-surgical-education-past-present-and-future/virtual-and-augmented-reality-in-medical-education
7. Trayanova N.A.: Custom cardiology: a virtual heart for every patient. Personalized computer models will let cardiologists test life-saving interventions. IEEE online (2014). http://www.ieee.org/about/index.html
8. Lopez-Perez, A., Sebastian, R., Izquierdo, M., Ruiz, R., Bishop, M., Ferrero, J.M.: Personalized cardiac computational models: from clinical data to simulation of infarct-related ventricular tachycardia. Front. Physiol. **10**, 580 (2019)
9. Quarteroni, A., Lassila, T., Rossi, S., Ruiz-Baier, R.: Integrated heart-coupling multiscale and multiphysics models for the simulation of the cardiac function. Comput. Meth. Appl. Mech. Eng. **314**, 345–407 (2017)
10. Hwang, M., Lim, C.H., Leem, C.H., Shim, E.B.: In silico models for evaluating proarrhythmic risk of drugs. APL Bioeng. **4**, 021–502 (2020)
11. Wilson, H.H., Feins, R.H., Heathcote, S.A., Sr., Caranasos, T.G.: A high-fidelity, tissue-based simulation for cardiac transplantation. Ann. Thorac. Surg. **109**(2), 147–148 (2020)
12. Makransky, G., Mayer, R.E., Veitch, N., Hood, M., Christensen, K.B., Gadegaard, H.: Equivalence of using a desktop virtual reality science simulation at home and in class. PLOS ONE **14**(4), e0214944 (2019)
13. Ong, C.S., et al.: Role of virtual reality in congenital heart disease. Congn. Heart Dis. **13**(3), 357–361 (2018)

14. Plasencia, J.D., et al.: The virtual heart transplant-the next step in size matching for pediatric heart transplantation. J. Heart Lung Transplant. **36**(4), S165 (2017)
15. Xie, T., Islam, M.M., Lumsden, A.B., Kakadiaris, I.A.: Holographic iRay: exploring augmentation for medical applications. In: IEEE International Symposium on Mixed and Augmented Reality (ISMAR-Adjunct), Nantes, pp. 220–222 (2017)
16. Gabor, D.: Holography, 1948–1971. Proc. IEEE **60**(6), 655–668 (1972)
17. Southworth, M., Silva, J.R., Silva, J.N.A.: Use of extended realities in cardiology. Trends Cardiovasc. Med. **30**(3), 143–148 (2020)
18. Mishra, S.: Hologram the future of medicine - from Star Wars to clinical imaging. Indian Heart J. **69**(4), 566–567 (2017)
19. Coelho, R.C., Lourenço, N.C.G.R., de Godoy, C.M.G.: A mobile device tool to assist the ECG interpretation based on a realistic 3D virtual heart simulation. SIMULATION **94**(6), 465–476 (2018)
20. Mauriello, D., Kirk, J., Fernsler, J.: Two novel approaches to visualizing internal and external anatomy of the cardiac cycle with a windowed virtual heart model. In: Proceedings of the 17th ACM SIGGRAPH, pp. 1–2 (2017)
21. Doost, S.N., et al.: Heart blood flow simulation: a perspective review. Biomed. Eng. Online **15**(101), 1–28 (2016)
22. Custom cardiology: a virtual heart for every patient. https://spectrum.ieee.org/biomedical/imaging/custom-cardiology-a-virtual-heart-for-every-patient
23. The visible heart laboratories. http://www.vhlab.umn.edu/
24. Heartworks. www.inventivemedical.com
25. Perez, A.L., Sebastian, R., Ferrero, J.M.: Three-dimensional cardiac computational modelling: methods, features and applications. Biomed. Eng. Online **14**(1), 35 (2015)
26. Sellers G., Wright, J., Richard, S., Haemel, N.: OpenGL superBible: Comprehensive Tutorial and Reference. Addison-Wesley (2013)
27. Shabtaie, S.A., Witt, C.M., Asirvatham, S.J.: Natural history and clinical outcomes of inappropriate sinus tachycardia. J. Cardiovasc. Electrophysiol. **31**(1), 137–143 (2020)
28. Sidhu, S., Marine, J.E.: Evaluating and managing bradycardia. Trends Cardiovasc. Med. **30**(5), 265–272 (2020)
29. Rokhsaritalemi, S., Sadeghi-Niaraki, A., Choi, S.M.: A review on mixed reality: current trends. Challenges and prospects. Appl. Sci. **10**(2), 636 (2020)
30. Patel, D., Bhalodiya, P.: 3D holographic and interactive artificial intelligence system. In: Proceedings of the International Conference on Smart Systems and Inventive Technology (ICSSIT), Tirunelveli, India, pp. 657–662 (2019)
31. Monaghan, D.S., et al.: Interactive holograms using pepper ghost pyramid. IJSRD - Int. J. Sci. Res. Develop. **4**(01), 1221–1224 (2016)

ADD-Net: Attention U-Net with Dilated Skip Connection and Dense Connected Decoder for Retinal Vessel Segmentation

Dongjin Huang[✉], Hao Guo, and Yue Zhang

Shanghai University, Shanghai, China
djhuang@shu.edu.cn

Abstract. Retinal vessel segmentation is an essential step in the diagnosis of many diseases. Due to the large number of capillaries and complex branch structure, efficient and accurate segmentation of fundus vessels faces a huge challenge. In this paper, we propose an improved U-shape network, aiming at the problem of complex vessel segmentation, especially those thin, obscure ones. Firstly, we propose a new attention module, including channel attention and spatial attention, to build the connection between channels and learn to focus on those crucial representations. Secondly, we improve the skip connection by adding dilated convolutions, which can not only coping with the problem of semantic gap between the low-dimension and high-dimension features but also extract rich context information in encoder. Finally, the idea of dense connection is adopted in the decoder to fuse the feature representations with low computation cost and parameters. Experimental results show that our method could efficiently obtain the accurate segmentation image and achieve state-of-the-art performance on the public datasets DRIVE and CHASE_DB1.

Keywords: Retinal vessel segmentation · Deep learning · U-Net · Attention mechanism

1 Introduction

Retinal vessel segmentation in fundus images plays an important role in computer aided diagnosis. As the only blood vessels that can be obtained without trauma, retinal blood vessels are of great significance for the detection of diseases such as diabetes, hypertension and retinopathy. However, manual segmentation of blood vessels is a time-consuming task and needs to be performed by professionally trained and experienced physicians. Therefore, it is necessary to accurately segment blood vessels in fundus images in order to make an efficient diagnosis of the disease.

Image segmentation is an important research direction in the field of computer vision. In the early years, traditional image processing methods were widely used, including the region-growing method, watershed transformation,

N. Magnenat-Thalmann et al. (Eds.): CGI 2021, LNCS 13002, pp. 327–338, 2021.
https://doi.org/10.1007/978-3-030-89029-2_26

thresholding method, edge detection, etc. These methods are mainly based on the mathematics and topology. The appearance of machine learning (ML) algorithms including K-NN, SVM and random forest greatly improves the segmentation results. The drawback of ML based methods is that their performances rely on how the features are constructed. With the rapid development of deep learning, CNN (Convolutional Neural Network) becomes one of the dominant methods and achieves excellent performance. Unlike those methods mentioned above, CNN can automatically learn features from images. Among them, fully convolutional neural network (FCN) [17], DeepLab [2–5], and other models were proposed in succession for segmentation tasks. However, these models do not perform well in the face of medical image processing with fewer datasets. The emergence of U-Net [20] effectively solves this problem. U-Net can use small data sets for training, and its encoding-decoding structure can accurately obtain the region of interest in various segmentation tasks.

For now, retinal vessel segmentation remains a challenging task due to: (1) Retinal vessels vary widely in shape and size. (2) a variety of tissues and lesions, such as optic disk, capillary and yellow spot appear in fundus images. (3) Limited by imaging technology, inadequate illumination or sensor noises may lead to the loss of essential information.

In this paper, we propose a novel network based on U-Net for accurate retinal vessel segmentation. We revise the encoder and decoder with attention module to contain the irrelevant features and strengthen the useful ones. Both spatial attention and channel attention are adopted to build relationship between the feature representations. Multi-scale dilated convolution are added to the skip connection to solve the problem of semantic gap and reuse the context information in encoder. To fuse features in different stages, pixelshuffle is employed as the upsample method to connect the feature in each decoder layer with those in deeper layers. We experiment on the public datasets DRIVE and CHASE_DB1 and compare with state-of-the-art methods.

2 Related Work

2.1 Traditional Image Processing

The traditional image processing methods do not need gold standard as a reference to segment blood vessels. These methods can be divided into matched filter, vascular tracking, and mathematical morphology methods. Cinsdikici [6] introduced a hybrid model where the result is the combination of the output of ant algorithm and match filter. In Mapayi's [18] work, vessels are detected by using fuzzy C-means and gray level co-occurrence matrix (GLCM). Median filter and morphological opening is utilized to repair the misclassification. Dash [7] proposed a morphological-based technology. The pre-processing pipeline consists of CLAHE, morphological opening and anisotropic diffusion filter. Segmentation is conducted with Kirsch's template and the final segmentation is refined by morphological cleaning as post-process.

2.2 Deep Learning

Recently, deep learning, as a branch of machine learning, has shown its promising performance in many computer vision tasks. U-Net is undoubtedly the milestone of biomedical image segmentation tasks. Its symmetric encoder-decoder structure has been widely used in medical image analysis.

Considering the elegant architecture of U-Net itself, many scholars focused on the combination of several U-Nets to achieve a better result. U-Net++ [25] redesigned the skip connection to embed four U-Nets of different depths into one model by nested skip connections. Zhuang [26] cascaded two U-Net with multiple paths for more efficient information flow. IterNet [15] added some refinery modules (mini-UNet) after U-Net to learn how to fix equivocal pixels close to the vessel boundary. These methods are relatively simple structures, and ignore the relationship between feature representations.

There are works attempting to replace the vanilla convolution block with some plug-and-play modules to extract features. For example, R2U-Net [1] stacked two recurrent convolution layers in one residual block. DUNet [13] employed deformable convolution which can automatically change the receptive field and focus on the blood vessels. However, simply replacing convolution operations may cause the great increasement of the amount of computation.

Besides, context information and multi-scale features are also the directions of many researchers. DEU-Net [22] proposed context path and feature fusion module (FFM) to encode spatial information and fuse them. Wang [23] proposed a feature pyramid cascade (FPC) module in RVSeg-Net to capture multi-scale features and aggregating information to improve connectivity. The performance of these methods usually depend on the settings of hyperparameters and is difficult to generalize.

Generative adversarial network (GAN) also attracts a lot of attention. RV-GAN [24] employed multi-scale generators and auto-encoders to extract both global and local features. In Sudgan [14], dense connection and short connection were used in generators to produce more confusing probability map. However, compared to CNN, GAN is harder to train due to its unstable training process.

3 Method

3.1 Network Structure

As shown in Fig. 1, our model is based on encoder-decoder structure. The network consists of four encoder blocks and four decoder blocks, the corresponding blocks are bridged by dilated skip connection. To avoid overfitting, we utilize DropBlock [9] as the regularization method. Different from dropout randomly dropping independent units, DropBlock discards a contiguous region of a feature map together. The new structured DropBlock conv unit is shown in Fig. 2, each convolutional layer is followed by a DropBlock, a batch normalization (BN) layer and a ReLU activation. After each encoder or decoder block, attention module is followed to enhance the feature representation. The first and the last two

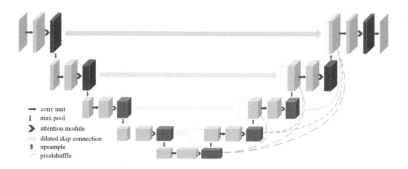

Fig. 1. Model structure.

attention modules contain both spatial attention and channel attention, while the rest contain channel attention only. In decoder, dense connection is used to connect the feature of different sizes. The last layer outputs the likelihood map calculated by Sigmoid. We use cross entropy as the loss function:

$$C = -\frac{1}{n}\sum_{x}^{n}[y_x\log\hat{y}_x + (1 - y_x)\log(1 - \hat{y}_x)] \tag{1}$$

where $y \in \{0, 1\}$ is the label from ground truth, $\hat{y} \in [0, 1]$ is the probability that the pixel belongs to the blood vessel.

3.2 Attention Module

Human attention mechanism is derived from intuition. It is a means by which humans use limited attention resources to quickly screen out high-value information from a large amount of information. The attention mechanism in deep learning is inspired by human attention, and is widely used in various types of deep learning tasks such as Natural Language Processing (NLP), image classification, and speech recognition.

Channel attention was proposed by SENet [11]. The main idea is modeling channel interdependencies to re-weight filter responses in two steps, squeeze and excitation. Squeeze is achieved by global average pooling (GAP) to embed global information. As shown in Fig. 3, the original feature tensor U_c is compressed to $Z_c \in R^{C \times 1 \times 1}$ through spatial dimension where the c-th element of z is calculated by:

$$Z_c = F_{sq}(U_c) = \frac{1}{H \times W}\sum_{i=1}^{H}\sum_{j=1}^{W}u_c(i, j) \tag{2}$$

Fig. 2. Structure of convolution unit.

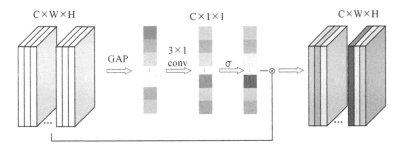

Fig. 3. Structure of the channel attention module.

To make use of the embedded information, we follow squeeze with excitation operation, aiming to capture channel-wise dependencies. In order to fully capturing local cross-channel interaction and make correspondence between channel and its weight, we make all channels share the same learnable parameters. Formally:

$$S = F_{ex}(z) = \sigma(C1D(z)) \tag{3}$$

where the C1D indicates 1D convolution, σ denotes Sigmoid. Finally, the output tensor through channel attention:

$$\hat{O}_c = F_{scale}(U_c, S_c) = u_c \cdot s_c \tag{4}$$

where $\hat{O}_c = [\hat{O}_1, \hat{O}_2, \ldots, \hat{O}_c]$ and F_{scale} refers channel-wise multiplication. Follow the same design paradigm, we propose the spatial attention. As is shown in Fig. 4, the original feature tensor $U_{i,j}$ is compressed to $Z_{i,j} \in R^{1 \times H \times W}$ through channel dimension instead of spatial dimension:

$$Z_{i,j} = F_{sq}(U_{i,j}) = \sum_{k=1}^{C} u_{i,j}(k) \tag{5}$$

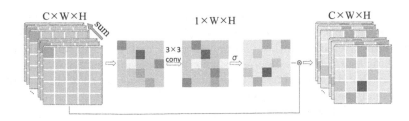

Fig. 4. Structure of the spatial attention module.

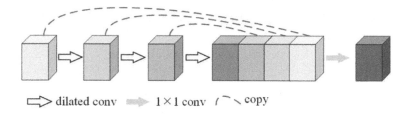

dilated conv ⟹ 1×1 conv ⌒⌒ copy

Fig. 5. Structure of dilated convolution skip connection.

Similar, 2D convolution is adopted to learn the corresponding spatial information:

$$S = F_{ex}(z) = \sigma(C2D(z)) \tag{6}$$

Finally, the output tensor through spatial attention:

$$\hat{O}_{i,j} = F_{scale}(U_{i,j}, S_{i,j}) = u_{i,j} \cdot s_{i,j} \tag{7}$$

where F_{scale} refers multiplication operation on the same spatial location. For
larger feature maps, we add both channel attention and spatial attention,
because the larger feature maps contain more detailed information. As the max
pooling downscales the feature maps to smaller ones, we remove spatial attention
in the middle layers, only the channel attention is retained.

3.3   Dilated Skip Connection

One of the reasons U-Net achieves accurate segmentation is the skip connection
structure, by concatenating the features in decoder and encoder, we can not only
reuse the features from the encoder, but also restore the lost detail information
due to the downsampling. However, concatenating the features directly ignores
the problem of semantic gap [12]. Take U-Net as an example, the first skip
connection cascades the encoder block before the first downsampling with the
decoder before output. However the features coming from the encoder block are
supposed to be low-level features as they are computed in the earlier layers of
the network, while the decoder features computed at deeper layers are supposed
to be higher level features.

   To solve this problem, we insert multiple convolution layers along the skip
connection. Its structure is shown in Fig. 5, the entire skip connection consists of
several dilated convolutions. Features are passed from encoder through a chain of
dilated convolutions, and the context information in different receptive fields is
aggregated by 1×1 convolution. Those convolutions layers can not only reduce
the semantic gap between different stages, but also maintain the relationship
between local and global context information. Considering that the size of features gradually halves as they goes deeper, we reduce the number of convolution
layers and the dilation rate of each convolution by the index of skip connection.
Compared with other methods [19] also applied dilated convolution in skip connection, our method would achieve larger receptive fields due to the successive

Fig. 6. Example of image pre-processing.

convolution layers. Taking Fig. 5 as an example, the dilate rate of each layer are $\{2, 4, 8\}$, and the receptive fields of features are $\{3, 5, 13, 29\}$ respectively, while other methods are $\{3, 5, 9, 17\}$.

3.4 Dense Connected Decoder

In many works, fusing features is an important means to improve segmentation performance. The low-level features usually contain more position and detail information but less semantical, while high-level features contain richer semantic information, but the spatial information is lost.

In order to obtain better segmentation results, we fuse feature maps of different sizes in the decoding stage, each feature map will be fused with a larger feature map. We adopt pixelshuffle [21] as upscale method. By rearranging the elements of $r^2 \times C \times H \times W$ tensor to a tensor of shape $C \times rH \times rW$, pixelshuffle can not only be parameter-free, but also reduce the number of channels after fusion. The dense connection of the decoder also effectively solves the problem of gradient disappearance in the process of back propagation.

4 Experiment Results and Analysis

We performed experiments on DRIVE [8] and CHASE_DB1 [10] datasets. In order to ensure that the training and test data have similar distributions, we used full images as input in the training and testing. As shown in Fig. 6, color images were converted to grayscale images before training, and then we exploited contrast limited adaptive histogram equalization (CLAHE) to improve contrast in images. After that, we applied rotation, translation, flip and noising to images for data augmentation.

The network is trained for a total of 30 epochs and Adam optimizer is adopted. We set initial learning rate to 0.0001 and adjust with reduceLROn-Plateau strategy. For DropBlock, the size of dropped feature is 7×7, and the drop rate is 0.15. Network construction and experimental tests were implemented based on Pytorch. The GPU configuration is Nvidia Titan Xp with cuda 10.1.

The retinal blood vessel segmentation can be seen as a binary classification problem where each pixel in the image is divided into blood vessel or background.

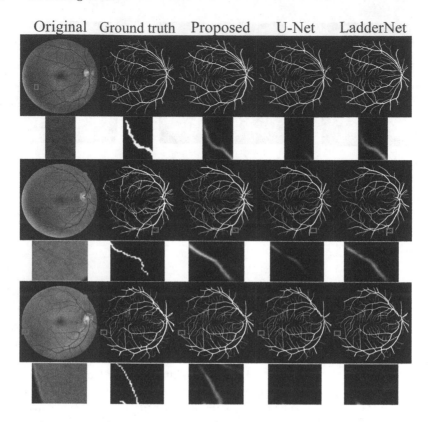

Fig. 7. Segment results on the DRIVE dataset

To make a qualitative evaluation of the experimental results, we use accuracy (ACC), sensitivity (SE), specificity (SP), F1-score and area under curve (AUC) as performance evaluation metrics.

Table 1 and 2 shows the comparison results of our model and other methods. On the DRIVE dataset, the sensitivity, accuracy, and AUC of the proposed method achieved the best results, reached 0.8221, 0.9856, 0.9688 respectively. Compared with other methods, F1 is lower than Liu [16]. On CHASE_DB1 dataset, our model obtained the best score of all five metrics, reached 0.8303, 0.8381, 0.9870, 0.9764, 0.9906. By analyzing these tables, we found our model tend to over-segment when it encounters more capillaries in the image, which results in the lower specificity in DRIVE dataset and indirectly lowers the F1 value.

Besides, we give the visualization of U-Net, LadderNet and our model on DRIVE and CHASE_DB1 datasets in Fig. 7 and 8. Our model can recognize the extremely thin vessels that other methods failed in low contrast. Figure 9 shows the precious-recall curve and ROC curve, area under the PR curve on DRIVE and CHASE_DB1 dataset reached 0.9077 and 0.9131 while area under the ROC curve reached 0.9856 and 0.9906.

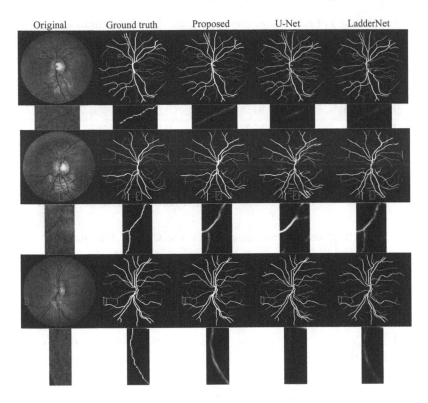

Fig. 8. Segment results on the CHASE_DB1 dataset.

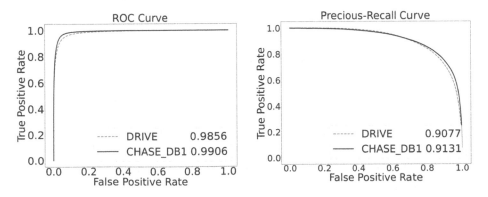

Fig. 9. PR curve and ROC curve of the DRIVE and CHASE_DB1 datasets.

In addition, Table 3 shows the compare of the operation time, number of parameters and FLOPs. The time consumption of our model is less than the most of models. The number of parameters of proposed method is more than LadderNet but less than others. Our model also has less FLOPs on these two datasets than the most of other models.

Table 1. Performance comparison on the DRIVE dataset.

Methods	Year	F1-score	SE	SP	ACC	AUC
U-Net [20]	2015	0.8142	0.7537	0.9820	0.9531	0.9755
R2U-Net [1]	2018	0.8171	0.7792	0.9813	0.9556	0.9784
RU-Net [1]	2018	0.8155	0.7751	0.9816	0.9556	0.9782
LadderNet [26]	2018	0.8202	0.7856	0.9810	0.9561	0.9793
Liu [16]	2019	0.8225	0.8072	0.9780	0.9559	0.9779
DEU-Net [22]	2019	**0.8270**	0.7940	0.9816	0.9567	0.9772
RVSeg-Net [23]	2020	–	0.8107	**0.9845**	0.9681	0.9817
Proposed	2021	0.8224	**0.8221**	0.9824	**0.9688**	**0.9856**

Table 2. Performance comparison on the CHASE_DB1 dataset.

Methods	Year	F1-score	SE	SP	ACC	AUC
U-Net [20]	2015	0.7783	0.8288	0.9701	0.9578	0.9772
R2U-Net [1]	2018	0.7982	0.7756	0.9712	0.9634	0.9815
RU-Net [1]	2018	0.7800	0.7726	0.9820	0.9553	0.9779
LadderNet [26]	2018	0.8031	0.7978	0.9818	0.9656	0.9839
DUnet [13]	2019	0.7853	0.8229	0.9821	0.9724	0.9863
DEU-Net [22]	2019	0.8037	0.8074	0.9821	0.9661	0.9812
RVSeg-Net [23]	2020	–	0.8069	0.9836	0.9726	0.9833
Proposed	2021	**0.8303**	**0.8381**	**0.9870**	**0.9764**	**0.9906**

Table 3. Compare of parameters, test time and FLOPs.

Methods	Params/M	DRIVE		CHASE_DB1	
		Time/s	Flops/G	Time/s	Flops/G
U-Net	34.5	2.92	327.5	8.28	954.1
LadderNet	3.5	1.78	55.2	4.43	160.1
RU-Net	39.1	6.51	328.6	18.04	957.7
Residual U-Net	13.0	3.11	472.57	9.16	994.7
R2U-Net	39.1	6.54	328.6	18.04	957.7
IterNet	13.6	3.73	209.2	11.47	608.3
Proposed	4.7	2.99	75.63	8.42	219.9

5   Conclusion

In this paper, we propose an improved U-Net based model, aiming to segment the retinal vessel in fundus images. Attention module is introduced to enhance the crucial features both in spatial and channel dimension. Convolutions with various dilation rates are inserted into skip connection to reduce the semantic gap and extract multi-scale context information from the encoder. In decoder, the feature of each layer is connected and fused with others. The pixelshflfe is adopted for upscaling which decreases the computation cost and parameters. Compared with state-of-the-art methods, our method achieves good performance.

In the next step, we will continue to improve our network, especially those incoherent and ambiguous pixels in the segmentation. Our work will further be extended to the segmentation of 3D data and integrated into the reconstruction work flow.

Acknowledgments. This work was supported by the Shanghai Natural Science Foundation of China under Grant No.19ZR1419100 and the National Natural Science Foundation of China under Grant No.61402278.

References

1. Alom, M.Z., Hasan, M., Yakopcic, C., Taha, T.M., Asari, V.K.: Recurrent residual convolutional neural network based on U-Net (R2U-Net) for medical image segmentation. arXiv preprint arXiv:1802.06955 (2018)
2. Chen, L.C., Papandreou, G., Kokkinos, I., Murphy, K., Yuille, A.L.: Semantic image segmentation with deep convolutional nets and fully connected CRFs. arXiv preprint arXiv:1412.7062 (2014)
3. Chen, L.C., Papandreou, G., Kokkinos, I., Murphy, K., Yuille, A.L.: DeepLab: semantic image segmentation with deep convolutional nets, atrous convolution, and fully connected CRFs. IEEE Trans. Pattern Anal. Mach. Intell. **40**(4), 834–848 (2017)
4. Chen, L.C., Papandreou, G., Schroff, F., Adam, H.: Rethinking atrous convolution for semantic image segmentation. arXiv preprint arXiv:1706.05587 (2017)
5. Chen, L.C., Zhu, Y., Papandreou, G., Schroff, F., Adam, H.: Encoder-decoder with atrous separable convolution for semantic image segmentation. In: Proceedings of the European Conference on Computer Vision (ECCV), pp. 801–818 (2018)
6. Cinsdikici, M.G., Aydın, D.: Detection of blood vessels in ophthalmoscope images using MF/ant (matched filter/ant colony) algorithm. Comput. Methods Program. Biomed. **96**(2), 85–95 (2009). https://doi.org/10.1016/j.cmpb.2009.04.005
7. Dash, J., Bhoi, N.: Retinal blood vessel extraction using morphological operators and Kirsch's template. In: Wang, J., Reddy, G.R.M., Prasad, V.K., Reddy, V.S. (eds.) Soft Computing and Signal Processing. AISC, vol. 900, pp. 603–611. Springer, Singapore (2019). https://doi.org/10.1007/978-981-13-3600-3_57
8. Fraz, M.M., Rudnicka, A.R., Owen, C.G., Barman, S.A.: Delineation of blood vessels in pediatric retinal images using decision trees-based ensemble classification. Int. J. Comput. Assist. Radiol. Surg. **9**(5), 795–811 (2013). https://doi.org/10.1007/s11548-013-0965-9
9. Ghiasi, G., Lin, T.Y., Le, Q.V.: DropBlock: a regularization method for convolutional networks. arXiv preprint arXiv:1810.12890 (2018)
10. Hoover, A., Kouznetsova, V., Goldbaum, M.: Locating blood vessels in retinal images by piecewise threshold probing of a matched filter response. IEEE Trans. Med. Imaging **19**(3), 203–210 (2000)

11. Hu, J., Shen, L., Sun, G.: Squeeze-and-excitation networks. In: Proceedings of the IEEE Conference on Computer Vision and Pattern Recognition, pp. 7132–7141 (2018)
12. Ibtehaz, N., Rahman, M.S.: MultiResUNet: rethinking the U-Net architecture for multimodal biomedical image segmentation. Neural Netw. **121**, 74–87 (2020)
13. Jin, Q., Meng, Z., Pham, T.D., Chen, Q., Wei, L., Su, R.: DUNet: a deformable network for retinal vessel segmentation. Knowl. Based Sys. **178**, 149–162 (2019)
14. Kamran, S.A., Hossain, K.F., Tavakkoli, A., Zuckerbrod, S.L., Sanders, K.M., Baker, S.A.: RV-GAN: retinal vessel segmentation from fundus images using multi-scale generative adversarial networks (2021)
15. Li, L., Verma, M., Nakashima, Y., Nagahara, H., Kawasaki, R.: IterNet: retinal image segmentation utilizing structural redundancy in vessel networks. In: Proceedings of the IEEE/CVF Winter Conference on Applications of Computer Vision, pp. 3656–3665 (2020)
16. Liu, B., Gu, L., Lu, F.: Unsupervised ensemble strategy for retinal vessel segmentation. In: Shen, D., Liu, T., Peters, T.M., Staib, L.H., Essert, C., Zhou, S., Yap, P.-T., Khan, A. (eds.) MICCAI 2019. LNCS, vol. 11764, pp. 111–119. Springer, Cham (2019). https://doi.org/10.1007/978-3-030-32239-7_13
17. Long, J., Shelhamer, E., Darrell, T.: Fully convolutional networks for semantic segmentation. In: Proceedings of the IEEE Conference on Computer Vision and Pattern Recognition, pp. 3431–3440 (2015)
18. Mapayi, T., Tapamo, J.R., Viriri, S.: Retinal vessel segmentation: a comparative study of fuzzy C-means and sum entropy information on phase congruency. Int. J. Adv. Rob. Syst. **12**(9), 133 (2015)
19. Moran, S., Leonardis, A., Mcdonagh, S., Slabaugh, G.: CURL: neural curve layers for global image enhancement (2019)
20. Ronneberger, O., Fischer, P., Brox, T.: U-Net: convolutional networks for biomedical image segmentation. In: Navab, N., Hornegger, J., Wells, W.M., Frangi, A.F. (eds.) MICCAI 2015. LNCS, vol. 9351, pp. 234–241. Springer, Cham (2015). https://doi.org/10.1007/978-3-319-24574-4_28
21. Shi, W., et al.: Real-time single image and video super-resolution using an efficient sub-pixel convolutional neural network. In: Proceedings of the IEEE Conference on Computer Vision and Pattern Recognition, pp. 1874–1883 (2016)
22. Wang, B., Qiu, S., He, H.: Dual encoding U-Net for retinal vessel segmentation. In: Shen, D., et al. (eds.) MICCAI 2019. LNCS, vol. 11764, pp. 84–92. Springer, Cham (2019). https://doi.org/10.1007/978-3-030-32239-7_10
23. Wang, W., Zhong, J., Wu, H., Wen, Z., Qin, J.: RVSeg-Net: an efficient feature pyramid cascade network for retinal vessel segmentation. In: Martel, A.L., et al. (eds.) MICCAI 2020. LNCS, vol. 12265, pp. 796–805. Springer, Cham (2020). https://doi.org/10.1007/978-3-030-59722-1_77
24. Yang, T., Wu, T., Li, L., Zhu, C.: SUD-GAN: deep convolution generative adversarial network combined with short connection and dense block for retinal vessel segmentation. J. Digit. Imaging **33**, 946–957 (2020)
25. Zhou, Z., Rahman Siddiquee, M.M., Tajbakhsh, N., Liang, J.: UNet++: a nested U-Net architecture for medical image segmentation. In: Stoyanov, D., et al. (eds.) DLMIA/ML-CDS -2018. LNCS, vol. 11045, pp. 3–11. Springer, Cham (2018). https://doi.org/10.1007/978-3-030-00889-5_1
26. Zhuang, J.: LadderNet: multi-path networks based on U-Net for medical image segmentation (2018)

BDFNet: Boundary-Assisted and Discriminative Feature Extraction Network for COVID-19 Lung Infection Segmentation

Hui Ding[1,2(✉)], Qirui Niu[1], Yufeng Nie[1], Yuanyuan Shang[1,2], Nianzhe Chen[1], and Rui Liu[1]

[1] College of Information Engineering, Capital Normal University, Beijing, China
dhui@cnu.edu.cn
[2] Beijing Advanced Innovation Center for Imaging Technology, Beijing, China

Abstract. The coronavirus disease (COVID-19) pandemic has affected billions of lives around the world since its first outbreak in 2019. The computed tomography (CT) is a valuable tool for the COVID-19 associated clinical diagnosis, and deep learning has been extensively used to improve the analysis of CT images. However, owing to the limitation of the publicly available COVID-19 imaging datasets and the randomness and variability of the infected areas, it is challenging for the current segmentation methods to achieve satisfactory performance. In this paper, we propose a novel boundary-assisted and discriminative feature extraction network (BDFNet), which can be used to improve the accuracy of segmentation. We adopt the triplet attention (TA) module to extract the discriminative image representation, and the adaptive feature fusion (AFF) module to fuse the texture information and shape information. In addition to the channel and spatial dimensions that are mainly used in previous models, the cross channel-special context is also obtained in our model via the TA module. Moreover, fused hierarchical boundary information is integrated through the application of the AFF module. According to experiments conducted on two publicly accessible COVID-19 datasets, COVID-19-CT-Seg and CC-CCII, BDFNet performs better than most cutting-edge segmentation algorithms in six widely used segmentation metrics.

Keywords: COVID-19 · Attention mechanism · Adaptive feature fusion · Medical image segmentation

1 Introduction

Since the outbreak of the novel Coronavirus Disease (COVID-19) [1] at the end of 2019, COVID-19 has become the largest global public health crisis. It has been reported that Chest CT and radiography play a crucial role in first-line diagnosis of COVID-19 [2]. From a clinical point of view, COVID-19 has rich imaging features in Computer Tomography (CT) [3], such as the lung consolidation and ground-glass opacity (GGO), which can accurately reflect the patient's infection region and degree of infection. Therefore,

© Springer Nature Switzerland AG 2021
N. Magnenat-Thalmann et al. (Eds.): CGI 2021, LNCS 13002, pp. 339–353, 2021.
https://doi.org/10.1007/978-3-030-89029-2_27

most hospitals have applied CT in research and later follow-up treatment. CT images are already the important basis for diagnosis and treatment of COVID-19 [4].

However, the researches related to the segmentation of the infection lesion from CT slices are relatively few.

By automatically highlighting lesion features and ROI (region of interest), the segmentation result of COVID-19 could provide doctors with many important information for accurate diagnosis and follow-up treatment plans. Dengping Fan et al. [5] proposed a novel deep network for COVID-19 lung infection segmentation named Inf-Net to identify lesion regions automatically by combing the implicit reverse attention and explicit edge-attention. Guotai Wang et al. [6] developed a novel deep neural segmentation network with a noise-robust dice loss to deal with the infection regions with various scales. In Yun Liu et al. [7], a lightweight deep learning model called MiniSeg, which combined with an attentive hierarchical spatial pyramid module, was used to segment infection regions from CT of COVID-19, and solve the problem of overfitting in network training.

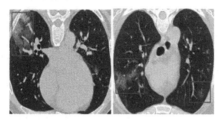

Fig. 1. An Examples of CT images. CT scan shows the areas (red frames) of GGO are irregular. (Color figure online)

Although, deep learning networks perform well in COVID-19. The segmentation is still a challenge: 1) The high accuracy and robustness of deep learning models requires training with sufficient annotated data, while the public available COVID-19 dataset is limited. 2) The infection lesions vary greatly in shape, size, and texture at different infection states and among different patients, such as GGO in the early infection stage and pulmonary consolidation in the late infection stage. For example, the boundaries of GGO have low contrast and irregular shape as shown in Fig. 1.

To address the above issues, we propose a novel boundary-assisted and discriminative feature extraction network named BDFNet, to segment COVID-19 lung infection from CT images. One branch consists of a discriminative feature by using the triplet attention (TA) module, and the other consists of a shape extraction. Then, the features extracted from the two branches are fused through the Adaptive Feature Fusion (AFF) module. The essential task is to exploit and extract the latent features in the training data and then make the prediction for each pixel of the image in the testing data, i.e., whether belonging to the COVID-19 infection lesion. Ours contributions are summarized as follows:

- The adaptive feature fusion (AFF) module is proposed, which can model the complementary relationship between texture features and shape features based on the location of the infected area and use boundary features as prior information to enhance the boundary of the segmented area.

- The triplet attention (TA) module is proposed to extract discriminative features from limited data for alleviating the shortage of annotation data. TA generates a discriminative feature by modeling interdependence in the spatial dimension, channel dimension, and cross spatial-channel dimension, respectively.

Especially, our network utilizes joint loss functions to improve the model learning capability and acquire a more precise segmentation result.

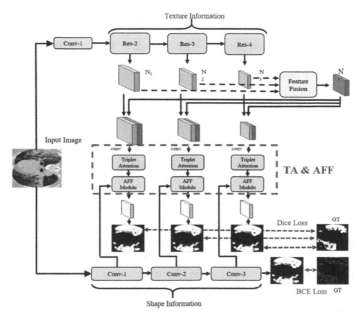

Fig. 2. A Structure of the BDFNet. The network extracts texture information and shape information from two branches, and then the AFF module models the complementary relationship between texture features and shape features by taking the boundary features as prior. The TA module is used to extract discriminative features.

2 Proposed Method

2.1 Architecture of BDFNet

In this section, we will describe the structure of the proposed COVID-19 segmentation network (BDFNet) in detail. As depicted in Fig. 2, BDFNet consists of two branches. The first branch of the network ("texture branch") is a regular segmentation convolutional neural network, and the second branch ("shape branch") processes the shape information in the form of the lesion region's boundaries. We enforce the shape branch to only extract boundary-related information by using a dedicated loss function as supervision. Finally, the representative features, especially those with precise boundaries is produced by fusing the texture features from the texture branch and shape features from the shape branch.

Mainbody. This texture branch uses ResNet-50 [8] as the feature extractor to obtain hierarchical texture features. The high-level layer's features mainly contain global information and it provide the infection regions' coarse location in a deep neural network. The integration of multi-level features has been demonstrated effective in the segmentation task [9, 10]. Inspired by these works, we utilize a parallel partial decoder [11] to aggregate high-level features.

At present, a lot of attention has been put forward. Misra et al. [12] proposed a kind of triplet attention. This attention can rotate the axis of different dimensions of the latitude rotation feature map, and then perform cascading and pooling operations. The difference is that the triplet attention used in this paper includes spatial attention, channel attention, and cross attention. After cascading the three operations, the final triplet attention mechanism is obtained.

Here, we feed CT images into texture branch and obtain high-level features denoted as N_s, where s indicates the texture branch architecture level. The fused features are computed by $N' = ppd(N_1, N_2, N_3)$, where $ppd(\cdot)$ means aggregate operations. Then feature N' combines with each of the feature maps at different levels, which is fed into the TA modules. This operation can be written as:

$$N_s'' = AttMod_s\left(Concat\left(N_s, N'\right)\right) \tag{1}$$

Where N_s'' denotes each feature generated from attention modules, and $AttMod_s(\cdot)$ represents each triplet attention module.

In the shape branch, three convolutional layers are used to extract shape features, which have larger spatial resolutions and contain more boundary-related information. Spatial resolution of conventional medical CT images is not intrinsically high, and the global features reduce the resolution. Therefore, just using only global features cannot satisfy to predict COVID-19 segmentation results.

Then, the AFF module is utilized to gradually fuse the learned feature maps at each layer of the shape branch, and combine with corresponding texture features. Finally, the generated features are fed into convolution layers to obtain output prediction. It is worth noting that we adopt the deep supervision for three output predictions, and the final segmentation prediction is the average of these three outputs.

Triplet Attention Module. Discriminative features can be extracted by building associations among pixels or features through the attention mechanism. TA module will obtain rich contextual dependencies and improve the feature representation, by modeling interdependence in the spatial dimension, channel dimension, and spatial-channel dimension. The cross spatial-channel attention is innovation.

The diagram of the proposed triplet attention (TA) module can be found in Fig. 3(a). The results are fused by three types of attention modules, which are position attention (PA) module, channel attention (CA) module and intersection attention (IA) module, to extract correlation from different dimensions. Accordingly, they obtain an enriched global dependency.

Given a local feature $\mathbf{X} \in \mathbb{R}^{C \times W \times H}$, where C denotes the number of channels, W and H are the input features' width and height. Firstly, it is fed into three attention modules to generate three new feature maps $\mathbf{P(X)}$, $\mathbf{C(X)}$ and $\mathbf{I(X)}$, respectively, where $\mathbf{P(X)}$, $\mathbf{C(X)}$, $\mathbf{I(X)} \in \mathbb{R}^{C \times W \times H}$.

Then, we concatenate them in $\mathbb{R}^{C \times W \times H}$, and apply a convolution layer to obtain the final output $\mathbf{Y} \in \mathbb{R}^{C \times W \times H}$:

$$\mathbf{Y} = Conv(Concat(\mathbf{P(X)}, \mathbf{C(X)}, \mathbf{I(X)})) \tag{2}$$

Where $Conv(\cdot)$ denotes the convolution operation and $Concat(\cdot)$ denotes the concatenate operation.

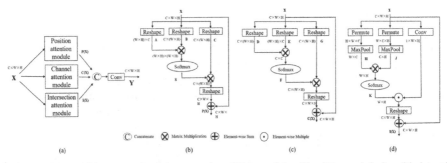

Fig. 3. (a) The architecture of triplet attention (TA) module. The TA module is added to the back of the feature that combines local and global information. This module uses three different attention extraction methods to extract contextual dependencies between features and improve feature representation. (b), (c), (d) are the architectures of position attention (PA) module, channel attention (CA) module, and intersection attention module (IA) in (a).

As illustrated in Fig. 3(b) and (c), we utilize a position attention (PA) module and a channel attention (CA) module to adaptively aggregate spatial dimensional dependency and channel dimensional dependency [13]. Through this operation, the network can model the correlation between two pixels of two features, and learn and use COVID-19 lesion regions' spatial information in any location thoroughly. Meanwhile, exploring the inter-dependencies among these activations could improve the representation of semantic features. However, in the process of obtaining position attention and channel attention, a loss of information is inevitable. For example, the interdependence of channel dimension is absent while computing position attention.

Therefore, we design the intersection attention (IA) module to build cross-dimension dependence between the channel dimension and the spatial dimension. As illustrated in Fig. 3(d). Firstly, the input features $\mathbf{X} \in \mathbb{R}^{C \times W \times H}$ was reshaped to $\mathbf{H} \in \mathbb{R}^{W \times C}$ and $\mathbf{J} \in \mathbb{R}^{C \times H}$ by permuting and maxpooling operations. Then, we apply matrix multiplication between H and J and calculate cross-dimension attention map $\mathbf{K} \in \mathbb{R}^{W \times H}$ by utilizing softmax layer:

$$K_{i,j} = \frac{exp(\mathbf{H_i} \cdot \mathbf{J_i})}{\sum_{i=1}^{W \times H} exp(\mathbf{H_i}, \mathbf{J_i})} \tag{3}$$

Where $K_{i,j}$ denotes the correlation between channel dimension and spatial dimension. Then, we perform element wise multiplication between the generated attention map with the feature generated from convolution layer. The output is applied to feature dimension adjustment and element-wise addition with original feature $\mathbf{X}$ to acquire $(\mathbf{X}) \in \mathbb{R}^{C \times W \times H}$:

$$I(\mathbf{X}) = Re(K \odot Conv(\mathbf{X})) + \mathbf{X} \tag{4}$$

Where $Re(\cdot)$ and $Conv(\cdot)$ denote feature dimension adjustment and convolution, respectively, and $\odot$ denotes element-wise multiplication.

Through obtaining the position attention, channel attention, and intersection attention separately, the triplet attention is used to fuse these branches to gain a global contextual dependency and achieve more accurate segmentation performance of COVID-19 infection regions.

Adaptive Feature Fusion Module. Since the accuracy of the segmentation result is closely related to the segmentation result's boundary, it is essential to use shape information in deep CNN effectively. Here, the second branch is used to capture rich shape-dependent information in parallel to the branch capturing texture information. The fusion of texture information with the shape information is done by the Adaptive feature fusion module.

As illustrated in Fig. 4. Given the texture features $\mathbf{M}_{\text{texture}} \in \mathbb{R}^{C \times W' \times H'}$ and the shape features $\mathbf{M}_{\text{shape}} \in \mathbb{R}^{C \times W \times H}$, here C is the number of channels; $\left(H, H'\right)$ and $\left(W, W'\right)$ are the height and width of the feature maps, respectively. First, the mapping function, L is obtained by the AFF module based on the shape features to produce a set of affine transformation parameters $\left(\varepsilon, \delta \in \mathbb{R}^{C \times W \times H}\right)$. It can be expressed as:

$$(\varepsilon, \delta) = L\left(\mathbf{M}_{\text{shape}}\right) \tag{5}$$

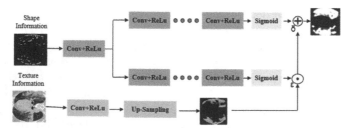

Fig. 4. Illustration of the proposed AFF module.

The mapping function is built by feeding the shape features into two parallel stacked convolution layers and sigmoid function. Then, we make the resolution of the texture features $\left(\mathbb{R}^{C \times W' \times H'}\right)$ same as the shape features $\left(\mathbb{R}^{C \times W \times H}\right)$ by up-sampling operation. Finally, the generated features are element-wise multiplied by ε and then element-wise summed by δ. Therefore, the output of each AFF module, $\mathbf{M}_{\text{output}} \in \mathbb{R}^{C \times W \times H}$, can be represented as follow:

$$\mathbf{M}_{\text{output}} = \mathbf{M}_{\text{texture}} \odot \varepsilon \oplus \delta \tag{6}$$

Where $\odot$ and $\oplus$ indicate the element-wise multiplication and element-wise addition, respectively. The AFF module learns pixel-wise affine transformation parameters and fuses the texture features and shape features through modulation operation adaptively.

Basing on the AFF module, the BDFNet could fuse texture information and shape information, and compensate for the lost infection boundary-related information to generate segment results with more precise boundaries.

2.2 Joint Loss Functions

To obtain the texture and shape features in an end-to-end fashion, we supervise boundary prediction and segmentation prediction during training simultaneously. Here, the boundary prediction is a binary image of all the outlines of infection regions in the CT image. Meanwhile, we adjust the all-prediction map's size to segmentation ground-truth map T before calculating training loss. Then, we use the standard Binary Cross Entropy (BCE) loss function to constrain the boundary prediction:

$$L_{boundary} = -\sum_{i=1}^{w}\sum_{j=1}^{H}\left[T_b log(P_b) + (1 - T_b)log(1 - P_b)\right] \tag{7}$$

Where W and H denote the weight and height of each map, respectively, and (i, j) is the pixel coordinate in the boundary prediction map P_b and boundary ground-truth map T_b. The T_b is obtained by calculating the gradient of ground-truth map T. The BCE loss function makes the probability distribution of the boundary segmentation prediction closer to the true distribution.

To learn the semantic representations of texture, Dice loss function is used for each segmentation outputs supervision, i.e.:

$$L_{dice}(P, T) = 1 - 2 \times \frac{\Sigma_{i=1}^{N}p_i t_i + \tau}{\Sigma_{i=1}^{N}p_i + \Sigma_{i=1}^{N}t_i + \tau} \tag{8}$$

Where summation is carried over the N pixels of the predicted map $p_i \in P$ and the ground-truth map $t_i \in T$, and τ is a minimal constant to prevent division by zero. Finally, we proposed the joint loss function which composed of the boundary segmentation loss and the segmentation output loss:

$$L_{joint} = L_{boundary} + \lambda\sum_{i=1}^{3}L_{dice}((P_s)_i, T_s) \tag{9}$$

Where λ is the weight to balance the different losses and be set to 1. Intuitively, the model trained with joint loss could learn to predict individual pixel values in infection regions boundaries correctly by $L_{boundary}$, and also learn to locate infection regions through L_{dice}.

3 Experiments

3.1 Implementation Details

We use the PyTorch1.3 framework to implement the proposed BDFNet. Adam optimizer is used to train with an initial learning rate of 1e-4. We train 100 epochs on the training set with a batch size of 24. For the fair comparison, we train all previous state-of-the-art segmentation networks that use the same settings as our BDFNet. All experiments are conducted on four TITAN RTX GPUs.

Datasets. In this experiment, we use two datasets for segmentation which are COVID-19-CT-Seg[1] and CC-CCII [14][2]. Both of them are open-access COVID-19 dataset for lung infection segmentation.

The COVID-19-CT-Seg dataset consists of 100 axial CT images in our experiments, which were collected by the Italian Society of Medical and Interventional Radiology from different COVID-19 patients. Each of the CT images has the segmentation mask of COVID-19 infection regions annotated by the radiologist. We select 50 CT images for training networks randomly, and another 50 CT images are utilized for performance evaluation.

Another dataset of the CT slice images is from the China Consortium of Chest CT Image Investigation (CC-CCII). A total of 750 CT slices from 150 COVID-19 patients were segmented into background, lung field, ground-glass opacity, and consolidation (CL). In order to highlight the segmentation of the lesion area, we preprocess the data which merged the lung and the background as well as the lesion area. We obtain the binary label of the lesion area and the non-lesion area, where 0 is the background and 1 is the lesion area. Due to the existence of unlabeled images in the dataset, in order to improve the usability of the data, we filter the data and finally got 549 usable high-quality images, which were randomly select 270 CT images for training networks, and another 279 CT images are utilized for performance evaluation.

Evaluation Metrics. Six widely used evaluation metrics are used to evaluate the performance of our method, including the Dice Similarity Coefficient (DSC), Specificity (Spec.), Sensitivity (Sen.), Structure Measure (S_α) [15], Enhance-alignment Measure (E_ϕ) [16] and Mean Absolute Error (MAE).

The DSC is a measure for calculating the overlap index between labeled ground-truth images and predicted images. The metrics of Spec. and Sen. measure the ability to correctly predict COVID-19 infected areas and the non-infected areas, respectively. Here, the S_α is used to measure the structural similarity between the ground-truth image and the predicted image. The E_ϕ is designed to evaluate both global and local similarities between the two images. Additionally, the MAE is utilized to measure the pixel-wise error between ground-truth images and prediction images.

3.2 Ablation Study

Effectiveness of Proposed Module. We conduct ablation studies on the different dataset to prove the effectiveness of the proposed components in BDFNet, including the Triplet Attention (TA) module and the Adaptive Feature Fusion (AFF) module.

Table 1 shows the segmentation performance of networks with different proposed components on COVID-19-CT-Seg dataset. We start with the ResNet-50 as the backbone,

---

[1] https://medicalsegmentation.com/covid19/.

[2] http://ncov-ai.big.ac.cn/download?lang=zh.

Table 1. Effectiveness of main components on COVID-19-CT-Seg dataset.

Models	DSC↑	Sen. ↑	Spec. ↑	Sα↑	E_ϕ↑	MAE↓
Backbone	0.534	0.697	0.841	0.646	0.704	0.161
Backbone + TA Module	0.739	0.733	**0.956**	0.747	0.913	0.066
Backbone + AFF Module	0.599	0.731	0.815	0.675	0.725	0.190
Backbone + TA + AFF Module	**0.756**	**0.751**	0.950	**0.760**	**0.923**	**0.060**

which has no TA module and AFF module. Adding the TA modules to the three output levels in the backbone, we achieve the improvement in all evaluation metrics, especially the improvement of DSC to 0.739, Spec. to 0.956 and E_ϕ to 0.913. It demonstrates the superiority of the triplet attention acquired from modeling inter-dependency in different dimensions. Then, we remove the TA modules and extend the backbone with the AFF modules, and such a dual-branch network increases the S_α to 0.675 and the E_ϕ to 0.725, which proves the importance of fusing shape information. At last, we continue to add the two proposed components to the backbone to recover BDFNet. And we achieve the DSC, Sen., S_α, E_ϕ, MAE of 0.756, 0.751, 0.760, 0.923, 0.060, respectively. The improvement is attributed to the accurate extraction of lesion features by the TA module and the fusion of shape and texture features by the AFF module.

Table 2. Effectiveness of main components on CC-CCII dataset

Models	DSC↑	Sen. ↑	Spec. ↑	Sα↑	E_ϕ↑	MAE↓
Backbone	0.623	0.803	0.883	0.592	0.810	0.087
Backbone + TA Module	0.701	0.747	0.933	0.803	0.904	0.006
Backbone + AFF Module	0.646	**0.807**	0.914	0.657	0.837	0.049
Backbone + TA + AFF Module	**0.709**	0.761	**0.934**	**0.807**	**0.908**	**0.006**

Table 2 shows different proposed components on CC-CCII dataset. After adding the TA module and the AFF module, the performance indicators have been significantly improved compared to the Backbone. We achieve the DSC to 0.709, Spec. to 0. 934, Sα to 0.807, E_ϕ to 0.908 and MAE to 0.006 which are best performance with other modules. These ablation studies prove that when the model combines the TA module and the AFF module at the same time, it can represent features from the texture information by modeling different dimensions of information, and can also integrate the edge information, which improve the model's segmentation effect on the lesion area.

Design of TA Module. Since the TA module is composed of PA, CA and IA, we also conducted ablation experiments inside the TA module to evaluate the effects of different modules.

Table 3. Design of triplet attention module in the BDFNet.

Models	DSC ↑	Sen. ↑	Spec. ↑	Sα↑	E_ϕ↑	MAE ↓
Channel Attention (CA)	0.709	**0.790**	0.921	0.716	0.875	0.083
Position Attention (PA)	0.715	0.700	**0.958**	0.734	0.894	0.067
Intersection Attention (IA)	0.734	0.781	0.938	0.743	0.896	0.069
Triplet Attention (TA)	**0.739**	0.733	0.956	**0.747**	**0.913**	**0.066**

First, we add the position attention module to the backbone. Then, we replace the positional attention module with the channel attention module to extract the interdependence of the channels. In addition, we also replace the channel attention module in the backbone with the intersection attention module. Finally, we combine the three modules to form our TA module. The results of the ablation experiment performed on the COVID-19-CT-Seg dataset are shown in Table 3. TA module has achieved a good performance on most evaluation metrics. Maybe the training data is not enough, and the proposed IA module already has strong feature extraction capabilities,it did not achieve the best results on the Sen. and Spec. metrics. TA module adds CA module and PA module on the basis of IA, which increases the risk of model overfitting.

3.3 Comparisons with State-of-the-Art Methods

For the COVID-19 infection area segmentation experiments, we compare the proposed BDFNet with previous state-of-the-art competitors based on two different dataset, including: U-net, Attention U-net, U-net++, Inf-Net, PraNet [17], SegNet [18] and SegAN [19].

Table 4. Quantitative results of infected areas on COVID-19-CT-Seg dataset.

Models	DSC ↑	Sen. ↑	Spec. ↑	Sα↑	Eφ↑	MAE ↓
U-Net	0.679	0.646	0.956	0.704	0.876	0.078
Attention U-Net	0.698	0.638	**0.973**	0.718	0.869	0.074
U-Net++	0.691	0.690	0.944	0.767	0.848	0.085
Inf-Net	0.681	0.701	0.935	**0.774**	0.834	0.090
PraNet	0.676	0.743	0.917	0.751	0.828	0.102
SegNet	0.560	0.544	0.930	0.637	0.723	0.114
SegAN	0.709	0.660	0.966	0.733	0.870	0.072
BDFNet (Ours)	**0.756**	**0.751**	0.950	0.760	**0.923**	**0.060**

Table 4 shows the evaluation results of BDFNet and other competitors on COVID-19-CT-Seg dataset. We achieve the DSC to 0.756, Sen. to 0.751,E_ϕ to 0.923 and MAE to 0.060 which are highest evaluation metrics compared to other moudles. We attribute this improvement to the designed TA module, which establishes a more comprehensive dimensional dependence. Additionally, the segmentation performance of the BDFNet in the evaluation metric Spec. and Sα is not as good as Attention U-Net and Inf-Net. The possible reason is that the feature extraction ability of the TA module in BDFNet is too strong. And the network pays more attention to the specific structure of the lesion area and consider more structures similar to the lesion area as segmentation targets.

Table 5. Quantitative results of infected areas on CC-CCII dataset.

Models	DSC ↑	Sen. ↑	Spec. ↑	Sα↑	Eφ↑	MAE ↓
U-Net	0.643	0.615	0.912	0.774	0.855	0.006
Attention U-Net	0.693	0.739	0.922	0.798	0.905	0.006
U-Net++	0.705	0.708	0.921	0.804	0.887	0.011
Inf-Net	0.643	**0.801**	0.926	0.686	0.847	0.030
PraNet	0.646	0.784	0.913	0.699	0.849	0.033
SegNet	0.538	0.578	0.861	0.599	0.777	0.084
SegAN	0.621	0.716	**0.952**	0.745	0.874	0.008
BDFNet (Ours)	**0.709**	0.761	0.934	**0.807**	**0.908**	**0.006**

Table 5 shows the evaluation results of BDFNet and other competitors on other datasets. We achieve the DSC to 0.709, Sα to 0.807, E$_\phi$ to 0.908 and MAE to 0.006 which are highest evaluation metrics compared to other moudles. But the segmentation performance of the BDFNet in the evaluation metric Sen. and Spec. is not as good as Inf-Net and SegAN. Inf-Net introduces a reverse attention mechanism that pays more attention to the edge information, so it has achieved the better performance on the Sen. metric. SegAN uses the Generative Adversarial Network (GAN) to generate external data and increases the diversity of data, so it has a higher Spec. score. But in general, BDFNet achieved the best performance on most evaluation metrics.

4 Conclusion

In this paper, we propose a novel boundary-assisted and discriminative feature extraction network (BDFNet) to segment COVID-19 infected areas from CT images. In order to solve the problems of difficult segmentation caused by drastic changes in the infected area, we utilize a triplet attention (TA) module to extract discriminative features for accuracy segmentation. Moreover, we provide an adaptive feature fusion (AFF) module to model the complementary relationship between shape information and texture information for clearer edge segmentation. Experiments on the publicly available COVID-19 dataset demonstrate that our network achieves better performance than most cutting-edge segmentation models in COVID-19 infected areas segmentation.

Appendix

In this section, we provide additional experiments and visualizations for the BDFNet model. Part A shows the visualization results of the heat map of the TA module and the AFF module. Part B compares the robustness differences between the TA module and other attention mechanisms. Part C shows the visual comparison of segmentation results between BDFNet and other advanced segmentation algorithms.

A. The Visualization Results on TA Module and AFF Module

In Sect. 3.2, the ablation experiments on the TA module and the AFF module demonstrate the effectiveness of the proposed module. To further validate the proposed TA module and AFF module's effectiveness intuitively, we randomly select some samples from COVID-19-CT-Seg dataset and use Grad-CAM [20] technology to visualize the gradients of segment prediction as a heat map, the bright area in the figure indicates the area participating in the segmentation.

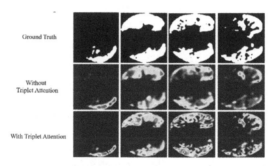

Fig. 5. The visualization results on TA module's gradients through Grad-CAM.

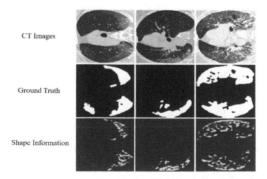

Fig. 6. The visualization results on AFF module's gradients through Grad-CAM.

As shown in Fig. 5, compared with the ground truth map, the TA module is able to capture more accurate and comprehensive COVID-19 infection regions from CT images.

In some cases, the network with the TA module can correctly identify the infected area that the original network misidentified.

Figure 6 shows the shape information captured by the network added with the AFF module. It can be seen from the figure that the obtained shape information basically depicts the outline of the infection area, which proves the AFF module's capability to capture richer and more precise shape information from infection regions.

B. The Compare of the Robustness for TA, PA, CA and IA

In Table 4 in Sect. 3.2, from the ablation experiment inside the TA module, it can be seen that although the TA module has achieved the best performance in multiple evaluation indicators, it does not lead too much. In order to verify the superiority of the proposed TA module, we performed a statistical analysis of the experimental results on the COVID-19-CT-Seg dataset, and the results are shown in Fig. 7.

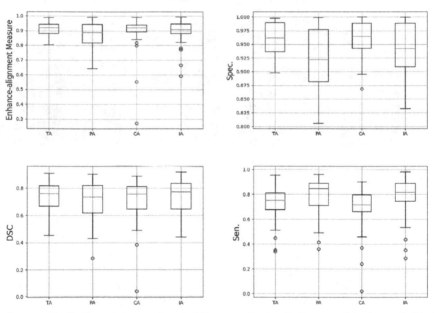

Fig. 7. The distribution of the results of different evaluation indicators of the internal ablation experiment in the TA module. The horizontal axis represents the network model that contains different attention mechanism modules, including TA module, PA module, CA module, IA module, and the vertical axis represents different evaluation indicators.

The fact is that the TA module achieves the best overall performance in COVID-19 infection regions segmentation, especially in terms of the metric of S_α, E_ϕ, and MAE. Figure 7 shows the evaluation distribution of the segmentation results of the four attention mechanism modules under dfferent evaluation metrics. From the figure, it can be seen that with the same evaluation parameters, the segmentation result obtained by the TA module is more stable. This shows that the TA module has a more robust segmentation ability for different test data. And it is not easy to be affected by extreme values in the segmentation results.

C. Visual Comparison of Segmentation Results

In Sect. 3.3, Fig. 4 and Fig. 5 show that no networks can lead consistently on all evaluation metrics. Therefore, by visually comparing the segmentation results, we can more intuitively verify the pros and cons of the segmentation results.

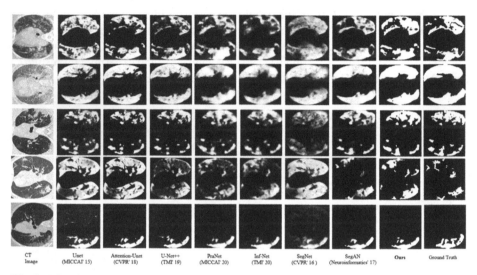

CT   Unet   Attention-Unet   U-Net++   PraNet   Inf-Net   SegNet   SegAN   Ours   Ground Truth
Image (MICCAI' 15) (CVPR' 18) (TMI' 19) (MICCAI' 20) (TMI' 20) (CVPR' 16) (Neuroinformatics' 17)

Fig. 8. Visual comparison of COVID-19 infected areas segmentation from different networks.

Figure 8 provide some comparison of COVID-19 infection regions segmentation results from different networks on COVID-19-CT-Seg dataset. As can be observed, the BDFNet yields segmentation results with more precise boundaries, especially in the subtle infected areas. From a medical point of view, it is very important to accurately distinguish the boundaries of the lesion area. It can help doctors determine the location and extent of the patient's infection and assist the doctor in diagnosis.

References

1. Wang, C., Horby, P.W., Hayden, F.G., Gao, G.F.: A novel coronavirus outbreak of global health concern. J. Lancet **395**, 470–473 (2020). https://doi.org/10.1016/S0140-6736(20)301 85-9
2. Zhao, W., Zhong, Z., Xie, X., Yu, Q., Liu, J.: Relation between chest CT findings and clinical conditions of coronavirus disease (COVID-19) pneumonia: a multicenter study. J. AJR Am. J. Roentgenol. **214**, 1072–1077 (2020). https://doi.org/10.2214/ajr.20.22976
3. Li, C., et al.: Asymptomatic novel coronavirus pneumonia patient outside Wuhan: the value of CT images in the course of the disease. J. Clin. Imaging **63**, 7–9(2020). 101016/j.clinimag.2020.02.008

4. Chen, Z., Wang, R.: Application of CT in the diagnosis and differential diagnosis of novel coronavirus pneumonia. J. CT Theor. Appl. **29**(3), 273–279 (2020). https://doi.org/10.15953/j.1004-4140.2020.29.03.02

5. Fan, D., et al.: Inf-Net: automatic COVID-19 lung infection segmentation. J. CT Images IEEE Trans. Med. Imaging **39**, 2626–2637 (2020). https://doi.org/10.1109/tmi.2020.2996645

6. Wang, G., et al.: A noise-robust framework for automatic segmentation of COVID-19 pneumonia lesions from CT images. J. IEEE Trans. Med. Imaging **39**, 2653–2663 (2020). https://doi.org/10.1109/tmi.2020.3000314

7. Qiu, Y., Liu, Y., Xu, J.: MiniSeg: an extremely minimum network for efficient COVID-19 segmentation. arXiv preprint arXiv:2004.09750 (2020)

8. He, K., Zhang, X., Ren, S., Sun, J.: Identity mappings in deep residual networks. In: Leibe, B., Matas, J., Sebe, N., Welling, M. (eds.) ECCV 2016. LNCS, vol. 9908, pp. 630–645. Springer, Cham (2016). https://doi.org/10.1007/978-3-319-46493-0_38

9. Hariharan, B., Arbelaez, P., Girshick R., et al.: Hypercolumns for object segmentation and fine-grained localization. In: 2015 IEEE Conference on Computer Vision and Pattern Recognition, pp. 447–456, IEEE Press, Boston (2015). https://doi.org/10.1109/CVPR.2015.7298642

10. Mostajabi, M., Yadollahpour, P., Shakhnarovich, G.: Feedforward semantic segmentation with zoom-out features. In: 2015 IEEE Conference on Computer Vision and Pattern Recognition, pp. 3376–3385, IEEE Press, Boston (2015). https://doi.org/10.1109/CVPR.2015.7298959

11. Wu, Z., Su, L., Huang, Q.: Cascaded partial decoder for fast and accurate salient object detection. In: 2019 IEEE/CVF Conference on Computer Vision and Pattern Recognition, pp. 3902–3911. IEEE Press, Long Beach (2019). https://doi.org/10.1109/CVPR.2019.00403

12. Misra, D., Nalamada, T., Arasanipalai, A.U., et al.: Rotate to attend: convolutional triplet attention module. arXiv preprint, arXiv:2010.03045 (2020)

13. Fu, J., et al.: Dual attention network for scene segmentation. In: 2019 IEEE/CVF Conference on Computer Vision and Pattern Recognition, pp. 3141–3149, IEEE Press, Long Beach (2019). https://doi.org/10.1109/CVPR.2019.00326

14. Zhang, K., Liu, X., et al.: Clinically applicable AI system for accurate diagnosis, quantitative measurements, and prognosis of COVID-19 pneumonia using computed tomography. J. Cell **181**, 1423–1433 (2020). https://doi.org/10.1016/j.cell.2020.04.045

15. Fan, D., Cheng, M., Liu, Y., Li, T., Borji, A.: Structure-measure: a new way to evaluate foreground maps. In: 2017 IEEE International Conference on Computer Vision, pp. 4558–4567, IEEE CS Press, Venice, Italy (2017). https://doi.org/10.1109/ICCV.2017.487

16. Zhang, J., et al.: UC-Net: uncertainty inspired RGB-D saliency detection via conditional variational autoencoders. In: 2020 IEEE/CVF Conference on Computer Vision and Pattern Recognition, pp. 8579–8588, IEEE Press, Seattle (2020). https://doi.org/10.1109/CVPR42600.2020.00861

17. Fan, D.-P., et al.: PraNet: parallel reverse attention network for Polyp segmentation. In: Martel, A.L., et al. (eds.) MICCAI 2020. LNCS, vol. 12266, pp. 263–273. Springer, Cham (2020). https://doi.org/10.1007/978-3-030-59725-2_26

18. Badrinarayanan, V., Kendall, A., Cipolla, R.: SegNet: a deep convolutional encoder-decoder architecture for image segmentation. J. IEEE Trans. Pattern Anal. Mach. Intell. **39**, 2481–2495 (2017). https://doi.org/10.1109/TPAMI.2016.2644615

19. Xue, Y., Xu, T., Zhang, H., Long, L.R., Huang, X.: SegAN: adversarial network with multi-scale L1 loss for medical image segmentation. Neuroinformatics **16**(3–4), 383–392 (2018). https://doi.org/10.1007/s12021-018-9377-x

20. Selvaraju, R.R., Cogswell, M., Das, A., et al.: Grad-CAM: visual explanations from deep networks via gradient-based localization. In: 2017 IEEE International Conference on Computer Vision, pp. 618–626, IEEE CS Press, Venice, Italy (2017). https://doi.org/10.1109/ICCV.2017.74

A Classification Network for Ocular Diseases Based on Structure Feature and Visual Attention

Yang Wen[1], Yupeng Xu[3], Kun Liu[3], Bin Sheng[1(✉)], Lei Bi[2], Jinman Kim[2], Xiangui He[3], and Xun Xu[3(✉)]

[1] Department of Computer Science and Engineering, Shanghai Jiao Tong University, Shanghai, China
{wenyang,shengbin}@sjtu.edu.cn
[2] School of Information Technologies, The University of Sydney, Sydney, Australia
{lei.bi,jinman.kim}@sydney.edu.au
[3] Department of Ophthalmology, Shanghai General Hospital, Shanghai Jiao Tong University School of Medicine, Shanghai, China
drxuxun@sjtu.edu.cn

Abstract. With the rapid development of digital image processing and machine learning technology, computer-aided diagnosis for ocular diseases is more active in the medical image processing and analysis field. Optical coherence tomography (OCT), as one of the most promising new tomography techniques, has been widely used in the clinical diagnosis of ophthalmology and dentistry. To overcome the lack of professional ophthalmologists and realize the intelligent diagnosis of different ocular diseases, we propose a convolutional neural network (CNN) based on structure feature and visual attention for ocular diseases classification. We firstly preprocess the OCT images according to the OCT data characteristics to enhance the OCT image quality. Meanwhile, we propose to use the CNN with structure prior to classify five kinds of ocular diseases, including age-related macular degeneration (AMD), diabetic macular edema (DME), normal (NM), polypoidal choroidal vasculopathy (PCV), and pathologic myopia (PM). Besides, the visual attention mechanism is also used to enhance the ability of the network to represent effective features. The experimental results show that our method can outperform most of the state-of-the-art algorithms in the classification accuracy of different ocular diseases on the OCT dataset.

Keywords: Classification of ocular diseases · Convolutional neural network · Visual attention

1 Introduction

The human visual system converts incoming light signals into biological signals, and its main sensory area is the macula located in the center of the retina. The macula processes light signals and detects light intensity, color, visual details,

© Springer Nature Switzerland AG 2021
N. Magnenat-Thalmann et al. (Eds.): CGI 2021, LNCS 13002, pp. 354–361, 2021.
https://doi.org/10.1007/978-3-030-89029-2_28

etc. through a special layer of photoreceptor nerve cells. The retina processes the information collected by the macula and sends it through the optic nerve to the brain to complete visual recognition. Eye diseases are a constant problem in everyone's life, especially threatening the health of the middle-aged and elderly population. In reality, the retina can be affected by a variety of pathological factors, including AMD and DME. In the case of age-related macular degeneration, for example, AMD causes blurring of the patient's visual field. Patients may see black spots in their vision or even no objects at all in the central area of their vision. In 2010, 23 million people worldwide had AMD, and in 2013, 13.4 million people had moderate to severe AMD [1,2]. In the United States, AMD is the leading cause of vision loss and blindness in people over the age of 50 [3]. Despite the serious impact of eye disease on the quality of life of patients, there is still a serious lack of professional ophthalmologists and medical diagnostic resources. Therefore, how to use computer-aided technology to effectively help doctors to make the intelligent diagnosis and reduce the workload has attracted the attention of many scholars.

Previous studies have shown that comprehensive eye examinations, as well as early intervention and treatment of eye diseases, can significantly reduce the rate of blindness [4,5]. OCT is one of the most promising and rapidly developing new tomographic imaging techniques for the treatment and diagnosis of ocular diseases. OCT imaging is able to capture biological tissue details very clearly and has profound implications for the early identification and treatment of retinal lesions. For ophthalmologists, interpretation of ocular diseases from OCT images is a time-consuming and tedious task. To reduce the diagnostic burden of physicians, various computer-aided diagnosis systems have been developed in recent years [6–12] for the semi/automatic processing and analysis of OCT image data, including OCT image curvature correction [6,7], retinal lesion area segmentation [13], and 2D or 3D OCT disease classification [14]. However, the existing methods cannot meet the practical needs due to the distribution of disease data and the quality of OCT images. At present, there are few appropriate classification algorithms to achieve accurate classification of most eye lesions, such as AMD and PCV diseases. On the one hand, the lesion structures of the two kinds of diseases are similar. On the other hand, there is a lack of professional doctors to provide the necessary medical knowledge. In addition, the classifier based on the neural network also needs to be further optimized. Differently, our proposed method can effectively help doctors distinguish the types of eye diseases and accelerate the speed of image reading, so as to provide professional technical support for timely follow-up treatment and intervention.

In this study, we propose a novel automatic classification system for macular region OCT ocular diseases. The proposed system includes OCT data preprocessing and a visual attention-based convolutional neural network for disease classification. In the preprocessing stage, we rely on image quality enhancement techniques and curvature correction algorithms in machine learning to eliminate retinal noise and capture the target region containing the lesions. In the classification step, the attention mechanism is used to improve the discrimination accuracy of the classification neural network for different ocular diseases.

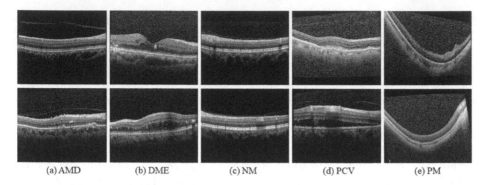

| (a) AMD | (b) DME | (c) NM | (d) PCV | (e) PM |

Fig. 1. Example B-scans from AMD, DME, NM, PCV and PM five ocular diseases subjects in our OCT dataset.

2   Material and Method

2.1   Dataset

For this ocular diseases classification research, we used five different OCT data sets (AMD, DME, NM, PCV, PM) provided by doctors for training and testing. We trained and tested with the OCT data set of 5 different disease types provided by doctors. The entire OCT dataset contains approximately 9500 OCT images, including 100 patients for each category and 19 OCT images for each patient. For each eye disease, we randomly selected all the images from 80 patients as the training set, and all the images from the remaining 20 patients as the test set. We use a unified procedure to pre-process the original OCT data and transform the original OCT images into new images of uniform size and form. Considering that the original OCT data contains different levels of noise and varies in size, the preprocessing algorithm we use needs to be as efficient and robust as possible. Figure 1 shows some example B-scans from AMD, DME, NM, PCV and PM five ocular diseases subjects in our OCT dataset.

2.2   Date Preprocessing

Due to the particularity and importance of medical image data, we preprocess the image first before completing the task of lesion classification. Figure 2 shows the image preprocess in our method. In the image preprocessing stage, we first binarize the original OCT image and median filter the binarized image to remove the black dots detached from the retina. Then, we keep only the maximum connected domain in the image, in order to eliminate small areas of noise and avoid interference with the preprocessing results. After that, we successively perform morphological open operations to eliminate the small bright spots in the OCT images and the white spots that existed alone in the retina. The morphological closed operation is also used to eliminate the possible holes in the OCT images, and to eliminate as many black dots as possible in the images. In addition, for

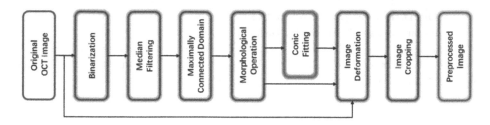

Fig. 2. OCT image preprocessing flow chart.

the obtained binary images, we find the midpoint of each bright line segment and fit all the obtained midpoints with a quadratic function. Finally, we translate each column of the original image and the binary image vertically, so that this quadratic curve becomes horizontal in the new image, which corrects the curvature of the retina itself. After a series of data preprocessing operations, we can reduce the unpleasant noise in the OCT data and extract more effective information about the focal area for improving the accuracy of the subsequent classification tasks. Figure 3 shows example B-scans from five ocular diseases subjects in our OCT dataset after preprocessing.

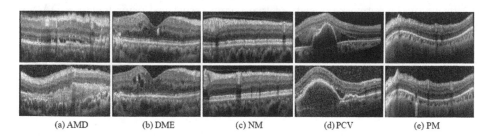

(a) AMD   (b) DME   (c) NM   (d) PCV   (e) PM

Fig. 3. Example B-scans from AMD, DME, NM, PCV and PM five ocular diseases subjects in our OCT dataset after preprocessing.

2.3 Structure Feature Extraction

Inspired by previous studies [15,16], high-level tasks such as classification and segmentation of OCT data are closely related to low-level features. Thus, we propose to classify OCT ocular diseases with the help of machine learning-based statistical features that are based on insignificant contrast, noise distribution and large background areas of the images. The DAISY [17] feature descriptor is used to generate a low-dimensional invariant descriptor feature for local image regions, which can be used for image matching and classification. Compared to GLOH [18] and SIFT [19] feature descriptors, the DAISY feature descriptor is faster [15,17] and it can compute the gradient efficiently on each pixel. Therefore, we use the DAISY feature to assist the CNN network to improve the accuracy of the ocular disease classification task. For each image, eight orientation maps O are computed by DAISY description. $O(x, y)$ denotes the image gradient at location (x, y) for one quantized direction. Specific explanations and calculations of DAISY are provided in [17].

$$G_\Sigma(x, y) = [O_1^\Sigma(x, y), ..., O_8^\Sigma(x, y)]^T \tag{1}$$

where $O_1^\Sigma(x, y), O_2^\Sigma(x, y), ..., O_8^\Sigma(x, y)$ denote the $\Sigma - convolved\ orientation$ $maps$. $G_\Sigma(x, y)$ is then normalized and denoted by $\widehat{G}_\Sigma(x, y)$. Then, structure feature $\widehat{G}_\Sigma(x, y)$ is combined with the original OCT image as input to the CNN network.

2.4   Classification Network

With the rapid development of deep learning technology, the convolutional neural network has shown unparalleled effects in high-level semantic analysis tasks such as image classification and segmentation. Although SVM and other traditional classification methods can achieve the basic task of image classification, in this paper, we implement the OCT classification task for different eye diseases based on the classical convolutional neural network Inception [20]. As shown in Fig. 4, the input of the network consists of two parts: structural prior features DAISY and OCT image features. The Inception layer consists of convolutional layers of sizes 3, 5 and 7, a pooling layer of size 3 and a NIN layer [21] for simplifying the network parameters. In this way, the network acquires feature information at different scales while increasing the perception field. Besides, we also use the attention module [22] which includes spatial and channel attention to enhance the ability of the network to extract important features.

3   Results and Discussion

To verify the accuracy of our method for automatic detection of five eye diseases, we perform all the training and testing experiments on the NVIDIA GTX 2080Ti using the PyTorch platform. In the experiment, the learning rate is 0.0001 and the batchsize is set to 16. All the OCT images are first preprocessed by the method in Sect. 2.2. At the same time, we also compare with many other classical classification methods [23,24] to verify the superiority of our proposed OCT classification algorithm. To be fair, all methods are performed under the same experimental environment and data conditions. Table 1 shows the classification accuracy of multiple classical methods for the different ocular diseases. The results in the Table 1 show that other algorithms generally have poor performance in judging PCV and AMD, which is mainly due to the similar structures of PCV and AMD lesions. However, our method can better improve the feature expression ability and lesion discriminant ability of the network with the help of additional structural prior features and visual attention mechanisms. Table 2

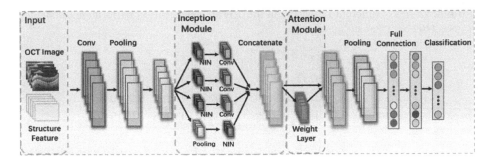

Fig. 4. The proposed OCT classification network based on structure feature and attention module for ocular diseases.

and Table 3 respectively show the impact of different learning rates and different batchsize settings on the performance of the OCT image classification task. According to Table 2 and Table 3, we can see that when the learning rate is 0.0001 and the batchsize is 16 for ResNet18 as an example, the OCT classification network can achieve the best performance. Therefore, in the actual experiment, we set the learning rate and batchsize as 0.0001 and 16, respectively.

Table 1. Classification accuracy of different methods for different ocular diseases.

Model	PM	AMD	PCV	DME	NM
ResNet18	0.9289	0.8526	0.871	0.9921	0.9711
ResNet34	0.8711	0.8553	0.9158	1.0000	0.9789
ResNet50	0.8789	0.8421	0.9184	1.0000	0.9658
VGG16	0.9079	0.8605	0.8816	1.0000	0.9895
VGG19	0.9132	0.8684	0.8763	1.0000	0.9868
Inception	0.9214	0.8631	0.8908	0.9954	0.9927
Our	0.9312	0.9031	0.9235	1.0000	0.9947

Table 2. Effects of different learning rates on the overall classification performance of ocular diseases (ResNet18 as an example).

Learning rate	ACC	Precision	Recall	F1	AUC
0.0001	0.9232	0.9233	0.9232	0.9230	0.9936
0.0003	0.9211	0.9216	0.9211	0.9207	0.9924
0.00005	0.9184	0.9169	0.9184	0.9185	0.9889

Table 3. Effects of different batchsize on the overall classification performance of ocular diseases (ResNet18 as an example).

Batchsize	ACC	Precision	Recall	F1	AUC
8	0.9232	0.9233	0.9232	0.9230	0.9936
4	0.9258	0.9260	0.9258	0.9258	0.9930
16	0.9347	0.9352	0.9347	0.9348	0.9919

4   Conclusion

In this paper, we propose an OCT classification network based on structure features and visual attention for ocular diseases. Our proposed OCT classification model captures structural features DAISY by machine learning approach to provide additional prior knowledge. Meanwhile, the visual attention module is used to enhance the feature representation capability of the network and to strengthen the extraction of effective classification features. Vast experiments have shown that our method can achieve accurate classification for different ocular diseases, especially for the indistinguishable PCV and AMD diseases, which show particularly superior performance. In the future, we will be committed to further improve the classification and location of special eye disease lesions, and provide more advanced technical support for the actual clinical needs of doctors.

Acknowledgement. This work was supported in part by the National Natural Science Foundation of China under Grants 62077037 and 61872241, in part by Shanghai Municipal Science and Technology Major Project under Grant 2021SHZDZX0102, in part by the Science and Technology Commission of Shanghai Municipality under Grants 18410750700 and 17411952600, in part by Shanghai Lin-Gang Area Smart Manufacturing Special Project under Grant ZN2018020202-3, and in part by Project of Shanghai Municipal Health Commission (2018ZHYL0230).

References

1. I.P. Collaborators: Global, regional, and national incidence, prevalence, and years lived with disability for 310 diseases and injuries, 1990c2015: a systematic analysis for the global burden of disease study 2015. LANCET, LONDON (2016)
2. Global, regional, and national incidence, prevalence, and years lived with disability for 354 diseases and injuries for 195 countries and territories, 1990c2017: a systematic analysis for the global burden of disease study 2017. Lancet (2018)
3. Lim, L.S., Mitchell, P.P., Seddon, J.M., Holz, F.G., Wong, T.Y.: Age-related macular degeneration. Nurse Pract. Forum **379**(9827), 1728–1738 (2012)
4. Engelgau, M.M., et al.: The evolving diabetes burden in the united states. Ann. Intern. Med. **140**(11), 945–50 (2004)
5. Rasti, R., Rabbani, H., Mehridehnavi, A., Hajizadeh, F.: Macular OCT classification using a multi-scale convolutional neural network ensemble. IEEE Trans. Med. Imaging **37**(4), 1024–1034 (2018)

6. Rabbani, H., Sonka, M., Abramoff, M.: Optical coherence tomography noise reduction using anisotropic local bivariate gaussian mixture prior in 3D complex wavelet domain. Int. J. Biomed. Imaging **2013**, 417491 (2013)
7. Kafich, R., Rabbani, H., Selesnick, I.: Three dimensional data-driven multi scale atomic representation of optical coherence tomography. IEEE Trans. Med. Imaging **34**(5), 1042–1062 (2015)
8. Amini, Z., Rabbani, H.: Statistical modeling of retinal optical coherence tomography. IEEE Trans. Med. Imaging **35**, 1544–1554 (2016)
9. Kafieh, R., Rabbani, H., Abramoff, M., Sonka, M.: Curvature correction of retinal OCTs using graph-based geometry detection. Phys. Med. Biol. **58**(9), 2925 (2013)
10. Karambakhsh, A., Kamel, A., Sheng, B., Li, P., Yang, P., Feng, D.D.: Deep gesture interaction for augmented anatomy learning. Int. J. Inf. Manag. **45**, 328–336 (2019)
11. Ertugrul, E., Li, P., Sheng, B.: On attaining user-friendly hand gesture interfaces to control existing GUIs. Virtual Reality Intell. Hardware **2**(2), 153–161 (2020). special issue on Visual interaction and its application
12. Nazir, A., et al.: OFF-eNET: an optimally fused fully end-to-end network for automatic dense volumetric 3D intracranial blood vessels segmentation. IEEE Trans. Image Process. **29**, 7192–7202 (2020)
13. Lou, L., et al.: Graph-based multi-surface segmentation of OCT data using trained hard and soft constraints. IEEE Trans. Med. Imaging **32**(3), 531–543 (2013)
14. Sun, Y., Shan, L., Sun, Z.: Fully automated macular pathology detection in retina optical coherence tomography images using sparse coding and dictionary learning. J. Biomed. Opt. **22**(1), 16012 (2017)
15. Ibrahim, M.R., Fathalla, K.M., Youssef, S.M.: HyCAD-OCT: a hybrid computer-aided diagnosis of retinopathy by optical coherence tomography integrating machine learning and feature maps localization. Appl. Sci. **10**(14), 4716 (2020)
16. Jin, Y.: Surrogate-assisted evolutionary computation: recent advances and future challenges. Swarm Evol. Comput. **1**(2), 61–70 (2011)
17. Tola, E., Lepetit, V., Fua, P.: A fast local descriptor for dense matching. In: Proceedings/CVPR, IEEE Computer Society Conference on Computer Vision and Pattern Recognition (2008)
18. Yang, Y.H., Xie, Y.Q.: Feature-based GDLOH deformable registration for CT lung image. Appl. Mech. Mater. **333–335**(1), 969–973 (2013)
19. Burger, W., Burge, M.J.: Scale-invariant feature transform (SIFT). In: Digital Image Processing. TCS, pp. 609–664. Springer, London (2016). https://doi.org/10.1007/978-1-4471-6684-9_25
20. Szegedy, C., Ioffe, S., Vanhoucke, V., Alemi, A.: Inception-v4, Inception-ResNet and the impact of residual connections on learning (2016)
21. Lin, M., Chen, Q., Yan, S.: Network in network, p. 10, December 2014
22. Woo, S., Park, J., Lee, J.-Y., Kweon, I.S.: CBAM: convolutional block attention module. In: Ferrari, V., Hebert, M., Sminchisescu, C., Weiss, Y. (eds.) ECCV 2018. LNCS, vol. 11211, pp. 3–19. Springer, Cham (2018). https://doi.org/10.1007/978-3-030-01234-2_1
23. Simonyan, K., Zisserman, A.: Very deep convolutional networks for large-scale image recognition. Computer Science (2014)
24. He, K., Zhang, X., Ren, S., Sun, J.: Deep residual learning for image recognition. In: 2016 IEEE Conference on Computer Vision and Pattern Recognition (CVPR), pp. 770–778 (2016)

Physics-Based Simulation

DSNet: Dynamic Skin Deformation Prediction by Recurrent Neural Network

Hyewon Seo[1]([✉]), Kaifeng Zou[1], and Frederic Cordier[2]

[1] ICube Laboratory, CNRS-Université de Strasbourg, Strasbourg, France
{seo,kaifeng.zou}@unistra.fr
[2] IRIMAS, Université de Haute-Alsace, Mulhouse, France
frederic.cordier@uha.fr

Abstract. Skin dynamics contributes to the enriched realism of human body models in rendered scenes. Traditional methods rely on physics-based simulations to accurately reproduce the dynamic behavior of soft tissues. Due to the model complexity, however, they do not directly offer practical solutions to domains where real-time performance is desirable. The quality shapes obtained by physics-based simulations are not fully exploited by example-based or more recent data-driven methods neither, with most of them having focused on the modeling of static skin shapes. To address these limitations, we present a learning-based method for dynamic skin deformation. At the core of our work is a recurrent neural network that learns to predict the nonlinear, dynamics-dependent shape change over time from pre-existing mesh sequences. After training the network delivers realistic, high-quality skin dynamics that is specific to a person in a real-time course. We obtain results that significantly saves the computational time, while maintaining comparable prediction quality compared to state-of-the-art.

Keywords: Dynamic skin deformation · Autoencoder · LSTM (Long short term memory) network · Person-specific skin dynamics

1 Introduction

Realistic skin or soft-tissue deformation for the human body model is a challenging task for many applications, which has a long tradition in computer graphics and computer animation. This is evidenced by the large amount of research done on geometric skin deformation, physics-based simulation, body shape capture and data-driven methods. The traditional skeleton driven skin deformation technique [17] and its variants are often widely practiced. Since these models mostly use linear transformations, it is difficult to model the nonlinear deformation such as bulging of muscles, not to mention the dynamic soft-tissue deformation on bodies under motion such as fat jiggling. These are crucial to capture and render the realism of a 3D body.

Physics-based models address the challenging problem of such nonlinear deformation and dynamics by adopting significantly more complex models

© Springer Nature Switzerland AG 2021
N. Magnenat-Thalmann et al. (Eds.): CGI 2021, LNCS 13002, pp. 365–377, 2021.
https://doi.org/10.1007/978-3-030-89029-2_29

[5,22,25,26]. A common strategy is to model bones, muscles, and fats as voxels, and to compute their time-varying deformation as the reaction to some external and internal forces by taking their physical properties into account. While these methods are well established in several domains like computer-aided medical intervention or computer aided design, and provide a possible solution to our problem, their model complexity and hence the heavy computation often make them impractical, especially for real-time applications.

Meanwhile, data driven methods have emerged as powerful models and seem to offer a good alternative. They seek for solutions to efficiently leverage realistic shapes coming either from interactive design by skilled designers, physically based simulation, or captured shapes of real people. Earlier works rely on the sparse set of captured or manually elaborated data [19,24], which have been gradually replaced by richer sets of captured shapes. Based on realistic shape datasets captured at high resolutions, mathematical models are learned to relate the model parameters to the detailed identity shapes and its deformation. Interestingly, data-driven models for the pose-dependent deformation [1,10,12,15] have been initially developed rather independently from the identity-dependent shape variation [2,21], whereas more recent models [3,4,7,14,18] incorporate both entities into a single, unifying framework. Although recent data-driven methods have shown to model person-specific and pose-dependent body shapes successfully, little attention has been paid to capturing and learning the dynamic skin- or soft-tissue deformations.

To address this problem, we pursue a new learning-based model for the realistic dynamic skin deformation. Our work is motivated by the fact that the skin dynamics is highly nonlinear yet significantly limited by kinematic constraints. Such an idea has been confirmed by the recent work Dyna [18], which has shown a successful application of data-driven approach to model such dynamics. There, the per-frame soft-tissue displacement is learned as a linear function of the static body shape, a few inertia parameters, and the function values of two previous frames. A similar spirit has been shown in a recent work by Casas and Otaduy [6], who have trained a neural network regressor to predict the nonlinear soft-tissue dynamics. We also deploy a deep neural network to learn the nonlinear approximator function for the dynamic skin behavior. However, our work differs from theirs in that we model the skin dynamics as a time-series entity, i.e., temporal evolution is explicitly modeled. Moreover, our model can learn the subject-specificity of the skin dynamics, predicting personalized skin dynamics for each body. More recent work by Santesteban et al. [20] has shown to approach the problem also by deploying a recurrent network. However, our model is simpler and lighter and thus more efficient to train and evaluate. Moreover, both the inertia parameters and the temporal scope of previous frames influencing the current frame are automatically learned, as part of the network training, rather than predefined by using a constant.

At the core of our work is a deep neural network to learn to approximate the detail and quality shapes of dynamic skin deformation from a dataset. After the training, the network enables the real-time regression of nonlinear skin dynamics, which can be added to the linear blended skinning to obtain high quality skin deformation. To make the training feasible over such high-resolution mesh, we build a low-dimensional latent space to approximate the soft tissue deformation by using an autoencoder, over which the prediction network is trained. Overall, our work makes the following contributions:

- DSNet that realistically predicts the nonlinear dynamics of skin deformation of a human body model under motion.
- A novel autoencoder that efficiently builds a low-dimensional latent space of the skin displacement of the body mesh, over which the predictor network is trained.
- A personalized skin dynamics simulation thanks to the learned function, producing distinct dynamic deformation according to the identity body shape.

2   Dynamic Skin Data and Representation

2.1   SMPL Model

We base our work on the previously developed body model SMPL [14]. It models an arbitrary posed body shape as a linear blend skinning [17] of a subject-specific body surface, given a set of subject-specific joint locations and the predefined vertex-to-joint blending weights. The subject-specific body surface is obtained by applying per-vertex displacements to a template model to capture the identity shape of the subject, and subsequent displacements to fix the artifacts of the linear blend skinning. The model is based on a linear subspace, which is found by the principle component analysis of thousands of 3D body scans coming from different subjects and poses. Formally, a surface body model $M = M(\beta, \theta)$ is represented as

$$M(\beta, \theta) = \mathcal{W}\left(\bar{M}(\beta, \theta), J(\beta), \theta, W\right) \tag{1}$$

$$\bar{M}(\beta, \theta) = \bar{T} + M_S(\beta) + M_P(\theta) \tag{2}$$

where $\mathcal{W}(M, J, \theta, W)$ is the linear blend skinning function that computes pose-dependent deformation of a body mesh M given the joint locations J, the pose vector θ, and the vertex-to-joint blending weight matrix W. J is a learned function to predict the joint locations from the subject-specific parameters β, shape coefficient vector encoding the coordinates of an identity shape in the shape subspace learned from datasets. The body surface in a rest pose $\bar{M}(\cdot)$ is obtained by adding vertex offsets computed by shape blend shape $M_S(\cdot)$, and subsequently adding those computed by pose blend shape $M_P(\cdot)$ to a learned rigged template mesh $\bar{T}$.

2.2   Datasets

We base our study on Dyna dataset [18] containing a variety of human shapes under motions revealing dynamic soft-tissue deformations, such as jumping and running in place. All subjects were all lightly clothed, while the motion duration varies across subjects and motions, from 2 to 15 s. Based on DMPL framework, an extension of SMPL (reviewed in the previous section), Dyna models come in the form of sequences of triangular meshes, each with $N = 6890$ vertices rigged to a skeleton hierarchy with $K_{Dyna} = 22$ joints excluding hands. Each joint has 3 rotational degrees of freedom (dof) parameterized with axis-angle representation, with an exception to the root joint that has 3 additional dof of translation. Thus, the pose vector θ has $22 \times 3 + 3 = 69$ parameters. To fully exploit Dyna dataset for the network training, and yet to be able to test the performance of the network, we used some of the skin-dynamics inducing motion sequences from Mosh [13] dataset, after some preprocessing to convert the frame rate (100 fps to 60 fps) and the orientation of the root joint (from z-up to y-up). Table 1 summarizes the two datasets used in this work.

Table 1. Dyna and Mosh datasets we used in this work for training and validation, respectively.

Dataset	Subjects	Motions	Fps	No. sequences (men/women)
Dyna	5 men, 5 women	10–14 motions for each subject: one-leg jumping, light hoping, chicken-wings, jumping jacks, shake hips, running in place, etc.	60	66/67
Mosh	Same subjects as above	Some skin-dynamics inducing motions (side-to-side hoping, basketball, kicking), with some others partly overlapping with Dyna.	100	24/30

2.3 Generation of Training Data

Since we are interested in modeling the nonlinear dynamic skin deformation, we extract the vertex displacements contributed by that deformation from each mesh surface S_t^j in the dataset, where j is the index for the subject. (More accurately it is $S_t^{j,m}$ but we will omit the motion index m, for the sake of simplicity). We do so by finding the body shape vector β^j that best matches the mesh at its first frame S_1^j, which is considered fixed throughout the rest of the motion sequence ($t = 2, \ldots$). Formally, we compute β^j by solving:

$$\min_{\beta^j, \theta_1} \left\| \mathcal{W} \left(\bar{T} + M_S \left(\beta^j \right), \theta_1 \right) - S_1^j \right\|_2 \tag{3}$$

Next, for each subsequent frame, we compute the pose vector θ_t that best aligns the model to the target mesh by solving:

$$\min_{\theta_t} \left\| \mathcal{W} \left(\bar{T} + M_S \left(\beta^j \right), \theta_t \right) - S_t^j \right\|_2 \tag{4}$$

The dynamic skin offset Δ_t is the displacement vector originated from the dynamic skin deformation and is computed by:

$$\Delta_t = \mathcal{W}^{-1} \left(S_t, \theta_t^* \right) - \left(\bar{T} + M_S \left(\beta^j \right) \right) \tag{5}$$

where $\mathcal{W}^{-1}$ denotes the unposing operation transforming a body mesh to its rest pose, and θ_t^* is the best matching pose vector at frame t. Note that both the nonlinear static deformation M_P and the dynamic deformation offset Δ is computed and added to body shape at its rest pose, similarly in [6]. We used stochastic gradient decent (SGD) for the parameter optimization with learning $rate = 0.0001$ and $momentum = 0.9$. Figure 1 shows some of the snapshots of mesh alignment results. We compute such dynamic skin offset Δ_t^m $(t = 1, ..T_m)$ for all motions $(m = 1, ... 67)$ in the dataset. The training data is a set of input and output pairs (θ_t^m, Δ_t^m), arranged in motion-major order. It is further processed: A dimension reduction of the dynamic skin offset vector by using an autoencoder (Sect. 3.1), and the uniformization of motion length (See Sect. 5) by tail-clipping or zero-padding.

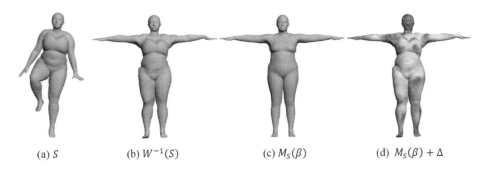

(a) S (b) $W^{-1}(S)$ (c) $M_S(\beta)$ (d) $M_S(\beta) + \Delta$

Fig. 1. The skin offset is found by computing the best (error-minimizing) alignment of the SMPL model $\mathcal{W}\left(\bar{T} + M_s\left(\beta\right), \theta\right)$ to the data mesh S. The residual deformation Δ as measured in the rest pose is considered as the dynamic skin deformation.

3   DSNet

Our goal is to regress soft-tissue dynamics that, when added to existing blend-shape models, will reproduce the nonlinear skin deformation effect. We leverage the well-known capability of a recurrent network to capture temporal information, to model the temporal evolution of the nonlinear skin dynamics. At the core of our work is an LSTM network that learns to generate realistic dynamics-dependent deformations from observations. At runtime, our model takes as input a character undergoing a motion, whose skin mesh is deformed by skeletal driven deformation. As noted in Dyna, the dynamic deformations depend on body shape, the amount and the distribution of fat in the body, in particular. Thus, we train our DSNet such that it learns to generate dynamic shapes depending on the shape identity coefficients.

3.1   Dimension Reduction by an Autoencoder

An LSTM with hidden state of dimensionality H takes feature vectors of dimensionality d as input uses parameters in the order of $4\left(dH + d^2\right)$ [23]. The effectiveness of such models can be largely improved by reducing the dimensionality of the input data. Given the large number of data dimension ($3 \times 6890 = 20,670$), it is desirable to reduce it into a compact, smaller sized latent representation. The majority of previous works use Principal Component Analysis, with an exception of [6] who use an autoencoder to make nonlinear dimension reduction. Here we also adopt an autoencoder, which compresses the original data to 100-dimensional latent space. The architecture of our autoencoder is shown in Fig. 2. The first two fully connected layers gradually increases the feature description of each vertex. The subsequent CNN layers outputs lower resolution representations of the mesh, while keeping the feature dimension. The last linear layer learns to map the lowest resolution representation to a feature vector $\delta \in \mathbb{R}^{100}$. The decoder takes the symmetric structure of the encoder and reconstructs the original mesh data $\tilde{\Delta}$ from the feature vector. The trained autoencoder can faithfully reconstruct the detailed shape of the original mesh, as shown in Fig. 3. The reconstruction error illustrated in colormap is measured as the per-vertex Euclidean distance between corresponding vertices. When compared to the autoencoder network by Casas and Otaduy [6], our network shows comparable performance, but it can be trained much more efficiently since it has much smaller number of parameters to be trained. We refer to the accompanying video [8] for a complete visual validation, and to Sect. 4 for the comparative analysis.

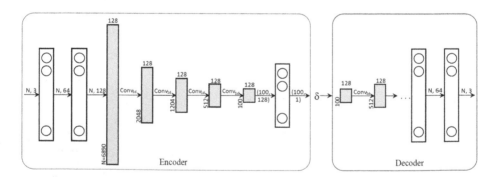

Fig. 2. Our mesh autoencoder reduces the dimension of the offset mesh $3N (3 \times 6890 = 20,670)$ to a vector of 100 dimensions, and reconstructs back the input offset mesh. The grey box represents the data, with its size denoted on top and bottom left.

3.2   Dynamic Skin Deformation Network

Our goal is to learn a function that, given a sequence of kinematic pose vectors θ_t ($t = 1 \ldots T$), predicts a sequence of dynamic skin offsets $\Delta_t (t = 1 \ldots T)$. Since

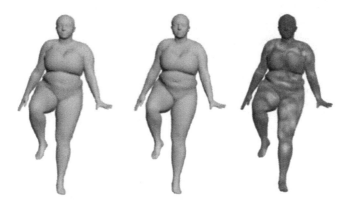

Fig. 3. The ground truth (left) and the reconstructed mesh with network output (middle) from our autoencoder. The per-vertex error is illustrated as a color map (right). (Color figure online)

we want to predict a time series, the results of each frame t depend not only on the kinematic parameters encoded in the pose vector θ_t, but also on the results of previous frames $t-1, \ldots t-l$. We should also consider the subject-specificity of the skin dynamics, which is related to the identity shape parameter β. Formally,

$$\Delta_t = f\left(\theta_t, f\left(\theta_{t-1}\right); \beta\right) \tag{6}$$

We model this with the long short term memory (LSTM) network, where the sequence of previous displacements is encoded as a fixed length hidden state memory. This memory is updated after seeing a new data (input and output pairs) by using non-linear functions. Note that this allows to learn an appropriate amount of history, i.e. how many previous frames to look back, to compute the skin offset in the current frame. This is contrary to the previous work where l has been set as a heuristically chosen constant (2 for example in [18]).

As shown in Fig. 4, our DSNet is composed of a single layer of LSTM network, padded with two dense (fully connected) layers at the beginning and one dense layer at the end. Adding more LSTM layers did not improve the results, as it tends to widen its temporal scope and overfit easily with the increased number of layers. Somewhat contrary to Vinyals et al. [27] on automatic image captioning where the encoded image feature is fed into the decoder only once at the beginning, we obtained better results by informing the decoder network about the subject-specific shape at each time step, rather than once at the beginning. DSNet takes the shape coefficient vector $\beta \in \mathbb{R}^{10}$ concatenated with the kinematic pose vector $\theta_t \in \mathbb{R}^{69}$ as input and learns to generate the kinematics-driven, subject-specific nonlinear dynamic skin deformation at each time step. The fully connected layers at the beginning learn to extract latent inertia features from θ_t, thus we do not need to compute the angular or linear velocity nor the acceleration unlike in previous work [6, 18, 20]. The dense layer at the end maps the output from the LSTM network to an output vector $\tilde{\delta}_t \in \mathbb{R}^{100}$, a low

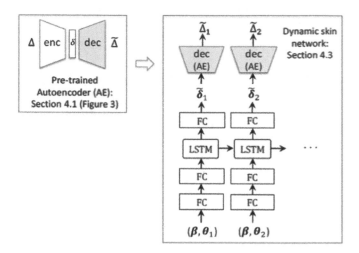

Fig. 4. The unrolled form of our DSNet architecture.

dimensional feature vector in the latent space of dynamic skin deformations that has been pre-constructed by the autoencoder. We use the output vector $\tilde{\delta}_t$ to evaluate the autoencoder (decoder part) to reconstruct the dynamic skin offset $\tilde{\Delta}_t$ to the body mesh in SMPL model.

Loss Function . To find the optimal parameters of the network to predict the dynamic deformation coefficients, we define the loss as the sum of L2-distances between the predicted dynamic coefficient vector $\tilde{\delta}_t$ and the ground truth in the latent space $\delta_t = AE_{enc}(\Delta_t)$ at each time step. The loss function $L(\cdot)$ is defined as:

$$L\left(\tilde{\delta}_t,\ \delta_t\right) = \sum_{t=1}^{T}\left(\tilde{\delta}_t - \delta_{t2}\right) \tag{7}$$

The above loss is minimized with respect to all the parameters of LSTM- and the dense-layers through backpropagation through time [16].

4   Implementation Details

Our network models have been implemented using Tensorflow 2.0 (Dynamic skin deformation network) and Pytorch (mesh alignment, autoencoder) in a python environment. Experiments including the network training have been carried out on a regular desktop PC running on Ubuntu environment, with Nvidia GeForce 2080 Super graphics card.

Frame Length Uniformization. Although spatially coherent (i.e. all meshes share a same topology), each motion sequence in Dyna database comes at different frame numbers. To feed in as input to the neural network, these sequence data need to be rearranged as a multidimensional tensor of a fixed shape, which means we need to uniformize the number of frames of all motion sequences. We heuristically chose a frame length, and zero-pad a sequence at the end if it is shorter or clip the tail out if it is longer. With most motion sequences having the frame lengths between 200 and 400, 300 has been chosen, as we want to avoid training the network with a dataset with too many 0's.

Autoencoder. All triangulated meshes available from Dyna dataset has been used. The training and validation sets consist of 15,051 (70%) and 6,451 (30%) meshes, respectively. The input data, i.e. the vertex coordinates have been normalized prior to input (so that their values vary within the range of $[-1, 1]$), and the network output has been denormalized. The network has been trained by using PyTorch implementation of the Adam optimizer [11], with a batch size of 64 and a learning rate of 0.0001. The total number of parameters are 33,626,606. Compared to the autoencoder from Casas and Otaduy [6], which has 3 fully connected layers of 6000, 3000, and 100 outputs each for the encoder and the symmetric decoder, this amounts to only 11.8% (=33,626,606/284,678,770) of parameters to be trained, which has been confirmed by several hours of training time saved and much less memory requirements.

Dynamic Skin Deformation Network. The first dense layer takes a 10-dimensional identity shape vector $(\beta \in \mathbb{R}^{10})$ concatenated with a 69-dimensional pose vector $(\theta_t \in \mathbb{R}^{69})$ as input and outputs a 64-dimensional vector, with a linear activation function. The second dense layer outputs a 128-dimensional vector with a tanh activation function, which is fed into the LSTM layer. The LSTM has 60 hidden units, and thus a 60-dimensional vector is produced as its output. This output vector goes through a batch normalization layer prior to the subsequent dense layer, so that its values vary within the range of $[-1, 1]$. We observed that it had a positive influence on the network performance in terms of error convergence.

Training Process. The end-to-end training has been conducted using the motion sequences in the training dataset. The training time took approximately 0.05 s per epochs. The decoder network runs at high speed, since we use only 69 parameters for the pose parameter and 100-dimensional feature vector to encode the dynamic skin offset. Batch size was set to 16. Thus, data block of input and output training data is $16 \times 300 \times 69$ (batch size, sequence length, pose parameter) and $16 \times 300 \times 100$ (batch size, sequence length, feature vector), respectively. The network has been trained via Tensorflow 2.0 implementation of Adam optimizer [11] with a learning rate of 0.0001.

5   Results

We have tested our DSNet to approximate the dynamic skin deformation on various unseen subjects or/and motions. Despite the rather limited size of training data, we have obtained very encouraging results. All our visual results including the comparison to the state of the art SoftSMPL [20] are provided in our accompanying video [8].

Skin Dynamics on Validation Data. Figure 5 shows the results we obtained on a validation data, a motion sequence that has not been used for training. The chosen subject ('50004')'s other motions, as well as the semantically identical motions ('one leg jump') from four other subjects had been used for training the network. The predicted dynamic skin offset, when added to the SMPL model (Fig. 5(d)), faithfully reproduces (Fig. 5(b)) the original skin shape (Fig. 5(a)).

Skin Dynamics Prediction on Unseen Motions or Unseen Subjects. Our DSNet can faithfully predict the skin dynamics for semantically new motions that have not been used for training. In the accompanying video [8], we visualize the dynamic skin deformation approximated for known and unknown subjects (framed in boxes) undergoing unobserved motions ('basketball dribble and shoot' 'side to side hopping') by our DSNet. These results confirm that our DSNet has successfully learned to predict quality skin dynamics for unseen motions and/or unseen subjects.

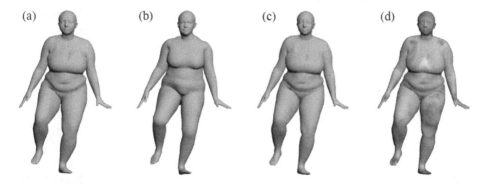

Fig. 5. Dynamic skin deformation predicted for a validation data by DSNet. (a) Ground truth; (b) SMPL model reconstructed by using the input parameters (β, θ); (c) SMPL model appended with the predicted dynamic skin deformation; and (d) a color map indicating the amount of skin deformation by the DSNet.

Note that DSNet can also predict different dynamic skin deformation according to the varying shapes of different individuals. In the accompanying video [8], we can see that DSNet has produced distinct skin dynamics for each subject, even for an unknown one (framed in boxes).

A Note on the Training Data. Ideally, the soft-tissue dynamics should be modeled solely by the residual mesh offset. However, we found that such dynamic shapes had been partly absorbed by the SMPL model. As shown in Fig. 6, the jiggling of breasts during 'jingle on toes' motion has been partly modeled by the oscillating rotation angle of 'spine2' joint during the per-frame based mesh aligning optimization. This is contrary to our visual inspection, which indicates the root and lower limbs are the only main contributors to the motion. The clear separation of the dynamics-dependent shapes from SMPL during the data generation is something that can be improved in the future.

6 Conclusion

We have presented a learning-based method to the estimation of quality dynamic skin deformation. The dynamic skin deformation has been modeled as a time series data, which is learned as a function of kinematic pose parameter, characteristics of body shape, and of the results of previous time steps. An LSTM-based network has been developed, which has been trained on sequences of high-quality triangular meshes captured from real people under diverse motions. Borrowing the SMPL human

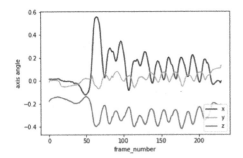

Fig. 6. The dynamics of bouncing breast has been partly modeled the rotation of the spine joint.

body shape representation, the dynamics-dependent skin deformation has been extracted from each frame mesh along with the pose parameters, which has been used as training data. Once trained, the network successfully predicts the nonlinear, dynamics-dependent shape changes over time, contributing to a high-quality skin dynamic of human body models under motion in a real-time course. Also developed has been an autoencoder, which builds a compact space for the intrinsic representation of dynamic skin offset and thereby allowing a very efficient operation of the dynamic skin deformation network. We have evaluated our model on various unseen motions and different individual shapes and shown that our model significantly saves the computational time and produces quality soft-tissue dynamics in real-time.

Acknowledgements. This work has been supported by ANR Human4D (ANR-19-CE23-0020) project by the French Agence Nationale de la Recherche.

References

1. Allen, B., Curless, B., Popovic, Z.: Articulated body deformation from range scan data. ACM Trans. Graph. **21**(3), 612–619 (2002)

2. Allen, B., Curless, B., Popovic, Z.: The space of human body shapes: reconstruction and parameterization from range scans. ACM Trans. Graph. **22**(3), 587–594 (2003)
3. Allen, B., Curless, B., Popovic, Z., Hertzmann, A.: Learning a correlated model of identity and pose-dependent body shape variation for real-time synthesis. In: Symposium on Computer Animation 2006, pp. 147–156 (2006)
4. Anguelov, D., Srinivasan, P., Koller, D., Thrun, S., Rodgers, J., Davis, J.: SCAPE: shape completion and animation of people. ACM Trans. Graph. **24**(3), 408–416 (2005)
5. Chadwick, J.E., Haumann, D.R., Parent, R.E.: Layered construction for deformable animated characters. In: SIGGRAPH 1989, pp. 243–252 (1989)
6. Casas, D., Otaduy, M.A.: Learning nonlinear soft-tissue dynamics for interactive avatars. Proc. ACM Comput. Graph. Interact. Tech. **1**(1), 10:1–10:15 (2018)
7. Hirshberg, D.A., Loper, M., Rachlin, E., Black, M.J.: Coregistration: simultaneous alignment and modeling of articulated 3D shape. In: Fitzgibbon, A., Lazebnik, S., Perona, P., Sato, Y., Schmid, C. (eds.) ECCV 2012. LNCS, vol. 7577, pp. 242–255. Springer, Heidelberg (2012). https://doi.org/10.1007/978-3-642-33783-3_18
8. https://youtu.be/7YDKFxCnprc
9. Hochreiter, S., Schmidhuber, J.: Long short-term memory. Neural Comput. **9**(8), 1735–1780 (1997)
10. Kry, P.G., James, D.L., Pai, D.K.: EigenSkin: real time large deformation character skinning in hardware. In: Symposium on Computer Animation 2002, pp. 153–159 (2002)
11. Kingma, D.P., Ba, J.: Adam: a method for stochastic optimization. ICLR (Poster) (2015)
12. Lewis, J.P., Cordner, M., Fong, N.: Pose space deformation: a unified approach to shape interpolation and skeleton-driven deformation. In: SIGGRAPH 2000, pp. 165–172 (2000)
13. Loper, M., Mahmood, N., Black, M.J.: MoSh: motion and shape capture from sparse markers. ACM Trans. Graph. **33**(6), 220:1–220:13 (2014)
14. Loper, M., Mahmood, N., Romero, J., Pons-Moll, G., Black, M.J.: SMPL: a skinned multi-person linear model. ACM Trans. Graph. **34**(6), 248:1–248:16 (2015)
15. Mohr, A., Gleicher, M.: Building efficient, accurate character skins from examples. ACM Trans. Graph. **22**(3), 562–568 (2003)
16. Mozer, M.C.: A focused backpropagation algorithm for temporal pattern recognition. Complex Syst. **3**(4) (1989)
17. Magnenat-Thalmann, N., Thalmann, D.: Human body deformations using joint-dependent local operators and finite-element theory. In: Badler, N., Barsky, B.A., Zeltzer, D. (eds.) Making Them Move, pp. 243–262. Morgan Kaufmann, San Mateo (1991)
18. Pons-Moll, G., Romero, J., Mahmood, N., Black, M.J.: Dyna: a model of dynamic human shape in motion. ACM Trans. Graph. **34**(4), 120:1–120:14 (2015)
19. Rose, C., Cohen, M.F., Bodenheimer, B.: Verbs and adverbs: multidimensional motion interpolation. IEEE Comput. Graph. Appl. **18**(5), 32–40 (1998)
20. Santesteban, I., Garces, E., Otaduy, M.A., Casas, D.: SoftSMPL: data-driven modeling of nonlinear soft-tissue dynamics for parametric humans. Comput. Graph. Forum **39**(2), 65–75 (2020)
21. Seo, H., Magnenat-Thalmann, N.: An automatic modeling of human bodies from sizing parameters. In: SI3D 2003, pp. 19–26 (2003)
22. Scheepers, F., Parent, R.E., Carlson, W.E., May, S.F.: Anatomy-based modeling of the human musculature. In: SIGGRAPH 1997, pp. 163–172 (1997)

23. Shi, Y., Fernando, B., Hartley, R.: Action anticipation with RBF kernelized feature mapping RNN. In: Ferrari, V., Hebert, M., Sminchisescu, C., Weiss, Y. (eds.) ECCV 2018. LNCS, vol. 11214, pp. 305–322. Springer, Cham (2018). https://doi.org/10.1007/978-3-030-01249-6_19
24. Sloan, P.-P.J., Rose, C.F., III., Cohen, M.F.: Shape by example. In: SI3D 2001, pp. 135–143 (2001)
25. Teran, J., Blemker, S.S., Ng-Thow-Hing, V., Fedkiw, R.: Finite volume methods for the simulation of skeletal muscle. In: Symposium on Computer Animation 2003, pp. 68–74 (2003)
26. Teran, J., Sifakis, E., Irving, G., Fedkiw, R.: Robust quasi static finite elements and flesh simulation. In: Symposium on Computer Animation 2005, pp. 181–190 (2005)
27. Vinyals, O., Toshev, A., Bengio, S., Erhan, D.: Show and tell: a neural image caption generator. In: CVPR 2015, pp. 3156–3164 (2015)

Curvature Analysis of Sculpted Hair Meshes for Hair Guides Generation

Florian Pellegrin[1,2,3]($\boxtimes$), Andre Beauchamp[2], and Eric Paquette[1]

[1] École de Technologie Supérieure, Montreal, Canada
`florian.pellegrin.1@ens.etsmtl.ca`
[2] Ubisoft La Forge, Montreal, Canada
[3] INSA Rennes, Rennes, France

Abstract. This paper proposes an approach that generates hair guides from a sculpted 3D mesh, thus accelerating hair creation. Our approach relies on the local curvature on a sculpted mesh to discover the direction of the hair on the surface. We generate hair guides by following the identified strips of polygons matching hair strands. To improve the quality of the guides, some are split to ensure they correspond to hairstyles ranging from straight to wavy, while others are connected so that they correspond to longer hair strands. In order to automatically attach the guides to the scalp of a 3D head, a vector field is computed based on the directions of the guides, and is used in a backward growth of the guides toward the scalp. This approach is novel since there is no state-of-the-art method that generates hair from a sculpted mesh. Furthermore, we demonstrate how our approach works on different hair meshes. Compared to several hours of manual work to achieve a similar result, our guides are generated in a few minutes.

Keywords: Hair synthesis · Hair modeling · Hair generation · 3D avatar · 3D computer graphics

1 Introduction

3D hair modeling is a complex task and is one of the difficult topics in the field of 3D character creation. Several types of representations are used for hair, namely, closed meshes, polygon strips and individual hair strands. Typically, artists work in two steps: first, they create hair guides, and then they either create other hair strands by interpolating the guides or they generate polygon strips along the guides. Sculpting a hair mesh with tools such as ZBrush is very efficient, as compared to the time-consuming process of manual hair guide creation. Since guide creation accounts for about fifty percent of the total time required to make a hairstyle, our goal is to automate the process by generating hair guides from a 3D hair mesh. Figure 1 illustrates the hair mesh (left) and the lines representing the hair guides (right). While 3D hair sculpting still calls for manual work, it gives freedom and control to the user in the creation process.

© Springer Nature Switzerland AG 2021
N. Magnenat-Thalmann et al. (Eds.): CGI 2021, LNCS 13002, pp. 378–397, 2021.
https://doi.org/10.1007/978-3-030-89029-2_30

Fig. 1. Example of a desired output for a given input.

Despite several methods currently exist, none of them is sufficient to meet our need. For example, Yuksel et al. [1] have proposed a method that generates individual hair strands from a 3D mesh. The method is used by some video game productions, but it is not entirely adequate since it calls for significant manual work. Other methods use images as inputs, which makes it hard to control the generated hair. Recently, several data-driven methods require the use of 3D surfaces with identical topologies. However, such a limitation is too constraining for a game production environment. More generally, current methods are not based on meshes and seek to generate a complete hairstyle, leaving little to no room for intervention by the user. Our approach uses two inputs, namely a 3D hair mesh and a 3D head onto which the generated guides will be connected. The hair mesh is analyzed to extract polygons along the hair stands based on the curvatures of the mesh. Guides are generated along these polygons. The curvature analysis is not perfect, and so we subsequently validate if consecutive guide curves can be connected together. We then use a signed distance field to push outward hair guides which intersect the 3D head mesh. Finally, hair guides are extended through a vector field generated from the guides' growing directions in order to connect the guides to the scalp of the head. Our contributions can be summarized as follows:

- First ever approach to convert a sculpted hair mesh into guide curves;
- Extraction of guide curves through a curvature analysis and curve connections;
- A signed distance field approach to push guides out of the 3D head mesh;
- A vector field approach to connect the guide curves to the hair root region.

2   Previous Work

Work related to hair generation generally falls under three categories [2]: physics-based methods, geometry-based methods, and finally, image-based methods. Physics-based methods [3–6] are no longer as popular as they used to be, because using them is difficult. Indeed, the selection of physical parameters to obtain a desired hairstyle is not intuitive.

For geometry-based methods, they favor the use of parametric representations as well as interactions with the user. Such methods are very similar to manual modeling techniques available to artists in the industry. These methods include the modeling of parametric surfaces using splines. Here, the splines are used to represent 2D surfaces [7] or a 3D mesh [8]. As an alternative to the use of splines, the methods of Yang et al. [9] and Choe and Ko [10] favor modeling by hair clusters and statistical distribution. Unlike these preceding methods which focus on the shape of an individual hair strand, Yuksel et al. [1] propose to model the outer surface of the hair. Since one of our goals is to use a mesh to generate a hairstyle, this method is therefore related to our approach. However, the mesh in the method of Yuksel et al. [1] must be created according to certain constraints and does not allow to use any user provided mesh which our approach allows.

Image-based modeling methods are comprised of two major types: those based on a single image and those based on multiple images. Satisfactory results can be obtained with multi-view methods [11–18]. However, due to the specialized hardware often required, these methods are harder to implement than those based on a single view. Many image-based methods rely on a 2D or 3D orientation field representing the hair flow. The field is usually built using a set of Gabor filters to detect the orientation. The method by Chai et al. [19] is based on a single image and uses 2D orientation maps. However, the individual hair strands generated by their method lack physical plausibility, and this was improved by Chai et al. [20]. These methods require the prior existence of images representing a desired hairstyle and do not allow an artist to slightly alter the input to achieve different results.

Another class of image-based methods try to reconstruct a 3D hairstyle using a data set of 3D meshes. Depending on the input provided by the user, a combination of several examples in the data set is made in order to create a new mesh. The use of a data set in order to combine multiple hairstyles based on user-drawn paths on the input image was introduced by Hu et al. [21], while the need for human interaction to determine hair orientation was mitigated by the work of Chai et al. [22], which introduced the use of a CNN to automatically segment the image and detect orientations. The method by Hu et al. [23] extracts the semantic features of a hairstyle in an image to select a subset of meshes sharing these attributes from the data set. The mesh closest to the image is then retrieved and adjusted to improve the correspondence. The methods by Chai et al. [22] and Hu et al. [23] have two major problems. The approaches call for the availability of the data set at runtime, which requires a large storage space. In addition, the hairstyles inside the data set are required to share an identical mesh topology. However, such a constraint is impractical when considering several projects and numerous artists in medium to large video game studios.

The need for a data set at run time is solved by neural network methods [24–26]. Indeed, these methods use neural networks to generate hair and only require the hair data set for training. Zhou et al. [26] propose an auto-encoder to generate hair directly from an image. In the method, the image is segmented and the hair orientation field is extracted. This 2D field is then provided to the network to generate 3D point sequences representing the coordinates of individual hair strands. Similarly, Zhang and Zheng [25] and Ye et al. [24] propose a generative antagonist network and an auto-encoder respectively. However the objective of these networks is to generate a 3D vector field, and not a set of hair strands directly. These methods present the same problems as those encountered using images to generate hair. Moreover some methods [24, 25] generate vector fields instead of hair, and rely instead on proper hair growing algorithms.

None of the methods presented fully satisfies our needs. The geometric methods are not very automated and require a significant user interaction. For their part, although promising, the methods based on one or more images are fundamentally contrary to our objective which is to use a 3D mesh as input. Finally, methods relying on a data set impose mesh topology constraints that are too limiting.

3   Hair Mesh Curvature Analysis

The proposed approach consists in generating hair guides from a sculpted 3D hair mesh (Fig. 1). The input mesh is a manifold with or without boundaries, and has enough polygons to allow visualizing smooth sculpted hair strands. Apart from the hair mesh, the user also provides a head mesh to which the guides will be "attached". To ensure that the approach is independent of the size of the hair and head, the user scales the sculpted mesh and the head mesh to their real sizes in millimeters before processing begins. The generation of the guides starts with a curvature analysis, which is used to extract regions of the mesh representing hair strands (Sect. 3.1). Then, splines are fitted along the regions extracted from the curvature analysis (Sect. 3.2). These guides are then analyzed to ensure that the strands correspond to hairstyles ranging from straight to wavy (Sect. 3.3). Some of these guides are then connected together as they should represent a single and longer hair strand (Sect. 3.5). We then fit the guides to a head mesh. Since the guides can intersect the head, the approach resolves these intersections by repulsion according to the signed distance field of the head (Sect. 3.6). Finally, the guides are extended through a vector field to be attached to the scalp of the head (Sect. 3.8).

3.1   Curvature Analysis

Our approach computes the curvature to find hair strands along the surface (Fig. 2). We compute the Weingarten equations and its determinant to obtain the Gaussian curvature. Triangles with their vertices having a curvature lower than 0.001 are retained. Thus, only the concave regions remain (Fig. 2(b)). The next step in the analysis is to separate the mesh into different groups based on the connectivity of the triangles, after which the groups are processed to remove those which are unlikely to represent hair strands. In this regard, we identify groups of connected triangles. These groups are randomly colored in Fig. 3(a). A group is deleted if the diagonal of its oriented bounding box is smaller than 15 mm. Furthermore, we identify groups that are unlikely to represent hair strands as they are too wide. We retain the groups for which the geodesic distance

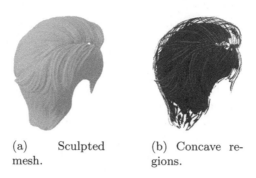

(a)   Sculpted mesh.

(b) Concave regions.

Fig. 2. Identification of strands from the curvature.

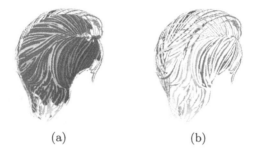

(a)   (b)

Fig. 3. Mesh connectivity. (a) Connectivity groups. (b) Mesh after deleting groups that are unlikely to represent hair strands.

from each internal vertex to a boundary vertex is less than a threshold set to 20 mm (Fig. 3(b)). This process also removes the inner part of the sculpted mesh (the part lying close to the scalp).

3.2   Generation of Guides

Our aim is to generate guides along the remaining parts of the mesh following the curvature analysis, and to that end, we implement two different strategies. Firstly, we detail the strategy to generate guides by computing the shortest path between the extremities of the groups. This approach works particularly well when the groups resulting from the analysis represent individual hair stands. Secondly, we describe an alternative way to obtain guides by computing a skeleton extraction on the parts of the mesh remaining after the curvature analysis. In our approach, both strategies are run and the output that generated the largest number of guides is automatically selected.

Shortest Path Strategy. For many of the groups in Fig. 3(b), we observe a correspondence between a group and a hair guide. The goal here is to find the extremities of these groups and to then fit a guide from one end to the other. We iterate over each connectivity group to generate one guide per group.

To find the extremities of the group, we compute the oriented bounding box. The extremities will be close to a corner of the box. Therefore, for each corner of the box we retrieve the nearest vertex of the group (Fig. 4(a)). As a result, we obtain eight vertices or less since multiple corners can share the same nearest vertex. Among these vertices, we identify the extremities by computing the shortest paths along the edges of the mesh from each vertex to all others. Thus, among the generated paths, the longest one allows to find the extremities (Fig. 4(b)). Each guide is computed by fitting a NURBS of order 6 to the selected path (Fig. 4(c)).

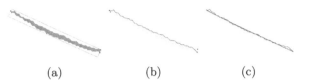

(a)   (b)   (c)

Fig. 4. Guide generation: (a) Selection of the nearest vertex for each corner of the bounding box; (b) Selected path (longest of the shortest paths between selected vertices); (c) Fitting of a spline to the vertices of the selected path.

Skeleton Extraction Strategy. One shortcoming of the shortest path strategy is that only one guide is generated per connectivity group. This implies a great loss of information when separate hair strands remain connected after the curvature analysis (Fig. 5). To overcome this, we have developed an alternative strategy using the mesh skeleton to generate the guides. We obtain the skeleton of the mesh using a mesh contraction method similar to that of Au et al. [27] (Fig. 6(a)). In order to generate splines from the skeleton, all joints connecting a bone to more than two other bones are removed (Fig. 6(b)). Then, NURBS of order 6 are fitted to the polyline of each bone.

Fig. 5. Mesh group representing multiple hair stands.

Our approach uses both the shortest path and the skeleton extraction strategies. In the case of a high-resolution mesh with fine details, the width and distance of their hair strands groups from each other are smaller than the mesh

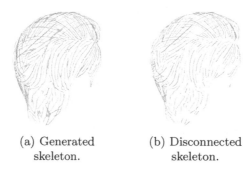

(a) Generated
skeleton.

(b) Disconnected
skeleton.

Fig. 6. Skeleton extracted from the mesh.

contraction fusing distance. Thus, the skeleton extraction fails at separating hair stands from each other. It is hard to predict which strategy will work best, as results depend on how the mesh was sculpted. However, it appears that the strategies are complementary: when one performs poorly, the other produces good results. Thus, one strategy is automatically chosen based on the one that generated the greatest number of guides.

3.3   Plausibility of Guides

After generating the guides, we check if they correspond to the expected shape of hair strands for straight to wavy hairstyles. We use the method proposed by Luo et al. [14] to detect U-shaped splines. In order to cut these splines, points are evenly sampled along them such that each segment's length is equal to 2 mm (guides are henceforth represented as polylines). Then, the local extrema of the curves are defined for each change of sign of the first derivative of the height values (with respect to the gravity vector). All the points labeled as extrema are then removed when the distance between two consecutive extrema is greater than 10 mm (Fig. 7(b)).

(a)   (b)

Fig. 7. Splitting of implausible curves.

3.4   Direction Analysis

We will now attempt to define the growing direction of each guide by setting one end as the root and the other as the tip. Most of the hair in a hairstyle is affected by gravity and is therefore oriented from top to bottom. However, some hair strands flow from bottom to top depending on the position of the hair parting line. This phenomenon can be seen in Fig. 8(a), where the guides above the parting line represent hair passing over the head going from bottom to top. In our approach, we use a parting line to determine the root of the guides that are close to it. The user manually paints the hair parting line on the sculpted mesh (Fig. 8(a)).

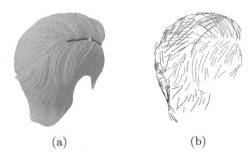

(a)   (b)

Fig. 8. Definition of the parting line: (a): the parting line painted on the mesh; (b): the guides affected by the parting line. (in red) (Color figure online)

For these guides, our approach firstly defines the root position as its closest end to the parting line. A guide is affected by the parting line when the distance between one of its ends and the parting line is less than a user-defined parameter ($\in [100, 180]$ mm for all of our examples, and specifically 110 mm for Fig. 8(b)). Secondly, the direction of the guides that are not affected by the parting line is determined according to the height value calculated from the polyline vertices in Sect. 3.3. For each guide, the root is associated with the highest end. The user chooses the global direction of the hair (falling or rising) beforehand in order to take into account the fact that a hairstyle may represent hair rising up. When hair is rising up, there is no parting line and the directions of the hair are reversed.

3.5   Connection of Guides

Notwithstanding the fact that the guides are usable as is, some of them could be connected together to match the hair of the sculpted mesh. We perform a connection analysis which includes a subset from the method proposed by Luo et al. [14]. We follow their method to detect potential connections, but we also propose our own strategy to decide which ones to connect. The detection of potential connections considers all pairs of guides whose ends are sufficiently close to each other (less than a threshold of 30 mm). A circle is fitted to the extremities of each pair of guides and the guides form a potential connection if the fitting error is below a given threshold. For each endpoint used to create a pair, its 9 neighboring points on the curve are used to form a set containing the 10 points closest to the end of the curve. Each pair forms a set Q of 20 points used to fit a plane. The plane fitting is done by a least squares fit. The points in Q are projected onto the fitted plane, and then the least squares method is used to fit a circle. The remaining potential connections are those for which the root mean squared error is below a threshold of 1.0 mm.

The above detection of potential connections is derived from the method of Luo et al. [14]. We now propose to sort all potential connections by increasing fitting error. We then iterate over each potential connection and connect the extremities of the guides if none of them is already connected. Since guides are represented as polylines (Sect. 3.2) we fit splines to all the points of a newly connected pair to ensure smooth connections between the guides. The splines of the newly connected guides are then converted back to polylines, as shown in Sect. 3.3. The result of this step can be seen in Fig. 9.

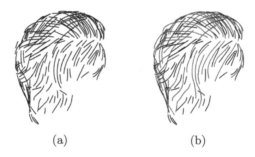

(a)   (b)

Fig. 9. Connection of guides: (a): guides before connection; (b) guides after connection where connected guides are represented in red. (Color figure online)

3.6   Repulsion of Guides

Our approach aims to generate hair guides from any sculpted 3D hair mesh. This implies that the sculpted mesh may not correctly fit the head intended to receive the guides, and intersections may occur between the generated guides and the head. Fitting to a 3D morphable head model [28] would also require adjusting for intersections. As a solution, we propose a method to repulse the guides penetrating the interior of the head using a signed distance field. First, it is easier to set the inside apart from the outside of a mesh when the mesh is a closed manifold. Since this is rarely the case for this type of mesh, we use standard mesh closure methods. Next, we transform the mesh into a VDB [29] voxel field (Fig. 10). We use a resolution fine enough to limit any loss of information during the discretization (each voxel is of size 1 mm). The VDB field is sampled to

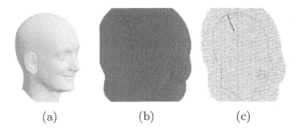

(a)   (b)   (c)

Fig. 10. Head voxelization with signed distance field. (b) represents the VDB field for the head in (a). (c) shows the segment representing the gradient multiplied by the signed distance of a given position. For visualization purposes, (b) and (c) show 4 mm voxels instead of the effective resolution of 1 mm we use.

obtain the signed distance of the nearest surface to any position in the field. In addition to the distance, the gradient of the signed distance function provides the normalized vector of the direction to the surface (Fig. 10(c). Since our guides are discretized with many points, repulsing only the points inside the head would have the effect of breaking the curved appearance of the guides. Our repulsion method mitigates this by temporarily converting the guides back to splines, as shown in Sect. 3.2, in order to repulse the control points penetrating the interior of the head rather than the points of the discretized guides. For each control point, the distance and gradient in the VDB volume are sampled at the position of the control point, and then the control point is projected onto the surface such that $\mathbf{p} = \mathbf{p} + f(\mathbf{p})\nabla f(\mathbf{p})$ where $\mathbf{p}$ is the position of the control point, f is the distance function and ∇f is the gradient of the function. Each control point is further translated by 0.2 mm along the normal of the vertex on the surface closest to the control point. Splines are then converted back to polylines, as shown in Sect. 3.3. The result of the repulsion process is shown in Fig. 11.

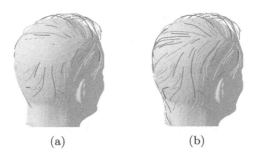

(a)   (b)

Fig. 11. Repulsion of guides: (a) shows the intersection of the guides with the head mesh, while (b) shows the result of the repulsion of the guides.

3.7   Vector Field Generation from Guides

With the objective of connecting the hair guides to the scalp, we compute a vector field describing the overall flow of the hairstyle based on the generated guides. We transform the hair mesh into a grid of voxels and we will associate these voxels with a growing direction. The generated guides do not cover the entire surface of the mesh and therefore provide sparse information about the hair directions. In order to fill in the areas of the field where no guides are detected, we describe a method to interpolate the directions within the field. After interpolation, the field could contain noise if the direction analysis (Sect. 3.4) partly failed, and thus has oriented some guides in the wrong direction. (i.e. some voxels in the field do not follow the general direction of their neighbors). To overcome this problem we present a smoothing approach using a median vector filter.

Similarly to what is provided in Sect. 3.6, the hair mesh is voxelized using the VDB structure.

For efficiency reasons, this time, the size of a voxel is set to 3.0 mm. The vector field is represented as a direction for each voxels. With the voxels $\{h_i\}$ of the field H and the points $\{g_j\}$ of the guides, the directions $d(h_i)$ are defined according to Eq. 1 where $\mathcal{N}(h_i)$ is the set of g_j inside voxel h_i.

$$d(h_i) = d \left(\operatorname*{argmin}_{g_j \in \mathcal{N}(h_i)} \|g_j - \mathrm{center}(h_i)\|_2^2 \right) \tag{1}$$

Fig. 12. Transfer of hair directions from the guides to the voxel field.

The directional field obtained (Fig. 12) contains sparse information: only a subset of voxels is associated with hair growth directions. In order to obtain a complete vector field, we leave the N voxels which were assigned a value by Eq. 1 unchanged, and we interpolate from these N known directions to the other voxels using Shepard's method [30] defined by Eq. 2:

$$\mathbf{d}'(h_i) = \frac{\sum_{j=1}^{N} w_j(h_i)\mathbf{d}(h_j)}{\sum_{j=1}^{N} w_j(h_i)}, \tag{2}$$

where $d'(h_i)$ is the interpolated direction for voxel h_i based on the known directions $d(h_j)$. Each direction is weighted by $w_j(h_i)$ where $p = 4$ defines the influence of the closest voxels:

$$w_j(h_i) = \frac{1}{\|\text{center}(h_i) - \text{center}(h_j)\|_2^p} \cdot \qquad (3)$$

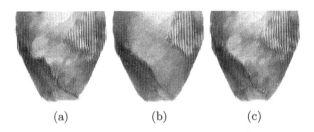

(a)   (b)   (c)

Fig. 13. (a) the interpolated directional field, (b) result after applying the median vector filter, and (c) result when the median vector filter is applied only when there is a strong change in direction.

As shown in Fig. 13(a), the interpolated field contains a little bit of noise related to a few guides having directions that are too different from that of their neighbors. To correct this type of artifact, we apply a median vector filter over the field. The objective of this filter is to find the median direction among the directions around the center of voxel h_i:

$$\mathbf{d}_m(h_i) = \underset{\mathbf{h} \in \mathcal{N}(h_i)}{\operatorname{argmin}} \sum_{\mathbf{h}_k \in \mathcal{N}(h_i)} \|\mathbf{d}'(h) - \mathbf{d}'(h_k)\|_2^2 \qquad (4)$$

where this time $\mathcal{N}(h_i)$ corresponds to the list of voxels h_k such that $\|\text{center}(h_k) - \text{center}(h_i)\|_2^2 < 30$ mm and $\mathbf{d}_m(h_i)$ is the median direction among the $\mathcal{N}(\langle\rangle)$ neighbors. With direction $\mathbf{d}_m(h_i)$ the result in Fig. 13(b) is obtained. Although the previously mentioned noise is eradicated, a loss can be noted in the variation of the directions. To overcome this, we define Eq. 5 such that:

$$\hat{\mathbf{d}}(h_i) = \begin{cases} \mathbf{d}_m(h_i) & \angle \mathbf{d}'(h_i), \mathbf{d}_m(h_i) > 18° \\ \mathbf{d}'(h_i) & \text{otherwise} \end{cases} . \qquad (5)$$

Thus, the median direction is used only when it is different enough from the interpolated direction.

3.8   Scalp Connection

A hairstyle without scalp connection looks unrealistic and makes hair simulation [31] difficult. Our last step grows the root of the guides up to the scalp. For this, the polygons belonging to the scalp are first defined by the user (Fig. 14(a)). Generally, the heads of the same project share the same mesh topology. Thus, the scalp identification can be transferred to all heads. Only the scalp polygons are kept, and then subdivided until the polygons have an area less than 8 mm^2 (Fig. 14(b)). The vector field S (Fig. 14(c)) represents the direction to the nearest vertex of the scalp, while the vector field H represents the direction of the hair in the hairstyle. The vector field S is composed of the same voxels as H. We then grow root ends of the guides through H and S. Until the scalp is reached, we iteratively add new points $\mathbf{p}_i$ to each guide, where $\mathbf{p}_1$ represents the root point of the guide and $\mathbf{d}_1$ is the reversed growing direction of the root point.

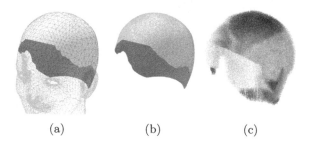

(a)   (b)   (c)

Fig. 14. Computation of directions to scalp.

The positions $\mathbf{p}_i$ and directions $\mathbf{d}_i$ of these points are calculated as:

$$\mathbf{d}_{i+1} = t[S(\mathbf{p}_i) - \frac{1}{2}H(\mathbf{p}_i)] + (1-t)\mathbf{d}_i \tag{6}$$

$$\mathbf{p}_{i+1} = \mathbf{p}_i + \delta\mathbf{d}_{i+1} \tag{7}$$

where t is the effect rate of the new direction $S(\mathbf{p}_i) - \frac{1}{2}H(\mathbf{p}_i)$ such that $t \in]0,1]$, δ is the step size, with $\delta > 0$, and $S(p)$ and $H(p)$ correspond to the direction of the closest point to p in each field. We use $t = 0.15$ with a step size $\delta = 2.0$ mm. To connect the guides exactly to the scalp surface, the extension of a guide stops when a point penetrates inside the head. This is detected using the signed distance field calculated in Sect. 3.7. Figure 15 shows the guides before and after they are connected to the scalp.

4   Results

We present the results of the entire process of our approach based on six different meshes in Figs. 16 and 17. These 3D sculpts were manually adjusted to a single head. The hairstyles represented are diverse: various hair lengths, with or without parting lines and different levels of detail. As shown in Fig. 18, the sculpting of more guides involves the use of a mesh with more polygons. For each example in Fig. 16 and 17 the user manually specified the parting line and adjusted

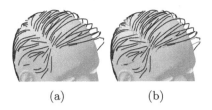

(a)   (b)

Fig. 15. Guides before and after the scalp attachment.

its influence distance (in the range of $[100, 180]$ mm). Apart from the manual adjustment related to the parting line, the guides are all generated with the same parameters. As our approach is the only one using sculpted meshes to generate hair our results can presently not be compared with those of state-of-the-art methods.

During the generation tests we used a computer with an Intel Xeon W-2135 processor, 64 GB of RAM and an NVIDIA GeForce RTX 2070 8 GB graphics card. Our method is implemented in the Houdini software and most of the code is written in VEX. All VEX code is automatically parallelized by Houdini when possible. The generation time varies between 17 and 124 s for the presented results. Specifically, Fig. 19 compares the time spent on the major steps of our approach.

In order to evaluate our approach, a qualitative survey was established and sent to a hair modeling expert working in the video game industry. The evaluation considered a complete hairstyle creation by an artist and thus considered the impact of using these guides to model a 3D hairstyle. According to the feedback, the time saved increases with the complexity of the hairstyle. Moreover, the method does not alter the creative process of the artists and allows to obtain good guides.

Our approach generates curves based on a shortest path and a skeleton extraction. Figure 20 compares curves generated with both approaches.

Although the results are satisfying, our approach has some limitations. As in the case with other recent research, our approach performs well for simple hairstyles, but would struggle for complex ones. For example, the hairstyle in Fig. 17(c) has hair sections that have opposite flow directions. In such a case, one could separate the hair in multiple meshes and apply our approach with the use of the parting line to orient the hair correctly. As our method is designed to provide control to the user at each step, for Fig. 17(c) we selected the incorrectly oriented guides and reversed their direction. Things get even worst for hairstyles with curly hair, as well as for hair tied in braids [32] or buns. Indeed, when the internal structure of the hair is not represented by the external structure of the mesh, the results will not be as useful.

The length of the guides is sometimes strongly heterogeneous. This is notably visible on Fig. 16(a), where neighboring guides can have significantly different lengths. On the other hand, in Fig. 17 the results obtained show that the step involving the connection of the guides to the scalp hardly works with long hair.

(a)

(b)

(c)

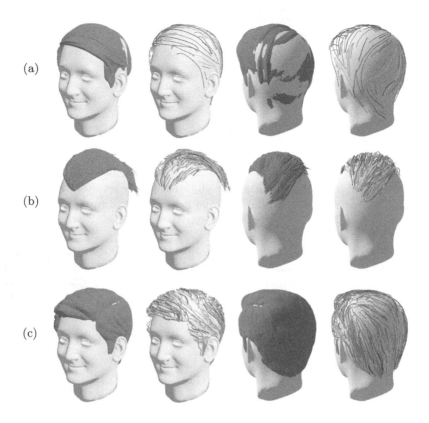

Fig. 16. Results of the approach for short hair.

Indeed, on Fig. 17(a), some guides are connected to the cheeks and the ears. On Fig. 17(c), several guides connect to the scalp before reaching the ponytail rallying area. Despite apparent flaws, the guides match the meshes well and follow their shapes correctly.

As a result of the curvature analysis, hair strands are sometimes too close to each other. Consequently, the skeleton extraction method (Sect. 3.2) is not able to contract each group individually. Therefore, after deleting points with more than two connections, there are sometimes a few segments left to generate guides. The result of this phenomenon is illustrated in Fig. 21(b). We propose an alternative that grows hair from the scalp to solve this situation. Indeed, guides can be traced through the vector field generated in Sect. 3.7, as shown in Fig. 21(c).

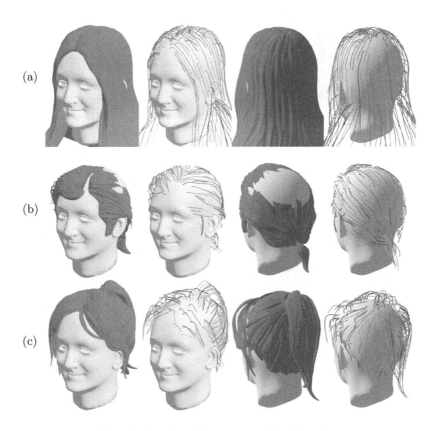

Fig. 17. Results of the approach for long hair.

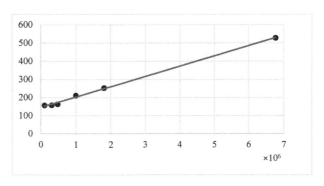

Fig. 18. Number of generated guides according to the number of triangles.

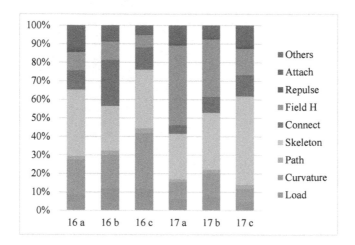

Fig. 19. Comparison of the generation time. The meshes used are those from Fig. 16(a–c) and Fig. 17(a–c).

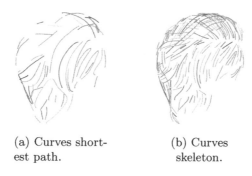

(a) Curves short-
est path.

(b) Curves
skeleton.

Fig. 20. Generated curves.

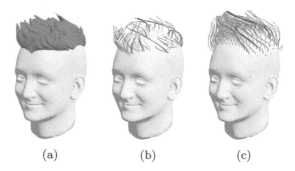

(a)   (b)   (c)

Fig. 21. Limitation of guide generation by direct curvature analysis and alternative solution.

5 Conclusion

Artists are able to quickly model hair using 3D sculpture software. The modeled hair represents the 3D volume of a hairstyle. The objective of our approach is to generate hair guides from the mesh of a hair volume. First, an analysis of curvature is performed to extract the polygons along hair strand regions. Then, two complementary strategies generate guides according to the polygons extracted from the curvature analysis. The first strategy separates the polygons into groups according to their connectivity and then uses the shortest path along edges to identify a guide for each group. The second strategy is based on the reconstruction of a skeleton for the extracted polygons to fit guides to the bones. The result with most guides between these two strategies is selected and used as input for the next steps. These guides are then analyzed to define their root ends. Then, they are connected together when possible. Beyond the generation of guides, we also perform the fitting of the guides to the mesh of a head. Indeed, our method corrects the guides to solve any collision with the head. This is done by pushing back the guides according to a signed distance field, obtained through a voxelization process of the head. Subsequently, a vector field is constructed by interpolating the directions of the guides, and is then used to trace connections from the guides to the scalp. Thus, this approach allows a user to obtain guides connected to a head. Moreover, these guides can be directly used in 3D software that uses guides to create dense hair.

During the generation process, we build a dense vector field representing the hair flow and use it to attach the guides to the scalp of a head. Nevertheless, it would be interesting to exploit this field for other purposes. Our method could loop on itself and use this generated field as new input information to improve the result of some steps. Also, this field together with an efficient hair growth algorithm would allow our approach to generate not only guides, but also individual hair strands from a mesh.

Acknowledgment. This work was supported by Ubisoft Inc. and École de technologie supérieure. We would also like to thank SideFX^{TM} for providing Houdini^{TM} licenses for research.

References

1. Yuksel, C., Schaefer, S., Keyser, J.: Hair meshes. ACM Trans. Graph. **28**(5), 1–7 (2009)
2. Ward, K., Bertails, F., Kim, T.Y., Marschner, S.R., Cani, M.P., Lin, M.C.: A survey on hair modeling: styling, simulation, and rendering. IEEE Trans. Visual Comput. Graph. **13**(2), 213–234 (2007)
3. Hadap, S., Magnenat-Thalmann, N.: Interactive hair styler based on fluid flow. In: Magnenat-Thalmann, N., Thalmann, D., Arnaldi, B. (eds.) Computer Animation and Simulation 2000. EUROGRAPH, pp. 87–99. Springer, Vienna (2000). https://doi.org/10.1007/978-3-7091-6344-3_7

4. Rosenblum, R.E., Carlson, W.E., Tripp, E., III.: Simulating the structure and dynamics of human hair: modelling, rendering and animation. J. Vis. Comput. Animat. **2**(4), 141–148 (1991)

5. Stam, J.: Multi-scale stochastic modelling of complex natural phenomena. Ph.D. thesis, University of Toronto (1996)

6. Yu, Y.: Modeling realistic virtual hairstyles. In: 9th Pacific Conference on Computer Graphics and Applications. Pacific Graphics 2001, pp. 295–304. IEEE (2001)

7. Liang, W., Huang, Z.: An enhanced framework for real-time hair animation. In: 11th Pacific Conference on Computer Graphics and Applications 2003, Proceedings, pp. 467–471. IEEE (2003)

8. Noble, P., Tang, W.: Modelling and animating cartoon hair with NURBS surfaces. In: Proceedings Computer Graphics International 2004, pp. 60–67. IEEE (2004)

9. Yang, X.D., Xu, Z., Yang, J., Wang, T.: The cluster hair model. Graph. Models **62**(2), 85–103 (2000)

10. Choe, B., Ko, H.S.: A statistical wisp model and pseudophysical approaches for interactive hairstyle generation. IEEE Trans. Visual Comput. Graph. **11**(2), 160–170 (2005)

11. Bao, Y., Qi, Y.: Realistic hair modeling from a hybrid orientation field. Visual Comput. **32**(6), 729–738 (2016). https://doi.org/10.1007/s00371-016-1240-1

12. Cao, C., Wu, H., Weng, Y., Shao, T., Zhou, K.: Real-time facial animation with image-based dynamic avatars. ACM Trans. Graph. **35**(4), 126:1–126:12 (2016)

13. Luo, L., Li, H., Paris, S., Weise, T., Pauly, M., Rusinkiewicz, S.: Multi-view hair capture using orientation fields. In: 2012 IEEE Conference on Computer Vision and Pattern Recognition, pp. 1490–1497. IEEE (2012)

14. Luo, L., Li, H., Rusinkiewicz, S.: Structure-aware hair capture. ACM Trans. Graph. **32**(4), 1–12 (2013)

15. Paris, S., Briceno, H.M., Sillion, F.X.: Capture of hair geometry from multiple images. ACM Trans. Graph. **23**(3), 712–719 (2004)

16. Paris, S., et al.: Hair photobooth: geometric and photometric acquisition of real hairstyles. ACM Trans. Graph. **27**(3), 30 (2008)

17. Wei, Y., Ofek, E., Quan, L., Shum, H.Y.: Modeling hair from multiple views. ACM Trans. Graph. **24**(3), 816–820 (2005)

18. Zhang, M., Chai, M., Wu, H., Yang, H., Zhou, K.: A data-driven approach to four-view image-based hair modeling. ACM Trans. Graph. **36**(4), 156–1 (2017)

19. Chai, M., Wang, L., Weng, Y., Yu, Y., Guo, B., Zhou, K.: Single-view hair modeling for portrait manipulation. ACM Trans. Graph. **31**(4), 1–8 (2012)

20. Chai, M., Wang, L., Weng, Y., Jin, X., Zhou, K.: Dynamic hair manipulation in images and videos. ACM Trans. Graph. **32**(4), 1–8 (2013)

21. Hu, L., Ma, C., Luo, L., Li, H.: Single-view hair modeling using a hairstyle database. ACM Trans. Graph. **34**(4), 1–9 (2015)

22. Chai, M., Shao, T., Wu, H., Weng, Y., Zhou, K.: AutoHair: fully automatic hair modeling from a single image. ACM Trans. Graph. **35**(4), 116:1–116:12 (2016)

23. Hu, L., et al.: Avatar digitization from a single image for real-time rendering. ACM Trans. Graph. **36**(6), 1–14 (2017)

24. Ye, Z., Li, G., Yao, B., Xian, C.: HAO-CNN: filament-aware hair reconstruction based on volumetric vector fields. Comput. Animat. Virtual Worlds **31**(4–5), e1945 (2020)

25. Zhang, M., Zheng, Y.: Hair-GAN: recovering 3D hair structure from a single image using generative adversarial networks. Visual Inform. **3**(2), 102–112 (2019)

26. Zhou, Y., et al.: HairNet: single-view hair reconstruction using convolutional neural networks. In: Ferrari, V., Hebert, M., Sminchisescu, C., Weiss, Y. (eds.) ECCV 2018. LNCS, vol. 11215, pp. 249–265. Springer, Cham (2018). https://doi.org/10.1007/978-3-030-01252-6_15
27. Au, O.K.C., Tai, C.L., Chu, H.K., Cohen-Or, D., Lee, T.Y.: Skeleton extraction by mesh contraction. ACM Trans. Graph. 27(3), 1–10 (2008)
28. Ghafourzadeh, D., et al.: Local control editing paradigms for part-based 3D face morphable models. Comput. Animat. Virtual Worlds e2028 (2021)
29. Museth, K.: VDB: high-resolution sparse volumes with dynamic topology. ACM Trans. Graph. 32(3), 1–22 (2013)
30. Shepard, D.: A two-dimensional interpolation function for irregularly-spaced data. In: Proceedings of the 1968 23rd ACM National Conference, pp. 517–524. Association for Computing Machinery, New York (1968)
31. Jiang, J., Sheng, B., Li, P., Ma, L., Tong, X., Wu, E.: Real-time hair simulation with heptadiagonal decomposition on mass spring system. Graph. Models 111, 101077 (2020)
32. Sun, C., Ramachandran, S., Paquette, E., Lee, W.S.: Single-view procedural braided hair modeling through braid unit identification. Comput. Animat. Virtual Worlds 32(3–4), e2007 (2021)

Synthesizing Human Faces Using Latent Space Factorization and Local Weights

Minyoung Kim and Young J. Kim[(⊠)]

Ewha Womans University, Seoul 03760, South Korea
minyoung.mia.k@ewhain.net, kimy@ewha.ac.kr

Abstract. We propose a 3D face generative model with local weights to increase the model's variations and expressiveness. The proposed model allows partial manipulation of the face while still learning the whole face mesh. For this purpose, we address an effective way to extract local facial features from the entire data and explore a way to manipulate them during a holistic generation. First, we factorize the latent space of the whole face to the subspace indicating different parts of the face. In addition, local weights generated by non-negative matrix factorization are applied to the factorized latent space so that the decomposed part space is semantically meaningful. We experiment with our model and observe that effective facial part manipulation is possible, and that the model's expressiveness is improved.

Keywords: Face synthesis · Generative models · Learning-based approach

1 Introduction

Various methods have been studied to develop three-dimensional(3D) geometric models to generate human faces and related research using deep learning is being actively pursued. However, most existing works are focused on a holistic generative approach to generate all parts at once and lack part details and manipulation. Previous part-based generative models exploit explicit segmentation data or labels for training their model or use several part decoders [1,2]. However, existing 3D facial mesh datasets barely have pre-segmented data.

Thus, we investigate an effective way to extract or present localized features from the whole data. Toward this goal, mesh segmentation might be one of the possible solutions. However, since human faces are often smooth, it is a challenge to segment the facial mesh explicitly. To bypass this, we exploit a generative approach that does not require additional segmentation data and makes the whole learning model simple. Furthermore, we explore a way for part control while exploiting holistic generation by learning localized features. In this paper, we propose a locally weighted 3D face generative model. Our approach can generate a rich variety of 3D face models beyond the training data using part manipulation with latent factorization. Latent space factorization enables manipulation

© Springer Nature Switzerland AG 2021
N. Magnenat-Thalmann et al. (Eds.): CGI 2021, LNCS 13002, pp. 398–405, 2021.
https://doi.org/10.1007/978-3-030-89029-2_31

of the local part of the face, and local weights make decomposed part spaces more semantically meaningful without additional segmentation labels. With a part-based representation of the data, our model is simpler and more straightforward than others and does not require any scmantic segmentation labels. As a basis model, we leverage Ranjan et al. [3]'s autoencoder with latent space factorization and apply local weights that partially influence the model during training. We also evaluate the performance of the proposed model in terms of part modification, part combination, and ablation tests to show the effect of each model component on the results.

Our main contributions are: (1) Locally weighted generative autoencoder for generating a whole human face geometric model; (2) End-to-end learning to learn local features without explicit facial feature segmentation data; (3) Experimentation and demonstration of the proposed model's performance in terms of generation and part manipulation. The majority of the materials contained in this paper are based on the same author's dissertation [4].

2   Related Work

There exist attempts to generate a new face with face segmentation and a local model to increase the model's expressiveness and achieve fine-scale modeling. Blanz and Vetter [5] demonstrated region-based modeling with 3D face morphable models (3DMMs) by manually dividing the face. Tena et al. [6] presented region-based linear face modeling with automatic segmentation by clustering.

CompoNet [1] presented a part-based generative neural network for shapes. They proved that the part-based model encourages the generator to create new data unseen in the training set. Dubrovina et al. [2] proposed decompose-composer network performing meaningful part manipulation and high-fidelity 3D shape generation. They used projection matrices to split full object encodings into part encodings and represent them as fully connected layers. To composite each part, both [1] and [2] compute per-part affine transformation. Since we pursue a holistic generation approach, our model does not computes affine transformation to combinate each part of the data.

3   Locally Weighted Autoencoder

We choose to represent 3D faces with triangular mesh due to its efficiency. Among previous approaches for applying mesh convolution operation, Ranjan et al. [3] proposed CoMA employing fast Chebyshev filters [7] with a novel mesh pooling method. More details are referred to [3]. Although their work has shown a decent performance of reconstructing 3D faces, we take one step further to improve generation ability and controllability by using per-part manipulation. Utilizing the basic generation ability of Ranjan et al. [3]'s model, we added two new methods: latent factorization and local weights.

Our model is based on the autoencoder [3] consisting of an encoder, projection, and a decoder, as illustrated in Fig. 1. The encoder and decoder learn

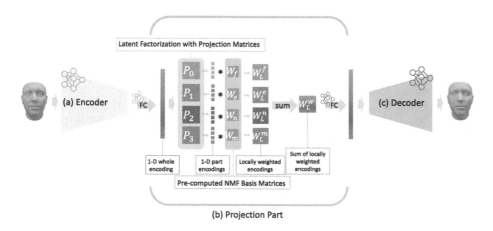

(b) Projection Part

Fig. 1. Locally weighted autoencoder architecture

how to compress and decompress the data, respectively. In between them, the projection part factorizes the latent space into the subspace and applies local weights to make the subspace semantically meaningful. More details on local weights and latent space manipulation will be explained in the following section.

3.1 Pre-Computed Local Weights from NMF

We use a part-based representation to extract the local part structure without segmented data or labels. The representation is used as weights, which have each vertex's influence on each divided facial part. To make a part-based representation of the whole data, we employ the non-negative matrix factorization(NMF), which is a robust feature factorization method to represent data as part-based ones. This method finds a low-rank approximation of a matrix V, where $V \approx WH$, when V, W, and H do not have non-negative values. Given a feature matrix, V, W is a basis matrix that contains basis elements of V, and H is a latent representation matrix. We call the matrix W local weights. To express local features more efficiently, we applied sparse NMF [8] enforcing sparsity on the column of H. This could improve the local separation of features [9]. We compute this with a sparsity constraint value of 7.5. The computed local weights serve as the influence of each vertex on a specific area. We expect that local weights would make the part encodings more semantically meaningful. Figure 2 shows the visualization of the local weights. The bright area shows how much each vertex influences the facial area.

Fig. 2. Pre-computed sparse NMF's basis matrix

3.2   Latent Space Manipulation

Projection Matrix Layer. Our encoder takes a whole shape as input and compresses to a low-dimensional representation, i.e., a latent vector. This encoding reflects the whole shape structure. When we factorize the whole encoding, we can generate part encodings corresponding to the shape structure of the part. Thereby, we disentangle different semantic part encodings from the encoding of the whole shapes. We then perform part-level shape manipulation. Similarly to [2], we use learnable projection matrices to transform the whole part encoding from the global latent space to the localized basis matrix space. We define part-specific projection matrices, where K is the number of semantic parts. Passing through the matrices, the whole part encodings from the encoder are divided into semantic part encodings.

For embedding parts, we implement projection matrices represented as K fully connected layers without biases and with the latent dimension size of $Z \times Z$. The input of the projection layers is a whole face encoding produced by the encoder, and their outputs are K part encodings. The K part encodings can be split unpredictably and have arbitrary meanings. To make them more semantically meaningful, we apply pre-computed local weights.

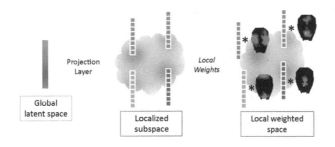

Fig. 3. Illustration of the projection part

Applying Local Weights to Factorized Part Encodings. Li et al. [10] proposed sketch, a combination of random noise and features of the original data, produced by transforming vectors from the noise space to a basis matrix space in NMF. Following [10], we apply the pre-computed local weights to the part encodings that are factorized by the projection matrices (Fig. 1-(b)). Each pre-computed local weight is multiplied by each latent vector. Thanks to this operation, each factorized latent vector has a localized weight, and the encodings lie on a part-based subspace. We describe this process schematically in Fig. 3.

4   Implementation

To obtain large facial mesh data, we used the AFLW2000-3D dataset [11] containing 2,000 3D faces having 53,215 vertices each face. All faces are in full correspondence and generated by the Basel Face Model [12] without pose variations. The dataset was divided into a training set and a test set with 1,780 faces and 220 faces, respectively. Our proposed synthesis model has a similar architecture like CoMA [3]. With the basic autoencoder architecture, we add the projection matrix layer that we explained in Sect. 3.2. To optimize the networks, we exploit the L_1 and cycle loss [2]. We trained our model for 300 epochs with a batch size of 32. The dimension of the latent vector was 64. We followed Ranjan et al. [3] in terms of other hyper-parameters. We used PyTorch [13] and PyTorch Geometric [14] to implement our model and conducted all experiments with NVIDIA Titan RTX GPU 24 GB.

5   Experimental Results

The experimental results of our proposed model are described in this section. We present the practicality of our model with generation tasks. In all experiments, we set the number of face parts, K, as 4. An extended version of this paper contains more implementation details and additional ablation test about the proposed model [4].

5.1   Generation Results

In this experiment, we tested the part manipulation results by applying interpolation between source and target as shown in Fig. 4. We interpolated the source's part encodings to the target's corresponding part encodings obtained by factorized latent vectors described in Sect. 3.2.

(a) Source   (b) Target

Fig. 4. Source and target face

Part Manipulation. Figure 5 shows that as the respective part of the face influence changes, the other parts of the face are not affected. Plus, we expected that each row's changing part matches each local weight in the same row. As a result, we observed that each variation area corresponds to each local weight in Fig. 5. Color gradients in the variation area included visualizing the Hausdorff distance between the first face ($\alpha = \frac{1}{9}$) and the last face ($\alpha = \frac{8}{9}$) in each row. Each of them displays a variation of each interpolation more clearly.

Diversity Visualization. To demonstrate the variety of data, we measured the diversity of generated data from our model. Using the trained encoder, we encoded 220 random faces from our training set and test set, respectively. Since our proposed model allows part manipulation and modification, we synthesized 220 faces by combining five source faces and 11 target faces for four parts. The result was visualized by projecting selected data onto a 2D plane using PCA and t-SNE [15], shown in Fig. 6. We displayed all encoded faces as markers and summarized them with ellipses. Here, there are three types of encoding: training set (red), test set (yellow), and part synthesis (green).

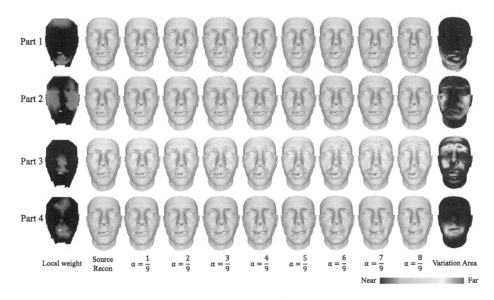

Fig. 5. Results of part interpolation

In Fig. 6-(a), we can discern that our synthesis sample area (green ellipse) involves both areas of the training set and test set (red and yellow ellipses) in the 2D PCA plane. Figure 6-(b) presents this result more distinctively as the synthesis samples are also located in a wider region as well as the region of the training set and test set. In our visualizations, our synthesis samples (green) cover wider areas in the encoding space. As a result, our proposed method shows a prominent performance to extend the model's representation ability.

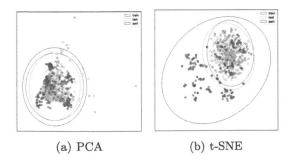

(a) PCA   (b) t-SNE

Fig. 6. Diversity visualization

5.2 Discussion

Although our proposed model performed notable part manipulation and synthesis using a holistic generative approach, there are a few points that need further discussion. First, the correlation between the changing area of faces and local weights should be better addressed. Most changing areas generally reflect corresponding local weights features, but some include another part or ignores them. One possible reason for this is that projection matrices would cover unassigned areas by transforming part encodings to local weight's space. The other is the natural quality of the dataset having correlations between facial features. In second, we multiply the part encodings in latent space and local weights in NMF. This approach seemed to work in our setting because the projection matrices transform part encodings to local weights' space. We have shown experimentally that our process works, but a more rigorous mathematical proof is still needed.

6 Conclusion

We proposed a locally weighted 3D generative face model using spectral convolution networks for a 3D mesh. Our model show improved expressiveness by manipulating the local parts of a face without explicit mesh segmentation. In future work, we would like to extend our model to apply other generative models i.e., VAE or GANs, to improve output's quality. Generating face textures with geometry also would express the quality of outcomes better. Besides, it would be worthwhile to study part-based representation to improve the proposed local weights to develop the model's synthesis ability.

Acknowledgements. This project was supported in part by the ITRC/IITP program (IITP-2021-0-01460) and the NRF (2017R1A2B3012701 and 2021R1A4A1032582) in South Korea. Y.-J. Kim is the corresponding author.

References

1. Schor, N., Katzir, O., Zhang, H., Cohen-Or, D.: Componet: learning to generate the unseen by part synthesis and composition. In: Proceedings of the IEEE/CVF International Conference on Computer Vision, pp. 8759–8768 (2019)
2. Dubrovina, A., Xia, F., Achlioptas, P., Shalah, M., Groscot, R., Guibas, L.J.: Composite shape modeling via latent space factorization. In: Proceedings of the IEEE/CVF International Conference on Computer Vision, pp. 8140–8149 (2019)
3. Ranjan, A., Bolkart, T., Sanyal, S., Black, M.J.: Generating 3d faces using convolutional mesh autoencoders. In: Proceedings of the European Conference on Computer Vision (ECCV), pp. 704–720 (2018)
4. Kim, M.: Face geometry synthesis using locally weighted autoencoder. Master's thesis, Ewha Womans University (2021)
5. Blanz, V., Vetter, T.: A morphable model for the synthesis of 3d faces. In Proceedings of the 26th Annual Conference on Computer Graphics and Interactive Techniques, pp. 187–194 (1999)

6. Tena, J.R., De la Torre, F., Matthews, I.: Interactive region-based linear 3d face models. In: ACM SIGGRAPH 2011 papers, pp. 1–10 (2011)
7. Defferrard, M., Bresson, X., Vandergheynst, P.: Convolutional neural networks on graphs with fast localized spectral filtering. arXiv preprint arXiv:1606.09375 (2016)
8. Potluru, V.K., Plis, S.M., Roux, J.L., Pearlmutter, B.A., Calhoun, V.D., Hayes, T.P.: Block coordinate descent for sparse nmf. arXiv preprint arXiv:1301.3527 (2013)
9. McGraw, T., Kang, J., Herring, D.: Sparse non-negative matrix factorization for mesh segmentation. Int. J. Image Graph. **16**(01), 1650004 (2016)
10. Li, W., et al.: Sketch-then-edit generative adversarial network. Knowl.-Based Syst. **203**, 106102 (2020)
11. Zhu, X., Lei, Z., Liu, X., Shi, H., Li, S.Z.: Face alignment across large poses: a 3d solution. In: Proceedings of the IEEE Conference on Computer Vision and Pattern Recognition, pp. 146–155 (2016)
12. Paysan, P., Knothe, R., Amberg, B., Romdhani, S., Vetter, T.: A 3d face model for pose and illumination invariant face recognition. In: 2009 sixth IEEE International Conference on Advanced Video and Signal Based Surveillance, pp. 296–301. IEEE (2009)
13. Paszke, A., et al. Pytorch: An imperative style, high-performance deep learning library. arXiv preprint arXiv:1912.01703 (2019)
14. Fey, M., Lenssen, J.E.: Fast graph representation learning with pytorch geometric. arXiv preprint arXiv:1903.02428 (2019)
15. Van der Maaten, L., Hinton, G.: Visualizing data using t-sne. J. Mach. Learn. Res. **9**(11), 2579–2605 (2008)

CFMNet: Coarse-to-Fine Cascaded Feature Mapping Network for Hair Attribute Transfer

Zhifeng Xie[1(✉)], Guisong Zhang[1], Chunpeng Yu[1], Jiaheng Zheng[1], and Bin Sheng[2]

[1] Shanghai University, Shanghai, China
zhifeng_xie@shu.edu.cn
[2] Shanghai Jiao Tong University, Shanghai, China

Abstract. Recently, GAN-based manipulation methods have been proposed to effectively edit and transfer facial attributes. However, these state-of-the-art methods usually fail to delicately manipulate hair attributes because hair does not own a concrete shape and varies a lot with flexible structure. Therefore, how to achieve high-fidelity hair attribute transfer becomes a challenging task. In this paper, we propose a coarse-to-fine cascaded feature mapping network (CFMNet), which can disentangle hair into coarse-grained and fine-grained attributes, and transform hair feature in latent space according to a reference image. The disentangled hair attributes consist of the coarse-grained labels, including length, waviness and bangs, and the fine-grained 3D model, including geometry and color. Next we design a cascaded feature mapping network to manipulate the attributes in a coarse-to-fine way between source and reference images, which can adjust and control hair feature more delicately. Moreover, we also construct an identity loss to avoid the destruction of identity information in source image. A variety of experimental results demonstrate the effectiveness of our proposed method.

Keywords: Hair attribute transfer · Latent space manipulation · GAN

1 Introduction

Hair attribute transfer is to manipulate hair attributes with definite target. Although a variety of attribute transfer methods are proposed to effectively manipulate facial feature, hair attribute transfer is still a challenging work due to the complexity of hair feature. With the achievement of generative adversarial networks (GANs) [7], some image-to-image translation methods are proposed for conditional image generation. CycleGAN [21] learns translation between two domains with unpaired data by employing the cycle consistency loss. StarGAN [6] further learns to translate images to more domains by applying attribute classification loss. AttGAN [8], taking an encoder-decoder architecture, translates image by attaching target labels to latent space. STGAN [15] further improves

© Springer Nature Switzerland AG 2021
N. Magnenat-Thalmann et al. (Eds.): CGI 2021, LNCS 13002, pp. 406–417, 2021.
https://doi.org/10.1007/978-3-030-89029-2_32

the encoder-decoder architecture by adding selective transfer units and replacing target labels with difference attribute vector. In above methods, images are embedded into latent space and then decoded to target domain, which are proved to be an efficient way to transfer coarse-grained attributes. However, feature of hair is more complex, which labels are too vague to present. Therefore, these image-to-image translation methods usually fail to transfer fine-grained attributes, which does not meet our expectation to delicately manipulate hair attributes.

Recently, StyleGAN [12,13] is proposed to generate high-quality images, over which a variety of methods are proposed to manipulate attributes in the intermediate latent space. StyleRig [19], a 3D-guided StyleGAN-based attribute transfer method, learns to transform face feature in latent space according to parameters of 3D face model, which enlightens us to manipulate hair attributes in latent space with 3D hair model. However, latent space of StyleGAN [12,13] is not sufficiently disentangled for hair attributes, which leads to the difficulty of delicate hair manipulation. MichiGAN [18] disentangles hair into four orthogonal attributes, with which desired hair are generated step by step. Inspired by this solution, we disentangle hair into coarse-grained and fine-grained attributes to delicately manipulate hair.

In this paper, we propose a coarse-to-fine cascaded feature mapping network (CFMNet), which can disentangle hair into coarse-grained and fine-grained attributes, and transform hair feature according to a reference image in latent space. CFMNet can be subdivided into three coarse-grained feature mapping subnetworks and two fine-grained feature mapping subnetworks. Coarse-grained feature mapping subnetworks are applied to manipulate coarse-grained attributes of hair length, waviness and bangs. Fine-grained feature mapping subnetworks are applied to manipulate fine-grained attributes which are 3D hair models of geometry and color. There are totally 1024 strands in each hair model and each strand is controlled by 100 points, which is delicate enough for our work to manipulate hair attributes in fine-grained part. As shown in Fig. 1, five subnetworks are cascaded to form a feature mapping network, which transforms hair feature from source to reference step by step. Label extraction modules, including length, waviness and bangs, and hair extraction modules, including 3D hair geometry and color, are constructed to extract hair feature for hair attribute transfer. We also predefine an identity extraction module for all subnetworks to avoid the destruction of identity from source image. Our contributions can be summarized as follow:

- We propose a novel attribute transfer framework to transform hair feature with identity preservation according to a reference image.
- We disentangle hair into coarse-grained attributes, including length, waviness and bangs, and fine-grained attributes, including geometry and color, based on which a cascaded feature mapping architecture is conducted to generate desired hair step by step.

– Strand-based 3D hair models are delicate enough for our work, with which fine-grained feature mapping subnetworks could transfer fine-grained hair attributes accurately.

2   Related Work

2.1   GAN-Based Attribute Manipulation

Generative adversarial Network (GAN) [7] works well on generating image from random noise. With further research on GAN technology, varieties of conditional image generation methods have been proposed for image-to-image translation. Pix2pix [11] learns to translate image from one domain to other domain with paired images by introducing "U-Net" to encoder-decoder architecture. Cycle-GAN [21] learns translation from unpaired images between two domains with cycle consistency loss. StarGAN [6] learns to translate images to more domains with only one model by applying attribute classification loss and cycle consistency loss. AttGAN [8] takes an encoder-decoder architecture and attach target labels to the decoder, making multi-domain translation more efficient. STGAN [15] improves the encoder-decoder architecture by attaching selective transfer units and replacing target labels with difference attribute vector. With labels guiding, above methods could manipulate coarse-grained attributes to different domain. However, images with the same labels may differ a lot, which causes details lost during hair attribute transfer. Although above methods could transfer attributes among domains, they do not meet our expectation to delicately manipulate hair.

StyleGAN [12,13] is proposed to be a high-quality image generation network, of which some works try to manipulate facial attribute in latent space. Style-Flow [2] simultaneously takes conditional continuous normalizing flows to edit facial attributes, which can transfer semantic feature in portrait. StyleRig [19] learns to transfer facial attribute by controlling parameters of 3D face model, which performs well on manipulation of fine-grained facial attributes. Their contributions inspire our work to manipulate hair based on StyleGAN [12,13] with 3D hair model. However, hair is so complex that delicate manipulation on hair is still a challenging work. MaskGAN [14] manipulates facial attribute by editing corresponding masks with a dense mapping network connecting images to semantic masks. Similarly, MichiGAN [18] disentangles hair into four orthogonal attributes, with which disentangled attributes are transferred in a cascaded way. Inspired by the disentanglement of hair, we disentangle hair into five attributes and apply coarse-to-fine attributes transfer with cascaded feature mapping.

2.2   3D Hair Reconstruction

Unlike 3D Morphable Model (3DMM) [3], working well on 3D face reconstruction, hair does not own a concrete shape and varies a lot. Luo et al. [16] reconstructs high-quality strand-based 3D model with 3D point cloud from multi-view

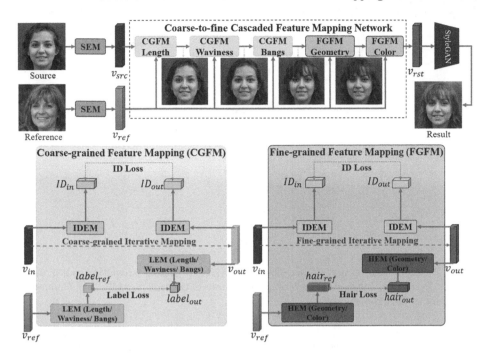

Fig. 1. The pipeline of CFMNet. The upper is the overall workflow. Source and reference image are firstly embedded into latent space and then manipulated by three coarse-grained feature mapping subnetworks (CGFMs) and two fine-grained feature mapping subnetworks (FGFMs). The bottom-left is structure of CGFM which iteratively manipulates coarse-grained hair attributes with identity extraction module (IDEM) and label extraction module (LEM). Similarly, the bottom-right is structure of FGFM which iteratively manipulates fine-grained hair attribute with identity extraction module (IDEM) and hair extraction module (HEM).

images. Chai et al. [5] proposes a strand tracing method to get frontal hair model from single-view image. Hu et al. [10] takes a data-driven method to retrieve 3D hair model from dataset. AutoHair [4] takes advantage of convolutional network to retrieve 3D hair model from larger dataset with manual operation. HairNet [20] is proposed to capture hair geometry from orientation image with convolutional encoder-decoder architecture. In this paper, we take advantage of HairNet [20] to generate hair geometry as part of fine-grained hair attributes.

3   Method

3.1   Overview

As shown in Fig. 1, based on W space which is the intermediate latent space of StyleGAN2 [13], we propose a cascaded feature mapping network to manipulate hair attribute. The first step of our work is to embed images to latent

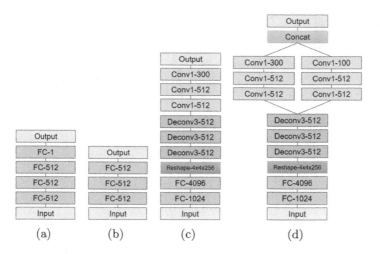

Fig. 2. Network architecture of modules in CFMNet. (a) Label extraction module. (b) Identity extraction module. (c) Color part of hair extraction module. (d) Geometry part of hair extraction module.

vector $w \in \mathbb{R}^{512}$ which is the output of mapping network in StyleGAN2 [13]. To prevent from confusing W space with other latent space, we name latent vector w as style vector. After embedded by the style embedding module (SEM) [1], a coarse-to-fine cascaded feature mapping network is applied to transform hair feature from source image to the reference. Two kinds of mapping models, coarse-grained feature mapping subnetwork (CGFM) and fine-grained feature mapping subnetwork (FGFM), are included in CFMNet.

3.2   Predefined Feature Extraction

Label Extraction Module (LEM). Labels of portrait are regarded as the coarse-grained feature in this paper. The portraits are tagged with hair labels of length, waviness and bangs. For each LEM, the input is a style vector, and the output is label of corresponding coarse-grained attribute. As shown in Fig. 2(a), we employ a four-layer Multi-Layer Perceptron (MLP) to classify hair attributes and apply cross-entropy loss for this module:

$$l_i = L_i(v, y_i) = -y_i \log(F_i(v)) \quad i \in \{1, 2, 3\}, \tag{1}$$

where $i \in \{1, 2, 3\}$ stands for hair attribute of length, waviness or bangs. F_i is the i-th LEM and v is the inputted style vector. $y_i \in \{0, 1\}$ is the i-th binary label of the sample. L_i is the loss function of i-th LEM and l_i is the loss of corresponding module.

Hair Extraction Module (HEM). In this step, 3D hair models, including geometry and color information of hair, are applied as the fine-grained attributes of hair. The dimension of hair geometry is $1024 \times 100 \times 4$ and dimension of 3D color is $1024 \times 100 \times 3$. Inspired by HairNet [20], we design a decoder to extract 3D geometry and color from style vector. As shown in Fig. 2(c) and Fig. 2(d), we firstly disentangle the style vector with two fully-connected layers, and then reshape it to $4 \times 4 \times 256$. With three deconvolutional layers, the scale of feature is enlarged. For the color part, shown in Fig. 2(c), three 1×1 convolutional layers are applied for extracting further feature; for the geometry part, another branch with three 1×1 convolutional layers are applied. ℓ_2 loss is used for training hair extraction module:

$$l_i = L_i(v, y_i) = \|y_i - F_i(v)\|_2^2 \quad i \in \{4, 5\}, \tag{2}$$

where $i \in \{4, 5\}$ respectively stands for geometry or color of hair. F_i is the i-th hair extraction module. v is the inputted style vector and y_i is the corresponding 3D hair model of the sample. L_i is the i-th loss function and l_i is the loss of hair extraction module.

Identity Extraction Module (IDEM). For identity preservation during hair manipulation, we propose IDEM to extract identity vector from style vector. As shown in Fig. 2(b), similar to LEM, we design a MLP for identity extraction. We apply cosine loss according to FaceNet [17] for this module:

$$l_{id} = L_{id}(v, y_{id}) = \frac{y_{id} \cdot D(v)}{\|y_{id}\|_2 \cdot \|D(v)\|_2}, \tag{3}$$

where v is the inputted style vector and y_{id} is the corresponding identity vector. D is the identity extraction module and L_{id} is the loss function and l_{id} is the loss of identity extraction module.

3.3 Coarse-to-Fine Cascaded Transfer

As shown in Fig. 1, there are five mapping subnetworks for hair attribute transfer, among which three are CGFMs and two are FGFMs. CGFMs focus on coarse-grained attributes, including hair length, waviness and bangs, which work on large-scale hair transformation. On the contrary, FGFMs are more concerned with detailed feature of hair geometry and color, thus fine-tuning hair at the strand level. Guided by the reference style vector v_{ref}, the source style vector v_{src} is manipulated to target style vector v_{rst} step by step. As shown in Fig. 1, we deploy the CFMNet in an iterative way. Each mapping subnetwork owns two essential parts, one of which is IDEM, applied to extract the identity of source image. The other part is LEM or HEM which is applied to extract hair attribute for hair feature manipulation. With IDEM, LEMs and HEMs pretrained, feature mapping subnetworks could work with iterative feature mapping. To make it available to delicately manipulate hair, we build an energy equation:

$$E_i(w, v_{in}, v_{ref}) = L_{id}(w, D(v_{in})) + \lambda_i L_i(w, F_i(v_{ref})), \tag{4}$$

where E_i is the energy function of i-th feature mapping subnetwork. v_{in} is the initial style vector to transform. v_{ref} is the reference style vector. v_{out} is the result of a single mapping step. w is the inputted style vector of energy function. λ_i is a fixed weight used to balance the energy from identity and feature. With the energy equation, the mapping process could be summarized as:

$$v_{out} = C_i(v_{in}, v_{ref}) = \arg\min_{w \in \mathbb{R}^{512}} E_i(w, v_{in}, v_{ref}) \tag{5}$$

C_i is i-th feature mapping step which transfers style vector to referential attribute. In practice, we take v_{in} as an initial value and then we take an optimizer to minimize the energy value $E_i(w, v_{in}, v_{ref})$.

All feature extraction modules would be pretrained before used for inference. We propose a cascaded structure to transfer hair attributes with cascaded feature mapping subnetworks, which could be summarized as:

$$v_i = C_i(v_{i-1}, v_{ref}) \quad v \in \{1, 2, 3, 4, 5\} \tag{6}$$

where v_i ($i \in \{1, 2, 3, 4, 5\}$) is the output of i-th feature mapping subnetwork. v_{ref} is the style vector of reference. v_0 is the style vector of source image and v_5 is the result style vector. With generator of StyleGAN2 [13], we could visualize v_5 to the result image and visualize v_1, v_2, v_3 and v_4 as intermediate image.

4   Experiments

4.1   Dataset and Pretraining

We select 28K images with long hair generated by StyleGAN2 [13]. All the selected images are saved with corresponding style vectors. Then the images are tagged with binary hair labels of length, bangs and waviness, which are regarded as the coarse-grained feature in our dataset.

For the fine-grained parts, HairNet [20] is used to generate geometry part of 3D hair models, with which 3D color information are sampled from the images. Each 3D hair model could be formulated as a matrix $P_{N*M*C_{hair}}$ ($N = 1024$, $M = 100$), which means each hair model is composed of 1024 strands, with each strand consisting of 100 points. $C_{hair} = 4$ for hair geometry, each point consists of 4 channels, among which 3 channels are coordinate of spatial position and 1 channel is curvature. $C_{hair} = 3$ for hair color, each point consists of color information of R, G and B. We extract identical vector with FaceNet [17] and the dimension of identity vector is 512. We take 19.5K samples for training, 5.6K for validation and 2.9K for test.

4.2   Result Analysis

We pretrain each feature extract module by Adam optimizer ($\beta_1 = 0.9$, $\beta_2 = 0.999$). Learning rate of LEM and IDEM is specified as 0.00001, and learning rate of HEM is 0.0001. At inference stage, we take Adam optimizer ($\beta_1 = 0.9$, $\beta_2 = 0.999$) as well. We assign $\lambda_1 = \lambda_2 = \lambda_3 = 100.0$ and learning rate of

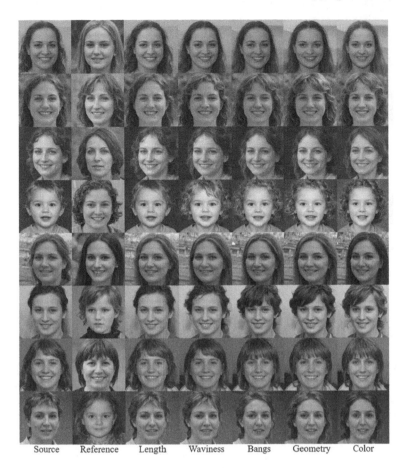

Source   Reference   Length   Waviness   Bangs   Geometry   Color

Fig. 3. Visualized image after each feature mapping subnetwork of CFMNet. With guidance of hair from reference image, cascaded feature mapping network transfer hair in five manipulation steps. Coarse-grained manipulation of length, waviness and bangs transforms large-scale hair attribute, while fine-grained manipulation of geometry and color pays more attention to detailed hair feature from reference. Each feature mapping subnetwork only focuses on corresponding attribute without changing other attribute, which demonstrates effectiveness of coarse-to-fine architecture.

0.01 for CGFMs. The iterative steps of CGFMs are 50, 40 and 40. We take $\lambda_4 = \lambda_5 = 1000000.0$ and learning rate of 0.003 for FGFMs. The iterative steps of FGFMs are 300 and 200.

To present the delicate manipulation on hair in our method, we visualize intermediate style vectors to intermediate images. As shown in Fig. 3, each feature mapping subnetwork only focuses on corresponding attribute without manipulating other attribute. The final result hair shares the same hair feature with reference hair and fits face and background naturally. Due to the inconsistence of light and face orientation between source and reference image, light direction, intensity and color are changed and face orientation is rotated during

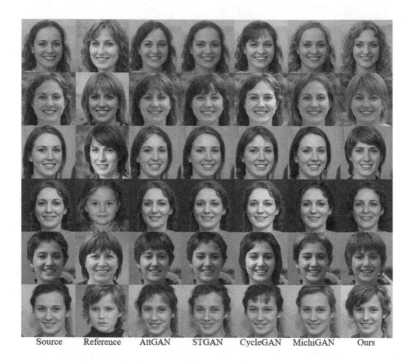

Source   Reference   AttGAN   STGAN   CycleGAN   MichiGAN   Ours

Fig. 4. Visual comparison with AttGAN [8], STGAN [15], CycleGAN [21] and Michi-GAN [18]. As shown in this figure, result hair of our method matches reference hair best. Methods of AttGAN [8], STGAN [15] and CycleGAN [21] fail to transfer detailed hair attributes. Generated hair of MichiGAN [18] is not photo-realistic due to the incompatible light directions between face and hair.

transferring process, causing some small changes on face which does not affect face identity nevertheless.

4.3   Comparison

Visual Comparison. We compare CFMNet with AttGAN [8], STGAN [15], CycleGAN [21] and MichiGAN [18]. Due to the lack of length label of original pretrained models, we train AttGAN [8], STGAN [15] and CycleGAN [21] in our dataset. For AttGAN [8] and STG AN [15], we extract reference labels as target. For CycleGAN [21], we train three individual models for every label. For MichiGAN [18], desired hair is generated with shape and background of source image, as well as structure and apperance of reference image. As shown in Fig. 4, our results look photo-realistic and match referential hair best. CycleGAN [21], AttGAN [8] and STGAN [15] are unable to manipulate detailed hair attributes. MichiGAN [18], lacking a method to compose target shape with referential hair, is unable to make hair longer or heavier without manual editing. Our method performs best to manipulate hair with referential hair, by which generated images of CFMNet gain the highest quality.

Table 1. Frecet Inception Distance (FID) score comparison for different methods. Our method gains the best FID score which means ours performs best in quantitative comparison

Method	CycleGAN [21]	AttGAN [8]	STGAN [15]	MichiGAN [18]	Ours
FID	66.565	132.117	107.782	49.515	31.559

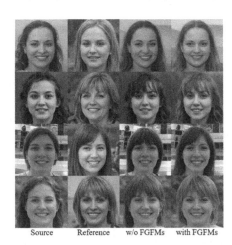

Source   Reference   w/o FGFMs   with FGFMs

Fig. 5. Ablation study for fine-grained feature mapping subnetworks. Some details, including detailed hair color, length, thickness and bangs, are only manipulated in FGFMs.

Quantitative Comparison. Frecet Inception Distance (FID) [9] is used to measure the difference between generated images and original images. The smaller FID score implies that generated images are more similar to the original. To verify that our results are best, we take FID for quantitative comparison. We get 570 result images with 30 source images and 19 reference images, resizing all result images to resolution of 256 × 256. As shown in Table 1, we achieve the best FID score, which shows generated images of our method are more similar to images from the dataset.

4.4 Ablation Study

Coarse-to-Fine Architecture. To draw the necessity of coarse-to-fine architecture, we obtain a variety of examples of different transferring stage. As shown in Fig. 5, CGFMs can manipulate attribute of larger scale, but it fails to transfer details like detailed hair waviness, thickness or bangs shape. With FGFMs attached, detailed attributes could be manipulated according to referential hair. It proves that CGFMs could only transfer large scale attributes, on which FGFMs could further manipulate detailed hair attributes and achieve the results to delicately manipulate hair attribute.

Source   Reference   w/o identity   with identity

Fig. 6. Ablation study for the importance of identity. The result shows that generated images without l_{id} may lose some facial identity feature.

Identity Loss. To evaluation the necessity of identity loss, we try to figure out the importance of identity loss l_{id}. As shown in Fig. 6, results without constrain of identity loss seem to have some facial identity destructions, which are changes on the shape of eyebow, mouth and eye, while results with identity loss could maintain the facial identity from source image. Results show that identity loss is effectively applied to get rid of facial identity destruction.

5   Conclusions

In this paper, we propose a novel method to delicately manipulate hair attribute to referential hair with preserving the facial identity. CFMNet disentangles hair into coarse-grained and fine-grained attributes and works well with a cascaded feature mapping structure which can effectively manipulate hair attribute in latent space of StyleGAN2 [13]. The disentangled hair attributes consist of the coarse-grained labels, including length, waviness and bangs, and the fine-grained 3D model, including geometry and color. From visualization of intermediate images, it is proved that the hair is well disentangled in our method. The cascaded feature mapping network manipulates hair step by step with guidance of referential hair and source identity. The results show that our method performs best to manipulate hair attributes with cascaded structure.

References

1. Abdal, R., Qin, Y., Wonka, P.: Image2stylegan: how to embed images into the stylegan latent space? In: Proceedings of the IEEE/CVF International Conference on Computer Vision, pp. 4432–4441 (2019)
2. Abdal, R., Zhu, P., Mitra, N.J., Wonka, P.: Styleflow: attribute-conditioned exploration of stylegan-generated images using conditional continuous normalizing flows. ACM Trans. Graph. (TOG) **40**(3), 1–21 (2021)
3. Blanz, V., Vetter, T.: A morphable model for the synthesis of 3d faces. In: Proceedings of the 26th Annual Conference on Computer Graphics and Interactive Techniques, pp. 187–194 (1999)
4. Chai, M., Shao, T., Wu, H., Weng, Y., Zhou, K.: Autohair: Fully automatic hair modeling from a single image. ACM Trans. Graph. **35**(4) (2016)

5. Chai, M., Wang, L., Weng, Y., Yu, Y., Guo, B., Zhou, K.: Single-view hair modeling for portrait manipulation. ACM Trans. Graph. (TOG) **31**(4), 1–8 (2012)
6. Choi, Y., Choi, M., Kim, M., Ha, J.W., Kim, S., Choo, J.: Stargan: unified generative adversarial networks for multi-domain image-to-image translation. In: Proceedings of the IEEE Conference on Computer Vision and Pattern Recognition, pp. 8789–8797 (2018)
7. Goodfellow, I.J., et al.: Generative adversarial networks. arXiv preprint arXiv:1406.2661 (2014)
8. He, Z., Zuo, W., Kan, M., Shan, S., Chen, X.: Attgan: facial attribute editing by only changing what you want. IEEE Trans. Image Process. **28**(11), 5464–5478 (2019)
9. Heusel, M., Ramsauer, H., Unterthiner, T., Nessler, B., Hochreiter, S.: Gans trained by a two time-scale update rule converge to a local nash equilibrium. arXiv preprint arXiv:1706.08500 (2017)
10. Hu, L., Ma, C., Luo, L., Li, H.: Single-view hair modeling using a hairstyle database. ACM Trans. Graph. (ToG) **34**(4), 1–9 (2015)
11. Isola, P., Zhu, J.Y., Zhou, T., Efros, A.A.: Image-to-image translation with conditional adversarial networks. In: Proceedings of the IEEE Conference on Computer Vision and Pattern Recognition, pp. 1125–1134 (2017)
12. Karras, T., Laine, S., Aila, T.: A style-based generator architecture for generative adversarial networks. In: Proceedings of the IEEE/CVF Conference on Computer Vision and Pattern Recognition, pp. 4401–4410 (2019)
13. Karras, T., Laine, S., Aittala, M., Hellsten, J., Lehtinen, J., Aila, T.: Analyzing and improving the image quality of stylegan. In: Proceedings of the IEEE/CVF Conference on Computer Vision and Pattern Recognition, pp. 8110–8119 (2020)
14. Lee, C.H., Liu, Z., Wu, L., Luo, P.: Maskgan: towards diverse and interactive facial image manipulation. In: Proceedings of the IEEE/CVF Conference on Computer Vision and Pattern Recognition, pp. 5549–5558 (2020)
15. Liu, M., Ding, Y., Xia, M., Liu, X., Ding, E., Zuo, W., Wen, S.: Stgan: a unified selective transfer network for arbitrary image attribute editing. In: Proceedings of the IEEE/CVF Conference on Computer Vision and Pattern Recognition, pp. 3673–3682 (2019)
16. Luo, L., Li, H., Rusinkiewicz, S.: Structure-aware hair capture. ACM Trans. Graph. (TOG) **32**(4), 1–12 (2013)
17. Schroff, F., Kalenichenko, D., Philbin, J.: Facenet: a unified embedding for face recognition and clustering. In: Proceedings of the IEEE Conference on Computer Vision and Pattern Recognition, pp. 815–823 (2015)
18. Tan, Z., Chai, M., Chen, D., Liao, J., Chu, Q., Yuan, L., Tulyakov, S., Yu, N.: Michigan: multi-input-conditioned hair image generation for portrait editing. arXiv preprint arXiv:2010.16417 (2020)
19. Tewari, A., et al.: Stylerig: rigging stylegan for 3d control over portrait images. In: Proceedings of the IEEE/CVF Conference on Computer Vision and Pattern Recognition, pp. 6142–6151 (2020)
20. Zhou, Y., et al.: Hairnet: single-view hair reconstruction using convolutional neural networks. In: Proceedings of the European Conference on Computer Vision (ECCV), pp. 235–251 (2018)
21. Zhu, J.Y., Park, T., Isola, P., Efros, A.A.: Unpaired image-to-image translation using cycle-consistent adversarial networks. In: Proceedings of the IEEE International Conference on Computer Vision, pp. 2223–2232 (2017)

Rendering and Textures

Dynamic Shadow Synthesis Using Silhouette Edge Optimization

Jihong Wang[1], Zhen Li[1], Saba Ghazanfar Ali[2], Bin Sheng[2(✉)], Ping Li[3], Xiaoyu Chi[4], Jinman Kim[5], and Lijuan Mao[1(✉)]

[1] Shanghai University of Sport,, Shanghai, People's Republic of China
maolijuan@sus.edu.cn
[2] Shanghai Jiao Tong University, Shanghai, People's Republic of China
shengbin@sjtu.edu.cn
[3] The Hong Kong Polytechnic University, Hong Kong, People's Republic of China
[4] Qingdao Research Institute of Beihang University, Qingdao 266000, China
[5] The University of Sydney, Sydney, Australia

Abstract. The shadow volume is utilized extensively for real-time rendering applications which includes updating volumes and calculating silhouette edges. Existing shadow volume methods are CPU intensive and complex occluders result in poor rendering efficiency. In this paper, we propose a hash-culling shadow volume algorithm that uses hash-based acceleration for the silhouette edge determination which is the most time-consuming processing in the traditional shadow volume algorithm. Our proposed method uses a hash table to store silhouette edge index information and thus reduces the time taken for redundant edge detection. The method significantly reduces CPU usage and improves algorithm time efficiency. Furthermore, for low hardware-level systems, especially embedded systems, it is still difficult to render dynamic shadows due to their high demand on the fill-rate capacity of graphics hardware. Our method has low hardware requirements and is easy to implement on PCs and embedded systems with real-time rendering performance with visual-pleasing shadow effects.

Keywords: Shaodow volume · Shadow synthesis · Shadow rendering · Hash · Dynamic · Optimization

1 Introduction

Shadow effects can help viewers to perceive the relative distance and position of objects, as well as the geometry of occluders and occludees [14]. However, rendering realistic shadows is difficult, and doing it in real-time is even more complicated. Offline rendering techniques such as ray tracing can generate shadows automatically; nonetheless, no standard approach to real-time shadow rendering currently exists. Among numerous shadow rendering methods used in the various applications, shadow volume has been prevalent and is efficient in its ability

© Springer Nature Switzerland AG 2021
N. Magnenat-Thalmann et al. (Eds.): CGI 2021, LNCS 13002, pp. 421–432, 2021.
https://doi.org/10.1007/978-3-030-89029-2_33

to generate accurate real-time shadows. When compared with shadow mapping with its aliasing artifacts problem, shadow volume is considered the better choice especially when there is a demand for high-quality shadows. However, the computation complexity of dynamic shadows in the shadow volume algorithm has been a long-standing problem since it is first introduced. Nowadays, graphics cards with stencil test support are omnipresent in the current computer hardware market [3,5,11]. Consequently, the shadow volume algorithm with a stencil test is utilized extensively in 3D games and other applications. The efficiency of the shadow volume algorithm is limited by two main procedures: determination of silhouette edges and shadow volume rendering. Because the number of silhouette edges has a significant impact on the stencil test time and ultimately determines the shadow rendering time, improving silhouette edge determination efficiency is our key objective. Furthermore, in recent years, 3D games have become prevalent, propelled by concomitant sharp increases in the usage of smartphones and tablets. However, the graphics hardware in smartphones and tablets is resource-constrained, and so efficient implementation of dynamic shadows for 3D games and other 3D applications is crucial. Thus, optimization of the classic shadow volume algorithm for use in such environments is imperative.

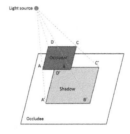

Fig. 1. Shadow volume created by single point light and square occluder.

We propose a hash-culling shadow volume algorithm that improves the efficiency of silhouette edge determination. In the proposed algorithm, according to the position of the light source and the mesh, all the faces of the mesh are tested to determine if they are front surfaces. Next, for all front surfaces, silhouette edges are recorded and each silhouette edge is extended away from the light source to infinity to form a shadow volume. We use shadow polygons to refer to polygons that form the bounds of the shadow volume. The efficiency of the search for the silhouette has a significant impact on the overall efficiency of the algorithm because it is the most time-consuming step. Conventionally the per-triangle method makes a high demand on the fill-rate capacity of graphics cards, which can result in process delays. Our proposed hash-culling shadow volume method is based on the per-object shadow volume concept, and therefore significantly reduces the stress on graphics cards without any meaningful increase in CPU usage. In our proposed algorithm, a hash map is used to improve the search performance of silhouette edges. Using this hash map, we can ensure that

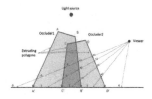

Fig. 2. Basic procedure of Z-Pass algorithm.

silhouette edges are distinguished once all front-surface edges are traversed, and our hash function guarantees that all silhouette edges are recorded. The results of timing tests conducted indicate that our method has significant advantages over classic methods. Our contributions include the following:

- Introducing a hash-culling method that greatly improves shadow volume time efficiency by reducing silhouette edge processing time and shadow volume rasterization time.
- Reducing hardware dependency of shadow volume to make it practical for an embedded system to run real-time shadows.
- Gaining the possibility that using the hash-culling method with other shadow volume culling and clamping method to further improve real-time shadow generating efficiency.

The remainder of this paper is organized as follows. Section 2 introduces related work on the shadow volume algorithm and stencil buffer. Section 3 presents our proposed efficient shadow volume algorithm, and Sect. 4 describes its implementation. Section 5 presents and discusses the results of experiments conducted to evaluate our proposed method. Finally, Sect. 5 concludes this paper.

2   Related Work

First described by Crow [7], shadow volume defines the shadow region of a specific occluder in space, with a given light source. Subsequent to Crow's work, many methods have been developed to improve the performance of the shadow volume algorithm. Brotman et al. proposed a software-based shadow algorithm with a depth buffer [6]. Hardware support for shadow volume evaluation is also supported in the Pixel Planes method [12]. Bergeron extended the shadow volume algorithm afterwards [4]. He clarified how to deal with open models and non-planar polygons. Further, he showed that close shadow volumes are necessary. Heidmann first implemented the shadow volume algorithm in graphics hardware. They used a stencil test to implement the shadow volume, and front and back surface tests to facilitate practical usage of the algorithm. Stencil buffer implementation of the shadow volume algorithm has subsequently become the most practical and widely-used real-time shadow-generating method [13]. The classic shadow volume algorithm is not very robust. To rectify this drawback, various algorithms have been proposed to help it adapt to various circumstances,

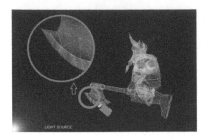

Fig. 3. Silhouette edges depicted with red lines on a mesh with one point light. (Color figure online)

such as the Z-fail, ZP+, and ++ZP algorithms. Batagelo et al. presented a shadow volume algorithm that uses Binary Space Partitioning (BSP) trees and stencil buffers [3]. Their algorithm combines the shadow volume technique with BSP trees and improves the efficiency of the shadow volume algorithm with graphics hardware support. Everitt and Kilgard [2,11] presented several solutions to reduce the fill-rate capacity demand for graphics cards. Kim et al. proposed techniques that extend the shadow volume to non-manifold meshes [16]. Aldridge et al. utilized a per-object shadow volume technique, thereby rectifying the high demand of the fill-rate problem [1]. Culling and clamping of the volumes are used to improve the robustness of this algorithm [10,17,19]. Most recently, the per-triangle shadow volume technique was used by Sintorn et al. with Compute Unified Device Architecture (CUDA) implementation [18] and proved to be robust and reduced pre-processing time for shadow volumes. A shadow volume is, in essence, a volume constructed with a light source and occluders. Several important concepts need to be clarified: Any object that casts a shadow is an occluder. Edges that connect front and back surfaces with consideration to the light source are silhouette edges. Extension of every silhouette edge away from the light source to infinity (usually a very large value in the actual implementation) can result in the formation of shadow polygons. Front and back caps of shadow volumes (faces on the object and their projection at infinity) should be added to form a closed volume. That infinity value should be sufficiently large because even if the light source is very close to the occluder, the shadow should be able to reach the occludee. Figure 1 illustrates the basic shadow volume idea.

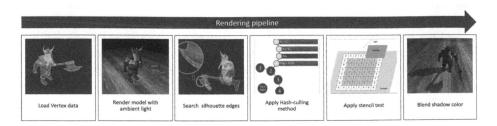

Fig. 4. Rendering pipeline for hash-culling method.

There are three basic steps in the construction of shadow volumes: (1) Find all silhouette edges, (2) extend all silhouette edges away from the light source to infinity, and (3) add front and back caps to form shadow volumes. After construction of a shadow volume, a stencil buffer is typically used to implement shadows. The two most commonly used techniques are depth-pass and depth-fail also called Z-pass and Z-fail because the depth buffer is often referred to as the Z-buffer [15]. The two most expensive operations in stencil shadow volume implementation are silhouette edge determination and shadow volume rendering [8]. In this paper, our proposed hash-culling technique is presented to address the first problem.

The shadow volume algorithm has several advantages over other shadow generating algorithms [9,19,20]: The shadow volume algorithm is more suitable for dynamic light sources, especially when light or objects change their positions frequently. It is also ideal for omnidirectional light sources and can obtain shadows with pixel accuracy. In addition, shadow volume can handle self-shadowing automatically. Computer hardware with stencil test functionality support is very common nowadays. With the standardization of OpenGL and DirectX's functionality, stencil-test-supported hardware is widespread, which makes the shadow volume algorithm easier to implement.

One of the problems associated with a stencil shadow volume implementation is the determination of silhouette edges. Every edge of the front surface, with respect to the light source, should be tested to decide whether it is a silhouette edge. This requires a significant amount of CPU resources. However, an effective way in which CPU usage can be reduced is to determine new silhouette edges only every two to four frames. This method is based on the fact that the position of the light source and objects will not change significantly within two to four frames. However, silhouette edge determination requires further optimization.

$$Key = (V_A^2 + V_B^2) \pmod{MAX}. \tag{1}$$

3   Hash-Culling Approach

In the classic shadow volume construction step, after extending silhouette edges away from the light source to infinity, front and back caps should be added to the shadow volume in order to form a closed volume. In the stencil test step, after shadow volume construction, when the light ray that originates from the viewer's eyes to a point in the scene passes through a front surface of a shadow volume, the stencil buffer is incremented by one. Conversely, when it passes through a back surface of a shadow volume, the stencil buffer is decremented by one. Figure 2 demonstrates this Z-pass mechanism which is used to conduct the stencil test. When viewport cuts through the shadow volume, Z-fail is used to obtain the correct result. Because these methods are not the focus of this paper, further details are omitted.

Algorithm 1. Adding an edge into hash table

1: **AddEdge**(hashtable H, hash-key K, vertex A, vertex B, loop N)
2: //Add edge when not occupied
3: **if** $H[K]$ is not occupied **then**
4:     $H[K]-> isOccupied = TRUE$
5:     $H[K]-> Vertex_A = A$
6:     $H[K]-> Vertex_B = B$
7: **else**
8:     //Remove redundant edge
9:     **if** $Edge(A, B)$ is in hash table **then**
10:         $H[K]-> isOccupied = FALSE$
11:     **else**
12:         //Map edge to another position
13:         $AddEdge(H, K + S, A, B, N + 1)$
14:     **end if**
15: **end if**

The front surfaces of the occluder typically must be projected to infinity. In this scenario, the back cap of the shadow volume is redundant. Since the back cap is at infinity, the receiver should always be covered by the shadow volume. Otherwise, the shadow will never reach the receiver, which is not the target effect. That is, no sight ray will pass through the back cap of the shadow volume before it reaches the occludee. Therefore, the back cap of the shadow volume can be cut.

As stated above, the determination of silhouette edges is a very time-consuming process. All edges of the front surfaces with respect to the light sources are added to the edge set used to generate the shadow volume. If we assume that we are using indexed mesh, then the silhouette edges are those edges that are shared by a front surface and a back surface. Figure 3 depicts the silhouette edges of a mesh with a given light source. The following steps are required for determination of silhouette edges: For every triangle of the mesh, if it faces the light source, add the three edges (pairs of vertices) to an edge array; check each of these three edges, respectively, to determine if it (or its reverse) has appeared in the array and, if yes, remove both edges.

$$(1 - p) \times n \times \sum_i^{(1-p)\times n} S_i \tag{2}$$

The complexity of S for each edge is $O(n)$. Consequently, the complexity of silhouette edge determination is $O(n^2)$.

We use a hash table to reduce the time complexity of the silhouette edge determination process and thereby improve the performance. Assume that we use indexed meshes, which means that there is an index array that decides every triangle of the mesh. The index of each vertex means the position for each vertex in vertex array, thus index for each vertex is unique. Every time a new edge is added into an array, we should not go through the whole array to decide whether

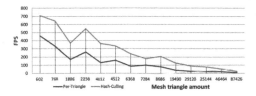

Fig. 5. Performance comparison between the Per-Triangle algorithm and our Hash-culling algorithm.

this edge has appeared or not. Instead, we can use a hash table to provide rapid searching and deleting performance when adding new edges. Each time a new edge is added into the hash table, we check whether it is a duplicate or not. In this way, we ensure that when two edges with the same vertices are added to the hash table, they map to the same position irrespective of the sequence of the vertices. For every hash element, it stores one unsigned integer that is used to store the key-value, two integers that are used to store vertex values, and one Boolean value that is used to store the occupation flag. Assume that MAX represents the size of the hash table, and V_A and V_B denote indices of two vertices. Then, the equation to calculate the key value is as follows: In this way, we ensure that when edges with identical vertices are added to the hash table, they map to the same position regardless of whether the vertex order is the same or reverse. When adding a new edge, the key value is calculated first, according to vertex indices. Then, the corresponding position in the hash table is checked. If the position is not occupied, the vertex index values are stored and the occupation flag set to $TRUE$. If the position is occupied, the vertex values are checked and, if the values are equal or reverse, which means that a redundant edge is found, the occupation flag is set to $FALSE$. If the vertex values are not equal or the reverse, S is added to the key value and the corresponding position's occupation flag checked again. Here, S can be any number standing for step length.

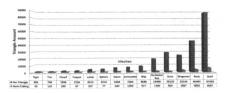

Fig. 6. Shadow volume triangle amount comparison between the Per-Triangle algorithm and our Hash-culling algorithm.

However, edges are added to the hash table, those edges with a $TRUE$ occupation flag are silhouette edges. Finally, we traverse the whole hash table to get all silhouette edges, then use them to render the shadow volume. In an actual implementation, the probability of collision is very low; therefore, the algorithm time efficiency is $O(n)$. Figure 4 demonstrates the rendering pipeline of our method, including loading vertices data, rendering model with ambient lights, searching silhouette edges, rendering shadow volume and doing stencil tests, finally blending shadow color to draw shadows.

4   Implementation

We implemented our proposed algorithm in C++ with OpenGL and conducted timing tests on a PC with an Intel i5 3210 2.5 GHz CPU, and an Intel 4000 HD graphics card, 8 GB RAM. In our implementation, all scenes were rendered with a resolution of 800 * 600 pixels, 16 bits RGBA color buffers, and 8-bit stencil buffers. For each scene, there was a single-point light source in a distinct place, and the same floor was used to conveniently observe shadows. We also implemented our method on several smartphones and tablets, however, timing tests are all conducted on PC.

Table 1. Comparison of performance for Kim's method and our hash-culling method.

Triangles	FPS	Our triangles	Our FPS
1120	703.4	2256	922
13576	193.1	19490	268
27736	35	29120	225
62724	41.4	87426	55

In the implementation, Z-pass was used to perform the stencil test and, when viewport cuts through shadow volume, Z-fail was used to obtain correct results. The pseudocode for our implemented hash-culling method is shown below.

Fig. 7. Test scenes on PC with different meshes.From left to right: (1) 25 Dwarfs, with 47400 triangles; (2) Chains, with 7128 triangles; (3) Airship, with 8698 triangles; (4) Occlusion Box, with 19490 triangles.

5 Results and Discussion

In this section, the results of the timing tests conducted on our hash-culling algorithm are presented. For comparison purposes, results for the per-triangle method, which is used in [15] with CUDA, are also presented. It is also a classic shadow volume method that is extensively utilized in various applications. In this timing test, we implemented it with software. In order to obtain convincing and comprehensive results, we used various meshes with a variety of shapes and structures. Transparent meshes are not tested since dealing with this is not the main purpose of our algorithm.

Through the timing tests for both classic per-triangle method and hash-culling method, we have those results and comparisons. Figure 5 helps to demonstrate the time efficiency (in frames per second (FPS)) gained by our hash-culling algorithm. Figure 6 shows the number of shadow volume triangles that needed to be rendered for both two algorithms respectively. Figure 7 and Fig. 9 depicts various test scenes used in our experiments on PC and embedded system, while Fig. 10 compares shadow rendering quality between two algorithms. Shadow volume can generate pixel-accurate shadow images thus aliasing is not the problem since shadow volume was introduced. The hash-culling method can render shadows whose quality is as good as the results of other shadow volume methods. The timing test that comparing our method with the per-triangle algorithm, which is commonly used in many games and applications, shows our method tremendously reduces the triangle amount of shadow volume. In most cases, the triangle amount of shadow volume decreases to less than 10% of the amount of per-triangle's. Generally speaking, the more complex the occluder is, the more the triangle amount will decrease. Since the majority of shadow rendering time is spent on shadow volume rasterization, decrease of triangle amount leads directly to the decrease of rendering time. With the hash-culling method, traversing all edges of front surfaces is necessary, just as it is in the per-triangle method. However, the hash-culling method records silhouette edges with no gain on time complexity. It has $O(n)$ time complexity and performs quite well in all tests. As a result, FPS for each scene increases over 200%. Good performance makes it possible to run real-time shadows on platforms with minimal hardware, such as embedded systems.

Fig. 8. Test scenes on embedded systems with different meshes. From left to right: (1) Dwarf, with 1896 triangles; (2) Car, with 6813 triangles; (3) Gun, with 5630 triangles; (4) Scanner arm, with 6116 triangles.

Compared with the results for Kim's [1] algorithm, which was implemented on a Pentium 3.0 GHz PC with NVIDIA GeForce 6800, from Table 1 we know that our method performed creditably in terms of FPS improvement with consideration to hardware difference. The first two columns display the number of triangles and the FPS for Kim's test case, while the last two columns display our test data. Our method can also be used to support non-manifold models. However, processing for model data and the determination of the non-manifold model is not the main topic of our paper thus these details are left out. Shadow effects for the non-manifold model can be found in Fig. 8. Our hash-culling method can achieve very similar performance as Sintorn's [15] method. We have not added support for transparent objects yet, this will require more resource and calculation, but considering the objective of our method that we want to implement dynamic shadow on different platforms and with low-level hardware, our performance is quite convincing and this method is practicable. The Hash-culling method is easy to implement since it doesn't require complex concurrent computation on GPU. Our method's CPU usage is as low as that of the classic per-triangle method. The hash method provides quick and accurate search performance for silhouette edges. We have tested our algorithm on several embedded systems, including Samsung Nexus S with 1GHz CPU, 512 Mb ram. The embedded systems have relatively low hardware capability, especially the incomplete graphic support, for example, the difference between OpenGL ES and OpenGL. Unlike other algorithms, our algorithm does not require programmable graphic pipeline, and do not use GPU for general concurrency calculation, meanwhile it does not require much CPU calculation. All these features make sure that it can be implemented on embedded systems with low hardware level. On the Nexus S platform, render a shadow for a model with more than 2000 triangles, we can still get more than 60 frames per second.

Fig. 9. Shadow rendering quality comparison between per-triangle method (left) and hash-culling method (right).

From the data and the graphs above, the improvement of our algorithm over the classic algorithm is evident. Using the hash-culling algorithm, the triangles that had to be rendered for the shadow volume decreased sharply without any additional burden on the CPU. As a result, the FPS of each scene significantly increased to a new level. Various hardware-dependent shadow volume algorithms have been proposed; however, to the best of our knowledge, none of them can be easily implemented, neither are they used extensively on embedded systems because of poor hardware support. In this scenario, our method can make a big difference when rendering dynamic shadows, which makes it very practical for generating dynamic shadow effects in embedded systems. Figure 10 depicts a number of scenes rendered using our proposed method on smartphones and tablets. Because one of our targets is to efficiently render dynamic shadows on smartphones and tablets, reducing hardware dependency can help the algorithm to become more robust.

Fig. 10. Test scenes of a manifold and non-manifold meshes.

6   Conclusion

In this paper, we presented a hash-culling shadow volume algorithm that can generate real-time shadows even for relatively complex meshes. Our algorithm is based on shadow volume and a stencil buffer is used in its implementation. As demonstrated by the implementation and test results, our algorithm improves the performance of various kinds of scenes, irrespective of whether the mesh is simple or complex. We improved performance primarily by simplifying silhouette edge determination, resulting in reduced shadow volume rendering time. In the future, graphics hardware may be able to support the two-side stencil test; in which case, only one render pass will be needed to render the shadow volume. This enhancement would advance the shadow volume algorithm to another level.

Acknowledgement. This work was supported in part by the National Natural Science Foundation of China under Grants 62077037 and 61872241, in part by Shanghai Municipal Science and Technology Major Project under Grant 2021SHZDZX0102, in part by the Science and Technology Commission of Shanghai Municipality under Grants 18410750700 and 17411952600, in part by Shanghai Lin-Gang Area Smart Manufacturing Special Project under Grant ZN2018020202-3, and in part by Project of Shanghai Municipal Health Commission(2018ZHYL0230).

References

1. Aldridge, G., Woods, E.: Robust, geometry-independent shadow volumes. In: Proceedings of the 2nd International Conference on Computer Graphics and Interactive Techniques in Australasia and South East Asia, pp. 250–253 (2004)
2. Arva, J., Aila, T.: Optimized shadow mapping using the stencil buffer. J. Graph. Tools **8**(3), 23–32 (2003)

3. Batagelo, H.C., Costa, I.: Real-time shadow generation using bsp trees and stencil buffers. In: XII Brazilian Symposium on Computer Graphics and Image Processing (Cat. No. PR00481), pp. 93–102. IEEE (1999)
4. Bergeron, P.: A general version of crow's shadow volumes. IEEE Comput. Graphics Appl. **6**(9), 17–28 (1986)
5. Breitenbach, C.S., Van Doren, D.C.: Value-added marketing in the digital domain: enhancing the utility of the internet. J. Consumer Mark. **15**(6), 558–575 (1998)
6. Brotman, L.S., Badler, N.I.: Generating soft shadows with a depth buffer algorithm. IEEE Comput. Graphics Appl. **4**(10), 5–14 (1984)
7. Crow, F.C.: Shadow algorithms for computer graphics. ACM siggraph Computer Graphics, vol. 11(2), pp. 242–248 (1977)
8. Dahlbom, M.: Stencil shadow volumes (2002)
9. Diefenbach, P.J., Badler, N.I.: Multi-pass pipeline rendering: Realism for dynamic environments. In: Proceedings of the 1997 Symposium on Interactive 3D Graphics, pp. 59-ff (1997)
10. Eisemann, E., Décoret, X.: Fast scene voxelization and applications. In: Proceedings of the 2006 Symposium on Interactive 3D Graphics and Games, pp. 71–78 (2006)
11. Everitt, C., Kilgard, M.J.: Practical and robust stenciled shadow volumes for hardware-accelerated rendering. arXiv preprint cs/0301002 (2003)
12. Fuchs, H., et al.: Fast spheres, shadows, textures, transparencies, and imgage enhancements in pixel-planes. In: ACM SIGGRAPH Computer Graphics, vol. 19(3), pp. 111–120 (1985)
13. Graphics, S.: Opengl-based real-time shadows (2002)
14. Hasenfratz, J.M., Lapierre, M., Holzschuch, N., Sillion, F., GRAVIR, A.: A survey of real-time soft shadows algorithms. In: Computer Graphics Forum, vol. 22, pp. 753–774. Wiley Online Library (2003)
15. Hook, E.W., III.: Remembering thomas parran, his contributions and missteps going forward: History informs us. Sex. Transm. Dis. **40**(4), 281–282 (2013)
16. Kim, B., Kim, K., Turk, G.: A shadow-volume algorithm for opaque and transparent nonmanifold casters. J. Graph. Tools **13**(3), 1–14 (2008)
17. Peers, P., Dutré, P.: Inferring reflectance functions from wavelet noise. In: Proceedings of the Sixteenth Eurographics Conference on Rendering Techniques, pp. 173–182. Eurographics Association (2005)
18. Sintorn, E., Olsson, O., Assarsson, U.: An efficient alias-free shadow algorithm for opaque and transparent objects using per-triangle shadow volumes. In: Proceedings of the 2011 SIGGRAPH Asia Conference, pp. 1–10 (2011)
19. Stich, M., Wächter, C., Keller, A.: Efficient and robust shadow volumes using hierarchical occlusion culling and geometry shaders. GPU Gems **3**, 239–256 (2007)
20. Woo, A., Poulin, P., Fournier, A.: A survey of shadow algorithms. IEEE Comput. Graphics Appl. **10**(6), 13–32 (1990)

DDISH-GI: Dynamic Distributed Spherical Harmonics Global Illumination

Julius Ikkala, Petrus Kivi$^{(\boxtimes)}$, Joel Alanko, Markku Mäkitalo,
and Pekka Jääskeläinen

Tampere University, P.O. Box 553, 33014 Tampere, Finland
petrus.kivi@tuni.fi

Abstract. We propose a real-time hybrid rendering algorithm that off-loads computationally complex rendering of indirect lighting from mobile client devices to dedicated ray tracing hardware on the server with a hybrid real-time computer graphics rendering algorithm. *Spherical harmonics* (SH) light probes are updated with path tracing on the server side, and the final frame is rendered with a fast rasterization-based pipeline that uses the light probes to approximate high quality indirect diffuse lighting and glossy specular reflections. That is, the rendering workload can be split to multiple devices across the network with a small bandwidth usage. It also benefits multi-user and multi-view scenarios by separating indirect lighting computation from camera positioning. Compared to simply streaming fully remotely rendered frames, the approach is more robust to network interruptions and latency. Furthermore, we propose a specular approximation for GGX materials via *zonal harmonics* (ZH). This alleviates the need to implement more computationally complex algorithms, such as screen space reflections, which was suggested in the state-of-the-art *dynamic diffuse global illumination* (DDGI) method. We show that the image quality of the proposed method is similar to that of DDGI, with a 23 times more compact data structure.

Keywords: Real-time rendering · Path tracing · Spherical harmonics · Photorealistic rendering · Distributed rendering · Global illumination

1 Introduction

Dedicated ray tracing acceleration in graphics hardware has become available on NVIDIA RTX GPUs since 2018 [19] and on AMD GPUs as of late 2020, including the recently released video game console generation with AMD graphics hardware [2]. Even though this has made real-time ray and path tracing possible with a high frame rate and screen resolution, high-quality path tracing is still not fast enough for real-time. Denoising methods can be used to make lower-spp path

Electronic supplementary material The online version of this chapter (https://doi.org/10.1007/978-3-030-89029-2_34) contains supplementary material, which is available to authorized users.

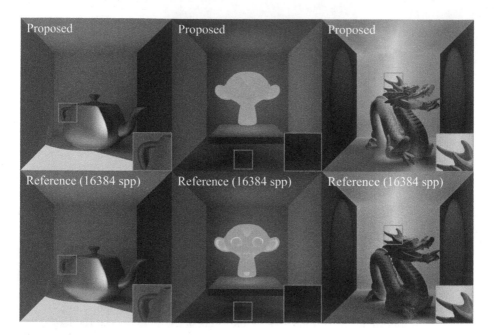

Fig. 1. Three example scenes highlighting different lighting phenomena simulated by DDISH-GI. From left to right: glossy reflections, emissive materials, and diffuse indirect lighting. The proposed method took 1.5 to 2.5 ms to render each image, while our hardware accelerated path tracer took 30 to 140 s for each 16384 spp reference image. The images are rendered at 1024 × 1024 with anti-aliasing implemented by 8×MSAA for DDISH-GI and equivalent box filter sampling for path tracing.

traced images plausible [14,22]. They rely on frame reprojection and suffer from the resulting camera-dependent artefacts, like ghosting artefacts and occlusion issues. Moreover, the lower hardware capabilities of mobile devices, such as standalone *head mounted displays* (HMD), do not offer the performance of desktop GPUs with highly dedicated hardware. Thus, it is interesting to distribute the rendering effort over the network, specifically with methods that use minimal bandwidth and are tolerant to latency issues.

Various systems for offloading the rendering effort from computationally restricted devices have been developed, including *PlayStation Now* [26] and *Google Stadia* [9]. These streaming services transfer the user input from the client side, update the game state accordingly, perform the actual rendering, and stream the output frames as image sequences back to the client. Even though the streamed frames are compressed with state-of-the-art techniques to lower the bitrate, bandwidth issues still become relevant with higher frame resolutions and refresh rates. Furthermore, the system is entirely reliant on the server and underutilizes the client hardware. In our case, we can fully rely on local rendering hardware if remote rendering resources become unavailable. The game streaming systems along with the rendering pipelines are inherently prone to network problems, including latency issues affecting the interactivity and immersion, as well as total network failure stopping the experience altogether. Moreover, providing photorealistic rendering on HMDs and other multi-view devices and techniques, such as light field displays, requires duplicating the rendering effort for multiple viewports. HMDs have a display for each eye with a typical resolution of 1440 × 1600 and a refresh rate 90 Hz [3]. Furthermore, high-end models, such as the Varjo VR-3 [29], exhibit two 1920 × 1920 and two 2880 × 2720 displays. For a near-eye light field display, a 5 × 5 array of 640 × 800 resolution viewports per eye was demonstrated in [11], yielding a total pixel count of over 25 million, which is 5 to 6 times the amount of a typical HMD. Lighting conditions are shared between the views and, thus, the view-independent aspects of the scene can be rendered irrespective of the viewports.

To tackle the presented challenges, we propose a real-time distributable rendering method that updates *spherical harmonics* (SH) light probes with *path tracing*, and uses them for *global illumination* (GI) approximation and glossy GGX-BRDF-based reflections. Figure 1 highlights some of the different lighting phenomena that the proposed method simulates. The heavy path tracing can be distributed to a server-side desktop system, which streams the dynamically updated SH probe coefficients to be used by a traditional rasterization pipeline on a lightweight mobile client device.

A key novelty of the proposed DDISH-GI method is in its use of the low-order SH basis for real-time path traced probes, which allows a very compact representation with rotational invariance, low network bandwidth and no high-frequency artefacts (Sect. 3). Another novel aspect is how it uses the light probes together with fitted *zonal harmonics* (ZH) representation of GGX (BRDF) lobes, specifically, for indirect glossy reflections (Appendix A), which reduces the need for heavy computation on the client side. We discuss how these aspects benefit distributed computing use cases in Sect. 4.

2   Related Work

A light probe is a representation of the lighting around a specified point in space. This information can then be used to approximate lighting for nearby surfaces. Environment maps are light probes that act as relatively high resolution globes of the surrounding environment.

A particular representation of a light probe is called a basis. One common basis used in computer graphics is the cubemap basis, which is good for storing precomputed high-resolution environment maps, but can be wasteful for shading rough surfaces. Alternatively, some other bases, like an SH basis or an octahedral basis, provide a more compact representation especially for lower-frequency data.

The SH are a set of special functions that form an orthonormal basis on the surface of a sphere and solve Laplace's equation. Hence, they are a widely used tool in many fields involving partial differential equations, and they also have a long history in real-time computer graphics, where the SH basis has been used to represent light probes since [21]. In particular, they have proved useful in video games, for precalculating indirect lighting (i.e., GI) for large and static scenes that have only few moving components.

Because games have been relying on light probes for a long time, dynamically updating light probes is an easy-to-integrate method for providing real-time GI. Hence, several rendering methods similar to DDISH-GI have been published.

Dynamic Diffuse Global Illumination (DDGI) is a method that updates light probes in real time using ray tracing, achieving impressive performance. However, in contrast to the proposed method, DDGI probes are limited to diffuse illumination, and a ray tracer is used to fill in glossy parts of the lighting as needed. DDGI uses an octahedral basis for its light probes, with additional visibility information used to improve interpolation [15]. The octahedral representation does not suffer from ringing, unlike SH; on the other hand, it is less compact than the SH representation requiring more bandwidth for distributing computations over a network. DDGI has since been extended to support probe-based glossy reflections as well, although it does not take surface roughness into account [16].

Signed Distance Fields Dynamic Diffuse Global Illumination (SDFDDGI) uses a signed distance field approximation of the scene, which can be used to quickly trace rays even without ray tracing hardware [10]. Like DDGI, this method uses an octahedral basis for the probes, as opposed to the SH in DDISH-GI. It has a fully automatic system for probe placement that relies on the SDF data structure. Probe placement is a challenge of its own, and automated probe placement is out of scope in this paper. Unlike in the proposed method, the probes are not used for reflections in SDFDDGI, and they suggest using other methods such as screen-space reflections or ray tracing for that part.

An SH-based approach for dynamic GI is presented in [23]. Probes are placed in the scene with an algorithm that ensures that each light receiver is visible in some probe. The method uses a real-time lightmap of direct illumination in order to update the probes. Since the probes are placed ahead of time, the contribution of the lightmap pixels to the probe can be precomputed. During runtime, the probes are then updated according to the state of the lightmap. The lighting from relevant probes is then interpolated to calculate lighting at the receiver. The interpolation takes advantage of precalculated visibility information to obtain high-quality lighting. Dynamic geometry is somewhat limited due to the amount of geometry-dependent precalculation needed, and is not directly comparable to the fully dynamic DDISH-GI as such. The method in [23] limits dynamic geometry to certain kinds of occluders and requires more precalculation, but seems to suffer from fewer artefacts and does not use ray tracing during runtime compared to the proposed method. Further, it does allow specular highlights from its probes unlike DDGI, but does this by approximating a directional light source from the probe and calculating the reflection from that.

3   Distributing SH Light Probe Updating and Usage

We propose a hybrid method where the indirect lighting is path traced onto an SH-based light probe approximation. This is used by a rasterization pipeline that handles the direct lighting and applies indirect lighting from the separately calculated light probes. The path tracing and rasterization parts are mostly independent of each other until their respective results are combined at the end of the rasterization pipeline. Communication between them is minimized by only transferring the SH light probe coefficients, which makes the method suitable for distributed rendering and remote path tracing.

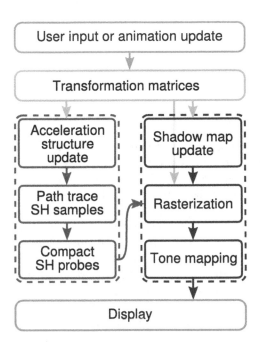

Fig. 2. The pipeline setup of DDISH-GI. The SH update (red) can run asynchronously relative to the SH usage (blue) with few negative effects. (Color figure online)

The full rendering pipeline is depicted in Fig. 2. User input and animation information, illustrated in green, is used to update all the transformation matrices describing the state of the scene, which is further fed to both the partial path tracing and rasterization pipelines. The path tracing pipeline (SH update), shown in red, updates the SH probes, and the rasterization pipeline (SH usage), shown in blue, renders direct lighting and combines it with the indirect lighting from the updated SH probes, and tone maps the result to be displayed. We explain the SH updating and usage parts in Sects. 3.1 and 3.2, respectively.

3.1 Path Tracing and SH Probe Update

In DDISH-GI, path tracing is used solely to update the SH probes that approximate the indirect lighting. This means that the amount of photorealism and accuracy can be flexibly chosen based on hardware capabilities and user preferences. For example, probe count, number of rays and samples used for each probe, and ray bounce depth can be configured. As the updated indirect lighting component is only needed at the end of the rasterization pipeline before tone mapping, the SH update part of the pipeline can be asynchronous to the SH usage part. Thus, distributing the SH update process to a remote server with dedicated ray tracing hardware over the network is easily achieved, providing computationally restricted mobile devices the capabilities of the server-side devices. Moreover, the indirect lighting does not suffer as much from bandwidth and latency issues due to the compact nature of the SH probe data. Even temporally stale indirect lighting is a decent approximation in the case of a total network failure if the scene, animations, and lighting do not change drastically.

3.2   Rasterization and SH Probe Usage

As in many rendering methods utilizing ray tracing [14,22], DDISH-GI also rasterizes direct lighting. Our rasterization pipeline is also used to combine all components into the final rendered image, because most GPU hardware is still very optimized to the pipeline steps needed in rasterization yielding a better performance than only using path tracing. The path tracer that updates the SH probes is configured separately from the rasterization, consequently making path tracing independent of the screen resolution. Moreover, the rasterization performance is not affected by the path traced sample count or bounce depth.

Producing direct lighting and realistic shadows with rasterization is not unambiguous and can be handled in many ways. In this publication, we do not propose a new method for rasterizing primary visibility and direct lighting. Rather, we refer to [32] which shows performant and power efficient rasterization on mobile devices. We used the method in [21] to implement diffuse indirect lighting.

It is possible to store and sample the coefficients of SH probes as volumes in 3D textures. GPUs traditionally have hardware accelerated operations to sample interpolated values from the textures, meaning trilinear interpolation in the case of a 3D texture. This acceleration can be naturally utilized in the case of the SH coefficients stored in the probes in 3D space, because values for SH coefficients in-between probes are valid when linearly interpolated. We do not use windowing for the SH approximation because while windowing helps to smooth out ringing in certain scenarios, it also produces less precise lighting data.

4   Distributed Computing

One of our main goals when designing DDISH-GI was to lower the amount of data transferred between the SH update and SH usage parts of the rendering pipeline. Our chosen L2 SH light probes use 56 bytes for the raw representation of one probe. Compared to the state-of-the-art DDGI system, which uses a minimum of 1280 bytes per probe, in our largest scene using a grid of 1024 probes, our

L2 SH basis only needs $57 \cdot 10^3$ bytes instead of $1.3 \cdot 10^6$ bytes, yielding a $23\times$ reduction in bandwidth. Considering the refresh rate 90 Hz on typical HMDs, updating indirect illumination for each frame would require a bandwidth of 5 MB/s in the proposed method, which is reasonable on current networking standards compared to 120 MB/s for DDGI if it were to be used in the same way. The benefit is exemplified on light field displays with dozens of individual viewports, such as [11], which can share the indirect lighting between viewports.

A secondary goal for utilizing distributability and remote hardware capabilities was to split the rendering effort such that the degradation or loss of a network connection to the remote server would not hinder the interactivity of the system. Simultaneously, the computationally most laborious rendering effort, global illumination, could be distributed separately to dedicated hardware. This was achieved with the pipeline structure presented in Sect. 3 and Fig. 2. The pipeline structure together with the view-independence of the SH probes also lends to multi-client use cases: the indirect lighting can be calculated only once to all users which independently rasterize their viewports with relatively lightweight local direct lighting calculations.

The two parts of the pipeline need not be synchronized. The only requirement for an interactive experience is client-side hardware capable of rendering the rasterization part of the pipeline, and the path tracing part of the pipeline can be utilized based on the network capabilities. Examples include situations where we have a large bandwidth and low latency connection, a high latency network, or no network at all. In the first case, the SH probes can easily be updated and transferred to the client side for each rasterized frame for indirect lighting updated in real time. In the second case, the SH probe coefficients can be asynchronously transferred when sufficient lighting or scene changes warrant an update. Precomputed SH probe indirect lighting suits the last case. Interactivity and frame rates are sustained irrespective of connection quality and only the plausibility of indirect lighting is affected by it.

Compared to interactive game streaming services that send controller inputs from the client side and receive fully rendered image sequences from the server side, DDISH-GI is not fully dependent on the server side producing the rendered frames. The streaming services are prone to latency issues manifesting as input-to-rendered-image-latency to the client or full termination of the service on network loss. Some of their latency issues could be mitigated through advances in low-latency compression techniques and their hardware support, for example by using the recent JPEG XS mezzanine compression standard [7] that allows for sub-frame latencies. However, such solutions have not received widespread adoption yet. Furthermore, they do not address the problem of possible network loss to the service. In the proposed method, total network connection loss results only in indirect lighting becoming static instead of dynamically updated.

A possible use case for our rendering method is as follows. A virtual reality headset or HMD with low-end rendering hardware, such as the Oculus Quest 2 [8], capable of running basic rasterization, can be utilized as the SH usage part of our pipeline. Then, a high-end desktop on the server side equipped with a GPU with dedicated ray tracing hardware can be used for the path tracing, or SH update, part of the pipeline. Because XR experiences are sensitive to latency in terms of immersion and user comfort [1], our scenario illustrates how occasional network latency issues will not affect the overall virtual experience – rather, it only influences the quality and plausibility of indirect lighting.

5 Results

DDISH-GI is compared to the closest equivalent method, DDGI, which is based on a different, less compact but more accurate octahedral probe basis. The original DDGI [15] did not support using the probes for glossy reflections, but the extension was added in [16]. They simply reuse the irradiance-filtered probe data instead of filtering the probes for each roughness value individually. They propose that this approximation be used only for second-order reflections, whereas the first-order reflection should be ray traced. We compare against this extended version of DDGI implemented in the G3D research framework [18].

Three commonly used test scenes are used for the measurements: the Sibenik Cathedral, Breakfast Room and Sponza scenes [17]. These scenes and the camera angles shown were selected such that indirect lighting has a major impact to the image output, which emphasizes the effects the compared methods have on the overall lighting. The irradiance volumes/probe grids are placed manually. The Sponza scene is rendered using $16 \cdot 8 \cdot 8 = 1024$ probes, Breakfast Room with $8 \cdot 4 \cdot 8 = 256$ probes and Sibenik Cathedral with $16 \cdot 8 \cdot 4 = 512$ probes. These probe densities were chosen such that they are not unrealistically dense, yet can represent most lower-frequency local lighting details to a visually acceptable degree. Some of the probes in the volumes are located inside geometry. The probes are placed in the exact same positions in both of the compared methods.

The quality of both methods is evaluated by comparing them against a 16384 spp path traced reference image of the test scene, using the PSNR and SSIM [31] metrics. Each ray was allowed to bounce a maximum of 32 times in the scene before termination. While DDGI technically models infinite bounces, we found that this number of bounces matches its output very closely. We use the implementation in the G3D framework for DDGI measurements, but the material code is modified to match the BSDF we use in these scenes. Furthermore, we use the DDGI glossy reflection approximation in first-order reflections, since both methods only use the probes for indirect lighting in this comparison.

All images are rendered at a resolution of 1920×1080 without anti-aliasing. A single NVIDIA RTX 3090 is used for all timing measurements. The L2 basis is used for DDISH-GI, as we found L3 and L4 significantly slower with negligible quality impact. DDGI is set to use 8×8 resolution for the irradiance data and 16×16 for the visibility data, as suggested in the paper. The proposed method is using 256 path traced samples per probe per frame, which are then temporally blended with data from previous frames. DDGI is given 256 rays per probe per frame, as it functions more similar to ray casting. A hysteresis parameter of $\alpha = 0.99$ is used in both methods. This parameter determines the ratio of reused data from the previous frame to the new data, which means that only 1% of new probe data is blended in with the old in each frame. We experimented with different values ranging from 0.80 to 0.99 (visualized in the supplemental video) and observed a trade-off between temporal flickering caused by the relatively low spp in probe path tracing and temporal staleness and "ghosting" due to data re-usage of indirect lighting. Because abrupt changes were much noticeable than slow lagging in indirect lighting, we decided to favor a much higher hysteresis parameter value. Furthermore, direct lighting is still unaffected by the parameter.

Because both compared rendering methods contain temporal components, the quality is measured after the lighting has visually stabilized. Performance measurements were averaged over 50 frames. While we have implemented a visibility-based interpolation scheme into our method, we choose not to use it in this comparison since it provides little quality benefit in these scenes but has a significant cost in the rasterization step. Instead, we use backface culling in probe updates, which prevents dark artefacts from occurring when probes are placed inside geometry. We enabled this same kind of backface culling for DDGI in Sponza and Sibenik Cathedral, because doing so results in better quality in those scenes, and some code for this option existed also in the G3D framework. Comparison images are shown in Appendix B.

Table 1. Quality and performance measurements for the Sponza scene.

Method	PSNR (dB)	SSIM	Probe update (ms)	Rasterization (ms)	Total (ms)
DDISH-GI	23.01	0.911	1.68	0.64	2.32
DDGI	19.05	0.843	5.29	1.14	6.43
16384spp PT	N/A	N/A	N/A	N/A	1866440

Table 2. Quality and performance measurements for the Breakfast Room scene.

Method	PSNR (dB)	SSIM	Probe update (ms)	Rasterization (ms)	Total (ms)
DDISH-GI	24.06	0.917	1.02	0.42	1.43
DDGI	20.41	0.907	3.76	0.90	4.66
16384spp PT	N/A	N/A	N/A	N/A	1114910

Table 3. Quality and performance measurements for the Sibenik Cathedral scene.

Method	PSNR (dB)	SSIM	Probe update (ms)	Rasterization (ms)	Total (ms)
DDISH-GI	23.44	0.873	0.97	0.43	1.40
DDGI	21.82	0.905	3.52	0.96	4.48
16384spp PT	N/A	N/A	N/A	N/A	521877

5.1   Quality

The obtained PSNR and SSIM results are presented in Tables 1, 2 and 3. Overall, the image quality produced by DDISH-GI is slightly better or on par with DDGI, with quite minimal differences in the Breakfast Room scene and close in terms of SSIM in the Sibenik Cathedral. The poor PSNR results for DDGI in the Sponza scene were assumed to be caused by us forcing the glossy approximation to occur in the first-order reflection, but this was not the case since disabling that resulted in a very similar but slightly lower PSNR score of 18.64 dB.

Because we had to modify the material model of G3D to match our rendering framework, we verified that they match by ensuring that we get the same results when rendering only direct lighting. Aside from very slight differences in shadow map pixel alignment and biasing (G3D uses a different type of shadow map biasing than our framework), we were able to produce the same image in both renderers and thus concluded that the material models match. Additional modifications had to be made to the glossy approximation, as it originally assumed an extended form of an isotropic variation of the Ashikhmin–Shirley BRDF model [5] instead of the GGX BRDF that we use. In terms of temporal flicker, DDGI was notably stabler with these settings in the Sibenik Cathedral scene and performed admirably in all scenes. Our method had some noticeable flicker in the Sibenik cathedral, but in the other two scenes temporal instability was barely visible through display color banding. This can be worked around by either taking more samples than 256 per probe or using a very aggressive hysteresis value such as $\alpha = 0.998$. Since DDGI reuses previous smooth probe lighting to render additional bounces, they do not have a similar noise source as our path tracing based approach. The downside of that approach is lower precision in lighting, as probe positioning and resolution directly affects secondary bounces as well. This spread of probe inaccuracy may be why the Sibenik Cathedral scene looks significantly more evenly lit in DDGI than the reference.

The main weakness we identify in our method is that the SH L2 basis used naturally blurs out sharp details when fit to the path traced indirect lighting. However, as indirect lighting is usually low-frequency in nature, the loss of high-frequency detail is not as noticeable as in direct lighting. In addition, our current implementation wastes some effort on keeping the SH probes active even if they are inside objects, and thus, not affecting the lighting. We have also experimented with adding a simple, visibility-based probe interpolation to tackle light leaking issues and saw negligible improvements in most scenes.

5.2   Performance

As shown in Tables 1, 2 and 3, DDISH-GI is significantly faster in both probe update (average 1.22 ms vs. 4.19 ms) and rasterization (average 0.50 ms vs. 1.00 ms) when compared to the DDGI implementation in G3D. The G3D framework uses a different graphics API (OpenGL) than our framework (Vulkan). OpenGL doesn't support ray tracing directly, so G3D uses the NVIDIA OptiX API [20] for this purpose. This interoperation may include buffer transfers that can slow down the probe update process. Further, we use forward rendering for the rasterization stage, which is less bandwidth-intensive than the deferred rendering used in G3D. The probe basis used in DDGI is also more complicated to filter than SH probes.

We found that the cost of probe interpolation in DDGI is significant and experienced a performance decrease when using interpolation based on visibility. We believe this is caused by the additional bandwidth and computation workload imposed by reading and interpolating probes manually. Some of this cost is avoided by storing probe data in a set of 3D textures and limiting to trilinear interpolation, where we can better utilize texture sampling hardware.

To match the infinite number of light bounces that DDGI simulates, we set the number of light bounces at 32. While realistic, this number is unreasonably high for plausible indirect lighting in general, and it should be sufficient to use just a few bounces in most scenes. Doing so would have a significant performance benefit in the probe update step of our method. Since our method is based on path tracing, most optimization techniques related to it are usable. We used *Russian roulette* sampling [4] to increase the performance of using so many bounces at the cost of some additional noise in individual samples.

6 Conclusion

We proposed a novel method of utilizing SH probes in a highly distributable rendering pipeline called DDISH-GI. Compared to the G3D implementation [18] of the state-of-the art method DDGI, the computational performance of our method was 3× as fast on the tested scenes and hardware, and the objective image quality was similar or slightly better. Moreover, our compact SH probe structure could be sent over a network connection to the client side with a 23× reduction in bandwidth compared to DDGI. Unlike approaches based on streaming image frames, it is also robust to network connection issues due to being view-independent and inherently falls back into static indirect lighting with fully local rendering if connection is fully lost.

We showed that our method excels in producing a highly compact representation of realistic indirect light with sufficient quality compared to the state-of-the-art, which can be utilized even in high-latency low-bandwidth server-client connection scenarios. For future work, discarding probes inside geometry and compressing the probe data before transfer would be interesting. It could also be beneficial to try a more robust probe interpolation method in conjunction with non-aligned grid-like probe placement.

Acknowledgements. This project has received funding from the ECSEL Joint Undertaking (JU) under Grant Agreement No 783162 (FitOptiVis). The JU receives support from the European Union's Horizon 2020 research and innovation programme and Netherlands, Czech Republic, Finland, Spain, Italy. The project is also supported in part by the Academy of Finland under Grant 325530.

Appendix A   GGX Approximation with ZH Lobes

ZH is a subset of SH that consists of the SH functions that are rotationally symmetric with respect to the z-axis. In particular, if we assume that our physically-based material model has rotationally symmetric BRDF lobes, we can represent those lobes more compactly and efficiently with the ZH functions instead of requiring a full SH representation. We refer the reader to [24] and [25] for general details on SH and ZH, respectively.

For the physically-based material model in our renderer, we chose to use the common GGX material model [30], also known as Trowbridge-Reitz distribution [28], to support the glTF 2.0 specification [27] as closely as possible. The GGX BSDF has parameters that allows it to be used for a large variety of different real-world materials with a good degree of realism [30]. It is quite fast to evaluate, which is why it has seen a lot of use in the real-time rendering industry.

SH has been previously used as an approximation for arbitrary BRDFs [13]. Hence, in addition to using an SH approximation for path traced indirect lighting, we also investigate using ZH for GGX-based rotationally invariant BRDF material approximations. The indirect lighting from the SH probes is convolved with the GGX material approximation for the final lighting contribution. As shown in [24], the convolution between a rotationally symmetric function g and some function f – in our case the ZH GGX basis and the SH light probe basis, respectively – has projection coefficients satisfying

$$(g * f)_l^m = \sqrt{\frac{4\pi}{2l + 1}} g_l^0 f_l^m, \qquad (1)$$

where the left-hand side of the equation denotes the projection coefficients of the basis of g convolved with f, m is the order of the basis function coefficient, and l is the degree of the basis function coefficient. Thus, a convolution of SH over the ZH is simple because it only amounts to scaling each degree of the SH basis with the respective ZH. On the other hand, the SH-over-SH convolution would require several multiplications added up for each coefficient.

Utilizing SH probes and SH approximation for surface materials was proposed in [6] for specular lighting. Their method uses several texture lookups and has to rotate the SH approximation, making it computationally challenging. As the SH probes are already an approximation for the indirect lighting components with smoothed expressiveness at lower degree coefficients, using a sharper convolution lobe for the material, like in [6], is wasteful and only highlights the low-frequency nature of the SH probes. Furthermore, our novel contribution is applying the ZH GGX approximation only for indirect glossy highlights from the SH probes. For the final indirect lighting contribution, we decided to adopt a less complex approach utilizing the *split sum approximation* published in [12]:

$$\int_\Omega \frac{L_i(\omega_i) f(\omega_i, \omega_o) n \cdot \omega_i)}{p(\omega_i, \omega_o)} d\omega_i \approx \left(\int_\Omega L_i(\omega_i) d\omega_i \right) \left(\int_\Omega \frac{f(\omega_i, \omega_o) n \cdot \omega_i}{p(d_k, v)} d\omega_i \right), \qquad (2)$$

where $L_i(\omega_i$ is the incoming radiance from the direction ω_i, $f(\omega_i, \omega_o)$ is the BRDF from direction ω_i to the direction ω_o, $n \cdot \omega_i$ is the angle between ω_i and the surface normal n, and $p(\omega_i, \omega_o)$ is the probability of sampling from ω_i to ω_o based on the BRDF. In our case, the left side integral of the product is calculated as the convolution between the nearest interpolated SH probes and our rotationally symmetric ZH approximation of the GGX specular lobe (similarly as in [12]). This convolution produces a new rotationally symmetric ZH function with coefficients calculated by Eq. 1. Furthermore, the right side integral of the split sum is evaluated as an *environment BRDF* which is encoded in a 2D 2-channel texture varying by surface roughness on one axis and $n \cdot \omega_i$ on the other

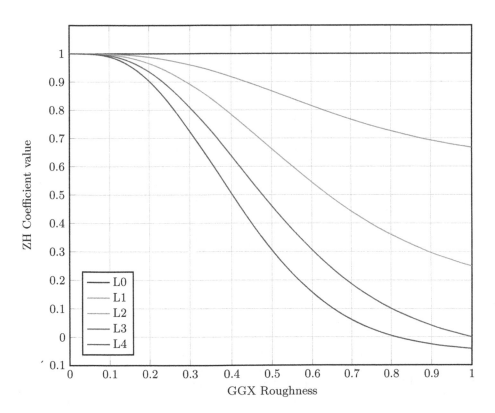

Fig. 3. Values of the precomputed ZH coefficients for approximating GGX specular lobes.

In order to use the ZH basis to approximate GGX materials with different roughnesses, we numerically integrated 1024 samples on the 0 to 1 roughness interval and fit a ZH basis function onto each GGX lobe value. The coefficients of the ZH basis are plotted as a function of the material roughness in Fig. 3. The figure shows how the specularity intensifies on smoother materials with large coefficients on the left, and dampens down to diffuse rough materials with small coefficients on the higher degrees. We experimented with different basis degrees from L0 to L4 and found that the L2 basis was a good trade-off between coefficient compactness and approximation quality. The fit is exactly correct to the Trowbridge-Reitz GGX lobe at the impulse direction of the surface normal.

Even though the split sum approximation doesn't take into account the skewness of the GGX lobe at grazing angles, it is an accepted trade-off in the industry and works well enough together with the SH-probes. In [12], the authors used Eq. 2 to compute the separate integrals in advance for environment maps on cubemap bases, whereas our novel contribution is applying this to an SH light probe basis for glossy specular highlights with the GGX lobe further approximated by a ZH basis. The split sum method constrains the materials' BRDF lobes to be axially symmetric, which means that in our implementation of the SH probe basis, we only consider the rotationally symmetric basis which is exactly the ZH basis. This provides us with the aforementioned faster SH-over-ZH convolution. In each degree of the SH basis, the ZH is unique and so, we can refer to the different degrees from L0 to L4 uniquely.

As discussed earlier, our SH probe approximations are only for the indirect lighting component produced by path tracing and do not consider effects from direct lights. In order to support specular highlights from direct lighting, we approximate direct lights as almost singular points and directly sample the BRDF, which is less accurate for larger lights. However, it serves as a decent approximation as long as the surface is not perfectly smooth and has some roughness present.

Appendix B   Comparison Images

We present comparison images between DDGI, the proposed method DDISH-GI, and a 16384 spp path traced reference from Sponza (Fig. 4), Breakfast Room (Fig. 5), and Sibenik Cathedral (Fig. 6). We observe that DDGI exhibits overly spread out indirect lighting in occluded areas whereas the proposed method is closer to the reference in those situations, as seen behind the benches of the Sibenik Cathedral. Both probe-based methods have challenges with high frequency detail in indirect lighting effects, such as in the corners of the Breakfast Room, due to the limited spatial resolution of the probes.

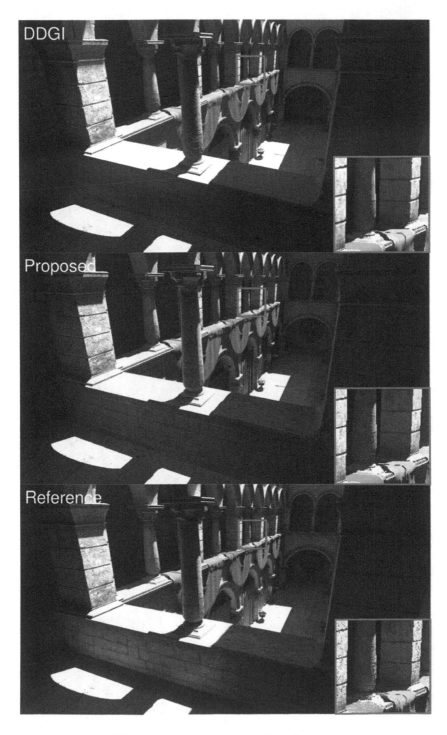

Fig. 4. Comparison images from Sponza.

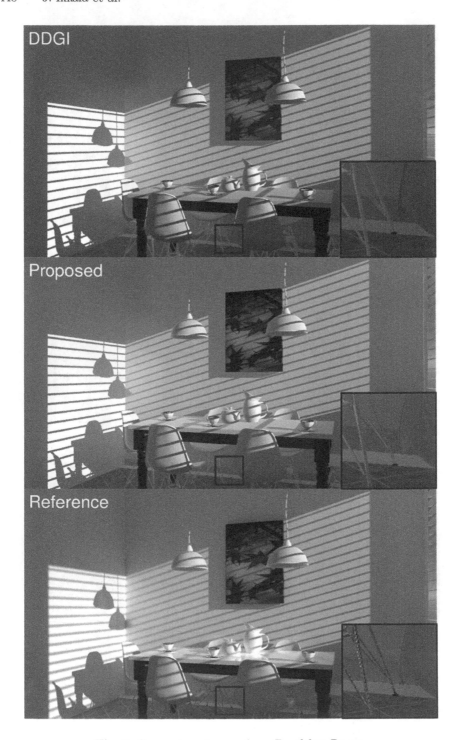

Fig. 5. Comparison images from Breakfast Room.

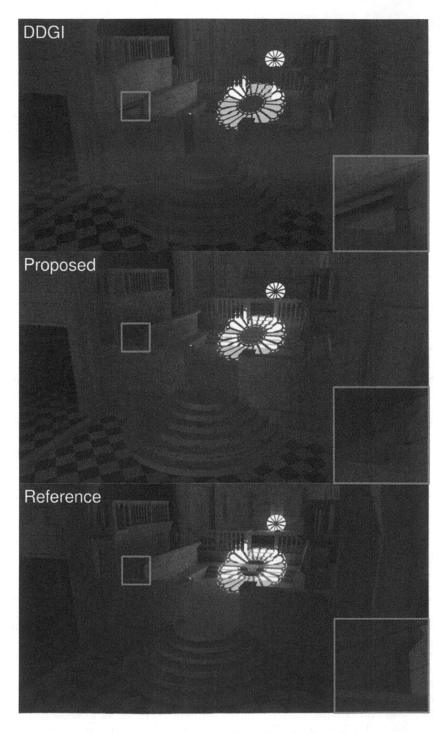

Fig. 6. Comparison images from Sibenik Cathedral.

References

1. Abrash, M.: What VR could, should, and almost certainly will be within two years. Steam Dev Days, Seattle 4 (2014)
2. Advanced Micro Devices Inc: RDNA 2 architecture. https://www.amd.com/en/technologies/rdna-2. Accessed 18 Oct 2020
3. Angelov, V., Petkov, E., Shipkovenski, G., Kalushkov, T.: Modern virtual reality headsets. In: Proceedings of the 2020 International Congress on Human-Computer Interaction, Optimization and Robotic Applications (HORA). IEEE (2020)
4. Arvo, J., Kirk, D.: Particle transport and image synthesis. In: Proceedings of the 17th Annual Conference on Computer Graphics and Interactive Techniques. SIGGRAPH 1990. ACM (1990)
5. Ashikhmin, M., Shirley, P.: An anisotropic Phong BRDF model. J. Graph. Tools 5(2), 25–32 (2000)
6. Chen, H., Liu, X.: Lighting and material of Halo 3. In: ACM SIGGRAPH 2008 Games. New York, NY, USA (2008)
7. Descampe, A., Keinert, J., Richter, T., Fößel, S., Rouvroy, G.: JPEG XS, a new standard for visually lossless low-latency lightweight image compression. In: Proceedings of the Applications of Digital Image Processing XL (2017)
8. Facebook Technologies LLC: Oculus quest 2. https://www.oculus.com/quest-2/features/, accessed: 2021–02-22
9. Google LLC: Stadia. https://stadia.google.com/. Accessed 18 Oct 2020
10. Hu, J., Yip, M., Alonso, G.E., Gu, S., Tang, X., Jin, X.: Signed distance fields dynamic diffuse global illumination. arXiv preprint (2020)
11. Huang, F.C., Luebke, D., Wetzstein, G.: The light field stereoscope. In: ACM SIGGRAPH 2015 Emerging Technologies. Association for Computing Machinery, New York (2015)
12. Karis, B., Games, E.: Real shading in unreal engine 4. In: Proceedings of Physically Based Shading in Theory and Practice, vol. 4, p. 3 (2013)
13. Kautz, J., Sloan, P.P., Snyder, J.: Fast, abitrary BRDF shading for low-frequency lighting using spherical harmonics. In: Proceedings of the 13th Eurographics Workshop on Rendering. EGRW 2002, Eurographics Association (2002)
14. Koskela, M., et al.: Blockwise multi-order feature regression for real-time pathtracing reconstruction. ACM Trans. Graph. 38(5), 14 (2019)
15. Majercik, Z., Guertin, J.P., Nowrouzezahrai, D., McGuire, M.: Dynamic diffuse global illumination with ray-traced irradiance fields. J. Comput. Graph. Tech. (JCGT) 8(2), June 2019. http://jcgt.org/published/0008/02/01/
16. Majercik, Z., Marrs, A., Spjut, J., McGuire, M.: Scaling probe-based real-time dynamic global illumination for production (2020)
17. McGuire, M.: Computer Graphics Archive, July 2017. https://casual-effects.com/data
18. McGuire, M., Mara, M., Majercik, Z.: The G3D innovation engine, January 2017. https://casual-effects.com/g3d, https://casual-effects.com/g3d
19. NVIDIA Corporation: Nvidia RTX ray tracing. https://developer.nvidia.com/rtx/raytracing. Accessed 18 Oct 2020
20. Parker, S.G., et al.: OptiX: a general purpose ray tracing engine. ACM Trans. Graph. 29(4), 13 (2010)
21. Ramamoorthi, R., Hanrahan, P.: An efficient representation for irradiance environment maps. In: Proceedings of the 28th Annual Conference on Computer Graphics and Interactive Techniques. SIGGRAPH 2001. ACM (2001)

22. Schied, C., et al.: Spatiotemporal variance-guided filtering: Real-time reconstruction for path-traced global illumination. In: Proceedings of High Performance Graphics. Association for Computing Machinery (2017)

23. Silvennoinen, A., Lehtinen, J.: Real-time global illumination by precomputed local reconstruction from sparse radiance probes. ACM Trans. Graph. 36(6), 1–13 (2017)

24. Sloan, P.P., Kautz, J., Snyder, J.: Precomputed radiance transfer for real-time rendering in dynamic, low-frequency lighting environments. ACM Trans. Graph. 21(3) (2002)

25. Sloan, P.P., Luna, B., Snyder, J.: Local, deformable precomputed radiance transfer, ACM Trans. Graph. 24(3) (2005)

26. Sony Interactive Entertainment LLC: Playstation Now https://www.playstation.com/en-us/ps-now/. Accessed 23 Feb 2021

27. The Khronos Group Inc.: glTF version 2.0 - specification. https://github.com/KhronosGroup/glTF/blob/master/specification/2.0/README.md

28. Trowbridge, T.S., Reitz, K.P.: Average irregularity representation of a rough surface for ray reflection. J. Opt. Soc. Am. 65(5) (May 1975)

29. Varjo Technologies Oy: Varjo VR-3. https://varjo.com/products/vr-3/. Accessed 16 Jan 2021

30. Walter, B., Marschner, S.R., Li, H., Torrance, K.E.: Microfacet models for refraction through rough surfaces. In: Proceedings of the 18th Eurographics Conference on Rendering Techniques, EGSR 2007, Goslar, DEU (2007)

31. Wang, Z., Bovik, A.C., Sheikh, H.R., Simoncelli, E.P.: Image quality assessment: from error visibility to structural similarity. IEEE Trans. Image Process. 13(4) (2004)

32. Zhang, Y., Ortin, M., Arellano, V., Wang, R., Gutierrez, D., Bao, H.: On-the-fly power-aware rendering. Comput. Graph. Forum 37(4) (2018)

Simplicity Driven Edge Refinement and Color Reconstruction in Image Vectorization

Zheng Zhang[1], Junhao Zhao[1], Shiqing Xin[1(✉)], Shuangmin Chen[2], Yuanfeng Zhou[1], Changhe Tu[1], and Wenping Wang[3]

[1] Shandong University, Qingdao, China
xinshiqing@sdu.edu.cn
[2] Qingdao University of Science and Technology, Qingdao, China
[3] The University of Hong Kong, Hong Kong, China

Abstract. Gestalt psychology indicates that simplicity is central to image vectorization, i.e., observers tend to perceive jagged raster edges as piecewise smooth curves and color changes as being either gradual (along edges) or abrupt (across edges). In this paper, we give a pair of simplicity-driven formulations to respectively cope with the two challenges. In detail, we formulate the underlying as-rigid-as-possible edges as the axes of symmetry of the edge saliency map, while reconstructing the color field by enforcing the fidelity and the smoothness at the same time (except on the detected boundaries). We finally convert a rasterized image into gradient-aware vector graphics whose base domain is a high-quality triangle mesh. On the one hand, the rigidity of the boundary curves is naturally achieved based on the assumption of simplicity, instead of by an empirically-grounded curve fitting operation; on the other hand, the color of near-boundary regions is inferred by Hessian energy (an extrapolation-like technique). Our vectorization method is able to yield more visually realistic results than existing approaches and is useful in flexible recoloring, shape editing, and hierarchical level-of-detail (HLOD) image representation.

Keywords: Image vectorization · Hessian energy · Centroidal voronoi diagram · Image reconstruction

1 Introduction

Both colors and shapes (points, lines, and curves) in a vector image are dictated by mathematical formulae, either explicitly or implicitly. It remains smooth and crisp, without introducing artifacts, even when sized up to massive dimensions, unlike a raster-based image that becomes pixelated and jagged when magnified. Image vectorization, i.e., converting raster images to vector graphics, becomes increasingly important due to its versatile applications in color editing, image

© Springer Nature Switzerland AG 2021
N. Magnenat-Thalmann et al. (Eds.): CGI 2021, LNCS 13002, pp. 452–463, 2021.
https://doi.org/10.1007/978-3-030-89029-2_35

embedding, and Image reconstruction. In this paper, we propose a pair of formulations to respectively cope with the two challenges, which is inspired by the simplicity principle of Gestalt psychology.

We first extract the edge saliency map from the raster image. The underlying vectorized edges are then identified as the axes of symmetry of the edge saliency map. Empirical evidence shows that the reconstructed polyline edges are with natural rigidity and smoothness. After that, we compute an edge-aligned centroidal Voronoi tessellation (CVT) to transform the domain into a well triangulated mesh $\mathcal{M}$. It's worth mentioning that $\mathcal{M}$ is sliced open by the detected edges, which facilitates representing color discontinuity. Finally, we integrate the smoothness requirement and the fidelity requirement of color changes into an energy minimization problem. In implementation, we enforce smoothness and fidelity at the same time for non-boundary regions but infer the color of the near-boundary regions by a Hessian energy (an extrapolation-like technique).

Our contributions are three-fold: 1) We propose a pair of simplicity-driven formulations to reconstruct vectorized edges and colors from a raster image. We identify the vectorized edges as the axes of symmetry of the edge saliency map while inferring the color of the near-boundary regions by Hessian energy. 2) We extend the famous centroidal Voronoi tessellation (CVT) technique to generate a high-quality triangulation of the image domain. The difference from the conventional CVT lies in that any cell belonging to a site cannot reside across the vectorized edges. 3) We creatively apply the proposed algorithm to several important occasions including flexible recoloring, shape editing, and hierarchical level-of-detail (HLOD) representation of vector graphics.

2   Related Work

2.1   Curve-Based Design of Vector Graphics

Prevost et al. [9] proposed to improve the technique of diffusion curves by leveraging an intermediate triangular representation with cubic patches to synthesize smooth images. Sun et al. [14] gave a fast multipole method for random-access evaluation of diffusion curve images (DCIs) and their algorithm achieves real-time performance for rasterization and texture-mapping DCIs of up to millions of curves. Hou et al. [5] presented Poisson vector graphics (PVG) for generating smooth-shaded images, which is an extension of diffusion curves. Roughly speaking, curve-based vectorization approximates the original image content with a set of diffusion-like curves, which facilitates artists to create artworks but is weak to produce a vectorized result with high fidelity.

2.2   Vectorization with Triangulation

The triangle mesh, as a popular form of geometric representation, is natively supported by standard vector graphics and triangle rasterization pipelines. Therefore, it can be naturally used for vectorization purposes. Swaminarayan and

Prasad *et al.* [15] found that polygonal representation of the domain, different from the curve-based vectorization, enables good visual quality and fidelity and can be displayed at various sizes and on various resolutions. Demaret *et al.* [3] proposed to recursively remove less significant pixels in a greedy way, and finally report a Delaunay triangulation w.r.t. a small set of significant pixels as the output. Xia *et al.* [17] observed that triangular patches, as a simplicial layout, are flexible in generating monolithic image decomposition and faithful to represent curvilinear features.

2.3   Vectorization with Quadrangulation

Considering that spline surfaces are the most popular form to represent smoothly varying colors but are often parameterized in a square domain, there are many research works that depend on quad decomposition. Price and Barrett [10] proposed a local greedy strategy to repeatedly refine an initial patch until the user-specified representation accuracy is satisfied and finally vectorize the given image with a collection of rectangular bicubic Bézier patches. Some other spline surfaces such that Ferguson patches [13] can also be used to create an optimal gradient mesh. In fact, the biggest challenge of quadrangulation-based vectorization lies in generating a boundary-aligned layout of a rectangular structure with as few as possible singularity points. Lai *et al.* [7] presented a topology-preserving gradient mesh representation that allows an arbitrary number of holes. Wei *et al.* [16] proposed to optimize a feature-aligned field to generate the quad layout. In this paper, we focus on how to better infer the real boundary curve and the color distribution of the near-boundary pixels, which has not been fully considered in the existing quadrangulation-based approaches.

3   Algorithm

We first give an overview of our algorithm that consists of three steps: (a) edge extraction and refinement, (b) converting the image domain into an edge-aligned well triangulated mesh, and (c) color reconstruction. See Fig. 1 for the algorithmic pipeline. In the first step, we identify edges as the axes of symmetry of edge saliency map. In the second step, we use the technique of centroidal Voronoi tessellation (CVT) to vectorize the base domain with a triangle mesh that conforms to the detected edges. Finally, we reconstruct the color field by simultaneously enforcing the smoothness requirement and the fidelity requirement.

3.1   Edge Extraction and Refinement

Imagine that when a vector image is rasterized, the color around the edges will be blurred and the gradients are degraded. It's much like what the Central Limit Theorem reveals, a Gaussian waveform is produced when a Dirac delta function is convolved with itself many times. In the implementation, we first compute the

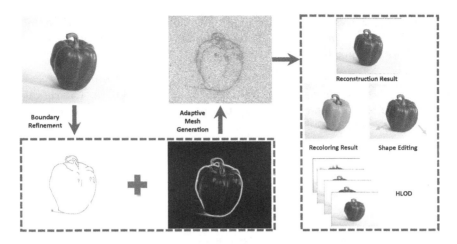

Fig. 1. The pipeline of our method, which consists of boundary extracting and color inferring.

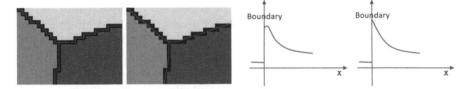

Fig. 2. Initial edge configuration and refined boundary edges.

Fig. 3. Reconstructed color field by the Laplacian energy and Hessian energy.

gradient based edge saliency map and then apply Canny's edge operator (excluding the hysteresis operation), which is a standard operation available in Matlab and OpenCV. In this way, we get a set of pixels that are labeled with an "ON-BOUNDARY" flag. The adjacency structure of ON-BOUNDARY pixels leads to a connection between the pixel centers $\{p_i\}_{i=1}^m$, which shall be used to initialize the vectorized boundary $\mathcal{C}^{(0)}$. See Fig. 2 (Left). Next, we refine $\mathcal{C}$ (may have branch points) until the edge saliency map can be approximately taken as a Gaussian waveform w.r.t. $\mathcal{C}$. See Fig. 2 (Right).

Symmetry. Since each pixel p_i contributes four corner points, we let $\{q_j\}_{j=1}^n$ be the corner point set on both sides of $\mathcal{C}$. Suppose that q_j' is the projection point of q_j on $\mathcal{C}$ and $d_j \triangleq d(q_j, \mathcal{C})$ is the distance from q_j to $\mathcal{C}$. We denote $\lambda(q_j')$ and $\sigma(q_j')$ be respectively the two unknown parameters to define the Gaussian function at q_j'. We use the following energy to measure how the edge saliency map is symmetric about $\mathcal{C}$.

$$E_{\text{Symmetry}}\left(\{p_i\}_{i=1}^m, \{\lambda_k\}_{k=1}^N, \{\sigma_k\}_{k=1}^N\right) = \sum_{\{q_j\}_{j=1}^n} \lambda(q_j') e^{-\frac{d_j^2}{2\sigma^2(q_j')}}, \qquad (1)$$

where $\{p_i\}_{i=1}^m$ defines the polyline representation of the potential boundary curve, and $\{\lambda_k\}_{k=1}^N, \{\sigma_k\}_{k=1}^N$ are defined per pixel (N is the total number of ON-BOUNDARY pixels).

Rigidity. Initially, $\mathcal{C}^{(0)}$ determines how the points $\{p_i\}_{i=1}^m$ are connected together. Generally, for each point $p_i \in \mathcal{C}^{(0)}$, it has two or more neighbors. The rigidity or smoothness of the boundary curve can be characterized by a discrete Dirichlet energy, i.e.

$$E_{\text{Rigidity}}\left(\{p_i\}_{i=1}^m\right) = \sum_{i=1}^m \sum_{p_j \text{ is neighboring to } p_i} \|p_i - p_j\|^2. \tag{2}$$

Refinement of Boundary Curve. By summarizing the above two requirements together, we transform the detection of boundary curve into a minimization problem with the following objective function:

$$E\left(\{p_i\}_{i=1}^m, \{\lambda_k\}_{k=1}^N, \{\sigma_k\}_{k=1}^N\right) = E_{\text{Symmetry}} + \mu E_{\text{Rigidity}}, \tag{3}$$

where μ is a balancing parameter and set to m by default. In implementation, we take each pixel as a quad and the underlying curve as a polyline passing through a sequence of quads. The point p_i lies on a quad edge and thus represented by the dividing ratio that is a floating number. Considering that the objective function continuously depends on the change of p_i, we use L-BFGS to find the point sequence. The optimization comes to termination if the gradient norm is less than 10^{-5}. Figure 2 shows an example of boundary curve refinement.

3.2 Adaptive Mesh Generation

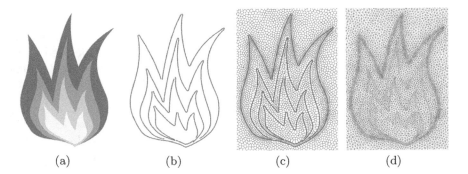

(a)   (b)   (c)   (d)

Fig. 4. (a) The input image. (b) The optimized edge. (c) The edge-aligned centroidal Voronoi tessellation. (d) The constrained Delaunay triangulation.

Centroidal Voronoi tessellations (CVTs) [4], as a special type of region decomposition, are proven to be useful in providing an exceedingly uniform point placement. It also supports density adaptive placement of points. In its essence, CVT is to find the best discrete point set that can well approximate the original continuous density function ρ with the minimum 2-Wasserstein distance. Given a set of sites $X = \{x_i\}_{i=1}^{k}$ in the image domain Ω as well as the corresponding Voronoi diagram $\{\Omega_i\}_{i=1}^{k}$, the objective function of CVT sums the second-order moment of each Voronoi sub-region together:

$$F_{\mathrm{CVT}}(X) = \sum_{i=1}^{k} \int_{\Omega_i} \rho(x)\|x - x_i\|^2 \mathrm{d}x. \tag{4}$$

However, it cannot be directly used for our purpose since we have to enforce the boundary alignment property, i.e., each Voronoi cell must reside on one side of the boundary curve. Therefore, we modify the definition of the Voronoi diagram. For the site $x_i \in \Omega_i$, the cell belonging to x_i is defined as follows: if $\|x - x_i\| \leq \|x - x_j\|$ holds for all the "visible" site x_j, x is deemed to dominated by x_i. Here "visible" means that the connection line segment $x_i x_j$ does not intersect the boundary curve $\mathcal{C}$. In Fig. 4, we respectively show the edge-aligned CVT and the corresponding edge constrained Delaunay triangulation $\mathcal{T}$.

3.3 Color Reconstruction

To this end, we have a triangle mesh $\mathcal{T}$ as the geometric domain to encode the color of the image. In order to guarantee that the color on one side of the boundary curve $\mathcal{C}$ is radically different from that on the other side, we slice $\mathcal{T}$ open along $\mathcal{C}$. Suppose that $\mathcal{T}$ contains a set of vertices $\{v_i\}_{i=1}^{M}$, and we need to infer the color at each vertex by considering fidelity, smoothness, and simplicity.

Choice of Color Models. Although R, G, and B channels are almost independent components of colors when shown on a screen, it is much different from how one perceives them. By contrast, after being mapped into the HSV color space, the three components including hue, saturation and value are more independent and consistent with human's color perception.

Fidelity. Let $H = (h_1^{\mathrm{old}}, h_2^{\mathrm{old}}, \cdots, h_M^{\mathrm{old}})$ be the hue channel, where M is the total number of vertices in $\mathcal{T}$. Since $\mathcal{T}$ aligns with boundary curve, we can classify the vertices in $\mathcal{T}$ into two groups: (1) on the boundary curve, and (2) off the boundary curve. We should enforce the fidelity requirement for those vertices of $\mathcal{T}$ that are not on the boundary curve $\mathcal{C}$. Therefore, we measure the overall fidelity as follows:

$$E_{\mathrm{Fidelity}} = \sum_{v_i \text{ is not on } \mathcal{C}} \|h_i^{\mathrm{new}} - h_i^{\mathrm{old}}\|^2. \tag{5}$$

Simplicity/Rigidity. The simplicity of H can be measured by the squared Laplacian energy like $E_{\mathrm{Simplicity}} = H \times L \times H^{\mathrm{T}}$ where L is the discrete squared Laplacian matrix. Since it is not necessary to enforce the fidelity for those vertices on $\mathcal{C}$, their color values are totally given by the prior assumption of simplicity and rigidity. However, the main disadvantage of the squared Laplacian energy lies in that it only emphasizes the smoothness, regardless of rigidity. In other words, it cannot be better infer the color at $\mathcal{C}$ based on the higher-order change of the potential field, which biases the real situation.

Recently, Stein *et al.* [12] proposed a new smoothness energy different from the squared Laplacian energy, named Hessian energy. The biggest difference lies in that the Hessian energy yields meaningful high-order boundary conditions and thus can infer perceptually consistent values across/near open boundaries, like the extrapolation technique. Technically, it rewrites L in the form of

$$L = \mathbf{G}^\mathbf{T}\mathbf{ADM}^{-1}\mathbf{D}^\mathbf{T}\mathbf{AG}, \qquad (6)$$

where $\mathbf{G},\mathbf{A},\mathbf{D},\mathbf{M}$ are respectively the discrete gradient operator, diagonal matrix of triangle areas, discrete matrix divergence operator and discrete mass matrix. See [12] for details. Here we use the Hessian energy to infer the color values of the vertices located on $\mathcal{C}$. Figure 3 visualize how crisp the color changes are across the boundary edge.

Optimization. We reconstruct the underlying hue component by minimizing

$$E_H = E_{\text{Simplicity}} + \nu E_{\text{Fidelity}}, \qquad (7)$$

where ν is set to 10^8 by default in our experiments. The above formulation of minimizing E_H can be finally transformed into a linear system with $H = (h_1, h_2, \cdots, h_M)$ being the variables. Similarly, the saturation and value components can be reconstructed.

4   Evaluation

All the experiments were conducted on a computer with an Intel® i5 core 2.80 GHz CPU and 16 GB RAM. We record the experimental statistics in Table 1.

Table 1. Experimental statistics

Image	Vertices	Timing (s)	Error	Error [16]	Storage (Kb)
1	4710	0.57	1.3	1.58	487/141
5	7267	0.80	2.3	3.81	622/173
6(a)	15400	1.70	3.2	3.77	1113/244
6(b)	35600	4.20	2.5	1.70	1584/398
6(c)	8320	0.63	1.3	1.26	673/207
6(d)	32700	4.03	3.5	5.24	1957/484
7	23736	3.30	1.4	1.44	1257/216
9	6045	0.67	2.3	2.48	558/158

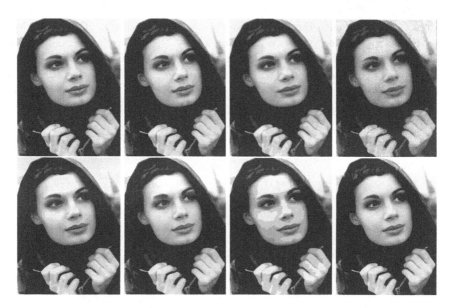

Fig. 5. Comparison with commonly used vectorization tools. The upper row (from left to right): Input raster image; AutoTrace; Inkscape; RaveGrid; The bottom row (from left to right): Scan2CAD; Vectormagic; Super Vectorizer; Ours.

There are many vectorization approaches as well as available vectorization tools. In Fig. 5, we compare our approach with the existing vectorization tools. We record the storage usage statistics in Table 1. Particularly, for the raster image as shown in Fig. 5. It's noted that our vectorized data can be further zipped into 173 KB. Besides, it can be seen from Table 1 that the fidelity is well preserved - the average color difference per pixel is less than 4 (each channel is between 0 to 255), which is an inconspicuous visual effect loss. Our optimization-driven algorithm, in its current form, is devised to vectorize a raster image with the complicated scene and doesn't have an advantage of run-time performance. We shall develop more techniques to further boost the implementation in the future.

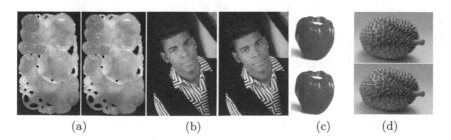

(a)   (b)   (c)   (d)

Fig. 6. Gallery of image vectorization based on our approach. Here we show three pairs, where each pair contains a raster image and its vectorized result.

Abrupt Color Change Across Boundary. As Fig. 7 shows, the traditional approaches [7] are easy to cause conspicuously visual artifacts near boundaries. In our approach, the strong boundaries are carefully extracted and the near-boundary color on the two sides is inferred respectively. To summarize, we enforce the fidelity requirement in the off-boundary area while borrowing the technique of Hessian energy to infer the color of near-boundary points. We give more examples of our vectorization approach in Fig. 6.

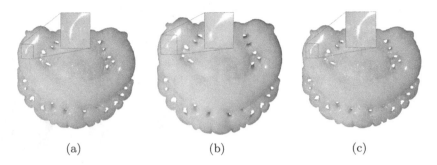

(a)   (b)   (c)

Fig. 7. Strong boundaries are central to guarantee the visual quality of image vectorization. (a) The original image. (b) The result of [7]. (c) Our result.

5   Applications

In this section, we give three separate interesting applications that can be easily handled by our algorithm. They include flexible recoloring, shape editing, and hierarchical level-of-detail (HLOD) image representation.

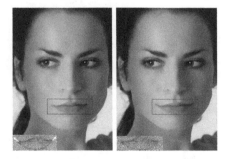

Fig. 8. Left: input image; Right: editing image. Shape editing on the vectorized image - users can simply drag a few mesh vertices to embed the vectorized image in a deformed mesh.

Fig. 9. Starting from a dense vectorization graphics, one can quickly establish a sequence of fine-to-coarse structure results, which defines a hierarchical level-of-detail (HLOD) representation.

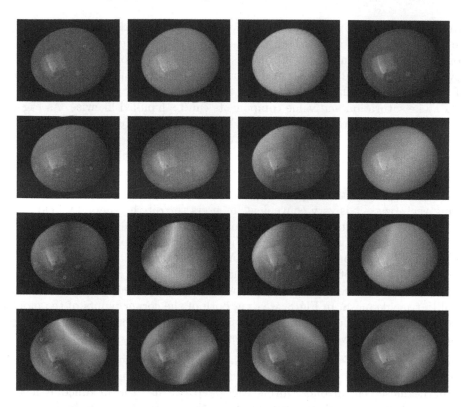

Fig. 10. Users can change the coloring style by simply specifying the color for just a few handle points (marked by red circles). The handle points remain the same for each row. Our approach is conducted in the HSV space and preserves the gradients as far as possible. (Color figure online)

Recoloring. The easiest way is to allow users to specify the color for just a few handle points and observe the recolored result in real time. We consider this problem in the HSV color space. Suppose that there are k handle vertices, $v_{i_1}, v_{i_2}, \cdots, v_{i_k} \in \mathcal{T}$, with user-specified color values. We measure the degree of how the gradients (w.r.t. hue, saturation and value respectively) are preserved by

$$\min_{h_i^{\text{new}}} \sum_{\substack{v_i \\ \text{is neighboring to } v_j}} \left((h_i^{\text{new}} - h_j^{\text{new}}) - (h_i^{\text{old}} - h_j^{\text{old}}) \right)^2 \tag{8}$$

$$\text{s.t.} \quad h_{i_1} = \overline{h}_{i_1}, h_{i_2} = \overline{h}_{i_2}, \cdots, h_{i_k} = \overline{h}_{i_k}$$

where $\overline{H} = (\overline{h}_{i_1}, \overline{h}_{i_2}, \cdots, \overline{h}_{i_k})$ defines the user-specified colors. It can be further rewritten in a linear system (based on the method of Lagrange multipliers):

$$\begin{bmatrix} \mathbf{A}^{\mathrm{T}}\mathbf{A} & \mathbf{S}^{\mathbf{T}} \\ \mathbf{S} & \mathbf{0} \end{bmatrix} \begin{bmatrix} H^{\text{new}} \\ \xi \end{bmatrix} = \begin{bmatrix} \mathbf{A}^{\mathrm{T}} H_{\text{diff}}^{\text{old}} \\ \overline{H}, \end{bmatrix} \tag{9}$$

where $\mathbf{A}_{ij} = 1, i < j$, for a pair of neighboring vertices v_i and v_j, $\mathbf{A}_{ij} = -1, i > j$, for the same neighboring vertex pair, and $\mathbf{A}_{ij} = 0$ otherwise. The matrix $\mathbf{S}$ consists of k rows, and the j-th row has a "1" at the i_j position; $\overline{H}$ also has k rows and encodes the user-specified colors; $H_{\text{diff}}^{\text{old}}$ is the column vector consisting of $\{h_i^{\text{old}} - h_j^{\text{old}}\}$; H is the hue component to be computed for all the mesh vertices of $\mathcal{T}$. The saturation and value components can be handled likewise. As Fig. 10 shows, users can change the coloring style by simply specifying the color of just a few handle points (highlighted by red circles).

Our approach aims at preserving image gradients and enforcing the user-specified color at handle points, and thus facilitates users to operate.

Shape Editing. Since the shape content has been embedded in a planar mesh after being vectorized, it is very convenient for users to edit the shape by deforming the base mesh. In fact, there is a large body literature [1,2,6,8,11] that conducts shape editing in this way. Here we use the as-rigid-as-possible mesh deformation approach [8] to perform shape editing. After users specify the region to deform and the movement of a few vertices, the deformed shape conforming to users' input can be observed immediately. In fact, our approach generates a high-quality triangle mesh. In Fig. 8, we drag both of the corner points of the mouth and get a visually natural smiling expression. It can be seen that the high triangle quality is still preserved after being deformed.

Hierarchical Level-of-Detail (HLOD). Given a dense triangulation of the image domain, we repeatedly simplify the triangulation by replacing a cluster of vertices with the most central one. During each step, we use the modified K-means algorithm to downsample the vertices by a ratio of α (we take α to be $1/4$ in our experiments), followed by a constrained Delaunay triangulation. Furthermore, we can keep the parent-child relationship between vertices and arrange them in a hierarchical structure. As Fig. 9 shows, we start from dense vectorization graphics, and then quickly establish a sequence of fine-to-coarse structure results. It can be seen that the loss of visual quality is often inconspicuous although the number of mesh vertices is greatly reduced.

6   Conclusions

In this paper, we propose a set of strategies to accomplish the task of image vectorization based on the prior assumption of simplicity. First, we formulate the as-rigid-as-possible edges as the axes of symmetry of the edge saliency map. Second, considering that the raster image is generally degraded around the boundary edges while the vectorized result should be crisper in the near-boundary area, we propose to infer the near-boundary color based on Hessian energy (an extrapolation-like technique). We further apply the proposed algorithm in three separate application scenarios including flexible recoloring, artifact-free shape editing, and hierarchical level-of-detail (HLOD) image representation. In the future, we shall investigate layered vectorization of a raster image to facilitate post-edit. Furthermore, we shall incorporate prior knowledge to produce more perpetually consistent vectorized results.

Acknowledgments. This work is supported by National Natural Science Foundation of China (61772016, 62002190) and NSF of Shandong Province (ZR2020MF036).

References

1. Botsch, M., Sorkine, O.: On linear variational surface deformation methods. IEEE Trans. Visual Comput. Graphics **14**(1), 213–230 (2007)
2. Chao, I., Pinkall, U., Sanan, P., Schröder, P.: A simple geometric model for elastic deformations. ACM Trans. Graph. **29**(4), 1–6 (2010)
3. Demaret, L., Dyn, N., Iske, A.: Image compression by linear splines over adaptive triangulations. Sig. Process. **86**(7), 1604–1616 (2006)
4. Du, Q., Gunzburger, M., Ju, L.: Advances in studies and applications of centroidal voronoi tessellations. Numer. Math. Theor. Methods Appl. **3**(2), 119–142 (2010)
5. Hou, F., et al.: Poisson vector graphics (pvg) and its closed-form solver. arXiv preprint arXiv:1701.04303 (2017)
6. Igarashi, T., Moscovich, T., Hughes, J.F.: As-rigid-as-possible shape manipulation. ACM Trans. Graph. **24**(3), 1134–1141 (2005)
7. Lai, Y.K., Hu, S.M., Martin, R.R.: Automatic and topology-preserving gradient mesh generation for image vectorization. ACM Trans. Graph. **28**(3), 1–8 (2009)
8. Levi, Z., Gotsman, C.: Smooth rotation enhanced as-rigid-as-possible mesh animation. IEEE Trans. Visual Comput. Graphics **21**(2), 264–277 (2014)
9. Prévost, R., Jarosz, W., Sorkine-Hornung, O.: A vectorial framework for ray traced diffusion curves. In: Computer Graphics Forum, vol. 34, pp. 253–264. Wiley Online Library (2015)
10. Price, B., Barrett, W.: Object-based vectorization for interactive image editing. Vis. Comput. **22**(9–11), 661–670 (2006)
11. Sorkine, O., Alexa, M.: As-rigid-as-possible surface modeling. In: Symposium on Geometry processing, vol. 4, pp. 109–116 (2007)
12. Stein, O., Grinspun, E., Wardetzky, M., Jacobson, A.: Natural boundary conditions for smoothing in geometry processing. ACM Trans. Graph. **37**(2), 1–13 (2018)
13. Sun, J., Liang, L., Wen, F., Shum, H.Y.: Image vectorization using optimized gradient meshes. ACM Trans. Graph. **26**(3), 11-es (2007)
14. Sun, T., Thamjaroenporn, P., Zheng, C.: Fast multipole representation of diffusion curves and points. ACM Trans. Graph. **33**(4), 53-1 (2014)
15. Swaminarayan, S., Prasad, L.: Rapid automated polygonal image decomposition. In: 35th IEEE Applied Imagery and Pattern Recognition Workshop (AIPR 2006), pp. 28–28. IEEE (2006)
16. Wei, G., Zhou, Y., Gao, X., Ma, Q., Xin, S., He, Y.: Field-aligned quadrangulation for image vectorization. In: Computer Graphics Forum, vol. 38, pp. 171–180. Wiley Online Library (2019)
17. Xia, T., Liao, B., Yu, Y.: Patch-based image vectorization with automatic curvilinear feature alignment. ACM Trans. Graph. **28**(5), 1–10 (2009)

Temporal-Consistency-Aware Video Color Transfer

Shiguang Liu$^{(\boxtimes)}$ and Yu Zhang

College of Intelligence and Computing, Tianjin University, Tianjin 300350, China
lsg@tju.edu.cn

Abstract. This paper proposes a new temporal-consistency-aware color transfer method based on quaternion distance metric. Compared with the state-of-the-art methods, our method can keep the temporal consistency and better reduce the artifacts. Firstly, keyframes are extracted from the source video and transfer the color from the reference image through soft segmentation based on Gaussian Mixture Models (GMM). Then a quaternion-based method is proposed to transfer color from keyframes to the other frames iteratively. Specifically, this method analyses the color information of each pixel along five directions to detect its best matching pixel through a quaternion-based distance metric. Additionally, considering the accumulating errors in frame sequences, an effective abnormal color correction mechanism is designed to improve the color transfer quality. A quantitative evaluation metric is further proposed to measure the temporal consistency in the output video. Various experimental results validate the effectiveness of our method.

Keywords: Color transfer · Temporal consistency · Video · Quaternion

1 Introduction

In daily life, people usually need to make their own amateur videos look as professional as the videos which are taken by professional photographer or come from a movie in either color palette, luminance or other attributes. Video color transfer techniques allow to transform the color palette of the reference images or videos to our own source videos automatically, which can be used in video processing of mobile devices such as mobile phone or tablet computer. However, the state-of-the-art techniques still fail to keep temporal consistency and may produce satisfactory results.

Many methods have been proposed to solve image color transfer problem [1–3,10,11]. In recent years, deep learning was also introduced to achieve automatic image style transfer [13–17]. However, these methods cannot be easily extended to video color transfer, since applying color transformation naively to every frame

S. Liu—This work was partly supported by the Natural Science Foundation of China under grant nos. 62072328 and 61672375.

N. Magnenat-Thalmann et al. (Eds.): CGI 2021, LNCS 13002, pp. 464–476, 2021.
https://doi.org/10.1007/978-3-030-89029-2_36

may easily lead to artifacts such as color bleeding and *temporal inconsistency* [4], and rely on a large amount of training data. It is the key problem in video color transfer to keep the temporal consistency between frames, the strong correlation between adjacent frames should be considered [5]. Bonneel et al. [6] smoothed the frame mapping by interpolation among keyframes. However, some of their results cannot get temporal consistency and some may lose contrasts and details because their methods cannot find the accurate corresponding among frames. To keep temporal consistency in video color transfer, an accurate measurement to detect the distance between pixels in two adjacent frame is necessary. Since Javier et al. [7] proposed an *image correction* method to correct image color by using SIFT algorithm on image shots of the same scene. However, this method is not suitable for color transfer task of general video. Therefore, Pei et al. [8] replaced the slow SIFT algorithm with quaternion [9] and can obtain pleasing color correction result between videos and had faster speed at the same time. However, their method can only solve videos from the same scene and suffer from flicker which results in temporal inconsistency, because their method naively relay a simply 3×3 matrix to transfer between videos. Recently, Niu et al. [12] proposed a stereoscopic video color correction method that handles global, local, and temporal color discrepancies.

Image sequence color transfer and video color transfer have also attracted researchers' attention. One of the main challenges is to ensure temporal consistency between frames. In the simplest case, a global transformation can be determined to apply in each frame. For instance, Hogervorst et al. [20,21] encoded the mapping between a given input image pair into a look-up table and then applied to all subsequent frames in the same way. Their purpose was to colorize night-vision imagery to change a daytime appearance. Xue et al. [22] proposed to learn a global mapping in terms of luminance, hue and saturation changes from a video collection, and then color palette could be applied to a given video. Wang and Huang [23] extended the statistical color transfer method [1] and colorized an image sequence with color palette borrowed from three user-given target images. However, all these methods apply the same pattern in the source videos or image sequences, which would generate temporal inconsistency results such as flickering. Yao et al. [24] employed patch matching to maintain the temporal consistency in re-colored videos, but their method suffers from processing large moving objects in the scene. If the reference is a video, small changes in the reference videos may not correspond to the content of the source videos, and thereby lead to artifacts. To solve this problem, Bonneel et al. [6] proposed to estimate a per-frame color transformation that mapped the color distributions of a reference video to the source video. Pei et al. [8] proposed to match the color palette between two videos from the same scene. Their algorithm is effective, but it can only process similar videos and may cause flickering. Recently, researchers began to seek solutions for video style transfer [18,19]. In contrast, this paper focuses on color transfer given examples.

In this paper, a video color transfer method is proposed which can keep better temporal consistency. Firstly, using a soft segmentation method, the color palette

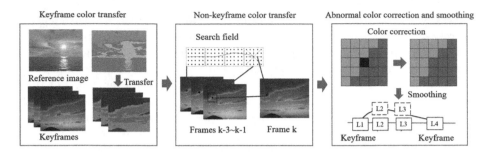

Fig. 1. The framework of our novel video color transfer method

is transferred between the reference image and the keyframes of the source video. Next, in order to keep temporal consistency, a novel quaternion-based scheme is developed to transfer color palette from keyframes to the other frames iteratively. Then, in order to remove some abnormal points to reduce artifacts, an effective abnormal color correction mechanism is designed. Finally, a smoothing filter is applied to remove flickers of the output videos. Additionally, a quantitative evaluation metric is proposed to measure the temporal consistency in the output video. Compared with the state-of-the-arts, our method enables better temporal consistency color transfer results and minimizes the artifacts both in objective evaluation and visual evaluation.

2   Our Method

Figure 1 illustrates our temporal-consistency-aware video color transfer framework. Given a reference image and a source video, the goal of video color transfer is to obtain an output video which maintains the content from source video and the color palette from the reference image.

2.1   Keyframe Color Transfer

Firstly, the input frame sequence is summarized with a few representative frames whose color distribution is representative of that of the entire video. Then the color distribution of the reference image can be transferred to the keyframes of the source video. Similarly to Bonneel et al.'s method [6], the K-medoids algorithm is run on the frames of the source video to extract the keyframes.

Then, color transfer would be performed for each frame. Global color transfer methods [10,11] which are too flexible such as full color histogram matching and estimate the full transformations may hardly retain the contrast especially in the images with clear segment between foreground and background. In our work, a method which can manipulate the videos with clear contrast [25] is needed. Therefore, the soft segmentation method is chosen to improve color transfer appearance.

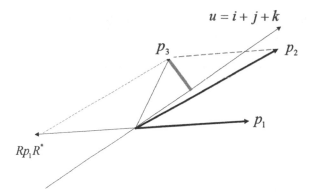

Fig. 2. Chromaticity distance between two pixels. Rp_1R^* represents a rotation of p_1 through an angle of $180°$ about the gray line μ. The blue line is vector p_3, and the red line shows the distance between p_3 and gray line indicates the chromaticity distance between p_1 and p_3. (Color figure online)

Gaussian Mixture Models (GMM) is applied to extract dominant colors in the image. The models assign each pixel a probability according to a given Gaussian distribution. In order to segment an image into regions, the expectation minimization (EM) optimization procedure is used. The number of regions is adjusted based on the complexity of scene content. After identifying the main colors in both the reference image and key frames of the source video, a Euclidean distance measure is used to match the regions:

$$\min \left(\sum_{n=1}^{k} w_n \, \|C_R^n - C_S^n\|\right)^2 \tag{1}$$

where k is the number of the clusters generated by the EM algorithm. w_n is the weight of the nth cluster. C_R^n and C_S^n are the nth main color in the reference image and key frames. Then for each region in key frames, if it has the minimal color distance with one region in reference image, they are matched. Then the pixels in the pair of regions are calculated with

$$P_O(x) = w(x)p_R, \quad w(x) = \exp(-\|p_S(x) - p_R(x)\|) \tag{2}$$

where p_R and p_S are the pixels in reference image and source video frames, respectively. p_O is the pixel after color transfer. After all pixels in the source image are processed, the recolored keyframes can be obtained. After transferring the color from reference image to keyframes of source video, we propagate the color palette of key frames to the other frames.

2.2 Video Interframe Color Transfer

To keep temporal consistency in video color transfer, an accurate measurement to detect the distance between pixels in two adjacent frames is necessary. It is found that using the channels in the uncorrelated color space is not adequate enough to judge the distance between pixels. So RGB color space is chosen and a quaternion-based distance metric is applied.

Given two pixels, the quaternion-based distance metric proposed by Jin et al. [9] is used to measure the difference between them. Some quaternion representations about pixels, p_1, p_2, and p_3 are computed as follows:

$$
\begin{aligned}
p_1 &= r_1 i + g_1 j + b_1 k, \quad p_2 = r_2 i + g_2 j + b_2 k \\
R &= (i + j + k)/\sqrt{3}, \quad p_3 = p_2 + R p_1 R^* = r_3 i + g_3 j + b_3 k
\end{aligned}
\tag{3}
$$

where r_i, g_i, b_i $(i = 1, 2, 3)$ stand for red, green, and blue colors, R represents a unit pure quaternion that is used as a transformation axis, and $R p_1 R^*$ represents a 3-D rotation of p_1 through an angle of $180°$ about the gray line $u = i + j + k$. p_3 is a vector and the Euclidean distance between and the gray line u stand for the chromaticity difference between p_1 and p_2 as is shown in Fig. 2. The color distance between p_1 and p_2 can be computed by

$$
\begin{aligned}
CD(p_1, p_2) &= w \left| Q(p_1, p_2) \right| + (1 - w) \left| I(p_1, p_2) \right| \\
Q(p_1, p_2) &= (r_3 - \tfrac{r_3 + g_3 + b_3}{3}) i + (g_3 - \tfrac{r_3 + g_3 + b_3}{3}) j + (b_3 - \tfrac{r_3 + g_3 + b_3}{3}) k \\
I(p_1, p_2) &= k_1 (r_2 - r_1) + k_2 (g_2 - g_1) + k_3 (b_2 - b_1)
\end{aligned}
\tag{4}
$$

where $Q(p_1, p_2)$ is chromaticity difference and $I(p_1, p_2)$ is luminance distance. $w \in [0, 1]$ represents the importance of chromaticity and luminance difference. If w is large, the influence of chromaticity in color distance is enhanced and that of luminance is suppressed. $k_i (i = 1, 2, 3)$ in $I(p_1, p_2)$ represent the contributions of red, green, and blue channels to luminance. In our experiment, $k_1 = 0.299$, $k_2 = 0.587$, and $k_3 = 0.114$.

In a video clip, there exits strong correlation between two adjacent frames, and only a few pixels in one frame are different from their adjacent frames [26]. In our experiment, as the first frame is assigned color distributions, it can be the second frame's reference. The rest can be deduced analogously: the current frame as the source image, and its former frame as the reference image. Assume that there are two kinds of pixels in source video frames, i.e., one is unchanging point $p(x, y)$ which has the same coordinate (x, y) with its best match pixel $p'(x, y)$ in reference image, so that the color of $p(x, y)$ can be directly transferred to $p'(x, y)$; the other kind of pixel is called changing point, its best match pixel p^* should be determined from its neighbourhood, and then transfer the color from p^* to p.

For a pixel p in source frame, p' is a pixel in reference image with the same coordinate with p. If p and p' satisfy $\left| I(p, p') \right| \leq \varepsilon$ then $p = p' = r'i + g'j + b'k$. ε is a given threshold. It is found that only a small amount of pixels are changing points.

The most difficult part in this step is to find the best match pixel p^* for the changing point p in source image. In our work, the directional samples are used to detect the best match pixels for changing point. In order to find the best matching pixel of the current pixel p, it should be taken into account that all the pixels in four directions: the horizontal, vertical, and two diagonal directions in the current frame. In addition, due to the strong correlation between neighboring frames, the pixels on motion trajectory should also be taken into account. To sum up, the color information along five directions are compared to detect the best matching pixel of the current pixel. Thus, it is necessary to choose reliable motion estimation. The optical flow estimation method in [27] is employed.

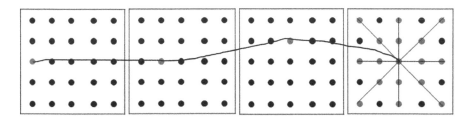

Fig. 3. Illustration of the target pixels along five directions (the pixels in the horizontal, vertical, and two diagonal directions in current frame, and the pixels of adjacent frames on the motion trajectory, all of which are marked in red). (Color figure online)

Assuming that the current changing pixel is $p(x, y, k)$ in the frame k, x and y are its horizontal coordinate and vertical coordinate. A 3-D window is used to determine the best match pixel of it. Here, the window size of the search field is set to be $5 \times 5 \times 4$. We denote the pixels along the five directions as

$$\Omega = \{p_{d,1}, p_{d,2}, ..., p_{d,n}\} \tag{5}$$

where $d = \{1, 2, 3, 4, 5\}$ represents the five directions, and n means the number of pixels, $p_{d,i}(i \in [1, n])$ denote the ith pixel in direction d. Figure 3 shows the search field. In the following, the pixel $\hat{p}$ which has the minimum distance with p. $\hat{p}$ can be defined as

$$\hat{p} = \arg \min_{p' \in \Omega} CD(p, p') \tag{6}$$

$\hat{p}$ is regarded as the best match pixel p^* in the search field, but directly transfer its color to the current pixel may lead to some artifacts. If the current pixel is originally an abnormal pixel on the boundary of one object, judging merely by the distance may match it with the pixel on the other object, which will cause mistaken transfer. Therefore, a constraint to determine p^* is added:

$$p^* = \begin{cases} \hat{p} & CD(p, \hat{p}) \leq Tol \\ p^{Correction} & Otherwise \end{cases} \tag{7}$$

where Tol is a threshold, $p^{Correction}$ denotes the correction result when p is judged to be an abnormal pixel.

2.3   Abnormal Color Correction

After the above processing, there may still exist some pixels which are mistakenly transferred colors or their best match cannot be found using the distance metric. Those pixels are denoted as abnormal color. It is observed that the abnormal color always appears in the changing point at the edge of some objects, but with the color transfer processing frame by frame, abnormal color spreads outward, which will lead to poor temporal consistency and cause unsatisfactory results. In order to further keep the temporal consistency, it is necessary to detect and remove the abnormal color.

Fig. 4. The procedure of the abnormal color correction. From left to right: some abnormal colors appear at the edge (see the rectangle area), finding a region around the abnormal colors based on neighbourhood similarity, the correction result.

Because the abnormal pixel has obvious color difference with the color around it, the neighbourhood similarity is used to detect abnormal color and correct it. Figure 4 shows our procedure of the abnormal color correction.

2.4   Luminance Smoothing

When all the frames are solved by the above steps, in order to remove flickers and keep the temporal consistency, a smoothing method is used to keep the luminance temporal in the output videos. A method similar to Wang et al.'s method [25] is used which smooths each frame by interpolating between every two keyframes to stabilize the video frames.

Given two keyframes F_m and F_n, the frames between them is defined to be linear. Ageneral form $y = ax + b$ is chosen. Thus, this function to determine the coefficients a and b can be obtained using the keyframes, $(x_1, y_1) = (m, F_m.c)$ and $(x_2, y_2) = (n, F_n.c)$, where c represents the mean of luminance in one keyframe. When a and b are evaluated, then the mean value of frames between F_m and F_n can be determined.

3   Experimental Results and Discussions

In the experiments, all input videos and images are processed in RGB color space. For interframe color transfer, the threshold ε for changing point judgement is set as 10. Tol, which is used to judge the abnormal color, is 10. In

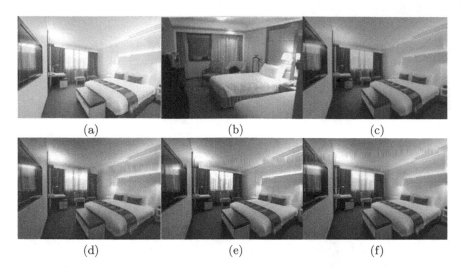

(a)   (b)   (c)

(d)   (e)   (f)

Fig. 5. The color transfer result comparison among the methods of Reinhard et al. [1], Nguyen et al. [28] and our method. (a) source image, (b) reference image, (c) result of Reinhard et al.'s method [1], (d) result of Nguyen et al.'s method [28], (e) result of Xiao et al.'s method [10], (f) result of our method.

abnormal color correction, the error threshold E_R and the Maximum neighborhood threshold M_N are set as 8 and 200, respectively. One of the input video size is normalized to 640 $\times$ 960 as the standard size of the video captured by mobile phone, and the video frame number is 235, and computing time of the video color transfer is 0.4635 s per frame.

Figure 5 shows a comparison of our method with Reinhard et al.'s method [1], Xiao et al.'s method [10], and Nguyen et al.'s method [28]. The source image displaces a content of a bedroom under white light, and the reference image shows a content of a bedroom under yellow light. All results of Reinhard et al.'s method [1] and Nguyen et al.'s method [28] didn't make the bedroom look like the reference image. Xiao et al.'s method [10] can preserve the color palette, but there are some artifacts in their results (see the blurring around the light). The whole color palette of our result looks more consistent with the reference image than other two methods.

Inspired by Chen et al.'s quantitative evaluation method [29], an evaluation method to measure the temporal consistency in video color transfer is proposed. If the variation of the adjacent frames difference in the output video is as similar to the difference in source video as possible, it is temporal consistency as the source video. Here, MSE is used to measure the difference between frames. The temporal consistency is computed by

$$w_{R,O} \cdot \|S(R_{MSE}) - S(O_{MSE})\|^2 \tag{8}$$

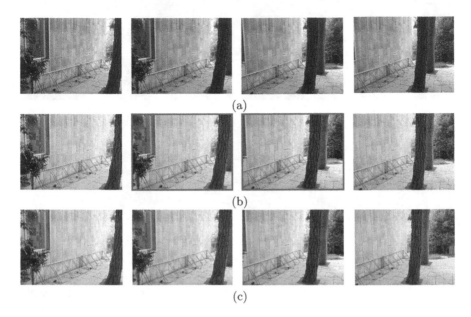

Fig. 6. The result comparison between our method and Pei et al.'s method [8]. (a) the 8th, 18th, 41th and 116th frame in the source video. (b) and (c) are the corresponding frames in Pei et al.'s result [8] and our result, respectively. Note that some flickers occur in the two frames with red rectangles in Pei et al.'s result. (Color figure online)

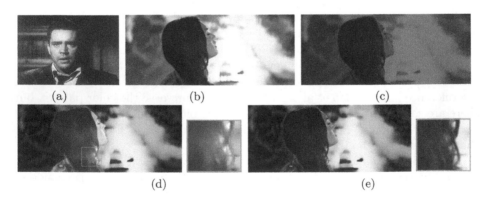

Fig. 7. The comparison of color transfer result by Reinhard et al.'s method [1], Bonneel et al.'s method [6], and our method. (a) reference image, (b) source image, (c) result of Reinhard et al.'s method [1] (note that the color distribution of this result still remains blue just like the reference image), (d) result of Bonneel et al.'s method [6] (note that artifacts in the background is transferred to hair as the zoomed region shows), and (e) our method (note that women's hair remains black).

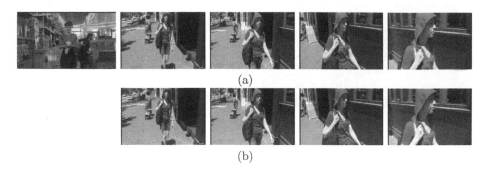

(a)

(b)

Fig. 8. Color transfer result using our method for the video "Lucie".

where R_{MSE} and S_{MSE} represent the frame difference in source video and output video, respectively. S is the variance components. $w_{R,O}$ is formulated as

$$w_{R,O} = \exp(\frac{\|\mu_R - \mu_O\|^2}{2\sigma^2}) \tag{9}$$

where μ_R and μ_O represent the mean values of the frame difference for source video and target video. In particular, the difference of the mean value between the source video and the output video receives high value, and the difference of the variance receives smaller weight. Figure 6 shows a comparison of our method with Pei et al.'s method [8]. The reference image is chosen to be the first frame in the result of Pei et al. [8]. Pei et al.'s [8] result generated some flickering just as the 18th and 41th frame show. In contrast, our result removes the flicking and makes the result video more steadily like the reference image. Table 1 demonstrates the temporal consistency measures between our method, Bonneel et al.'s method [6], and Pei et al.'s method [8]. As our method can better keep temporal consistency than other methods, the measure of our method is lower than the other two methods.

Figure 7 shows a comparison of our method with Bonneel et al.'s method [6] and Reinhard et al.'s method [1]. The reference image is a black-and-white image, and the source video comes from the movie "Transformers" [6]. Since the source frame and reference image have clear foreground and background segment, Reinhard et al.'s method [1] and other global transformations remain the blue color palette. Bonneel et al.'s method [6] adopt a segment of foreground and background and transferred color separately, the result of their method lead to color bleeding. For instance, the color of the women's hair is transferred with the color of the background. In our result, the women's hair still remains black, because our method transfers the right part of the reference image's background to there. Figure 8 shows two videos named "Lucie".

Table 1. The temporal-consistency-evaluation comparison

Methods	Example 1	Example 2
Our method	**0.1023**	**0.2531**
Method of [6]	0.1982	–
Method of [8]	–	0.3823

4   Conclusion and Future Work

In this paper, a temporal-consistency-aware video color transfer method has been proposed. Firstly, based on a soft-segmentation method, the color palette of reference image is transferred to the keyframes of source video. Then a quaternion-based interframe color transfer method was designed to transfer color from keyframes to non-keyframes. An effective abnormal color correction mechanism is specially designed to improve the color transfer quality. Moreover, the flicker has been removed so as to keep the temporal consistency by luminance smoothing. Our new method can achieve better temporal consistency and fewer artifacts both in objective evaluation and visual evaluation. However, our method also has some limitations. The abnormal color correction method processes the video per-pixels, thus the correction mechanism needs optimization. Furthermore, it is interesting to devise a parallel processing scheme to speed up our color transfer computation. It is another direction to choose more advanced quantification and similarity evaluation metric [30]. In the future, we will also estimate video temporal consistency by exploiting the modern deep learning techniques [31] and introduce super-resolution techniques [32], so that the quality of video color transfer results can be further optimized.

References

1. Reinhard, E., Ashikhmin, M., Gooch, B., Shirley, P.: Color transfer between images. IEEE Comput. Graph. Appl. **21**(5), 34–41 (2001)
2. Song, Z., Liu, S.: Sufficient image appearance transfer combining color and texture. IEEE Trans. Multimedia **19**(4), 702–711 (2017)
3. Liu, S., Sun, H., Zhang, X.: Selective color transferring via ellipsoid color mixture map. J. Vis. Commun. Image R. **23**(1), 173–181 (2012)
4. Faridul, H.S., et al.: Colour mapping: a review of recent methods, extensions and applications. Comput. Graph. Forum. **35**(1), 59–88 (2005)
5. Song, C., Zhao, H., Jing, W.: Robust video stabilization based on particle filtering with weighted feature points. IEEE Trans. Consum. Electron. **58**(2), 570–577 (2012)
6. Bonneel, N., Sunkavalli, K., Paris, S., Pfister, H.: Example-based video color grading. ACM Trans. Graph. **32**(4), 1–12 (2013)
7. Vazquezcorral, J., Bertalmio, M.: Color stabilization along time and across shots of the same scene, for one or several cameras of unknown specifications. IEEE Trans. Image Process. **23**(10), 4564–4575 (2014)

8. Pei, S., Hsiao, Y.: Simple effective image and video color correction using quaternion distance metric. In: Proceedings of IEEE International Conference Image Process, pp. 2920–2924 (2015)
9. Jin, L., Liu, H., Xu, X., Song, E.: Quaternion-based impulse noise removal from color video sequences. IEEE Trans. Circuits Syst. Video Technol. **23**(5), 741–755 (2013)
10. Xiao, X., Ma, L.: Gradient-preserving color transfer. Comput. Graph Forum. **28**(7), 1879–1886 (2009)
11. Papadakis, N., Provenzi, E., Caselles, V.: A variational model for histogram transfer of color images. IEEE Trans. Image Process. **20**(6), 1682–1695 (2011)
12. Niu, Y., Zheng, X., Zhao, T., Chen, J.: Visually consistent color correction for stereoscopic images and videos. IEEE Trans. Circuits Syst. Video Technol. **30**(3), 697–710 (2020)
13. Liu, S., Song, Z., Zhang, X., Zhu, T.: Progressive complex illumination image appearance transfer based on CNN. J. Vis. Commun. Image R. **64**, 1–11 (2019)
14. Liao, J., Yao, Y., Lu, Y., Hua, G., Kang, S.B.: Visual attribute transfer through deep image analogy. ACM Trans. Graph. **36**(4), article no. 120 (2017)
15. Zhu, T., Liu, S.: Detail-preserving arbitrary style transfer. In: Proceedings of the IEEE International Conference on Multimedia and Expo, pp. 1–6 (2020)
16. He, M., Liao, J., Yuan, L., Sander, P.V.: Neural color transfer between images. In: Proceedings of IEEE Conference on Computer Vision and Pattern Recognition, pp. 1–14 (2017)
17. Luan, F., Paris, S., Shechtman, E., Bala, K.: Deep photo style transfer. In: Proceedings of IEEE Conference on Computer Vision and Pattern Recognition (CVPR), pp. 6997–7005 (2017)
18. Zabaleta, I., Bertalmío, M.: Photorealistic style transfer for video. Sig. Process. Image Commun. **95**, 116240 (2021)
19. Liu, S, Zhu, T.: Structure-guided arbitrary style transfer for artistic image and video. IEEE Trans. Multimedia **23** (2021, early access). https://doi.org/10.1109/TMM.2021.3063605
20. Hogervorst, M.A., Toet, A.: Method for applying daytime colors to nighttime imagery in realtime. In: Proceedings of SPIE, pp. 6974–6984 (2013)
21. Hogervorst, M.A., Toet, A.: Fast natural color mapping for night-time imagery. Inf. Fusion **11**(2), 69–77 (2010)
22. Xue, S., Agarwala, A., Dorsey, J., Rushmeier, H.: Learning and applying color styles from feature films. Comput. Graph. Forum **32**(7), 255–264 (2013)
23. Wang, C.M., Huang, Y.H., Huang, M.L.: An effective algorithm for image sequence color transfer. Math. Comput. Model. **44**(7), 608–627 (2006)
24. Yao, C.H., Chang, C.Y., Chien, S.Y.: Example-based video color transfer. In: Proceedings of IEEE International Conference Multimedia Expo, pp. 1–6 (2015)
25. Jeong, J.Y., Kim, H.J., Wang, T.S.: Real-time video re-coloring algorithm considering the temporal color consistency for the color-blind. IEEE Trans. Consum. Electron. **58**(2), 721–729 (2012)
26. Gu, X., He, M., Leung, H., Gu, X.: Fast colorization for single-band thermal video sequences. Neurocomputing **17**(1), 1146–1157 (2016)
27. Liu, C., Freeman, W.T.: A high-quality video denoising algorithm based on reliable motion estimation. In: Proceedings of European Conference on Computer Vision, pp. 706–719 (2010)
28. Nguyen, R.M.H., Kim, S.J., Brown, M.S.: Illuminant aware gamut-based color transfer. Comput. Graph. Forum **33**(7), 319–328 (2014)

29. Chen, D., Liao, J., Yuan, L., Yu, N., Hua, G.: Coherent online video style transfer. In: Proceedings of IEEE Computer Vision and Pattern Recognition, pp. 1114–1123 (2017)
30. Aouaidjia, K., Sheng, B., Li, P., Kim, J., Feng, D.: Efficient body motion quantification and similarity evaluation using 3-D joints skeleton coordinates. IEEE Trans. Syst. Man Cybern. Syst. **51**(5), 2774–2788 (2021)
31. Lai, W.S., Huang, J.B., Wang, O., Shechtman, E., Yumer, E., Yang, M.H.: Learning blind video temporal consistency. In: Proceedings of the European Conference on Computer Vision (ECCV), pp. 170–185 (2018)
32. Wen, Y., Sheng, B., Li, P., Lin, W., Feng, D.: Deep color guided coarse-to-fine convolutional network cascade for depth image super-resolution. IEEE Trans. Image Process. **28**(2), 994–1006 (2019)

An Improved Advancing-front-Delaunay Method for Triangular Mesh Generation

Yufei Guo[1]([✉]), Xuhui Huang[1], Zhe Ma[1], Yongqing Hai[2], Rongli Zhao[1], and Kewu Sun[1]

[1] X Lab, The Second Academy of China Aerospace Science And Industry Corporation, Beijing 100854, China
yfguo@pku.edu.cn
[2] Department of Mechanics and Engineering Science, Peking University, Beijing 100871, China

Abstract. The triangular mesh is widely used in computer graphics. The advancing-front-Delaunay method is a mainstream method to generate the triangular mesh. However, it generates interior nodes on the basis of the segment front and needs to manage and update the generation segment front set carefully. This paper describes an improved advancing-front-Delaunay method that generates interior nodes based on the node front. The idea of node front can be implemented easily by our disk packing algorithm and does not need a complicated management strategy. Besides, unlike the traditional advancing-front-Delaunay method that generates interior node and the mesh at the same time, the method generates all the nodes firstly by the disk packing method, then generates the mesh. Hence, the method can be more efficient using these more efficient algorithms for a given fixed node-set to generate Delaunay triangular meshes or these more efficient algorithms with a carefully designed insertion sequence to insert the interior nodes. Four examples are given to show the effectiveness and robustness of the improved advancing-front-Delaunay method.

Keywords: Mesh generation · Advancing-front-delaunay method · Disk packing · Triangular mesh.

1 Introduction

Triangular meshes play an important role in many fields, such as computer graphics, finite element analysis, computer vision, biomedicine, virtual reality, and computer-aided design. The triangular mesh generation is an important topic in the field of mesh generation [1,2]. Considering the efficiency of the algorithm, the quality of the generated mesh, and the development history, the advancing front method, the Delaunay triangulation method, and the advancing-front-Delaunay method are currently popular mesh generation methods.

The advancing front method is a greedy algorithm that generates mesh nodes from boundaries to interior gradually and executes recursively. Each recursive

© Springer Nature Switzerland AG 2021
N. Magnenat-Thalmann et al. (Eds.): CGI 2021, LNCS 13002, pp. 477–487, 2021.
https://doi.org/10.1007/978-3-030-89029-2_37

process is divided into three steps: select a line segment from the generation segment front set which splits the meshed domain and unmeshed domain, and the selected segment is called the base segment as it will form the basis for the creation of a new triangle element; connect a new mesh node or an existing mesh node to the base segment to generate a high-quality triangle element; and update the generation segment front set and triangle elements. The advancing front method can generate high-quality mesh, but it involves a lot of geometric calculations and the algorithmic efficiency is low [3].

For a given non-overlapping point set $P = \{P_1, P_2, \cdots, P_n\}$ in the Euclidean 2D plane $\mathbb{R}^2$, the plane can be divided by a set of polygons $V = \{V_1, V_2, \cdots, V_n\}$ [4], as shown in Fig. 1a, where

$$V_i = x \in \mathbb{R}^2 : ||x - P_i|| < ||x - P_j||, \forall j \neq i \qquad (1)$$

and $||x - P||$ represents the distance from point x to point P. V_i represents a region that any point in it is nearer to the point P_i than to any other point in the given point set. V_i is called the Voronoi polygon whose boundaries are the perpendicular bisectors of the lines connecting node P_i and node P_j of neighboring polygons V_j. The collection of Voronoi polygon V is called the Dirichlet tessellation of the point set P or Voronoi diagram [5]. Delaunay [6] pointed out that a Delaunay triangulation corresponding to the Voronoi diagram can be obtained dually, as shown in Fig. 1b. The nodes of the Delaunay triangulation are the given point set. Delaunay triangulation has an important property that among all triangulations of a set of points in 2D, the Delaunay triangulation maximizes the minimum angle and minimizes the maximum angle of these triangulations. Based on this property, given a set of points with a reasonable distribution, a high-quality mesh can be obtained by constructing the Delaunay triangulation. The Delaunay triangulation method has a sound theoretical foundation and is very efficient. However, it only considers how to connect a given node set and how to generate nodes requires additional algorithms support. The quality of the generated mesh is greatly affected by the quality of the generated nodes.

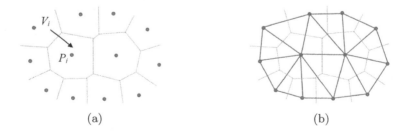

(a)   (b)

Fig. 1. Delaunay triangulation corresponding to the Voronoi diagram. (a) The Voronoi diagram. (b) A Delaunay triangulation.

Since the advancing front method can generate a higher quality mesh than the Delaunay triangulation method and the Delaunay triangulation method is faster and more robust than the advancing front method, a direct idea is to put them together to form an overall more efficient method, that is the advancing-front-Delaunay method, in which the robustness and speed of the Delaunay triangulation method and the quality in the generation of interior nodes of the advancing front method can all be retained [7–11]. These two methods can be put together in a natural manner such that the given mesh generation domain is partitioned into two regions: the unmeshed domain and the meshed domain. At the beginning, the unmeshed domain is a constrained Delaunay triangulation of the entire domain bounded by all the boundary segments. The boundary segments are seen as the initial generation segment front set. Based on a selected line segment as the base segment, an interior node is generated and inserted into the unmeshed domain following the Delaunay criterion. The meshed domain grows gradually by taking one triangle element at a time from the unmeshed domain as in the advancing front method until there is no more region remaining in the unmeshed domain. As interior nodes are generated by the advancing front method and the triangle elements are formed following the Delaunay criterion, the resulting triangular mesh is high-quality.

However, the advancing-front-Delaunay method still needs to manage and update the generation segment front set, and when there are a large number of segment fronts, the efficiency of the method will be affected. Moreover, the insertion of interior nodes is a dynamic process of the method, hence it can not use these more efficient algorithms for a given fixed node set to generate Delaunay triangular meshes, such as the Divide-and-Conquer algorithm [12]. And the insertion order is the generation order of the interior nodes of the method, hence it can not use these more efficient algorithms with a carefully designed insertion sequence to insert the interior nodes [13–17].

To address the above problems, an improved advancing-front-Delaunay method is proposed in this paper. The improvement of the method is to replace the segment front with the node front to generate interior nodes. It is like changing *the advancing-segment-front-Delaunay method* to *the advancing-node-front-Delaunay method*. The idea of node front can be implemented easily by a disk packing algorithm. The algorithm iterates each generated node as the base node and generates its neighborhood nodes. All interior nodes will be generated after traversing all generated nodes. Meanwhile, the node generation and node insertion are two independent processes in the method. Compared with the traditional advancing-front-Delaunay method, the method has the following advantages:

1. The method uses the idea of node front rather than segment front to generate interior nodes. It only needs to traversal the generated nodes sequentially and needs not to manage and update the generation front set. Hence, it is more efficient to generate the interior nodes.
2. Different from the traditional advancing-front-Delaunay method, which generates interior node and the mesh at the same time, the method generates all the interior nodes firstly then generates the mesh. Hence, the method can be more efficient using these more efficient algorithms for a given fixed node set to

generate Delaunay triangular meshes or these more efficient algorithms with a carefully designed insertion sequence to insert the interior nodes [13–17].

The rest of the paper is organized as follows. We start by introducing the idea of our method in Sect. 2 and then give a brief overview of our method in Sect. 3. The detail of node generation of the method is introduced in Sect. 4. After presenting some experimental results in Sect. 5, we conclude our method and mention some possible future research in Sect. 6.

2   The Idea of Our Method

Considering a uniform mesh, the advancing front method will identify an optimal interior node C for the base generation segment front Γ on where the interior node will form a regular triangular element with Γ without considering the influence of other elements and nodes, as shown in Fig. 2. When all the interior nodes are generated, an ideal case is that every interior node is surrounded by six nodes or six regular elements. In this case, a regular mesh will be generated. If we center disks of the same radii at the nodes, the set of disks will pack the domain compactly and uniformly, as shown in Fig. 3. A node surrounded by six nodes is corresponding to a disk surrounded by 6 disks.

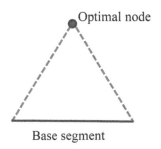

Fig. 2. An optimal interior node generation of the advancing front method.

Based on the above observation, we replace the idea of the segment front in the advancing front method with the idea of the node front. Our method iterates each generated node as the base front and generates its neighborhood nodes. All interior nodes will be generated after traversing all generated nodes. In this way, our method can avoid the problem of managing and updating the generation segment front set in the advancing front method which is some complicated. Meanwhile, the processes of node generation and node insertion can be implemented independently in our method. Hence, the method can use these more efficient algorithms for a given fixed node-set to generate Delaunay triangular meshes or these more efficient algorithms with a carefully designed insertion sequence to insert the interior nodes. Since nodes and disks correspond one to one, the problem of node generation can be seen as disk generation. This paper

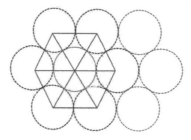

Fig. 3. A node surrounded by six nodes is corresponding to a disk surrounded by 6 disks.

focuses on how to traverse each disk to pack the surrounding disks compactly and uniformly. The disk packing needs to satisfy two criteria:

1. The disks should be packed as close to one another as possible so that the gaps between them are minimized. However, it is difficult to pack them densely for a graded mesh because the radius for a given disk is related to the corresponding position and does not always fit its neighbors. Hence, the center and radius of the generating disk have to be adjusted several times to obtain a dense packing.
2. There should be no or little overlapping between any two disks. If the distance between 2 centers of the disks is within 1.8 times of sum of the radii of the two disks, we call them overlapping disks.

3   Overall Method

The paper first introduces the overall process of the method, and then introduces the specific details of the method. At the beginning of the mesh generation, all the boundary nodes are seen as the initial generation node front set NS. Each node is selected from NS in turn as the base node to arrange its adjacent nodes, and all the neighbor nodes are recorded in NS too. Thereby, all the nodes will be generated after traversing all nodes. Then, a high-quality mesh will be generated by the Delaunay triangulation method and be optimized by a mesh optimization method. The essential steps for the generation of meshes over a 2D domain are given in the following.

- Step1. Generate all the nodes based on a disk packing algorithm.
- Step2. Generate a high-quality mesh using the efficient Divide and Conquer algorithm[12], which is suitable to generate Delaunay triangular meshes for a given fixed node set.
- Step3. Recover boundary.
  - Step3.1. Recover the boundary of the domain in DT.
  - Step3.2. Remove the elements in DT which are outer of the boundary of the domain.
- Step4. Optimize the DT.

4   Node Generation

In this section, we first focus on packing disks with a radius r for a uniform mesh with element size $2r$. For a given 2D bounded domain, we shelter disks at vertices first and then subdivide edges and shelter disks on edges. After the boundary is subdivided and covered with disks, the disks in the interior of the domain are sheltered, as shown in Fig. 4.

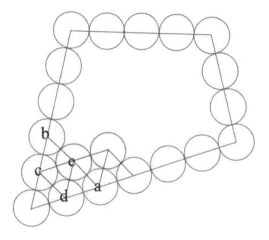

Fig. 4. Node generation by our disk packing algorithm.

Sheltering disks on vertices and edges are simple and similar to sheltering disks in the interior of the domain, hence we present the specific process for generating interior nodes. The initial generation node front set NS is composed of all the boundary nodes and will be updated during the packing process. Figure 4 shows that the boundary nodes have been generated and covered with blue disks, the center of the red disk is selected as the base node a, and the light blue disks are the generated neighbor disks for the red disk and their centers represent the generated neighbor nodes for a. Nodes within a distance of $4r$ from the base node may determine the positions of the newly generated nodes together with the base node. As can be seen from Fig. 4, The newly generated node e may be generated by the base node a and the existing nodes b, c, or d. Based on the observation, we first traverse all nodes within $4r$ from the base node and make node pairs with the base node and these nodes respectively. Then we cover the two nodes from each node pair with two disks with a radius of r and place a new disk tangent to the two disks. The center of the newly placed disk is corresponding to the position of the newly generated node. A node pair can generate two disks with no constraints. However, like the traditional advancing-front-Delaunay method, the newly generated node needs to determine whether to satisfy the no overlapping criteria, and it will not be accepted if it is too close to other nodes.

The method only needs to traversal the generated nodes sequentially as the base front and generates its neighborhood nodes. All interior nodes will be generated after traversing all generated nodes. Compared with the traditional advancing-front-Delaunay method, the method needs not to select the base elaborately and needs not to manage and update the generation segment front set. Hence, it is more efficient to generate the interior nodes.

We then introduce to generate a grading mesh with a specified element size. The sizes of the triangular elements are controlled by packing disks with different radii. For the base disk pair that is considered to generate new nodes or disks, we denoted the two disks as S_1 and S_2. The radii of the two disks are determined according to a given size control function. We use the parameter γ described below to show how close two disks are

$$\gamma_{S_1 S_2} = min(\lambda, 1/\lambda) \quad with \quad \lambda(r_1 + r_2)/d \tag{2}$$

where r_1 and r_2 are the radii of the disk S_1 and disk S_2, and d is the distance between the two nodes or the two centers of disk S_1 and disk S_2. The bigger $\gamma_{S_1 S_2}$, the closer are the two disks. When $d = r_1 + r_2$, that is $\gamma_{S_1 S_2} = 1$, the two disks are touching each other.

A new disk S can be packed to S_1 and S_2 following the steps.

- Step1. Pack a disk S at point P tangent to S_1 and S_2 and suppose $r_s = (r_1 + r_2)$, where r_s denotes the radius of disk S.
- Step2. Calculate the radius r at point P according to the size control function.
- Step3. Calculate $\gamma = \gamma_{S_1 S}\gamma_{S_2 S}$ at point P using Eq. (2).
- Step4. If $\gamma > 0.90$, the disk at point P can be fitted to disk S_1 and disk S_2, end; otherwise.
- Step5. Move the disk S to a new point P tangent to S_1 and S_2 and suppose $r_s = r$, where r_s denotes the radius of disk S.
- Step6. Go to step3.

According to the above procedure, the disk S moves towards a suitable point P and is tangent with disk S_1 and disk S_2 gradually as shown in Fig. 5.

5   Results and Discussion

Four meshes are chosen to demonstrate the performance of our improved advancing-front-Delaunay method and the results are discussed in this section. We program our method and a traditional advancing-front-Delaunay method in C++. For surface meshes, we compare our method with NetGen [19] which is a famous and state-of-the-art mesh generator that has been developed for many years. Table 1 shows the statistics of the example meshes. We use the angle and aspect ratio quality metric [18] to describe the triangle quality. Aspect ratio quality metric is as follows:

$$\gamma = (4\sqrt{3} \times S)/(l_1{}^2 + l_2{}^2 + l_3{}^2) \tag{3}$$

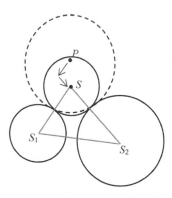

Fig. 5. Node generation for a grading mesh.

Table 1. The statistics of the four examples.

Model	Nodes	time/(s)	Min. $\theta/(°)$	Avg. Min. $\theta/(°)$	Min. γ	Avg. γ
Example 1(our method)	217	0.006	59.911	59.960	1.000	1.000
Example 1(traditional method)	217	0.009	59.934	59.945	1.000	1.000
Example 2(our method)	339	0.009	33.751	53.018	0.776	0.971
Example 2(traditional method)	336	0.013	36.786	52.143	0.784	0.965
Example 3(our method)	1407	0.050	29.857	52.442	0.654	0.964
Example 3(NetGen)	1338	0.097	25.132	51.809	0.601	0.932
Example 4(our method)	3936	0.162	25.190	52.239	0.537	0.961
Example 4(NetGen)	3651	0.286	19.457	51.517	0.392	0.945

where l_i represents the length of $i-th$ edge of the triangular element and S represents area of the triangle element. The worst value of this metric is 0 and the optimal value of the metric is 1.

Example 1 shows a planar regular triangular mesh with 217 nodes. It can be seen in Fig. 6 that our method can generate high-quality regular mesh for this kind of planar domain with regular boundaries as the traditional advancing-front-Delaunay method. However, our method is more efficient.

Example 2 is a planar grading triangular mesh with 339 nodes as shown in Fig. 7. The variable size is specified by a distance function. The disk packing algorithm is applied to generate closely packed disks of specified sizes to cover the entire domain as shown in Fig. 6. By treating the centers of disks as node positions, a grading triangular mesh is obtained by our improved advancing-front-Delaunay method as shown in Fig. 7. It can be seen that our method can still generate a high-quality mesh efficiently.

The next examples are about the application of planar meshing to curved surfaces. We use the two examples to show the performance of our disk packing algorithm. In general, we can extend the disk packing in a plane to the sphere packing in a surface. Figure 8a and 8b and Fig. 9a and 9b show the sphere packings and the corresponding triangular meshes. The surface meshes are generated by an advancing front method. It can be seen that sphere packing algorithm can

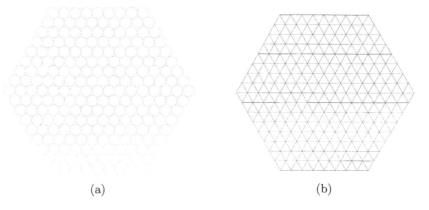

(a)   (b)

Fig. 6. Example 1. (a) Disk packing. (b) Final triangular mesh.

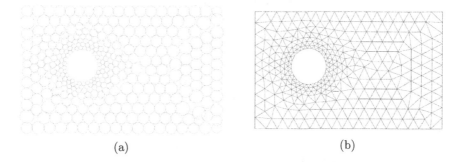

(a)   (b)

Fig. 7. Example 2. (a) Disk packing. (b) Final triangular mesh.

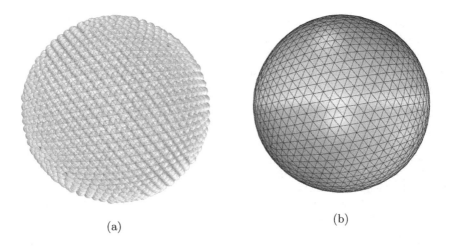

(a)   (b)

Fig. 8. Example 3. (a) Sphere packing. (b) Final triangular mesh.

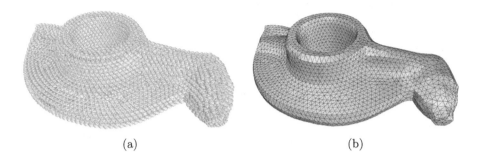

(a)   (b)

Fig. 9. Example 4. (a) Sphere packing. (b) Final triangular mesh.

still generate a high-quality node configuration and a high-quality mesh can be generated by the node configuration. The results show that our method is more effective and efficient compared with NetGen.

The proposed method uses the idea of node front rather than segment front to generate interior nodes. It only needs to traversal the generated nodes sequentially and needs not to manage and update the generation segment front set. Hence, it is more efficient to generate the interior nodes. The method generates all the interior nodes firstly then generates the mesh. Hence, the method can be more efficient using these more efficient algorithms for a given fixed node-set to generate Delaunay triangular meshes or these more efficient algorithms with a carefully designed insertion sequence to insert the interior nodes [13–17]. Overall, the proposed method in this paper has an efficiency advantage and can generate a high-quality mesh.

6   Conclusions and Future Research

In this paper, an improved advancing-front-Delaunay method for the generation of finite element meshes is presented. based on a disk packing algorithm, a high-quality mesh can be generated efficiently. The extension of the method for mesh generation based on a sphere packing algorithm over a three-dimensional domain is under investigation.

References

1. Shewchuk, J.R.: Delaunay refinement algorithms for triangular mesh generation. Comput. Geom. Theor. Appl. **47**(1–3), 741–778 (2014)
2. Liu, F., Feng, R.: Automatic triangular grid generation on a free-form surface using a particle self-organizing system. Eng. Comput. **36**(1), 377–389 (2019). https://doi.org/10.1007/s00366-019-00705-4
3. Lohner, R., Parikh, P.: Generation of three-dimensional unstructured grids by the advancing-front method. Int. J. Numer. Meth. Fluids **8**(10), 1135–1149 (1988)

4. Dirichlet, P.G.L., Kronecker, L.G.: lejeune dirichlets werke: Ueber die reduction der positiven quadratischen formen mit drei unbestimmten ganzen zahlen. Journal Fr Die Rne Und Angewandte Mathematik **1850**(40), 209–227 (1850)
5. Voronoi, G.: Nouvelles applications des paramtres continus la thorie des formes quadratiques. J. Reine Angew. Math. **133**, 97–178 (1907)
6. Delaunay, B.: Sur la sphere vide. a la memoire de georges voronoi, Bulletin De Lacad & Eacutemie Des Sciences De Lurss. Classe Des Sciences Math & Eacutematiques Et Na 793–800 (1934)
7. Yu, F., Zeng, Y., Guan, Z., Lo, S.: A robust delaunay-aft based parallel method for the generation of large-scale fully constrained meshes. Comput. Struct. **228**, 106–170 (2020)
8. Borouchaki, H., Laug, P., George, P.-L.: Parametric surface meshing using a combined advancing front generalized delaunay approach. Int. J. Numer. Methods Eng. **49**(1–2), 233–259 (2000)
9. Mavriplis, D.J.: An advancing front delaunay triangulation algorithm designed for robustness. J. Comput. Phys. **117**(1), 90101 (1995)
10. Li, S.S., Shi, J.Z.: Algorithms for automatic generating interior nodal points and delaunay triangulation using advancing front technique. Commun. Numer. Methods Eng. **22**(5), 467–474 (2006)
11. El-Hamalawi, A.: A 2d combined advancing front-delaunay mesh generation scheme. Finite Elem. Anal. Des. **40**(9/10), 967–989 (2004)
12. Dwyer, R.A.: A faster divide-and-conquer algorithm for constructing delaunay triangulations. Algorithmica **2**(1–4), 137–151 (1987)
13. Zhou, S., Jones, C.B.: Hcpo: an efficient insertion order for incremental delaunay triangulation. Inf. Process. Lett. **93**(1), 37–42 (2005)
14. Su, T., Wang, W., Lv, Z., Wu, W., Li, X.: Rapid delaunay triangulation for randomly distributed point cloud data using adaptive hilbert curve. Comput. Graph. **54**, 65–74 (2015)
15. Buchin, K.: Constructing delaunay triangulations along space filling curves. In: European Symposium on Algorithms (2009)
16. Lo, S.H.: Delaunay triangulation of non-uniform point distributions by means of multi-grid insertion. Finite Elements in Analysis & Design **63**(4), 8–22 (2013)
17. Wang, W., Su, T., Wang, G.: Rapid 2d delaunay triangulation algorithm for random distributed point cloud data **27**, 1653–1660 (2015)
18. Munson, T.: Mesh shape-quality optimization using the inverse mean-ratio metric. Math. Program. **110**(3), 561–590 (2007)
19. SchoBerl, J.: Netgen an advancing front 2d/3d-mesh generator based on abstract rules. Comput. Vis. Sci. **1**, 41–52 (1997)

Robotics and Vision

Does Elderly Enjoy Playing Bingo with a Robot? A Case Study with the Humanoid Robot Nadine

Nidhi Mishra[1](✉), Gauri Tulsulkar[1], Hanhui Li[1],
Nadia Magnenat Thalmann[1,2], Lim Hwee Er[3], Lee Mei Ping[3],
and Cheng Siok Khoong[4]

[1] Institute for Media Innovation, Nanyang Technological University,
Singapore, Singapore
[2] MIRALab, University of Geneva, Geneva, Switzerland
[3] Goshen Consultancy Services, Singapore, Singapore
[4] Bright Hill Evergreen Home, Singapore, Singapore

Abstract. There are considerable advancements in medical health care in recent years, resulting in a rising older population. As the workforce for such a population is not keeping pace, there is an urgent need to address this problem. Having robots to stimulating recreational activities for older adults can reduce the workload for caretakers and give them time to address the emotional needs of the elderly. In this paper, we investigate the effects of the humanoid social robot Nadine as an activity host for the elderly. We propose to evaluate this by placing Nadine humanoid social robot in a nursing home as a caretaker where she hosts bingo game. We record sessions with and without Nadine to understand the difference and acceptance of these two scenarios. We use computer vision methods to analyse the activities of the elderly to detect emotions and their involvement in the game. Our results present positive enforcement during recreational activity, Bingo, in the presence of Nadine. This research is in line with all ethical recommendations as shown in our Annex.

Keywords: Social robotics · Social Assistive Robotics (SAR) · Robot companions · Social robot Nadine · Human-humanoid interaction · Computer vision · Graphical human-computer interaction

1 Introduction

Many nursing and elderly homes face the challenges of balancing costs and quality due to an increased demand for long-term care for the elderly. Besides, most nursing homes focus on medical and nursing procedures because they lack human resources and expertise to address the psychosocial well-being demands. As such, there is greater demand for quality services and resources, in addition to the existing challenges of human-resource shortages, limited expertise, and rising

© Springer Nature Switzerland AG 2021
N. Magnenat-Thalmann et al. (Eds.): CGI 2021, LNCS 13002, pp. 491–503, 2021.
https://doi.org/10.1007/978-3-030-89029-2_38

costs of healthcare and social care. To bridge the gap caused by resource short-ages, we propose to deploy a social robot in nursing homes, taking advantage of AI technologies.

This research aims to apply the human-robot interaction (HRI) technology to draw the attention of the elderly and stimulate their interest. As discussed in [9] entertainment by robots constitutes a relevant and promising area of appli-cation in HRI that needs to address many different populations, including older adults. [2], and [1] discuss those game activities with robots that can help the cognitive stimulation of the elderly. Bingo is one such fun and popular activ-ity that triggers long-term memory, making it one of the more stimulating brain games for the elderly. In this paper, we like to present a human-robot interaction study where a Humanoid Social Robot Nadine [24] facilitates multiple sessions of Bingo games for a group of elderly.

Before Nadine was deployed at the nursing home, the nursing home's care staff used to host the Bingo sessions. We recorded two of these sessions as our baseline for the study. We studied several Bingo sessions between profes-sional care staff and the elderly, using them to define appropriate and proactive behaviour in Nadine. We developed and deployed a module that helped Nadine host the Bingo game. Nadine can carry the game by calling out the Bingo num-bers, verifying winning Bingo players, and celebrating with the winners.

To obtain a comprehensive understanding of the effects of Nadine, we use objective tools for data analysis. The objective tools are based on cutting-edge computer vision techniques, such as Deep Neural Networks (DNNs), to automat-ically evaluate the emotional states and the residents' quality of engagement.

The rest of the paper is organized as follows: We provide related work for humanoid robots assisting in the nursing home. in Sect. 2. In Sect. 3, we explain the experimental setup and adaptation technique of the Nadine social robot at the nursing home. We also describe the ethical protocol we have followed as well as the Covid-19 prevention measures. We include the details of our data collection methods, and we provide details of our framework to analyze the data collected in Sect. 4. In Sect. 5, we present and discuss the data analysis's experimental results. We provide conclusions in Sect. 6.

2   Related Work

Efforts have been made to enhance the overall mental health of the elderly by providing robots as companions. These robots can help the elderly live in their own homes and communities, safely and independently, by providing assistance or services [13]. Participants in the nursing homes engaged more frequently in the presence of different types of stimuli, such as moderate levels of sound and small groups of people [8].

Social assistive-robot-based systems with the abilities to perform activities, play cognitive games, and socialize, can be used to stimulate the physical, cog-nitive, and social conditions of older adults and restrain deterioration of their cognitive state [20].

Tangy robot was used to facilitate a multi-player Bingo game with seven elderly residents in a LTC facility [15, 17, 18, 29]. The robot would autonomously call out the bingo numbers and check individual cards of the players to provide help or let them know if they had won Bingo. The results of the studies showed that they had high levels of compliance and engagement during the games facilitated by the robot. Tangy was humanlike, however the appearance was not that of a realistic humanoid. The study conducted was for a short duration, which resulted in us being unable to see if the robot could hold the interest over a course of time. Also, the number of participants in each session was low, which raises the question of "if Tangy can hold the interest of a larger group?".

Interactions with Stevie the robot can improve the enjoyability of the games and can be used for cognitive stimulation by playing Bingo for the elderly [27]. The robot, Matilda was used to improve the emotional wellbeing of the elderly in three care facilities with 70 participants in Australia [12]. The authors found that a Bingo game activity with Matilda positively engaged the elderly and increased their social interaction. Some participants wanted Matilda to participate in all the group activities as she rewarded the winner by singing and dancing.

Paro robot was placed at nursery homes [6], and in everyday elderly care [26]. These studies found that the extended use of Paro brought about a steady increase in the physical interaction between the elderly and the robot and also led to a growing willingness among the participants to interact with it. An increase in sociability within the group of elderly as well as other social benefits [25]. When Paro took part in group activities, it positively influenced mood change, reduced loneliness, and resulted in a statistically significant increase in interactions.

Silbot robot was hosting Bingo as part of a brain fitness instructor in an elderly care facility in Denmark [5]. The author had highlighted hardware and software problems and mentioned battery problems, usability problems, and multiple use case issues. It was studied for two years long, and many of the issues with having for the long term were highlighted, which can be the base of our study.

Table 1. Summary of the robots for recreational activity for elderly care where (a) Humanoid realistic appearance, (b) Residents information, (c) Empathy, (d) Facial expressions, (e) Gestures, (f) Multilingual, (g) Computer Vision based analysis, (h) Internet of Things and (i) Gazing

Paper	(a)	(b)	(c)	(d)	(e)	(f)	(g)	(h)	(i)
Pepper [15]	X	X	✓	✓	✓	✓	X	✓	✓
Zora [21]	X	X	✓	N/A	✓	N/A	X	✓	✓
Tangy [17]	X	X	✓	✓	✓	N/A	X	✓	✓
Silbot [5]	X	✓	✓	✓	✓	N/A	X	✓	✓
Zora [11]	X	X	✓	✓	✓	X	X	✓	✓
Zora [30]	X	X	✓	✓	✓	X	X	✓	✓
Stevie [27]	X	✓	✓	X	✓	X	X	✓	✓
Matilda [12]	X	✓	✓	X	✓	N/A	X	X	✓
Nadine	✓	✓	✓	✓	✓	✓	✓	✓	✓

In the Table 1, we classify the available state of the art robots based on similar studies with robots conducting a recreational activity where '✓' indicates the presence and 'X' indicates the absence of those characteristics.

In most studies, robots used are not realistic as Nadine humanoid robot. Nadine can emote natural human communication with its humanlike features, as reported in [3]. Nadine can give facial expression, respond with gestures, make eye contact with the elderly, and compare these with other robots. Studies have shown that the interaction is stimulating with face and arm movements and could arouse curiosity and interest [13]. We also classify Whether the robot can speak and understand speech; if yes, is it multilingual? Next, for functionalities, we address different aspects of the vision-based capabilities of Robots. We study whether the robot can understand the environment to gaze at the elderly and understand their facial emotions. We examine if previously studied robots could control and interact with the devices (such as TV, speakers, temperature control, etc.) to facilitate the recreational activity. Further, our classification builds upon the analysis method used for the statistical results in previous studies. Specifically, if they were, AI or ML enabled.

The above parameters are deduced from the table that has not been taken into account in the literature so far. We believe that our study could be a step forward in introducing the humanoid social Nadine robot with humanlike characteristics in appearance and its mimic of human behaviour.

3   Experimental Setup

For our study we used Nadine Humanoid robot. Nadine was seated in a ward's activity area in the nursing home, where she hosts Bingo games to interact with the elderly. Nadine is a socially intelligent, realistic humanoid robot with natural skin, hair, and appearance. She has 27 DOF, which enables her to make facial movements and gesticulate effectively, as documented in [32] and [4]. Nadine can be considered a part of human-assistive technology [19], as she can assist people over a continuous period without any breaks. She has previously worked at different places that required her to work for long hours [22].

Nadine's architecture consists of three layers: perception, processing, and interaction. Nadine receives audio and visual stimuli from microphones, 3D cameras, and web cameras to perceive user characteristics and her environment, sent to the processing layer. The processing layer receives all results about the environment from the perception layer and acts upon them. This layer includes various submodules, such as dialogue processing, affective system, and Nadine's memory of previous encounters with users. Finally, the action layer consists of a dedicated robot controller, including emotion expression, lip synchronization, and gaze generation. Nadine can recognize people she has met before and engage in a flowing conversation.

3.1 Adaptation

The studies [23] and [14] stated that most robots designed for the elderly do not fulfil the needs and requirements to perform their best. For Nadine to perform her best at nursing homes, we updated some previous models and developed new modules recommended in previous studies [7] (Fig. 1).

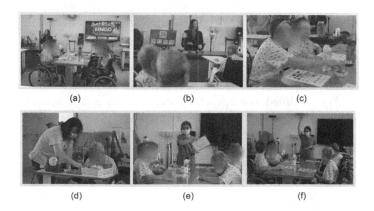

Fig. 1. Nadine hosting bingo session VS Care-staff hosting bingo session. (a) Nadine starting Bingo with Encouragement, (b) Nadine displaying number on the TV, (c) Elderly pressing buzzer on getting Bingo, (d) Care-staff and elderly Start running Bingo, (e) Care-staff going to each elderly table to announce number and (f) Care-staff raising hand for elderly on getting Bingo

Bingo Game: Before Nadine deployment at the nursing home, care staff use to host bingo sessions for the elderly. They would announce the number and use a small whiteboard to display the number for residents with hearing impairment. To do the same task of hosting the Bingo game, a new module was developed. This module enables Nadine to do the following:

– Start the session with greetings and weather information.
– Call out the bingo numbers in English and Mandarin.
– Call numbers in specific time duration and repetitions.
– Enables her to display the current number and four previous number on the TV screen.
– The numbers called out are also accompanied by hand gestures, facial expressions, gazing, and background music.
– It also allows care staff to control and customize Nadine's Bingo sessions using an attached touch screen.
– Let's Nadine verify winning players and applaud them.

Fabricated in-house buzzers were provided to the residents to press when they win the game. Nadine also played a cheering sound upon confirming a Bingo call from the residents.

Update in Nadine's Existing Module: As a social humanoid robot, Nadine has an emotion engine that controls her emotions, personality, and mood during the interaction, enabling her to perceive the situation (user and environment) and adjust her emotions and behaviour accordingly. As a result, Nadine can generate different emotions such as pleasure, arousal, and dominance. For Nadine to perform best at nursing homes, she needs to appear patient and show no negativity or anger. Therefore, Nadine should exhibit a positive temperament only. A configuration file was set to different parameters that allow Nadine to stay positive and behave accordingly, even when the resident is frustrated, angry or upset with her.

Another important aspect is to reveal positive emotions in Nadine's speech synthesis output. This mainly relates to changing the pitch, tone, and speed modulations. We modified the speech synthesizer to adapt speech output so that Nadine speaks slower and louder and in a low tone to make it easier for residents to understand her.

3.2 Participants

Twenty-nine participants aged 60 years above participated in our research. The experiment took place at Bright Hill Evergreen Nursing Home in Singapore. NTU Institutional Review Board has approved this study. A detailed consent form was signed before the onset of the procedure, followed by a detailed explanation of the experiment. We ensured that our participants had no previous experience with robots or any advanced technology. All the sessions were monitored by nursing home care staff. Overall, we recorded 24 sessions with Nadine hosting Bingo and 2 with care-staff hosting Bingo.

4 Data Collection and Analysis

To fully comprehend the effects of Nadine's presence in the nursing home, the whole session was recorded by five cameras from different angles. Objective tools based on cutting-edge computer vision techniques were considered. We used deep neural networks (DNNs) to evaluate the emotional and physical states of the elderly automatically. The following three evaluation metrics were focused on:

- *Happiness*, which is the satisfaction level of residents during the Bingo game.
- *Movement*, which reflects Nadine's effect on the physical movement of the elderly during the game.
- *Activity*, which is the overall care staff physical movement during the Bingo game hosted by Nadine.

To provide a quantitative analysis concerning these three metrics, the advantages of DNNs in efficient video processing were exploited. Particularly, we applied four different networks for this study: a face detector[1], an expression

---

[1] http://dlib.net/.

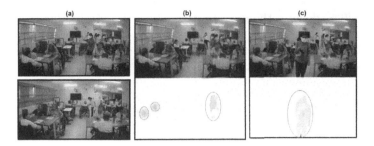

Fig. 2. Example results from computer vision methods. (a) Elderly faces detected in red box with smiling faces in green box, (b) Elderly body movement in three small patches and (c) staff movement in one patch (Color figure online)

recognizer, an action detector[2] and an optical flow estimator [28]. The roles and detailed implementations of these networks are as follows:

The face detector estimates the locations of faces in a given frame. Moreover, as all residents are in wheelchairs, their relative locations can be inferred based on their face locations. Also, only elderly faces are detected since the nursing care staff were wearing medical masks throughout their intervention in Nadine's Bingo sessions. We adopted the Dlib library with its pre-trained convolutional neural network (CNN) to implement the face detector.

The expression recognizer categorizes the expression of a detected face. We consider two classes in our case, i.e., smiling and neutral, and constructed a CNN with ResNet-50 [10] as the backbone. The expression recognizer is trained on the CelebA dataset [16] until convergence.

The action detector is a method to measure the motions and actions of the detected faces. It generates action proposals, which are the locations and confidences of detecting an action. We implement the action detector based on the pre-trained temporal segment network [31] provided in the MMAction2 library. The action detector informs us of the movement of the elderly during the Bingo game session as the face detector detected only their faces.

The optical flow estimator aims at discovering moving targets. We propose to estimate dense optical flow via the recurrent all-pairs field transformation network. At this moment, for an arbitrary region in each frame, the average magnitude of the estimated optical flow in the region can be used to measure the intensity of movement of care staff during the Bingo game sessions.

With the above DNNs, we are now ready to define the quantitative measures of *Happiness*, *Movement* and *Activity*:

Happiness is closely related to expressions of smiling and laughing. Hence, given a target video of L frames we define group happiness h as:

$$h = \frac{1}{L} \sum_{l=1}^{L} \frac{1}{n_l} \sum_{t=1}^{n_l} p_t, \tag{1}$$

---

[2] https://github.com/open-mmlab/mmaction2.

where $p_t \in [0, 1]$ denotes the probability of the t-th detected face in l-th frame belonging to the smiling class, which is estimated by the expression recognizer.

Movement of elderly is defined using action detector in the following equation where d_t is the confidence of detecting an action:

$$b = \frac{1}{L} \sum_{l=1}^{L} \frac{1}{n_l} \sum_{t=1}^{n_l} d_t \qquad (2)$$

For *Activity* of the care staff, we use the optical flow estimator as following equation where o_t is the average magnitude of optical flow:

$$f = \frac{1}{L} \sum_{l=1}^{L} \frac{1}{n_l} \sum_{t=1}^{n_l} o_t \qquad (3)$$

Using the above analyses (example shown in Fig. 2), we obtained the data for every video across all sessions and further studied it using statistical methods to get meaningful comparisons.

5   Results

In order to determine whether the presence of Nadine hosting bingo games has any effect on the elderly, the video material is analyzed. Four aspects of the video material (smile, neutral, body score, optical flow) were compared between the sessions in which Nadine hosted the games and the sessions in which the caretakers hosted the games. After cleaning the footage, there were 24 sessions with 29 elderly participating in each game in which Nadine was the host and 2 sessions in which the caretakers hosted the games. For each of the sessions, there were multiple camera angles that generated the footage. The analyses were conducted by comparing all the footage from each of the available cameras without compressing them into single averages for the sessions.

Table 2. Descriptive statistics of the relevant variables in the two situations.

Variable	Situation	Mean	Standard deviation	SD error mean
Smile	Nadine present	0.019	0.015	0.002
	Nadine absent	0.010	0.006	0.002
Neutral	Nadine present	0.947	0.179	0.024
	Nadine absent	0.990	0.006	0.002
Body score	Nadine present	0.154	0.053	0.007
	Nadine absent	0.172	0.015	0.005
Optical flow	Nadine present	0.181	0.133	0.018
	Nadine absent	0.288	0.081	0.029

To compare the scores for when Nadine hosted the games and the sessions in which the caretakers hosted the games, an independent samples t-test was conducted. The test results can be seen in Table 3, while the means and the standard deviations of the four variables in the two situations can be seen in Table 2. Before conducting the t-tests, Levene's test of equality of variance was conducted to check for the assumption of homoscedasticity. It was determined that two of the variables had unequal variance (variables smile and body score). Therefore, for these two variables, modified degrees of freedom were used.

Table 3. Results of the t-tests.

Variable	t	df	Sig. (2-tailed)	Mean difference
Smile	3.341	23.122	0.003	0.009
Neutral	−0.678	63	0.500	−0.043
Body score	−2.123	38.275	0.040	−0.019
Optical flow	−2.211	63	0.031	−0.107

Variable	Std. error difference	95% confidence interval of the difference	
		Lower	Upper
Smile	0.003	0.004	0.015
Neutral	0.064	−0.171	0.084
Body score	0.009	−0.036	−0.001
Optical flow	0.049	−0.204	−0.010

As can be seen from Table 3, three of the variables showed significant differences between the two situations: the smile variable was significantly higher in the Nadine group, while the body score and the optical flow variables were higher in the no-Nadine group. There were no differences in the neutral measurement between the two groups.

In order to determine whether or not the reactions of the elderly changed through time, bivariate correlations were calculated between the four variables and the serial number of the session. The higher the serial number is, the later the session was, so a correlation would imply a linear change in the variables with time. The results of the correlational analysis are presented in Table 4.

Table 4. Bivariate correlations between serial number of the session and the four variables.

Variable	Pearson correlation	Significance
Smile	0.249	0.062
Neutral	−0.241	0.071
Body score	−0.069	0.609
Optical flow	0.113	0.403

6   Conclusion

In this study, the effects of a humanoid robot, Nadine, on the behaviour of elderly in a nursing home were investigated. The sessions and tracked through video material obtained from several different angles in the nursing home.

The results indicated three significant differences in the bingo sessions in which Nadine was present compared to those in which she was not. The elderly was smiling more, they were moving around less, and the optical flow, which primarily relates to how many nursing home's care staff had to move, was also lower. Therefore, it can be concluded that the situation in the nursing home was better when Nadine was present: the residents were calmer and happier, while the staff had less work to do. This is in line with previous research [7–11], all of which have shown the potential positive effects of employing robotic assistance in nursing homes. Since Nadine has a humanoid appearance and the ability to communicate, read and exert facial expressions related to emotions, it is logical to assume that her presence can improve the states of the residents of nursing homes while simultaneously unloading the nursing home staff. This study confirms that this may be the case since all the changes in the measured variables between the situations in which Nadine was present and those in which she was not point in that direction.

On the other hand, there were no significant changes in the variables through time. This may be due to the nature of the variables: since the effects of Nadine are that the elderly is more concentrated, happier, and less needy (seen through the lower movement of the staff), it is plausible that these effects did not change over time. Furthermore, this means that the positive effects of Nadine's presence can be seen very early and that no period of adaptation is needed to achieve the changes. Therefore, her presence can bear immediate positive changes in a nursing home or a similar facility.

7   Discussion and Future Work

Our experiments demonstrate the need for socially assistive robots to operate in environments with multiple users. As this study shows, social robots can support overloaded care staff during recreational activities. In further research, we will develop a multi-party interaction system. Our findings also provide an excellent opportunity to design and develop a mobile social robot that increases accessibility and interaction opportunities. A roving robot could serve as an enhancement to the workforce by moving around to generate more personal engagement and interaction.

The realism of Nadine's appearance and interactions are of paramount importance for her usage in human interactions, especially amongst the elderly. Since they are not used to technology, it is beneficial to bridge this gap by using robots who look like humans for more natural and common communication. In these situations, all the benefits of having people do a particular job can be combined with the benefits of using robots, which leads to the best possible outcomes for both users and organizations. That is why the research on humanoid robots is so important and why it needs to be developed further. Our study, which showed that the usage of Nadine in a bingo sessions setting is very beneficial to the residents of the nursing home, is a step in that direction. Future studies should continue to investigate these issues and determine all the settings in which humanoid robots' usage could be an asset for improving the quality of life of the elderly.

References

1. Agrigoroaie, R., Tapus, A.: The outcome of a week of intensive cognitive stimulation in an elderly care setup: a pilot test. In: 2018 27th IEEE International Symposium on Robot and Human Interactive Communication (RO-MAN), pp. 814–819. IEEE (2018)
2. Agrigoroaie, R., Tapus, A.: Physiological differences depending on task performed in a 5-day interaction scenario designed for the elderly: a pilot study. In: Ge, S.S., et al. (eds.) ICSR 2018. LNCS (LNAI), vol. 11357, pp. 192–201. Springer, Cham (2018). https://doi.org/10.1007/978-3-030-05204-1_19
3. Baka, E., Vishwanath, A., Mishra, N., Vleioras, G., Thalmann, N.M.: "Am I talking to a human or a robot?": a preliminary study of human's perception in human-humanoid interaction and its effects in cognitive and emotional states. In: Gavrilova, M., Chang, J., Thalmann, N.M., Hitzer, E., Ishikawa, H. (eds.) CGI 2019. LNCS, vol. 11542, pp. 240–252. Springer, Cham (2019). https://doi.org/10.1007/978-3-030-22514-8_20
4. Beck, A., Zhijun, Z., Magnenat-Thalmann, N.: Motion control for social behaviors. In: Magnenat-Thalmann, N., Yuan, J., Thalmann, D., You, B.-J. (eds.) Context Aware Human-Robot and Human-Agent Interaction. HIS, pp. 237–256. Springer, Cham (2016). https://doi.org/10.1007/978-3-319-19947-4_11
5. Blond, L.: Studying robots outside the lab: HRI as ethnography. Paladyn J. Behav. Robot. **10**(1), 117–127 (2019). https://doi.org/10.1515/pjbr-2019-0007
6. Chang, W., Šabanovic, S., Huber, L.: Use of seal-like robot PARO in sensory group therapy for older adults with dementia. In: 2013 8th ACM/IEEE International Conference on Human-Robot Interaction (HRI), pp. 101–102 (2013)
7. Chang, W.L., Šabanović, S.: Exploring Taiwanese nursing homes as product ecologies for assistive robots. In: 2014 IEEE International Workshop on Advanced Robotics and its Social Impacts, pp. 32–37. IEEE (2014)
8. Cohen-Mansfield, J., Dakheel-Ali, M., Marx, M.S.: Engagement in persons with dementia: the concept and its measurement. Am. J. Geriatr. Psychiatry **17**(4), 299–307 (2009)
9. Correia, F., Alves-Oliveira, P., Petisca, S., Paiva, A., et al.: Social and entertainment robots for older adults (2017)
10. He, K., Zhang, X., Ren, S., Sun, J.: Deep residual learning for image recognition. In: Proceedings of European Conference on Computer Vision, pp. 770–778 (2016)
11. Huisman, C., Kort, H.: Two-year use of care robot Zora in Dutch nursing homes: an evaluation study. Healthcare **7**, 31 (2019). Multidisciplinary Digital Publishing Institute
12. Khosla, R., Chu, M.T.: Embodying care in Matilda: an affective communication robot for emotional wellbeing of older people in Australian residential care facilities. ACM Trans. Manag. Inf. Syst. (TMIS) **4**(4), 1–33 (2013)

13. Law, M., et al.: Developing assistive robots for people with mild cognitive impairment and mild dementia: a qualitative study with older adults and experts in aged care. BMJ Open **9**(9), e031937 (2019)
14. Lee, H.R., Tan, H., Šabanović, S.: That robot is not for me: addressing stereotypes of aging in assistive robot design. In: 2016 25th IEEE International Symposium on Robot and Human Interactive Communication (RO-MAN), pp. 312–317. IEEE (2016)
15. Li, J., Louie, W.Y.G., Mohamed, S., Despond, F., Nejat, G.: A user-study with tangy the bingo facilitating robot and long-term care residents. In: 2016 IEEE International Symposium on Robotics and Intelligent Sensors (IRIS), pp. 109–115. IEEE (2016)
16. Liu, Z., Luo, P., Wang, X., Tang, X.: Large-scale CelebFaces attributes (CelebA) dataset (2018). Accessed 15 Aug 2018
17. Louie, W.Y.G., Li, J., Mohamed, C., Despond, F., Lee, V., Nejat, G.: Tangy the robot bingo facilitator: a performance review. J. Med. Devices **9**(2) (2015)
18. Louie, W.-Y.G., Nejat, G.: A social robot learning to facilitate an assistive group-based activity from non-expert caregivers. Int. J. Soc. Robot. **12**(5), 1159–1176 (2020). https://doi.org/10.1007/s12369-020-00621-4
19. Magnenat Thalmann, N., Zhang, Z.: Social robots and virtual humans as assistive tools for improving our quality of life. In: 2014 5th International Conference on Digital Home, pp. 1–7. IEEE (2014)
20. Martinez-Martin, E., Escalona, F., Cazorla, M.: Socially assistive robots for older adults and people with autism: an overview. Electronics **9**(2), 367 (2020)
21. Melkas, H., Hennala, L., Pekkarinen, S., Kyrki, V.: Impacts of robot implementation on care personnel and clients in elderly-care institutions. Int. J. Med. Inform. **134**, 104041 (2020)
22. Mishra, N., Ramanathan, M., Satapathy, R., Cambria, E., Magnenat Thalmann, N.: Can a humanoid robot be part of the organizational workforce? A user study leveraging sentiment analysis. In: 2019 28th IEEE International Conference on Robot and Human Interactive Communication (RO-MAN), pp. 1–7. IEEE (2019)
23. Neven, L.: 'But obviously not for me': robots, laboratories and the defiant identity of elder test users. Sociol. Health Illness **32**(2), 335–347 (2010)
24. Ramanathan, M., Mishra, N., Thalmann, N.M.: Nadine humanoid social robotics platform. In: Gavrilova, M., Chang, J., Thalmann, N.M., Hitzer, E., Ishikawa, H. (eds.) CGI 2019. LNCS, vol. 11542, pp. 490–496. Springer, Cham (2019). https://doi.org/10.1007/978-3-030-22514-8_49
25. Šabanović, S., Bennett, C.C., Chang, W.L., Huber, L.: PARO robot affects diverse interaction modalities in group sensory therapy for older adults with dementia. In: 2013 IEEE 13th International Conference on Rehabilitation Robotics (ICORR), pp. 1–6. IEEE (2013)
26. Šabanović, S., Chang, W.L.: Socializing robots: constructing robotic sociality in the design and use of the assistive robot PARO. AI Soc. **31**(4), 537–551 (2016)
27. Studies, B.C.: Meet Stevie the social robot that holds bingo lessons in a care home (2020). https://businesscasestudies.co.uk/meet-stevie-the-social-robot-that-holds-bingo-lessons-in-a-care-home/
28. Teed, Z., Deng, J.: RAFT: recurrent all-pairs field transforms for optical flow. In: Proceedings of the IEEE Conference on Computer Vision and Pattern Recognition (2020)

29. Thompson, C., Mohamed, S., Louie, W.Y.G., He, J.C., Li, J., Nejat, G.: The robot tangy facilitating trivia games: a team-based user-study with long-term care residents. In: 2017 IEEE International Symposium on Robotics and Intelligent Sensors (IRIS), pp. 173–178. IEEE (2017)
30. Tuisku, O., Pekkarinen, S., Hennala, L., Melkas, H.: Robots do not replace a nurse with a beating heart. Inf. Technol. People **32**, 47–67 (2019)
31. Wang, L., et al.: Temporal segment networks for action recognition in videos. IEEE Trans. Pattern Anal. Mach. Intell. **41**(11), 2740–2755 (2018)
32. Xiao, Y., Zhang, Z., Beck, A., Yuan, J., Thalmann, D.: Human-robot interaction by understanding upper body gestures. Presence Teleoperators Virtual Environ. **23**(2), 133–154 (2014)

Resilient Navigation Among Dynamic Agents with Hierarchical Reinforcement Learning

Sijia Wang[1,2], Hao Jiang[1,2(✉)], and Zhaoqi Wang[1,2]

[1] Institute of Computing Technology, Chinese Academy of Sciences, Beijing, China
jianghao@ict.ac.cn
[2] University of Chinese Academy of Sciences, Beijing, China

Abstract. Behaving safe and efficient navigation policy without knowing surrounding agents' intent is a hard problem. This problem is challenging for two reasons: the agent need to face high environment uncertainty for it can't control other agents in the environment. Moreover, the navigation algorithm need to be resilient to various scenes. Recently reinforcement learning based navigation has attracted researchers interest. We present a hierarchical reinforcement learning based navigation algorithm. The two-level structure decouples the navigation task into target driven and collision avoidance, leading to a faster and more stable model to be trained. Compared with the reinforcement learning based navigation methods in recent years, we verified our model on navigation ability and the resilience on different scenes.

Keywords: Reinforcement learning · Navigation

1 Introduction

Navigating in crowded space with high efficiency and safety is a challenging task. Traditional approaches often need to adjust theirs parameters manually for different scenes, which restricts the application environment [10,18]. In order to perform adaptive and resilient behaviors for diverse scenes, navigation algorithm needs to understand different environment semantic.

To address the above issues, some work attempt to learn navigation behaviors from data. According to the source of data, the approaches can be divided into imitation learning and reinforcement learning (RL). Imitation learning [6,12,14, 17,20] learns navigation policy based on human walking trajectory data from real word, resulting in that the agent can perform similar behaviors to humans. However, the application of imitation learning restrict to the scenes of collected data.

In recent years, RL shows the level of human beings in go and games [15,16]. More and more researchers try to apply RL to navigation. Reinforcement learning does not depend on real data sets, it can continuously obtain training data

© Springer Nature Switzerland AG 2021
N. Magnenat-Thalmann et al. (Eds.): CGI 2021, LNCS 13002, pp. 504–516, 2021.
https://doi.org/10.1007/978-3-030-89029-2_39

through the virtual environment. Moreover, the optimization goal of RL is the cumulative environmental feedback signal. Compared with imitation learning, instead of simply imitating the real data, RL thinks about what strategies will make the cumulative environmental feedback higher. In recent years, the RL based navigation methods have achieved good results [3–5,13], which verify the effectiveness of RL.

To address this, we propose to use hierarchical RL to generate plausible and collision free trajectories. The main contributions of our work include:

1) We built an effective and novel HRL framework to guide the agent to reach the destination efficiently. By using hierarchical RL framework, the navigation task is decoupled into target driving and collision avoidance, so that a stable and robust model can be trained, which can quickly adapt to a new environment.

2) Through comparisons with state-of-the-art RL-based methods, our model achieves superior performance, especially in various challenging resilient experiments.

2   Related Work

In this section, we review related works on navigation and hierarchical RL which our work refers to.

2.1   Conventional Methods for Navigation

Helbling et al. [9,10] proposed social forces model to describe interactions among pedestrians. The model is based on a potential field in which attractive forces lead agents to the destination and repulsive forces block the surrounding obstacles. Reactive model predicts the collision time based on the current velocity. The representing work is ORCA [21], which is based on RVO [2]. ORCA seeks joint obstacle avoidance velocities under reciprocal assumptions. These models which are designed elaborately by researchers behave well in the specific application scene, while they rely on hand-craft functions and can not generalize well to various scenes.

2.2   Deep Reinforcement Learning Methods for Navigation

Earlier works [8,23] was limited by calculate capability, thus researches tried to simplify problems when applying RL to the navigation problem. The combination of RL and deep learning enables processing data with higher dimensions and larger state space. Recent work of navigation by deep reinforcement learning can be divided into two categories according to the algorithm.

One is value based reinforcement learning, which decomposes the action space into discrete velocity set V according to speed and direction. The method CADRL [5] first applied DRL to navigation, which adapted two-agent to the multi-agent case through maximin operation to pick up the best action. Chen et al. [4] proposed SARL which rethinks human-robot pairwise interactions with a self-attention mechanism.

One is policy-based reinforcement learning, whose action space is continuous. Long et al. [13] directly mapped raw sensor measurements to desired collision avoidance policy and presented a multi-scene multi-stage training framework for adapting to different scenes. Based on [7,13] learned safer and more resilient behaviors for navigation by integrating uncertainty estimation.

2.3   Hierarchical Reinforcement Learning

Hierarchical reinforcement learning (HRL) is inspired by divide-and-conquer, decoupling task to reduce training difficulty. Bacon et al. [1] proposed Option-Critic Framework which decouples the problem into two levels. The high policy is responsible for choosing an option. The low level do the low-level policy following the option until meet the option's termination condition.

Vezhnevets [22] proposed FuUdal Networks where two levels of hierarchy within an agent communicate via explicit goals. Both the high level and low level are deep learning model and no gradients are propagated between two levels. The Manager receives its learning signal from the environment alone. Our model takes inspiration from the design of FeUdal Networks.

3   Approach

3.1   Overview

In this work, we consider the problem that an agent navigates towards a goal on the ground where N dynamic obstacles exists. Both the agent and N dynamic obstacles are modeled as discs with the same radius. The agent can not communicate with other dynamic obstacles. Therefore at each time t the agent's observation is N obstacles' positions $p_i^t = [p_x^t, p_y^t] \in P, P^t = \{p_1^t, p_2^t, \cdots, p_n^t\}$ and velocities $v_i^t = [v_x^t, v_y^t] \in V, V^t = \{v_1^t, v_2^t, \cdots, v_n^t\}$.

Figure 1 shows the overview of method, our model takes inspiration from feudal reinforcement learning [22] where levels of hierarchy communicate via explicit goals. The high-level module aims to optimize long term interest, whose output is the sub-goal $g_t = (p_x^{t+c}, p_y^{t+c})$ for the future. The low-level module aims to safely and efficiently navigate to the sub-goal, whose output is primitive actions which is 2-dimensional velocity $a_{t+i} = (v_x^{t+i}, v_y^{t+i})$. The low-level is the module that actually interacts with the environment.

Both of high-level and low-level are constructed by deep RL models and optimize their policy respectively on the reward received from the environment. Similar to the FeUdal Networks [22], there are no gradient between two levels. The information that agent can get from the environment, x_t contains last six consecutive observations: $x_t = \{P^{t-5}, V^{t-5}, \cdots, P^t, V^t\}$. As Fig. 2 shows, our model converts the change of obstacles' positions into the 360-degree laser form

o_z^t, the shape of which is 6×360. The high-level and low-level modules don't use the same neural network but share the same neural network architecture as the Fig. 3 shows. Based on the current velocities of the obstacles, we predict the obstacles' positions in next 3 time steps by linear interpolation and convert the future positions to the laser form o_p^t. θ_t is the current agent's orientation and o_{z+p}^t is a slice of o_z^t and o_p^t chosen by θ_t: $o_{z+p}^t = o_z^t[\theta_t] + o_p^t[\theta_t]$. p_g^t is the agent's final goal (for high-level) or sub-goal (for low-level). v_t is the agent's current velocity. Both high and low level take the agent's position as the origin for the local coordinate every time step, high-level's y-axis points toward the final goal and low-level's y-axis points toward the sub-goal.

Here we introduce the transition between the high-level and low-level. Every c time steps, the high-level module calculates the sub-goal g_t for the future c time steps and conveys it to the low-level module. c is a hyper-parameter which we set 20. Low-level receives the sub-goal and starts the loop of calculating the primitive action, two-dimensional velocity v_t. The low-level module will not stop until meeting the terminal conditions. The terminal conditions contain three situations, the first one is the agent arrives the sub-goal, the second one is the agent collides with other obstacle, the third one is the agent have performed low-level action c times.

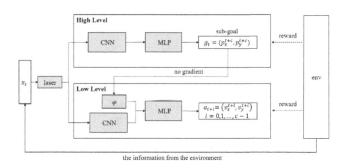

Fig. 1. The overview of our model. There are two levels in our model. The high-level module aims to optimize long term interest, whose output is the sub-goal $g_t = (p_x^{t+c}, p_y^{t+c})$ for the future. The low-level module aims to safely and efficiently navigate to the sub-goal, whose output is primitive actions which is 2-dimensional velocity $a_{t+i} = (v_x^{t+i}, v_y^{t+i})$.

3.2   High-Level Module

Above all, low-level module actually interacts with the environment while high-level module interacts with environment by directing low-level module. The responsibility for high-level module is giving low-level module a good sub-goal which can balance the need of the reaching final goal and safety. Therefore, we estimate high-level policy by the trajectory that the low-level module actually performed in loop after receiving the sub-goal from high-level.

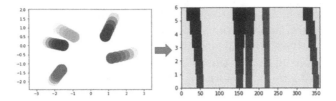

Fig. 2. In our model, the agent processes the environment observation to the form of laser.

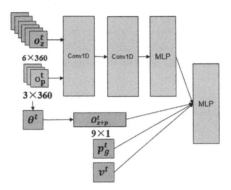

Fig. 3. The neural network shared by high-level and low-level module.

We first introduce the notations of the trajectory that the low-level module generated, then introduce the estimation criteria on the trajectory. After the low-level received sub-goal, assume that low-level performed c^L times before meeting the terminal condition, $c^L \leq c$. Then the agent's trajectory is $\{p_t, p_{t+1}, \cdots, p_{t+c^L}\}$, the minimal distances between the agent and obstacles are $\{d_t, d_{t+1}, \cdots, d_{t+c^L}\}$.

Let the displacement during c^L times be $p_{t+c^L} - p_t$ and the travelled distance be $\sum_{k=1}^{k=c^L} \|p_{t+k} - p_{t+k-1}\|$. Let the agent's final goal be g, then $g - p^t$ is the relative vector from the final goal to the agent's position at the beginning of the loop.

We define d_{goal} to represent the relative distance that the agent navigate to the final goal during the c^L times and the relative distance the agent move per unit time is $UnitGoal$.

$$d_{goal} = \frac{(p^{t+c^L} - p^t)(g - p^t)}{\| g - p^t \|} \tag{1}$$

$$UnitGoal = \frac{d_{goal}}{c^L} \tag{2}$$

If the agent's minimal distance to the obstacles is less than 0.25 m, then the reward function will give a penalty signal for being too close to obstacles, which is $-0.25+d$. Formula 3 is the sum of the distance penalty $CloseDist$, $1_{d<0.25}(d)$ is an indicator function.

$$CloseDist = \sum_{t=1}^{c^L} 1_{d<0.25}(d) * (-0.25 + d) \tag{3}$$

We define $ExtraPath$ to represent the difference between the travelled distance and displacement.

$$ExtraPath = \sum_{k=1}^{k=c^L} \|p_{t+k} - p_{t+k-1}\| - \|p^{t+c^L} - p^t\| \tag{4}$$

Formula 5 is the high-level reward function, which takes $UnitGoal$, $CloseDist$, and $ExtraPath$ into account. w_1, w_2, w_3 is weighting parameters which are set 0.5, −0.5 and 0.5 at the beginning for dimensional homogeneity. Then these parameters were gradually adjusted by persistent attempts to $w_1 = 0.8$, $w_2 = -0.5$, $w_3 = 0.4$.

$$R_t = w_1 UnitGoal + w_2 ExtraPath + w_3 CloseDist \tag{5}$$

High-level module is responsible for giving a good sub-goal, therefore we train the module to maximize the one step interest. We refer to the training design of DDPG [11], a policy based RL algorithm, and transform the design to optimize one step interest. There are three neural networks, a policy network $Actor$ for giving out the sub-goal, two value networks $Critic$ and $Critic_{target}$ for describing the state value. The network structure of $Critic$ and $Critic_{target}$ is the same. The task of $Critic_{target}$ is to provide policy's value without gradient, thus it won't be optimized when training, the parameters of $Critic_{target}$ will periodically copy from $Critic$. The loss for $Critic$ is shown as Formula 6, whose aim is minimizing the value estimated by $Critic$ and the real reward. The loss for $Actor$ is shown as Formula 7, whose aim is maximizing the state value that the Actor can bring.

$$critic\ loss = (Critic(s_t, g_t) - r_t)^2 \tag{6}$$
$$actor\ loss = -Critic_{target}(s_t, Actor(s_t)) \tag{7}$$

3.3   Low-Level Module

The responsibility for low-level module is navigating to the sub-goal safely, this task is similar to the mono-layer RL work [4,13]. The termination condition of low-level is reaching sub-goal or colliding with obstacles or the executions is over c. Formula 8 shows the low-level reward function which awards navigating to the sub-goal and penalizes collisions.

If the agent collides with other obstacles, we will give penalty $r_{collision} = -3$. If the agent is too close to other obstacles (the distance to other obstacles is less than 0.2 m), we will give penalty on the uncomfortable distance: $-0.6 + d_{min}/2$. Otherwise, we will give the award for navigating to the sub-goal: $-w_g (\|p^{t-1} - g\| - \|p^t - g\|)$, where $w_g = 2.5$. Our reward function doesn't award for reaching the final goal specially like the mono-layer RL method [4,13], because low-level can end up with reaching the final goal or reaching the sub-goal or timeout so that awarding the final goal will induce the inequality. Previous discount factor γ in [4,13] is over 0.9. However the collision influence doesn't need be so far, thus the discount factor γ in our model is 0.6.

$$r_t = \begin{cases} r_{collision} & p^t - p_j^t < 2R \\ -0.6 + d_{min}/2 & d_{min} < 0.2 \\ -w_g(\|p^{t-1} - g\| - \|p^t - g\|) & otherwise \end{cases} \quad (8)$$

Low-level module is trained using Deep Deterministic Policy Grading (DDPG) [11], a policy based method. Compare to the stochastic policy search of Proximal Policy Optimization (PPO) [19], the deterministic policy of DDPG accelerates convergence on navigation problem. When navigating in the crowded environment, low-level module will frequently collide with other obstacles, which possibly leading to the training lies in local minimum. For improving this problem, low-level module uses two tricks. The first is controlling the ratio of success and fail trajectories in the data set, which we set 0.6:0.4 in our paper. The second is adding protect for the low-level policy, the 2-d velocity. The conventional method ORCA has robust collision avoidance ability, whose input is the prefer velocity. After the low-level policy network outputs the velocity v_t, we use ORCA to reduce the collision probability by taking v_t as the prefer velocity. In other words, we treat the low-level model's output as the prefer velocity for ORCA to increase security.

4   Experiment

4.1   Scene Design

The scenes should be able to verify the model's navigation ability, we design the scenes from two aspect: First, the agent should be able to maintain navigation ability when the scene's size changed. Second, the agent should be able to maintain navigation ability when the scene change to dissimilar scene.

Therefore, this paper train and test on following three scenes which are easy to change size. Figure 4 shows the diagram of these three scenes, the red disc represents the agent and the blue disc represents the human, the stars with the corresponding color represents the agent's or humans' goals. Fig(a) is scene *Squeeze*, where an agent and a human randomly positioned on a circle of radius of rm and their goal positions are on the opposite side of the same circle. (b) is scene *Circle*, its design is similar to *Squeeze*, the only difference is *Circle* has one agent and five humans. (c) is scene *Square*, an agent and five humans randomly positioned on a square whose side length is w m.

We design two kinds of experiment. Experiment 1 compares the models' navigation, where the train and test scene is the same. Experiment 2 compares the models' resilience from two aspect: compare the resilience explicitly on scene size and scene type.

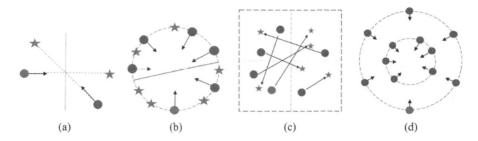

Fig. 4. The scenes that we use in this paper to verify the effectiveness of our model.

4.2 Perform Metrics

To fairly compare our model with other models, every test scene is evaluated for 100 repeats. We use the three performance metrics. Success rate represents the ratio that the agent successfully arrived the destination without collision. Collision rate represents the ratio that the agent collide with other obstacles. Average navigation time represents the average navigation time of the successful trajectories.

4.3 Navigation Ability Comparison

We compared with the representative models which are based on RL. As expected, the CADRL and the SARL have low collision rate due to their training algorithm is value based, which cautiously enumerates all the discrete actions. Long et al. [13] uses policy-based algorithm which action space is continuous, which exploration space is further higher than the value based. With the scene's complexity increase, Long et al. fails to avoid the obstacles. The collision rates of *Squeeze*, *Circle* and *Square* are 0.24, 0.3, 0.47 respectively. Our model's hierarchical structure decouples the navigation task into target-driven task and collision avoidance task, each layer concentrates on the its own responsibility and our low-level module add ORCA policy to protect, thus our model has the highest success rate among three scenes.

As for the average navigation time, the value-based methods' has longer time than the policy-based methods on *Circle* and *Square*. Because the value-based methods' action space is discrete, which means its trajectories are less smooth than the policy-based trajectories. We also make a statistic on the trajectories' kinetic energy, we compute the minimum, mean value and maximum of 100 trajectories' energy. As the fifth row in Table 1 shows, our model has the lowest value among *Circle* and *Square*.

4.4   Resilience Comparison

Table 1. Testing the learning ability of the model: train and test on the same scene.

Metrics	Method	Squeeze	Circle	Square
SuccessRate	CADRL	0.95	–	–
	SARL	0.93	0.93	0.96
	Long et al.	0.76	0.7	0.53
	Our model	**0.96**	**0.96**	**1.0**
CollisionRate	CADRL	0.05	–	–
	SARL	0.07	0.01	0.0
	Long et al.	0.24	0.3	0.47
	Our model	**0.04**	0.04	**0.0**
AvgNavTime	CADRL	9.96	–	–
	SARL	9.77	10.93	8.23
	Long et al.	10.25	8.8	5.61
	Our model	**8.5**	**9.66**	6.76
Energy	CADRL	(31.2,36.8,51.6)	–	–
	SARL	(32.5,38.0,49.0)	(32.7,37.9,46.4)	(6.0,29.6,68.3)
	Long et al.	(37.3,37.3,37.3)	(30.6,30.6,30.6)	(4.9,16.3,43.0)
	Our model	(29.5,32.5,41.0)	**(23.3,28.8,38.0)**	**(2.8,22.4,41.0)**

Resilience on Scene Size. In this experiment, we train the model on *Squeeze* with diameter 8 m, then test the model on *Squeeze* with diameter 16 m. The same configuration for *Circle* and *Square*. The test results are shown in Table 2 (3rd, 4th and 5th column). Above all, the value-based model CADRL and SARL behaved bad on scene *Squeeze* and *Circle*, the success rates of which are 0.03 and 0 respectively. Because *Square* changes little with its side length increases, the SARL still retains 0.49 success rate. This is because, the value-based method chooses policy by the formula $a_t \leftarrow \arg\max_{a_t \in A} R(s_t, a_t) + \gamma V(\hat{s}_{t+1})$ which highly depends on the accurate estimation on the state value, $V(\hat{s}_{t+1})$. If the value network hasn't seen the state s_{t+1} before, it is hard for value-based method to choose a reasonable action.

The policy-based method uses the policy network to learn the relation of environment state and the action. Therefore, even if the method meets the unfamiliar environment state, the policy network still knows the general direction of the action. As the second row in Table 2 shows, the success rates of the Long et al. are 0.76, 0.7 and 0.53 explicitly, which are apparently higher than value-based method. However, it has higher collision rate with the complexity of the scene increases. Our model retains high success rate when the scene size increased, where the success rates are 0.96, 0.95, and 0.92 explicitly. Our high-level module helps to avoid the relative crowded area by choosing temporal destination.

Resilience on Scene Type. For testing the resilience on scene type, we train the model on *Squeeze* with diameter 8 m, then test on *Circle* with diameter 8 m and *Square* with side length 8 m. Thus the scene sizes of train and test are the same. The test results are shown in Table 2 (6th and 7th column). Face to the unfamiliar scene with the same size, the CADRL and SARL retain some navigation ability, whose success rates are over 0.65. The SARL behaves better than CADRL for its value network can process crowd while the CADRL can only process pair-wise relationship. The success rate of our model on *Circle* and *Square* are 0.99 and 0.92, apparently behaves better than other models.

Table 2. Testing the resilience of the model: train and test on different scenes.

Metrics	Method	Resilience on scene size			Resilience on scene type	
		Squeeze (8 m→16 m)	Circle (8 m→16 m)	Square (8 m→16 m)	Squeeze→Circle	Squeeze→Square
SuccessRate	CADRL	0.03	–	–	0.65	0.67
	SARL	0	0	0.49	0.83	0.89
	Long et al.	0.88	0.71	0.54	0.82	0.79
	Our model	**0.96**	**0.95**	**0.92**	**0.99**	**0.92**
CollisionRate	CADRL	0.02	–	–	0.03	0.03
	SARL	0.05	0.05	0.00	0.17	0.11
	Long et al.	0.12	0.29	0.31	0.18	0.21
	Our model	**0.04**	**0.00**	**0.00**	**0.00**	**0.00**
AvgNavTime	CADRL	20.08	–	–	12.94	7.40
	SARL	–	–	10.73	8.48	6.60
	Long et al.	21.50	17.00	11.88	8.25	6.40
	Our model	**18.07**	18.07	12.62	9.54	8.92
Energy	CADRL	(79.3,82.9,86.3)	–	–	(25.7,103.4,165.9)	(6.0,25.2,61.5)
	SARL	–	–	(9.0,57.2,77.0)	(31.5,33.4,43.5)	(6.0,24.8,47.6)
	Long et al.	(82.4,82.4,82.4)	(64.6,64.6,64.6)	(2.9,43.2,76.0)	(30.4,30.4,30.4)	(3.0,21.0,41.6)
	Our model	(66.3,70.5,74.9)	(48.7,64.2,70.8)	(11.1,49.6,76.2)	(25.3,29.7,39.3)	(1.1,23.8,57.1)

Table 3. Test the navigation ability of the model: train and test in Concentric scene.

	Success	Collision	AvgNavTime
Mono-layer	0.18	0.82	19.05
Our model	0.99	0.00	20.21

4.5 Ablation Experiment

To verify the effectiveness of our hierarchical architecture, we compare our model with mono-layer RL model. The reward function and train configuration of mono-layer RL is same to our model's low-level module, except the low-level module calculate velocity policy based on sub-goal while our model based on final goal. We compare the two models under the scene Concentric (the Fig(d) in Fig. 4). The radius of two circles are 8 m and 16 m. The test result is shown in Table 3. The success rate of our model is 0.99 which are much higher than the mono-layer's 0.18. As the Fig. 5 shows, mono-layer model's policy (the left trajectory) is aggressive that the agent walks straight to the final goal. Although the agent tried to avoid the nearby obstacles, the high-density led to collision at last. Our policy (the right trajectory) avoid the high-density by sub-goals which are represented as red stars in Fig. 5.

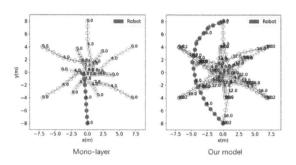

Fig. 5. Train and test the models on Concentric scene. (Color figure online)

5   Conclusion

In this paper, we propose a hierarchical reinforcement learning based navigation algorithm, which decouple navigation task into target-driven and collision avoidance. We evaluated our approach by comparing the trajectories taken by the agent with previous methods. Our experimental results suggest that our approach produces motion that is more resilience in different scenes.

Acknowledgments. This work was supported by National Key Research and Development Program of China (No. 2018AAA0103002 and 2017YFB1002600) and National Natural Science Foundation of China (No. 61702482 and 62002345).

References

1. Bacon, P., Harb, J., Precup, D.: The option-critic architecture. CoRR abs/1609.05140 (2016)
2. Van den Berg, J., Lin, M., Manocha, D.: Reciprocal velocity obstacles for real-time multi-agent navigation. In: 2008 IEEE International Conference on Robotics and Automation, pp. 1928–1935. IEEE (2008)
3. Chen, C., Hu, S., Nikdel, P., Mori, G., Savva, M.: Relational graph learning for crowd navigation. arXiv preprint arXiv:1909.13165 (2019)
4. Chen, C., Liu, Y., Kreiss, S., Alahi, A.: Crowd-robot interaction: crowd-aware robot navigation with attention-based deep reinforcement learning. In: 2019 International Conference on Robotics and Automation (ICRA), pp. 6015–6022. IEEE (2019)

5. Chen, Y.F., Liu, M., Everett, M., How, J.P.: Decentralized non-communicating multiagent collision avoidance with deep reinforcement learning. In: 2017 IEEE International Conference on Robotics and Automation (ICRA), pp. 285–292. IEEE (2017)

6. Fahad, M., Chen, Z., Guo, Y.: Learning how pedestrians navigate: A deep inverse reinforcement learning approach. In: 2018 IEEE/RSJ International Conference on Intelligent Robots and Systems (IROS), pp. 819–826. IEEE (2018)

7. Fan, T., Long, P., Liu, W., Pan, J., Yang, R., Manocha, D.: Learning resilient behaviors for navigation under uncertainty. In: 2020 IEEE International Conference on Robotics and Automation (ICRA), pp. 5299–5305. IEEE (2020)

8. Godoy, J., Chen, T., Guy, S.J., Karamouzas, I., Gini, M.: ALAN: adaptive learning for multi-agent navigation. Autonomous Robots **42**(8), 1543–1562 (2018)

9. Helbing, D., Farkas, I., Vicsek, T.: Simulating dynamical features of escape panic. Nature **407**(6803), 487–490 (2000)

10. Helbing, D., Molnar, P.: Social force model for pedestrian dynamics. Phys. Rev. E **51**(5), 4282 (1995)

11. Lillicrap, T.P., et al.: Continuous control with deep reinforcement learning. arXiv preprint arXiv:1509.02971 (2015)

12. Liu, Y., Xu, A., Chen, Z.: Map-based deep imitation learning for obstacle avoidance. In: 2018 IEEE/RSJ International Conference on Intelligent Robots and Systems (IROS), pp. 8644–8649. IEEE (2018)

13. Long, P., Fan, T., Liao, X., Liu, W., Zhang, H., Pan, J.: Towards optimally decentralized multi-robot collision avoidance via deep reinforcement learning. In: 2018 IEEE International Conference on Robotics and Automation (ICRA), pp. 6252–6259. IEEE (2018)

14. Long, P., Liu, W., Pan, J.: Deep-learned collision avoidance policy for distributed multiagent navigation. IEEE Robot. Autom. Lett. **2**(2), 656–663 (2017)

15. Mnih, V., et al.: Playing Atari with deep reinforcement learning. arXiv preprint arXiv:1312.5602 (2013)

16. Peng, X.B., Abbeel, P., Levine, S., van de Panne, M.: DeepMimic: example-guided deep reinforcement learning of physics-based character skills. ACM Trans. Graph. (TOG) **37**(4), 1–14 (2018)

17. Pfeiffer, M., et al.: Reinforced imitation: sample efficient deep reinforcement learning for mapless navigation by leveraging prior demonstrations. IEEE Robot. Autom. Lett. **3**(4), 4423–4430 (2018)

18. Reynolds, C.W.: Flocks, herds and schools: a distributed behavioral model. In: Proceedings of the 14th Annual Conference on Computer Graphics and Interactive Techniques, pp. 25–34 (1987)

19. Schulman, J., Wolski, F., Dhariwal, P., Radford, A., Klimov, O.: Proximal policy optimization algorithms. arXiv preprint arXiv:1707.06347 (2017)

20. Tai, L., Zhang, J., Liu, M., Burgard, W.: Socially compliant navigation through raw depth inputs with generative adversarial imitation learning. In: 2018 IEEE International Conference on Robotics and Automation (ICRA), pp. 1111–1117. IEEE (2018)

21. Van Den Berg, J., Guy, S.J., Lin, M., Manocha, D.: Reciprocal n-body collision avoidance. In: Robotics Research, pp. 3–19. Springer (2011). https://doi.org/10.1007/978-3-642-19457-3_1

22. Vezhnevets, A.S., et al.: Feudal networks for hierarchical reinforcement learning. In: International Conference on Machine Learning, pp. 3540–3549. PMLR (2017)
23. Zhang, C., Lesser, V.: Coordinating multi-agent reinforcement learning with limited communication. In: Proceedings of the 2013 International Conference on Autonomous Agents and Multi-Agent Systems, pp. 1101–1108 (2013)

Visual Analytics

MeshChain: Secure 3D Model and Intellectual Property management Powered by Blockchain Technology

Hunmin Park, Yuchi Huo, and Sung-Eui Yoon[✉]

KAIST, Daejeon, South Korea
95phm@kaist.ac.kr

Abstract. The intellectual value of digitized 3D properties in scientific, artistic, historical, and entertaining domains is increasing. However, there has been less attention on designing an immutable, secure database for their management. We propose a secure 3D property management platform powered by blockchain and decentralized storage. The platform connects various 3D modeling tools to a decentralized network-based database constructed on blockchain and decentralized storage technologies and provides the commit and checkout of the 3D model to that network. This structure provides 3D data protection from damages and attacks, intellectual property (IP) management, and data source authentication. We analyze its performance and show its applications to cooperative 3D modeling and IP management.

1 Introduction

3D models have become one kind of valuable property in many domains. For example, many scientific studies are targeting the study of 3D structures of microorganisms. Modern artists materialize their thoughts as 3D model artworks. Designers claim authorities to 3D models as the products of their intellectual endeavors. The scanning of relics and celebrities bestows 3D models' historical values. In the domain of computer graphics, the 3D model is one of the primary inputs and outputs for different subjects, such as rendering, geometry, and animation [2,17,18,34,36].

While 3D models have become nonnegligible intellectual properties of society, organizations, and individual persons, there has been less attention on designing immutable secure mechanisms to preserve, manage, cooperatively produce, and authenticate 3D models.

Beyond the actual 3D data, the intellectual rights of the authors are even more vulnerable. Nowadays, the internet is the most popular repository to disseminate digital data, including 3D models. While people spread and share 3D models through web pages or social networks, the data is vulnerable to tampering and plagiarizing. A reliable platform to authenticate the 3D data and track down the history of the data will help the creators protect their intellectual properties.

© Springer Nature Switzerland AG 2021
N. Magnenat-Thalmann et al. (Eds.): CGI 2021, LNCS 13002, pp. 519–534, 2021.
https://doi.org/10.1007/978-3-030-89029-2_40

The process of creating 3D models also requires data security and intellectual rights management, but those issues have rarely been studied. Nowadays, the 3D models used in movies and games are becoming complex, which sometimes overwhelms individual designers. So collaborative modeling has gained increased attention and became one of the standard workflows. Currently, the existing 3D model platforms are local or based on centralized networks. For example, some collaborative 3D modeling platforms [1,26] use centralized networks that depend on the central point (central node or central group of nodes) to connect the 3D modeling tools. In such a network, all data in a network should pass through the central point.

Building a 3D management platform on a classic centralized network enjoys the advantage of simple deployment. However, platforms on centralized networks have their limitations. First, maintaining the central nodes is expensive and not suitable for flexible collaborations within communities. Second, the network and data are vulnerable to network attacks or physical disasters. Third, there is no strong protection mechanism to prevent the tampering of integrity, security, and property of the intellectual asset from the central nodes.

Our contribution in this paper is the proposal of a decentralized 3D property management platform. The decentralized platform, powered by blockchain and decentralized storage techniques, connects various 3D modeling tools to local clients. Specifically, we adopt the blockchain technique for managing intellectual properties and the decentralized storage technique for storing the (large) 3D data safely. Such design gives the following benefits to 3D property management:

- Flexibility enabling various applications of the platform.
- Decentralized 3D data, transparent intellectual property (IP) management, and IP protection.
- Invulnerability to network failures and physical disasters.

In this paper, we also show the implementation of our method built on Ethereum [6] and Swarm [10]. We analyze its performance overhead and show its applications to 3D collaborative modeling.

2 Related Work

In this section, we discuss decentralized data security, cooperative 3D modeling, and decentralized version control that are related to our work.

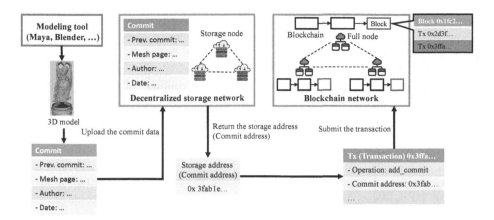

Fig. 1. The overall structure of the proposed platform and the fundamental operations. The platform contains three parts: the local client, index blockchain network, and decentralized mesh network. Nodes within the index blockchain network and decentralized storage network connect through peer-to-peer connections (dotted lines).

2.1 Decentralized Data Security

One common method of protecting crucial digital data is decentralizing the data. Blockchain is one of the hottest decentralized techniques in recent years [32,33, 35]. It started from building a digital currency system on the P2P network that provides the immutability of data without depending on a central organization [24]. Technologies like smart contracts enabled blockchain to store more complex structures such as a code and its execution history [6], and the blockchain became a tool for building a general-purpose application on a decentralized network.

Another important decentralized technology is decentralized storage [3], such as IPFS [29] and Swarm [10]. It is a distributed data storage on a decentralized network built on blockchain technology. Unlike the traditional distributed network, it uses the content of the file, e.g., file hash, instead of the node's IP address to locate the file. It makes it easier to integrate the storage network into the blockchain network that consists of anonymous nodes. It uses unused hardware spaces of people to store the data and usually uses a cryptocurrency incentive system to let them manage the data. It is becoming an alternative method to centralized cloud storage for storing large files since its decentralized structure helps protect attacks and decreases data management costs.

Our work utilizes a decoupled approach to using the blockchain network and decentralized storage together for efficiently supporting cooperative 3D modeling.

2.2 Cooperative 3D Modeling

There have been prior approaches to enable collaboration in 3D modeling in different directions. MeshGit proposes diffing and merging algorithms for 3D polygonal meshes to enable version control of 3D models [8]. SceneGit constructs a version control system for the various components of the 3D scene, such as shapes, materials and textures, which is based on a heuristic method that is robust and efficient for the large 3D scenes [7]. MeshHisto supports sharing and merging mesh version histories for real-time 3D modeling collaboration [31].

Pixar proposes a format (language) for describing complex 3D scenes, which uses a layered structure for enabling collaboration [28]. CoMaya shows that we can connect users of the 3D modeling tool without modifying the source code of the tool [1]. Conflict resolution of different 3D model versions is addressed by separating conflict into multiple types [9]. Omniverse constructs a cloud-based collaboration modeling platform that provides data exchange between multiple kinds of 3D modeling tools to allow the designers to use multiple tools [26].

These prior approaches focus on developing management and the exchange of 3D modeling data to connect the 3D modeling tools through the network. However, these techniques paid less attention to the security of the data and intellectual property. Since the 3D model has become a valuable asset, its security should be considered critical for a database. These previous techniques use a centralized network to connect the 3D modeling tools and manage 3D modeling data, which is vulnerable to network attacks, physical disasters, and internal tempering. Instead, we propose a decentralized network powered by blockchain and decentralize storage to provide state-of-the-art security in practice.

2.3   Decentralized Version Control

There are approaches applying blockchain technology to version control. Gitchain [30] and Mango [4] are two implementations of using the blockchain network as a backend for Git, a version control system for code.

Similar to code cooperation, cooperative 3D modeling or database also relies on a version control algorithm. However, it is a more challenging problem due to the need for much larger and more frequent real-time data transactions. Therefore, we propose a specific format (called 'mesh page') for decreasing the data size by adopting 3D data compression on the difference between two versions of the 3D model. The simple technique reduces the network load and helps improve the performance of uploading and downloading the 3D models.

2.4   Decentralized Technologies in Computer Graphics

There are some computer graphics techniques incorporated into decentralized technologies. Besançon et al. [5] proposed a data representation of 3D assets for enabling blockchain-based data exchange in 3D applications such as video games. OTOY [27] and Golem [14] proposed a distributed GPU rendering system on the blockchain, which allows the participants to perform rendering tasks submitted by others (end-users) and receive the proper amount of cryptocurrency. OTOY [27] pointed out that incorporating blockchain technology would help to protect intellectual rights.

Departing from those prior approaches, our platform tracks the history of the cooperative modeling process. It also provides matching 3D models, which can protect the intellectual rights of cooperative 3D property and authenticate data sources.

3 Overview

To realize a secure database for 3D models and intellectual properties, we consider recent advances in the distributed system field. Blockchain is a distributed append-only ledger, i.e., a database of transactions on a peer-to-peer network. It stores the transactions on distributed network nodes with append-only (immutable, once written) modification records. Its security mechanism is practically unbreakable. However, blockchain is appropriate for managing small data such as numbers and text rather than managing large data such as a 3D model due to the synchronization cost. Therefore, we use the blockchain network to manage the 3D models' intellectual properties and indices. Also, to store the actual 3D data, we use a decentralized storage network that is appropriate for storing large data on a decentralized network.

Figure 1 illustrates an overview of our platform with fundamental operation blocks. The platform contains three components, the local client, a blockchain network (called 'index blockchain network'), and a decentralized storage network (called 'decentralized mesh network'). The local client provides basic UI for editing, uploading, and downloading models for different applications. The index blockchain network provides efficient and immutable management of the intellectual property and data structure. The decentralized mesh network can safely store the large-size 3D models by distributing the data to the decentralized network.

We explain four different applications that can be supported by MeshChain:

- **Data registering and storing.** Users can update the data to the decentralized mesh network and the intellectual information to the index blockchain network for the purpose of 3D property protection.
- **Intellectual property management.** Since we record every submission on the blockchain, we use that data to calculate the contribution of each author.
- **Data authentication.** Users can download the models to authenticate a model. The local client calculates and shows the geometry and visual similarities for matching models. (Fig. 3)
- **Cooperative modeling.** For committing a model, local clients calculate mesh pages representing the difference between the prior and current commits (Sect. 4) and commit them as a new, single transaction. For checkout, the local client queries the latest block from the index blockchain network for the latest version or trackbacks the chain to get different branches. The mesh is downloaded from the decentralized mesh network according to the storage address. We also construct 'commit incentive', a cryptocurrency paid to the author when the author submits a commit. It encourages users to participate

in the modeling project and improves the 3D model. Such a feature might be especially useful in community-driven projects. (Fig. 2)

4 Cooperative Modeling

In this section, we describe main components of our method for enabling cooperative modeling based on the blockchain.

4.1 Commit and Checkout

Various applications mentioned above require two main operations: the commit and checkout of 3D models. As illustrated in Fig. 1, the local client, index blockchain network, and decentralized mesh network cooperates to accomplish the operations of commit and checkout.

For the commit operation, users can import and edit 3D models using 3D modeling tools, such as Blender, 3ds Max, and Maya. The local client then performs the creation and submission of a transaction. Before creating a transaction, the local client calculates the difference between the current mesh and the previous commit, called 'mesh page' for efficient communication to the blockchain network, and submits it to the decentralized mesh network. Given the storage address on the decentralized mesh network, the local client creates a transaction that records the previous commit ID, the storage address, tags (keywords for searching), the author's address (the author's blockchain account), date, and additional data.

The local client submits the transaction to nearby 'full nodes' of the blockchain network. Full nodes are the blockchain network nodes that are maintaining the entire blockchain in their local storage by creating the blocks and verify incoming transactions and blocks. The full nodes broadcast the new transaction to each other and verify it. Several verified transactions are merged into a new block, which is linked to the end of the blockchain as an immutable record.

For the checkout, the local client first queries the commit information such as storage address from the index blockchain network. Then the local client downloads actual geometry data from the decentralized mesh network and provides the expected mesh to the user.

4.2 Mesh Page

In order to reduce the network load and network operation overhead, we propose a 3D-specific strategy called 'mesh page'.

When we submit a commit, we store only the difference between the mesh of the current commit and the mesh of the previous commit, instead of storing the whole mesh. In addition, the time of storing the data on the decentralized storage increases almost linearly for the small number of triangles, but it becomes larger than expected if the number of triangles is very large (Table 2). So we partition the set of triangles into multiple pieces and then compress each piece by using the 3D compression algorithm such as OpenCTM [13]. We show that how much performance boosts these steps can make in Sect. 6.1.

Specifically, we stored each piece to the decentralized storage and its address to the index blockchain network and continue to process the next piece of the 3D model. In this iterative process, we measured the total time spent on storing the data on the decentralized storage network and the separate time & total time spent on storing its address on the blockchain network. We can observe that the blockchain's overhead is significantly larger than the overhead of storing the data on the decentralized storage network (Fig. 5).

Specifically, when storing the (compressed) pieces of the 3D model, we first store all the pieces to the storage network, and then merge their addresses into one string and store that string to the blockchain at once, to reduce the overhead of accessing the blockchain network.

5   Intellectual Property Management

Calculating and managing intellectual property is an important challenge in software management. Similarly, cooperative 3D modeling and public 3D model databases face the challenge of calculating the contributions among the participants. While the demands for cooperative modeling and large-scale public 3D database keep increasing, there have been few studies on the intellectual management of the 3D property. Besides the evaluation metric, the transparency and consistency of intellectual management are also important, especially for the cooperation of communities.

5.1   Mesh Incentive

Inspired by SLOC (Source Lines of Code) [19,25], the number of newly modified triangles (let's call it 'effective triangles') can be a unit of measurement for the work effort of modeling. Modern blockchains such as Ethereum [6] supports stacking the cryptocurrency on the network via smart contract [11]. Based on these ideas, we propose 'mesh incentive', an incentive distributed to the contributors of a 3D modeling project, which can be considered as a metric of 3D modeling contribution.

Simply in our work, mesh incentive, I, regards the number of effective triangles as the contribution:

$$I \propto |T_{\text{eff}}|, \tag{1}$$

where T_{eff} is a set of effective triangles. T_{eff} is defined as:

$$T_{\text{eff}} = T \setminus \bigcup_{k=1}^{n} T_k, \tag{2}$$

where T is a set of all mesh triangles modified (added & removed) by a user and $T_1, \cdots, T_n$ are the modified triangles in each past commit operation. Since T_{eff}

excludes all the triangles submitted in the past, it prevents the user to abuse the incentive system, e.g., submitting the same data repeatedly to get a lot of incentive.

Suppose that the incentive supply, say r, is stacked on the blockchain. We need to guarantee $I < r$ so that the platform will not run out of incentive for new contributions. Additionally, we also have to balance the distribution of incentives to the participants of the project. To solve these issues, we set I like this:

$$I = \frac{|T_{\text{eff}}|}{|T|} \times \frac{r}{u+1}, \tag{3}$$

where r is the remaining incentive supply, u is the current number of participants in the modeling project. (In our implementation, we count u by just considering everyone who commits at least once to the network as an author.) Since $|T_{\text{eff}}| \leq |T|$ and $u + 1 > 1$, we have $I < r$. As a result, a user can always get an incentive if the user adds at least one new triangle to the mesh. After the blockchain gives I to the user, the supply r will decrease to $r - I$. Our implementation (Sect. 6) uses this version (Eq. (3)) of the mesh incentive.

We can extend this formula to handle the 'importance' of each triangle. There have been several methods for measuring the importance of each triangle, called 'mesh saliency' [21, 22]. Let $s(t)$ the saliency (importance) of the triangle $t \in T$. We regard the saliency as 'weight' of each triangle in T_{eff}:

$$I = \frac{\sum_{t \in T_{\text{eff}}} w(t)}{|T|} \times \frac{r}{u+1}. \quad \left(w(t) = \frac{s(t)}{\sum_{t \in T} s(t)} \right) \tag{4}$$

Since $\sum_{t \in T_{\text{eff}}} w(t) \leq \sum_{t \in T_{\text{eff}}} 1 \leq |T_{\text{eff}}|$, we still have $I < r$.

5.2   Data Authentication

Since the Internet became the most popular repository for digital data, the data authentication problem has been getting increasing attention. 3D models and designs are vulnerable to tampering, plagiarism, or piracy while being propagated. The important data, such as the author information associated with the models, can also be easily modified. We thus suggest using a transparent, decentralized, and immutable platform to register and authenticate important 3D properties.

Since 3D models are stored immutably on our network, we can apply the similarity of 3D models to compare the relationship between two models, such as the model stored in the network and the model which looks similar to it (Fig. 3). Measuring visual and geometric similarity has been an active research topics [12, 15], but we adopt simple approaches as a proof-of-concept for our approach. We may have to adopt more complex approaches such as learning-based geometrical similarity [12] to implement real-world application of our idea. In our approach, geometry similarity simply computes the ratio of common triangles between the two models. Visual similarity measures a visual matching rate. Visual clue provides high-level information about the appearance of the 3D model and retains robustness even if the low-level geometry details are changed.

Models may have different geometry details or formats, but they can be visually similar if they stem from the same design. In this regard, the visual similarity provides a metric to match models from the design perspective.

6   Results

In this section, we discuss the results of our approach with various tested applications built on top of our prototype.

We implemented our approach using Ethereum blockchain [6] and Swarm decentralized storage [10]. The client, written in Kotlin, communicates with Blender modeling tool via RPC (Remote Procedure Call), Ethereum via Web3j [23], and Swarm via HTTP (Fig. 4). The client reads/writes the information from those tools and performs 3D operations. For example, when the user creates the commit, it reads the 3D model from Blender, calculates the mesh page, stores the data on Swarm, calculates the mesh incentive, and creates a transaction to Ethereum. Then the smart contract (executable code on the blockchain) stores the commit address on the Ethereum network and pays the mesh incentive to the author. The client provides calculating the visual similarity of the 3D model of a commit and the external 3D model. We used match3d library [16] for performing visual similarity, and used OpenCTM [13] for 3D compression. The code and demonstration video of our platform are available at https://github.com/Avantgarde95/MeshChain-publish. The video is also available at https://youtu.be/xLU79JfRdbQ.

We built a small test network on the servers connected by LAN, where each server runs its own instances of Ethereum and Swarm clients. For the performance analysis, we used the localhost network (i.e., single computer) to minimize the overhead of the network.

6.1   Decentralized Storage and Mesh Page

We compare the performance of using different techniques of the proposed platform when conducting commit/checkout of a 3D model.

In Table 1, the first approach (Blockchain) submits the mesh data directly to the blockchain network. The second approach (+ Storage) stores the mesh data on the integrated decentralized storage network, and the blockchain holds its storage address instead. The third approach (+ Mesh page) additionally applies the mesh difference and mesh compression of our mesh page technique. The commit time is decomposed into two parts: the time of committing to the decentralized storage network and to the blockchain network.

Since the blockchain network has to synchronize and store a complete copy of the blocks in every full nodes' local storage, the blockchain usually sets the synchronization cost (called 'GAS'), whose value is related to the size of data. The large data size of the 3D model can cause the blockchain's synchronization cost to exceed an internal limit (called 'GAS limit') set by the network initiator; in the real world, the GAS limit is about 8,000,000 gwei, and in our test network, we set the limit to 1,000,000,000 gwei for testing bigger models.

As shown in Table 1, unless the 3D model is very small, using only the blockchain itself is unable to support 3D models. By using decentralized storage together, we can handle such models. Furthermore, compressing the mesh reduces the storage requirement by a factor of 3 to 40 times and gives the performance boost for the large models. Note that in this scenario (submitting a new model), mesh difference does not help boost the performance, so for the small models ($< 10K$ triangles) the processing time for commit does not decrease.

The mesh difference technique in our mesh page shows its power when we modify the already submitted model. In Fig. 6, we assume that a 3D model of 69K triangles is stored on the network, and an author wants to modify some triangles of the model. The mesh page technique clearly reduces the operation times, especially the checkout time. The commit time decreases by 3.6% on average, and the checkout time decreases by 90.2% on average. The commit time decreases relatively less because of the blockchain's overhead of verifying and applying the new data.

Partitioning the Mesh. We now check whether applying the mesh separation in our mesh page gives us a performance boost or not. As a simple test, we separate the mesh into just two pieces. We measure the time to store the mesh on the network Table 2. We can clearly see that the mesh separation and compression give a performance boost, especially for large models.

7   Conclusion and Discussion

We have proposed a secure 3D model and intellectual property management platform powered by blockchain and decentralized storage techniques. The platform can support various applications, including cooperative modeling, intellectual property management, 3D data authentication, and 3D data protection. More importantly, both the 3D data and the intellectual property can be protected by a decentralized and immutable system. The mesh page technique reduces the workload of the system.

There are some limitations in the current implementation, which also enlightens possible future works. Currently we don't apply any kind of encryptions to the 3D models. Adapting secure rendering through remote rendering [20] to our platform will enable performing confidential 3D projects on our platform. Handling not only the triangles but also the material information such as texture and color will enable more flexible cooperative modeling. More sophisticated geometry feature extraction techniques can improve the performance of geometry matching.

Acknowledgements. This work was supported in part by NRF (2019R1A2C3002833) and Starlab (IITP-2015-0-00199).

Appendix

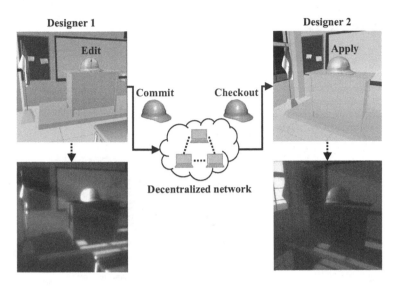

Fig. 2. Example of cooperative modeling. Designer 1 adds a model (colored by green) on the scene and submits its commit to the network. Designer 2 can then perform checkout to download the model added by designer 1. So, both designers can share and render the model. (Color figure online)

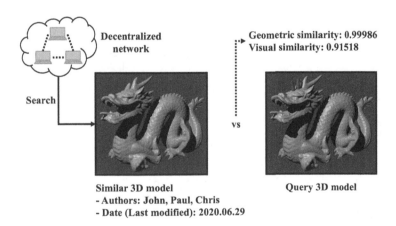

Fig. 3. Example of data authentication. Since the decentralized network securely holds the 3D data and important information (e.g., author, date, etc.), a designer can search 3D models that are similar to the query model. The designer can also find which part of a similar 3D model infringes the intellectual right by comparing those models.

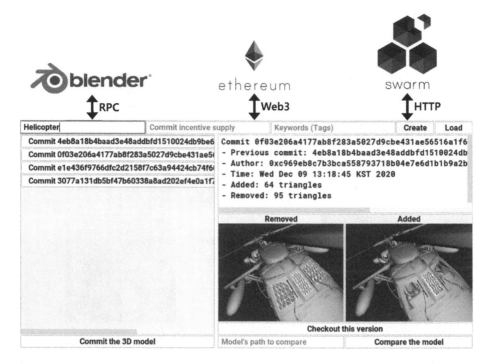

Fig. 4. Our prototype is built on Blender modeling tool, Ethereum blockchain, and Swarm decentralized storage. Applications introduced in this paper are realized via the client code and the smart contract code.

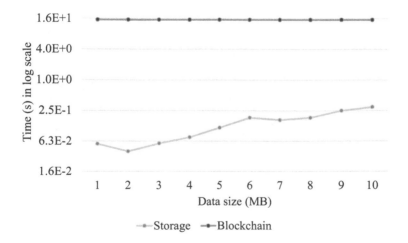

Fig. 5. Time of storing the data on the Swarm [10] storage and storing its storage address on the Ethereum [6] blockchain. The graph shows that the blockchain overhead is significantly larger than the storage overhead. The average time is reported out of 10 different tests.

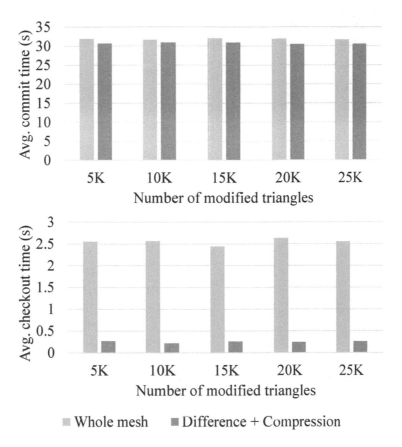

Fig. 6. Comparison in terms of commit and checkout times between using the whole mesh and using mesh pages, when we modify different portions of a bunny model consisting of 69 K triangles. The average is computed out of four different tests.

Table 1. The performances of storing and restoring different models by using only the blockchain network, additionally using the decentralized storage network, and using the mesh difference and mesh compression of our mesh page method.

Model (# of Δ)	Blockchain Commit (s) Checkout (s) Storage (MB)	+ Storage Commit (s) Checkout (s) Storage (MB)	+ m.d. & m.c Commit (s) Checkout (s) Storage (MB)
Cube (12)	30.104	30.234	30.538
	0.149	0.184	0.137
	0.001 MB	0.001 MB	0.0003 MB
Table (1,267)	N.A	30.120	30.113
	N.A	0.159	0.098
	N.A.	0.176 MB	0.009 MB
Copter (46,703)	N.A	31.667	31.745
	N.A	0.951	0.196
	N.A.	6.356 MB	0.324 MB
House (427,647)	N.A	37.404	31.730
	N.A	7.797	1.001
	N.A.	61.959 MB	1.568 MB

Table 2. Results w/ and w/o using separation & compression of mesh page.

# of triangles	427,647	2,000,000
Store the model to the storage	6.5 s	103.4 s
Store the model's address to the blockchain	15.1 s	15.0 s
Whole process	21.5 s	118.4 s
Size of each piece	213,824	1,000,000
Store each piece to the storage	2.5 s	33.7 s
Store the pieces' address to the blockchain	15.0 s	15.0 s
Whole process	**20.0 s**	**82.4 s**
Compress & store each piece to the storage	1.2 s	3.1 s
Store the pieces' address to the blockchain	15.0 s	15.0 s
Whole process	**17.4 s**	**21.1 s**

References

1. Agustina, Liu, F., Xia, S., Shen, H., Sun, C.: CoMaya: incorporating advanced collaboration capabilities into 3D digital media design tools, pp. 5–8 (2008)
2. Bargteil, A.W., Cohen, E.: Animation of deformable bodies with quadratic bézier finite elements. ACM Trans. Graph. (TOG) **33**(3), 1–10 (2014)

3. Benisi, N.Z., Aminian, M., Javadi, B.: Blockchain-based decentralized storage networks: a survey. J. Netw. Comput. Appl. **162**, 102656 (2020)
4. Beregszaszi, A.: Mango (2016). https://github.com/axic/mango
5. Besançon, L., Da Silva, C.F., Ghodous, P.: Towards blockchain interoperability: improving video games data exchange. In: 2019 IEEE International Conference on Blockchain and Cryptocurrency (ICBC), pp. 81–85 (2019)
6. Buterin, V.: Ethereum: a next-generation smart contract and decentralized application platform (2014). Accessed 22 Aug 2016
7. Carra, E., Pellacini, F.: SceneGit: a practical system for diffing and merging 3D environments. ACM Trans. Graph. (TOG) **38**(6), 1–15 (2019)
8. Denning, J.D., Pellacini, F.: MeshGit: diffing and merging meshes for polygonal modeling. ACM Trans. Graph. **32**(4), 35:1–35:10 (2013)
9. Doboš, J., Steed, A.: 3D diff: an interactive approach to mesh differencing and conflict resolution. In: SIGGRAPH Asia 2012 Technical Briefs, SA 2012, pp. 20:1–20:4. ACM, New York, NY, USA (2012)
10. Ethereum Foundation: Swarm: storage and communication for a sovereign digital society (2017). https://swarm.ethereum.org/
11. Ethereum Foundation. Solidity (2016). https://docs.soliditylang.org/
12. Furuya, T., Ohbuchi, R.: Deep aggregation of local 3D geometric features for 3D model retrieval. In: BMVC, vol. 7, p. 8 (2016)
13. Geelnard, M.: Openctm (2009). http://openctm.sourceforge.net/
14. Golem Factory GmbH: The golem project. Technical report (2016)
15. Gordo, A., Almazán, J., Revaud, J., Larlus, D.: Deep image retrieval: learning global representations for image search. In: Leibe, B., Matas, J., Sebe, N., Welling, M. (eds.) ECCV 2016. LNCS, vol. 9910, pp. 241–257. Springer, Cham (2016). https://doi.org/10.1007/978-3-319-46466-4_15
16. Henderson, R.: match3D (2016). https://github.com/ascribe/match3d
17. Huo, Y., Wang, R., Zheng, R., Hualin, X., Bao, H., Yoon, S.-E.: Adaptive incident radiance field sampling and reconstruction using deep reinforcement learning. ACM Trans. Graph. (TOG) **39**(1), 1–17 (2020)
18. Kalogerakis, E.: Session details: learning geometry. ACM Tran. Graph. (TOG) **37**(6) 2018
19. Kelleher, T.: Five core metrics-the intelligence behind successful software management. Softw. Qual. Prof. **6**(2), 44 (2004)
20. Koller, D., et al.: Protected interactive 3D graphics via remote rendering. ACM Trans. Graph. **23**(3), 695–703 (2004)
21. Lavoué, G., Cordier, F., Seo, H., Larabi, M.-C.: Visual attention for rendered 3D shapes. In: Computer Graphics Forum, vol. 37, pp. 191–203. Wiley Online Library (2018)
22. Lee, C.H., Varshney, A., Jacobs, D.W.: Mesh saliency. ACM Trans. Graph. **24**(3), 659–666 (2005)
23. Web3 Labs Ltd.: Solidity (2018). https://www.web3labs.com/web3j-sdk
24. Nakamoto, S.: Bitcoin: a peer-to-peer electronic cash system (2009). http://bitcoin.org/bitcoin.pdf
25. Nguyen, V., Deeds-Rubin, S., Tan, T., Boehm, B.: A SLOC counting standard. In: COCOMO II forum, vol. 2007, pp. 1–16. Citeseer (2007)
26. NVIDIA: Omniverse (2019). https://developer.nvidia.com/nvidia-omniverse
27. OTOY: Render token (RNDR) whitepaper. Technical report (2017)
28. Pixar. USD (universal scene description) (2016). https://graphics.pixar.com/usd/docs/index.html

29. Protocol Labs. IPFS(interplanetary file system): content addressed, versioned, P2P file system (2015). https://ipfs.io/
30. Rashkovskii, Y.: Gitchain (2020). http://gitchain.org/
31. Salvati, G., Santoni, C., Tibaldo, V., Pellacini, F.: MeshHisto: collaborative modeling by sharing and retargeting editing histories. ACM Trans. Graph. **34**(6), 205:1–205:10 (2015)
32. Swan, M.: Blockchain: Blueprint for a new economy. O'Reilly Media, Inc. Sebastopol (2015)
33. Underwood, S.: Blockchain beyond bitcoin (2016)
34. Yoon, S-E.: Rendering. First edition (2018)
35. Zheng, Z., Xie, S., Dai, H.-N., Chen, X., Wang, H.: Blockchain challenges and opportunities: a survey. Int. J. Web Grid Services **14**(4), 352–375 (2018)
36. Zoss, G., Bradley, D., Bérard, P., Beeler, T.: An empirical rig for jaw animation. ACM Trans. Graph. (TOG) **37**(4), 1–12 (2018)

Image Emotion Analysis Based on the Distance Relation of Emotion Categories via Deep Metric Learning

Guoqin Peng, Hao Zhang, and Dan Xu[✉]

Yunnan University, Kunming 650504, China
danxu@ynu.edu.cn

Abstract. Existing deep learning-based image emotion analysis methods regard image emotion classification as a usual classification task in which the semantics of categories are clear. Nevertheless, the semantics of emotion categories are fuzzy, leading to that people are ambiguous between emotions of similar semantic distance when observing images. Considering the semantic distance of emotion categories, that is, far or near distance relations between them, we design a similarity decline rule to first pre-process the similarities of sample pairs making them comparable. Then, image emotion analysis is performed through deep metric learning. For key issues in deep metric learning, that is, sampling and weighting, we design adaptive decision boundaries for sampling and a double-weighted mechanism for sampled pairs which is integrated in our proposed emotion constraint loss, which learns more information contributing to update model by boasting the weights. Therefore, more expressive embedding features are learned from embedding space. Thus, the similarity of pairs from adjacent categories is larger than that from far away ones. The experimental results demonstrate that our proposed method outperforms the state-of-the-art methods. In addition, the ablation experiments show that it is necessary to consider the semantic distance of emotion categories in image emotion analysis.

Keywords: Image emotion analysis · Category distance · Similarity decline rule · Emotion constraint loss · Deep metric learning

1 Introduction

Psychological studies have shown that visual content (such as images and videos) can evoke various emotional responses of observers [1]. Meanwhile, the public are also becoming increasingly interested in expressing their ideas and feelings by uploading images to social media platforms, such as Weibo and Twitter. Understanding the emotions conveyed by the images, that is, image emotion analysis, is meaningful and important, and can be applied widely in many domains, such as emotional semantic image retrieval. Thus, image emotion analysis has been a hot topic in computer vision.

With the great success of convolutional neural networks (CNNs) in computer vision, CNN-based deep learning methods show better performance than that of handcrafted

N. Magnenat-Thalmann et al. (Eds.): CGI 2021, LNCS 13002, pp. 535–547, 2021.
https://doi.org/10.1007/978-3-030-89029-2_41

methods based on art and psychology theories for image emotion analysis. In these methods, the affective categories are independent of each other, similar to object recognition of the usual classification. Nevertheless, emotion is fuzzy naturally, mainly due to the relevance of emotional semantics and the subjectivity and complexity of emotional cognition of humans. Humans may be ambiguous between emotions of similar semantic distance, or have completely different emotion responses to the same image, as shown in Fig. 1. The line chart on the right part represents the annotation statistics of left images. For example, half of the observers labeled the top-right image with surprise, and the other half labeled it with joy. This suggests that the emotion semantic boundaries are not clear. Thus, it is difficult to distinguish among those emotions whose semantic distance is close. Moreover, some observers label the bottom right image with sadness, while most label it with surprise. Nevertheless, sadness and surprise are completely different polar emotions. However, the existing works seldom consider the essential fuzzy relation, that is the far or near distance relation of emotions.

Fig. 1. Illustration the ambiguity of image emotion semantics.

In this work, considering the distance relation of emotions, we develop a novel emotion similarity constraint (ESC) loss via deep metric learning for image emotion analysis. More discriminative embedded features are learned in the embedded space by fully considering the far or near relation of emotions. So that the similarity of an image pair from adjacent categories is greater than that of a pair from distant categories, while the similarity of one from the same category is largest. The framework of our method is illustrated in Fig. 2. First, the similarity of the sample pair is pre-processed according to the Mikels' emotion wheel [2]. Second, we designed sampling mechanism with adaptive decision boundaries, so that informative pairs are selected for training, while uninformative pairs are discarded. Then, a double-weighted mechanism which is integrated in our emotion ESC loss is proposed. According to the current status of sample pairs, the greater weights are set to more informative pairs.

The main contributions of this paper are as follows:

1. We consider the essential distance relation of emotion categories, i.e., the far or near distance relation. We develop the similarity decline rule (SDR) to pre-process the similarities to a comparable rank. The ablation experiments show that it is necessary to consider the distance relation of emotion categories for image emotion analysis.

2. For the two key factors in deep metric learning, i.e., sampling and weighting, we design a sampling mechanism with adaptive decision boundaries which are adaptively updated with the optimization of the model. Therefore, more image pairs which can contribute to update model are sampled.

3. A double-weighted mechanism which is fused into the emotion similarity constraint is designed to accelerate model convergence by enhancing the contribution of more informative sample pairs. The gradient weight of emotion similarity constraint loss with respect to parameter of the model is exaggerated by a weight coefficient which is adaptively set according to the extent of violation to the target.

4. The experimental results demonstrate the effectiveness of our proposed method. The embedded features are more representative and discriminative according to the performances of classification and retrieval.

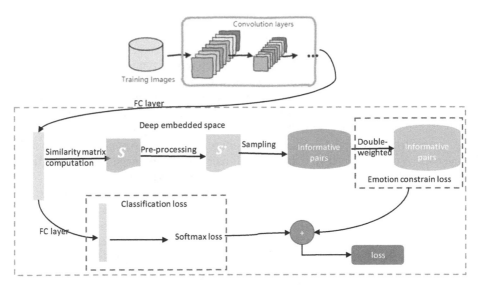

Fig. 2. The framework of the proposed method.

2 Related Works

2.1 Image Emotion Analysis

Inspired by psychology, art and color theories, researchers developed handcrafted features of images and trained them with traditional machine learning methods for image emotion analysis. Low-level features (such as color and texture) [3], and mid-level features [4] based on principle-of-art and high-level adjective noun pairs (ANPs) [5] are extracted for image emotion analysis. Recently, CNN-based deep learning methods have demonstrated their excellence in emotional feature extraction. Thus, they have been widely used in image emotion analysis and have achieved great success [6]. Based on the pre-trained on large-scale dataset for object recognition [7], CNN is fine-tuned for visual emotion analysis. Peng et al. [8] developed a regression CNN model for image emotion analysis based on Euclidean loss. Yang et al. [9] and Zhao et al. [10] revealed the extent to which each label describes each sample image by label distribution learning [11] in which each sample is mapped into a label distribution. Yang et al. [12] proposed jointly optimized image emotion classification and distribution learning in a framework, demonstrating better performance. Xiong et al. [13] exploited the structured and sparse characteristic of emotion by grouping and ordering effectively to solve the issue of label ambiguity. These methods seldom consider the distance between emotion categories, or at most the polar character of emotion is explored, viewing image emotion classification as a usual object classification task in which distances among categories are equal. Nevertheless, image emotion analysis is different from common computer vision tasks, there is a far or near nature relation of distance between emotions, which is considered in this paper.

2.2 Deep Metric Learning

Metric learning has been widely used in pattern recognition for decades. With the excellent performance of deep learning, deep metric learning methods have been proposed. The goal of metric learning is to learn an embedded space, where the sample pairs from the same category are encouraged to be closer, while the ones from different categories are pushed apart from each other. The pairs which violate the goal of deep metric learning can contribute to update model, called informative pairs. An image pair from the same class is called a positive sample pair (P-pair), while an image pair from different classes is a negative sample pair (N-pair), an anchor image is selected firstly.

Researchers have developed several loss functions i0n deep metric learning. The contrastive loss [14] and triplet loss [15] are two basic loss functions. In contrast loss, some N-pairs whose distances are larger than a margin are discarded. Triplet loss enforces the similarity of a N-pair to be smaller than that of a randomly selected P-pair over a given margin. In both losses, the weights of all sample pairs are equal. Later, lifted structure loss [16] and n-pair loss [17] introduce new weighting mechanisms in which more informative pairs have greater weight. Binomial deviance loss [18] evaluates the cost between labels and similarity by using a binomial deviance, which emphases harder pairs. Wang et al. [19] proposed to cast sampling into a general pair weighting (GPW) formulation, in which hard-pair mining and weighing which are two key issues in deep metric learning are conducted by considering multi-similarity. Based on the intuition that if a similarity score deviates far from the optimum, it should be emphasized, Sun et al. [20] proposed circle loss, which is named due to its circular decision boundary.

Yang et al. [21] firstly extended triplet loss to a hierarchical structure triplet constraint for image emotion analysis. Nevertheless, the problems of triplet loss itself are brought into. First, not all the triplet relations of images are represented. Second, all pairs are considered equally. In this work, for the two key issues in deep metric learning, we propose an effective sampling and weighting mechanism, aiming at learning from more informative pairs and exaggerating their contributions to model updating.

3 Method

The key in deep metric learning is to learn from rich informative pairs. Thus, the first step is to identify informative pairs, i.e., sampling. Then, more information that is beneficial to the model is learned from these sampled informative pairs by weighting mechanism. Nevertheless, due to the far or near distance relation of emotions as shown in Fig. 3, it is problematic to compare the similarities directly. Thus, we first pre-process the similarities of sample pairs. The framework of our method is illustrated in Fig. 2.

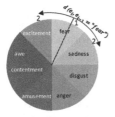

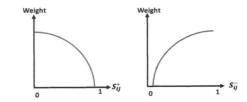

Fig. 3. Mikels' emotion wheel and the distance of emotions

Fig. 4. The weight varieties according the similarity itself

Let $X = \{x_i | x_i \in \mathbb{R}^d\}_{i=1}^m$ be the training dataset, where m is the size of the dataset. $Y = \{y_i\}_{i=1}^m$ is the corresponding labels, $y_i \in \{1, 2, \cdots, C\}$ is the label of x_i, and C is the number of emotion categories. C is 8 in this paper. In embedded space, x_i is mapped into an l-d embedded feature vector $f(\cdot, \theta) : \mathbb{R}^d \to \mathbb{R}^l$, where f is parametrized with θ. Then, $f(\cdot, \theta)$ is normalized, the similarity of images x_i and x_j is defined as $s_{ij} = <f(x_i, \theta), f(x_j, \theta)>$, where $<\cdot, \cdot>$ denotes the dot product. Therefore, the optimal similarity of a P-pair is 1, while that of a N-pair is 0. The similarities of all sample pairs in a mini batch (batch-size is n) compose the similarity matrix $S \in \mathbb{R}^{n \times n}$.

3.1 Pre-processing

The similarities of sample pairs from near emotion categories are naturally larger than that of pairs from far away categories, so they are not comparable. Therefore, based on the Mikels' emotion wheel, we first pre-process the similarities to a comparable rank, and then carry out deep metric learning for image emotion analysis.

The farther the distance between categories, the smaller the emotional similarity should be. Thus, the similarity of a pair declines with the increasing of distance between the emotion categories which the pair images belong to, that is:

$$s_{ij}^* = f(d)s_{ij} \tag{1}$$

Where d is the distance between emotion categories y_i and y_j, which are the corresponding labels of images x_i and x_j, respectively. d is defined as the step from one emotion category to the other in Mikels' emotion wheel adding 1. For example, in Fig. 3, the numbers illustrate the distance from "fear" to the other categories. $f(d)$ is a function with respect to the distance d. In this paper, according to the rate of decline in similarity, we define two types of SDRs. One is that the rate of decline is a uniform distribution, i.e.,

$f(d) \sim U(0, d)$. The other is that it obey the Gaussian distribution is considered, i.e., $f(d) \sim N(\mu, \sigma^2)$. μ is 0. The rate of decline is based on the variance σ. The smaller σ is, the faster the descent, so the similarity score of sample pairs from more distant emotion categories is smaller. Therefore, we can control the strength of the similarity between sample pairs from different emotions by adjusting the variance σ. We will discuss the results of the two distributions in Sect. 4.3.

3.2 Sampling Mechanism

Following circle loss, adaptive decision boundaries are proposed to continuously extract more informative sample pairs in this paper. Nevertheless, circle loss did not sample pairs, thus, the informative pairs may be overwhelmed in non-informative pairs.

Assuming that the decision boundary of the P-pair is O_P, while that of the N-pair is O_N. If the similarity of a pair approaches to its decision boundary with a margin, it is non-informative and discarded. Otherwise, the pair is selected for training. Specifically, a P-pair $s_{ij}^* < O_P - m_1$ is selected, the N-pair $s_{ij}^* > O_N + m_2$ is selected. All selected P-pairs and N-pairs of x_i comprise its positive sample set P_i and negative sample set N_i, respectively.

The similarity of a P-pair should be greater than that of any N-pair. Therefore, if the similarity of a P-pair is less than that of any N-pair, it should be selected. Thus, the decision boundary of P-pairs is set as the max similarity of N-pair, that is:

$$O_P = \max_{x_j \in N_i} s_{ij}^*, \forall_i \tag{2}$$

Similarly, the decision boundary of N-pairs is:

$$O_N = \min_{x_j \in P_i} s_{ij}^*, \forall_i \tag{3}$$

The definitions show that the decision boundaries can adaptively update with the optimization of the model. With the convergence of the model, the standard of sampling becomes higher, which means that the model learns from the harder pairs, while firstly learning from hard pairs. This is also a general way to solve problems.

3.3 Double-Weighted Mechanism

In this paper, a double-weighted mechanism is proposed. First, a weight coefficient is designed. Then, the weight coefficient is combined to gradient weight to exaggerate the contribution of the informative pairs to the model updating.

Weight Coefficient. Intuitively, the weight coefficient is the distance from the similarity to its optimal state, that is:

$$
\begin{aligned}
a_{ij}^+ &= \left[1 - s_{ij}^*\right]_+, \ if \ y_i == y_j \\
a_{ij}^- &= \left[s_{ij}^* - 0\right]_+, \ if \ y_i \neq y_j
\end{aligned}
\tag{4}
$$

Where $[\cdot]_+$ is the "cut-off at zero" operation, which ensures that a_{ij}^+ and a_{ij}^- are non-negative weight coefficients of a P-pair and an N-pair, respectively. Further away from the optimal state, the greater the weight coefficient is. a_{ij}^+ and a_{ij}^- are multiplied by the similarities themselves, that is, $a_{ij}^+ s_{ij}^*$ and $a_{ij}^- s_{ij}^*$, respectively, boosting the loss. Since the goal of the P-pair is the larger the similarity, the better is. So, the smaller the similarity is, the heavier the penalty is, as shown in Fig. 4. The weight of a N-pair is opposite, the smaller the similarity the greater weight is.

Gradient Weight. The gradient weight reflects the gradient which affect the pace of updating the parameter θ of the model. It depends on loss function. Our proposed emotion similarity constraint (ESC) loss is formulated as:

$$L_{ESC} = \frac{1}{m}\sum_{i=1}^{m}\left\{\log\left[1 + \sum_{x_k \in N_i} e^{a_{ik}^-(s_{ik}^* - m_2)}\right] + \log\left[1 + \sum_{x_k \in P_i} e^{-a_{ik}^+(s_{ik}^* - m_1)}\right]\right\} \quad (5)$$

The gradient of ESC loss with respect to an N-pair is derived as follows:

$$w_{ij}^- = \frac{\partial L_{ESC}}{\partial s_{ij}^*} = a_{ij}^- \frac{1}{\exp\left(a_{ij}^-\left(m_2 - s_{ij}^*\right)\right) + \sum_{x_k \in N_i} \exp\left(a_{ik}^-\left(s_{ik}^* - s_{ij}^*\right)\right)} \quad (6)$$

And the gradient with respect to a P-pair is:

$$w_{ij}^+ = \frac{\partial L_{ESC}}{\partial s_{ij}^*} = a_{ij}^+ \frac{1}{\exp\left(-a_{ij}^+\left(m_1 - s_{ij}^*\right)\right) + \sum_{x_k \in P_i} \exp\left(-a_{ik}^-\left(s_{ik}^* - s_{ij}^*\right)\right)} \quad (7)$$

Where the w_{ij}^- and w_{ij}^+ are the gradient weighs of a N-pair and a P-pair, respectively.

Based on the chain rule in backpropagation, the gradient of L_{ESC} with respect to parameter θ is:

$$\frac{\partial L_{ESC}}{\partial \theta} = \sum_{i=1}^{m}\left(\sum_{x_j \in N_i} w_{ij}^- \frac{\partial s_{ij}^*}{\partial \theta} + \sum_{x_j \in P_i} w_{ij}^+ \frac{\partial s_{ij}^*}{\partial \theta}\right) \quad (8)$$

For an N-pair, the denominator of w_{ij}^- is composed of the weight of similarity itself and the similarity difference between the other N-pair with the same anchor and this N-pair, that is, the so-called relative similarity in Multi-similarity loss. The relative similarity of an N-pair decreases, even when its self-similarity does not change. As the relative similarity decreases, it becomes closer to optimum. Thus, the weight is small, which react as the value of w_{ij}^- decreases. The analysis of the weight of a P-pair is similar. This is consistent with our expectation of weighting mechanism.

Therefore, the gradient weight w_{ij} is affected not only by the similarity itself but also by the similarity of other adjacent sample pairs. In addition, the weight coefficient is used to stretch the contribution of the gradient weight. Therefore, the richer the informative pair is, the greater the weight and the faster the pace of the network parameter updating. It is beneficial to accelerate the convergence of the model. Otherwise, the pace of updating the parameter is slow, which prevents model zigzag. However, in multi-similarity loss, the weigh cooperates with a constant coefficient. Thus, all weights are exaggerated with the same degree. Therefore, in our double-weight mechanism, every sample pair optimized the model at its own pace.

Loss. For classification tasks, the cross-entropy loss is optimized to maximize the probability of correctly classified samples. The soft-max loss of classification is L_C. The final loss L is the cooperative emotion similarity constraint loss and soft-max loss:

$$L = (1 - \alpha)L_C + \alpha l_{ESC} \tag{9}$$

Where α is the ratio. Stochastic gradient decent (SGD) optimization is used. As more representative information is learned, the classification performance improves a lot.

4 Experiment

The pre-trained ResNet34 is adopted as the backbone structure. The last average pool feature of ResNet34 is input into a fully connect layer, resulting in embedded feature vector f. The input images are cropped to 224×224 and augmented by random horizontal flip. The hyper parameters $m_1 = 0.1$, $m_2 = 0.2$ and $\alpha = 0.6$ in all experiments.

Sine there are fewer 8-class emotion image datasets available, our experiments are performed on the ArtPhoto and Abstract datasets created by Machajdik and Hurbary [3]. The ArtPhoto consists of 806 artistic photos taken by professional artists with the goal of evoking the observers' specific emotions by adjusting light, color and composition parameters. The ground-truth label is provided by photo-creators. The Abstract consists of 280 peer rated art painting with only colors and textures. The two datasets are randomly split into 80% training and 20% testing.

4.1 Performance Analysis

The proposed ESC is compared with baseline handcrafted detection methods, common fully connected CNN (FC-CNN) methods and deep metric learning methods, in which the multi-similarity loss and circle loss are transferred for image emotion analysis by cooperating with SDR. The results on testing dataset are shown in Table 1. On Art-Photo, considering the SDR, the accuracy of multi-similarity and circle loss outperforms the state-of-the-art triple sentiment by 2% and 2.5%, respectively. The performances on Abstract also improve a lot. Comparing with multi-similarity and circle loss, ESC improves the accuracy by 1.2% and 1.8% on two datasets, respectively. Comparing with the most related and the state-of-the-art deep metric learning method for image emotion analysis, i.e., triple sentiment, the accuracy improves by approximately 4% and 4.6% on two datasets, respectively. Since the 8-class emotion classification task is hard, it is truly a performance breakthrough to improve the accuracy so much. The results demonstrate that our proposed ESC is effective.

Table 1. Accuracy comparison of several methods

Method		Acc. (%)	
		ArtPhoto	Abstract
Baseline	SIFT	21.12	20.29
	HOG	19.44	20.86
	Gabor	15.77	21.71
	SentiBnak	25.07	29.14
	DeepSentiBank	30.15	32.29
FC-CNN	GoogleNet	35.21	35.14
Deep Metric Learning	Triple Sentiment	39.72	38.29
	Circle loss + SDR	41.62	39.29
	Multi-similarity loss + SDR	42.24	41.07
	ESC + SDR	**43.48**	**42.86**

To further illustrate the effectiveness of the proposed method, the image emotion retrieval is conducted on both ArtPhoto and Abstract. Since both datasets are small, each image acting as a test image to retrieve emotion images from the remaining images of its own dataset. Some results illustrate in Fig. 5 (amusement-amuse, excitement-excite, contentment-content). The similarity score and ground-truth label are marked on the retrieved images. In the first 4 rows, the categories of the retrieved top-3 images are consistent with the categories of the retrieval images. Although in the last two row, not all of the top-3 retrieved images are from the category of the input image. However, they are from neighboring categories, not from far away ones. This demonstrates that the proposed ESC is effective in learning embedded space, that is, the similarity of the similarity of pairs from adjacent categories is larger than that from far away ones, in addition to the similarity of pairs from the same category is largest. The confusion matrixes on the whole dataset in Fig. 6 further show that the embedded feature vectors of pairs from the same emotions are closer, while pairs from different emotions are pushed apart from each other. Therefore, the maximum value is all on the diagonal.

4.2 Ablation

To further demonstrate the importance and necessity of considering the emotion category distance in image emotion analysis, we carry out the ablation experiment. As can be seen in Table 3, all methods with SDR are superior to those without SDR. The results further show that it is necessary to pre-process the similarity based on the far or near distance relation between emotions.

(a) Input image   (b) Retrieved top-3 images

Fig. 5. Visualization of the top-3 retrieval results.

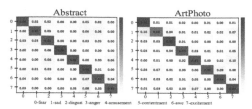

Fig. 6. Confusion matrix of prediction.

Table 2. Performance (Acc.%) of different SDRs.

	Uniform	Gaussian
ArtPhoto	42.85	43.48
Abstract	41.07	42.86

Table 3. Ablation analysis of SDR

Method		Acc.(%)	
		ArtPhoto	Abstract
Multi-similarity loss	Without SDR	40.37	37.50
	With SDR	42.24	41.07
Circle loss	Without SDR	39.76	37.50
	With SDR	41.62	39.29
ESC(ours)	Without SDR	42.23	39.29
	With SDR	43.48	42.86

4.3 Similarity Decline Rule

As described in Sect. 3.1, two SDRs are designed, and their experiment results are shown in Table 2. In the Gaussian strategy, the standard deviation σ affects the rate of decent. The max step of emotion categories is 5 in Mikels' wheel, setting $2\sigma = 5$. The performances of Gaussian strategy are better. Thus, all experiments adopt this strategy.

5 Conclusion

As 8-class emotion analysis is quite challenging, researchers have been devoted to achieving breakthroughs. Our emotion similarity constraint fully considers the distance relation of emotions, which is the essential character of emotion semantics. The ablation experiments also show that it is necessary to consider the distance relation of emotions. For the two key issues of deep metric learning, i.e., sampling and weighting, an adaptive sampling mechanism where the decision boundaries vary gradually with the model optimization is propose to select informative sample pairs for training. A double-weighted mechanism which is integrated into emotion similarity constraint loss is also designed for these selected sample pairs. Therefore, a larger weigh coefficient is applied to the more informative sample pair to exaggerate the its contribution to model optimization. In other word, the sample pairs optimize the model on its own space, more informative pairs do more contribution at faster speeds while less informative pairs do contribution at mild pace. The experiment results demonstrate that ESC outperforms the state-of-the-art methods.

Acknowledgments. This work is supported by the National Natural Science Foundation of China under Grant No. 61163019 and No. 61540062, the Yunnan Applied Basic Research Key Project under Grant No. 2014FA021, and the Scientific Research Project of Yunnan Province Education Department under Grant No. 2021J0029 and 2021Y027.

References

1. Detenber, B.H., Simons, R.F., Bennett, G.G., Jr.: Roll'em!: the effects of picture motion on emotional responses. Broadcast. Electr. Media **42**(1), 113–127 (1998)
2. Mikels, J., Fredrickson, A., Larkin, B.L., et al.: Emotional category data on images from the international affective picture system. Behav. Res. Methods **37**(4), 626–630 (2005)
3. Machajdik, J., Hanbury, A.: Affective image classification using features inspired by psychology and art theory. In: International Conference on Multimedia, pp. 83–92. ACM, Firenze (2010)
4. Zhao, S., Gao, Y., Jiang, X., et al.: Exploring principles-of-art features for image emotion recognition. In: The ACM International Conference on Multimedia, pp. 47–56. ACM, Orlando (2014)
5. Borth, D., Ji, T., Chen, T., et al.: Large-scale visual sentiment ontology and detectors using adjective noun pairs. In: ACM Multimedia Conference, pp. 223–232. ACM, Barcelona (2013)
6. Zhao, S., Zhao, X., Ding, G., et al.: Emotiongan: unsupervised domain adaptation for learning discrete probability distributions of image emotions. In: ACM Multimedia Conference on Multimedia Conference, pp. 1319–1327. ACM, Seoul (2018)
7. Deng, J., Dong, W., Socher, R., et al.: ImageNet: a large-scale hierarchical image database. In: IEEE Computer Society Conference on Computer Vision and Pattern Recognition, pp. 248–255. IEEE, Florida (2009)
8. Peng, K.C., Chen, T., Sadovnik, A., et al.: A mixed bag of emotions: model, predict, and transfer emotion distributions. In: IEEE Conference on Computer Vision and Pattern Recognition, pp. 860–868. IEEE, Boston (2015)
9. Yang, J., Sun, M., Sun, X.: Learning visual sentiment distributions via augmented conditional probability neural network. In: AAAI Conference on Artificial Intelligence, pp. 224–230. AAAI, California (2017)
10. Zhao, S., Ding, G., Gao, Y., et al.: Discrete probability distribution prediction of image emotions with shared sparse learning. IEEE Trans. Affect. Comput. **11**(4), 574–587 (2020)
11. Geng, X.: Label distribution learning. IEEE Trans. Knowl. Data Eng. **28**(7), 1734–1748 (2016)
12. Yang J., She D., Sun M.: Joint image emotion classification and distribution learning via deep convolutional neural network. In: International Joint Conference on Artificial Intelligence, pp. 3266–3272. Melbourne (2017)
13. Xiong, H., Liu, H., Zhong, B., et al.: Structured and sparse annotations for image emotion distribution learning. In: AAAI Conference on Artificial Intelligence, pp. 363–370. AAAI, Hawaii (2019)
14. Hadsell, R., Chopra, S., LeCun, Y.: Dimensionality reduction by learning an invariant mapping. In: IEEE Computer Society Conference on Computer Vision and Pattern Recognition, pp. 1735–1742. IEEE, New York (2006)
15. Hoffer, E., Ailon, N.: Deep metric learning using triplet network. In: International Conference on Learning Representations, pp. 84–92. Sprinter, San Diego (2015)
16. Oh Song, H., Xiang, Y., Jegelka, S., et al.: Deep metric learning via lifted structured feature embedding. In: IEEE Conference on Computer Vision and Pattern Recognition, pp. 4004–4012. IEEE, Las Vegas (2016)
17. Sohn, K.: Improved deep metric learning with multi-class n-pair loss objective. In: Advances in Neural Information Processing Systems, pp. 1849–1857. Barcelona (2016)
18. Yi, D., Lei, Z., Li, S.Z.: Deep metric learning for practical person re-identification. arXiv: 1407.4979 (2014)
19. Wang, X, Han, X.T., Huang, W.L., et al.: Multi-similarity loss with general pair weighting for deep metric learning. In: IEEE Conference on Computer Vision and Pattern Recognition, pp. 5022–5030. IEEE, Long Beach (2019)

20. Sun, Y., Cheng, C., Zhang, Y., et al.: Circle loss: a unified perspective of pair similarity optimization. In: IEEE Conference on Computer Vision and Pattern Recognition, pp. 6397–6406. IEEE, Seattle (2020)
21. Yang, J., She, D, Lai, Y., et al.: Retrieving and classifying affective images via deep metric learning. In: AAAI Conference on Artificial Intelligence, pp. 491–498. AAAI, New Orleans (2018)

How Much Do We Perceive Geometric Features, Personalities and Emotions in Avatars?

Victor Araujo$^{(\boxtimes)}$, Bruna Dalmoro, Rodolfo Favaretto, Felipe Vilanova, Angelo Costa, and Soraia Raupp Musse

Pontifical Catholic University of Rio Grande do Sul, Porto Alegre, Brazil
victor.flavio@acad.pucrs.br, soraia.musse@pucrs.br

Abstract. The goal of this paper is to evaluate the human perception regarding geometric features, personalities and emotions in avatars. To achieve this, we used a dataset that contains pedestrian tracking files captured in spontaneous videos which are visualized as identical virtual human beings. The main objective is to focus on individuals motion, not having the distraction of other features. In addition to tracking files containing pedestrian positions, the dataset also contains emotion and personality data for each pedestrian, detected through computer vision and pattern recognition techniques. We are interested in evaluating whether participants can perceive geometric features such as density levels, distances, angular variations and speeds, as well as cultural features (emotions and personality traits) in short video sequences (scenes), when pedestrians are represented by avatars. With this aim in mind, we propose two questions to be answered through this analysis: *i)* "Can people perceive geometric features in avatars?"; and *ii)* "Can people perceive differences regarding personalities and emotions in virtual humans without body and facial expressions?". Regarding the participants, 73 people volunteered for the experiment in order to answer the two mentioned questions. Results indicate that, even without explaining to the participants the concepts of cultural features and how they were calculated (considering the geometric features), in most cases the participants perceived the personality and emotion expressed by avatars, even without faces and body expressions.

Keywords: Human perception · Geometric features · Personalities · Emotions · Points of view · Avatars

1 Introduction

Human behavior is widely studied as a topic that attracts many scientific interests and probably an inexhaustible source of research [19]. Due to its importance in many applications, automatic analysis of this behavior has been a very popular research focus in recent decades [1]. In the literature, there are work involving

© Springer Nature Switzerland AG 2021
N. Magnenat-Thalmann et al. (Eds.): CGI 2021, LNCS 13002, pp. 548–567, 2021.
https://doi.org/10.1007/978-3-030-89029-2_42

visualization and analysis of cultural features (emotions, personality traits, etc.), such as analyzing the impact of groups of people on crowds through human perceptions [25], visualizing interactions between virtual agents in crowd simulations and pedestrians in real video sequences [20], perceptual analysis of cultural features in virtual humans with body expressions [8], and others [7,26]. Lately, studies have used geometric features to analyze cultural features in crowds. Favaretto et al. [10] used group behaviors to detect cultural features according to Hofstede [17]. In other investigations, Favaretto and his colleagues investigated cultural features using controlled experiment videos (related to Fundamental Diagram [5]) and spontaneous videos from various countries, using geometrical features [11], Big-Five personality model [12] and OCC emotion [13] models.

In this sense, the aim of this paper is to investigate how people perceive geometric features (for example, density levels, distances, angular variation and velocities) and cultural features (for example, personality traits and emotions) in avatars (virtual humans and cylinders). We used the videos of *Cultural Crowds*[1] dataset [10], which contains sequences from different countries, with pedestrians walking in different scenarios. Therefore, the dataset contains tracking files with pedestrian positions and also provides personality and emotion information of these pedestrians, which was obtained using GeoMind Model [14]. Interest in the field of crowd perception has increased a lot in recent years in science. The study of crowd perception is important for understanding group behavior, where human beings can observe interpersonal interaction on a collective level [22]. There are many proposed methods in this area, in which some explore the perception of different character models in crowd simulations [23], perception of average emotion in a crowd through ensemble coding [15,22], among others. However, few studies [3] focus on perceptions about geometric and cultural features obtained from videos of real crowds, and simulated from avatars. With that, we created two hypotheses: $H0_1$: Defines that people can not perceive geometric features in avatars; $H0_2$: Defines that people can not perceive cultural features in avatars without traditional expressions (body, facial, etc.).

For our experiments, we used the tracked positions to animate avatars. In a simulated environment, they can be visualized as humanoids or cylinders. The goal is to focus on behavior and not be distracted by other features. In our analysis, participants were asked to answer questions to identify whether they could perceive geometric features (density, speed, angular variation and distance) as well as cultural features (emotions and personality traits) in scenes. In the present work, our focus is on the perception of information based on space and geometry. Even when we investigate emotion and personality, we are interested in pure geometric manifestations, that is, avatars presenting emotions through movement (for example, walking and running). Thus, the main objective of this article is to evaluate human perception regarding geometric and cultural features through the following questions: *i)* "Can people perceive geometric features in avatars?"; and *ii)* "Can people perceive cultural features in virtual humans without body and facial expressions?".

---

[1] (Available at: http://www.inf.pucrs.br/vhlab).

2   Related Work

This section discusses some related work to pedestrian and crowd behavioral analysis, focusing on personality traits, emotion and perception. Durupinar et al. [7] also used OCEAN to visually represent personality traits. Visual representation of agents is given in various ways, for example, the animations of agents are based on these two cultural features (OCEAN and emotion). If an agent is sad, the animation will represent that emotion. Yang et al. [25] conducted a study analyzing perception to determine the impact of groups at various densities, using two points of view: top and first-person. Unlike the work by Yang et al. [25], we used three viewpoints and two types of avatars. In addition, we do not want to assess the difference between densities from different viewpoints, but whether people perceive features. In the work of Araujo et al. [3], the authors evaluated perceptions about geometric features in different types of cameras and types of avatars. One of the results indicated that different points of view can influence the perception of geometric features. As in the work of Araujo et al. [3], we want to assess the perception of geometric and cultural features.

Regarding the detection of personalities and emotions in crowd pedestrians, Favaretto et al. [10] proposed a method to identify groups and characterize them to evaluate aspects of cultural differences by mapping Hofstede's dimensions [18]. A similar idea, although using computer simulation and not focused on computer vision, is proposed by Lala et al. [21]. Gorbova et al. [16] introduced an automatic personality screening system from video presentations to decide whether a person should be invited to a job interview based on visual, audio and lexical tips. In other work proposed by Favaretto et al. [12], the authors presented a model to detect personality features based on OCEAN model using individuals behaviors automatically detected in video sequences. Several models have been developed to explain and quantify basic emotions in humans. One of the most cited is proposed by Paul Ekman [9] which considers the existence of six universal emotions based on cross-cultural facial expressions (anger, disgust, fear, happiness, sadness and surprise). In [13], the authors proposed a way to detect pedestrian emotions in videos, based on OCC emotion model. The OCC (Ortony, Clore, and Collins) emotional model indicate the susceptibility of each five personality factors to feeling every emotion. To detect emotions of each pedestrian, the authors used OCEAN as inputs, as proposed by Saifi [24]. In our approach, we proceed with an analysis to assess if participants can perceive geometric features, as well as emotions and personalities in scenes when pedestrians are represented by avatars. The next section presents the methodology used to perform the analysis.

3   Methodology

In this work, personality and emotion traits are calculated based on psychological hypotheses [12]. Next sections detail all processes. Note: the application of the questionnaire is presented in Appendix A.3.

3.1   Data Extraction

Based on the tracking input file, Favaretto et al. [12] compute information for each pedestrian i at each time step: $i)$ 2D position x_i (meters); $ii)$ speed s_i (meters/frame); $iii)$ angular variation α_i (degrees) w.r.t. a reference vector $\mathbf{r} = (1,0)$; $iv)$ isolation level φ_i; $v)$ socialization level ϑ_i; and $vi)$ collectivity ϕ_i. To compute the collectivity affected in individual i from all n neighbors, Favaretto proposed $\phi_i = \sum_{j=0}^{n-1} \gamma e^{(-\beta \varpi(i,j)^2)}$, where the collectivity between two individuals (i,j) was calculated as a decay function of $\varpi(i,j) = s(s_i, s_j).w_1 + o(\alpha_i, \alpha_j).w_2$, considering s and o respectively the speed and orientation differences between two people i and j, and w_1 and w_2 are constants that should regulate the offset in meters and radians.

3.2   Features Extraction

To compute the socialization level ϑ, Favaretto et al. [11] used an artificial neural network (ANN) with a Scaled Conjugate Gradient (SCG) algorithm in the training process to calculate the socialization ϑ_i level for each individual i. The ANN has 3 inputs (collectivity ϕ_i of person i, mean Euclidean distance from a person i to others $\bar{d}_{i,j}$ and the number of people in the Social Space[2] according to Hall's proxemics [4] around the person i). The isolation level corresponds to inverse of socialization, $\varphi_i = 1 - \vartheta_i$. For more details about that, please refer to [11,12]. For each individual in a video, we computed the average of all parameters for frames and generate a vector $\mathbf{V_i}$ of extracted data where $\mathbf{V_i} = \left[\bar{x}_i, \bar{s}_i, \bar{\alpha}_i, \bar{\varphi}_i, \bar{\vartheta}_i, \bar{\phi}_i\right]$.

3.3   Personality and Emotion Extraction

To detect the five dimensions of OCEAN model for each pedestrian, Favaretto et al. [12] used the NEO PI-R [6] that is the standard questionnaire measure of the Five Factor Model. They firstly selected NEO PI-R items related to individual-level crowd features and the corresponding OCEAN-factor. For example: "Like being part of crowd at sporting event" corresponding to the factor "Extraversion". As described in details in [12], they proposed a series of empirically defined equations to map pedestrian features to OCEAN dimensions. Firstly, they selected 25 from the 240 items from NEO PI-R inventory that had a direct relationship with crowd behavior. In order to answer the items with data coming from real video sequences, they proposed equations that could represent each one of the 25 items with features extracted from videos, as described in Sect. 3.2. In the work presented in [13], the authors proposed a way to map OCEAN dimensions of each pedestrian in OCC Emotion model, regarding four emotions: Anger, Fear, Happiness and Sadness.

---

[2] Social space is related to 3.6 m [4].

3.4   Video Characteristics

This section provides some information about the videos from Cultural Crowds dataset [10] and the scenes generated from them. The last two columns of Table 1 in Appendix A.2 shows relations of all dataset videos that were used in this work, with information about the Country where the video was recorded, number of pedestrians and density level (low, medium, or high). Each video was chosen based on features of each questionnaire question (which is explained in the next section). For example, the videos used for speed questions were chosen based on pedestrian speed data. Thus, the videos $BR - 15$, $BR - 25$ and $BR - 34$ were only used in scenes referring to questions of geometric features. The other videos were used in scenes of cultural features questions, however, the video $BR - 01$ was also used in speed questions. All data are visualized as shown in the Appendix A.1, represented by cylinder or humanoid type avatars, which can be seen respectively in Fig. 2(b) and (c). Table 1 presents all scenes used in questions, the type of camera used, type of avatar, and the Cultural Crowds video for each of them.

4   Results

This section presents results from the participants' perceptions about geometric data, personality traits and emotions represented by virtual humans. Regarding the participants, 73 people volunteered for the experiment: 62.66% men and 37.33% women; 65.33% under 31 years old; and 48% had at least a undergraduate degree. In all statistical analysis, we used a significance level of 5% (paired and independent T-tests, and *Logistic Regression*). In addition, for all questions presented in Appendix A.3, we analyzed answers between right (1) and wrong (0). In all cases, we analyzed the answers of participants in general, between genders, ages, and levels of education. Table 4, in the Appendix A.1, shows the average score of right answers for all questions.

4.1   Geometric Features Perception

Density Perception Analysis. Regarding density questions, as shown in the second column of Table 4, both in $D1$ and $D5$ (control questions) the majority of all participants answered according to ground truth, i.e., they could correctly classify the high density scene. In the case of $D2$, $D3$, $D4$ and $D6$, the averages of right answers were less than 0.5, that is, different types of avatars, types of cameras, and walls influenced density perceptions. With regard to gender analysis, as can be seen in the third and fourth columns of Table 4, men had higher averages of right answers in questions $D1$ and $D5$ (control questions), and in question $D4$. Women had higher averages in questions $D2$, $D3$ and $D6$. In order to assess which factors have a statistically significant effect on the correctness of the density questions, a simple logistic regression was performed associating the independent variable gender with each of the questions $D1$ to $D5$ individually, using the right and wrong dichotomous response variable. However, no significant gender association with density questions was identified. Men had the highest overall average of right answers to density questions, while women had the highest average when we excluded control questions. However, comparing these two cases between women and men, we found no significant results, that is, **gender did not impact the density perception.** In age analysis (fifth and sixth columns of Table 4), participants under 31 years old only had higher averages in control questions, while other participants had higher averages in the remaining questions. Regarding the age group, a significant association of age with the response variable $D1$ was identified, with an odds ratio of 0.2174, that is, participants over 31 years correctly answered question D1 78.26% more than participants under 31. Overall, participants over 31 years old had higher averages of right answers than participants under 31, with and without questions $D1$ and $D5$. We found a significant p-value (.01) only in the second case. Thus, excluding control questions, **we can say that the density feature was more correctly perceived by participants over 31 than participants under 31.** Regarding the analysis of educational level (seventh and eighth columns of Table 4), participants with schooling up to complete high school had higher average scores only in $D3$ and $D4$, while participants with at least a complete undergraduate had higher average questions remaining. However, no significant association was identified. Overall, undergraduate participants had the highest average, while non-undergraduate had the highest average when we excluded control questions. However, we did not find any significant results, that is, **educational level did not impact the perception of density.**

Speed Perception Analysis. In such videos there were no analysis of speed perceptions using the camera in the first person, since we observed that such videos did not allow a good vision of the scene. Regarding the perception of density of all participants, as you can see in Table 4, all the averages of correct responses were below 0.5, $S3$ having the highest average. So, our descriptive results indicate that the camera point of view and type of avatar impacts in the speed perception. In gender analysis, men only had higher averages in $S3$ and $S4$, while women had higher averages in the others, and also a higher overall average. In this case, we did not identify any significant association using Simple Logistic Regression, and we did not find any significant results using independent T-test. Therefore, **there was no gender effect on the perception of speed.** Regarding age analysis, as well as men, participants under 31 years old only had higher averages in $S3$ and $S4$, while participants over 31 had higher averages in the others, and also a higher overall average. Simple logistic regression identified a significant association of age with question $S6$, with an odds ratio of 6.4533, that is, participants over 31 years correctly answered question S6 545.33% more than participants under 31. In this case, through the independent T-test, we found a significant result (.04). With that, **we can say that the speed feature was perceived more correctly by participants over 31 years old than by participants under 31 years old.** In the education level analysis, the non-undergraduate participants had higher averages in $S1$, $S3$ and $S6$, while the other participants had higher averages in the other questions. In this case, we did not identify any significant association. In addition, **we found no statistical evidence between the averages of the two levels of education in general averages.**

Angular Variation Perception Analysis. Analyzing the perceptions of all participants about angular variation, we can also see that the averages of the right answers were also low (less than .35, as shown in Table 4). So, our descriptive results also indicate that the camera point of view and type of avatar impacts in the angular variation perception. In gender analysis, women had the highest overall average and the highest averages on all questions. In this case, we did not identify any significant association. We compared the general averages between women and men, and found a significant result (.02). With that, **we can say that the angular variation feature was perceived more correctly by women than by men.** As with women, in age analysis, participants over 31 had the highest overall average and the highest averages on all questions. Simple logistic regression identified a significant association between age and the question $A4$, with an odds ratio of 4.0303, and with the question $A5$, with an odds ratio of 2.86. In other words, participants over 31 years answered the question $A4$ 303.03% and the question $A5$ 186.00% more correctly than participants under 31. We also compared the general averages, and we also found a significant value ($< .001$). With that, **we can say that angular variation was more correctly perceived by participants over 31 than by participants under 31.** Regarding the level of education analysis, undergraduate participants had higher averages in first three questions, non-undergraduate participants had a higher average in last question, and in question $A4$ both groups of participants had the same average. We did not identify any significant association. In addition, undergraduate participants had the highest overall average. However, we found no significant value when comparing general averages, that is, **the perception of angular variation was not affected by the educational level.**

Distance Perception Analysis. As in the analysis of the perception of angular variation, the distance averages were below .35. So, our descriptive results also indicate that the camera point of view and type of avatar impacts in the distance perception. Regarding gender analysis, women had the highest overall average and the highest averages on questions $E1$, $E4$ and $E5$, while men had the highest averages on questions $E2$ and $E3$. We did not identify any significant association, and we did not find a significant result among general averages, that is, **there was no gender effect on the perception of distance.** Regarding age analysis, participants over 31 had the highest overall average and the highest averages for all questions. Simple logistic regression identified a significant association of age with question $E3$, with odds ratio of 3.8095, with question $E4$, with odds ratio of 8.3611, and with question $E5$, with odds ratio of 3.5972. That is, participants over 31 years answered $E3$, $E4$ and $E5$ 280.95%, 736.11% and 259.72% respectively, more than participants under 31. Comparing the general averages, we obtained a significant value ($<$ .001). With this, **we can say that the distance feature was perceived more correctly by participants over 31 years old than by participants under 31 years old.** Regarding the analysis of educational level, the non-undergraduate participants only had a higher average in the first question. We did not identify any significant association. In addition, undergraduate participants had the highest overall average. Thus, we found a significant p-value (.01). So, **we can say that the distance feature was perceived more correctly by the undergraduate participants than by the non-undergraduate ones.**

Comparison Between Geometric Features. In this section we compare general averages of right answers between geometric features. Initially, we excluded general averages that contained questions $D1$ and $D5$, because they were control questions and had different formats from other density questions. With regard to all participants, we only found a significant result (.04) when comparing the general average speed with the general average angular variation. With that, **we can say that the participants had more correctly perception of speed than angular variation.** Regarding gender analysis, on men, we found significant results in the comparisons between the general average of angular variation and general averages of speed (.02) and distance (.01). With that, **we can say that men had more correctly perception about speed and distance than angular variation.** We found no significant results on women. However, we found a significant p-value (.04) when comparing the general averages of all geometric features (as shown in Table 4) between women and men. With that, **we can say that, in general, women perceived more correctly about geometric features than men.** Regarding the age analysis, on participants under 31, we found significant results in comparisons between general average of speed and general averages of angular variation (.003) and distance (.02). With that, **we can say that participants under 31 had more correctly perception about speed than about angular variation and distance.** Regarding participants over 31, we did not find any significant results. However, we found a significant p-value ($<$ .001) when comparing general averages of all geometric features between participants under 31 and over 31. With that, **we can say that, in general, participants over 31 had more correctly perception about geometric features than participants under 31.** Regarding the analysis of education level, on undergraduate participants, we only found a significant result (.009) when comparing the general average of angular variation and the general average of distance. With this, **we can say that undergraduate participants had more correctly perception about distance speed than about angular variation.** We did not find any more significant results, neither on the non-undergraduate participants, nor between undergraduate participants and non-undergraduate participants.

4.2   Personality and Emotion Perceptions

This section presents the results regarding people's perceptions of cultural features (emotions and personality traits) in virtual humans without facial and body expressions. The last eight lines of Table 4 present the averages of right answers to questions about cultural features. Analyzing all participants, in $Q1$ and $Q2$, it was interesting to see that more than half of participants answered according to the ground truth. The pedestrian highlighted in red was the most neurotic and angry, according to Favaretto and his colleagues [13]. The pedestrian was isolated, had low angular variation, low speed, low socialization and low collectivity. So, participants who do think that no agent was neurotic were certainly thinking about the psychological point of view, while we are analyzing based on space relationship. Still on $Q1$ (Neuroticism) and $Q2$ (Anger), men had higher averages of right answers than women, participants under 31 had higher averages than participants with over 31, and undergraduate participants had higher averages than other participants. Regarding questions $Q3$ and $Q4$, results also show that most participants correctly chose the yellow pedestrian as the most opened to experiences in the first, and correctly chose the red pedestrian as having fear in the second. According to Favaretto et al. [13], a pedestrian opened to new experiences is related to a high value for angular variation feature. Geometrically speaking, a person who allows himself/herself to change objectives (direction) while walking is more subject to new experiences. Fear, in turn, is linked to the fact that the person is isolated from others and walks at lower speeds. Still on $Q3$ (Openness) and $Q4$ (Fear), women had the highest average of right answers in $Q3$ and men in $Q4$, participants over 31 had the highest average in $Q3$ and participants under 31 in $Q4$, and non-undergraduate participants had a higher average in $Q3$ and undergraduate participants in $Q4$. Regarding question $Q5$, less than half responded according to ground truth. Geometrically, our hypothesis is that a happy person is not isolated and can present high levels of collectivity and socialization. Pedestrian highlighted in yellow presented that characteristics, however, it was not identified correctly by the participants. In question $Q6$, less than half of the participants answered correctly according to ground truth (Extraversion), indicating that the participants were not very sure about perceiving such characteristic. We thought that the $Q6$ question caused a greater variety of perceptions from part of the participants due to the fact that we did not explain any concept when asking the questions, nor did we mention that the perceptions would be given from a geometric point of view, considering the position of pedestrians in space. Many of the participants, when asked about Extraversion, may have been influenced by the movements and appearances of the humanoids, and not by the geometric features. In this sense, in question $Q7$, instead of which pedestrian was more extroverted, we asked which pedestrian appeared to be more sociable. With this, most participants responded according to the model proposed by [13]. Still on $Q5$ (Happiness), $Q6$ (Extraversion) and $Q7$ (Sociability), women had the highest average of right answers in the last two and men in the first. Participants under 31 had a higher average in $Q6$, participants over 31 in $Q7$, and had the same average in $Q5$. Non-undergraduate participants had higher averages in $Q5$ and $Q6$, and undergraduate participants in $Q7$.

In addition, we also performed statistical analysis, and we found significant results in the comparisons between the averages of $Q5$ and $Q6$ with the averages of $Q1$ (.01 and $<$ .001), $Q2$ (.003 and $<$ .001), $Q3$ (.006 and $<$ .001) and $Q4$ (.006 and $<$ .001). We did not find any significant results regarding $Q7$. With that, **we can say that the participants perceived more correctly Neuroticism, Anger, Openness and Fear than Happiness and Extraversion.** We also found a significant p-value ($<$ .001) when compare the general average of right answers about cultural features and the general average of geometric features (without control questions $D1$ and $D5$). So, **we can also say that the participants perceived more correctly cultural than geometric features.** With regard to gender analysis, for women, again through the paired T-test, we only found significant results when comparing the averages of right answers from $Q3$ to the averages of $Q5$ (.008) and $Q6$ (.01). So, **we can say that women perceived more correctly Openness than Happiness and Extraversion.** For men, we found significant p-values in the comparisons between $Q5$ and $Q6$ with $Q1$ (.03 and $<$ .001), $Q2$ (.02 and .001) and $Q4$ (.04 and .003). With that, **we can say that men perceived Neuroticism, Anger and Fear more correctly than Happiness and Extraversion.** In addition, using independent T-tests, for both women ($<$ .001) and men ($<$ .001), we found significant results between the general averages of right answers on cultural features and the general averages of geometric features. Then, **we can say that women and men perceived more correctly cultural rather than geometric features.** In comparisons of participants under 31 and over 31, we found significant results between cultural features and geometric features (without density control questions). So, **we can also say that participants under 31 ($<$ .001) and over 31 (.02) also perceived more correctly cultural than geometric features.** We did not identify any significant association, and we also found no significant results in comparing general averages between ages. Comparing general averages, both for non-undergraduate and undergraduate participants, we found significant results between cultural features ($<$ .001) and geometric features ($<$ .001). So, **we can also say that undergraduate and non-undergraduate participants also perceived more correctly cultural than geometric features.**

5   Final Considerations

This paper evaluated people's perceptions of geometric (density, velocity, angular variation, and distance) and cultural (personality traits and emotions) features to answer two questions: $i)$ "Can people perceive geometric features in avatars?", and $ii)$ "Can people perceive cultural features in avatars without body and facial expressions?". For this, we proposed two hypotheses ($H0_1$, defining that people cannot perceive geometric features in avatars); $H0_2$, defining that people cannot perceive cultural features in avatars without traditional expressions (body, facial, etc.). We used geometric and cultural data from *Cultural Crowds* dataset, proposed by Favaretto et al. [10].

Regarding $H0_1$, we can see that averages of right answers had low values. In the analysis of data from all people, only the density control questions (D1 and D5) had results above the average (0.5). Separating people into demographics, in addition to the control questions, only men and people under 31 in S3, and people over 31 in A4, E4 and E5 had above-average results. So, these results are in line with our hypothesis $H0_1$. These results also imply that different viewpoints (which is in line with the work by Yang et al.[25], which the authors found the main viewpoint effect, but only about density) and avatars influenced the perception of geometric features. In addition, the results indicated that there was an effect of age in all geometric features, both in general and separately (density, speed, angular variation and distance), where participants over 31 perceived geometric features more correctly than participants under 31. There was also a gender effect, where women perceived geometric features more correctly than men. Women also perceived more correctly angular variation than men. Answering our research question, our results indicate that in some cases people can perceive geometric features (in general, almost 30% of the participants), but the variation of viewpoints and avatars can negatively influence this perception.

Regarding $H0_2$ and our second research question, in most cases, participants had more right answers (averages greater than 0.5 in Table 4), which may indicate that people can perceive cultural features in virtual humans without body and facial expressions, that is, refuting our second hypothesis. Overall, people perceived more Neuroticism, Anger, Openness and Fear, than Happiness and Extraversion. In addition, they perceived cultural features more than geometric ones. This can be explained by the fact that different avatars and cameras are used in the analysis of geometric features. Interestingly, even without explaining to the participants the concepts of personality or emotion, most of them noted the cultural features expressed by virtual humans, according to our approach. Of course, this last aspect is much more intangible and the missing explanations that we were interested about spatial manifestation and not trying to "figure out" if the person is social or open in a psychological point of view is certainly one aspect we want to deal in a future work.

Acknowledgments. The authors would like to thank CNPq and CAPES for partially funding this work.

A   Appendix

A.1   Visualization of Geometric Features

Our viewer was developed using Unity3D[3] engine, with $C\#$ programming language. The viewer allows users to rewind, accelerate and stop the scene through a time controller and can focus on something interesting multiple times at any time. Figure 1 shows the main window of the viewer. As identified in Fig. 1, the viewer is divided in five parts, as follows: *1)* time controller, where is possible

---

[3] Unity3D is available at https://unity3d.com/.

to start, stop and continue simulation playback; *2) ChangeScene* and *Restart-CamPos* buttons to respectively load data file of another video and restart the camera position for first person view; *3)* a window that shows the top view of the environment; *4)* first-person view of a previously selected agent (this agent is highlighted in area *3)*; and *5)* which contains the resource panel, where users can enable the visualization of data related to agents' emotion, socialization and collectivity.

This viewer has three modes of visualization: *(i)* first-person camera, *(ii)* top camera, and *(iii)* an oblique camera. Figure 2 shows an example of each type of camera viewpoint in a video available in Cultural Crowds dataset. In addition to these different viewpoints, it is possible to observe all pedestrians present at each frame f. Pedestrians are represented by a humanoid or cylinder type avatar. Each pedestrian i present in frame f has a position (X_i, Y_i) (already converted from image coordinates to world coordinates). In addition to positions, it is also possible to know if the pedestrian is walking, running or stopped in frame f through the current speed s_i. If in a certain frame the current speed is greater than or equal to $\frac{0.08m}{f}$, which is equivalent to $\frac{2m}{s}$, considering $\frac{24f}{s}$, then the avatar is running. It was defined based on the Preferred Transition Speed PTS [2] to change from walk to run, for instance. The values of the transitions can be seen in Eq. 1, considering the current speed of the agent s_i.

$$Animation = \begin{cases} \textbf{Idle,} & \text{when } s_i == 0; \\ \textbf{Walk,} & \text{when } 0 < s_i < \frac{0.08m}{f}; \\ \textbf{Run,} & \text{when } s_i \geq \frac{0.08m}{f}. \end{cases} \tag{1}$$

Also, for the humanoid avatar type, each speed transition is accompanied by an animation transition, for example, if the current speed $s_i = 0$, then it does not change animation (remaining stationary), but if its speed is $0 < s_i < \frac{0.08m}{f}$, then the animation changes for walking as well as if $s_i \geq \frac{0.08m}{f}$, the animation of avatar changes to running.

A.2   Table of Scenes

The Table 1 shows all scenes used in all questions in survey.

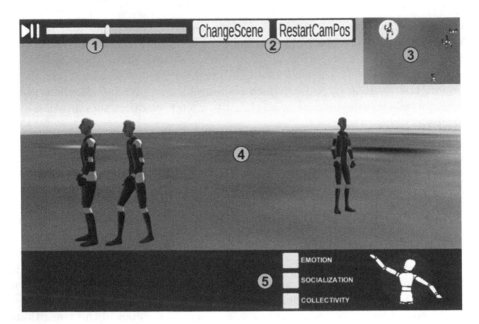

Fig. 1. Main window of the viewer.

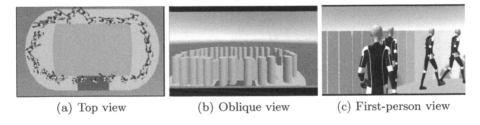

(a) Top view   (b) Oblique view   (c) First-person view

Fig. 2. Types of visualization: (a) top view, (b) oblique and (c) first-person view.

A.3   Questions

The Questionnaire. We formulated a questionnaire to evaluate human perceptions, divided into two stages: *i)* The first aims to assess whether participants can perceive geometric features in avatars and from different points of view; and *ii)* the second aims to assess whether participants can perceive emotions and personality traits geometrically, extracted in real videos and represented in avatars. Before the questionnaire, we notified the participants that they could withdraw at any time and for any reason. We do not collect personal data. Before each question, participants saw two to three of the scenes (shown in Table 1) referring to geometric or cultural feature presented in the question. No explanation of the content of the survey was provided to try to avoid bias. In addition, we used Google Forms to apply the questionnaire on social networks, so all participants were volunteers. Next sections described the evaluated aspects.

Table 1. Walls were added in scenes 4 and 9 to evaluate density perception with and without walls. In addition, this table also shows the camera and avatar type of each scene, the video identification, and the density level.

Scene	Camera	Avatar	Questions	Video	Number of Pedestrian	Density
Scene 1	Oblique	Humanoid	D1, S2 S3, S5	BR-15	15	Low
Scene 2	Oblique	Humanoid	D1	BR-25	25	Medium
Scene 3	Oblique	Humanoid	D1, D2 A1, A4 E1, E4	BR-34	34	High
Scene 4	FirstPerson	Humanoid	D2, D4 D5, D6 A1, A5 E1, E5	BR-34	34	High
Scene 5	Top	Humanoid	D2, A1 A3, E1 E3	BR-34	34	High
Scene 6	Oblique	Cylinder	D3, A2 A4, E2 E4	BR-34	34	High
Scene 7	FirstPerson	Cylinder	D3, D4 A2, A5 E2, E5	BR-34	34	High
Scene 8	Top	Cylinder	D3, A2 A3, E2 E3	BR-34	34	High
Scene 9	FirstPerson	Humanoid	D5	BR-15	15	Low
Scene 10	Oblique	Humanoid	S1, S3 Q3, Q4	BR-01	16	Low
Scene 11	Top	Humanoid	S1, S4	BR-01	16	Low
Scene 12	Top	Humanoid	S2, S4 S6	BR-15	15	Low
Scene 13	Oblique	Cylinder	S5	BR-15	15	Low
Scene 14	Top	Cylinder	S6	BR-15	15	Low
Scene 15	Oblique	Humanoid	Q1, Q2	AE-01	12	Low
Scene 16	Oblique	Humanoid	Q5, Q6 Q7	AT-03	10	Low

Geometric Features. The first part of the questionnaire contains twenty-two questions, as shown in Table 2, six related to density, six to speed, five to angular variation and five to distance. Table 2 also presents the possible answers, and the right ones highlighted in bold. In all density questions (Table 2) we asked **in which of the short sequences the participant observed the highest density level.** The first question ($D1$) represented a control question, i.e., we wanted to assess whether participants could perceive density variation: low, medium and high density video scenes of pedestrians in crowds. Questions

$D2$ and $D3$ aimed to assess whether different points of view (camera types) would influence participants' density perception. Our goal was to assess whether density perception would change due to the camera's point of view and the way agents were displayed. As shown in Table 2, both questions $D2$ and $D3$ scenes were applied after same scene, but displayed with different points of view, and different avatars. Before question $D4$, two scenes are presented with same density and same point of view, but changing avatar type. Those evaluations aimed to assess whether different types of avatars and point of view would influence density perception. In $D5$ and $D6$, walls were added around scenes (4 and 9). $D5$ had the same objective as $D1$, i.e., control question. $D6$ aimed to assess whether walls would influence density perception using first person camera.

Table 2. All questions related to geometric features and possible answers. Right answers highlighted in bold.

Density questions	D1	D2	D3	D4	D5	D6
In which scene did you observe the highest density?	a) Scene 1	a) Scene 3	a) Scene 6	a) Scene 4	a) Scene 9 (walls)	a) Scene 4
	b) Scene 2	b) Scene 4	b) Scene 7	b) Scene 7	b) Scene 4 (walls)	b) Scene 4 (walls)
	c) Scene 3	c) Scene 5	c) Scene 8	c) No difference	c) No difference	c) No difference
	d) No difference	d) No difference	d) No difference	d) I don't know	d) I don't know	d) I don't know
	e) I don't know	e) I don't know	e) I don't know			
Speed questions	S1	S2	S3	S4	S5	S6
In which video did you observe the higher speed?	a) Scene 10	a) Scene 1	a) Scene 10	a) Scene 11	a) Scene 1	a) Scene 12
	b) Scene 11	b) Scene 12	b) Scene 1	b) Scene 12	b) Scene 13	b) Scene 14
	c) No difference	c) No difference	c) No difference	c) No difference	c) No difference	c) No difference
	d) I don't know	d) I don't know	d) I don't know	d) I don't know	d) I don't know	d) I don't know
Angular variation questions	A1	A2	A3	A4	A5	–
In which scene did you observe the greatest angular variation performed by agents?	a) Scene 3	a) Scene 6	a) Scene 5	a) Scene 3	a) Scene 4	
	b) Scene 4	b) Scene 7	b) Scene 8	b) Scene 6	b) Scene 7	
	c) No difference	c) No difference	c) No difference	c) No difference	c) No difference	
	d) I don't know	d) I don't know	d) I don't know	d) I don't know	d) I don't know	
Distance questions	E1	E2	E3	E4	E5	–
In which scene did you observe the greatest distance between agents?	a) Scene 3	a) Scene 6	a) Scene 5	a) Scene 3	a) Scene 4	
	b) Scene 4	b) Scene 7	b) Scene 8	b) Scene 6	b) Scene 7	
	c) No difference	c) No difference	c) No difference	c) No difference	c) No difference	
	d) I don't know	d) I don't know	d) I don't know	d) I don't know	d) I don't know	

Regarding speed perception, all questions had low density. The purpose of these questions was to assess whether participants were able to perceive different speed levels (presented in Eq. 1) in different points of view and types of avatars. The first-person camera was not evaluated for speed questions, as avatars' first-person views had a lot of variation. The questions $S1 - S4$ aimed to evaluate speed perception over points of view (top and oblique camera). $S1$ presented two scenes with "run" speed on oblique and top cameras. Same process for $S2$ but with the "walk" speed. Both $S3$ and $S4$ presented two scenes with both speed types. Finally, both $S5$ and $S6$ (which aimed to assess the influence of avatar on speed perception) presented two scenes containing two types of avatars using walk speed, one with top camera and one with oblique.

Regarding angular variation and distance, all questions used $BR - 34$ (high density) video scenes. $A1$, $A2$, $E1$ and $E2$ aimed to assess whether points of view could influence perceptions of angular variation and distance. $A1$ and $E1$ presented three scenes with humanoids in three types of cameras. Similar process for $A2$ and $E2$, with cylinder type avatars. Finally, $A3$, $A4$, $A5$, $E3$, $E4$ and $E5$ presented, both for angular variation and for distance, two scenes containing two different avatars with top, oblique and first person cameras. These questions aimed to assess whether the types of avatars would influence perceptions.

Cultural Features. The second stage of the questionnaire contains seven questions related to emotions and personality traits. In all scenes presented, two avatars of different colors (red and yellow) were highlighted to be perceptual focus questions, as illustrated in Fig. 3. All questions related to cultural features with their answers (right answers are highlighted in bold) are presented in Table 3. We used as ground truth the results obtained by the approach proposed by Favaretto et al. [13]. In the example of Fig. 3, the initial and final frames of *scene*15 (shown in Table 1) are shown, where there is a group of pedestrians (represented by avatars) on the right part of the scene. The avatar highlighted in yellow is part of this group and the avatar highlighted in red walk trough the group with a higher speed.

This scene is related to $Q1$ and $Q2$, questions that questioned which avatars (yellow or red) were, respectively, neurotic and angry. $Q3$ and $Q4$, related to *scene*10, aimed to assess, respectively, whether the participants would perceive which highlighted avatar was open to new experiences and which one was afraid. *Scene*10 shows a yellow highlighted avatar interacting with a group of avatars and a red highlighted avatar standing alone with no interaction. Finally, $Q5$, $Q6$ and $Q7$ aimed to assess happiness, extraversion and sociability. $Q7$ was proposed

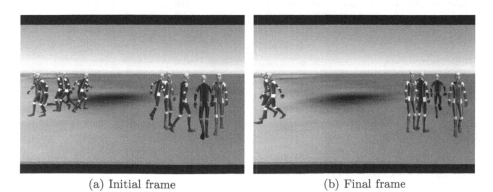

(a) Initial frame   (b) Final frame

Fig. 3. Initial (a) and final (b) frames from *Scene*15.

Table 3. Cultural questions and answers. Correct answers are highlighted in bold, according to Favaretto et al. [13].

Cultural questions	Possible answers
Q1: In your opinion, which of the two pedestrians highlighted in the video has a neurotic personality, yellow or red?	*a*) Yellow pedestrian; *b*) **Red pedestrian**; *c*) Both pedestrians; *d*) Neither of them; *e*) I don't know.
Q2: In your opinion, which of the two pedestrians highlighted in the video is angry, yellow or red?	*a*) Yellow pedestrian; *b*) **Red pedestrian**; *c*) Both pedestrians; *d*) Neither of them; *e*) I don't know.
Q3: In your opinion, which of the two pedestrians highlighted in the video is more openness to experiences, yellow or red?	*a*) **Yellow pedestrian**; *b*) Red pedestrian; *c*) Both pedestrians; *d*) Neither of them; *e*) I don't know.
Q4: In your opinion, which of the two pedestrians highlighted in the video is afraid, yellow or red?	*a*) Yellow pedestrian; *b*) **Red pedestrian**; *c*) Both pedestrians; *d*) Neither of them; *e*) I don't know.
Q5: In your opinion, which of the two pedestrians highlighted in the video is happier, yellow or red?	*a*) **Yellow pedestrian**; *b*) Red pedestrian; *c*) Both pedestrians; *d*) Neither of them; *e*) I don't know.
Q6: In your opinion, which of the two pedestrians highlighted in the video is more extroverted, yellow or red?	*a*) **Yellow pedestrian**; *b*) Red pedestrian; *c*) Both pedestrians; *d*) Neither of them; *e*) I don't know.
Q7*: In your opinion, which of the two pedestrians highlighted in the video seems to be more sociable, yellow or red?	*a*) **Yellow pedestrian**; *b*) Red pedestrian; *c*) Both pedestrians; *d*) Neither of them; *e*) I don't know.

after analyzing the results of question $Q6$, so it is explained in Sect. 4.2. These questions are related to *scene*16, which contains a yellow highlighted avatar walking with a group of avatars and a red highlighted avatar walking alone, in the opposite direction to all other avatars.

A.4   Table of Results

The Table 4 presents the averages of right answers for each question of our work.

Table 4. In addition, the table also presents general averages for each question category: density (with and without control questions), speed, angular variation, distance, all geometric features (with and without density control questions), and all cultural features.

All Questions	All (Avg)	Women (Avg)	Men (Avg)	Under 31 (Avg)	Over 31 (Avg)	Not undergraduate (Avg)	Undergraduate+ (Avg)
D1	0.88	0.78	0.93	0.98	0.76	0.85	0.88
D2	0.29	0.32	0.27	0.22	0.42	0.23	0.31
D3	0.33	0.39	0.29	0.26	0.46	0.38	0.31
D4	0.25	0.21	0.27	0.22	0.3	0.28	0.24
D5	0.85	0.78	0.89	0.87	0.8	0.76	0.88
D6	0.2	0.25	0.17	0.18	0.23	0.19	0.2
Density (Avg)	0.46	0.45	0.47	0.45	0.5	0.45	0.47
Density without D1 and D5 (Avg)	0.27	0.29	0.25	0.22	0.35	0.27	0.26
S1	0.33	0.39	0.29	0.26	0.46	0.38	0.31
S2	0.28	0.32	0.25	0.24	0.34	0.23	0.29
S3	0.48	0.42	0.51	0.53	0.38	0.47	0.48
S4	0.33	0.32	0.34	0.36	0.26	0.28	0.35
S5	0.18	0.21	0.17	0.12	0.3	0.14	0.2
S6	0.21	0.32	0.14	0.1	0.42	0.23	0.2
Speed (Avg)	0.3	0.33	0.28	0.27	0.36	0.29	0.3
A1	0.16	0.21	0.12	0.1	0.26	0.09	0.18
A2	0.2	0.21	0.19	0.14	0.3	0.19	0.2
A3	0.24	0.28	0.21	0.16	0.38	0.23	0.24
A4	0.33	0.42	0.27	0.22	0.53	0.33	0.33
A5	0.28	0.39	0.21	0.2	0.42	0.33	0.25
Angular Variation (Avg)	0.24	0.3	0.2	0.16	0.38	0.23	0.24
E1	0.22	0.28	0.19	0.18	0.3	0.23	0.22
E2	0.26	0.25	0.27	0.2	0.38	0.19	0.29
E3	0.28	0.25	0.29	0.18	0.46	0.14	0.33
E4	0.26	0.28	0.25	0.12	0.53	0.14	0.31
E5	0.34	0.39	0.31	0.24	0.53	0.23	0.38
Distance (Avg)	0.27	0.29	0.26	0.18	0.44	0.19	0.31
All Geometric Features Without D1 and D5 (Avg)	0.27	0.29	0.24	0.21	0.38	0.25	0.28
Q1 (Neuroticism)	0.57	0.5	0.61	0.61	0.5	0.47	0.61
Q2 (Anger)	0.58	0.57	0.59	0.65	0.46	0.57	0.59
Q3 (Openness)	0.6	0.64	0.57	0.59	0.61	0.61	0.59
Q4 (Fear)	0.58	0.57	0.59	0.59	0.57	0.47	0.62
Q5 (Happiness)	0.38	0.35	0.40	0.38	0.38	0.4	0.33
Q6 (Extraversion)	032	0.35	0.29	0.32	0.3	0.33	0.31
Q7 (Sociability)	0.52	0.54	0.5	0.37	0.58	0.37	0.58
Cultural Features (Avg)	0.5	0.5	0.51	0.52	0.48	0.46	0.52

References

1. Alameda-Pineda, X., Ricci, E., Sebe, N.: Multimodal Behavior Analysis in the Wild: Advances and Challenges. Elsevier Science, London (2018)
2. Alexander, R.M.: A model of bipedal locomotion on compliant legs. Phil. Trans. R. Soc. Lond. B **338**(1284), 189–198 (1992)
3. Araujo, V., Migon Favaretto, R., Knob, P., Raupp Musse, S., Vilanova, F., Brandelli Costa, A.: How much do you perceive this?: an analysis on perceptions of geometric features, personalities and emotions in virtual humans. In: Proceedings of the 19th ACM International Conference on Intelligent Virtual Agents, pp. 179–181. ACM (2019)
4. Calvin, S., Hall, G.L., Campbell, J.B.: Theories Of Personality, 4th edn. John Wiley & Sons, New Jersey (1998)
5. Chattaraj, U., Seyfried, A., Chakroborty, P.: Comparison of pedestrian fundamental diagram across cultures. Adv. Complex Syst. **12**(03), 393–405 (2009)
6. Costa, P., McCrae, R.: Revised NEO Personality Inventory (NEO PI-R) and NEO Five-Factor Inventory (NEO-FFI). PAR (1992)
7. Durupınar, F., Güdükbay, U., Aman, A., Badler, N.I.: Psychological parameters for crowd simulation: from audiences to mobs. IEEE TVCG **22**(9), 2145–2159 (2016)
8. Durupinar, F., Kapadia, M., Deutsch, S., Neff, M., Badler, N.I.: Perform: perceptual approach for adding ocean personality to human motion using laban movement analysis. ACM Trans. Graph. (TOG) **36**(1), 1–16 (2016)
9. Ekman, P., Friesen, W.V.: Constants across cultures in the face and emotion. JPSP **17**(2), 124 (1971)
10. Favaretto, R.M., Dihl, L., Barreto, R., Musse, S.R.: Using group behaviors to detect hofstede cultural dimensions. In: ICIP, pp. 2936–2940. IEEE (2016)
11. Favaretto, R.M., Dihl, L., Musse, S.R.: Detecting crowd features in video sequences. In: Proceedings of Conference on Graphics, Patterns and Images (SIBGRAPI), pp. 201–208. IEEE Computer Society, São José dos Campos (2016)
12. Favaretto, R.M., Dihl, L., Musse, S.R., Vilanova, F., Costa, A.B.: Using big five personality model to detect cultural aspects in crowds. In: Graphics, Patterns and Images (SIBGRAPI), pp. 223–229. IEEE (2017)
13. Favaretto, R.M., Knob, P., Musse, S.R., Vilanova, F., Costa, Â.B.: Detecting personality and emotion traits in crowds from video sequences. Mach. Vision Appl. **30**(5), 999–1012 (2018). https://doi.org/10.1007/s00138-018-0979-y
14. Favaretto, R.M., Musse, S.R., Costa, A.B.: Emotion, personality, and cultural aspects in crowds. In: Emotion, Personality and Cultural Aspects in Crowds, pp. 23–33. Springer, Cham (2019). https://doi.org/10.1007/978-3-030-22078-5_3
15. Goldenberg, A., Weisz, E., Sweeny, T.D., Cikara, M., Gross, J.J.: The crowd-emotion-amplification effect. Psychol. Sci. **32**(3), 437–450 (2021)
16. Gorbova, J., Lüsi, I., Litvin, A., Anbarjafari, G.: Automated screening of job candidate based on multimodal video processing. In: CVPRW (2017)
17. Hofstede, G.: Culture's Consequences: Comparing Values, Behaviors, Institutions and Organizations Across Nations. Sage publications, Thousand Oaks (2001)
18. Hofstede, G.: Dimensionalizing cultures: the hofstede model in context. Online Read. Psychol. Cult. **2**(1), 8 (2011)
19. Jacques Junior, J., Musse, S.R., Jung, C.: Crowd analysis using computer vision techniques. IEEE Signal Process. Mag. **27**, 66–77 (2010)
20. Knob, P., de Andrade Araujo, V.F., Favaretto, R.M., Musse, S.R.: Visualization of interactions in crowd simulation and video sequences. In: Brazilian Symposium on Computer Games and Digital Entertainment (2018)

21. Lala, D., Thovuttikul, S., Nishida, T.: Towards a virtual environment for capturing behavior in cultural crowds. In: 6th ICDIM, pp. 310–315 (2011)
22. Lamer, S.A., Sweeny, T.D., Dyer, M.L., Weisbuch, M.: Rapid visual perception of interracial crowds: racial category learning from emotional segregation. J. Exp. Psychol. Gener. **147**(5), 683 (2018)
23. McDonnell, R., Larkin, M., Dobbyn, S., Collins, S., O'Sullivan, C.: Clone attack! perception of crowd variety. In: ACM SIGGRAPH 2008 papers, pp. 1–8. ACM (2008)
24. Saifi, L., Boubetra, A., Nouioua, F.: An approach for emotions and behavior modeling in a crowd in the presence of rare events. AB **24**(6), 428–445 (2016)
25. Yang, F., Shabo, J., Qureshi, A., Peters, C.: Do you see groups?: the impact of crowd density and viewpoint on the perception of groups. In: IVA, pp. 313–318, ACM (2018)
26. Zhao, J., Gou, L., Wang, F., Zhou, M.: Pearl: an interactive visual analytic tool for understanding personal emotion style derived from social media. In: VAST, pp. 203–212. IEEE (2014)

High-Dimensional Dataset Simplification by Laplace-Beltrami Operator

Chenkai Xu[1] and Hongwei Lin[1,2]

[1] School of Mathematical Sciences, Zhejiang University, Hangzhou, China
{ckxu,hwlin}@zju.edu.cn
[2] State Key Laboratory of CAD&CG, Zhejiang University, Hangzhou, China

Abstract. With the development of the Internet and other digital technologies, the speed of data generation has become considerably faster than the speed of data processing. Because big data typically contain massive redundant information, it is possible to significantly simplify a big dataset while maintaining the key information. In this paper, we develop a high-dimensional (HD) dataset simplification method based on the eigenvalues and eigenfunctions of the Laplace-Beltrami operator (LBO). Specifically, given a dataset that can be considered as an unorganized data point set in an HD space, a discrete LBO defined on the HD dataset is constructed, and its eigenvalues and eigenvectors are calculated. Then, the local extremum and saddle points of the eigenvectors are proposed to be the feature points of the HD dataset, constituting a simplified dataset. Moreover, we develop feature point detection methods for the functions defined on an unorganized data point set in HD space, and devise metrics for measuring the fidelity of the simplified dataset to the original set. Finally, examples and applications are demonstrated to validate the efficiency and effectiveness of the proposed methods, demonstrating that the developed HD dataset simplification method is feasible for processing a maximum-sized dataset using a limited data processing capability.

Keywords: Dataset simplification · High-dimensional data · Laplace-Beltrami operator · Feature point detection

1 Introduction

It is well known that big data concerns large-volume, complex, and growing datasets with multiple sources [35]. With the development of the Internet and other digital technologies, increasingly larger amounts of data are generated at a speed considerably greater than the data processing speed of human beings. Because big data typically contain massive redundant information, it is possible to significantly simplify a big dataset while maintaining the key information it contains. Therefore, dataset simplification is a feasible method to process a maximum-sized dataset using a limited data processing capability. However,

© Springer Nature Switzerland AG 2021
N. Magnenat-Thalmann et al. (Eds.): CGI 2021, LNCS 13002, pp. 568–585, 2021.
https://doi.org/10.1007/978-3-030-89029-2_43

HD dataset simplification is a difficult problem, and there is a little method nowadays.

The purpose of data simplification is to maintain the maximum amount of information a dataset contains, while deleting the maximum amount of redundant information. In this paper, the dataset we handled is considered as an unorganized point. We developed an HD dataset simplification method by classifying the points in an HD dataset as *feature* points and *trivial* points, and then considering the feature point set as the simplification of the HD dataset because it contains a majority of the information that the original HD dataset contained.

Feature point detection is a fundamental problem in numerous research fields, including signal processing, computer vision, and computer graphics. These fields focus on the process of 1D and 2D manifolds, such that one of the main tools for the feature point detection is the curvature, including both Gaussian and mean curvature. However, in the HD space, the definition of curvature is complicated, and practical computational methods for calculating the curvature of an HD manifold are not available. Therefore, it is necessary for HD data processing to develop practical and efficient methods for detecting feature points in HD datasets.

The eigenvalues and eigenvectors of a Laplace-Beltrami operator (LBO) defined on a manifold are closely related to its geometry properties. Moreover, whatever the dimension of the manifold, after discretization, the discrete LBO becomes a matrix. That is, the discrete LBO is unrelated to the dimension of the manifold where it is defined. Therefore, the eigenvalues and eigenvectors of LBOs and the related heat kernel functions are desirable tools for studying the geometric properties of HD datasets, including detecting feature points.

In this paper, we develop an HD dataset simplification method based on feature point detection using the eigenvectors of an LBO. Moreover, three metrics are devised for measuring the fidelity of the simplified dataset to the original dataset. Finally, the capability of the proposed HD data simplification method is extensively discussed using several examples and applications.

1.1   Related Work

Computation and Applications of the LBO. To calculate the eigenvalues and eigenfunctions of an LBO defined on a HD dataset, it must first be discretized. Belkin & Niyogi proposed the Laplace for HD dataset in [4], where the weight is generalized from Laplace in Euclidean space. Furthermore, the point cloud data Laplace is proposed in [5], which converges faster than other Laplacians.

The LBO has been extensively employed in spectral mesh processing and shape analysis. By first modulating the eigenvalues and eigenvectors on a mesh and then reconstructing the shape of the mesh model, mesh editing tasks can be fulfilled, including mesh smoothing, shape detail enhancement, and change of model posture [33]. Using the isometry-invariant property of the LBO, the eigenvalues and eigenvectors are designed as shape descriptors, such as *Shape DNA* [28] and *HKS* [30]. These shape descriptors have been successfully applied in shape retrieval, point matching [23], and non-rigid shape recognition. More importantly, the LBO has been successfully applied in the HD data processing. A well-known application is Laplacian eigenmaps [4]. To appropriately represent HD data for machine learning and pattern recognition, Belkin & Niyogi proposed a locality-preserving method for nonlinear DR using the LBO eigenfunctions, which has a natural connection to clustering and can be computed efficiently.

Feature Point Detection. In image processing, a series of feature point detection methods were proposed using the difference of Gaussians(DoG) [10,19]. Similarly, geometric function-based methods have been proposed. Two widely known surface descriptors based on surface geometry are 3D spin images [16] and 3D shape contexts [17]. Another kind of feature point detection approach is based on geometric diffusion equation, such as heat kernel signature (HKS) [30]. For 2D surface quadrangulation, Shen et al. [12] used the extremes of the Laplacian eigenfunctions to build a Morse-Smale complex and construct a well-shaped quadrilateral mesh.

In recent years, deep networks have achieved excellent success in feature point detection [24,34]. Luo et al. [20] proposed a novel face parser approach by detecting faces at both the part- and component-levels, and then computing the pixel-wise label maps, where the feature points can then be easily obtained from the boundary of the label maps. Sun et al. [31] presented an approach for detecting the positions of face key-points with three-level carefully designed convolution networks.

Dataset Simplification. In statistics, data sampling selects a subset from a given dataset to estimate the characteristics of the whole dataset. The most commonly used sampling methods include simple random sampling, systematic sampling, stratified sampling, and cluster sampling [22]. Data sampling technology has been widely used in big data context to effectively reduce the amount of data and help speed up data processing [18]. As stated in [1], data sampling can improve big data analysis and will become a preprocessing step in big data processing in the future.

In recent years, topological simplification methods have been successfully employed in data analysis and data visualization. The methods extract the topological structure of a given dataset through a scalar or 'multi-' field defined on the dataset. Representative methods based on scalar fields include *Reeb graph* [27], *Contour tree* [9] and *Morse-Smale complex* [15]. On the other hand, for multi-field methods, there are *Reeb spaces* [14], *Joint contour nets* [8], and *Mapper* [29] that are expanded from the scalar methods.

2   High-Dimensional Dataset Simplification

2.1   Spectrum of LBO and Feature Points

Let M be a Riemannian manifold (differentiable manifold with Riemannian metric), and $f \in C^2$ be a real-valued function defined on M. The LBO Δ on M is defined as

$$\Delta f = \mathbf{div}(\nabla f), \tag{1}$$

where ∇f is the gradient of f, and $\mathbf{div}(\cdot)$ is the divergence on M.

The eigenvalues and eigenfunctions of the LBO (1) can be calculated by solving the Helmholtz equation:

$$\Delta f = -\lambda f, \tag{2}$$

where λ is a real number. The spectrum of LBO is a list of eigenvalues: $0 \leq \lambda_0 \leq \lambda_1 \leq \lambda_2 \leq \dots \leq +\infty$, with the corresponding eigenfunctions $\phi_0(x), \phi_1(x), \phi_2(x), \cdots$, which are orthogonal. In the case of a closed manifold, the first eigenvalue λ_0 is always zero. Moreover, the eigenvalues specify the discrete frequency domain of an LBO, and the eigenfunctions are the extensions of the basis functions in Fourier analysis to a manifold. Eigenfunctions of larger eigenvalues contain higher frequency information.

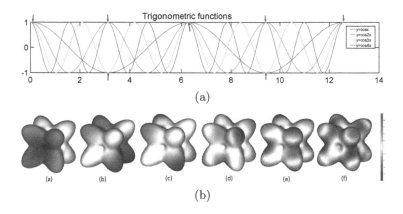

Fig. 1. The local extrema of the eigenfunctions on $\mathbb{R}$ and 2D manifolds.

It has been shown in [7,30] that when the time t approaches 0^+ sufficiently close, the heat kernel [30] $H(x, x, t)$ can be represented as

$$H(x, x, t) = \sum_{i=0}^{\infty} e^{-\lambda_i t} \phi_i^2(x) = \frac{1}{4\pi t} + \frac{K(x)}{12\pi} + O(t), \tag{3}$$

where $K(x)$ is the scalar curvature at point x on M. From Eq. (3), we can see that the eigenfunctions are closely related to the scalar curvature of the manifold. In the trigonometric function system, the local extrema of a trigonometric function with a lower frequency hold in the trigonometric function with a higher frequency (Fig. 1(a)). This property is preserved by the eigenfunctions on manifolds. In Fig. 1(b), the eigenfunctions of an LBO defined on a 2D manifold are illustrated with their local extrema. We can observe that the local extrema in the lower frequency eigenfunctions remain the local extrema in the higher frequency eigenfunctions. Because the local extrema of $\phi_i(x)$ hold in $\phi_j(x), j < i$, and the heat kernel (Eq. (3)) is a weighted sum of $\phi_i^2(x)$, the local extrema of $\phi_i(x)$, especially the eigenfunctions with low frequency, are the candidates of the local extrema of the heat kernel $H(x, x, t)$ and the scalar curvature $K(x)$. In conclusion, the local extrema of the eigenfunctions contain the features of the manifold where the LBO is defined. Therefore, in this paper, we use the local extrema of the eigenfunctions of the LBO defined on an HD dataset as its *feature points*, which constitute the simplified dataset.

2.2   Discrete Computation

To calculate the eigenvalues and eigenfunctions of the LBO, Eq. (2) must be discretized into a linear system of equations. In this paper, we address an unorganized data point set in an HD space, where the connectivity information is missing. We use the discretization method developed in [4] to construct the discrete LBO. The LBO discretization method contains two steps:

1. Adjacency graph construction. We use k-nearest neighbors (*KNN*) to construct an adjacency graph: For any vertex v, its *KNN*'s set N_v is determined using KD-tree. Then, the connection between the vertex v and each neighbor $v_i \in N_v$ is established, thus constructing the adjacency graph. Because the *KNN* are not symmetric for sure, i.e., it is possible that the vertex v_i is in the *KNN* of the vertex v_j, yet, v_j is not in the *KNN* of v_i, the weight matrix (see below) constructed by the *KNN* method is not guaranteed to be symmetric.

2. Weight computation. Using the adjacency graph for each point v_i in the given dataset, the connections between point v_i and the other points in the dataset are established. Based on the adjacency graph, the weights between point v_i and each of the other points can be calculated as follows:

$$w_{ij} = \begin{cases} -e^{-\frac{\|v_i - v_j\|^2}{t}}, & \text{if } i, j \text{ are adjacent,} \\ \sum_{k \neq i} -w_{ik}, & \text{if } i = j, \\ 0, & \text{otherwise .} \end{cases} \tag{4}$$

Because only the Euclidean distance $\|v_i - v_j\|$ is required in the computation of w_{ij}, it is appropriate for addressing HD datasets.

As stated above, the weight matrix $\bar{W} = [w_{ij}]$ constructed by the *KNN* method is not symmetric, so we take the matrix $W = \frac{\bar{W} + \bar{W}^T}{2}$ as the weight matrix, which is a symmetric matrix. Moreover, we construct a diagonal matrix $A = diag(a_1, a_2, \cdots, a_n)$, where $a_i = w_{ii}$ (refer to Eq. (4)), and n is the number of data points. Then the LBO can be discretized into the matrix $L = A^{-1}W$, whatever the dimension of the space the LBO defined on. Meanwhile, the Helmholtz Eq. (2) is discretized as $L\varphi = A^{-1}W\varphi = \lambda\varphi$, where λ is the eigenvalue of the Laplace matrix L, and φ is the corresponding eigenvector. So it is equivalent to

$$W\varphi = \lambda A\varphi. \tag{5}$$

Because the matrix W is symmetric, and the matrix A is diagonal, the eigenvalues λ are all non-negative real numbers satisfying $0 = \lambda_1 \leq \lambda_2 \leq \cdots \leq \lambda_n$ and the corresponding eigenvectors are orthogonal, i.e., $\langle \varphi_i, \varphi_j \rangle_A = \varphi_i^T A \varphi_j = \delta_{ij}$.

2.3   Dataset Simplification by Feature Point Detection

By solving Eq. (5), the eigenvalues $\lambda_1 \leq \lambda_2 \leq \cdots \leq \lambda_n$ and the corresponding eigenvectors $\varphi_i, i = 1, 2, \cdots, n$ are determined. The local maximum, minimum, and saddle points of the eigenvectors are used as the feature points. The dataset simplification algorithm first detects the feature points of the eigenvector φ_1, and adds them to the simplified dataset. Then, it detects and adds the feature points of φ_2 to the simplified dataset. This procedure is performed iteratively until the simplified dataset satisfies a preset fidelity threshold to the original data point set, according to the metrics defined in Sect. 2.4.

Because the eigenvectors are defined on an unorganized HD point set, the detection of the maximum, minimum, and saddle points on the defined function is not straightforward. Suppose $\omega(x)$ is a scalar function defined on each point of an unorganized data point set. For each point x in the dataset, we construct its neighbor N_x using the *KNN* algorithm, discussed previously in Sect. 2.2. The methods for detecting the maximum, minimum, and saddle points of the function $\omega(x)$ are elucidated in the following.

Maximum and Minimum Point Detection: For a data point x in the dataset and any data point $y \in N_x$, if $\omega(y) < \omega(x)$, $\forall y \in N_x$, the data point x is a local maximum point of $\omega(x)$. Conversely, if $\omega(y) > \omega(x)$, $\forall y \in N_x$, the data point x is a local minimum point of $\omega(x)$.

Saddle Point Detection: To detect the saddle points of $\omega(x)$ defined on an unorganized HD data point set, the points of the set are projected into a 2D plane, using the DR methods [4]. The data point projected into a 2D plane continues to be denoted as x. For a point x, the points in its *KNN*: N_x comprise its one-ring neighbors R_x (see Fig. 2). Each point x_r in R_x has a sole previous point x_r^{prev} and a sole next point x_r^{next} in a counter-clockwise direction. As illustrated in Fig. 2, if $\omega(x) \geq \omega(x_r)$, the point x_r is labeled as $\ominus$; otherwise, it is labeled as $\oplus$. Now, we initialize a counter $sum = 0$ and traverse the one-ring neighbors R_x of point x from an arbitrary point. If the signs of two neighbor points in R_x are different (marked with dotted lines), $sum = sum + 1$. Finally, if the counter $sum \geq 4$, point x is a saddle point; otherwise, it is not a saddle point. Examples of saddle points and non-saddle points are demonstrated in Fig. 2.

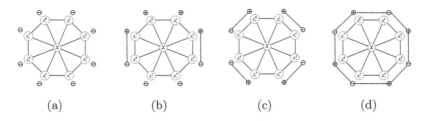

(a)   (b)   (c)   (d)

Fig. 2. Saddle point detection. Dotted line indicates the change of signs between neighbor points. While the points x in (a) and (b) are not saddle point, the points x in (c) and (d) are saddle point.

2.4   Measurement of Fidelity of the Simplified Dataset

As stated in Sect. 2.3, the simplified dataset adds the feature points iteratively, until the simplified dataset satisfies a preset threshold of fidelity to the original dataset. In this section, three metrics are devised to measure the fidelity of the simplified dataset S to the original dataset $\mathcal{H}$; these are the Kullback-Leibler(KL)-divergence-based metric [25], Hausdorff distance [13], and volume of convex hull [3]. They measure the fidelity of S to $\mathcal{H}$ from three aspects:

1. entropy of information (KL-divergence-based metric),
2. distance between two sets (Hausdorff distance), and
3. 'volume' of a dataset (volume of convex hull).

For the detailed calculation methods of the three metrics, see Appendix 1.

3   Results and Discussion

In this section, the proposed method is employed to simplify four well-known HD datasets, including the *swiss roll* dataset with 2000 points in 3D space, *MNIST* handwritten digital dataset which contains 60000 gray-images (28×28) of handwritten digits from '0' to '9', *human face* dataset which includes 698 gray-images (64×64) of a plaster head sculpture, and *CIFAR-10* classification dataset with 50000 RGB-images ($32 \times 32 \times 3$).

The proposed method is implemented using C++ with OpenCV and ARPACK, and executes on a PC with a 3.60 GHz Intel Core $i7-4790$ CPU, GTX 1060 GPU, and 16GB memory. We employed the OpenCV function 'cv::flann' to perform the *KNN* operation and ARPACK to solve the sparse symmetric matrix eigen-equation (Eq. (5)).

3.1   Simplification Results

In this section, we will illustrate several data simplification results.

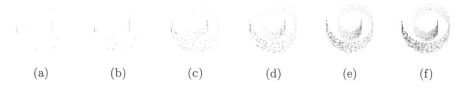

(a)   (b)   (c)   (d)   (e)   (f)

Fig. 3. The intuitive data simplification procedure of the *swiss roll* dataset. In (a)-
(e), the simplified datasets consist of $24, 62, 397, 612, 1286$ data points, generated by
detecting the feature points of the first $5, 10, 30, 50, 100$ eigenvectors, respectively. (f)
is the original data with 2000 points. (Color figure online)

In Fig. 3, we use the *swiss roll* dataset in 3D space to illustrate the intuitive simplification procedure by the proposed data simplification algorithm. In
Fig. 3(a), the simplified dataset is generated by detecting the feature points of
the first five eigenvectors, which captures the critical points at the head and
tail positions of the roll (marked in red and blue colors). In Figs. 3(b)–3(e),
by detecting higher frequency eigenvectors, more feature points are increasingly
added into the simplified dataset and it approaches increasingly closer to the
original dataset (Fig. 3(f)).

The simplification procedures on the *MNIST* and *human face* dataset are
shown in Appendix 2. Similarly, increasingly more critical points of the dataset
were added into the simplified dataset as a consequence of the simplification
procedure. The dataset *CIFAR-10* was also simplified by the proposed method.
Since it is difficult to visualize the *CIFAR-10* in 2D-plane, we use the fidelity of
the simplified datasets to show its simplified procedure in next section.

Finally, in Table 1, the running time of the proposed method is listed. It can
be seen that the operations of *KNN* and eigen-solving consume the majority of
the time, and the data simplification time ranges from 0.044 to 4.759 seconds.

Table 1. Running time (seconds) of the proposed method

Dataset	Data size	KNN	Eigen	Simplification
Swiss roll	2000×3	5.535	6.986	0.044
MNIST	60000×784	57.579	178.933	6.544
Human face	698×4096	3.604	1.079	0.035
CIFAR-10	50000×3072	115.919	146.113	4.759

3.2 Quantitative Measurement of the Fidelity

In this section, the fidelity of the simplified dataset S to the original dataset $\mathcal{H}$ is
quantitatively measured by the three metrics developed in Sect. 2.4. Specifically,
for the data simplification procedure of each dataset mentioned above, a series of
simplified datasets $\{S_i, i = 1, 2, \cdots, n\}$ was first generated. Then, we calculated

the *simplification rate* $r_i = \frac{Card(\mathcal{S}_i)}{Card(\mathcal{H})}$, i.e., the ratio between the cardinality of each $\mathcal{S}_i$ and that of $\mathcal{H}$, and the three metrics $d_{KL}(\mathcal{H},\mathcal{S}_i)$, $d_H(\mathcal{H},\mathcal{S}_i)$ and $d_V(\mathcal{H},\mathcal{S}_i)$, which were normalized into $[0,1]$. Finally, the diagrams of 'r_i v.s. $d_{KL}(\mathcal{H},\mathcal{S}_i)$', '$r_i$ v.s. $d_H(\mathcal{H},\mathcal{S}_i)$', and '$r_i$ v.s. $d_V(\mathcal{H},\mathcal{S}_i)$' were plotted as displayed in Fig. 4.

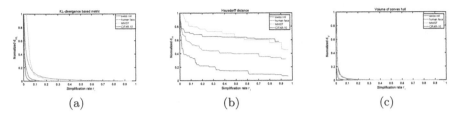

(a)   (b)   (c)

Fig. 4. Quantitative Measurement of the Fidelity. (a) Diagram of r_i v.s. the normalized $d_{KL}(\mathcal{H},\mathcal{S}_i)$. (b) Diagram of r_i v.s. the normalized $d_H(\mathcal{H},\mathcal{S}_i)$. (c) Diagram of r_i v.s. the normalized $d_V(\mathcal{H},\mathcal{S}_i)$. Here, $i = 1, 2, \cdots, n$. (Color figure online)

KL-Divergence-Based Metric: Fig. 4(a) displays the diagram of 'r_i v.s. $d_{KL}(\mathcal{H},\mathcal{S}_i)$' of the four datasets. It can be observed that in the simplification procedures of all of four datasets, the metric $d_{KL}(\mathcal{H},\mathcal{S})$ is rapidly reduced to a small value (less than 0.1), when $r_i = 0.1$, approximately, i.e., $\mathcal{S}_i$ contains approximately 10% of the data points of $\mathcal{H}$. Using the dataset *swiss roll* as an example (blue line) when $\mathcal{S}$ is composed of 5% of the data points of $\mathcal{H}$ (i.e., $r_i = 0.05$), the normalized $d_{KL}(\mathcal{H},\mathcal{S})$ is less than 0.1; when $r_i = 0.2$ ($\mathcal{S}$ contains 20% of the data points of $\mathcal{H}$), the normalized $d_{KL}(\mathcal{H},\mathcal{S})$ is close to 0, meaning that $\mathcal{S}$ contains virtually all of the information embraced by $\mathcal{H}$.

The Hausdorff Distance: In Fig. 4(b), the diagram of 'r_i v.s. $d_H(\mathcal{H},\mathcal{S}_i)$' is illustrated. Because $d_H(\mathcal{H},\mathcal{S}_i)$ and $d_H(\mathcal{H},\mathcal{S}_{i+1})$, $i = 1, 2, \cdots, n-1$, are possibly the same, the diagrams demonstrated in Fig. 4(b) are step-shaped. Based on Fig. 4(b), in the data simplification procedures of the four datasets, the Hausdorff distances $d_H(\mathcal{H},\mathcal{S})$ decrease when increasingly more data points are contained in the simplified datasets. Moreover, the convergence speed of $d_H(\mathcal{H},\mathcal{S}_i)$ with respect to r_i is related to the intrinsic dimension of the dataset: The lower the intrinsic dimension of a dataset, the faster the convergence speed. For example (refer to Fig. 4(b)), the intrinsic dimension of the dataset *swiss roll* is 2 (the smallest of the four datasets), and the convergence speed of the diagram for the simplification procedure of *swiss roll* is the fastest. The intrinsic dimension of the dataset *human face* is 3, greater than that of *swiss roll*, and the convergence speed of its diagram is slower than that of *swiss roll*. The intrinsic dimensions of the datasets *MNIST* and *CIFAR-10* are greater than those of *swiss roll* and *human face*, and the convergence speeds of their diagrams are the slowest.

The Metric of Volume of Convex Hull: In Fig. 4(c), the diagram of $'r_i$ v.s. $d_V(\mathcal{H}, \mathcal{S}_i)'$ is illustrated. It can be observed that in the simplification procedures of all of four datasets, the metric $d_V(\mathcal{H}, \mathcal{S})$ is rapidly reduced to a small value (less than 0.1), when $r_i = 0.05$ or so. It means that our method can fast capture the geometric features of the dataset under low sampling rate ($r_i < 0.05$). And with increasingly more data points inserted into the simplified dataset (i.e., with increasingly greater r_i), the diagrams of all four datasets converge to zero. Considering the dataset *MNIST* (the yellow curve) as an example, when the simplified dataset contains 10% of the data points of the original dataset ($r_i = 0.1$), the metric $d_V(\mathcal{H}, \mathcal{S})$ (8) is nearly zero, meaning that the 'volume' of the simplified dataset has approached that of the original dataset very closely.

3.3   Comparisons

In this section, the proposed HD dataset simplification method is compared with the simple random sampling (SRS) method [22]. The goal of random sampling is to obtain representative small subsets that can be processed efficiently to explore and analyze the data. Although random sampling has a long history of use in databases, it is becoming more important in the big data era, when handling an entire dataset all at once may not be possible [21]. Specifically, we compare the $'r_i$ v.s. metric$'$ curves of our method with the average $'r_i$ v.s. metric$'$ curves of the SRS method. To generate the curves of the SRS method, we run SRS 200 times. The comparison is performed on the dataset *human face*, and illustrated in Fig. 5. It can seen from Fig. 5 that, with the two metrics d_H and d_V, the $'r_i$ v.s. metric$'$ curves of our methods are below those of the SRS methods, meaning the better performance of our method. That is, with the same simplification rate, the simplified datasets by our method are more fidelity to the original dataset than the SRS method. The comparison results are similar on the other datasets.

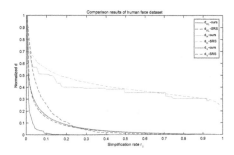

Fig. 5. The comparison results on dataset *human face*. The metric curves of our method and the average results of simple random sampling are demonstrated by solid lines and dotted lines, respectively.

However, with the metric d_{KL}, the performance of our method is similar to that of the SRS method. To compare the two methods in more detail, we add an additional comparison in Appendix 3. Besides, we also compare the proposed method with the topological simplification methods, and discuss the advantages of the proposed method.

4 Conclusion

In this paper, we proposed an HD data simplification method by detecting the feature points of the eigenvectors of an LBO defined on the dataset. The time complexity of our method is independent of the dimensions of data, the simplification rate is easy to control, and the data representation is not changed. Moreover, three metrics were developed to measure the fidelity of the simplified dataset to the original dataset from three perspectives, i.e., information theory, distance and volume. Finally, the proposed method was validated by simplifying some HD datasets. Two applications of the simplified dataset were demonstrated in Appendix 4, including the speedup of DR and training data simplification. These demonstrated that the simplified dataset can capture the main features of the original dataset and can replace the original dataset in data processing tasks, thus improving the data processing capability significantly.

Acknowledgments. This work is supported by the National Natural Science Foundation of China under Grant Nos. 61872316, 61932018, and the National Key R&D Plan of China under Grant No. 2020YFB1708900.

Appendix 1. The Detailed Calculation of Metrics

KL-divergence-Based Metric. KL-divergence, also called relative entropy, is typically employed to measure the difference between two discrete probability distributions $P = \{p_i\}$ and $Q = \{q_i\}$, i.e., $D_{KL}(P\|Q) = \sum_i p_i log\left(\frac{p_i}{q_i}\right)$. To define the KL-divergence-based metric, the original dataset $\mathcal{H}$ and simplified dataset $\mathcal{S}$ are represented as $M_{\mathcal{H}} \in \mathbb{R}^{n \times d}$ and $M_{\mathcal{S}} \in \mathbb{R}^{m \times d}$, where n and m ($n > m$) are the number of data points in $\mathcal{H}$ and $\mathcal{S}$, respectively. Each row of the matrices stores a data point in $\mathbb{R}^d$. First, we calculate the probability distribution $P^{(k)} = \{p_i^{(k)}, i = 1, 2, \cdots, l\}$ for the kth dimension of the data points in $\mathcal{H}$, corresponding to the kth column of matrix $M_{\mathcal{H}}$. To do this, the kth column elements of matrix $M_{\mathcal{H}}$ are normalized into the interval $[0, 1]$, which is divided into l subintervals, (in our implementation, we set $l = 100$). By counting the number of elements of the kth column of matrix $M_{\mathcal{H}}$ whose values lie in the l subintervals, the value distribution histogram is generated, which is then used as the probability distribution $P^{(k)} = \{p_i^{(k)}, i = 1, 2, \cdots, l\}$ of the kth column of matrix $M_{\mathcal{H}}$. Similarly, the probability distribution $Q^{(k)} = \{q_i^{(k)}, i = 1, 2, \cdots, l\}$ of the kth column of matrix $M_{\mathcal{S}}$ can be calculated. Then, the KL-divergence for the kth column elements of matrix $M_{\mathcal{H}}$ and $M_{\mathcal{S}}$ is $D_{KL}(P^{(k)}\|Q^{(k)}) = \sum_i p_i^{(k)} log\left(\frac{p_i^{(k)}}{q_i^{(k)}}\right)$.

And the KL-divergence-based metric is defined as

$$d_{KL}(\mathcal{H}, \mathcal{S}) = \sqrt{\sum_{k=1}^{d}(D_{KL}(P^{(k)}\|Q^{(k)}))^2}. \tag{6}$$

The KL-divergence-based metric (6) transforms the HD dataset into its probability distribution, and measures the difference between the probability distributions of the original and simplified datasets. As the simplified dataset $\mathcal{S}$ becomes increasingly closer to the original dataset $\mathcal{H}$, the KL-divergence-based metric d_{KL} becomes increasingly smaller. When $\mathcal{S} = \mathcal{H}$, $d_{KL} = 0$.

Hausdorff Distance. The Hausdorff distance measures how far two sets are away from each other. Suppose $\mathcal{X}$ and $\mathcal{Y}$ are two dataset in d-dimensional space, and denote $D(\mathcal{X}, \mathcal{Y}) = \sup_{x \in \mathcal{X}} \inf_{y \in \mathcal{Y}} d(x, y)$ as the maximum distance from an arbitrary point in set $\mathcal{X}$ to set $\mathcal{Y}$, where $d(x, y)$ is the Euclidean distance between two points x and y. The Hausdorff distance between $\mathcal{H}$ and $\mathcal{S}$ is defined as $d_H(\mathcal{H}, \mathcal{S}) = max\{D(\mathcal{H}, \mathcal{S}), D(\mathcal{S}, \mathcal{H})\}$. Note that the simplified dataset $\mathcal{S}$ is a subset of the original dataset $\mathcal{H}$, and then, $D(\mathcal{S}, \mathcal{H}) = 0$. Therefore, the Hausdorff distance between $\mathcal{H}$ and $\mathcal{S}$ can be calculated by

$$d_H(\mathcal{H}, \mathcal{S}) = D(\mathcal{H}, \mathcal{S}) = \sup_{x \in \mathcal{H}} \inf_{y \in \mathcal{S}} d(x, y). \tag{7}$$

That is, the Hausdorff distance is the maximum distance from an arbitrary point in the original dataset $\mathcal{H}$ to the simplified dataset $\mathcal{S}$.

Volume of Convex Hull. As the third metric, we use the difference of the volumes of the convex hulls to measure the fidelity of $\mathcal{S}$ to $\mathcal{H}$, i.e.,

$$d_V(\mathcal{H}, \mathcal{S}) = |V(\mathcal{H}_{conv}) - V(\mathcal{S}_{conv})|, \tag{8}$$

where $\mathcal{H}_{conv}$ and $\mathcal{S}_{conv}$ are the convex hulls of $\mathcal{H}$ and $\mathcal{S}$, and $V(\mathcal{H}_{conv})$ and $V(\mathcal{S}_{conv})$ are their volumes. Because the volume of a convex hull in an HD space is difficult to calculate, we first perform the DR operation [4] to project the datasets into 3D space. Afterwards, we employ the quickhull algorithm [3] to construct the convex hulls of the two datasets, and calculate their volumes correspondingly.

Appendix 2. The Simplification Procedures on MNIST and Human Face Dataset

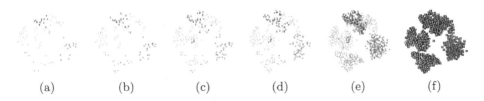

(a)   (b)   (c)   (d)   (e)   (f)

Fig. 6. Simplification of the dataset *MNIST*. (a–d): The simplified datasets by detecting the first 5, 10, 20, 30 LBO eigenvectors, which consist of 82, 120, 196, 280 data points. (e,f): The DR result (using t-SNE) of the original dataset, illustrated by colorful digits (e) and original images (f). (Color figure online)

MNIST: For clarity of the visual analysis, we selected 900 units of the gray-images for the digits '0' to '4', from the *MNIST* dataset, and resized each image as 8×8. The selected images were projected into the 2D-plane using the t-SNE. Whereas in Fig. 6(e), colorful digits are placed at the projected 2D points, in Fig. 6(f), the images themselves are located at the projected points. The simplified datasets are displayed in Fig. 6(a)–6(d). For illustration, their positions in the 2D-plane are extracted from the dimensionality reduced dataset (Fig. 6(e)). In the simplified dataset in Fig. 6(a), which has 82 data points (approximately 9% of the points of the original dataset), all five categories of the digits are represented. In the simplified dataset in Fig. 6(c), which has 196 data points (approximately 22% of the points of the original dataset), virtually all of the key features of the dataset are represented, including the subset of digit '2' in the class of digit '1'. In Fig. 6(d), the simplified dataset contains 280 data points (approximately 31% of the points of the original dataset). We can observe that the boundary of each class of data points has formed (Fig. 6(d)), and the geometric shape of each class is similar to that of the corresponding class in the original dataset (Fig. 6(e)).

Human Face: The *human face* dataset contains 698 gray-images(64×64) of a plaster head sculpture. The images of the dataset were captured by adjusting three parameters: up-down pose, left-right pose, and lighting direction. Therefore, the images in the dataset can be regarded as distributing on a 3D-manifold. Thus, as illustrated in Fig. 7, after the *human face* dataset is dimensionally reduced into a 2D-plane using PCA, it can observed that the longitudinal axis represents the sculpture's rotation in the right-left direction, and the horizontal axis indicates the change of lighting.

In Fig. 7, the images marked with red frames constitute the simplified dataset. In the simplified dataset in Fig. 8(a), the critical points at the boundary are

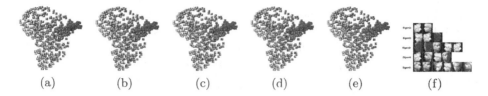

(a)   (b)   (c)   (d)   (e)   (f)

Fig. 7. The simplified datasets of the *human face* dataset, after DR by PCA. Each simplified dataset is comprised of the images marked with red frames. (a–e) The simplified datasets by detecting the first 5, 10, 20, 30, 50 LBO eigenvectors, which consist of 16, 40, 95, 150, 270 data points, respectively. (f) The feature points of the first 5 eigenvectors. (Color figure online)

captured. In Figs. 8(b)–8(d), increasingly more critical points at the boundary and interior are added into the simplified datasets. In Fig. 8(e), virtually all of the images at the boundary are added into the simplified set. For clarity, we display the feature points of the first five LBO eigenvectors in Fig. 7(f), which indeed capture several 'extreme' images in the *human face* dataset. Specifically, the two feature points of the first eigenvector, ϕ_1, are two images with 'leftmost pose + most lighting' and 'rightmost pose + most lighting'. In the feature point set of the second eigenvector, ϕ_2, an image with 'leftmost pose + fewest lighting' is added. Similarly, in the feature point sets of the eigenvectors ϕ_3, ϕ_4, and ϕ_5, there are more 'extreme' images of the pose and lighting (Fig. 7(f)).

Appendix 3. Additional Comparisons

To compare the two methods in more detail, the simplified datasets by the SRS method with the best performance in the 200 times of samplings are visualized in Fig. 8, after DR by PCA. Compared with the simplified datasets generated by our method in Fig. 7, the simplified datasets by our method contain more data points on the boundaries. It is well known that the boundary points are more important than the inner points of a dataset, so the simplified datasets generated by our method contain more important information than those by the SRS method.

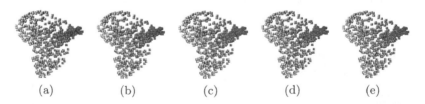

(a)   (b)   (c)   (d)   (e)

Fig. 8. The simplified datasets of the *human face* dataset generated by the SRS method, after DR by PCA. Each simplified dataset is comprised of the images marked with red frames. (a–e) The simplified datasets which consist of 16, 40, 95, 150, 270 data points, respectively. (Color figure online)

Compared with other existing statistical sampling methods, the proposed method can be applied to a broader range of dataset types. For some sampling methods, such as stratified sampling [2], 'Tomek links' [32], and 'SMOTE' [11], data classification is required as supplementary information. However, when the data classification labels are missing, the above methods cannot be implemented. Compared with the topological dataset simplification methods, such as *Reeb spaces* [14], *Joint contour nets* [8], and *Mapper* [29], our method also has obvious advantages. For our method, the size of the simplified dataset is easier to control than those of topological methods. More importantly, in some cases, topological methods may generate new data points whose 'legality' cannot be guaranteed. For example, the simplified *human face* dataset obtained by topological methods can not guarantee that each data point is a 'correct' plaster photo. Therefore, topological simplification methods are suitable for extracting the topological structure of a given dataset, but unsuitable for generating simplified datasets with specified numbers.

Appendix 4. Additional Applications

Speedup of DR : The computation of the DR algorithms for an HD dataset is typically complicated. Given an original dataset $\mathcal{H}$, if we first perform the DR on the simplified dataset $\mathcal{S}$, and then employ the 'out-of-sample' algorithm [6] to calculate the DR coordinates of the remaining data points, the computation requirement can be reduced significantly. Because the simplified dataset $\mathcal{S}$ captures the feature points of the original dataset, the result generated by *DR on simplified set + 'out-of-sample'* is similar as that by *DR on the original set*. In Table 2, the running time for the methods 'DR on simplified set + out-of-sample' and 'DR on original set' are listed. The running-time savings of one orders of magnitude.

Table 2. Timing for speedup of DR (in seconds).

Dataset	Simplification	DR (PCA)	Out-of-sample	Total
Human face	/	7.975	/	7.975
Simplified data	0.467	0.079	0.001	0.547

Training Data Simplification: With the increase of the use of training data in supervised learning, the cost of manual annotation has become increasingly more expensive. Moreover, repeated samples or 'bad' samples can be added into the training dataset, adding confusion and complication into the training data, and influencing the convergence of the training. Therefore, in supervised and active learning, simplifying the training dataset by retaining the feature points and deleting the repeated or 'bad' samples can lighten the burden of the manual annotation, reduce the number of epochs, and the save storage space.

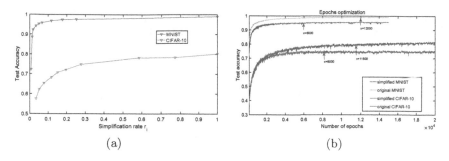

(a)   (b)

Fig. 9. a) The diagram of simplification rate r_i v.s. test accuracy; (b) The diagram of number of epochs v.s. test accuracy, the arrows indicate the places where the training processes stop.

First, we studied the relationship between the simplification rate and test accuracy on *MNIST* and *CIFAR-10*. In Fig. 9(a), the diagram of the simplification rate r_i v.s. test accuracy is illustrated. For the dataset *MNIST*, when $r_i = 0.177$, the test accuracy achieves 97.4%, which is close to the test accuracy of 98.98% using the original training data. For the dataset *CIFAR-10*, when $r_i = 0.584$, the test accuracy is 78.2%, whereas using the original training images, the test accuracy is 80.2%. Therefore, with the proposed simplification method, the simplified dataset is sufficient for training in the two image classification tasks.

Furthermore, with the simplified training set, the training process can terminate earlier than that with the original training set, thus reducing the number of epochs. In Fig. 9(b), the diagrams of the number of epochs v.s. test accuracy are illustrated. The 'early stopping' criterion proposed in [26] was used to determine the stopping time (indicated by arrows). For the dataset *MNIST*, the training process with the original training set stopped at 12000 epochs, with a test accuracy 99.07%. With the simplified training set, the training process stopped as early as at 6000 epochs, with a test accuracy 95.25%. For the dataset *CIFAR-10*, the training process stopped at 8000 epochs with the simplified training set, whereas the training process with the original training set stopped at 11500 epochs. Therefore, with the simplified training dataset, the training epochs can be reduced significantly.

References

1. Albattah, W.: The role of sampling in big data analysis. In: Proceedings of the International Conference on Big Data and Advanced Wireless Technologies, pp. 1–5 (2016)
2. Aoyama, H.: A study of the stratified random sampling. Ann. Inst. Stat. Math. **6**(1), 1–36 (1954)
3. Barber, C.B., Dobkin, D.P., Huhdanpaa, H.: The quickhull algorithm for convex hulls. ACM Trans. Math. Softw. **22**(4), 469–483 (1996)
4. Belkin, M., Niyogi, P.: Laplacian eigenmaps for dimensionality reduction and data representation. Neural Comput. **15**(6), 1373–1396 (2003)

5. Belkin, M., Sun, J., Wang, Y.: Constructing Laplace operator from point clouds in $\mathbb{R}^d$. In: Proceedings of the twentieth annual ACM-SIAM symposium on Discrete algorithms, pp. 1031–1040. SIAM (2009)
6. Bengio, Y., Paiement, J.F., Vincent, P., Delalleau, O., Roux, N.L., Ouimet, M.: Out-of-sample extensions for LLE, isomap, MDS, eigenmaps, and spectral clustering. In: Advances in Neural Information Processing Systems, pp. 177–184 (2004)
7. Benko, K., Kothe, M., Semmler, K.D., Simon, U.: Eigenvalues of the Laplacian and curvature. In: Colloquium Mathematicum, vol. 42, pp. 19–31. Institute of Mathematics Polish Academy of Sciences (1979)
8. Carr, H., Duke, D.J.: Joint contour nets. IEEE Trans. Vis. Comput. Graph. **20**(8), 1100–1113 (2014)
9. Carr, H., Snoeyink, J., Van De Panne, M.: Simplifying flexible isosurfaces using local geometric measures. In: IEEE Visualization 2004, pp. 497–504 (2004)
10. Castellani, U., Cristani, M., Fantoni, S., Murino, V.: Sparse points matching by combining 3d mesh saliency with statistical descriptors. Comput. Graph. Forum **27**(2), 643–652 (2008)
11. Chawla, N.V., Bowyer, K.W., Hall, L.O., Kegelmeyer, W.P.: SMOTE: synthetic minority over-sampling technique. J. Artif. Intell. Res **16**, 321–357 (2002)
12. Dong, S., Bremer, P.T., Garland, M., Pascucci, V., Hart, J.C.: Spectral surface quadrangulation. ACM Trans. Graph. **25**(3), 1057–1066 (2006)
13. Dubuisson, M.P., Jain, A.K.: A modified hausdorff distance for object matching. In: Proceedings of 12th International Conference on Pattern Recognition, vol. 1, pp. 566–568 (1994)
14. Edelsbrunner, H., Harer, J., Patel, A.K.: Reeb spaces of piecewise linear mappings. In: Proceedings of the Twenty-Fourth Annual Symposium on Computational Geometry, pp. 242–250 (2008)
15. Gyulassy, A., Bremer, P.T., Hamann, B., Pascucci, V.: A practical approach to morse-smale complex computation: scalability and generality. IEEE Trans. Vis. Comput. Graph. **14**(6), 1619–1626 (2008)
16. Johnson, A.E., Hebert, M.: Using spin images for efficient object recognition in cluttered 3d scenes. IEEE Trans. Pattern Anal. Mach. Intell. **21**(5), 433–449 (1999)
17. Körtgen, M., Park, G.J., Novotni, M., Klein, R.: 3d shape matching with 3d shape contexts. In: The 7th Central European Seminar on Computer Graphics, vol. 3, pp. 5–17. Budmerice (2003)
18. Liu, Z., Zhang, A.: Sampling for big data profiling: a survey. In: IEEE Access, p. 1 (2020)
19. Lowe, D.G.: Distinctive image features from scale-invariant keypoints. Int. J. Comput. Vision **60**(2), 91–110 (2004)
20. Luo, P., Wang, X., Tang, X.: Hierarchical face parsing via deep learning. In: 2012 IEEE Conference on Computer Vision and Pattern Recognition, pp. 2480–2487 (2012)
21. Mahmud, M., Huang, J., Salloum, S., Emara, T., Sadatdiynov, K.: A survey of data partitioning and sampling methods to support big data analysis. Big Data Min. Anal. **3**, 85–101 (2020)
22. Nassiuma, D.K.: Survey Sampling: Theory and Methods. Nairobi University Press, Nairobi (2001)
23. Ovsjanikov, M., Mérigot, Q., Mémoli, F., Guibas, L.: One point isometric matching with the heat kernel. Comput. Graph. Forum **29**(5), 1555–1564 (2010)
24. Peng, X., Feris, R.S., Wang, X., Metaxas, D.N.: RED-Net: a recurrent encoder-decoder network for video-based face alignment. Int. J. Comput. Vision **126**(10), 1103–1119 (2018)

25. Pérez-Cruz, F.: Kullback-Leibler divergence estimation of continuous distributions. In: 2008 IEEE International Symposium on Information Theory, pp. 1666–1670 (2008)
26. Prechelt, L.: Automatic early stopping using cross validation: quantifying the criteria. Neural Netw. **11**(4), 761–767 (1998)
27. Reeb, G.: Sur les points singuliers dune forme de pfaff compltement intgrable ou dune fonction numrique. Comptes Rendus Hebdomadaires des Sances de lAcadmie des Sciences **222**, 847–849 (1946)
28. Reuter, M., Wolter, F.E., Peinecke, N.: Laplace-Beltrami spectra as 'shape-DNA' of surfaces and solids. Comput.-Aided Des. **38**(4), 342–366 (2006)
29. Singh, G., Mémoli, F., Carlsson, G.E.: Topological methods for the analysis of high dimensional data sets and 3d object recognition. In: SPBG, pp. 91–100 (2007)
30. Sun, J., Ovsjanikov, M., Guibas, L.: A concise and provably informative multi-scale signature based on heat diffusion. Comput. Graph. Forum **28**(5), 1383–1392 (2009)
31. Sun, Y., Wang, X., Tang, X.: Deep convolutional network cascade for facial point detection. In: Proceedings of the IEEE Conference on Computer Vision and Pattern Recognition, pp. 3476–3483 (2013)
32. Tomek, I.: Two modifications of CNN. IEEE Trans. Syst. Man Cybern. **6**, 769–772 (1976)
33. Vallet, B., Lévy, B.: Spectral geometry processing with manifold harmonics. Comput. Graph. Forum **27**(2), 251–260 (2008)
34. Wang, N., Gao, X., Tao, D., Yang, H., Li, X.: Facial feature point detection: a comprehensive survey. Neurocomputing **275**, 50–65 (2018)
35. Wu, X., Zhu, X., Wu, G.Q., Ding, W.: Data mining with big data. IEEE Trans. Knowl. Data Eng. **26**(1), 97–107 (2013)

VR/AR

Characterizing Visual Acuity in the Use of Head Mounted Displays

Vladimir Soares da Fontoura (ID) and Anderson Maciel(✉) (ID)

Federal University of Rio Grande do Sul (UFRGS) – Institute of Informatics (INF),
Porto Alegre 91501-970, Brazil
amaciel@inf.ufrgs.br
http://www.inf.ufrgs.br/cg

Abstract. In the real world, the sense of sight is dominant for humans, and having a normal vision is essential to perform well in many common tasks. There, ophthalmology has several tools to assess and correct a person's vision. In VR, when wearing an HMD, even a user with normal vision is challenged by additional hurdles that affect the virtual environment's perceptual acuity, negatively impacting their performance in the application task. Display resolution, but also soiled lenses and bad vergence adjustment are examples of possible issues. To better understand and tackle this problem, we provide a study on assessing visual acuity in a VR setup. We conducted an experimental evaluation with users and found out, among other results, that visual acuity in VR is significantly and considerably lower than in real environments. Besides, we found several correlations of the measured acuity and task performance with difficulty adjusting the HMD and use of prescription glasses.

Keywords: Perception in VR · Head-mounted display · Virtual reality · Visual acuity · Snellen

1 Introduction

Head mounted displays (HMDs) were conceived in the early 1960's, at the very foundation of computer graphics. However, only recently the display technology attained levels of quality and cost-effectiveness to allow their deployment to the general consumer. This, combined with the outstanding advancement of computer graphics, enabled immersion in highly realistic virtual worlds.

Still, oftentimes the user experience in VR is undermined by factors dependent of the HMD construction and use. While an HMD is a display, it is also an input device which sensors define the head pose. Thus, the whole human vestibulo-oculomotor system is stimulated, in such way that any discrepancies cause some level of discomfort and perception issues that may hinder the user performance. Nausea, disorientation and eye-strain, among other symptoms, are grouped under the cybersickness umbrella. Previous works approached the problem of cybersickness, demonstrating that it can be fairly predicted and avoided

N. Magnenat-Thalmann et al. (Eds.): CGI 2021, LNCS 13002, pp. 589–607, 2021.
https://doi.org/10.1007/978-3-030-89029-2_44

by controlling such parameters (although some of them are difficult to control) [11]. However, another phenomenon has been extensively overlooked: the variability of the perceptual accuracy among users and systems. Arguably, pixel size, lens aberration, contrast and size of the displayed objects all potentially influence the ability of the user to accurately perceive visual elements.

In the real world, ophthalmologists can measure any deviation from the average quality of the visual perception in a patient. Many types of deviation are very common and well known, such as myopia, hyperopia, astigmatism, cataract, etc. They are caused by either optical or neural factors. The disability caused by these deviations is grouped under the term low vision or low visual acuity. Visual acuity (VA) is the ability to recognize small details with precision, and is a measure relative to the normal vision. The VA is said to be normal, 6/6 or 20/20 when the individual discriminates two contours separated by 1 arc minute (or 1.75 mm) at 6 m (or 20 ft) [21]. In the Appendix 1 we present an overview of the approaches used in ophthalmology to assess visual acuity.

In VR, the visual acuity experienced by an individual with normal vision in a given session wearing an HMD is dependent on a number of additional factors, e.g. rendering technique, display resolution, focus, vergence, lens quality. While some factors are system dependent and are constant for the same system among different sessions and users, such as rendering and display resolution, other factors such as focus, vergence and transparency of the lenses vary considerably between sessions due to human influence. When putting on the HMD, people soil the lenses, do not fasten enough or fasten too much the straps, do not understand how to setup vergence, cannot judge if they are seeing as well as possible. These factors potentially affect the perceived acuity in some way, disturbing the experience. To our knowledge, visual acuity has not been characterized for HMD-based VR. In our research, we are especially concerned by the lack of control in the experimental conditions of task-based studies in VR. Our premise is that researchers do not know to which extent the results of their experiments are affected by the studied variables, e.g. an interaction technique, or by the user ability to see the elements necessary to accomplish the task.

In this paper, we investigate visual acuity in VR for the first time. Our primary contribution is to define the problem of lower acuity in terms of the relevance of each potential cause. We then propose a methodology to measure acuity adapting known ophthalmology techniques to VR, which is a second contribution. This method, we expect, can be used by researchers in the future to ensure each subject is experiencing a suitable level of visual acuity necessary to fulfill a task, or to normalize the collected user performance data according to a measured level of visual acuity. Finally, we contribute with an experiment to verify the variability of acuity among users and sessions.

2   Related Work

While we could not find previous works in VR where the researchers consider acuity as one of the variables in their task-based studies, we could find previous works related to visual perception in the use of head mounted displays.

Perception in VR was investigated as a function of distance estimation [5]. The research overviews methods and techniques used to measure perceived distance concluding that in AR underestimation of distances are less likely to happen than in VR. Another work [7] assessed HMDs through visual performance metrics. They developed a prototype HMD to analyze the resolution of visual acuity as a function of contrast using three different light levels and two different types of projection materials. Similarly, Kooi and colleagues [17] conducted a test at a virtual distance of 3 m using three HMDs (Iodisplay, Kaiser and Sony). The test correlated display resolution with stereoscopic acuity. They found that the HMDs provide better stereo acuity than presented in the scientific literature, which was attributed to the target used, which is much more representative of real world scenes unlike the typical static 'fine line' targets often used.

Another previous work studied the relationship between color mode and environmental lighting relative to visual acuity and fatigue in VR when using HMDs [6]. Two letter schemes were used, one characterized by light letters on a dark background (dark mode) and another with dark letters on a light background (light mode). As a result, the dark background in dark mode provided a significant advantage in terms of reducing visual fatigue and increasing visual acuity in dark virtual environments on current HMDs. Meanwhile, Matsuura et al. [20] discussed the difficulty caused in a walkthrough and its interference in viewing information on HMDs, as well as the format of fonts to minimize the effect of this problem. In the end, the authors found that fonts with very thin horizontal and vertical lines should not be presented in HMDs.

More recently, visual acuity and contrast sensitivity were evaluated using two types of HMD (Oculus Rift and HTC Vive Pro) [30]. The research findings indicate that visual acuity and contrast sensitivity experienced in VR are lower than those experienced in real-world scenarios. The study presented a quantitative approach to characterize the limitations of VR with respect to visual acuity and contrast sensitivity. Also on contrast, Goudé et al. [10] proposed a new Tone Mapping Operator that takes advantage of vision-dependent tone mapping that improves contrast and a Tone Mapping Operator applied to the entire 360° image that preserves global coherence by being adapted to the human eye's perception of luminance on head-mounted displays.

Some previous works also studied how to test and correct natural loss of acuity using HMDss [24, 31]. Ong et al. [22] evaluated the performance and identified the limitations of an automated HMD for visual acuity testing. They developed a head-mounted display (HMD) to automate these tests and thus increase its efficiency.

Despite our efforts to survey the literature for other works investigating visual acuity in VR, we could not find a previous work on the characterization of visual acuity. In the present work, we look at visual acuity in the virtual world in a similar way it is seen in the real world by ophthalmologists.

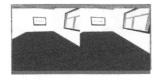  

Fig. 1. Test scenarios. Upper row: the virtual ophtalmologist room used for the virtual Snellen, contrast sensitivity and glare tests (binocular view). Middle and bottom rows: daytime and nighttime monocular views of the virtual shooting range used for the shooting test.

3 Methodology

To characterize visual acuity for HMDs, we propose the adaptation of typical acuity tests from ophthalmology. These are the four tests described in Appendix 1. Each of the tests will measure one of the dimensions of acuity selected: focus (Snellen), contrast (Pelli-Robson), central glare and peripheral glare. We hypothesize that the acuity in VR is significantly different than that in the physical world. More than that, we hypothesize that the variability of acuity among users is high. To test these hypotheses and characterize how acuity varies, we implemented these tests and applied them in an experiment with human subjects. We present the tests design (Sect. 3.3 to 3.6) and the experimental protocol for the user study in this section.

Furthermore, we hypothesize that other characteristics of VR applications, such as type of task and attention focus, modulate the effect of acuity over user performance. To analyze the factorial influence of acuity with visual and motor tasks, we designed another experimental setup consisting of a shooting stand where the users are asked to shoot under different visual conditions. This setup and experiment are described in Sect. 3.7.

3.1   Hardware and Software Setup

We created a common immersive scenario using the Unity 3D Engine and an Oculus Rift to support the 4 acuity tests. This scenario consists of a room (Fig. 1a) where the subject is seated at a certain distance from the wall in front of them. On the wall, we present the four tests in sequence. At the end of these tests, we transport the subject to another scenario for the shooting stand test (Fig. 1b). There, they will stand up and perform a series of shots at a target placed at a distance in front of them.

3.2   Study Protocol

The participants were invited by email and 23 people volunteered to take part in the experiment. The procedures performed in our studies involving human participants were in accordance with the ethical standards of the institutional and national research committee and with the 1975 Helsinki Declaration and its later amendments or comparable ethical standards. We scheduled an appointment for each participant in a separate time-slot. Upon arrival they were informed of task to be performed and that they could decide to stop at any time. They were then invited to fill an informed consent form and a profiling questionnaire.

A session consisted of performing the sequence of four acuity tests in the same order, following with the shooting-stand test. The participant sits on a fixed chair and puts on the HMD. They are encouraged and instructed to adjust the HMD until they feel comfortable before starting. They are informed that the first two tests will be performed initially with the right eye and then with the left eye. A completely dark image is displayed to the other eye. During these two tests (Snellen and Pelli-Robson), the researcher asks the volunteer: "Which is the letter or set of letters that is underlined in red?", and if the volunteer answers the letter or set of letters correctly, the researcher moves on to the next one, until the participant does not identify correctly what is being shown underlined. The last successful response is registered for a later analysis. After performing the first four tests seated, the volunteers are asked to stand for the shooting test. They were not allowed to remove the HMD before the end of the experimental session unless, of course, they decide not to continue the experiment. In this case, their data would be excluded from the population.

Quantitative dependent variables are collected from the oral responses given to the experimenter during the visual acuity tests (Snellen, Pelli-Robson and Glare). During the shooting test, the system logs all events with the respective details and timestamps for subsequent analysis, in such a way that no oral response is necessary.

At the end of the session of all tests performed, just after removing the HMD, the participants were asked to fill a form based on the NASA TLX (Task Load Index) multidimensional assessment tool [12].

3.3   Snellen Test

To reproduce the Snellen test (Sect. 3.3) in VR, we placed a virtual chart (Fig. 6) containing the optotypes on the wall opposite to the user location in the VE at a distance of 6 m. We took care to make the appearance and size of the characters and spaces following the same standards used in the real-world Snellen. We used the data in Table 3 to determine the size of the optotypes based on the visual angle of 0.5 arc-minutes viewed from a distance of 6.10 m (20 Paris Feet).

The participant views the scene with only one eye at a time. Nevertheless, they have freedom do move the head naturally as in the real world. We recorded the resulting visual acuity as the decimal number in the last row where the volunteer could discriminate more than half of the optotypes.

3.4   Pelli-Robson Contrast Sensitivity Test

To build an equivalent of the Pelli-Robson test in VR, we assembled two tables of character triplets following the Pelli-Robson key to the contrast sensitivity chart (see Table 5), one for each eye.

The participant sits at 3 m from the table, so that their vision is directed to the center of the table. Two different tables (Table 5 right) are used for each eye so that the participants do not memorize the sequence of letters.

The values collected from the test are the numbers on each side of the table, given in logarithmic unit (log unid.), and correspond to each group of three letters (e.g.: $0.60 = (1/10^{0.60} = 0.25 = 25\%)$.

3.5   Central Glare

In our adaptation of the glare test to VR, a set of five optotypes of the same size, in black color is shown on a white background on a frame at the wall in front of the participants at 6 m away (Fig. 5).

Besides, a white light-source is placed above the board and directed to the center of the participant's eyes. The letters from Table 4 column *peripheral* are presented.

Directional Light was set to realtime mode with intensity 0.22. Shadow type soft, realtime, strength 1, bias 0.05, normal bias 0.4, near plane 0.2. The cooke size 10, none flare, render mode auto, culling mask everything.

Contrarily to the previous tests, here the participant is allowed to use both eyes simultaneously to try and identify the optotypes.

The brightness in the environment is set to almost total darkness. In our Unity3D implementation, the parameter in Lighting/Scene/Environment Lighting/ Intensity Multiplier was set to 2.47 to obtain this effect. The participant then reads the letters and, if the response is correct, the next row from Table 4 column *central* is presented. This is repeated until the participant misses 3 or more optotypes in the same row.

The result of the recorded visual acuity is the decimal index of the last row the volunteer can see more than half of the optotypes.

3.6   Peripheral Glare

This test is similar to the central glare (Sect. 3.5), with two differences. Here, the room is brightly lit and there is no directional light toward the participant's eyes (Fig. 5).

The result of the recorded visual acuity is, again, the decimal index of the last row the volunteer can see more than half of the optotypes.

3.7   Shooting Test

While the previous tests are based on ophtalmology approaches for assessing visual acuity while wearing an HMD, in this section we present a task-based user performance assessment in VR. This strategy assumes that task-performance correlates with visual acuity, as the task, target shooting, requires vision to aim at the target. Besides, lighting conditions vary during the task execution, in such a way that contrast variation and glare effects impose challenges comparable to those of the previous test. Finally, as the task requires balance and motor actions from the users, this test is arguably more comprehensive in terms of the elements to be tested.

The virtual environment consists of a shooting range (Fig. 2 based on a model designed for a military unit of our country's Army[1]. The stand has a shooting module, inside which the shooter is positioned to perform their shots, two overhead baffles and a target (International Shuting Sport Federation (ISSF) - Standard ISSF Rimfire/Centrefire Target) (Fig. 2 placed at 20 m. The result of each shot is shown on a scoreboard positioned to the right of the shooter in the VE for a prompt feedback.

The environment simulates day and night (Fig. 1 middle and bottom) with gradual transitions including sunrise and sunset. This ensures that the shooting task is performed with varying brightness. The time-slots for each shot are controlled by the system. Between shots, a green light located above the overhead baffle lights up and authorizes the shot.

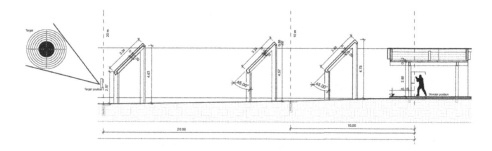

Fig. 2. Schematic of the shooting range and target

Before starting, an expert shooter and VR researcher explains the task and provides basic shooting instructions to each participant. This includes: how to hold the Oculus Rift controller, how to control breathing, that they must close the left eye to aim since the gun will be on their right hand, stand in a comfortable position to perform the shots, the importance of accuracy in the shot, that after each shot, they must lower the hand and restart the procedure, always keeping calm. They are also informed that they may interrupt the test at any time.

The shooting test is applied just after the previous 4 acuity tests for each participant, who are then sitting on a chair. At this moment, the researcher helps the participant to stand up for the shooting test. The participant's HMD is not removed. They will be told that they must perform a series of ten shots on the target, and that the result is shown on the scoreboard. The maximum time duration to complete the ten shots is 1 min and 20 s, divided into 10 slots of 12 s. The sun and lighting conditions complete one day cycle during the session

---

[1] Reference removed for blind review.

of 80 s, starting and ending at noon, in such a way that the first three and the last two shots are taken with daylight, and the other five without.

At the end of the ten shots, the researcher helps the volunteer to remove the HMD and invite them to fill a form with questions about their experience during each of the tests and about the participation as a whole.

4   Results

A total of twenty-three participants completed the tests (six women) with ages ranging from 15 to 30 years, with a mean of 21.5 and standard deviation (SD) of 2.3. Twelve reported visual conditions, being the most cited myopia, hyperopia and astigmatism. As for the use of prescription glasses, eleven answered they use them regularly, and among these, only seven preferred to perform the tests wearing their glasses. None of the participants reported having had some kind of eye surgery, or any disease that could influence their vision (hypertension, diabetes or autoimmune disease). About previous experience with virtual reality glasses (HMD), eleven participants responded positively. When asked if they had any previous experience with firearms (shooting stand, hunting, armed forces, etc.), six responded yes.

4.1   Objective Results

The Snellen Test results show that 11 participants were able to visualize the 20/80 optotypes with both the left and right eye, 8 participants were successful in discriminating up to the 20/100 row of optotypes with the right eye and 9 with the left eye.

The results of the Pelli-Robson Contrast Sensitivity Test show that 15 subjects had contrast sensitivity of 2.10 with both eyes. Besides, 2 participants attained a contrast sensitivity of 2.25 with the right eye and one with the left eye.

The results of the Glare Test - Peripheral show that 14 participants were able to visualize the 20/80 optotypes. Other 4 participants were able to discriminate 20/100 optotypes.

The results of the Glare Test - Central show that fourteen subjects could visualize up to the 20/100 optotypes only. Five participants could identify the 20/80 optotypes.

In the shooting test, a perfect performance would be 100 points overall, with 50 points in daytime and another 50 in nighttime. The participants obtained a mean of 17.22, $sd = 13.03$ points for the daytime shots, and a mean of 20.04, $sd = 13.49$ in nighttime. The overall average was 37.26 points with $sd = 25.21$.

In their first daytime shot, eleven subjects missed the target completely, but in their last daytime shot only six missed. Similarly, eight participants missed the first nighttime shot and only five missed the last nighttime shot.

4.2   Subjective Results

When questioned whether they had difficulty adjusting the HMD, 11 participants responded they had none and 2 that they had slight difficulty. Eight participant reported having considerable difficulty. The average of the ratings is 2.35, where 1 means *no difficulty* and 5 means *considerable difficulty*. Figure 7a shows all the responses. These and other questionnaire data are in Appendix 3.

We also asked the participants about comfort and presence in the virtual environment with a single question. The ratings average to 3.65, where 5 is maximum comfort and presence (Fig. 7(b)).

The remainder of the subjective results come from the analysis of workload. The raw NASA TLX results are shown in Fig. 8 with the mean score for each statement.

The unweighted TLX score ($max = 100$) was assessed as 26.04 for the Snellen Test, 23.52 for Pelli-Robson Contrast Sensitivity Test, 24.09 for Glare - Peripheral Test, 25.39 for Glare - Central Test, and 27.48 for Shooting Test.

4.3   Discussion

The eight participants who reported difficulty in adjusting the HMD also scored low on the target shooting, although two of them had previous experience with firearms. This suggests that correct HMD adjustment has an effect on visual acuity. Among the thirteen subjects who had no difficulty adjusting the HMD ten of them were better at night shooting than day shooting, characterizing the importance of correct HMD adjustment, although three of them stressed that they were not comfortable in an immersive environment.

All five subjects who were better in daytime than nighttime shooting had grade 2.10 on the Pelli-Robson test in both eyes and 20/80 on the Peripheral Glare test. Also, none of them had difficulty adjusting the HMD. Similarly, all the five subjects who did not achieve any points in the first and last daytime shots had 20/80 on the Peripheral Glare test and four of them had 20/100 on the Central Glare test. They were also all comfortable in the virtual environment, which may, in a future test with more participants, be proven a pattern.

From the five subjects with worse performance in the night shooting, four wore prescription glasses, all had 20/100 on the central Glare test and on the Pelli-Robson test, four had 2.10 on the right eye, which may be due to the choice of the wrong eye to aim at, since the dominant eye in the shot should always be the eye opposite to the hand that holds the gun [33].

Among the subjects who did not wear prescription glasses but have a vision problem (Myopia), two scored 20/200 in the Snellen test in both eyes, and in the Pelli-Robson test 1.25 and 1.20 (very low) with the left-eye. In addition, they had difficulty adjusting the HMD and preferred to perform the test without their prescription glasses. Both obtained a score of 50 pts on the shooting (the average was 37 points). In myopia, light rays entering the eye are focused in front of the retina, rather than directly on it, so that distant objects appear blurry [14]. As the HMD screen is very close to the eye, myopia has no potential effect on acuity for VR. This differential may have helped these participants to outperform their counterparts, which should be further investigated.

5   Conclusion

The presented work investigated visual acuity in VR and had its main focus on concerns about the lack of control, by an experimenter, of the acuity experienced by participants in their in test conditions.

Our results brought evidence that some factors such as using appropriate eyeglasses for hyperopia and astigmatism, correct HMD adjustment and the subject being comfortable in the immersive environment correlate with good results in the Snellen, Pelli-Robson, peripheral and Central Glare tests. Consistently, measured acuities correlate with performance in a target shopoting task in VR. Notice that all variations could be detected even using the same HMD, with the same physical parameters (resolution, optics, rendering system).

The ophtalmology acuity tests that we adapted to VR helped us to substantiate the importance of the factors presented above, which can serve as a basis for research for new technologies, devices more capable and less demanding in the vision correction of its users. But essentially, our developments demonstrate that sub-normal acuity impacts the task performance in VR. The virtual shooting test demonstrated to predict the acuity experienced during a session wearing an HMD. Thus, an important lesson learned from our work is that a brief visuo-motor task performed before an experimental session in VR can help to understand the effect that acuity is causing on the dependent variables of the experiment for that specific participant in that session instante. This allows to remove contributions from bad acuity which otherwise mask the measures of interest.

In future work we can delve deeper into tests with subjects who present specific eye conditions, such as myopia, compare the outcome of different devices and rendering systems, as well as the influence of the dominant eye in the simulation of shooting or other specific tasks.

Acknowledgements. This work was funded by the Brazilian funding agencies Coordenação de Aperfeiçoamento de Pessoal de Nível Superior (CAPES) - Finance Code 001, Conselho Nacional de Desenvolvimento Científico e Tecnológico (CNPq) project 311251/2020-0, and FAPERGS PqG 17/2551-0001192-9.

Appendix 1 – Background on Visual Acuity in Ophthalmology

Visual acuity refers to the clarity of vision and the ability to distinguish details in objects. Anatomically, it is the ability of the eye to focus the image on the retina [30]. It is also the capability of the eye to distinguish small details appearing on the visual field at a specified distance [23]. Acuity can also be split into two types:

static, when the object is perceived stationary; dynamic, when the observer, the object or both are in motion [27].

Standard objects used to assess acuity are often called optotypes. The most common set of optotypes used to measure static VA are the Snellen chart and the Landolt C, also known as a Landolt ring. Both were created more than 100 years ago. There are also other more recent optotypes in use today [8, 26]. We present them and their different uses for visual acuity assessment in the next subsections.

Snellen-Type Optotype

Herman Snellen, in 1862 [29] created a Table 1 composed by letters of different sizes (optotypes - Table 1) representing a visual angle of 5 min of arc (5') at a distance of 5 m. The letters are composed by elements of $\frac{1}{5}$ of this measure.

Table 1. Snellen-type optotype dimensions.

Dimension	Size in mm
I	67.891
II	136.107
III	203.999
IV	272.215
V	340.106
VI	408.323
VII	476.214
VIII	544.105
...	...

In his study [29], Snellen specifies the dimensions of the characters and the spaces that separate them. The visual acuity (V) is the maximum distance at which the optotype is recognized (d) divided by the distance at which it should be to form an angle of 5 arc-minutes (D) [29] as in Eq. 1:

$$V = \frac{d}{D} \tag{1}$$

If d and D are equal and the optotype is visible at 20 Paris feet[2], then $V = \frac{20}{20} = 1$ is defined as a normal visual acuity.

In the Snellen proposal, the minimum resolution angle is 1 arc-minute, as seen in Fig. 3. To determine the size of an optotype in the Snellen chart, the formula of Eq. 2 is used:

$$H = 14.6 \frac{D}{V} \tag{2}$$

---

[2] 1 Paris foot is equivalent to 324.8393 mm. 1 Paris foot = 1.06575 feet.

$$u = \text{arc tan} (1.45 / 5000) = \text{arc tan} (0.00029) = 0.01662 \text{ deg.}$$
$$u' = 0.01662° \times 60 = 0.997 \text{ min arc} \approx 1 \text{ min arc;} => AV = 1 / 1 = 1;$$

Fig. 3. Calculation of the Static Visual Acuity (SVA) in a Snellen-type optotype. It is assumed that the observer looks at the letter from a distance of 5 m ($d = 5$ m). Therefore, the height of the letter will be 7.25 mm and the thickness of the horizontal feature will be $s = 1.45$ mm [27].

where H is the height of the optotype (in mm), D is the presentation distance (in meters), V is the visual acuity (in tenths) and the constant 14.6 represents the tangent of 5 multiplied by 10,000 to compensate for the use of millimeters and tenths in the other components.

In a Snellen chart, some letters are more easily readable than others and each row has a different number of letters. This causes the phenomena of non-proportional grouping and spacing between letters and rows, making reliability and reproducibility of using a Snellen chart low. Nevertheless, it is widely used and universally accepted.

Pelli-Robson Contrast Sensitivity

Besides the high-contrast VA measurement (black optotypes on a white background) provided by Snellen charts, other contrast levels can also be used to obtain a second measure of acuity. The principle is to use gray optotypes on the same white background, showing successively lighter and lighter grays.

Contrast is defined as the relative difference of luminance between a target and the background. The whole human visual system (HVS) is involved in object detection, meaning that while the eyes capture and convert light into electric signals, the brain processes and makes the decisions about the visual perception of objects [1, 32]. Contrast is used to determine what is detectable by the HVS. The objects are visible if they have a contrast greater than the contrast sensitivity (CS) [16, 32], which is defined as the minimum contrast necessary to detect a grid in some specified spatial frequency

CS was first measured in 1889 [28], but its value was recognized only after Bodis-Wolner work in 1972 [4].

Pelli et al. [25, 26] first proposed a chart with variable contrast letters sized at half a degree that can measure the CS of an individual with spatial frequencies between 3 and 5 c/deg. That is the best interval to determine whether an individual has a loss of sensitivity in the spatial frequency. Later, they came up with a new chart with single sized letters that change in contrast at each row to obtain information about the contrast sensitivity of any individual. Hence, they created a model that allows to choose the best parameters to accurately maximize the measurements provided by the test [25,26].

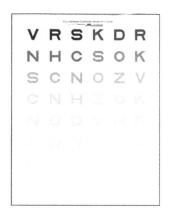

Fig. 4. Miniature Pelli-Robson Letter-Sensitivity Chart

The most widely used chart presents a set of Sloan font letters with size of 0.5° at a distance of 3 m, although it can be used at shorter distances to assess individuals with subnormal vision. The chart is read from left to right, from top to bottom. Each row contains two groups of three letters. The letters within each group have the same contrast, while each successive group has lower contrast than the previous one. As seen in Fig. 4, there is a total of 48 optotypes on a white background, divided in 16 groups. The first group is black (contrast is 100%), and each subsequent group has a contrast reduction factor of 0.707 (0.15 log units). Thus, the contrast of the last group is 0.56% (2.25 log units below 100% [35].

The Pelli-Robson chart is considered a suitable technique to asses the visual function [19].

Glare and Disability Glare

Glare is a light phenomenon that causes difficulty, and may even disable, viewing of an object due to very bright light of artificial or natural origin. The light scatters in opacified regions of the eye capsule, causing ofuscating bright regions to appear in the field of view. Cataract is the most associated condition with glare testing. While most vision quality analyses are performed in a fixed viewing position and direction, glare depends on the viewing position and direction within a space [3], in such a way that specific central and peripheral glare tests are used. Lacava [18] concluded that the glare test associated with the contrast sensitivity test shows that the visual acuity provided by the Snellen Table does not correspond to everyday vision. Although the measurement of visual acuity using contrast sensitivity is not unanimous, it is considered more informative than the measurement of visual acuity using onkly the Snellen chart [35].

Hoskins [13] states that glare testing and contrast sensitivity play a role in quantifying or describing visual impairment in some patients.

Luminance, Contrast, Resolution and Field of View

In modern optics, the ability of the eye to resolve a line pair is one of many ways to determines the human eye-plus-brain acuity. This acuity is measured in the fovea zone as $1/a = 1.7$, where a is the number of arc minutes of field of view necessary to discriminate the two lines. This is roughly $0.59'$ (arc minutes), or $171.62\,\mu$rad microradian. As two pixels are necessary to see the two lines, it is said that the resolution of the human eye in good light conditions is about $1'$ arc minute ($290.89\,\mu$rad microradians. Outside the fovea zone, the resolution of the eye decreases considerably [29], so a moderate variation in contrast or illumination will reflect very little on the person's visual acuity. Visual perception is rather influenced by the difference in intensity between the object and the background (contrast), the spatial frequency (inverse of the line thickness in regular optotypes) and the area of the object. As for the field of view, there is no consensus and it varies among people, but it is accepted that it is somewhere above $180°$ horizontally, limited at $220°$. The binocuar vision is, in turn, limited to the central $120°$ of the total field of view (FoV).

When referring to displays, the term *resolution* is often used to mean either display pixel pitch or pixel count, which may be confusing. When referring to HMDs, resolution more accurately refers to cycles (or lines) per unit angle that can be resolved [34], as seen above for the human vision. Typical VR optics have a focal length of about $40\,\text{mm}$ [9], which amplifies the pixel size. So, HMDs use a larger amount of smaller pixels when compared to screens to try and increase both the perceived angular resolution and the FoV. An estimation is that to provide 60 pixels per degree (1 pixel per arc minute) or Snellen acuity of 20/20 for a FoV of $150°$, an HMD would require 9600×9000 pixels per eye [34].

Besides resolution, the luminance and contrast provided by a display are other items that could impact acuity. Luminance is the amount of visible light emitted per unit projected area of the display. It is relative to the amount of light emitted by the display system being expressed in candelas per squared meter (cd/m^2) [15]. Contrast, on the other hand, is the ratio between the highest and lowest luminance provided by the display.

Luminance is sometimes confused with brightness. In the real world, it can reach much higher values than in display systems, such as 1.6×10^9 cd/m^2 for the sun at noon versus 50–300 cd/m^2 at a maximum resolution on a computer monitor [15].

Table 2. A representative list of HMD display characteristics [2, 15]

Model	Pixels (per eye)	FoV (diagonal)	Res.* (arc min)	Lum. max (cd/m^2)
Oculus Rift	1080 × 1200	94°	1.14	176
HTC Vive	1080 × 1200	110°	0.98	183
PlayStation VR	960 × 1080	100°	0.96	NA
Dell Visor	1440 × 1440	110°	1.23	NA
Lenovo Explorer	1440 × 1440	110°	1.23	NA
Samsung Odyssey	1440 × 1600	110°	1.3	NA
Asus HC102	1440 × 1440	95°	1.43	NA
HTC Vive Pro	1440 × 1600	110°	1.30	NA
Pimax 8K	3840 × 2160	200°	1.47	NA
Oculus Rift S	1280 × 1440	110°	1.17	NA
Oculus Quest 2	1832 × 1920	100	1.77	NA

* arc min necessary to fit a pixel pair.

The technology used in today's HMDs construction is based on two approaches [2]. The first, similar to the display of smartphones, televisions and computer monitors, is based on liquid crystals (LCD - Liquid-Crystal Displays), while the other is based on OLED (Organic Light-Emitting Diode). These technologies allow for different ranges in terms of luminance, color, contrast, refresh rate, etc., which combined with optical lenses and design decisions compose the final experience and acuity of these displays. In Table 2 we present a comparison of the technical specifications of some popular HMDs.

Appendix 2 – Virtual Charts and Optotypes Used

Fig. 5. A row of optotypes as they are seen in the Peripheral and central glare test.

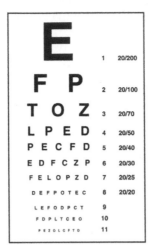

Fig. 6. Our virtual reproduction of the Snellen chart. An individual with normal visual acuity must be able to discriminate the characters until the line 8 (20/20 visual acuity).

Table 3. Acuity and corresponding sizes of each row of optotypes in our virtual snellen chart [29].

Acuity	Height (mm)	
20/200	88.72	
20/100	44.36	
20/80	35.49	
20/60	26.62	
20/50	22.11	
20/40	17.74	
20/30	13.24	
20/20	8.87	NORMAL
20/15	6.69	
20/10	4.44	

Table 4. Progressive sequence of letters used in the glare tests.

Index	Peripheral	Central	Acuity
1	V S R K D	Z R K D C	20/200
2	H C S O K	D N C H V	20/100
3	S C N O Z	C D H N R	20/80
4	N H Z O K	R V Z O S	20/50
5	N O D V H	O S D V Z	20/40
6	D N Z S V	N O Z C D	20/30
7	K C H O D	R D N S K	20/15
8	S Z H V R	O K S V Z	20/10

Table 5. Key to the Pelli-Robson contrast sensitivity chart [26] (left), and letters used with the left-eye and the right-eye (right) in the contrast sensitivity test.

log 0.00	**HSZ DSN**	log 0.15		HSZ DSN	VRS KDR
log 0.30	**CKR ZVR**	log 0.45		CKR ZVR	NHC SOK
log 0.60	**NDC OSK**	log 0.75		NDC OSK	SCN OZV
log 0.90	**OZK VHZ**	log 1.05		OZK VHZ	CNH ZOK
log 1.20	**NHO NRD**	log 1.35		NHO NRD	NOD VHR
log 1.50	**VRC OVH**	log 1.65		VRC OVH	CDN ZSV
log 1.80	**CDS NDC**	log 1.95		CDS NDC	KCH ODK
log 2.10	**KVZ OHR**	log 2.25		KVZ OHR	RSZ HVR

Appendix 3 – Raw Data from Questionnaires

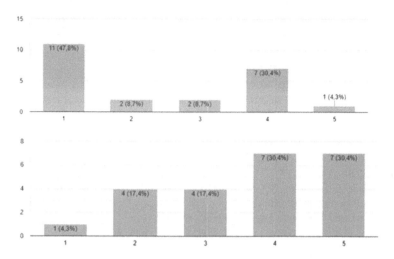

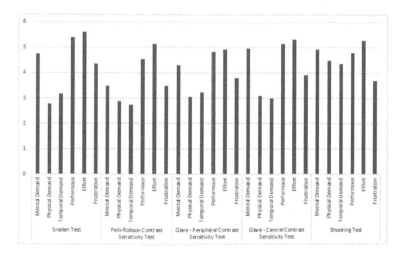

Fig. 7. Participants' agreement with the following statements: (a) I found it was difficult to adjust the headset; (b) I felt comfortable as if I was actually at the virtual place where the tasks were performed.

Fig. 8. Results from the administration of the NASA Task-load Index questionnaire.

References

1. Barten, P.G.: Contrast Sensitivity of the Human Eye and Its Effects on Image Quality. SPIE Press (1999)

2. Benkhaled, I., Marc, I., Lafon-Pham, D., Jeanjean, L.: Evaluation of colorimetric characteristics of head-mounted displays. In: Stephanidis, C. (ed.) HCI 2016. CCIS, vol. 617, pp. 175–180. Springer, Cham (2016). https://doi.org/10.1007/978-3-319-40548-3_29
3. Bian, Y., Leng, T., Ma, Y.: A proposed discomfort glare evaluation method based on the concept of 'adaptive zone'. Build. Environ. **143**, 306–317 (2018)
4. Bodis-Wollner, I.: Visual acuity and contrast sensitivity in patients with cerebral lesions. Science **178**(4062), 769–771 (1972)
5. El Jamiy, F., Marsh, R.: Survey on depth perception in head mounted displays: distance estimation in virtual reality, augmented reality, and mixed reality. IET Image Proc. **13**(5), 707–712 (2019)
6. Erickson, A., Kim, K., Bruder, G., Welch, G.F.: Effects of dark mode graphics on visual acuity and fatigue with virtual reality head-mounted displays. In: 2020 IEEE Conference on Virtual Reality and 3D User Interfaces (VR), pp. 434–442. IEEE (2020)
7. Fidopiastis, C., Fuhrman, C., Meyer, C., Rolland, J.: Methodology for the iterative evaluation of prototype head-mounted displays in virtual environments: visual acuity metrics. Presence **14**(5), 550–562 (2005)
8. Ginsburg, A.P.: A new contrast sensitivity vision test chart. Optom. Vis. Sci. **61**(6), 403–407 (1984)
9. Goradia, I., Doshi, J., Kurup, L.: A review paper on Oculus Rift & project Morpheus. Int. J. Curr. Eng. Technol. **4**(5), 3196–3200 (2014)
10. Goudé, I., Cozot, R., Le Meur, O.: A perceptually coherent TMO for visualization of 360° HDR images on HMD. In: Gavrilova, M.L., Tan, C.J.K., Chang, J., Thalmann, N.M. (eds.) Transactions on Computational Science XXXVII. LNCS, vol. 12230, pp. 109–128. Springer, Heidelberg (2020). https://doi.org/10.1007/978-3-662-61983-4_7
11. Guo, J., Weng, D., Duh, H.B.L., Liu, Y., Wang, Y.: Effects of using HMDs on visual fatigue in virtual environments. In: 2017 IEEE Virtual Reality (VR), pp. 249–250. IEEE (2017)
12. Hart, S.G., Staveland, L.E.: Development of NASA-TLX (task load index): results of empirical and theoretical research. In: Advances in Psychology, vol. 52, pp. 139–183. Elsevier (1988)
13. Hoskins, D.H., Jr.: Cataract surgery: maintaining the excellence. J. Cataract Refract. Surg. **22**(6), 643–644 (1996)
14. Kaur, K., Gurnani, B., Kannusamy, V., et al.: Myopia: current concepts and review of literature. TNOA J. Ophthalmic Sci. Res. **58**(4), 280 (2020)
15. Kemeny, A., Chardonnet, J.-R., Colombet, F.: Getting Rid of Cybersickness. Springer, Cham (2020). https://doi.org/10.1007/978-3-030-59342-1
16. Koenderink, J.J., Van Doorn, A.J.: Illuminance texture due to surface mesostructure. JOSA A **13**(3), 452–463 (1996)
17. Kooi, F.L., Bijl, P., Padmos, P.: Stereo acuity and visual acuity in head mounted displays. In: Proceedings of the Human Factors and Ergonomics Society Annual Meeting, vol. 50, pp. 2693–2696. SAGE Publications Sage CA: Los Angeles (2006)
18. Lacava, A.C., Centurion, V.: Teste de sensibilidade ao contraste e teste de ofuscamento no paciente portador de catarata. Arq. Bras. Oftalmol. **62**(1), 38–43 (1999)
19. Lasa, M.S.M., Datiles, M.B., III., Podgor, M.J., Magno, B.V.: Contrast and glare sensitivity: association with the type and severity of the cataract. Ophthalmology **99**(7), 1045–1049 (1992)

20. Matsuura, Y., Terada, T., Aoki, T., Sonoda, S., Isoyama, N., Tsukamoto, M.: Readability and legibility of fonts considering shakiness of head mounted displays. In: Proceedings of the 23rd International Symposium on Wearable Computers, pp. 150–159 (2019)

21. Messina, E., Evans, J.: Standards for visual acuity. National Institute for Standards and Technology (2006)

22. Ong, S.C., et al.: A novel automated visual acuity test using a portable head-mounted display. Optom. Vis. Sci. **97**(8), 591–597 (2020)

23. Panfili, L.: Effects of VR-displays on visual acuity

24. Parra, J.C.O., Pujol, J., Garcia, R.B., Sánchez-Magan, A., Muñoz, J.M.: New system based on HMD to objectively and automatically assess visual function and to perform visual therapy. Invest. Ophthalmol. Vis. Sci. **55**(13), 755 (2014)

25. Pelli, D.G., Rubin, G.S., Legge, G.E.: Predicting the contrast sensitivity of low vision observers (A). J. Opt. Soc. Am. A **3**, P56 (1986)

26. Pelli, D., Robson, J., et al.: The design of a new letter chart for measuring contrast sensitivity. In: Clinical Vision Sciences. Citeseer (1988)

27. Quevedo Junyent, L.J., Aznar-Casanova, J.A., da Silva, J.A.: Dynamic visual acuity. Trends Psychol. **26**(3), 1283–1297 (2018)

28. Regan, D.: Low-contrast letter charts and sinewave grating tests in ophthalmological and neurological disorders. Clin. Vision Sci. **2**(3), 235–+ (1988)

29. Snellen, H.: Letterproeven, tot bepaling der gezigtsscherpte, vol. 1. J. Greven (1862)

30. Sproule, D., Jacinto, R.F., Rundell, S., Williams, J., Perlmutter, S., Arndt, S.: Characterization of visual acuity and contrast sensitivity using head-mounted displays in a virtual environment: a pilot study. In: Proceedings of the Human Factors and Ergonomics Society Annual Meeting, vol. 63, pp. 547–551. SAGE Publications Sage CA: Los Angeles (2019)

31. Stevens, R., Rhodes, D., Hasnain, A., Laffont, P.Y.: Varifocal technologies providing prescription and VAC mitigation in HMDS using Alvarez lenses. In: Digital Optics for Immersive Displays, vol. 10676, p. 106760J. International Society for Optics and Photonics (2018)

32. Sukumar, V., Hess, H.L., Noren, K.V., Donohoe, G., Ay, S.: Study on threshold patterns with varying illumination using 1.3 m imaging system. Intell. Inf. Manag. **2**(1), 21–25 (2010)

33. Thibodeaux, J.R.: Shotgun sighting device. US Patent 6,598,331, 29 July 2003

34. Vieri, C., et al.: An 18 megapixel 4.3ï443 ppi 120 Hz OLED display for wide field of view high acuity head mounted displays. J. Soc. Inf. Display **26**(5), 314–324 (2018)

35. Williamson, T., Strong, N., Sparrow, J., Aggarwal, R., Harrad, R.: Contrast sensitivity and glare in cataract using the Pelli-Robson chart. Br. J. Ophthalmol. **76**(12), 719–722 (1992)

Effects of Different Proximity-Based Feedback on Virtual Hand Pointing in Virtual Reality

Yujun Lu[1], BoYu Gao[1(✉)], Huawei Tu[2], Weiqi Luo[1], and HyungSeok Kim[3]

[1] College of Information Science and Technology/Cyber Security,
Jinan University, Guangzhou, China
bygao@jnu.edu.cn
[2] Department of Computer Science and Information Technology,
La Trobe University, Melbourne, Australia
h.tu@latrobe.edu.au
[3] Department of Computer Science and Engineering, Konkuk University,
Seoul, South Korea
hyuskim@konkuk.ac.kr

Abstract. Virtual hand pointing is a natural interaction method, however, suffers from the issue of depth perception in virtual environments. The proximity feedback cues, which deliver intensity information once the pointer is getting closer to the target, may improve virtual hand pointing performance in virtual environments. However, less is known about the effects of such feedback cues on the depth movement phases of virtual hand pointing task. Therefore, this work focuses on the effects of different feedback cues (either visual (**V**), auditory (**A**), haptic (**H**), or any combinations of them) on a virtual hand pointing task in view and lateral directions in virtual environments. Results show that compared with other feedback types, haptic feedback cue significantly reduced movement time, particularly in a larger visual depth. We further analyzed the sub-movement time phases (e.g. ballistic and correction), and found that the participants achieved the shortest ballistic time with A+H and A+H+V, and shortest correct time with H. However, no significant differences of feedback conditions on the speed, error rate, and throughout were found. In addition, we discuss the implications based on the findings and present the future work.

Keywords: Proximity feedback cues · 3D hand pointing · Visual depth perception · Virtual reality

1 Introduction

Virtual hand pointing is a fundamental and natural interaction technique for virtual environments, where users can acquire targets located within arm reach using virtual hands [22,23], (e.g. picking color in arm menu for VR conceptual

© Springer Nature Switzerland AG 2021
N. Magnenat-Thalmann et al. (Eds.): CGI 2021, LNCS 13002, pp. 608–620, 2021.
https://doi.org/10.1007/978-3-030-89029-2_45

design). However, the perceptual limitations of stereo display systems (e.g. the vergence-accommodation conflict or diplopia) in currently popular VR head-mounted displays (HMDs) may negatively affect user ability to localize the targets using virtual hand pointing [2]. For example, Machuca et al. [2] confirmed the negative effect of stereo display deficiencies on virtual hand pointing with a reciprocal pointing task, revealing that target depth was found to exert a significant influence on movement time for targets with stereoscopic viewing. More recently, Katzakis et al. [19] evaluated 3D pointing accuracy in the fovea and periphery with head-mounted displays, the target arrangement included the various target depths. The findings of these work [2,3,12] emphasize the importance of taking account for perceptual limitations associated with depth perception when modeling virtual hand pointing tasks in VR.

Multimodal feedback has been showed its effectiveness when providing additional spatial and/or temporal information for 3D interactions, for example, Ariza et al. [14] proposed a proximity-based multimodal feedback, in which the feedback intensity can be matched with the spatial distance between target and virtual cursor, for 3D selection in immersive virtual environments. However, target arrangement involving depth perception on virtual hand pointing task was not considered in VR. It is unknown that how such proximity feedback can improve the virtual hand pointing tasks in VR.

Previous works investigated the multimodal feedback for target acquisition in 2D or 3D user interfaces [8,14,21], and concluded with the benefits of multimodal feedback, compared with unimodal feedback. However, it seems that providing more information from multi-channels is not ideal in some situations. For example, increasing the quality of visual feedback seems does not necessarily improve user performance [15], and might even reduce selection performance. Thus, whether uni-modal proximity cue is enough to enhance efficiency and accuracy, comparing with multimodal feedback, is also unknown to virtual hand pointing interaction in depth directions for VR.

In this work, we focus on the effects of proximity feedback cues on virtual hand pointing task in depth direction. The task is based on the ISO 9241-411 [11], a Fitts' Law setting on horizontal plane at eyes' level in VR [2,3], targeting on the feedback cues (8 feedback conditions: none, V, A, H, V+A, V+H, A+H, and V+A+H) on virtual hand pointing in view and lateral directions (Fig. 1).

The contributions of this work are that we systematically analyze various combination of proximity feedback cues (visual, audio, and haptic) on virtual hand pointing along depth and lateral directions at participants' eye level in VR. We present design implications based on the findings, and validate the effects of proximity feedback on virtual hand pointing tasks in depth direction.

2   Related Work

2.1   Depth Perception in Virtual Hand Pointing

Estimation of depth perception is one of fundamental requirements to 3D interactions in VR (e.g. reaching, grasping). However, one of leftover problems for current popular VR devices is the perceptual limitation due to imperfect of stereoscopic displays [5–7]. For example, Willemsen et al. [6,7] studied the effects of stereo viewing conditions, e.g., real world, image-based, and traditional virtual environments, on perceived ego-distance or distance perception. Lin et al. [19,20] found that distance overestimation of virtual targets to participants, and even better performance for targets farther away (150 cm, 88.2%) than that at closer distance (65 cm, 78.8%).

For the consideration of the distance in peri-personal space, the issue of depth perception negatively impacts the movement time of virtual hand pointing tasks. For example, Grossman et al. [17] investigated the pointing performance to 3D targets in virtual environments, where they designed a reciprocal Fitts' law task, with participants alternating selections between two targets, constrained to the xz-plane, and oriented in the depth direction. They found that target depth and width, direction of movement, and distance to target all had a significant effect on movement time. In particular, movements in the depth direction were found to be the most error-prone.

More recently, Machuca et al. [2] investigated the effect of stereo display deficiencies on virtual hand pointing in both real world and virtual environment settings, and found longer movement time for paired 3D targets in virtual environment than that in real world, revealing the effects of depth issue on virtual hand pointing with stereoscopic displays. However, Batmaz et al. [3] found that no significant difference between VR and AR head-mounted displays for virtual hand pointing performance. Clark et al. [12] also calculated a new extension of Fitts' law model in virtual environments, covering a common target arrangement with consideration of depth perception. The change of target depth contributes to the movement time of virtual hand pointing in the view direction.

2.2 Feedback Cues for 3D Selections

The use of additional sensory information for 3D interaction becomes effective, e.g., 3D hand pointing [14,16], 3D manipulation [21]. For example, Teather et al. [16] utilized visual aids (highlighting) to improve 3D selection accuracy, increasing movement speed, while decreasing error rate. However, no significant impact on throughput was found. Corbett et al. [9] studied the effects of haptic feedback on pointing task when the visual distraction was available, and confirmed the role of haptic feedback in enhancing pointing performance even with a complex virtual environment.

Except for unimodal sensory information, multiple sensory information combined for 3D selections has been also explored in virtual environments. For example, El-Shimy et al. [8] investigated the 3D target acquisition with multimodal feedback (visual, audio and tactile). Ariza et al. [14] analyzed the proximity-based multimodal feedback for 3D selection, consistent with previous work [8], the experimental results showed that binary feedback outperformed continuous feedback, resulting in higher effective throughput and less undershooting. More recently, Batmaz et al. studied the effects of auditory error feedback on fitts' law tasks [24,25]. Note that this 3D target arrangement remained in vertical plane, the various target depths in z axis were not considered. Little work is known on the effects of proximity feedback on virtual hand pointing in depth direction.

3 Experiment

3.1 Participants

We recruited 16 participants (age: 18 and 25 years old, M: 21.5) from the local campus (9 female and 7 male). All of them were corrected to normal or normal version, four of them worn the glasses during the experiments. Six of them had experience using HTC Vive VR device, but only a few times for each of them. In addition, all participants measured normal when testing the perceptual ability of listening the audio and viewing targets with VR device, and they used right hand for task selection. 10 dollars were paid to each participant after the experiment.

3.2 Apparatus

The apparatus used in our experiment was windows PC with Inter Core i7 with GTX 1060 graphics card and 16 GB RAM. The VR device used was HTC Vive Pro headset and controller, the field of view (FOV) is 110°. The display resolution of both eyes for the headset is 2880 × 1600 pixels with a refresh rate 90 Hz. No observable latency for this VR headset and controller was found.

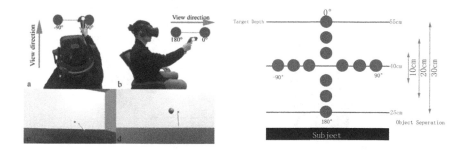

Fig. 1. Experimental setup with VR HMDs, (a) select targets in the lateral direction (−90 to 90°), (b) select targets in the view direction (180 to 0°), (c) select target using the virtual cursor, (d) closer view of selecting target using the virtual cursor. The top view of target arrangement with object separation is illustrated (right). (Color figure online)

3.3 Material

First, we utilized the discrete proximity feedback cues, as mentioned its advantages in related work [14]. We chosen the vibration intensity of haptic feedback, as it enables users to adjust their action when acquiring targets. The amplitude of sound was used to provide additional temporal information when approaching the target [10]. For the visual aid [16], we set the active color as red, the initial color of the target was gray, as the red color is a warning cue. In our experiment, the largest value of haptic and auditory feedback 1500 Hz and 50db respectively. For the coupling feedback with the target, the relationship of intensity of haptic, auditory, visual and spatial distance between the target and the cursor is illustrated in Fig. 2. Once the cursor was inside the target, the corresponding feedback would be rendered.

Second, the designation of virtual cursor contributed to virtual hand pointing performance. For example, the size or shape of virtual cursor affects the movement time and accuracy of target acquisition [18]. The size of the virtual controller was larger than that of the target, which would negatively affect the performance of acquisition. In order to accurately calculate the performance of target selection, we designed a virtual cursor (Fig. 1 d) with a virtual sphere and cylinder, and the diameter of the virtual sphere (10 cm) was smaller than that (15 cm, 25 cm, and 35 cm) of the target (Fig. 1 c and d). The action of virtual cursor was synchronized with the movement of virtual controller in the virtual environment.

We implemented a virtual scene, including a cube-style room with four white walls and one dark gray floor (Fig. 1), to keep the scene as simple as possible. The target was located at the center of the virtual room. We resized target and separation of target to test the selection performance with different IDs.

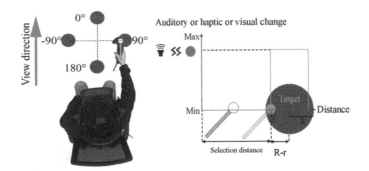

Fig. 2. Illustration of relationship of intensity of auditory, haptic, visual and the spatial distance between the target and the cursor, the diameter of target R was 15, 25, and 35 cm in the experiment, and the diameter of the cursor r is 10 cm. Once the cursor is inside the target, the feedback becomes active status. (Color figure online)

3.4   Experimental Design

Each participant was asked to perform a reciprocal pointing task under each feedback condition. In order to simplify the experimental design, and focus on the effects of feedback cues on virtual hand pointing task in depth direction, we designed three object separations (OS3: 10, 20, and 30 cm) only in view and lateral directions (four target positions in each IDs (TP4 : 0°, 180°, −90°, and

$90°))$ (Fig. 2). There were four groups of target depth. In addition, the target size was also considered as an important factor to movement time. Consistent with ISO 9241-411 task [1], we defined three Target Sizes (TS3: 1.5, 2.5, and 3.5 cm). There were 9 levels of index of difficulty (3 target size ×3 object separation, ID: 1.94, 2.32, 2.74, 2.93, 3.16, 3.25, 3.7, 3.84). We utilized a within-subject design, with a FC8 × TS3 × OS3 × TP4.

3.5 Task Procedure

Before the experiment, all participants were asked to fill in a biography questionnaire and a consent form. Then they were instructed to get familiar with VR device, and to practice until comfortable and confident. The study was approved by the ethics committee of local university.

During the experiment, the participant was asked to sit 40 cm (the distance between the center of target layout and the participant) away from the eye view. The participants were required to select two targets reciprocally, and asked to perform lateral direction acquisition after finishing all trials in view direction. At the beginning of each trial, a gray sphere flowing in front of them and a controller with yellow cursor can be seen. Then they were asked to select targets trial by trial as quickly and accurately as possible. For one ID, there were 12 trials in view direction and 12 trials in lateral direction (6 trials per each target position). Once they missed a target (yellow cursor outside of target when acquisition), no feedback was provided, which was recorded as an incorrect one. Each feedback condition contained 9 IDs. A 3-minutes-break was given after finishing every trial in an ID. The size and separation of target were changed randomly in each ID. Once they finished all trials in a movement direction, the task was changed to another direction immediately, counterbalanced across all participants. The experiment duration lasted about one and half hours for each participant, including the questionnaire and subjective interview. It is important to note that the participants were free to stop during the experiment.

Overall, each participant was asked to complete FC8 × TS3 × OS3 × TP4 × 6 = 1728 trials (16 participants × 1728 trials = 27648 trials).

3.6 Metrics

The objective metrics selected for performance evaluation from [2,3] were movement time (seconds, s), throughput (bits per second, bps), error rate (percentage of missed target), the number of entry target, speed of cursor (m/s), ballistic time (seconds, s) and correction time (seconds, s) [4]. The correction time referred to the confirmation phase of target selection, while the ballistic time involved the duration of movement before correction phase. The subjective evaluation employed the NASA-TLX questionnaire.

4 Result and Analysis

The repeated measure ANOVA with the post-hoc test (Bonferonni Correction) was employed to analyze objective measures, and the Kruskal-Wallis H test for

Table 1. Average Movement Time (MT), Throughputs (TP), Error Rate (ER), Entry (E), Speed (S), Bal-listic Time (BT), Correction Time (CT) across change of target depth (CTD), ID and feedback condition.

	Movement direction				CTD (cm)			ID(bits)								
	180°	0°	−90°	90°	10	20	30	1.95	2.32	2.75	2.94	3.17	3.26	3.70	3.84	4.39
MT	1.13	1.25	1.07	1.04	0.92	1.11	1.27	0.74	0.85	0.91	1.23	1.03	1.04	1.19	1.43	1.61
TP	2.98	2.78	3.16	3.30	2.89	3.20	3.21	2.96	3.04	3.36	2.68	3.34	3.37	3.35	2.90	2.92
ER	8.7	12.0	9.1	9.8	34.1	37.7	39.8	11.2	26.8	14.8	64.3	31.7	16.9	32.7	66.5	68.6
E	1.37	1.34	1.34	1.27	1.31	1.33	1.34	1.07	1.16	1.07	1.07	1.15	1.09	1.21	1.76	1.72
S	0.22	0.19	0.22	0.23	0.15	0.22	0.27	0.18	0.16	0.27	0.11	0.23	0.33	0.28	0.16	0.20
BT	0.59	0.57	0.61	0.62	0.50	0.61	0.68	0.47	0.50	0.58	0.54	0.60	0.65	0.68	0.64	0.71
CT	0.56	0.70	0.46	0.43	0.41	0.47	0.54	0.20	0.29	0.25	0.73	0.35	0.31	0.44	0.81	0.88

subjective rating. If ANOVA's sphericity assumption was violated (Mauchly's test $p < .05$), Greenhouse–Geisser adjustments were therefore performed.

For the collected experimental data, we excluded the outliers when the acquisition time of these trials were more than 3 times of average in each ID (Index of difficulty) (the amounts of outlier were: Baseline:8.7%, A:13.1%, H:10.0%, V:15.9%, A+H:14.3%, A+V:11.3%, H+V:12.6%, A+H+V:13.2%).

4.1   Factor Analysis

Movement Time: As expected, there was a significant main effect for feedback conditions on movement time ($F_{7,105} = 2.245$, $p < .05$). The post-hoc test revealed that participants spent longer time in visual condition than that in H, A+H, H+V and A+H+V conditions ($p < .05$). In addition, significant effect between A+V and H+V ($p < .05$), A+V and A+H+V ($p < .05$) was found, indicating that haptic feedback helped reduce the movement time among these multiple channels. Consistent with previous work [2,3], a significant main effect of directions ($F_{3,45} = 36.018$, $p < .001$) and IDs ($F_{8,120} = 140.063$, $p < .001$) on

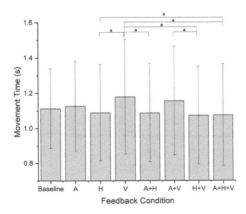

Fig. 3. Movement time under different feedback conditions, the significant effect between two conditions was marked.

movement time was found. The participants spent more time in acquiring far-ther targets in view direction than that in lateral direction (p <.001). Means of movement time in each position were as follows: 18°: 1.27s, SD: .250; 0°: 1.40s, SD: .320; −90°: 1.16s, SD : .236; 90°: 1.13s, SD: .217. The post-hoc test revealed a significant effect between each pair of ID (p <.001) except the pair between ID 4 and ID 8, ID 5 and ID 9.

Ballistic Time: There were significant main effects for movement direction ($F_{3,45}$ = 14.773, p <.001), ID ($F_{8,120}$ = 339.677, p <.001) and feedback condi-tions ($F_{7,105}$ = 4.528, p <.001) on ballistic time. For feedback conditions, the post-hoc test revealed that significant effect was found between the following pairs (Baseline and A, H, A+H, H+V, A+H+V), (H and V), (V and A+H, H+V, A+H+V) and (A+V and H+V) (Fig. 4a). The participants spent the shortest ballistic time with the combination of feedback cues (A+H, A+H+V). In move-

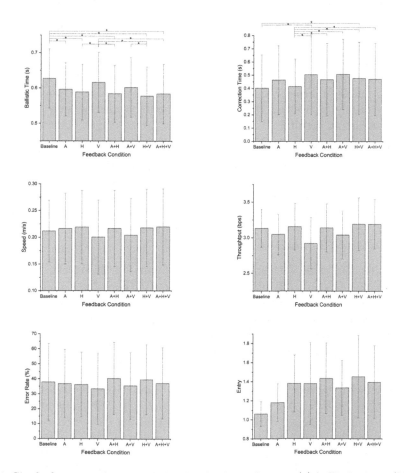

Fig. 4. Single factor analysis result for feedback conditions. (a) ballistic time, (b) cor-rection time, (c) speed, (d) throughput, (e) error rate, (f) entry. —— means that there was significant difference between each pair of these feedback conditions. with *** for p <0.001, ** for p <0.01, * for p <0.05.

ment directions, post-hoc test manifested that significant differences were found for any pairs of position except for $-90°$ and $180°$.

Correction Time: As with ballistic time, significant effects for movement direction ($F_{3,45} = 37.493$, p $<.001$), ID ($F_{8,120} = 110.486$, p $> .001$) and feedback conditions ($F_{7,105} = 2.705$, p $> .05$) on correction time were found. As expected, the correction time under baseline condition was shorter than any other feedback conditions. The post-hoc test showed there was a significant effect between (Baseline and V, H+V), (H and V, A+H, A+V, H+V, A+H+V) (p $> .05$). The haptic feedback allowed the shortest correction time compared with other combinations of feedback and visual feedback only. In Fig. 4b, the correction time decreased for the sequence $0°$, $180°$, $-90°$, $90°$. The $0°$ was at the further location. Post-hoc tests showed that significant effect was found in all pairs, except the pair $-90°$ and $90°$. The participants spent more time on the correction stage instead of the ballistic stage when acquiring the target at further location.

Speed: There were significant effects for movement directions ($F_{3,45} = 35.928$, p $<.001$) and ID ($F_{8,120} = 257.909$, p $<.001$), but feedback conditions ($F_{7,105} = 1.742$, p $= .107 > .05$) on speed of virtual hand pointing. Post-hoc test also revealed significant effect between ($180°$ and $0°$), ($0°$ and $-90°$), ($0°$ and $90°$) and ($-90°$ and $90°$). From Fig. 4c, we found that the speed at $0°$ was lower than other 3 positions, indicating that the participants tended to slow down when pointing at further depth.

Throughput: As with speed, significant effects for movement directions ($F_{3,45} = 56.951$, p $<.001$) and IDs ($F_{8,120} = 69.922$, p $<.001$) on throughput were found, while no significant effect for feedback conditions ($F_{7,105} = 1.369$, p $= .226 > .05$). The post-hoc tests showed no significant effects were found between each feedback condition on throughput. From Fig. 4, the results showed that throughput in lateral direction was larger than that in view direction (the value was the highest at $90°$, and the smallest at $0°$).

Error Rate: The same with speed and throughput, significant effects for movement direction ($F_{3,45} = 25.169$, p $<.001$) and ID ($F_{8,120} = 74.367$, p $<.001$) but feedback conditions ($F_{7,105} = 1.828$, p $= .089 > .05$) were found. Post-hoc tests showed no significant effect between them. As expected, participants had the highest error rate at $0°$ position, and lowest error rate at $180°$. It's not surprising that participants had the worst performance in ID 1, 2, 3, which target diameter was only 1.5 cm, the mean of error rate reached 66.47%.

Entry: As with movement time, there were significant effects for movement direction ($F_{3,45} = 3.917$, p $<.05$), ID ($F_{8,120} = 16.258$, p $<.001$) and feedback conditions ($F_{7,105} = 6.508$, p $<.001$) on entry times during the target selection. For feedback conditions, post-hoc test demonstrated that any pairs of feedback conditions were significantly different (p $<.05$) except for the pair between baseline and auditory feedback. Participants performed the least number of entry times with auditory feedback condition (1.18), the most entry times was under H+V feedback (1.45) (Fig. 4). For movement directions, the post-hoc test revealed significant effect between (180° and 90°), (0° and 90°) and (−90° and 90°) (p <.05). The participants had less entry times at 90° (1.27) compared to other 3 positions (180° :1.37, 0° :1.33, −90° :1.34).

4.2 Subjective Evaluation

The H test results showed that no significant effects were found on every dimension of NASA-TLX (p > .05). However, most participants reported that feedback information only plays a supplementary role with perception of relative spatial distance. The most popular feedback condition were haptic feedback and A+H+V condition from the collection of participants' interview. However, three participants pointed out the visual information made them tired in mental attention, while tactile and pitch feedback gave the negative side effect, making them annoying. Some participants reported that the visual feedback had positive correction with target size, and the vibration intensity from the controller worked well for selection action by hand directly when the participants hold on the controller.

5 Discussion

The experimental results showed that significant effects for feedback conditions and movement directions on movement time, correction time and ballistic time (See Subsect. 4.1). The movement time in the lateral and viewing directions was consistent with previous work [2,3], the participants spent more time in view direction than that in lateral, as expected. Importantly, the additional sensory feedback did contribute to the efficiency, other than accuracy of virtual hand pointing, from the analysis of our experimental results. In particular, most participants reported the preference of A+H+V feedback. However, there was no interaction effect on each metric between feedback conditions and movement directions, between feedback conditions and change of target depth. From the subjective evaluation, most participants reported that feedback information plays a supplementary role in the perception of relative spatial distance when approaching targets.

The Findings: (1). Inconsistent with [14], the haptic feedback was faster than multimodal feedback on movement time, particularly for larger target depth in view direction, which reveals that multimodal feedback information sometimes made worse performance. (2). The participants spent more time on the correction stage instead of the ballistic stage when acquiring the target at further location. (3). There was no interaction effect between movement directions and feedback conditions on virtual hand pointing performance. Most probably, the target arrangement could be one of main reasons to make different results, compared with previous works [24, 25].

Design Implications: First, additional sensory cues could give accurate and efficient selection performance. For example, "Minecraft" is a popular game, allowing the users to acquire the cube stacked in front of them, in such a situation, our study showed that use of proximity feedback can offer a more efficient way of acquiring the targets. Second, for 3D spatial menus in VR, the participants used to acquire the items with eyes-engaged manner, in order to reduce the frequency of head rotation, in such a case, the proximity feedback can provide users with more spatial information. It is also possible to allow the efficient eyes-free interaction in VR [10].

Future Work: Although the participants preferred the haptic feedback, we suspected that the vibration from the controller would be an important confounding factor to the virtual hand pointing performance, compared with auditory or visual feedback. The vibration on the hand or arm may lead to different performances. In future, we will there-fore focus on the design of vibration on different locations of body to further explore the haptic feedback on 3D pointing performance in virtual environments. Second, we will investigate this research question with AR device, and the depth perception in AR device also existed. It is worth investigating the proximity feedback cues with AR device, and checking whether such feedback cues performed the similar results. This future work will guide the AR virtual hand interaction with additional feedback cues.

6   Conclusion

This work presented the first investigation into using proximity feedback cues on virtual hand pointing in view and lateral directions at eyes' level in VR. We conducted an experiment to evaluate seven proximity feedback conditions on virtual hand pointing task in VR. In summary, significant effects of the feedback conditions on movement time, ballistic and correction time were found, however, no interaction effect between feedback cues and movement directions was found. The findings of this work were discussed along with the suggested guidelines and possible implications. The results of this work provided suggestion of using feedback cues to enhance virtual hand interaction in VR.

Acknowledgements. This work was supported by the National Science Foundation of China (61902147, 61877029, 61932011), Guangdong Province (2021A1515012629, 2019B1515120010), Guangzhou Applied and Basic Applied Foundation (20210202 1131), and by the Bio-Synergy Research Project (2013M3A9C4078140) of the Ministry of Science, ICT and Future Planning through the National Research Foundation.

References

1. ISO 9241–400:2007 Ergonomics of human-system interaction - Part 400: Principles and requirements for physical input devices (2015)
2. Barrera Machuca, M.D., Stuerzlinger, W.: The effect of stereo display deficiencies on virtual hand pointing. In: ACM CHI 2019, 207 (2019)

3. Batmaz, A.U., Machuca, M.D.B., Pham, D.M., Stuerzlinger, W., et al.: Do head-mounted display stereo defi-ciencies affect 3D pointing tasks in AR and VR?. In: IEEE VR 2019, pp. 585–592 (2019)
4. Nieuwenhuizen, K., Liu, L., van Liere, R., et al.: Insights from dividing 3D goal-directed movements into meaningful phases. IEEE Comput. Graph. Appl. **29**(6), 44–53 (2009)
5. Armbruster, C., Wolter, M., Kuhlen, T., et al.: Depth perception in virtual reality: distance estimations in peri-and extrapersonal space. Cyberpsychology Behav. **11**(1), 9–15 (2008)
6. Willemsen, P., Gooch, A.A., Thompson, W.B., et al.: Effects of stereo viewing conditions on distance perception in virtual environments. Presence Teleoperators Virtual Environ. **17**(1), 91–101 (2008)
7. Willemsen, P., Gooch, A.A.: Perceived egocentric distances in real, image-based, and traditional virtual environments. In: IEEE VR 2002, pp. 275–276 (2002)
8. El-Shimy, D., Marentakis, G., Cooperstock, J.R.: Multimodal feedback in 3D target acquisition. In: IEEE 3DUI 2009, pp. 95–98 (2009)
9. Corbett, B., Nam, C.S., Yamaguchi, T.: The effects of haptic feedback and visual dis-traction on pointing task performance. IJHCI **32**(2), 89–102 (2016)
10. Gao, B.Y., Lu, Y., Kim, H.S., Kim, B., Long, J.: Spherical layout with proximity-based multimodal feedback for eyes-free target acquisition in virtual reality. In: Chen, J.Y.C., Fragomeni, G. (eds.) HCII 2019. LNCS, vol. 11574, pp. 44–58. Springer, Cham (2019). https://doi.org/10.1007/978-3-030-21607-8_4
11. MacKenzie, I.S., Buxton, W.: Extending Fitts' law to two-dimensional tasks. In: ACM CHI 1992, pp. 219–226 (1992)
12. Clark, L.D., Bhagat, A.B., Riggs, S.L.: Extending Fitts' law in three-dimensional virtual environments with current low-cost virtual reality technology. IJHCS **139**, 102413 (2020)
13. Luciano, C., Banerjee, P., DeFanti, T.: Haptics-based virtual reality periodontal training simulator. Virtual Reality **13**(2), 69–85 (2009)
14. Ariza, O., Bruder, G., Katzakis, N., Steinicke. F., Analysis of proximity-based multimodal feedback for 3D selection in immersive virtual environments. In: IEEE VR, pp. 327–334 (2018)
15. Poupyrev, I., Ichikawa, T., Weghorst, S., Billinghurst, M.: Egocentric object manipulation in virtual environments: empirical evaluation of interaction techniques. Comput. Graph. Forum **17**(3), 41–52 (1998)
16. Teather, R., Stuerzlinger, W.: Visual aids in 3D point selection experiments. In: ACM SUI 2014, pp. 127–136 (2014)
17. Grossman, T., Balakrishnan, R.: Pointing at trivariate targets in 3D environments. In: ACM CHI 2004, pp. 447–454 (2004)
18. Lu, Y., Yu, C., Shi, Y.: Investigating bubble mechanism for ray-casting to improve 3D target acquisition in virtual reality. In: IEEE VR, pp. 35–43 (2020)
19. Lin, C.J., Woldegiorgis, B.H.: Egocentric distance perception and performance of direct pointing in stereoscopic displays. Appl. Ergon. **64**, 66–74 (2017)
20. Lin, C.J., Woldegiorgis, B.H.: Interaction and visual performance in stereoscopic displays: a review. J. Soc. Inf. Disp. **23**(7), 319–332 (2015)
21. Marquardt, A., et al.: Audio-Tactile proximity feedback for enhancing 3D manipulation. In: ACM VRST 2018, Article No.2, pp. 1–10 (2018)
22. Argelaguet, F., Andujar, C.: A survey of 3D object selection techniques for virtual environments. Comput. Graph. **37**(3), 121–136 (2013)
23. Lubos, P., Bruder, G., Steinicke, F.: Analysis of direct selection in head-mounted display environment. In: IEEE 3DUI, pp. 11–18 (2014)

24. Batmaz, A.U., Stuerzlinger, W.: Effects of different auditory feedback frequencies in virtual reality 3D pointing tasks. In: IEEE VRW, pp. 189–194 (2021)
25. Batmaz, A.U., Stuerzlinger, W.: The effect of pitch in auditory error feedback for fitts' tasks in virtual reality training systems. In: IEEE VR, pp. 85–94 (2021)

Virtual Scenes Construction Promotes Traditional Chinese Art Preservation

Hui Liang[1]([⊠]), Fanyu Bao[1], Yusheng Sun[1], Chao Ge[1], and Jian Chang[2]

[1] Zhengzhou University of Light Industry, Zhengzhou, China
hliang@zzuli.edu.cn
[2] Bournemouth University, Poole, UK

Abstract. Chinese traditional opera is a valuable and fascinating heritage assert in the world as one of the most representative folk art in Chinese history. Its characteristic of 'suppositionality' in stage scenery provides a possibility of preservation of cultural heritage by digitization means, e.g., 3D Animation and Virtual Reality-based art show. In this novel digitization art form, the construction of virtual scenes is an important pillar--variety of created models should be accommodated to provide a vivid performance stage, including stage props and background. However, the generation of scenes based on traditional manual 3D virtual props modelling method is a tedious and strenuous task. In this paper, a novel shadow puppetry virtual stage scenes construction approach based on semantic and prior probability is proposed for the generation of compositional virtual scenes. First, primitive models based on semantics text segmentation and retrieval is provided for scene composition; and then, scene placement algorithm based on prior probability is conducive to assign these 3D models within virtual scene. This method is tested by generating the virtual performance stage for our shadow puppetry prototype system, within which various traditional art-specific 3D models are assembled. Its ease of use can assist artists to create visually plausible virtual stage without professional scene modelling skill. The user study indicates our approach's effectiveness and its efficiency.

Keywords: Virtual scenes construction · Traditional Chinese art · Semantic

1 Introduction

With a long history, the Chinese culture has always been a shining pearl in the history of mankind. As one of the unique traditional entertainment items in China, Chinese opera is an important part of traditional Chinese culture and known as the treasure of Chinese culture [1]. Shadow puppetry [2], figure silhouette made of animal skin or cardboard to tell folk stories, carries and contains the Chinese culture inherited from our ancestors. However, the form of shadow puppetry is more and more out of step with the rapid development of the times [3, 4]. The inheritance of cultural heritage faces great challenges. New possibilities of heritage protection are provided for cultural digitization. Firstly, the digitized cultural heritage can be watched by users for a long time without interruption. Secondly, the loss, destruction and theft of historical relics can

© Springer Nature Switzerland AG 2021
N. Magnenat-Thalmann et al. (Eds.): CGI 2021, LNCS 13002, pp. 621–632, 2021.
https://doi.org/10.1007/978-3-030-89029-2_46

be prevented, so as to achieve the universality and permanent accessibility of cultural heritage [5]. Hence, we can realize the protection of traditional art through digital forms of expression [6].

The construction of virtual environment uses computer technology, multimedia technology, image processing technology and other technologies [7, 8]. 3D shadow puppetry stage Scene Generation is the core of the puppetry show, which will produce a better cultural heritage preservation effort by providing a vivid virtual scene art effect. With the introduction of digital technology, the construction of virtual scene is faced with the problems of complex technology, long production cycle and so on [9]. Our goal is to design scene placement algorithm based on semantic analysis and prior probability, improved the efficiency of scene automation construction.

The rest of this paper is structured as follow. Section 2 presents a background in compositional virtual scenes generation and some related works. Section 3 focuses on the design of scene primitive model generation and scene placement algorithm. Section 4 mainly discusses implementation of prototype system. Section 5 invited 30 college students of opera major volunteers to evaluate this system. Finally, Sect. 6 presents our main conclusions and some ideas for future work.

2 Related Work

The UK Culture Secretary, David Lammy, announced in Bristol the European Collaborative Action Plan on Digitisation of Cultural and Scientific Content to ensure better access to Europe's cultural heritage through the Internet [10]. The Central Opera House and The Beijing Institute of Technology set up the "Digital Stage Joint Laboratory". They use virtual reality to set the opera stage [11]. George Tsypin, as a master of international stage art design, has integrated 3D into the stage. An 8.2 m (27 ft) high and 27.4 m (90 ft) long semicircular ultrathin LED screen wall is used on the stage to further enhance the sense of reality and movement [12]. In the cultural heritage domain, one of the applications of virtual reality (VR) is the virtual reconstruction of the Forum of Augustus [13]. An interesting application is Arkaevision Arkeo. It is aimed at finding the temple of Hera in Paestum Posidona. During the game, users come to understand the culture of the Magnogreek city in the 5th Century BC [14].

In image reconstruction, Remondino et al. described a method that uses a multistage image modeling approach for digital heritage preservation [15]. Song et al. [16] is the author of Semantic Scene Completion from a Single Depth Image. This method of automatic scene construction is commonly used in current animation scene generation.

Photogrammetry is used to generate scenario. When generate 3D reconstructed images, techniques such as SfM (Structure from Motion) and CRP (Close Range Photogrammetry) could be used to enhance the quality [17]. Balletti developed a system based on SfM and re-created a 3D model with digital camera [18].

Automatically generate scenarios using natural language processing. NLP (Natural Language Processing) within the AI programs dates back to the end of 80s. The SHRDLU system used natural language to move various objects around in a closed virtual world [19]. An NLP-based 3D scene generation system for children with autism or mental retardation [20] offers great opportunities for disabled children to communicate with others.

To the best of our knowledge, one of the most innovative ways for 3D animation scene generation is the natural language processing [21]. In 2005, the 3DSV (3D Story Visualiser) system [22] was proposed by Zeng et al. They implemented an interactive 3D animation interface that builds a scene from a story text with simple constraints. Spika et al. [23] describe AVDT (Automatic Visualization of Descriptive Texts) for advanced scene production. Chang et al. (2014) [24] is the developer of a text-to-scene system, they focused on learning dimension special by lots of indoor scenes. In their system, users can adjust models to match the text. Other than these, the WordsEye Text-to-Scene System has been developed about twenty years.

WordsEye [25] is a system which can automatically convert a natural language text into 3D scene representing. After two decades of development, the system has become very mature. A survey of the system is given in Ulinski and Coyne [26], shows that WordsEye has good performance. S2S is like WordsEye in countenancing entirely natural linguistic expressions as input. Nonetheless, S2S compared to WordsEye, it generates fairly less complicated scenarios [27].

In 2014, Stanford University proposed a scene generation system that can infer the implicit relationship in the text, and proposes to use conditional probability to obtain the relatively common model placement patterns [28]. For example, a static scene is generated with the statement "There is a room with a poster bed and a poster." (Fig. 1).

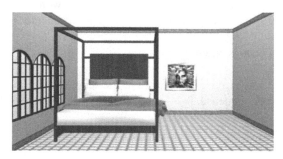

Fig. 1. Generated scene for "There is a room with a poster bed and a poster."

With the emergence of new technologies such as neural networks and machine-learning, natural language processing has enjoyed a continuous development. Natural language processing is a fusion of linguistics, computer science and artificial intelligence. It assists computers as close to human language, as possible to understand tasks. However, natural language processing has been widely used in text processing, it is still difficult to analyze specific text. The ignorance of internal semantic information would generate the semantic gap between input text and generated scene. In order to make generated scene suitable for the text which we input, we chose semantic analysis to process the text.

This paper we use the semantic analysis for model generation and prior probability-based algorithm for scene generation. Our method enables to generate scene easily and also advance in bridging the aforementioned semantic gap, and provides a new method for cultural protection.

3   Method

3.1   Scene Primitive Model Generation Based on Semantics

Scene primitive model generation based on semantics mainly consists of semantics text segmentation, model library, model generation and placement. Word segmentation algorithm is used for the semantic understanding and the acquisition of key words. Key words are imported into the model library to search for and automatically generate the desired model. The scene construction is completed through our proposed automatic placement algorithm of priori probability model suitable for traditional Chinese dramatic scenes.

The accuracy of text semantic understanding is the key to the success of the generation. The key words obtained from text segmentation directly determine the accuracy and correctness of the generation model. Due to the exquisite and sophisticated design of objects in the scene, the overall modeling effect is general, and the details cannot be highlighted. We use the semantic decomposition-combination method to build automatically. Relative to the use of spaces for word separation in English text, Chinese text will produce semantic noise when semantically segmented, which can easily produce multiple segmented results and cause ambiguity. Therefore, we use statistical word segmentation to build a Bi-Gram statistical model to count the frequency of text occurrence, and then use Hidden Markov Model (HMM) to extract key words correctly by learning and counting the occurrence of the same vocabulary in different texts several times.

(1)   Text semantic statistics based on Bi-Gram

Assuming that J represents a piece of text, the length is n, and it is composed of $(M_1, M_2, \ldots M_n)$ word sequence, then the probability of representing J is:

$$P(J) = P(M_1, M_2 \ldots M_n) = P(M_1) * P(M_2 \mid M_1) * \ldots * P(M_n \mid M_1, M_2 \ldots M_{n-1}) \tag{1}$$

Binary means that the word M_n appearing in the nth is related to historical word M_{n-1} Bi-Gram Mode:

$$P(M_1, M_2 \ldots M_i) = \prod_n^i P(M_n \mid M_{n-1}) \tag{2}$$

(2)   Word segmentation based on Hidden Markov Model (HMM) The HMM is a quintuple containing:
- Set of state values $Q = \{q_1, q_2, \ldots, q_N\}$, N: possible number of states.
- Set of observations $V = \{v_1, v_2, \ldots, v_M\}$, M: possible number of observations.
- Transition probability matrix $A = [a_{ij}]M * N$, a_{ij}: probability of transition from state i to state j.
- Observation probability matrix $B = [b_j(k)]M * N$, $b_j(k)$: Probability of generating observation vk under the condition of state value j.
- Initial state distribution π.

We use HMM for word segmentation. First, set the state value set Q to $\{B, E, M, S\}$ to indicate the beginning, end, middle of a word, and the character-independent word (single). Then, for the string $C = \{c_1 \ldots c_n\}$ to solve the maximum conditional probability: $maxP(t_1 \ldots t_n \mid c_1 \ldots c_n)$. $t1$ denotes the state corresponding to the character c1. Equation (3) can get through Bayesian processing:

$$P(t_1 \ldots t_n \mid c_1 \ldots c_n) = P(c_1 \ldots c_n \mid t_1 \ldots t_n) P(t_1 \ldots t_n) \tag{3}$$

Make a finite historic assumption: assume that the ci of the received signal at moment i is determined only by the transmitted signal t_i Eq. (4):

$$P(c_1 \ldots c_n \mid t_1 \ldots t_n) = P(c_1 \mid t_1) P(t_1) \ldots P(c_n \mid t_n) P(t_n \mid t_{n-1}) \tag{4}$$

Finally, Viterbi algorithm is used to find the final optimal word segmentation sequence.

$$\delta_{t+1}(i) = max[\delta_t(j)a_{ij}]b_i(c_t + 1) \tag{5}$$

$\delta_t(j)$: Maximum probability of state i at time t.

In the scene of 'The Emperor and the Assassin', Mrs. Xu's dagger is an important primitive model. The short sword, which is divided into three parts: the body of the dagger is a short silver edge, the handle is brown, and the tip of the dagger is golden yellow. So, the Chinese text to be analyzed is '我需要一柄银色的剑身 (I need a sword with silver sword body), 棕色的剑柄 (brown sword handle), 金黄色的剑梢的剑 (golden sword tip)'. The '银色的剑 (Silver sword)', '棕色的剑 (Brown sword)', '金黄色的剑 (Golden sword)' are text ambiguities. By building a Bi-Gram Model, we get P (剑身 (Sword body)| 银色 (Silver)), P (剑柄 (Sword handle) | 棕色 (Brown)), P (剑梢 (Sword tip) | 金黄色 (Golden)), and P(剑(Sword)| 银色 (Silver)), P(剑(Sword)| 棕色 (Brown)), P(剑(Sword)|金色 (Golden)). Then use the Chinese word breaker corpus for training HMM, through supervised learning, get silver-white modified sword body, not modified sword. Finally, use the trained HMM treatment to get '我 (I) / 需要 (need) / 一柄 (a) / 银色的 (Silver) / 剑身 (Sword body) /, /棕色的 (Brown) / 剑柄 (Sword handle)/, / 金黄色的 (Golden) / 剑梢 (Sword tip) / 的(a) / 剑 (Sword)/。'.

Table 1. Attribute information of primitive model

Attribute information	
Name	剑身
Towards	towards.x, towards.y, towards.z
Color	银色
Size	Length, width, height
Format	Obj, 3ds, stl, fbx, mb, stp, igs, max, 3ds, ma, vtk
Position	Position.x, Position.y, Position.z

The key words are extracted from the semantic understanding, then the three- dimensional model library of the stored entity is searched by the keywords. We store the basic information of the primitive model in a JSON file format for easy export of accurate primitive models. The fields of the primitive model information table include: Name, Towards, Color, Format. The primitive model information table is shown in Table 1.

Primitive model generation searches the model library for keyword matches based on entity names extracted from the previous section. The primitive model is automatically generation as shown in Fig. 2.

Fig. 2. Primitive model is automatically generation

3.2 Scene Placement Algorithm Based on Priori Probability

In view of the particularity of Chinese traditional opera scene, there are a lot of common sense logical spatial relations in the scene that match with the prior probability algorithm model. Based on the statistics of the basic placement and spatial relationship of the primitive model in the scene, the data probability model is designed. On this basis, the model placement algorithm based on prior probability is proposed innovatively. The spatial model is transferred to the spatial model as a prior spatial model through JSON. The model space area table is shown in Table 2.

Table 2. Three-dimensional spatial area table.

Spatial region	
Center	Center.x, Center.y, Center.z
RelPos	relPos.x, relPos.y, relPos.z
Semantics	上
Probability	0.68

This paper analyzes the text semantics of spatial relations of primitive models and extracts the spatial relations of matched indoor scenes [29]. Spatial relations are the orientation relations between models. Because the spatial positions generally need three points to be determined, a triple set between primitive models is constructed. For example: Mrs. Xu's dagger is on the top of the map of the state of Yan, and the table for offering is under the map of the state of Yan. The table is located in the north of the hall, and to the west is a carved screen. It forms a triple set.

{
(map of Yan state, upper part, Mrs. Xu's dagger),
(Altar, map of Yan state),
(Altar, north side, Audience Hall),
(Altar, west side, screen).
}.

First, the coordinate system needs to be determined, with the spatial Cartesian coordinate system generated by the spatial relationship of the scene as the world coordinate system, the absolute orientation. Converts the obtained spatial location to a JSON file in the same format as Table 1 and matches the strings; matches the successful output file and translates the spatial shift to the specified location by converting the JSON file to model information. Failed matching queries several locations of related models in Table 1, compares probability attributes, and outputs the maximum probability [30]. The resulting scene description file JSON format is converted:

{
File information: {version number, type},
Scene type: {The palace of the Qin Dynasty, Audience Hall}
Scene: {
        Name: 'Altar',
        Scene: 'Audience Hall', Position: {x, y, z}
        Size: {x, y, z},
        }
}

Finally, the generated scene description file is submitted to Three.js to analyze. Three.js to analyze the JSON file and querying the model information contained in the file, in order to improve the efficiency of model loading, the system will first determine whether the model is contained in the local cache. If it exists, it will be called directly. If not, it needs to be obtained from the server. Then the size and coordinate position information in JSON file is combined with the model to render and display in the page. Figure 3 shows the result after parsing the statement '卧室的墙边有一张床 (There is a bed by the wall of the bedroom)'. As can be seen from the figure, for the common objects, the system can achieve the expected results.

{"FileInfo": {"version": 1.0, "type": "JSON"},
"GroundType": "flat",
"Object": {"Name": "床",
"Scene": "客厅",
"Position": {"x": 1.33, "y": 2.66, "z": 3.67},
"Scale": {"x": 1, "y": 1, "z": 1},
"Rotation": {"rot": 0, "yaw": 0, "pitch": 0}}}.

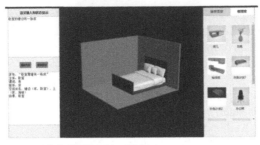

Fig. 3. Generated scene for '卧室的墙边有一张床 (There is a bed by the wall of the bedroom)'

4   Implementation

Chinese traditional opera is a stage performance art that combines literary, music, martial arts, performance, acrobatics and other elements. Performers, on a specific stage, talk about China's long history through the combination of singing and action. Stage scene layout is very important to the success of a dramatic performance.

4.1   Realization of Scene Primitive Model

Use the word segmentation algorithm to obtain keywords which the information about the placement of objects in the scene, such as subject, object, predicate, spatial orientation relationship, scale ratio in the text, and find similar characters in the model library. We choose The Emperor and The Assassin as an example of placing objects in the scene. In the process of scene modeling, the spatial relationship between different objects is the focus of our placement. We have made a statistic on the placement relation between common objects, which is convenient for reference later, so as to improve the accuracy of object placement, enhance the practicability of the system, and the interactivity of users. For example, the input text '我需要戴着红色的戏帽翎 (I need to wear the plume of the red opera hat's plumes), 黄色的戏帽顶 (the top of the yellow opera hat's top), 红色的戏帽檐的帽子头部 (the head of the red opera hat with the red opera hat's brim), 下面身体是红色黄色为主的戏服的人 (and the body below is the person in the costume with the main color of red and yellow)。'. The text analysis and generation objects are shown in the figure below. P (戏帽翎 (Opera hat's plumes) | 红色 (Red)), P (戏帽顶 (Opera hat's top) | 黄色 (Yellow)), P (戏帽檐 (Opera hat's brim) | 红色 (Red)) 和P (戏帽 (Opera hat) | 红色 (Red)), P (戏帽 (Opera hat) | 黄色 (Yellow)), P (戏帽 (Opera hat) | 红色 (Red)) are gained through Bi-Gram text statistics. Through HMM word segmentation processing, I finally got '我 (I) /需要 (need to) /戴 (wear) /着 (the) /红色的(red) /戏帽翎 (opera hat's plumes) /, /黄色的 (yellow) /戏帽顶(opera hat's top) /, /红色的(red) /戏帽檐 (opera hat's brim) /的 (of)/帽子 (hat)/头部(heat)/, /下面 (below) /身体 (the body) /是(is) /红色(red) /黄色 (yellow) /为 (with) /主 (main) /的 (of) /戏服 (costume) /的 (of) /人(person)/。'. Import keywords such as '戏帽翎 (Opera hat's plumes), 黄色的 (Yellow), 戏帽顶 (Opera hat's top), 红色的 (Red), 戏帽檐 (Opera hat's brim), 帽子 (Hat)' and other keywords into the model library, and finally obtain the required model (Fig. 4).

Fig. 4. Text analysis and model generation

4.2 Scene Placement

Scene placement is the top priority in scene construction, which directly reflects the effect presented by the scene. The corresponding model is found in the model library according to the objects in the text, and the coordinate information of each model is calculated by using prior probability according to the spatial relationship between objects, and then the coordinate information is combined with the model attribute information extracted previously. With the shadow puppetry of China's intangible cultural heritage as the background, we get an unordered set of Triple through prior probability:

(PanLong column, East, King Qin).

(King Qin, East, Jing Ke).

(Screen, North, Jing Ke).

Then convert it into a JSON file and import it into the database for string matching, and finally export the required placement position. 'The Emperor and the Assassin' is completed as shown in Fig. 5.

Fig. 5. 'The Emperor and the Assassin' scene generation

5 Experiment and Discussion

We use Leap Motion to track and control the gesture of hand movement, and gesture replaces the bamboo stick in Chinese traditional opera to directly control the movement of shadow puppetry [31–33]. The realization of human-computer interaction can not only restore image and speech, but also realize multi-angle and multi-directional viewing. Digital shadow puppetry provides us with new ideas and methods to solve the problem of high production difficulty and long-term preservation.

A set of questions is designed to assess student's understanding of traditional opera, their acceptance of virtual reality, the effect of virtual scene construction, the operation, etc.. 30 college students of opera major volunteers were invited to experience our prototype for evaluation. After the experiment, questionnaire surveys were sent to all the participants to give feedback on the practicability of the digital stage. The findings in Fig. 6 show that some students may be new to virtual reality games and are not very proficient in virtual reality games. Compared with traditional opera performance, they are more like the novel and immersive VR-based performance environment. Most of the students think that the digital stage enhances the stage performance and is helpful to the study of opera culture.

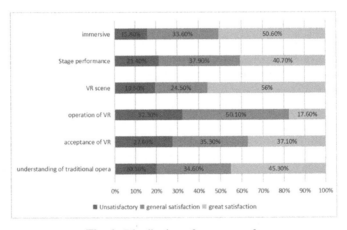

Fig. 6. Distribution of survey results

Combining all the feedback from the questionnaire leave message, users' suggestions can be summarized into three positive points, which are

- The combination of VR and opera is more attractive to students;
- It provides a new possibility for the inheritance of Chinese traditional opera culture;
- construction effect of virtual scene is remarkable and provides a good stage performance.

6 Conclusion

We use semantic-based scene original model generation and our prior probability- based scene placement algorithm to complete the scene generation. According to the generated results, the output scene and the demo text are highly similar. Experiments have proved that the scene placement algorithm based on prior probability can save time and reduce the difficulty of modeling. However, due to the limited number of models in the model library, it is difficult for some objects to find a fully corresponding model, and only the closest feature can be selected object. In the future research process, we plan to establish a community where everyone can upload and download models from the website to solve the problem of insufficient models in the model library. We will continue to combine more fields with advanced technology to enrich digital content.

References

1. Yan, S., Qiang, W.: The experience design of shadow puppet culture based on tangible interaction. In: Proceedings of 2016 Nicograph International, pp. 64–67. (2016)
2. Dostal, C., Yamafune, K.: Photogrammetric texture mapping: a method for increasing the Fidelity of 3D models of cultural heritage materials. Archaeol. Sci. Reports **18**, 430–436 (2018)
3. Zhang, Y., Fangbemi, A.: "Third-Person" augmented reality-based interactive chinese drama, In: Proceedings of 2015 International Conference on Culture and Computing (Culture Computing), pp. 41–46. (2015).
4. York, Q.Y., Shen J.H., Yang, Y.: How 'dama' becomes drama—assessing the ideological forces underlying open air group dances by Chinese senior females. Lsure Studies, 1–10 (2019)
5. Porte, B.D.L., Higgs, R.: Challenges in digitisation of cultural heritage material in the Western Cape, South Africa. SA J. Inf. Manage. **21**(1), 1–11 (2019)
6. Haval, N.: Three-dimensional documentation of complex heritage structures. IEEE Multimedia **7**(2), 52–55 (2000)
7. Wang, Y., Hu, X.: Wuju opera cultural creative products and research on visual image under VR technology. IEEE Access **8**, 161862–161871 (2020)
8. Deng, F., Gan, B.: Research on the application of 3D virtual simulation technology in ancient village restoration. In: Proceedings of 2019 4th International Conference on Mechanical, Control and Computer Engineering (ICMCCE), pp. 1050–10503 (2019)
9. Bastug, E., Bennis, M., et al.: Toward interconnected virtual reality. Opportunities, challenges, and enablers. IEEE Commun. Mag. **55**(6), 110–117 (2017)
10. Francesco, G.D.: Towards an agreed European common platform for digitisation of cultural and cientific heritage: The ministerial network for valorising activities in digitisation (MINERVA). Rev. National Center Digitization, 2–11 (2005)
11. Zhang, Y.X., Zhu, Z.Q.: On stage interactive spatial AR for drama performance. In: Proceedings of 2016 IEEE International Symposium on Mixed and Augmented Reality (ISMAR-Adjunct), pp. 280–283 (2016)
12. Zhang, F., Ding, G., et al.: Research of simulation of creative stage scene based on the 3DGans technology. Inf. Hiding Multimedia Signal Process. **9**(6), 1430–1443 (2018)
13. Ferdani, D., Fanini, B., et al.: 3D reconstruction and validation of historical background for immersive VR applications and games: The case study of the Forum of Augustus in Rome. Cult. Heritage **43**, 129–143 (2020)
14. Bozzelli, G., Raia, A., et al.: An integrated vr/ar framework for user-centric interactive experience of cultural heritage: the arkaevision project, Digital Applications in Archaeology and Cultural Heritage **15** (2019)
15. Remondino, F., El-Hakim, S.F., et al.: Turning images into 3D model. IEEE Signal Process. Mag. **25**(4), 55–65 (2008)
16. Song, S., Yu, F., Zeng, A., et al.: Semantic scene completion from a single depth image. In: Proceedings of 2017 IEEE Conference on Computer Vision and Pattern Recognition (CVPR), pp. 190–198 (2017)

17. Fonstad, M.A., Dietrich, J.T., et al.: Topographic structure from motion: a new development in photogrammetric measurement. Earth Surf. Proc. Land. **38**(4), 421–430 (2013)
18. Balletti, C., Guerra, F.: The survey of cultural heritage: a long story. Rendiconti Lincei **26**(1), 115–125 (2015). https://doi.org/10.1007/s12210-015-0411-8
19. Winograd, T.: Understanding natural language. Massachusetts Inst. Technol. **3**(1), 115–125 (1972)
20. Kılıçaslan, Y., Uçar, Ö., Güner, E.S.: An NLP-based 3D scene generation system for children with autism or mental retardation. In: Rutkowski, L., Tadeusiewicz, R., Zadeh, L.A., Zurada, J.M. (eds.) ICAISC 2008. LNCS (LNAI), vol. 5097, pp. 929–938. Springer, Heidelberg (2008). https://doi.org/10.1007/978-3-540-69731-2_88
21. Coyne, B., Sproat, R.: WordsEye: an automatic text-to-scene conversion system. In: Proceedings of 28th Annual Conference on Computer Graphics and Interactive Techniques (SIGGRAPH 2001), pp. 487–496 (2001)
22. Zeng, X., Mehdi, Q., Gough, N.: From visual semantic parameterization to graphic visualization. In: Proceedings of Ninth International Conference on Information Visualisation (IV'05), pp.488–493 (2005)
23. Liu, D., Bober, M., Kittler, J.: Visual semantic information pursuit: a survey. IEEE Trans. Pattern Anal. Mach. Intell. **43**(4), 1404–1422 (2021)
24. Chang, A.X., Savva, M., Manning, C.D.: Semantic parsing for text to 3D scene generation. In: Proceedings of Association for Computational Linguistics (ACL) Workshop on Semantic Parsing, pp. 17–21 (2014)
25. Spika, C., Schwarz, K., et al.: AVDT - automatic visualization of descriptive texts. In: Proceedings of the Vision, Modeling, and Visualization Workshop 2011, pp. 129–136 (2011)
26. Ulinski, M., Coyne, B., Hirschberg, J.: Evaluating the WordsEye text-to-scene system: imaginative and realistic sentences. In: Proceedings of the Eleventh International Conference on Language Resources and Evaluation (LREC 2018), pp. 1493–1499 (2018)
27. Milliet, Q.: Virtual reality and 3D animation in forensic visualization. Forensic Sci. **55**(5), 1227–1231 (2011)
28. Chang, A.X., Savva, M., Manning, C.D.: Learning spatial knowledge for text to 3D scene generation. In: Proceedings of the 2014 Conference on Empirical Methods in Natural Language Processing (EMNLP), pp. 2028–2038 (2014)
29. Lin, Y., François, C.: Chinese opera and the international market. Arts Manage. **20**(3), 75–82 (2018)
30. Brunetaud, X., Janvier, R., et al.: The valmod project: historical and realistic 3D models for the touristic development of the château de chambord. In: Proceedings of Euro-Mediterranean Conference, vol. 10059, pp. 53–60 (2016)
31. Liang, H., Chang, J., et al.: Hand gesture based interactive puppetry system to assist storytelling for children. Vis. Comput. **33**(3), 31–15 (2017)
32. Liang, H., Zhang, Q., et al.: Surface modelling of Jun ware based on ordinary differential equations. Traitement du Signal **36**(1), 53–58 (2019)
33. Wu, F.L., Liang, H., et al.: Semantic framework promotes interactive puppetry animation production to assist storytelling training. Inf. Sci. Eng. **36**(6), 1179–1189 (2020)

A Preliminary Work: Mixed Reality-Integrated Computer-Aided Surgical Navigation System for Paranasal Sinus Surgery Using Microsoft HoloLens 2

Sungmin Lee[1] , Hoijoon Jung[2] , Euro Lee[1] , Younhyun Jung[1(✉)] ,
and Seon Tae Kim[3]

[1] School of Computing, Gachon University, Seonam-si, Republic of Korea
{yugioh1118,younhyun.jung}@gachon.ac.kr
[2] School of Computer Science, University of Sydney, Sydney, Australia
hjun6058@uni.sydnet.edu.au
[3] Department of Otolaryngology-Head and Neck Surgery, College of Medicine, Gachon
University, Gil Medical Center, Incheon, Korea

Abstract. Paranasal sinus surgery has high demands for minimal invasion and safety. Computer-aided surgical navigation (CSN) applications have been recognized as the standard of the surgical practice; the operations of a user can be guided with visually complementary data such as preoperative medical imaging. The introduction of new innovation from mixed reality head mounted display (MR-HMD) technologies is a promising research direction for enhanced usability of paranasal sinus CSN applications. The combined use of MR-HMD with CSN provides a physically unified environment where a user's field of view in intraoperative sites can be augmented with complementary preoperative data, thereby enhancing their situational awareness. In this study, we present an early phase of the MR introduction for paranasal sinus surgery. We developed an alpha version of a commercial paranasal sinus CSN application using 3D Slicer, a dominant opensource clinical software development platform, and then implemented a scene sharing extension module. We refer to it as MR-CSN system. It enables a user wearing MR-HMD networked to equip with their MR-enhanced navigation; their navigation using surgical instruments in the intraoperative sites can be aided with the real-time information from the CSN application. The feasibility of our MR-CSN system was evaluated by experimenting a paranasal sinus surgical simulation with a phantom model.

Keywords: Mixed reality · Computer-aided surgical navigation · Paranasal sinus surgery · 3D Slicer

1 Introduction

1.1 A Subsection Sample

Computer-aided surgical navigation (CSN) applications have been recognized as the gold standard in surgical treatment for a variety of diseases [1, 2]. They visually associate

© Springer Nature Switzerland AG 2021
N. Magnenat-Thalmann et al. (Eds.): CGI 2021, LNCS 13002, pp. 633–641, 2021.
https://doi.org/10.1007/978-3-030-89029-2_47

preoperative image data, such as computer tomography (CT) or magnetic resonance (MR) images, with regions of interest (e.g., intraoperative sites). A user can navigate surgical instruments with the aid of an aligned three-dimensional (3D) image view of the intraoperative sites through the monitoring display in real-time. Over the past decade, it has experienced tremendous technological innovations, resulting in enhanced quality, reliability, and efficiency of surgical treatment [3].

The current form of CSN applications, however, still has room to be further optimized towards real clinical settings. One of the technological challenges for better adoption lies in the lack of the full, natural integration of the preoperative data, (e.g., medical images, surgical path planning, and the display of risk areas) into intraoperative sites. The visualization space of the preoperative data, mainly through the monitoring display, and the interaction space of a user (i.e., the intraoperative site) are separated and often have physical distance. This can prevent the user from keeping both the spaces in their field of view and limit their visual perception that they have to shift their attention from the intraoperative sites to the monitoring display for guidance; it thus potentially leads to the adverse effects of attention shifting, such as impacting the continuity of surgery.

Mixed reality (MR) is an intermixed presence where the physical sites of a user are seamlessly superimposed by relevant virtual contents. One of the key capabilities provided by MR is to enable a unification of visualization and interaction spaces; the user views and interacts with virtual contents within the same space. The application of MR to a CSN can help increase their situational awareness by mapping the visualization of preoperative data directly onto the intraoperative sites. Furthermore, the current generation of MR devices, such as Microsoft HoloLens 2[1], introduce new innovations using an MR-head mounted display (MR-HMD) freeing hands for the user to operate the surgical instruments. It aids the continuity of surgery together with relevant virtual preoperative guidance being exposed.

Multiple evidence has been observed to develop the merits of MR-HMD technologies in a variety of surgical practices using a CSN application [4–7]. Li et al. [4] applied MR-HMD technology to laparoscopic nephrectomy by augmenting 3D visualization of preoperative CT images to intraoperative laparoscopic images on the monitoring display using Microsoft HoloLens 1 to enhance a spatial perception of renal tumor. The comparative user study with 100 patient cases – 50 for a user group with MR-HMD and another 50 without it – demonstrated the MR-HMD user group with enhanced surgery performance, such as shortened operative time and reduced side effects. Incekara et al. [5] suggested an MR-integrated CSN application and augmented the preoperative MR images to the head of the patient for brain tumor neurosurgery. Consistent with the findings from Li et al. [4], their results showed improved understanding of the tumor location related to the brain and skull. For other different applications of CSN application integrated with MR technologies, we refer the readers to recent technological surveys [6, 7].

The aim of this study is to present preliminary progress on the provision of MR-HMD technologies to the CSN application for paranasal sinus surgery. The use of the CSN application is a well-established clinical practice for paranasal sinus surgery [8], but its integration with MR-HMD is hardly investigated. Sinus surgery requires minute

---

[1] https://www.microsoft.com/en-us/hololens.

and exquisite insertion of surgical instruments through the narrow ethmoidal precham-bers to the frontal and maxillary sinuses. The complimentary presentation of surgical instruments with preoperative CT images of the nasal wall in the user's field of view has been proven to be an ideal surgical guidance approach. As such, the CSN application for sinus surgery can be improved with enhanced situational awareness and minimal attention dispersion available when MR-HMD is adopted.

We developed an alpha version of a commercial CSN application for paranasal sinus surgery using 3D Slicer [9], a well-established personal computer (PC) open-source clinical software development platform, as a baseline. We further developed an MR extension module that can be directly plugged into the commercial CSN application. It streams real-time scenes of the CSN application to the MR-HMD, Microsoft HoloLens 2, and projects the scenes in the proximity of the face of the patient, where the paranasal sinus surgical operation is conducted, using a marker-based tracking method. We refer to it as MR-CSN system and evaluated the feasibility and utility of our MR-CSN system by experimenting a paranasal sinus surgical simulation with a phantom model.

2 Method

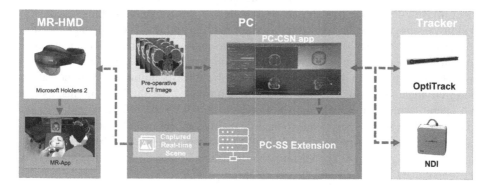

Fig. 1. Overview of MR-CSN system with software components.

Our MR-CSN system consists of three major components – PC-CSN app, PC-Streamer Stream (PC-SS) extension, and MR app - and three devices – a PC, two trackers, and a Microsoft HoloLens 2 MR-HMD - as shown in Fig. 1. The two trackers include (i) OptiTrack[2] using vision and (ii) NDI[3] using a magnetic field. The PC-CSN app is the alpha version of the commercial CSN application we developed for paranasal sinus surgery, and it runs on a typical PC environment. It tracks the surgical instruments using a hybrid tracking method with the two trackers and their locations are shown accordingly in the preoperative CT images of the patient. The PC-SS extension, added to the PC CSN app, continuously captures its real-time scenes (i.e., the preoperative CT images with the location of the surgical instruments) and transmits the scenes to the MR-HMD through a secured network connection. The MR app - an application running on

---

[2] https://optitrack.com/cameras/v120-trio/.

[3] https://www.ndigital.com/products/aurora/.

Microsoft HoloLens 2 MR-HMD - provides an integrated environment in the user's field of view by augmenting the received scenes as well as additional guide information in the proximity of the intraoperative site of the face of the patient. Here, the additional guide information was the visual indicator of the insertional point of the surgical instruments.

2.1 PC-CSN App

The 3D Slicer baseline platform [9] equips with a set of built-in functions of medical image processing and visualization which is essential for developing CSN applications. We used built-in digital imaging and communications in medicine (DICOM) module to extract and display the biological information of the patient from their preoperative data, including name, gender, age, identification number, and study date, and load the paired CT images. The standard data format of DICOM was used as the input of preoperative data for compatibility, but other data formats can also be supported. The typical quarter view visualization was used for displaying the preoperative CT images. It contains a set of two-dimensional (2D) cross-sectional axial, coronal, and sagittal view alongside with 3D view rendered using direct volume rendering (DVR) technique.

Our PC-CSN app registered the preoperative CT images to the intraoperative site of the patient face through a two-stage registration procedure with the two trackers. The slicer image-guided therapy (SlicerIGT) module [10] was included in the procedure to exploit various calculation algorithms used for the registration. The two-stage registration procedure consists of an initial coarse stage and a subsequent refinement stage. Point-to-point registration was performed in the initial coarse stage. A user was required to define 7 key points in the 3D DVR view, and the corresponding points in the patient face were identified using the surgical instrument tracked. As the 7 key points, medial and lateral canthus in the left and right eye, the center of the philtrum, and both the corners of the lip were chosen due to their distinctive appearances and locations on the patient face. The correspondences were calculated using the singular value decomposition (SVD) algorithm [11], generating an intermediate coarse transformation matrix between the 3D DVR view and the patient face.

The refinement stage refined the intermediate coarse transformation matrix using the surface-to-surface registration to improve the registration accuracy. The face surface in the 3D DVR view was matched with that of the patient. 100 sample points from the face surface of the patient were collected by scratching it randomly and gently using the surgical instrument; the corresponding points in the 3D DVR view were concurrently obtained using the coarse transformation matrix. The correspondences were calculated with the iterative closest point (ICP) algorithm [12], resulting in a refined final transformation matrix.

Our PC-CSN app used the open network for image-guided therapy interface (OpenIGTLinkIF) module [13] to locate and track the surgical instruments. The location of the surgical instruments was synchronized with the quarter view visualization of the preoperative CT images using the refined final transformation matrix. OpenIGTLinkIF module enables communication with a variety of commercial trackers. Among the two trackers used, we primarily relied on OptiTrack due to its superior tracking accuracy. When the OptiTrack-based tracking was not available due to visibility loss of the surgical instrument to the OptiTrack, Our PC-CSN app automatically switched the tracking mode to NDI which was independent of the visibility but had inferior tracking accuracy. Once OptiTrack got back to being operatable, it became the primary for the tracking. This hybrid tracking method ensured the integrity of surgical instrument localization and ultimately, surgery continuity maintenance.

2.2 PC-SS Extension

PC-SS extension established a scene transmission pipeline between the PC-CSN app and MR app by implementing a server-client model based on standard hypertext transfer protocol over secure socket layer (HTTPS) [14]. We note that the PC-SS extension could be easily integrated into any existing CSN applications based on 3D Slicer, not limited to our PC-CSN app. It captured real-time scenes of the PC-CSN app every 200 ms (i.e., 5 frames per second (FPS)); the capture rate was experimentally pre-defined to balance between the rate and computational intensity. It contained an internal web server where the captured scenes were instantly uploaded through the loopback network interface. The internal webserver only kept the latest captured scene and transmitted it to the MR app based upon its HTTPS request. This approach was used to ensure the data integrity of transmitting scenes by preventing them from being overwritten by newer captured scenes during the transmission.

2.3 MR App

MR app, as the network client of PC-SS extension, updated the received real-time scenes to a holographic quadrangle. The holographic scene augmentation was automatically positioned using a maker-based tracking method. MR app tracked a pre-defined quick response (QR) code [15] as a marker and placed the scene hologram relatively to the position of the marker. The position of the scene hologram was pre-defined to be approximately 10 cm above the head of the patient; it ensured keeping the scene hologram in a user's field of view with the interoperative sites. The position of the additional guide information is pre-determined during surgical planning and was rendered as a red arrow.

2.4 Experimental Setting

A simulated experiment using a phantom model was conducted to evaluate the feasibility and utility of our MR-CSN system for paranasal sinus surgery. The experimental setting is illustrated in Fig. 2. We placed the OptiTrack tracker (Fig. 2a) in a distance that its field of view fully covered its tracking reference unit (Fig. 2b) and the possible movement variation of the surgical instrument (Fig. 2f) being tracked. Similarly, the location of the NDI tracker (Fig. 2c) was set in the proximity where the surgical instrument could be accurately sensed by the magnetic field. A phantom model of the human face (Fig. 2e) was prepared with its preoperative CT images before the experiment. The phantom model was stably anchored onto the fixed support fixture. A laptop (Intel i5-6300HQ with 16 GB RAM; Fig. 2d) running PC-CSN app and PC-SS extension was in the same wireless network with Microsoft HoloLens 2 MR-HMD (Fig. 2g) for the real-time scene transmission and sharing. A user wearing Microsoft HoloLens 2 running MR app continued to navigate the phantom model using the surgical instrument.

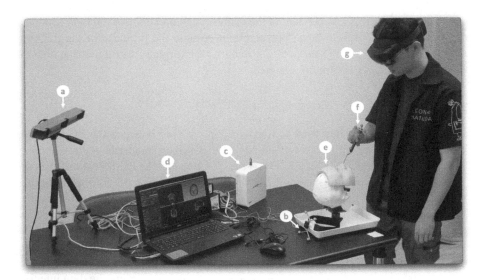

Fig. 2. Experiment environment with the user and varying components: (a) OptiTrack tracker; (b) the tracking reference module; (c) NDI tracker; (d) the laptop; (e) a phantom model of the human face; (f) the surgical instrument; and (g) the Microsoft HoloLens 2 MR-HMD.

3   Results

The result of our MR-CSN system using the experimental phantom model is shown in Fig. 3. PC-CSN app (Fig. 3a) displayed the quarter view visualization of the preoperative CT images alongside the control panel. A user's field of view (Fig. 3b) contained the same scene augmented in the proximity of the phantom model of the intraoperative site. It enabled the user to obtain instant access to the location of the surgical instrument in the preoperative CT images. This localization could be timely updated accordingly with the user's instrument navigation in the phantom model. The user could simultaneously confirm the results from their instrument navigation, thereby enabling their improved situational awareness. A demo video trailer of our MR-CSN system is accompanied in the Appendix.

In Fig. 4, we show how the two-stage registration can be effectively performed under an integrated environment provided by our MR-CSN system. When the user attempted the initial point-to-point coarse state (Fig. 4a), the key points in 3D DVR were provided in the user's field of view. It enabled the user to intuitively specify the corresponding points in the phantom model using the surgical instrument with the same field of view. Similarly, the surface-to-surface refinement stage (Fig. 4b) can be performed by gently scratching the surface of the phantom model while confirming the corresponding points in 3D DVR visualization.

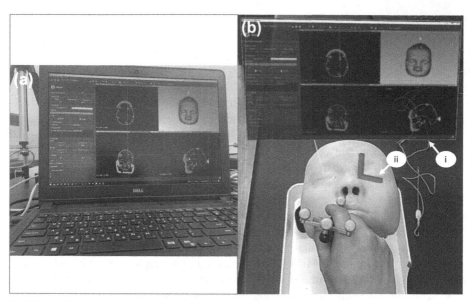

Fig. 3. (a) PC-CSN app running on a laptop, and (b) the field of view from the user wearing Microsoft HoloLens 2 MR-HMD where there are (i) the same real-time scene of PC-CSN app as well as (ii) the additional insertional point guide for the surgical instrument (rendered as the red arrow). (Color figure online)

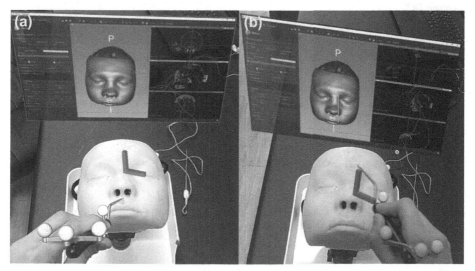

Fig. 4. Our two-stage registration in MR-HMD navigation: (a) the initial point-to-point coarse stage and (b) its subsequent surface-to-surface refinement stage. The position of the surgical instrument in the phantom model corresponds to the yellow spheres in 3D DVR. (Color figure online)

4   Discussion

Our results showed that our MR-CSN system could provide useful visual guidance in the user's field of view during the two important functionalities of a paranasal sinus CSN application – the preprocess registration and real-time instrument navigation.

Initial informal feedback from a domain expert clinician for his use of the MR-CSN system was positive. Presenting the real-time scenes of preoperative CT images to his field of view was effective in keeping his attention on the intraoperative site and maintaining the continuity of the surgical practice. Clinical performance in paranasal sinus surgery with the use of our MR-CSN system, however, was not identified yet, and a formal user study needs to be conducted to thoroughly assess it.

The current form of our approach is with secured and stable sharing of PC-CSN app scenes using MR-HMD. This simple but effective design was deliberately chosen. The current generation of MR-HMDs, including Microsoft HoloLens 2, have their own development environment, which prevents the existing PC-based CSN applications from being integrated with MR-HMD technologies without re-implementing the whole systems from scratch. This re-implementation is time-consuming and cumbersome work to be achieved. As such, our use of the public 3D Slicer platform for CSN application development with modular MR implementation can minimize an effort for the re-implementation and enables the rapid adoption of MR-HMD technologies to CSN applications.

Another advantage from our scene sharing approach relates to the limited computing capacity of MR-HMDs. With our approach, the demanding computation of CSN can be offloaded to a powerful PC and MR-HMDs prioritize visualizing the scenes transmitted from the PC.

In our experiment, we constrained the capture rate to 5 FPS to minimize the negative effect of the user experience with MR-HMDs. A higher capture rate means a more frequent update of the holographic display of MR-HMDs requiring intensive computation, and drifting (lags) of the holographic display may occur when the capture rate is above a certain level. The experimentally predefined rate largely addressed the negative effects. Our current implementation, however, is in a prototype, and we could expect further enhanced user experience via pipeline optimization.

5   Conclusion and Future Works

We presented the research progress on developing the MR-CSN system for paranasal sinus surgery. The results of our study showed the MR integrated navigation can provide potential benefits of reduced attention dispersion and enhanced situational awareness during paranasal sinus surgery. The current form of our MR-CSN system, however, is in an early phase of MR integration, and our future study will have to pursue full integration of MR technologies by overcoming technical challenges, for example, the augmentation of the preoperative scenes through the minimal use of the marker-based tracking method that inevitably needs several manual pre-processing steps. Clinical user studies with domain experts to identify the surgical outcomes of our MR-CSN system in paranasal sinus surgical practices should be the final milestone of future research.

References

1. Citardi, M.J., Batra, P.S.: Intraoperative surgical navigation for endoscopic sinus surgery: rationale and indications. Curr. Opin. Otolaryngol. Head Neck Surg. **15**(1), 23–27 (2007)
2. Weber, R., Hosemann, W.: Comprehensive review on endonasal endoscopic sinus surgery. GMS Curr. Top. Otorhinolaryngol. Head Neck Surg. (14), 08 (2015)
3. Strau, G., et al.: Evaluation of a navigation system for ENT with surgical efficiency criteria. Laryngoscope **116**(4), 564–572 (2006)
4. Li, G., et al.: The clinical application value of mixed-reality-assisted surgical navigation for laparoscopic nephrectomy. Cancer Med. **9**(15), 5480–5489 (2020)
5. Incekara, F., et al.: Clinical feasibility of a wearable mixed-reality device in neurosurgery. World Neurosurgery **118**, e422–e427 (2018)
6. Teatini, A., Kumar, R.P., Elle, O.J., Wiig, O.: Mixed reality as a novel tool for diagnostic and surgical navigation in orthopaedics. Int. J. Comput. Assist. Radiol. Surg. **16**(3), 407–414 (2021). https://doi.org/10.1007/s11548-020-02302-z
7. Vujjini, D.T., et al. Survey on real-time tracking and treatment of infectious diseases using mixed reality in visualisation technique with autoimmune therapy. In: 2020 5th International Conference on Innovative Technologies in Intelligent Systems and Industrial Applications (CITISIA). IEEE (2020)
8. Galletti, B., et al.: Endoscopic sinus surgery with and without computer assisted navigation: a retrospective study. Auris Nasus Larynx **46**(4), 520–525 (2019)
9. Fedorov, A., et al.: 3D Slicer as an image computing platform for the Quantitative Imaging Network. Magn. Reson. Imaging **30**(9), 1323–1341 (2012)
10. Ungi, T., Lasso, A., Fichtinger, G.: Open-source platforms for navigated image-guided interventions. Med. Image Anal. **33**, 181–186 (2016)
11. Van Loan, C.F.: Generalizing the singular value decomposition. SIAM J. Numer. Anal. **13**(1), 76–83 (1976)
12. Chetverikov, D., et al. The trimmed iterative closest point algorithm. In: Object Recognition Supported by User Interaction for Service Robots. IEEE (2002)
13. Tokuda, J., et al.: OpenIGTLink: an open network protocol for image-guided therapy environment. Int. J. Med. Robot. Comput. Assist. Surg. **5**(4), 423–434 (2009)
14. Bhiogade, M.S.: Secure socket layer. In: Computer Science and Information Technology Education Conference. Citeseer (2002)
15. Marchand, E., Uchiyama, H., Spindler, F.: Pose estimation for augmented reality: a hands-on survey. IEEE Trans. Visual Comput. Graphics **22**(12), 2633–2651 (2015)

Engage

Algorithms for Multi-conditioned Conic Fitting in Geometric Algebra for Conics

Pavel Loučka and Petr Vašík$^{(\boxtimes)}$ ⓘD

Brno University of Technology, Technická 2896/2, 616 69 Brno, Czech Republic
{Pavel.Loucka,Petr.Vasik}@vutbr.cz

Abstract. We introduce implementations of several conic fitting algorithms in Geometric algebra for conics. Particularly, we incorporate additional conditions into the optimisation problem, such as centre point position at the origin of coordinate system, axial alignment with coordinate axes, or, eventually, combination of both. We provide mathematical formulation together with the implementation in MATLAB. Finally, we present examples on a sample dataset and offer possible use of the algorithms.

Keywords: Conic fit · Geometric algebra · Clifford algebra · Centre position · Axial alignment

1 Introduction

We present mathematical formulation and MATLAB implementation of conic fitting algorithms in Geometric algebra for conics (GAC), [4,5]. Let us stress that we use the notation of [5] and, in Sect. 2, we recall the original fitting algorithm. Consequently, we summarise the modifications to this algorithm, particularly, we impose additional geometric conditions on the fitted conic such as centre point position at the origin of coordinate system, axial alignment with coordinate axes, or, eventually, combination of both. Let us note that precise formulations together with proofs of the appropriate theorems may be found in [7] together with different solutions leading to the same results. An example of a more general constraint and alternative approach to its solution, see [10]. For elementary fitting algorithms using geometric algebra see e.g. [8], for classical ones see [2]. For more accurate introduction to Geometric algebra for conics see [4]. We recall that formulation of a fitting problem in GAC introduced new normalisation condition and allowed an eigenvalue-based approach to the solution of the optimisation problem.

2 Conic Fitting in GAC - Original Algorithm

Altogether, GAC is constituted as a Clifford algebra $Cl(5,3)$ with an embedded point P and the IPNS representation of a general conic section Q_I of the vector forms

---

The research was supported by a grant no. FSI-S-20-6187.

N. Magnenat-Thalmann et al. (Eds.): CGI 2021, LNCS 13002, pp. 645–657, 2021.
https://doi.org/10.1007/978-3-030-89029-2_48

$$P = \begin{pmatrix} 0 & 0 & 1 & x & y & \frac{1}{2}(x^2 + y^2) & \frac{1}{2}(x^2 - y^2) & xy \end{pmatrix}^T, \tag{1}$$

$$Q_I = \begin{pmatrix} \bar{v}^{\times} & \bar{v}^{-} & \bar{v}^{+} & v^1 & v^2 & v^+ & 0 & 0 \end{pmatrix}^T, \tag{2}$$

together with an associated bilinear form given by a matrix

$$B = \begin{pmatrix} 0_{3 \times 3} & 0_{3 \times 2} & -I_3 \\ 0_{2 \times 3} & E_2 & 0_{2 \times 3} \\ -I_3 & 0_{3 \times 2} & 0_{3 \times 3} \end{pmatrix}, \quad \text{where } I_3 = \begin{pmatrix} 0 & 0 & 1 \\ 0 & 1 & 0 \\ 1 & 0 & 0 \end{pmatrix} \text{ and } E_2 = \begin{pmatrix} 1 & 0 \\ 0 & 1 \end{pmatrix}. \tag{3}$$

Using GAC, we define a conic fitting problem as follows: For a conic represented by a vector Q of the form (2) and for given points represented by vectors P_i of the form (1), we assume the objective function to be given by

$$Q \mapsto \sum_i (P_i \cdot Q)^2, \tag{4}$$

where $\cdot$ denotes the inner product between vectors in GAC. The best conic fitting the points w.r.t. this function is represented by the Q that minimises this function. The geometrically meaningless minimum $Q = 0$ is not of the interest and thus the authors of [5] consider the natural geometric (normalisation) constraint

$$Q^2 = 1. \tag{5}$$

Using the matrix of bilinear form (3), the objective function (4) then reads

$$Q \mapsto \sum_i (P_i B Q)^2 = \sum_i Q^T B P_i P_i^T B Q = Q^T P Q,$$

and thus it is a quadratic form on $\mathbb{R}^{5,3}$ with the matrix

$$P = \sum_i B P_i P_i^T B. \tag{6}$$

To formulate the solution to the optimisation problem (4), (5), it is advantageous to decompose this matrix into following blocks:

$$P = \begin{pmatrix} P_0 & P_1 & 0 \\ P_1^T & P_c & 0 \\ 0 & 0 & 0 \end{pmatrix}, \tag{7}$$

where P_0 is a 2×2 matrix, P_1 is a 2×4 matrix and P_c is a 4×4 matrix. The subscript c denotes that this block corresponds to the CRA part in GAC. Similarly, B_c denotes the middle 4×4 part of B and it coincides with the matrix of the inner product in CRA, [3], denoted as B_c. Moreover, after defining a vector $v = \begin{pmatrix} \bar{v}^+ & v^1 & v^2 & v^+ \end{pmatrix}^T$, the normalisation constraint (5) can be reformulated simply as

$$v^T B_c v = 1. \tag{8}$$

Consequently, the desired solution is acquired according to following Proposition.

Proposition 1. *The solution to the optimisation problem* (4), (5) *for conic fitting in GAC is given by* $Q = \begin{pmatrix} w & v & 0 \end{pmatrix}^T$, *where* $v = \begin{pmatrix} \bar{v}^+ & v^1 & v^2 & v^+ \end{pmatrix}^T$ *is an eigenvector corresponding to the minimal non-negative eigenvalue of the operator*

$$P_{con} = B_c(P_c - P_1^T P_0^{-1} P_1) \tag{9}$$

and $w = \begin{pmatrix} \bar{v}^\times & \bar{v}^- \end{pmatrix}^T$ *is a vector acquired as*

$$w = -P_0^{-1} P_1 v. \tag{10}$$

Let us note that inversion in (10) exists up to the case when all points lie on a single line, such case must be detected and treated separately.

2.1   Implementation

The original fitting algorithm is very easy to implement due to the matrix formulation of Proposition 1. We summarise the procedure in seven steps, each of them followed by the corresponding MATLAB code. Let us just remark that all the algorithms described in the text use input data in the form of point matrix p, with i-th point $p_i = (x_i, y_i)^T$ constituting the i-th column.

Algorithm Q

---

1. Definition of matrix B for GAC inner product according to (3) and its 4×4 submatrix B_c.

```
B = zeros(8);
I3 = [0 0 1; 0 1 0; 1 0 0];
B(1:3,6:8) = -I3;
B(4:5,4:5) = eye(2);
B(6:8,1:3) = -I3;
Bc = B(3:6,3:6);
```

2. Formation of data matrix D of size $8 \times N$, where i-th column is the GAC vector P_i representing the i-th point from the data set according to (1).

```
D = zeros(8,N);
D(3,:) = ones(1,N);
D(4:5,:) = p;
D(6,:) = 1/2*(p(1,:).^2 + p(2,:).^2);according to

D(7,:) = 1/2*(p(1,:).^2 - p(2,:).^2);
D(8,:) = p(1,:).*p(2,:);
```

3. Computation of the symmetric matrix P for the objective function by (6) and the definition of its blocks P_0, P_1 and P_c according to (7).

```
P = 1/N*B*(D*D')*B';
Pc = P(3:6,3:6);
P0 = P(1:2,1:2);
P1 = P(1:2,3:6);
```

4. Formation of matrix P_{con} according to (9) and computation of its eigenvalues and eigenvectors.

```
Pcon = Bc*(Pc-P1'*(P0\P1));
[EV,ED] = eig(Pcon);
EW = diag(ED);
```

5. Finding the eigenvector v corresponding to the least non-negative eigenvalue of P_{con}.

```
k_opt = find(EW == min(EW(EW>0)));
v_opt = EV(:,k_opt);
```

6. Normalisation of the optimal vector v according to constraint (8)

```
kappa = v_opt'*Bc*v_opt;
v_opt = 1/sqrt(kappa)*v_opt;
```

7. Computation of w by (10) and forming the optimal vector Q according to Proposition 1.

```
w = -P0\P1*v_opt;
Q = [w;v_opt;0;0];
```

Let us note that the obtained optimal conic given by the vector Q can be equivalently represented by a matrix

$$
A = \begin{pmatrix}
-\frac{1}{2}(\bar{v}^+ + \bar{v}^-) & -\frac{1}{2}\bar{v}^\times & \frac{1}{2}v^1 \\
-\frac{1}{2}\bar{v}^\times & -\frac{1}{2}(\bar{v}^+ - \bar{v}^-) & \frac{1}{2}v^2 \\
\frac{1}{2}v^1 & \frac{1}{2}v^2 & -v^+
\end{pmatrix},
$$

from which the extraction of the internal parameters of the conic is possible and well known (see e.g. [6]). For detailed information about conic sections see e.g. [9]. Let us also remark that the code in the Algorithm **Q** may be further optimised by modification of steps 1. and 2. Namely, we can see that the first two rows of the data matrix D are by definition zero, resulting then in a block of 0's in the matrix P, while this block is not further used in the subsequent computation. The redundant zero block in the matrix P is not that critical itself, but the computation of the matrix P described in step 3. uses multiplication of matrix D with its transpose and thus constitutes both unnecessary element multiplications and storage of useless zero rows of matrix D. Therefore, by removing first two elements from the vector (1) we can define the i-th reduced GAC point vector $\hat{P}_i$ of the form

$$
\hat{P}_i = \begin{pmatrix} 1 & x_i & y_i & \frac{1}{2}(x_i^2 + y_i^2) & \frac{1}{2}(x_i^2 - y_i^2) & x_i y_i \end{pmatrix}^T
$$

and create the corresponding reduced data matrix $\hat{D}$ of size $6 \times N$, where the i-th column is $\hat{P}_i$. Additionally, by removing the first two columns and the last two rows from the matrix B of the form (3), we also define a reduced matrix for GAC inner product

$$\hat{B} = \begin{pmatrix} 0_{3\times1} & 0_{3\times2} & -I_3 \\ 0_{2\times1} & E_2 & 0_{2\times3} \\ -1 & 0_{1\times2} & 0_{1\times3} \end{pmatrix}, \quad \text{where} \quad I_3 = \begin{pmatrix} 0 & 0 & 1 \\ 0 & 1 & 0 \\ 1 & 0 & 0 \end{pmatrix} \quad \text{and} \quad E_2 = \begin{pmatrix} 1 & 0 \\ 0 & 1 \end{pmatrix}.$$

Consequently, steps 1. and 2. of Algorithm **Q** can be respectively replaced by

1*
```
B = zeros(6);
I3 = [0 0 1;0 1 0; 1 0 0];
B(1:3,4:6) = -I3;
B(4:5,2:3) = eye(2);
B(6,1) = -1;
Bc = B(3:6,1:4);
```

2*
```
D = ones(6,N);
D(2:3,:) = p;
D(4,:) = 1/2*(p(1,:).^2 + p(2,:).^2);
D(5,:) = 1/2*(p(1,:).^2 - p(2,:).^2);
D(6,:) = p(1,:).*p(2,:);
```

As a result, the matrix P computed in the step 3. does not contain the zero blocks as in (7) and takes the form of a reduced 6×6 matrix

$$\hat{P} = \begin{pmatrix} P_0 & P_1 \\ P_1^T & P_c \end{pmatrix}.$$

Moreover, the rest of the algorithm remains unaffected by this change, so the steps 3.−7. stay the same. Let us note that we can also analogously omit zeroes in the GAC conic vector of the form (2), and thus create a reduced conic vector

$$\hat{Q} = \begin{pmatrix} \bar{v}^\times & \bar{v}^- & \bar{v}^+ & v^1 & v^2 & v^+ \end{pmatrix}^T,$$

and then compute the objective function (4) equivalently as

$$\hat{Q} \mapsto \hat{Q}^T \hat{P} \hat{Q}.$$

3   Conic Fitting in GAC - Additional Conditions

One of the main features of the original algorithm is that the sought conic is not limited in advance by any prescribed geometric condition. In other words, parameters of the fitted conic such as its axial tilt or centre point position in the plane are not known beforehand, being just a result of the optimisation process.

While this general type of fit may be useful in some cases, there are problems demanding a fit with one or more additional geometric conditions constraining the output conic. In this section we focus on forming three types of fitting algorithms, each resulting in either of following conics:

1. *conic having its axes aligned with coordinate axes*
2. *conic having its centre point at the coordinate system origin*
3. *conic satisfying both 1. and 2.*

After inspecting the meaning of the coefficients of IPNS conic Q of the form (2) and using part of the conic section theory, it can be shown that either of conics of types 1.−3. can be obtained from the vector representation (2) simply by setting some of the coefficients to zero, namely, according to Theorem 1:

Theorem 1. *Conic Q represented in the form of vector* (2) *is*

1. **axes-aligned** $\Leftrightarrow \bar{v}^{\times} = 0$,
2. **origin-centred** $\Leftrightarrow (v^1 = 0)$ *and* $(v^2 = 0)$,
3. **axes-aligned origin-centred** $\Leftrightarrow (\bar{v}^{\times} = 0)$ *and* $(v^1 = 0)$ *and* $(v^2 = 0)$.

In other words, after denoting the mentioned conics respectively as Q^{al}, Q^0 and $Q^{al,0}$, their general forms are:

$$Q^{al} = \begin{pmatrix} 0 & \bar{v}^- & \bar{v}^+ & v^1 & v^2 & v^+ & 0 & 0 \end{pmatrix}^T, \tag{11}$$

$$Q^0 = \begin{pmatrix} \bar{v}^{\times} & \bar{v}^- & \bar{v}^+ & 0 & 0 & v^+ & 0 & 0 \end{pmatrix}^T, \tag{12}$$

$$Q^{al,0} = \begin{pmatrix} 0 & \bar{v}^- & \bar{v}^+ & 0 & 0 & v^+ & 0 & 0 \end{pmatrix}^T. \tag{13}$$

Consequently, we may formulate an optimisation problem almost identical to the original problem of minimising objective function (4) subject to (5), however, instead of searching for a general conic Q of the form (2) we will assume the optimal conic to be of one of the forms (11)–(13). If we further denote any of these conic vectors by Q^*, the objective function and the constraint for any of these conics with additional geometric conditions read

$$Q^* \mapsto \sum_i (P_i \cdot Q^*)^2, \tag{14}$$

$$\text{s.t. } Q^{*2} = 1. \tag{15}$$

As in the case of the original algorithm, here we can also rewrite the objective function (14) into matrix notation, yielding

$$Q^* \mapsto Q^{*T} P Q^*,$$

where P is thus again a matrix of a quadratic form w.r.t. the vector Q^*. Since some of the coefficients of the vector Q^* are known to be zero, we are not interested in the rows and columns of the matrix P corresponding to such zero elements and hence we may decompose it in a way different to decomposition (7).

For instance, if we denote the (generally) non-zero entries of symmetric matrix P as p_{ij} and use Q^{al} with the 1st zero entry as Q^*, we get a decomposition

$$P = \begin{pmatrix} p_{11} & p_{21} & p_{31} & p_{41} & p_{51} & p_{61} & 0 & 0 \\ p_{21} & p_{22} & p_{32} & p_{42} & p_{52} & p_{62} & 0 & 0 \\ p_{31} & p_{32} & p_{33} & p_{43} & p_{53} & p_{63} & 0 & 0 \\ p_{41} & p_{42} & p_{43} & p_{44} & p_{54} & p_{64} & 0 & 0 \\ p_{51} & p_{52} & p_{53} & p_{54} & p_{55} & p_{65} & 0 & 0 \\ p_{61} & p_{62} & p_{63} & p_{64} & p_{65} & p_{66} & 0 & 0 \\ 0 & 0 & 0 & 0 & 0 & 0 & 0 & 0 \\ 0 & 0 & 0 & 0 & 0 & 0 & 0 & 0 \end{pmatrix} = \left(\begin{array}{c|c|cccc|cc} p_{11} & p_{21} & p_{31} & p_{41} & p_{51} & p_{61} & 0 & 0 \\ \hline p_{21} & P_0^{al} & & P_1^{al} & & & 0 & 0 \\ \hline p_{31} & & & & & & 0 & 0 \\ p_{41} & P_1^{al^T} & & P_c & & & 0 & 0 \\ p_{51} & & & & & & 0 & 0 \\ p_{61} & & & & & & 0 & 0 \\ \hline 0 & 0 & 0 & 0 & 0 & 0 & 0 & 0 \\ 0 & 0 & 0 & 0 & 0 & 0 & 0 & 0 \end{array} \right)$$

Analogously, we consider decompositions of matrix P for vectors Q^0 and $Q^{al,0}$, respectively, as:

$$P = \left(\begin{array}{cc|c|cc|c|cc} & & \sim & p_{41} & p_{51} & \sim & 0 & 0 \\ & P_0 & & p_{42} & p_{52} & & 0 & 0 \\ & & \sim & & & \sim & 0 & 0 \\ \wr & \wr & \bullet & p_{43} & p_{53} & \bullet & 0 & 0 \\ \hline p_{41} & p_{42} & p_{43} & p_{44} & p_{54} & p_{64} & 0 & 0 \\ p_{51} & p_{52} & p_{53} & p_{54} & p_{55} & p_{65} & 0 & 0 \\ \hline \wr & \wr & \bullet & p_{64} & p_{65} & \bullet & 0 & 0 \\ \hline 0 & 0 & 0 & 0 & 0 & 0 & 0 & 0 \\ 0 & 0 & 0 & 0 & 0 & 0 & 0 & 0 \end{array} \right) = \left(\begin{array}{c|c|c|cc|c|cc} p_{11} & p_{21} & p_{31} & p_{41} & p_{51} & p_{61} & 0 & 0 \\ \hline p_{21} & P_0^{al} & \approx & p_{42} & p_{52} & \approx & 0 & 0 \\ \hline p_{34} & \wr & \bullet & p_{43} & p_{53} & \bullet & 0 & 0 \\ \hline p_{41} & p_{42} & p_{43} & p_{44} & p_{54} & p_{64} & 0 & 0 \\ p_{51} & p_{52} & p_{53} & p_{54} & p_{55} & p_{65} & 0 & 0 \\ \hline p_{61} & \wr & \bullet & p_{64} & p_{65} & \bullet & 0 & 0 \\ \hline 0 & 0 & 0 & 0 & 0 & 0 & 0 & 0 \\ 0 & 0 & 0 & 0 & 0 & 0 & 0 & 0 \end{array} \right).$$

The cells inscribed with $\sim$ indicate the elements of matrix P_1^0 consisting of two mutually isolated columns (due to the symmetry of matrix P, the cells with $\wr$ stand for the matrix $P_1^{0^T}$), the isolated elements designated with $\bullet$ comprise matrix P_c^0 and, similarly to P_1^0, the cells inscribed with $\approx$ indicate the elements of vector $P_1^{al,0}$, so the matrices and the vector read

$$P_1^0 = \begin{pmatrix} p_{31} & p_{61} \\ p_{32} & p_{62} \end{pmatrix}, \quad P_c^0 = \begin{pmatrix} p_{33} & p_{63} \\ p_{63} & p_{66} \end{pmatrix}, \quad P_1^{al,0} = \begin{pmatrix} p_{32} & p_{62} \end{pmatrix}.$$

Moreover, we can also simplify the normalisation constraint (15) for the vectors Q^0 and $Q^{al,0}$. After defining a vector $v^0 = \begin{pmatrix} \bar{v}^+ & v^+ \end{pmatrix}^T$ and a matrix

$$B_c^0 = \begin{pmatrix} 0 & -1 \\ -1 & 0 \end{pmatrix},$$

the constraint (15) can be rewritten as

$$v^{0^T} B_c^0 v^0 = 1.$$

Thanks to the derived decompositions of matrix P and overall similarities between the matrix formulations of the original conic fitting problem and the conic fitting with additional geometric conditions, we can describe the solution to optimisation problem (14), (15) using basically the same formulae as in Proposition 1.

Proposition 2. *The solution to the optimisation problem* (14), (15) *for conic fitting in GAC is given by a conic vector Q^* containing vector v^* and w^*, where v^* is an eigenvector corresponding to the minimal non-negative eigenvalue of*

$$P^*_{con} = B^*_c (P^*_c - P^{*T}_1 P^{*-1}_0 P^*_1), \tag{16}$$

and w^* is a real number or a vector acquired as

$$w^* = -P^{*-1}_0 P^*_1 v^*. \tag{17}$$

The particular choice of the elements that substitute for the starred elements in Eqs. (16), (17) depends on the type of conic we want to fit. An overview of the substitution rules for each conic type is given by the following table:

Q^*	v^*	w^*	B^*_c	P^*_{con}	P^*_0	P^*_1	P^*_c
Q^{al}	$v = \left(\bar{v}^+ \ v^1 \ v^2 \ v^+ \right)^T$	$w^{al} = \bar{v}^-$	B_c	P^{al}_{con}	P^{al}_0	P^{al}_1	P_c
Q^0	$v^0 = \left(\bar{v}^+ \ v^+ \right)^T$	$w = \left(\bar{v}^\times \ \bar{v}^- \right)^T$	B^0_c	P^0_{con}	P_0	P^0_1	P^0_c
$Q^{al,0}$	$v^0 = \left(\bar{v}^+ \ v^+ \right)^T$	$w^{al} = \bar{v}^-$	B^0_c	$P^{al,0}_{con}$	P^{al}_0	$P^{al,0}_1$	P^0_c

Let us point out the existence of inversions in (17): P^{-1}_0 does not exist when all data points lie on a single line, while $P^{al\,-1}_0$ does not exist when all data points lie on a double line $x^2 - y^2 = 0$. Such cases must be detected and treated separately.

3.1   Implementation

In this subsection we present three novel MATLAB algorithms based on Proposition 2. Each of the algorithms results in one of the conic vectors Q^{al}, Q^0 or $Q^{al,0}$, with name corresponding to the output conic type.

The algorithms have a form very similar to Algorithm **Q**, containing only a few adjustments to the involved matrices, therefore, the individual steps are only numbered, without comments repeating. Let us stress that for the sake of code optimisation, we follow the example of Algorithm **Q** and employ the reduced forms of vectors and matrices in the first steps of the algorithms.

Algorithm QAL

1.
```
B = zeros(5);
I2 = [0 1; 1 0];
B(1:2,4:5) = -I2;
B(3:4,2:3) = eye(2);
B(5,1) = -1;
Bc = B(2:5,1:4);
```

2.
```
D = ones(5,N);
D(2:3,:) = p;
D(4,:) = 1/2*(p(1,:).^2 + p(2,:).^2);
D(5,:) = 1/2*(p(1,:).^2 - p(2,:).^2);
```

3.
```
P = 1/N*B*(D*D')*B';
Pc = P(2:5,2:5);
P0 = P(1,1);
P1 = P(1,2:5);
```

4.
```
Pcon = Bc*(Pc-P1'*1/P0*P1);
[EV,ED] = eig(Pcon);
EW = diag(ED);
```

5.
```
k_opt = find(EW == min(EW(EW>0)));
v_opt = EV(:,k_opt);
```

6.
```
kappa = v_opt'*Bc*v_opt;
v_opt = 1/sqrt(kappa)*v_opt;
```

7.
```
w = -1/P0*P1*v_opt;
Q = [0;w;v_opt;0;0];
```

Algorithm Q0

1.
```
B = zeros(4);
I2 = [0 1; 1 0];
B(1:2,3:4) = -I2;
B(3:4,1:2) = -I2;
Bc = -I2;
```

2.
```
D = ones(4,N);
D(2,:) = 1/2*(p(1,:).^2 + p(2,:).^2);
D(3,:) = 1/2*(p(1,:).^2 - p(2,:).^2);
D(4,:) = p(1,:).*p(2,:);
```

3.
```
P = 1/N*B*(D*D')*B';
Pc = P(3:4,3:4);
P0 = P(1:2,1:2);
P1 = P(1:2,3:4);
```

4.
```
Pcon = Bc*(Pc-P1'*(P0\P1));
[EV,ED] = eig(Pcon);
EW = diag(ED);
```

| 5. | ```
k_opt = find(EW == min(EW(EW>0)));
v_opt = EV(:,k_opt);
``` |
| 6. | ```
kappa = v_opt'*Bc*v_opt;
v_opt = 1/sqrt(kappa)*v_opt;
``` |
| 7. | ```
w = -P0\P1*v_opt;
Q = [w;v_opt(1);0;0;v_opt(2);0;0];
``` |

Algorithm QAL0

| 1. | ```
B = [0 0 -1; 0 -1 0; -1 0 0];
Bc = B(2:3,1:2);
``` |
| 2. | ```
D = ones(3,N);
D(2,:) = 1/2*(p(1,:).^2 + p(2,:).^2);
D(3,:) = 1/2*(p(1,:).^2 - p(2,:).^2);
``` |
| 3. | ```
P = 1/N*B*(D*D')*B';
Pc = P(2:3,2:3);
P0 = P(1,1);
P1 = P(1,2:3);
``` |
| 4. | ```
Pcon = Bc*(Pc-P1'*1/P0*P1);
[EV,ED] = eig(Pcon);
EW = diag(ED);
``` |
| 5. | ```
k_opt = find(EW == min(EW(EW>0)));
v_opt = EV(:,k_opt);
``` |
| 6. | ```
kappa = v_opt'*Bc*v_opt;
v_opt = 1/sqrt(kappa)*v_opt;
``` |
| 7. | ```
w = -1/P0*P1*v_opt;
Q = [0;w;v_opt(1);0;0;v_opt(2);0;0];
``` |

4 Experimental Results and Applications

Finally, we apply each of the presented algorithms (including the original Algorithm $\mathbf{Q}$) on a sample dataset of 10 points listed by Table 1. After doing so, we compare the resulting conics both visually and by values of the corresponding objective functions. The resulting conics sorted by type and used algorithm can be seen in Figs. 1, 2, 3 and 4. It is obvious that in our case the new conic fitting

Table 1. Fitted points

x_i	-3	-3	-2	-3	-6	-7	-9	-10	-9	-7
y_i	3	4	6	7	8	8	7	4	2	1

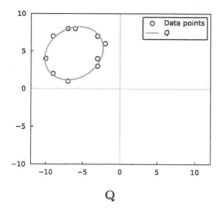

Q

Fig. 1. General conic Q

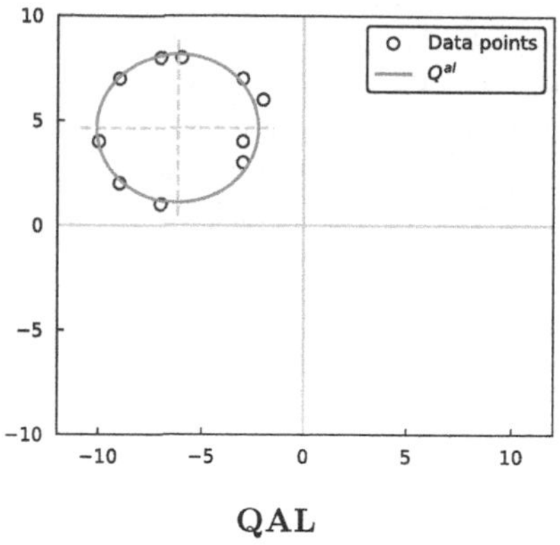

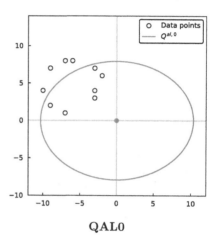

QAL

Fig. 2. Axes-aligned conic Q^{al}

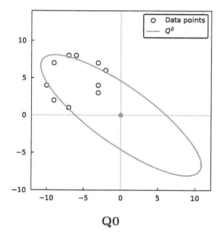

Q0

Fig. 3. Origin-centred conic Q^0

QAL0

Fig. 4. Axes-aligned origin-centred conic $Q^{al,0}$

methods with additional geometric constraints produce conics with greater total distance from the data points than general conic Q acquired by Algorithm **Q**. Even though the difference is not that evident when comparing conics Q and Q^{al}, one cannot overlook the increase of total distance from the data points to conic Q^0, let alone the case of conic $Q^{al,0}$. Consequently, we can conclude that the ability to achieve a tight fit is decreasing with the fitted conic's degree of freedom reduction (at least for our dataset), in other words, value of the objective function is inversely proportional to the degrees of freedom (d.f.). Indeed, we can see this trend in Figs. 1-4: a general conic Q has five d.f. in total; an axes-aligned conic Q^{al} has one less d.f. due to the fixed tilt of axes; an origin-centred conic Q^0 loses two d.f. because of the fixed position of its centre-point; finally, a conic $Q^{al,0}$ has three d.f. less than a general conic Q, since it has both the tilt of axes and the centre-point position fixed. The fits depicted in Figs. 1, 2, 3 and 4 are characterised by the corresponding conic type, the value of the objective function and the degrees of freedom in Table 2. The residual value is comparable to the standard approaches, see [5]. Due to the layout of the points in the used dataset, conics Q^0 and $Q^{al,0}$ are not exactly tightly fitted, nonetheless, such fits can be conveniently used for data consisting of points that approximately lie on an origin-centred, or axes-aligned origin-centred conic, respectively. For an application to integral curve construction for so called *switched systems*, see [1].

Table 2. Objective function & geometric freedom

Conic	Value of objective function	Degrees of freedom
Q	0.0245	5
Q^{al}	0.0871	4
Q^0	1.0369	3
$Q^{al,0}$	4.3361	2

5   Conclusion

At the beginning of the text, we briefly recalled the basic GAC elements together with the original conic fitting algorithm and specific normalisation constraint [5]. Subsequently, we presented three novel methods of fitting conics with one of three additional geometric properties, in particular: axial alignment, origin-centring, and, eventually, two previous properties combined.

Each of the presented fitting methods (including the original one) is followed by the corresponding MATLAB algorithm, resulting in one of four geometrically (un)constrained types of conics. Moreover, redundant elements used in the derivations of the fitting methods were mostly omitted in the described algorithms, thus reducing the computational demands on both time and memory.

All the methods were tested on a sample dataset and the resulting conics were analysed visually and by the values of the corresponding objective functions. In particular, our empirical results showed a relationship between a fitted conic's degrees of freedom and tightness of the fit to the data points: the more degrees of freedom, the tighter the fit. We point out that all GAC fitting algorithms are not invariant under translation, which is a natural property due to the structure of GAC. A translation invariant algorithm is a subject of further research.

References

1. Derevianko, A.I., Vašík, P.: Solver-free optimal control for Linear Dynamical Switched System by means of Geometric Algebra. arXiv:2103.13803 [math.OC]

2. Fitzgibbon, A.W., Fisher, R.B.: A buyer's guide to conic fitting. In: Proceedings of the 6th British Conference on Machine Vision, vol. 2, pp. 513–522 (1995)
3. Hildenbrand, D.: Introduction to Geometric Algebra Computing. CRC Press, Taylor & Francis Group (2019)
4. Hrdina, J., Návrat, A., Vašík, P.: Geometric algebra for conics. Adv. Appl. Clifford Algebras **28**(3), 1–21 (2018). https://doi.org/10.1007/s00006-018-0879-2
5. Hrdina, J., Návrat, A., Vašík, P.: Conic fitting in geometric algebra setting. Adv. Appl. Clifford Algebras **29**(4), 1–13 (2019). https://doi.org/10.1007/s00006-019-0989-5
6. Korn, G.A., Korn, T.M.: Mathematical Handbook for Scientists and Engineers. McGraw-Hill Book Company (1961)
7. Loučka, P., Vašík, P.: On multi-conditioned conic fitting in Geometric algebra for conics. arXiv:2103.14072 [math.NA]
8. Perwass, Ch.: Geometric Algebra with Applications in Engineering. Springer (2009)
9. Richter-Gebert, J.: Perspectives On Projective Geometry: a guided tour through real and complex geometry. Springer (2016)
10. Waibel, P., Matthes, J., Gröll, L.: Constrained ellipse fitting with center on a line. J. Math. Imaging Vision **53**(3), 364–382 (2015). https://doi.org/10.1007/s10851-015-0584-x

Special Affine Fourier Transform for Space-Time Algebra Signals

Eckhard Hitzer[✉]

International Christian University, Mitaka, Tokyo 181-8585, Japan
hitzer@icu.ac.jp

Abstract. We generalize the space-time Fourier transform (SFT) [9] to a special affine Fourier transform (SASFT, also known as offset linear canonical transform) for 16-dimensional space-time multivector $Cl(3,1)$-valued signals over the domain of space-time (Minkowski space) $\mathbb{R}^{3,1}$. We establish how it can be computed in terms of the SFT, and introduce its properties of multivector coefficient linearity, shift and modulation, inversion, Rayleigh (Parseval) energy theorem, partial derivative identities, a directional uncertainty principle and its specialization to coordinates.

Keywords: Clifford's geometric algebra · Space-time · Space-time algebra · Special affine Fourier transform · Uncertainty principle

1 Introduction

In signal processing and optics the special affine Fourier transforms have been introduced in 1994 [1,2] as a vast generalization of Fourier transforms, and other known signal transforms like the fractional Fourier transform. A further notable trend has been the introduction of hypercomplex (quaternionic and Clifford) Fourier transforms [14]. A species of Fourier transform particularly relevant to signal processing, navigation and physics is the space-time Fourier transform (SFT) [5,6,9,10] that transforms signals defined on the domain of (special relativistic) space-time (Minkowski space) $\mathbb{R}^{3,1}$ with range in the corresponding geometric (Clifford) algebra of space-time (space-time algebra STA) $Cl(3,1)$. Apart from electromagnetic waves and light it can be applied in any area of physics, including electro-magnetism, special relativity, satellite navigation, optics and quantum mechanics (e.g. to spinor wave functions). It is therefore on the applied

---

This work is dedicated to 70 year old London Pastor John Sherwood who was arrested on 23 April 2021 by police in Uxbridge for preaching publicly about these verses in Genesis: *So God created man in His own image; in the image of God He created him; male and female He created them. Then God blessed them, and God said to them, 'Be fruitful and multiply; fill the earth and subdue it; have dominion over the fish of the sea, over the birds of the air, and over every living thing that moves on the earth.'*, Genesis 1:27+28, NKJV, Biblegateway [18]. Please note that this research is subject to the Creative Peace License [13].

© Springer Nature Switzerland AG 2021
N. Magnenat-Thalmann et al. (Eds.): CGI 2021, LNCS 13002, pp. 658–669, 2021.
https://doi.org/10.1007/978-3-030-89029-2_49

side also of interest to quantum bit computations and quantum computing in general. A steerable split of quaternions [15] is found to have a natural algebraic analogue in STA as space-time split, defined by the time vector and its dual trivector (the three-dimensional space volume element). Applied to any space-time signal, it naturally generates two wave packages, one traveling to the left and one to the right, classical solutions of relativistic wave equations.

With this backdrop we undertake to generalize the SFT to a special affine Fourier transform. This automatically generates (for special parameter settings) a fractional SFT, a linear canonical SFT, a lens transformation SFT, a free-space propagation SFT and a magnification SFT, amongst others. We thus create a set of potentially powerful new tools for physics, signal processing, optics, quantum mechanics, quantum computing, space navigation, etc.

This paper is structured as follows. Section 2 introduces the necessary background of space-time algebra and the space-time Fourier transform (SFT). Section 3 then defines the special affine space-time Fourier transform (SASFT) generalization and establishes several of its properties. This includes in Subsect. 3.3 the uncertainty principle for the SASFT in a general directional form and a specific coordinate system related form. The paper concludes with Sect. 4 and a list of references.

2   Background

For a general introduction to Clifford's geometric algebras see [11], for geometric calculus based on geometric algebra see [17].

2.1   Space-Time Algebra

Space-time of Einstein's special relativity is a four-dimensional non-Euclidean quadratic space $\mathbb{R}^{3,1}$ equipped with the orthonormal vector basis[1]

$$\{e_t, e_1, e_2, e_3\}, \qquad -e_t^2 = e_1^2 = e_2^2 = e_3^2 = 1. \tag{1}$$

Space-time algebra [4,8] (isomorphic to Dirac algebra of quantum mechanics) is Clifford's geometric algebra $Cl(3,1)$ generated by all geometric products of $\mathbb{R}^{3,1}$, also called (flat) Minkowski space, with a 16-dimensional algebra basis of scalar, vector, bivector, trivector, and pseudoscalar elements:

$$\{1, e_t, e_1, e_2, e_3, e_{t1}, e_{t2}, e_{t3}, e_{23}, e_{31}, e_{12}, e_{123} = i_3, e_{t31}, e_{t23}, e_{t12}, e_{t123} = i_{st}\}, \tag{2}$$

where we used the conventional index notation $e_{t1} = e_t e_1$, $e_{123} = e_1 e_2 e_3$, etc. The even subalgebra $Cl^+(3,1)$ of the space-time algebra has the eight-dimensional basis

$$\{1, e_{t1}, e_{t2}, e_{t3}, e_{12}, e_{23}, e_{31}, e_{t123} = i_{st}\}, \tag{3}$$

---

[1] The signature $(+---)$ chosen in [8] would also be possible, but then the important quaternionic subalgebra (4) would be absent. The possibility of our $(-+++)$ is also indicated in Footnote 15 on page 22 of [8].

and is isomorphic to the Clifford algebra of space $Cl(3,0)$, also known as Pauli algebra, if we identify (denoting $Cl(3,0)$ elements with bold e)

$$1 = 1, \quad \boldsymbol{e}_k = e_{tk}, \quad \boldsymbol{e}_{jk} = e_{jk}, \quad \boldsymbol{e}_{123} = i_{st}, \quad k, j \in \{1,2,3\}, k \neq j. \quad (4)$$

Furthermore we have the important four-dimensional subalgebra of space-time algebra isomorphic to quaternions with basis[2]

$$\{1, e_t, i_3, i_{st}\}, \qquad e_t^2 = i_3^2 = i_{st}^2 = -1. \quad (5)$$

Left multiplication with e_t and right multiplication with its space-time dual $i_3 = e_t^* = e_t i_{st}^{-1}$ is a form of space-time duality mapping for basis elements of grade k to grade $4 - k$, $0 \leq k \leq 4$:

$$e_t\{(2)\}i_3 =$$
$$\{i_{st}, -i_3, e_{t23}, e_{t31}, e_{t12}, -e_{23}, -e_{31}, -e_{12}, -e_{t1}, -e_{t2}, -e_{t3}, -e_t, e_1, e_2, e_3, 1\}, \quad (6)$$

A useful tool for us will be the following split [9] of multivectors and multivector functions

$$M_\pm = \frac{1}{2}(M \pm e_t M i_3), \qquad M = M_+ + M_-, \quad (7)$$

with the convenient property that

$$e_t M_\pm = \mp M_\pm i_3. \quad (8)$$

Using the principal reverse (reverse product order combined with changing the sign of every basis vector of negative square) [16], we have for any two multivectors $M, N \in Cl(3,1)$ that

$$M * \overline{N} = \langle M\overline{N} \rangle_0 = \sum_A M_A N_A, \quad (9)$$

where index A ranges over all indexes in (2) and in addition index 0 is for the scalar part: $M_0 = \langle M \rangle_0$, $N_0 = \langle N \rangle_0$. Then we can define the *multivector norm*

$$|N| = \sqrt{N * \overline{N}} = \sqrt{\sum_A N_A^2}. \quad (10)$$

Note that the split (7) results in the norm identity

$$|M|^2 = |M_+|^2 + |M_-|^2. \quad (11)$$

---

[2] Note that this four-dimensional subalgebra of STA is spatially isotropic, i.e. invariant under spatial rotations.

2.2   Space-Time Fourier Transform (SFT)

For background on Fourier transforms we refer to [3,7] and for Clifford Fourier transforms to [12].

For functions $f : \mathbb{R}^{3,1} \to Cl(3,1)$ and $1 \leq a < \infty$, we introduce the linear spaces

$$L^a(\mathbb{R}^{3,1}; Cl(3,1)) = \left\{ \mathbb{R}^{3,1} \to Cl(3,1) : \|f\|_a = \left(\int_{\mathbb{R}^{3,1}} |f(\mathbf{x})|^a \, d^4x \right)^{1/a} < \infty \right\}. \tag{12}$$

Definition 1. *The space-time Fourier transform (SFT) [9] maps 16-dimensional space-time algebra functions $f \in L^1(\mathbb{R}^{3,1}; Cl(3,1))$ to 16-dimensional spectrum functions $\mathcal{F}_{SFT}\{f\} : \mathbb{R}^{3,1} \to Cl(3,1)$. It is defined as*

$$\mathcal{F}_{SFT}\{f\}(\omega) = \int_{\mathbb{R}^{3,1}} e^{-e_t t \omega_t} f(\mathbf{x}) e^{-i_3 \overrightarrow{x} \cdot \overrightarrow{\omega}} d^4x, \tag{13}$$

with space-time vectors $\mathbf{x} = t e_t + \overrightarrow{x} \in \mathbb{R}^{3,1}$, $\overrightarrow{x} = x e_1 + y e_2 + z e_3 \in \mathbb{R}^3$, infinitesimal space-time volume $d^4x = dt\,dx\,dy\,dz$ and space-time frequency vector $\omega = \omega_t e_t + \overrightarrow{\omega} \in \mathbb{R}^{3,1}$, $\overrightarrow{\omega} = \omega_1 e_1 + \omega_2 e_2 + \omega_e e_3 \in \mathbb{R}^3$.

The SFT is invertible, compare (72) of [9] or Lemma 2.5 of [6].

Theorem 1. *For $f, \mathcal{F}_{SFT}\{f\} \in L^1(\mathbb{R}^{3,1}; Cl(3,1))$, the inverse of the SFT is*

$$f(\mathbf{x}) = \frac{1}{(2\pi)^4} \int_{\mathbb{R}^{3,1}} e^{e_t t \omega_t} \mathcal{F}_{SFT}\{f\}(\omega) e^{i_3 \overrightarrow{x} \cdot \overrightarrow{\omega}} d^4\omega, \quad d^4\omega = d\omega_t d\omega_1 d\omega_2 d\omega_3. \tag{14}$$

We will need the following anisotropic scaling property, a special case of the general linear transformation property Theorem 5.4 of [9].

Lemma 1. *For $\alpha_t, \alpha_1, \alpha_2, \alpha_3 \in \mathbb{R} \setminus \{0\}$, $f \in L^1(\mathbb{R}^{3,1}; Cl(3,1))$, we have*

$$\mathcal{F}_{SFT}\{f(\alpha_t t e_t + \alpha_1 x_1 e_1 + \alpha_2 x_2 e_2 + \alpha_3 x_3 e_3)\}(\omega)$$
$$= \frac{1}{|\alpha_t \alpha_1 \alpha_2 \alpha_3|} \mathcal{F}_{SFT}\{f\}(\frac{\omega_t}{\alpha_t} e_t + \frac{\omega_1}{\alpha_1} e_1 + \frac{\omega_2}{\alpha_2} e_2 + \frac{\omega_3}{\alpha_3} x_3). \tag{15}$$

We will furthermore need the SFT Rayleigh (or SFT Parseval) energy theorem, see Corollary 16 of [5].

Lemma 2. *For $f \in L^2(\mathbb{R}^{3,1}; Cl(3,1))$, we have*

$$\int_{\mathbb{R}^{3,1}} |\mathcal{F}_{SFT}\{f\}(\omega)|^2 d^4\omega = (2\pi)^4 \int_{\mathbb{R}^{3,1}} |f(\mathbf{x})|^2 d^4x. \tag{16}$$

We also need the following lemma (Lemma 13 in [5]) on partial derivatives.

Lemma 3. *For* $f, \frac{\partial}{\partial t} f, \frac{\partial}{\partial x_k} f \in L^1(\mathbb{R}^{3,1}; Cl(3,0))$, $k = 1, 2, 3$, *provided that the derivatives exist, we obtain*

$$\mathcal{F}_{SFT}\left\{\frac{\partial}{\partial t} f(\mathbf{x})\right\}(\omega) = \omega_t e_t \mathcal{F}_{SFT}\{f(\mathbf{x})\}(\omega), \tag{17}$$

$$\mathcal{F}_{SFT}\left\{\frac{\partial}{\partial x_k} f(\mathbf{x})\right\}(\omega) = \mathcal{F}_{SFT}\{f(\mathbf{x})\}(\omega) i_3 \omega_k. \tag{18}$$

We note the following directional uncertainty principle for the SFT (Theorem 7.2 of [10]).

Theorem 2. *For two arbitrary space-time vectors* $\mathbf{c}, \mathbf{d} \in \mathbb{R}^{3,1}$ *and* $f, |\mathbf{x}|^{1/2} f \in L^2(\mathbb{R}^{3,1}; Cl(3,0))$ *we have*

$$\int_{\mathbb{R}^{3,1}} (c_t t - \overrightarrow{c} \cdot \overrightarrow{x})^2 |f(\mathbf{x})|^2 d^4 x \int_{\mathbb{R}^{3,1}} (d_t \omega_t - \overrightarrow{d} \cdot \overrightarrow{\omega})^2 |\mathcal{F}_{SFT}\{f\}(\omega)|^2 d^4 \omega$$

$$\geq \frac{(2\pi)^4}{4}\left[(c_t d_t - \overrightarrow{c} \cdot \overrightarrow{d})^2 F_-^2 + (c_t d_t + \overrightarrow{c} \cdot \overrightarrow{d})^2 F_+^2\right], \tag{19}$$

with energies of the left- and right traveling wavepackets

$$F_\pm = \int_{\mathbb{R}^{3,1}} |f_\pm(\mathbf{x})|^2 d^4 x, \qquad \int_{\mathbb{R}^{3,1}} |f(\mathbf{x})|^2 d^4 x = F_- + F_+. \tag{20}$$

3   Special Affine Space-Time Fourier Transform (SASFT)

3.1   Defining the SASFT

We now want to vastly extend the SFT to a special affine Fourier transform (SASFT) following the approach in [1,2]. For this purpose we introduce two special affine phase space transformations given by matrixes and vectors

$$\begin{pmatrix} a & b \\ c & d \end{pmatrix}, \begin{pmatrix} m \\ n \end{pmatrix}, \qquad \begin{pmatrix} A & B \\ C & D \end{pmatrix}, \begin{pmatrix} \overrightarrow{M} \\ \overrightarrow{N} \end{pmatrix},$$

$$a, b, c, d, m, n, A, B, C, D \in \mathbb{R}, \qquad \overrightarrow{M}, \overrightarrow{N} \in \mathbb{R}^3, \tag{21}$$

with the lossless area- and power-preserving unit determinants

$$\det\begin{pmatrix} a & b \\ c & d \end{pmatrix} = ad - bc = 1, \qquad \det\begin{pmatrix} A & B \\ C & D \end{pmatrix} = AD - BC = 1. \tag{22}$$

We modify the left and the right kernel factors of (13) to[3]

$$k(t, \omega_t) = \frac{1}{\sqrt{2\pi b}} e^{\frac{e_t}{2b}\left(at^2 + 2mt + d\omega_t^2 - 2(t + dm - bn)\omega_t\right)},$$

$$K(\overrightarrow{x}, \overrightarrow{\omega}) = \frac{1}{(2\pi B)^{3/2}} e^{\frac{i_3}{2B}\left(A\overrightarrow{x}^2 + 2\overrightarrow{M} \cdot \overrightarrow{x} + D\overrightarrow{\omega}^2 - 2(\overrightarrow{x} + D\overrightarrow{M} - B\overrightarrow{N}) \cdot \overrightarrow{\omega}\right)}, \tag{23}$$

---

[3] Note that Abe and Sheridan adopt in their 1994 papers that introduce the SAFT slightly different sign conventions in (61) of [1] and in (3) of [2]. For consistency, we use the conventions specified in (3) of [2].

Remark 1. Note that we need to choose the quantities $\overrightarrow{M}, \overrightarrow{N}$ as vectors in $\mathbb{R}^3$, otherwise we would not be able to obtain a scalar phase factor in the exponent of $K(\overrightarrow{x}, \overrightarrow{\omega})$. A more elaborate alternative would be to construct $K(\overrightarrow{x}, \overrightarrow{\omega})$ as the product of three kernel factors $K_1(x, \omega_1)$, $K_2(y, \omega_2)$, $K_3(z, \omega_3)$, and use three (2×2) matrices and three (2×1) vectors for their construction in analogy to $k(t, \omega_t)$. But this approach would introduce eight extra parameters.

We now define the special affine space-time Fourier transform.

Definition 2. *The special affine space-time Fourier transform (SASFT) maps 16-dimensional space-time algebra functions $f \in L^1(\mathbb{R}^{3,1}; Cl(3,1))$ to 16-dimensional spectrum functions $\mathcal{F}\{f\} : \mathbb{R}^{3,1} \to Cl(3,1)$. It is defined as*

$$\mathcal{F}\{f\}(\omega) = \int_{\mathbb{R}^{3,1}} k(\omega_t, t) f(\mathbf{x}) K(\overrightarrow{x}, \overrightarrow{\omega}) d^4 x, \tag{24}$$

with kernel factors (23).

Remark 2. Note that we obtain the SFT [9] by setting $a = d = m = n = 0$, $b = -c = 1$ and $A = D = 0$, $B = -C = 1$, $\overrightarrow{M} = \overrightarrow{N} = \overrightarrow{0}$. By setting only $m = n = 0$ and $\overrightarrow{M} = \overrightarrow{N} = \overrightarrow{0}$ we obtain a *linear canonical transform*[4] generalization of the SFT without offsets. By choosing $b = -c = -\sin\vartheta$, $a = d = \cos\vartheta$, $m = n = 0$ and $B = -C = -\sin\theta$, $A = D = \cos\theta$, $\overrightarrow{M} = \overrightarrow{N} = \overrightarrow{0}$ we get a generalization of the SFT to a *fractional Fourier transform*. Including translations $m, n \neq 0$ and $\overrightarrow{M}, \overrightarrow{N} \neq \overrightarrow{0}$, we obtain SASFT generalizations of special known cases of interest [2] in optics as the *lens transformation*[5] with $a = d = 1$, $c = \xi$, $b = 0$ and $A = D = 1$, $C = \Xi$, $B = 0$; the *free-space propagation* with $a = d = 1$, $c = 0$, $b = \eta$ and $A = D = 1$, $C = 0$, $B = \Gamma$; and *magnification*[6] with $a = e^\alpha$, $d = e^{-\alpha}$, $c = b = 0$ and $A = e^\Lambda$, $D = e^{-\Lambda}$, $C = B = 0$. Any property of the SASFT of Definition 2 will therefore automatically apply to all the special cases listed in this remark.

3.2   Properties of the SASFT

Convenient for computations, it is possible to pull out parts of the kernel factors to the left and right of the integral in Definition 2 that do not depend on the integration variable $\mathbf{x} \in \mathbb{R}^{3,1}$.

Lemma 4.

$$\mathcal{F}\{f\}(\omega) = \frac{1}{\sqrt{2\pi b}} e^{\frac{e_t}{2b}\left(d\omega_t^2 + 2(bn-dm)\omega_t\right)} \int_{\mathbb{R}^{3,1}} e^{\frac{e_t}{2b}\left(at^2 + 2(m-\omega_t)t\right)} f(\mathbf{x})$$
$$e^{\frac{i_3}{2B}\left(A\overrightarrow{x}^2 + 2(\overrightarrow{M}-\overrightarrow{\omega})\cdot\overrightarrow{x}\right)} d^4 x \; e^{\frac{i_3}{2B}\left(D\overrightarrow{\omega}^2 + 2(B\overrightarrow{N}-D\overrightarrow{M})\cdot\overrightarrow{\omega}\right)} \frac{1}{(2\pi B)^{3/2}}. \tag{25}$$

---

[4] The SASFT is therefore more general than the linear canonical SFT, obtained by setting for the SASFT the translation offsets to zero: $m = n = 0$ and $\overrightarrow{M} = \overrightarrow{N} = \overrightarrow{0}$.

[5] As [2] points out on page 1802, for the lens transformation a degenerate version of the SAFT is required, see also [1].

[6] As pointed out related to equation (13) on page 1802 of [2], a special limit for $b \to 0$ formula will need to be used in this case.

The next lemma shows, that we can reduce the computation of the SASFT to that of the SFT. By defining the function

$$g(\mathbf{x}) = e^{\frac{e_t}{2b}(at^2+2mt)} f(\mathbf{x})\, e^{\frac{i_3}{2B}(A\vec{x}^2+2\vec{M}\cdot\vec{x})}, \tag{26}$$

we can reduce the computation of the SAFT to

$$\mathcal{F}\{f\}(\omega) = \frac{1}{\sqrt{2\pi b}} e^{\frac{e_t}{2b}\left(d\omega_t^2+2(bn-dm)\omega_t\right)} \int_{\mathbb{R}^{3,1}} e^{-\frac{e_t}{b}\omega_t t} g(\mathbf{x})\, e^{-\frac{i_3}{B}\vec{\omega}\cdot\vec{x}} d^4x$$
$$e^{\frac{i_3}{2B}\left(D\vec{\omega}^2+2(B\vec{N}-D\vec{M})\cdot\vec{\omega}\right)} \frac{1}{(2\pi B)^{3/2}}. \tag{27}$$

Lemma 5. *The SASFT can be computed from the SFT of $g(\mathbf{x})$, defined in* (26), *by*

$$\mathcal{F}\{f\}(\omega) = \frac{1}{\sqrt{2\pi b}} e^{\frac{e_t}{2b}\left(d\omega_t^2+2(bn-dm)\omega_t\right)} \mathcal{F}_{SFT}\{g\}\left(\frac{\omega_t}{b}e_t + \frac{\vec{\omega}}{B}\right)$$
$$e^{\frac{i_3}{2B}\left(D\vec{\omega}^2+2(B\vec{N}-D\vec{M})\cdot\vec{\omega}\right)} \frac{1}{(2\pi B)^{3/2}}. \tag{28}$$

We further note useful relationships between the functions f and g of (26).

Lemma 6. *For g defined according to* (26) *in terms of f, we have*

$$|g(\mathbf{x})| = |f(\mathbf{x})|, \qquad |g_\pm(\mathbf{x})| = |f_\pm(\mathbf{x})|. \tag{29}$$

Proof. For the proof we observe that by its definition $g = e^{e_t\alpha} f e^{i_3\beta}$ for some scalar functions α, β, see (26). Therefore

$$|g(\mathbf{x})|^2 = \langle g(\mathbf{x})\overline{g(\mathbf{x})}\rangle_0 = \langle e^{e_t\alpha} f(\mathbf{x}) e^{i_3\beta} e^{-i_3\beta}\overline{f(\mathbf{x})} e^{-e_t\alpha}\rangle_0$$
$$= \langle f(\mathbf{x})\overline{f(\mathbf{x})}\rangle_0 = |f(\mathbf{x})|^2, \tag{30}$$

where we used for the third identity the cyclic commutation property of the scalar part $\langle abc\rangle_0 = \langle cab\rangle_0$, for any $a,b,c \in Cl(3,1)$. Because by construction

$$g_\pm = \left(e^{e_t\alpha} f e^{i_3\beta}\right)_\pm = e^{e_t\alpha} f_\pm e^{i_3\beta}, \tag{31}$$

we also have $|g_\pm(\mathbf{x})| = |f_\pm(\mathbf{x})|$.   □

In analogy to Theorem 3.3 of [6], where in the quaternionic setting the SAFT is referred to by another popular name of *offset linear canonical transform*, we can establish the following properties, which are noted here without proof.

Theorem 3. *The SASFT is left linear for multivector coefficients that commute with e_t*

$$\alpha = \alpha_0 + \alpha_t e_t + \alpha_{12} e_{12} + \alpha_{23} e_{23} + \alpha_{31} e_{31} + \alpha_{t12} e_{t12} + \alpha_{t23} e_{t23} + \alpha_{t31} e_{t31} \tag{32}$$

and right linear for coefficients that commute with i_3

$$\beta = \beta_0 + \beta_1 e_1 + \beta_2 e_2 + \beta_3 e_3 + \beta_{12} e_{12} + \beta_{23} e_{23} + \beta_{31} e_{31} + \beta_{123} i_3. \tag{33}$$

That is

$$\mathcal{F}\{\alpha f + \alpha' g\} = \alpha \mathcal{F}\{f\} + \alpha' \mathcal{F}\{g\}, \qquad \mathcal{F}\{f\beta + g\beta'\} = \mathcal{F}\{f\}\beta + \mathcal{F}\{g\}\beta'. \tag{34}$$

Furthermore, we have

$$\lim_{|\omega| \to 0} |\mathcal{F}\{f\}(\omega)| = 0. \tag{35}$$

Finally, $\mathcal{F}\{f\}$ is uniformly continuous on $\mathbb{R}^{3,1}$.

We further obtain the following shift and modulation properties and the inverse transform.

Theorem 4. *For $f \in L^1(\mathbb{R}^{3,1}; Cl(3,1))$, $\mathbf{x}, \omega \in \mathbb{R}^{3,1}$, and constant vector $\mathbf{k} = k e_t + \overrightarrow{K} \in \mathbb{R}^{3,1}$ we have*

$$\mathcal{F}\{f(\mathbf{x} - \mathbf{k})\}(\omega) = e^{e_t(-\frac{1}{2}ack^2 - cmk + ck\omega_t + ank)} \, \mathcal{F}\{f(\mathbf{x})\}\left(\omega - (ak e_t + A\overrightarrow{K})\right)$$

$$e^{i_3(-\frac{1}{2}AC\overrightarrow{K}^2 - C\overrightarrow{M} \cdot \overrightarrow{K} + C\overrightarrow{K} \cdot \overrightarrow{\omega} + A\overrightarrow{N} \cdot \overrightarrow{K})}. \tag{36}$$

Theorem 4 can be proved by straightforward computation using substitution $\mathbf{x}' = \mathbf{x} - \mathbf{k}$ under the integral and applying the determinant conditions (22) for simplification.

Theorem 5. *For $f \in L^1(\mathbb{R}^{3,1}; Cl(3,1))$, $\mathbf{x}, \omega \in \mathbb{R}^{3,1}$, and constant vector $\mu = \mu_t e_t + \overrightarrow{\mu} \in \mathbb{R}^{3,1}$ we have*

$$\mathcal{F}\{e^{c_t t\mu_t} f(\mathbf{x}) e^{i_3 \overrightarrow{x} \cdot \overrightarrow{\mu}}\}(\omega) = e^{-e_t\left(\frac{1}{2}d(b\mu_t^2 - 2\mu_t \omega_t) + \mu_t(dm - bn)\right)}$$

$$\mathcal{F}\{f(\mathbf{x})\}\left(\omega - (b\mu_t e_t + B\overrightarrow{\mu})\right) e^{-i_3\left(\frac{1}{2}D(B\overrightarrow{\mu}^2 - 2\overrightarrow{\mu} \cdot \overrightarrow{\omega}) + \overrightarrow{\mu} \cdot (D\overrightarrow{M} - B\overrightarrow{N})\right)}. \tag{37}$$

Theorem 5 can be proved by straightforward computation.

Theorem 6. *For $f, \mathcal{F}\{f\} \in L^1(\mathbb{R}^{3,1}; Cl(3,1))$, we obtain the inverse transform as*

$$f(\mathbf{x}) = \int_{\mathbb{R}^{3,1}} \overline{k(\omega_t, t)} \, \mathcal{F}\{f\}(\omega) \, \overline{K(\overrightarrow{x}, \overrightarrow{\omega})} \, d^4\omega, \tag{38}$$

with overbar denoting the principal reverse [16], i.e. $\overline{e_t} = -e_t$, $\overline{i_3} = -i_e$.

Theorem 6 can be proved using the relationship of the SASFT to the SFT of Lemma 5 and the inverse of the SFT of Theorem 1.

For the SASFT we have the following Rayleigh (Parseval) energy theorem.

Theorem 7. *A space-time algebra signal $f \in L^2(\mathbb{R}^{3,1}; Cl(3,1))$ and its SASFT $\mathcal{F}\{f\}$ satisfy the energy identity*

$$\|\mathcal{F}\{f\}\|_2 = \|f\|_2. \tag{39}$$

For the proof one needs Lemmas 5, 1 and 2.

In analogy to Lemma 3.7 of [6] we can establish relationships between signal derivatives and multiplication with frequency components of the SASFT.

Lemma 7. *For* $f, \frac{\partial}{\partial t} f, \frac{\partial}{\partial x_k} f \in L^2(\mathbb{R}^{3,1}; Cl(3,0))$, $k = 1, 2, 3$, *provided that the derivatives exist, we obtain*

$$\int_{\mathbb{R}^{3,1}} \omega_t^2 |\mathcal{F}\{f\}(\omega)|^2 d^4\omega = b^2 \int_{\mathbb{R}^{3,1}} |e_t(\frac{a}{b}t + \frac{m}{b}) f(\mathbf{x}) + \frac{\partial}{\partial t} f(\mathbf{x})|^2 d^4 x, \quad (40)$$

$$\int_{\mathbb{R}^{3,1}} \omega_k^2 |\mathcal{F}\{f\}(\omega)|^2 d^4\omega = B^2 \int_{\mathbb{R}^{3,1}} |(\frac{A}{B}x_k + \frac{M_k}{B}) f(\mathbf{x}) i_3 + \frac{\partial}{\partial x_k} f(\mathbf{x})|^2 d^4 x. \quad (41)$$

For the proof of Lemma 7 one needs Lemmas 3 and 5, and the multivector norm (10). We note that on the right side the extra factors of $f(\mathbf{x})$ in the first term under the integral arise from differentiating $g(\mathbf{x})$ defined in (26).

3.3   Uncertainty Principle for the SASFT

We now establish the directional uncertainty principle for the SASFT. The uncertainty principle specifies how precisely a signal can be measured in space as well as in its spectral (frequency) domain, and is therefore of universal importance in quantum theory, optics and signal processing.

Theorem 8. *For two arbitrary constant space-time vectors* $\mathbf{c}, \mathbf{d} \in \mathbb{R}^{3,1}$ *and* $f, |\mathbf{x}|^{1/2} f \in L^2(\mathbb{R}^{3,1}; Cl(3,0))$ *we have*

$$\int_{\mathbb{R}^{3,1}} (c_t t - \overrightarrow{c} \cdot \overrightarrow{x})^2 |f(\mathbf{x})|^2 d^4 x \int_{\mathbb{R}^{3,1}} (d_t \omega_t - \overrightarrow{d} \cdot \overrightarrow{\omega})^2 |\mathcal{F}\{f\}(\omega)|^2 d^4 \omega$$

$$\geq \frac{1}{4}\left[(c_t d_t' - \overrightarrow{c} \cdot \overrightarrow{d}')^2 F_-^2 + (c_t d_t' + \overrightarrow{c} \cdot \overrightarrow{d}')^2 F_+^2\right], \quad (42)$$

with $\mathbf{d}' = b d_t e_t + B \overrightarrow{d}$, *and energies of the left- and right traveling wavepackets*

$$F_\pm = \int_{\mathbb{R}^{3,1}} |f_\pm(\mathbf{x})|^2 d^4 x. \quad (43)$$

Proof. We observe that according to (26) and Lemma 5

$$|\mathcal{F}\{f\}(\omega)|^2 = \frac{1}{(2\pi)^4 b B^3} |\mathcal{F}_{SFT}\{g\}(\omega')|^2, \qquad \omega' = \frac{\omega_t}{b} e_t + \frac{\overrightarrow{\omega}}{B}. \quad (44)$$

Therefore,

$$\int_{\mathbb{R}^{3,1}} (d_t \omega_t - \overrightarrow{d} \cdot \overrightarrow{\omega})^2 |\mathcal{F}\{f\}(\omega)|^2 d^4 \omega$$

$$= \frac{1}{(2\pi)^4 b B^3} \int_{\mathbb{R}^{3,1}} (d_t \omega_t - \overrightarrow{d} \cdot \overrightarrow{\omega})^2 |\mathcal{F}_{SFT}\{g\}(\omega')|^2 d^4 \omega$$

$$= \frac{b B^3}{(2\pi)^4 b B^3} \int_{\mathbb{R}^{3,1}} (d_t' \omega_t' - \overrightarrow{d}' \cdot \overrightarrow{\omega}')^2 |\mathcal{F}_{SFT}\{g\}(\omega')|^2 d^4 \omega' \quad (45)$$

with $\mathbf{d}' = bd_t e_t + B\vec{d}$, such that $d_t \omega_t - \vec{d} \cdot \vec{\omega} = d_t' \omega_t' - \vec{d}' \cdot \vec{\omega}'$, and $d^4\omega = bB^3 d^4\omega'$. Relabeling $\omega' \to \omega$ in the last integral of (45), and using $|f(\mathbf{x})| = |g(\mathbf{x})|$ of Lemma 6, we obtain

$$\int_{\mathbb{R}^{3,1}} (c_t t - \vec{c} \cdot \vec{x})^2 |f(\mathbf{x})|^2 d^4 x \int_{\mathbb{R}^{3,1}} (d_t \omega_t - \vec{d} \cdot \vec{\omega})^2 |\mathcal{F}\{f\}(\omega)|^2 d^4 \omega$$

$$= \int_{\mathbb{R}^{3,1}} (c_t t - \vec{c} \cdot \vec{x})^2 |g(\mathbf{x})|^2 d^4 x \frac{1}{(2\pi)^4} \int_{\mathbb{R}^{3,1}} (d_t' \omega_t - \vec{d}' \cdot \vec{\omega})^2 |\mathcal{F}_{SFT}\{g\}(\omega)|^2 d^4 \omega$$

$$\geq \frac{1}{4} \left[(c_t d_t' - \vec{c} \cdot \vec{d}')^2 F_-^2 + (c_t d_t' + \vec{c} \cdot \vec{d}')^2 F_+^2 \right], \tag{46}$$

where we applied the directional uncertainty principle of the SFT (Theorem 2) for the inequality, and replaced $G_\pm = \int_{\mathbb{R}^{3,1}} |g_\pm(\mathbf{x})|^2 d^4 x = F_\pm$, i.e. finally applying Lemma 6 to the left- and right traveling energy integrals for g.

For coordinate directions we get the following specialization.

Corollary 1. *For any two space-time and frequency coordinates x_λ, ω_μ, with $\lambda, \mu \in \{t, 1, 2, 3\}$, $x_t = t$, and $f, |\mathbf{x}|^{1/2} f \in L^2(\mathbb{R}^{3,1}; Cl(3,0))$ we have*

$$\int_{\mathbb{R}^{3,1}} x_\lambda^2 |f(\mathbf{x})|^2 d^4 x \int_{\mathbb{R}^{3,1}} \omega_\mu^2 |\mathcal{F}\{f\}(\omega)|^2 d^4 \omega \geq \frac{\delta_{\lambda,\mu}}{4} \beta^2 F^2, \tag{47}$$

with Kronecker symbol $\delta_{\lambda,\mu}$ equal 1 if $\mu = \lambda$ and zero otherwise, $\beta = b$ for $\mu = t$ and $\beta = B$ for $\mu \in \{1, 2, 3\}$, and total signal energy (see (11))

$$F = \int_{\mathbb{R}^{3,1}} |f(\mathbf{x})|^2 d^4 x = \int_{\mathbb{R}^{3,1}} [|f_-(\mathbf{x})|^2 + |f_+(\mathbf{x})|^2] d^4 x = F_- + F_+. \tag{48}$$

4   Conclusion

After giving some background on space-time algebra and reviewing the space-time Fourier transform (SFT) and some of its properties, we have defined the special affine space-time Fourier transform as a vast generalization of the SFT on the one hand, which now includes new transforms such as a fractional SFT and others. On the other hand this generalization means also to lift the classical special affine Fourier transforms, with their primary relevance for optics [1,2], to the level of high dimensional hypercomplex (Clifford) integral transforms. We expect that a series of theoretical and applied research on this new class of hypercomplex transforms may ensue in fields like physics, electro-magnetism, optics, signal processing, GPS, space navigation and quantum computing, including quantum internet related signal processing.

Acknowledgments. The author wishes to thank God: *In the beginning God created the heavens and the earth. The earth was without form, and void; and darkness was on the face of the deep. And the Spirit of God was hovering over the face of the waters. Then God said, "Let there be light"; and there was light.* (NKJV, Biblegateway). He further thanks his colleagues B. Mawardi. Y. El Haoui, and S.J. Sangwine, as well as the organizers of the ENGAGE 2021 workshop at CGI 2021, and the organizers of CGI 2021.

References

1. Abe, S., Sheridan, J.T.: Generalization of the fractional Fourier transformation to an arbitrary linear lossless transformation an operator approach. J. Phys. A Math. Gen. **27**(12), 4179–4187 (1994)
2. Abe, S., Sheridan, J.T.: Optical operations on wave functions as the Abelian subgroups of the special affine Fourier transformation. Opt. Lett. **19**(22), 1801–1803 (1994)
3. Bracewell, R.: The Fourier Transform and Its Applications, 3rd edn. Mc Graw Hill India, Gautam Buddha Nagar (2014)
4. Doran, C., Lasenby, A.: Geometric Algebra for Physicists. Cambridge University Press, Cambridge (2003)
5. El Haoui, Y., Hitzer, E., Fahlaoui, S.: Heisenberg's and Hardy's uncertainty principles for special relativistic space-time fourier transformation. Adv. Appl. Clifford Algebras **30**, 69 (2020). https://doi.org/10.1007/s00006-020-01093-5
6. El Haoui, Y., Hitzer, E.: Generalized uncertainty principles associated with the quaternionic offset linear canonical transform. Complex Var. Elliptic Eq., 1–20 (2021). https://doi.org/10.1080/17476933.2021.1916919
7. Folland, G.B.: Fourier Analysis and Its Applications. American Mathematical Society, Rhode Island (2009)
8. Hestenes, D.: Space-Time Algebra, 2nd edn. Birkhäuser, Basel (2015)
9. Hitzer, E.: Quaternion Fourier transform on quaternion fields and generalizations. Adv. Appl. Clifford Algebras **17**(3), 497–517 (2007). https://doi.org/10.1007/s00006-007-0037-8
10. Hitzer, E.: Directional uncertainty principle for quaternion Fourier transform. Adv. Appl. Clifford Algebras **20**(2), 271–284 (2010). https://doi.org/10.1007/s00006-009-0175-2
11. Hitzer, E.: Introduction to Clifford's geometric algebra. SICE J. Control Meas. Syst. Integr. **51**(4), 338–350 (2012). Preprint: http://arxiv.org/abs/1306.1660. Accessed 22 May 2020
12. Hitzer, E., Sangwine, S.J. (eds.): Quaternion and Clifford Fourier Transforms and Wavelets. Trends in Mathematics, vol. 27. Birkhäuser, Basel (2013)
13. Hitzer, E.: Creative Peace License. https://gaupdate.wordpress.com/2011/12/14/the-creative-peace-license-14-dec-2011/. Accessed 31 May 2021
14. Hitzer, E.: New developments in Clifford Fourier transforms. In: Mastorakis, N.E., Pardalos, P.M., Agarwal, R.P., Kocinac, L.: (eds.) Advances in Applied and Pure Mathematics, Proceedings of the 2014 International Conference on Pure Mathematics, Applied Mathematics, Computational Methods (PMAMCM 2014), Santorini Island, Greece, 17–21 July 2014. Mathematics and Computers in Science and Engineering Series, vol. 29, pp. 19–25 (2014). http://inase.org/library/2014/santorini/bypaper/MATH/MATH-01.pdf. Preprint: http://viXra.org/abs/1407.0169
15. Hitzer, E.: The orthogonal planes split of quaternions and its relation to quaternion geometry of rotations. In: Brackx, F., De Schepper, H., Van der Jeugt, J. (eds.) Proceedings of the 30th International Colloquium on Group Theoretical Methods in Physics (group30), Ghent, Belgium, 14–18 July 2014. IOP Journal of Physics: Conference Series (JPCS), vol. 597, p. 012042 (2015). https://doi.org/10.1088/1742-6596/597/1/012042. Open Access: http://iopscience.iop.org/1742-6596/597/1/012042/pdf/1742-6596_597_1_012042.pdf. Preprint: http://viXra.org/abs/1411.0362

16. Laville, G., Ramadanoff, I.: Stone-Weierstrass theorem. Preprint: https://arxiv.org/pdf/math/0411090.pdf. Accessed 27 May 2021
17. Macdonald, A.: Vector and geometric calculus, May 2020 Printing. CreateSpace Independent Publishing Platform, Scotts Valley, CA, USA (2020)
18. Simpson, P.: Marched off to the cells for preaching God's word, 27 April 2021. https://www.conservativewoman.co.uk/marched-off-to-the-cells-for-preaching-gods-word/. Accessed 30 May 2021

On Explicit Formulas for Characteristic Polynomial Coefficients in Geometric Algebras

Kamron Abdulkhaev[1](✉) and Dmitry Shirokov[1,2]

[1] HSE University, 101000 Moscow, Russia
ksabdulkhaev@edu.hse.ru, dshirokov@hse.ru
[2] Institute for Information Transmission Problems of the Russian
Academy of Sciences, 127051 Moscow, Russia
shirokov@iitp.ru

Abstract. In this paper, we discuss characteristic polynomials in (Clifford) geometric algebras $\mathcal{G}_{p,q}$ of vector space of dimension $n = p + q$. For the first time, we present explicit formulas for all characteristic polynomial coefficients in the case $n = 5$. The formulas involve only the operations of geometric product, summation, and operations of conjugation. For the first time, we present an analytic proof of the corresponding formulas in the case $n = 4$. We present some new properties of the operations of conjugation and grade projection and use them to obtain the main results of this paper. The results of this paper can be used in different applications of geometric algebras in computer graphics, computer vision, engineering, and physics. The presented explicit formulas for characteristic polynomial coefficients can also be used in symbolic computation.

Keywords: Geometric algebra · Clifford algebra · Characteristic polynomial

1 Introduction

In this paper, we discuss characteristic polynomials in (Clifford) geometric algebras. In [19], explicit formulas for all characteristic polynomial coefficients in geometric algebras $\mathcal{G}_{p,q}$, $p + q = n \leq 4$ are presented. These formulas involve only the operations of geometric product, summation, and operations of conjugation (the grade involution, the reversion, and one additional operation of conjugation $\triangle$). In this paper, we generalize results obtained in [19] to the case $n = 5$. Also we present an analytic proof of the formulas in the case $n = 4$ (some of the formulas were proved using computer calculations in [19]). We present some new properties of operations of conjugation and grade projection and use them to obtain the main results of this paper. The presented explicit formulas for characteristic polynomial coefficients can be used in symbolic computation using different software [1,9,18,25].

© Springer Nature Switzerland AG 2021
N. Magnenat-Thalmann et al. (Eds.): CGI 2021, LNCS 13002, pp. 670–681, 2021.
https://doi.org/10.1007/978-3-030-89029-2_50

The geometric algebras of vector spaces of dimensions $n = 4$ and 5 are important for different applications. The space-time algebra $\mathcal{G}_{1,3}$ is widely used for applications in physics [6,11,15], the conformal geometric algebra $\mathcal{G}_{4,1}$ is widely used in computer science and engineering [3,7,12,16].

The characteristic polynomial and related concepts (eigenvectors, eigenvalues) are widely used in computer vision (see, for example, on eigenfaces and the computer vision problem of human face recognition [4,26,27]). The characteristic polynomial coefficients are used to solve the Sylvester and Lyapunov equations in geometric algebra [20,21].

2   Grade Projections and Operations of Conjugation in Geometric Algebras

Let us consider the (Clifford) geometric algebra $\mathcal{G}_{p,q}$, $p + q = n$ [11,15,17] with the generators $e_1, e_2, \ldots, e_n$ and the identity element e. The generators satisfy the conditions

$$e_a e_b + e_b e_a = 2\eta_{ab} e, \qquad a, b = 1, \ldots, n,$$

where $\eta = (\eta_{ab}) = \operatorname{diag}(1, \ldots, 1, -1, \ldots, -1)$ is the diagonal matrix with its first p entries equal to 1 and the last q entries equal to -1 on the diagonal.

We call the subspace of $\mathcal{G}_{p,q}$ of elements, which are linear combinations of the basis elements

$$e_{a_1 \ldots a_k} := e_{a_1} \cdots e_{a_k}, \qquad a_1 < a_2 < \cdots < a_k, \qquad k = 0, 1, \ldots, n, \qquad (1)$$

with multi-indices of length k, the subspace of grade k and denote it by $\mathcal{G}_{p,q}^k$. Elements of grade 0 are identified with scalars $\mathcal{G}_{p,q}^0 \equiv \mathbb{R}, e \equiv 1$. The projection of any element $U \in \mathcal{G}_{p,q}$ onto the subspace $\mathcal{G}_{p,q}^k$ is denoted by $\langle U \rangle_k$ (or U_k to simplify notation) in this paper. We have

$$\langle U + V \rangle_k = \langle U \rangle_k + \langle V \rangle_k, \qquad \langle \lambda U \rangle_k = \lambda \langle U \rangle_k, \qquad \lambda \in \mathbb{R}, \quad U, V \in \mathcal{G}_{p,q}. \qquad (2)$$

An arbitrary element $U \in \mathcal{G}_{p,q}$ can be written in the form

$$U = \sum_{k=0}^{n} \langle U \rangle_k, \qquad \langle U \rangle_k \in \mathcal{G}_{p,q}^k. \qquad (3)$$

The scalar $\langle U \rangle_0$ is called the scalar part of U. We have the property

$$\langle UV \rangle_0 = \langle VU \rangle_0, \qquad \forall U, V \in \mathcal{G}_{p,q}. \qquad (4)$$

Definition 1 ([19]). Any operation of the form

$$U \mapsto \sum_{k=0}^{n} \lambda_k \langle U \rangle_k, \qquad \lambda_k = \pm 1 \qquad (5)$$

is called *an operation of conjugation* in $\mathcal{G}_{p,q}$.

Note that the operation of conjugation is an involution: the square of each operation equals the identical operation. The operations of conjugation commute with each other. We have three classical operations of conjugation: the grade involution, the reversion, and the Clifford conjugation[1]:

$$\hat{U} = \sum_{k=0}^{n} (-1)^k \langle U \rangle_k, \quad \tilde{U} = \sum_{k=0}^{n} (-1)^{\frac{k(k-1)}{2}} \langle U \rangle_k, \quad \widehat{\tilde{U}} = \sum_{k=0}^{n} (-1)^{\frac{k(k+1)}{2}} \langle U \rangle_k. \quad (6)$$

These operations have the following properties

$$\widehat{UV} = \hat{U}\hat{V}, \qquad \widetilde{UV} = \tilde{V}\tilde{U}, \qquad \widehat{\widetilde{UV}} = \widehat{\tilde{V}}\widehat{\tilde{U}}, \qquad \forall U, V \in \mathcal{G}_{p,q}. \quad (7)$$

Definition 2 ([19]). We call an operation of conjugation of the form

$$U^\triangle = \sum_{k=0}^{n} (-1)^{\frac{k(k-1)(k-2)(k-3)}{24}} \langle U \rangle_k \quad (8)$$

an additional operation of conjugation in $\mathcal{G}_{p,q}$ (or $\triangle$-conjugation).

Note that we have $(UV)^\triangle \neq U^\triangle V^\triangle$ and $(UV)^\triangle \neq V^\triangle U^\triangle$ in the general case. However, the operation $\triangle$ has the following weaker property by Lemma 1 and (4):

$$\langle (UV)^\triangle \rangle_0 = \langle U^\triangle V^\triangle \rangle_0 = \langle V^\triangle U^\triangle \rangle_0, \quad \forall U, V \in \mathcal{G}_{p,q}. \quad (9)$$

We widely use the operation $\triangle$ in this paper.

We need the following two lemmas to prove the main results of this paper.

Lemma 1. *We have the following properties*

$$\langle UV^\star \rangle_0 = \langle U^\star V \rangle_0, \quad \forall U, V \in \mathcal{G}_{p,q}, \quad (10)$$
$$\langle U^\star V^\star \rangle_0 = \langle UV \rangle_0, \quad \forall U, V \in \mathcal{G}_{p,q}, \quad (11)$$

where $\star$ is any operation of conjugation (3);

$$\langle U \rangle_0 = \langle U^\bullet \rangle_0, \quad \forall U \in \mathcal{G}_{p,q}, \quad (12)$$
$$\langle U^\bullet V^\bullet \rangle_0 = \langle (UV)^\bullet \rangle_0, \quad \forall U, V \in \mathcal{G}_{p,q}, \quad (13)$$

where $\bullet$ is any operation of conjugation (3) that does not change the sign of grade 0 (i.e. $\lambda_0 = +1$).

---

[1] The Clifford conjugation is a superposition of the grade involution $\hat{}$ and the reversion $\tilde{}$. Note that some authors [17] denote the Clifford conjugation by $\overline{}$. We do not use separate notation for the Clifford conjugation in this paper and write the combination of the two symbols $\hat{}$ and $\tilde{}$.

Proof. If

$$U = X + x, \qquad \text{where} \qquad (X + x)^\star = X - x,$$
$$V = Y + y, \qquad \text{where} \qquad (Y + y)^\star = Y - y,$$

then

$$\langle Xy \rangle_0 = \langle Yx \rangle_0 = 0, \tag{14}$$

because the elements X and y are of different grades (similarly for the elements Y and x) by construction. Using (14) and (2), we get

$$\langle UV^\star \rangle_0 = \langle (X + x)(Y - y) \rangle_0 = \langle XY - Xy + xY - xy \rangle_0 = \langle XY - xy \rangle_0, \tag{15}$$
$$\langle U^\star V \rangle_0 = \langle (X - x)(Y + y) \rangle_0 = \langle XY + Xy - xY - xy \rangle_0 = \langle XY - xy \rangle_0. \tag{16}$$

From the equality of the right-hand sides of the expressions (15), (16), we get the equality of the left-hand sides (10). Substituting $U^\star$ for U in (10), we get (11). Substituting e for V in (10) and using $e^\bullet = e$, we get (12)[2]. Using (11) and (12), we get (13). □

In the next lemma, we discuss the relation between the operations of conjugation (left-hand sides of the equalities) and the grade projections (right-hand sides of the equalities). Note that the same left-hand sides of equalities are used in [19] to realize the scalar part operation $\langle \ \rangle_0$ in the cases of smaller dimensions n. For example, the left-hand side of (18) is equal to $4\langle U \rangle_0$ in the cases $n \leq 6$.

Lemma 2. *For $n \leq 7$, the following equalities hold*

$$U + \widehat{\widetilde{U}} = 2(U_0 + U_3 + U_4 + U_7), \tag{17}$$

$$U + \widehat{\widetilde{U}} + \widehat{U}^\triangle + \widetilde{U}^\triangle = 4(U_0 + U_7), \tag{18}$$

$$U + \widehat{U} + \widetilde{U}^\triangle + \widehat{\widetilde{U}}^\triangle = 4(U_0 + U_6), \tag{19}$$

$$U + \widetilde{U} + \widehat{U}^\triangle + \widehat{\widetilde{U}}^\triangle = 4(U_0 + U_5), \tag{20}$$

$$U + \widehat{U} + \widetilde{U} + \widehat{\widetilde{U}} = 4(U_0 + U_4), \tag{21}$$

where the simplified notation U_k is used for $\langle U \rangle_k$.

Proof. The proof is by direct calculation. For example, from (3) and (6), we have

$$U = U_0 + U_1 + U_2 + U_3 + U_4 + U_5 + U_6 + U_7, \tag{22}$$
$$\widehat{\widetilde{U}} = U_0 - U_1 - U_2 + U_3 + U_4 - U_5 - U_6 + U_7. \tag{23}$$

Summing (22) and (23), we obtain the expression (17) from Lemma 2

$$U + \widehat{\widetilde{U}} = 2U_0 + 2U_3 + 2U_4 + 2U_7.$$

Similarly one can prove all the other equalities from Lemma 2. □

---

[2] Note that the property (12) is also follows from the definition of $\bullet$ and the fact that grade projections commute with operations of conjugation.

3   Characteristic Polynomials in Geometric Algebras

Characteristic polynomials in geometric algebras $\mathcal{G}_{p,q}$, $n = p + q$, are discussed in [10] and [19]. We use the notation $N := 2^{[\frac{n+1}{2}]}$, where square brackets mean taking the integer part.

Definition 3 ([19]). Let us consider an arbitrary element $U \in \mathcal{G}_{p,q}$. We call *the characteristic polynomial* of U

$$\varphi_U(\lambda) := \det(\beta(\lambda e - U)) = \mathrm{Det}(\lambda e - U) =$$
$$= \lambda^N - C_{(1)}\lambda^{N-1} - \cdots - C_{(N-1)}\lambda - C_{(N)} \in \mathcal{G}_{p,q}^0, \tag{24}$$

where $C_{(j)} = C_{(j)}(U) = c_{(j)}(\beta(U)) \in \mathcal{G}_{p,q}^0 \equiv \mathbb{R}, j = 1, \ldots, N$ can be interpreted as constants or as elements of grade 0 and are called *characteristic polynomial coefficients* of U. Here $c_{(j)}(\beta(U))$ are the ordinary characteristic polynomial coefficients of the matrix $\beta(U)$ and

$$\beta : \mathcal{G}_{p,q} \to \beta(\mathcal{G}_{p,q}) \subset M_{p,q} := \begin{cases} \mathrm{Mat}(2^{\frac{n}{2}}, \mathbb{C}), & \text{if } n \text{ is even,} \\ \mathrm{Mat}(2^{\frac{n-1}{2}}, \mathbb{C}) \oplus \mathrm{Mat}(2^{\frac{n-1}{2}}, \mathbb{C}), & \text{if } n \text{ is odd,} \end{cases}$$

is a representation of $\mathcal{G}_{p,q}$ (of not minimal dimension, see the details in [19]).

Note that the trace $\mathrm{Tr}(U) = C_{(1)}$ and the determinant $\mathrm{Det}(U) = -C_{(N)}$ are particular cases of characteristic polynomial coefficients. The explicit formulas for the determinant allow us to calculate the adjugate $\mathrm{Adj}(U)$ and the inverse U^{-1} in $\mathcal{G}_{p,q}$ (see [2,13,19]).

We use the following recursive formulas for the characteristic polynomial coefficients $C_{(k)}$, $k = 1, \ldots, N$, $N = 2^{[\frac{n+1}{2}]}$ from [19]. The elements $U_{(k)} \in \mathcal{G}_{p,q}$, $k = 1, \ldots, N$, are auxiliary.

Theorem 1 ([19]). *Let us consider an arbitrary element* $U \in \mathcal{G}_{p,q}$, $n = p + q$, $N = 2^{[\frac{n+1}{2}]}$. *Setting* $U_{(1)} = U$, *we have*

$$U_{(k+1)} = U(U_{(k)} - C_{(k)}), \qquad C_{(k)} = \frac{N}{k}\langle U_{(k)}\rangle_0, \quad k = 1, \ldots, N, \tag{25}$$

$$\mathrm{Det}(U) = -U_{(N)} = -C_{(N)} = U(C_{(N-1)} - U_{(N-1)}), \tag{26}$$

$$\mathrm{Adj}(U) = C_{(N-1)} - U_{(N-1)}, \qquad U^{-1} = \frac{\mathrm{Adj}(U)}{\mathrm{Det}(U)}. \tag{27}$$

4   The Cases $n \leq 4$

The explicit formulas for all characteristic polynomial coefficients in $\mathcal{G}_{p,q}$, $n = p + q \leq 4$ were presented in [19]. These formulas were obtained using the algorithm from Theorem 1. The formulas (29) and (30) were proved in [19] using computer calculations, all other formulas from Theorem 2 were proved analytically. We present an analytic proof of the formulas (29) and (30) for the first time in this paper.

Theorem 2. *In the cases* $n = 1, 2, 3, 4$, *we have the following explicit formulas for the characteristic polynomial coefficients* $C_{(k)} \in \mathcal{G}_{p,q}^0$, $k = 1, 2, \ldots, N$:

$$n = 1, \qquad C_{(1)} = U + \widehat{U}, \qquad C_{(2)} = -U\widehat{U};$$

$$n = 2, \qquad C_{(1)} = U + \widehat{\widetilde{U}}, \qquad C_{(2)} = -U\widehat{\widetilde{U}};$$

$$n = 3, \qquad C_{(1)} = U + \widehat{U} + \widetilde{U} + \widehat{\widetilde{U}},$$

$$C_{(2)} = -(U\widetilde{U} + U\widehat{U} + U\widehat{\widetilde{U}} + \widehat{U}\widehat{\widetilde{U}} + \widetilde{U}\widehat{\widetilde{U}} + \widehat{U}\widetilde{U}),$$

$$C_{(3)} = U\widehat{U}\widetilde{U} + U\widehat{U}\widehat{\widetilde{U}} + U\widetilde{U}\widehat{\widetilde{U}} + \widehat{U}\widetilde{U}\widehat{\widetilde{U}}, \quad C_{(4)} = -U\widehat{U}\widetilde{U}\widehat{\widetilde{U}};$$

$$n = 4, \qquad C_{(1)} = U + \widehat{\widetilde{U}} + \widehat{U}^\triangle + \widetilde{U}^\triangle, \tag{28}$$

$$C_{(2)} = -(U\widehat{\widetilde{U}} + U\widehat{U}^\triangle + U\widetilde{U}^\triangle + \widehat{\widetilde{U}}\widehat{U}^\triangle + \widehat{\widetilde{U}}\widetilde{U}^\triangle + (\widehat{U}\widetilde{U})^\triangle), \tag{29}$$

$$C_{(3)} = U\widehat{\widetilde{U}}\widehat{U}^\triangle + U\widehat{\widetilde{U}}\widetilde{U}^\triangle + U(\widehat{U}\widetilde{U})^\triangle + \widehat{\widetilde{U}}(\widehat{U}\widetilde{U})^\triangle, \tag{30}$$

$$C_{(4)} = -U\widehat{\widetilde{U}}(\widehat{U}\widetilde{U})^\triangle. \tag{31}$$

Proof (of (29)). Our analytical proof of the formula (29) for $C_{(2)}$ in the case $n = 4$ is in two steps. Step 1: we prove that the projection of the expression (29) onto the subspace of grade 0 is equal to $C_{(2)}$ from (25). Step 2: we prove that the expression (29) belongs to $\mathcal{G}_{p,q}^0$.

Step 1: Using (25), (28), and (2), we get

$$C_{(2)} = 2\langle U(U - C_{(1)})\rangle_0 = -2\langle U(\widehat{\widetilde{U}} + \widehat{U}^\triangle + \widetilde{U}^\triangle)\rangle_0$$

$$= -\langle U\widehat{\widetilde{U}}\rangle_0 - \langle U\widehat{U}^\triangle\rangle_0 - \langle U\widetilde{U}^\triangle\rangle_0 - \langle U\widehat{\widetilde{U}}\rangle_0 - \langle U\widehat{U}^\triangle\rangle_0 - \langle U\widetilde{U}^\triangle\rangle_0.$$

Using the properties (10) and (12) for the operations $\widehat{}$, $\widetilde{}$, and $\triangle$, we get

$$\langle U\widehat{\widetilde{U}}\rangle_0 = \langle \widehat{U}\widetilde{U}\rangle_0 = \langle (\widehat{U}\widetilde{U})^\triangle\rangle_0, \quad \langle U\widehat{U}^\triangle\rangle_0 = \langle \widehat{\widetilde{U}}\widetilde{U}^\triangle\rangle_0, \quad \langle U\widetilde{U}^\triangle\rangle_0 = \langle \widehat{\widetilde{U}}\widehat{U}^\triangle\rangle_0.$$

Finally, we obtain

$$C_{(2)} = -\langle U\widehat{\widetilde{U}} + U\widehat{U}^\triangle + U\widetilde{U}^\triangle + \widehat{\widetilde{U}}\widehat{U}^\triangle + \widehat{\widetilde{U}}\widetilde{U}^\triangle + (\widehat{U}\widetilde{U})^\triangle\rangle_0, \tag{32}$$

which differs from (29) only by the scalar part operation.

Step 2: Using the properties (7), we conclude that the expression $U\widehat{\widetilde{U}} + (\widehat{U}\widetilde{U})^\triangle$ does not change under the operations $\widehat{\widetilde{}}$ and $\widehat{\triangle}$:

$$U\widehat{\widetilde{U}} + (\widehat{U}\widetilde{U})^\triangle = (U\widehat{\widetilde{U}} + (\widehat{U}\widetilde{U})^\triangle)^{\widehat{\widetilde{}}} = (U\widehat{\widetilde{U}} + (\widehat{U}\widetilde{U})^\triangle)^{\widehat{\triangle}}. \tag{33}$$

This means that the sum of the first and the last two terms of (29) belongs to the subspace of grade 0:

$$U\widehat{\widetilde{U}} + (\widehat{U}\widetilde{U})^\triangle \in \mathcal{G}_{p,q}^0. \tag{34}$$

For the other four terms of (29), using (17), we get[34]

$$U\widehat{U}^{\triangle} + \widehat{\widetilde{U}}\widetilde{U}^{\triangle} + U\widetilde{U}^{\triangle} + \widehat{\widetilde{U}}\widehat{U}^{\triangle} = (U + \widehat{\widetilde{U}})(U + \widehat{\widetilde{U}})^{\widetilde{\triangle}}$$
$$= 4(U_0 + U_3 + U_4)(U_0 - U_3 - U_4)$$
$$= 4(U_0^2 - U_3^2 - U_4^2 - \{U_3, U_4\} - [U_0, U_3 + U_4])$$
$$= 4(U_0^2 - U_3^2 - U_4^2) \in \mathcal{G}_{p,q}^0, \tag{35}$$

because $U_0^2, U_3^2, U_4^2 \in \mathcal{G}_{p,q}^0$ and $\{U_3, U_4\} = 0$ (see, for example, [22]). Summing (34) and (35), we conclude that the expression (29) belongs to $\mathcal{G}_{p,q}^0$.   □

Proof (of (30)). The analytical proof of the formula (30) for $C_{(3)}$ is in two steps.

Step 1: Using the properties (4), (10), and (12) for the operations $\widehat{}$, $\widetilde{}$, and $\triangle$, we get

$$\langle U\widehat{\widetilde{U}}\widehat{U}^{\triangle}\rangle_0 = \langle U\widehat{\widetilde{U}}\widetilde{U}^{\triangle}\rangle_0 = \langle U(\widehat{U}\widetilde{U})^{\triangle}\rangle_0 = \langle \widehat{\widetilde{U}}(\widehat{U}\widetilde{U})^{\triangle}\rangle_0. \tag{36}$$

Using (25), (2), (28), (29), and (36), we get

$$U_{(2)} = U(U - C_{(1)}) = -(U\widehat{\widetilde{U}} + U\widehat{U}^{\triangle} + U\widetilde{U}^{\triangle}),$$

$$C_{(3)} = \frac{4}{3}\langle U(U_{(2)} - C_{(2)})\rangle_0 = \frac{4}{3}\langle U\widehat{\widetilde{U}}\widehat{U}^{\triangle} + U\widehat{\widetilde{U}}\widetilde{U}^{\triangle} + U(\widehat{U}\widetilde{U})^{\triangle}\rangle_0$$

$$= \langle U\widehat{\widetilde{U}}\widehat{U}^{\triangle} + U\widehat{\widetilde{U}}\widetilde{U}^{\triangle} + U(\widehat{U}\widetilde{U})^{\triangle} + \widehat{\widetilde{U}}(\widehat{U}\widetilde{U})^{\triangle}\rangle_0, \tag{37}$$

which differs from (30) only by the scalar part operation.

Step 2: Let us prove that the expression (30) belongs to $\mathcal{G}_{p,q}^0$. It can be represented in the form

$$(\widehat{U}\widetilde{U})\widehat{}(U + \widehat{\widetilde{U}})^{\widehat{\triangle}} + (U + \widehat{\widetilde{U}})(\widehat{U}\widetilde{U})^{\triangle} = \widehat{A}\widehat{B}^{\triangle} + BA^{\triangle}, \tag{38}$$

where we use the notation $A := \widehat{U}\widetilde{U}$ and $B := U + \widehat{\widetilde{U}}$. Using $\widehat{\widetilde{A}} = A$ and (17), we get

$$A = A_0 + A_3 + A_4, \qquad B = B_0 + B_3 + B_4, \qquad \text{where} \quad A_i, B_i \in \mathcal{G}_{p,q}^i.$$

Therefore, the expression (38) is equal to

$$(A_0 - A_3 + A_4)(B_0 - B_3 - B_4) + (B_0 + B_3 + B_4)(A_0 + A_3 - A_4)$$
$$= \{A_0, B_0\} - [A_0, B_3] - [A_0, B_4] - [A_3, B_0] + \{A_3, B_3\} + \{A_3, B_4\} + [A_4, B_0]$$
$$-\{A_4, B_3\} + \{A_4, B_4\} = \{A_0, B_0\} + \{A_3, B_3\} + \{A_4, B_4\},$$

which belongs to $\mathcal{G}_{p,q}^0$ because $\{U_{n-1}, V_n\} = 0$ for even n and the expressions $\{U_0, V_0\}$, $\{U_{n-1}, V_{n-1}\}$, $\{U_n, V_n\}$ belong to $\mathcal{G}_{p,q}^0$ (see, for example, [22][5]). Therefore the expression (30) belongs to $\mathcal{G}_{p,q}^0$.   □

---

[3] The commutator and anticommutator of two arbitrary elements $U, V \in \mathcal{G}_{p,q}$ are denoted by $[U, V] = UV - VU$ and $\{U, V\} = UV + VU$ respectively.

[4] We remind that we use the simplified notation $U_k := \langle U\rangle_k$ in this paper.

[5] Alternatively, we can use the quaternion type classification of Clifford algebra elements [23, 24] to prove this.

5   The Case $n = 5$

In this section, we present explicit formulas for all characteristic polynomial coefficients in the geometric algebras $\mathcal{G}_{p,q}$, $n = p + q = 5$. The formula (46) for $C_{(8)} = -\mathrm{Det}(U)$ is presented in [19] and in some another form in [2]. The formula for $C_{(1)} = \mathrm{Tr}(U)$ is also presented in [19]. The explicit formulas for $C_{(2)}$, $C_{(3)}$, $C_{(4)}$, $C_{(5)}$, $C_{(6)}$, $C_{(7)}$ are presented in this paper for the first time.

Theorem 3. *In the case $n = 5$, we have the following explicit formulas for the characteristic polynomial coefficients $C_{(k)} \in \mathcal{G}_{p,q}^0$, $k = 1, 2, \ldots, 8$:*

$$C_{(1)} = U + \widehat{\widetilde{U}} + \widehat{U} + \widetilde{U} + \widehat{U}^\triangle + \widetilde{U}^\triangle + U^\triangle + \widehat{\widetilde{U}}^\triangle, \tag{39}$$

$$\begin{aligned}
C_{(2)} = -(&U\widehat{\widetilde{U}} + U\widehat{U} + U\widetilde{U} + U\widehat{U}^\triangle + U\widetilde{U}^\triangle + UU^\triangle + U\widehat{\widetilde{U}}^\triangle \\
&+ \widehat{U}\widetilde{U} + \widehat{\widetilde{U}}\widetilde{U} + \widehat{\widetilde{U}}\widehat{U} + \widehat{\widetilde{U}}\widetilde{U}^\triangle + \widehat{\widetilde{U}}\widehat{U}^\triangle + \widehat{U}\widehat{U}^\triangle + \widehat{U}U^\triangle \\
&+ (\widehat{U}\widetilde{U})^\triangle + (\widehat{U}U)^\triangle + (\widehat{U}\widehat{\widetilde{U}})^\triangle + \widetilde{U}\widehat{\widetilde{U}}^\triangle + \widetilde{U}U^\triangle + \widetilde{U}\widetilde{U}^\triangle + \widehat{U}\widetilde{U}^\triangle \\
&+ (U\widehat{\widetilde{U}})^\triangle + (\widetilde{U}\widehat{\widetilde{U}})^\triangle + (\widetilde{U}U)^\triangle + \widehat{U}U^\triangle + \widehat{U}\widehat{\widetilde{U}}^\triangle + \widehat{\widetilde{U}}\widehat{\widetilde{U}}^\triangle + \widetilde{U}\widehat{U}^\triangle),
\end{aligned} \tag{40}$$

$$\begin{aligned}
C_{(3)} = \ &U\widehat{\widetilde{U}}\widehat{U} + U\widehat{\widetilde{U}}\widetilde{U} + U\widehat{U}\widetilde{U} + \widehat{\widetilde{U}}\widehat{U}\widetilde{U} + U\widehat{\widetilde{U}}\widehat{U}^\triangle + U\widehat{\widetilde{U}}\widetilde{U}^\triangle + U\widehat{U}U^\triangle \\
&+ U\widehat{U}\widehat{U}^\triangle + U\widehat{U}\widetilde{U}^\triangle + U\widehat{U}U^\triangle + U\widehat{U}\widehat{\widetilde{U}}^\triangle + U\widehat{U}\widetilde{U}^\triangle + \widehat{\widetilde{U}}\widehat{U}\widehat{U}^\triangle + \widehat{\widetilde{U}}\widehat{U}\widetilde{U}^\triangle \\
&+ \widehat{U}\widetilde{U}\widehat{U}^\triangle + \widehat{U}\widetilde{U}\widetilde{U}^\triangle + \widehat{U}\widetilde{U}U^\triangle + \widehat{U}\widetilde{U}\widehat{\widetilde{U}}^\triangle + U\widetilde{U}\widehat{U}^\triangle + U\widetilde{U}U^\triangle + U\widehat{U}\widehat{\widetilde{U}}^\triangle \\
&+ \widehat{\widetilde{U}}\widehat{U}U^\triangle + \widehat{\widetilde{U}}\widehat{U}\widehat{\widetilde{U}}^\triangle + \widehat{\widetilde{U}}\widetilde{U}\widehat{U}^\triangle + \widehat{\widetilde{U}}\widetilde{U}\widetilde{U}^\triangle + \widehat{\widetilde{U}}\widetilde{U}U^\triangle + \widehat{\widetilde{U}}\widetilde{U}\widehat{\widetilde{U}}^\triangle + U\widehat{\widetilde{U}}\widehat{\widetilde{U}}^\triangle \\
&+ \widehat{U}(\widehat{U}U)^\triangle + U(\widehat{U}\widetilde{U})^\triangle + U(\widehat{U}U)^\triangle + U(\widehat{U}\widehat{\widetilde{U}})^\triangle + U(\widehat{U}U)^\triangle + U(\widehat{U}\widetilde{U})^\triangle \\
&+ U(U\widehat{\widetilde{U}})^\triangle + \widehat{\widetilde{U}}(\widehat{U}\widetilde{U})^\triangle + \widehat{\widetilde{U}}(\widehat{U}U)^\triangle + \widehat{\widetilde{U}}(\widehat{U}\widehat{\widetilde{U}})^\triangle + \widehat{\widetilde{U}}(\widetilde{U}U)^\triangle + \widehat{\widetilde{U}}(\widetilde{U}\widehat{\widetilde{U}})^\triangle \\
&+ \widehat{\widetilde{U}}(U\widehat{\widetilde{U}})^\triangle + \widehat{U}(\widehat{U}\widetilde{U})^\triangle + \widehat{U}(\widehat{U}\widehat{\widetilde{U}})^\triangle + \widehat{U}(\widetilde{U}U)^\triangle + \widehat{U}(\widehat{U}U)^\triangle + \widehat{U}(U\widehat{\widetilde{U}})^\triangle \\
&+ \widetilde{U}(\widehat{U}\widetilde{U})^\triangle + \widetilde{U}(\widehat{U}U)^\triangle + \widetilde{U}(U\widehat{\widetilde{U}})^\triangle + \widetilde{U}(\widetilde{U}U)^\triangle + \widetilde{U}(\widehat{\widetilde{U}}\widetilde{U})^\triangle + \widetilde{U}(U\widehat{U})^\triangle \\
&+ (\widehat{U}\widetilde{U}U)^\triangle + (\widehat{U}\widetilde{U}\widehat{\widetilde{U}})^\triangle + (\widehat{U}U\widehat{\widetilde{U}})^\triangle + (\widetilde{U}U\widehat{\widetilde{U}})^\triangle,
\end{aligned} \tag{41}$$

$$\begin{aligned}
C_{(4)} = -(&U\widehat{\widetilde{U}}\widehat{U}\widetilde{U} + U\widehat{\widetilde{U}}\widehat{U}U^\triangle + U\widehat{\widetilde{U}}\widehat{U}\widetilde{U}^\triangle + U\widehat{\widetilde{U}}\widehat{U}U^\triangle + U\widehat{\widetilde{U}}\widehat{U}\widehat{\widetilde{U}}^\triangle + U\widehat{\widetilde{U}}\widetilde{U}U^\triangle \\
&+ U\widehat{\widetilde{U}}\widetilde{U}U^\triangle + U\widehat{\widetilde{U}}\widetilde{U}U^\triangle + U\widehat{\widetilde{U}}\widetilde{U}\widehat{\widetilde{U}}^\triangle + U\widehat{U}\widetilde{U}U^\triangle + U\widehat{U}\widetilde{U}U^\triangle + U\widehat{U}\widetilde{U}U^\triangle \\
&+ \widehat{\widetilde{U}}\widehat{U}\widetilde{U}U^\triangle + \widehat{\widetilde{U}}\widehat{U}\widetilde{U}U^\triangle + \widehat{\widetilde{U}}\widehat{U}\widetilde{U}\widehat{\widetilde{U}}^\triangle + U\widehat{U}\widetilde{U}\widehat{\widetilde{U}}^\triangle + \widehat{\widetilde{U}}\widehat{U}(\widehat{U}\widetilde{U})^\triangle + \widehat{\widetilde{U}}\widehat{U}(\widehat{U}U)^\triangle \\
&+ U\widehat{\widetilde{U}}(\widetilde{U}U)^\triangle + U\widehat{\widetilde{U}}(\widetilde{U}\widehat{\widetilde{U}})^\triangle + U\widehat{\widetilde{U}}(U\widehat{\widetilde{U}})^\triangle + U\widehat{\widetilde{U}}(\widehat{U}\widetilde{U})^\triangle + U\widehat{\widetilde{U}}(\widehat{U}U)^\triangle + U\widehat{\widetilde{U}}(\widehat{U}\widehat{\widetilde{U}})^\triangle \\
&+ U\widehat{U}(\widehat{U}\widetilde{U})^\triangle + U\widehat{U}(\widehat{U}U)^\triangle + U\widehat{U}(\widehat{U}\widehat{\widetilde{U}})^\triangle + U\widehat{U}(\widetilde{U}U)^\triangle + U\widehat{U}(\widehat{U}\widetilde{U})^\triangle + \widehat{\widetilde{U}}\widehat{U}(\widehat{U}\widetilde{U})^\triangle \\
&+ U\widehat{U}(U\widehat{\widetilde{U}})^\triangle + U\widetilde{U}(\widehat{U}\widetilde{U})^\triangle + U\widetilde{U}(\widehat{U}U)^\triangle + U\widetilde{U}(U\widehat{\widetilde{U}})^\triangle + U\widetilde{U}(\widetilde{U}U)^\triangle + U\widetilde{U}(\widehat{\widetilde{U}}\widetilde{U})^\triangle \\
&+ U\widetilde{U}(U\widehat{\widetilde{U}})^\triangle + U(\widehat{U}\widetilde{U}U)^\triangle + U(\widehat{U}\widetilde{U}\widehat{\widetilde{U}})^\triangle + U(\widehat{U}U\widehat{\widetilde{U}})^\triangle + U(\widetilde{U}U\widehat{\widetilde{U}})^\triangle + \widehat{\widetilde{U}}\widehat{U}\widetilde{U}U^\triangle \\
&+ \widehat{\widetilde{U}}\widehat{U}(\widetilde{U}U)^\triangle + \widehat{\widetilde{U}}\widehat{U}(\widetilde{U}\widehat{\widetilde{U}})^\triangle + \widehat{\widetilde{U}}\widehat{U}(U\widehat{\widetilde{U}})^\triangle + \widehat{\widetilde{U}}\widehat{U}(\widehat{U}U)^\triangle + \widehat{\widetilde{U}}\widehat{U}(\widehat{U}U)^\triangle + \widehat{\widetilde{U}}\widehat{U}(\widehat{U}\widehat{\widetilde{U}})^\triangle \\
&+ \widehat{\widetilde{U}}\widetilde{U}(\widehat{U}U)^\triangle + \widehat{\widetilde{U}}\widetilde{U}(\widehat{U}\widehat{\widetilde{U}})^\triangle + \widehat{\widetilde{U}}\widetilde{U}(U\widehat{\widetilde{U}})^\triangle + \widehat{\widetilde{U}}(\widehat{U}\widetilde{U}U)^\triangle + \widehat{\widetilde{U}}(\widehat{U}\widetilde{U}\widehat{\widetilde{U}})^\triangle + \widehat{\widetilde{U}}(\widehat{U}U\widehat{\widetilde{U}})^\triangle \\
&+ \widehat{\widetilde{U}}(\widetilde{U}U\widehat{\widetilde{U}})^\triangle + \widehat{U}\widetilde{U}(\widehat{U}U)^\triangle + \widehat{U}\widetilde{U}(\widehat{U}U)^\triangle + \widehat{U}\widetilde{U}(U\widehat{\widetilde{U}})^\triangle + \widehat{U}\widetilde{U}(\widetilde{U}U)^\triangle + \widehat{U}\widetilde{U}(\widehat{\widetilde{U}}\widetilde{U})^\triangle \\
&+ \widehat{U}\widetilde{U}(U\widehat{\widetilde{U}})^\triangle + \widehat{U}(\widehat{U}\widetilde{U}U)^\triangle + \widehat{U}(\widehat{U}\widetilde{U}\widehat{\widetilde{U}})^\triangle + \widehat{U}(\widehat{U}U\widehat{\widetilde{U}})^\triangle + \widehat{U}(\widetilde{U}U\widehat{\widetilde{U}})^\triangle + \widetilde{U}(\widehat{U}\widetilde{U}U)^\triangle
\end{aligned}$$

$$+ \widetilde{U}(\widehat{U}\widetilde{U}\widehat{U})^\triangle + \widetilde{U}(\widehat{U}U\widehat{\widetilde{U}})^\triangle + \widetilde{U}(\widetilde{U}U\widehat{\widetilde{U}})^\triangle + (\widehat{U}\widetilde{U}U\widehat{\widetilde{U}})^\triangle), \tag{42}$$

$$C_{(5)} = U\widehat{\widetilde{U}}\widehat{U}\widetilde{U}\widehat{U}^\triangle + U\widehat{\widetilde{U}}\widehat{U}\widetilde{U}\widetilde{U}^\triangle + U\widehat{\widetilde{U}}\widehat{U}\widetilde{U}U^\triangle + U\widehat{\widetilde{U}}\widehat{U}\widetilde{U}\widehat{\widetilde{U}}^\triangle + U\widehat{\widetilde{U}}\widehat{U}(\widehat{U}\widetilde{U})^\triangle$$

$$+ U\widehat{\widetilde{U}}\widehat{U}(\widehat{U}U)^\triangle + U\widehat{\widetilde{U}}\widehat{U}(\widehat{U}\widehat{\widetilde{U}})^\triangle + U\widehat{\widetilde{U}}\widehat{U}(\widetilde{U}U)^\triangle + U\widehat{\widetilde{U}}\widehat{U}(\widehat{\widetilde{U}}\widehat{U})^\triangle + U\widehat{\widetilde{U}}\widehat{U}(U\widehat{\widetilde{U}})^\triangle$$

$$+ U\widehat{\widetilde{U}}\widetilde{U}(\widehat{U}\widetilde{U})^\triangle + U\widehat{\widetilde{U}}\widetilde{U}(\widehat{U}U)^\triangle + U\widehat{\widetilde{U}}\widetilde{U}(\widehat{U}\widehat{\widetilde{U}})^\triangle + U\widehat{\widetilde{U}}\widetilde{U}(\widetilde{U}U)^\triangle + U\widehat{\widetilde{U}}\widetilde{U}(\widehat{\widetilde{U}}\widehat{U})^\triangle$$

$$+ U\widehat{\widetilde{U}}\widetilde{U}(U\widehat{\widetilde{U}})^\triangle + U\widehat{U}(\widehat{U}\widetilde{U}U)^\triangle + U\widehat{U}(\widehat{U}\widehat{\widetilde{U}}\widehat{U})^\triangle + U\widehat{U}(\widehat{U}U\widehat{\widetilde{U}})^\triangle + U\widehat{U}(\widetilde{U}U\widehat{\widetilde{U}})^\triangle$$

$$+ U\widehat{U}\widetilde{U}(\widehat{U}\widetilde{U})^\triangle + U\widehat{U}\widetilde{U}(\widehat{U}U)^\triangle + U\widehat{U}\widetilde{U}(\widehat{U}\widehat{\widetilde{U}})^\triangle + U\widehat{U}\widetilde{U}(\widetilde{U}U)^\triangle + U\widehat{U}\widetilde{U}(\widehat{\widetilde{U}}\widehat{U})^\triangle$$

$$+ U\widehat{U}\widetilde{U}(U\widehat{\widetilde{U}})^\triangle + U\widehat{U}(\widehat{U}\widetilde{U}U)^\triangle + U\widehat{U}(\widehat{U}\widehat{\widetilde{U}}\widehat{U})^\triangle + U\widehat{U}(\widehat{U}U\widehat{\widetilde{U}})^\triangle + U\widehat{U}(\widetilde{U}U\widehat{\widetilde{U}})^\triangle$$

$$+ U\widetilde{U}(\widehat{U}\widetilde{U}U)^\triangle + U\widetilde{U}(\widehat{U}\widehat{\widetilde{U}}\widehat{U})^\triangle + U\widetilde{U}(\widehat{U}U\widehat{\widetilde{U}})^\triangle + U\widetilde{U}(\widetilde{U}U\widehat{\widetilde{U}})^\triangle + U(\widehat{U}\widetilde{U}U\widehat{\widetilde{U}})^\triangle$$

$$+ \widehat{\widetilde{U}}\widehat{U}\widetilde{U}(\widehat{U}\widetilde{U})^\triangle + \widehat{\widetilde{U}}\widehat{U}\widetilde{U}(\widehat{U}U)^\triangle + \widehat{\widetilde{U}}\widehat{U}\widetilde{U}(\widehat{U}\widehat{\widetilde{U}})^\triangle + \widehat{\widetilde{U}}\widehat{U}\widetilde{U}(\widetilde{U}U)^\triangle + \widehat{\widetilde{U}}\widehat{U}\widetilde{U}(\widehat{\widetilde{U}}\widehat{U})^\triangle$$

$$+ \widehat{\widetilde{U}}\widehat{U}\widetilde{U}(U\widehat{\widetilde{U}})^\triangle + \widehat{\widetilde{U}}\widehat{U}(\widehat{U}\widetilde{U}U)^\triangle + \widehat{\widetilde{U}}\widehat{U}(\widehat{U}\widehat{\widetilde{U}}\widehat{U})^\triangle + \widehat{\widetilde{U}}\widehat{U}(\widehat{U}U\widehat{\widetilde{U}})^\triangle + \widehat{\widetilde{U}}\widehat{U}(\widetilde{U}U\widehat{\widetilde{U}})^\triangle$$

$$+ \widehat{\widetilde{U}}\widetilde{U}(\widehat{U}\widetilde{U}U)^\triangle + \widehat{\widetilde{U}}\widetilde{U}(\widehat{U}\widehat{\widetilde{U}}\widehat{U})^\triangle + \widehat{\widetilde{U}}\widetilde{U}(\widehat{U}U\widehat{\widetilde{U}})^\triangle + \widehat{\widetilde{U}}\widetilde{U}(\widetilde{U}U\widehat{\widetilde{U}})^\triangle + \widetilde{U}(\widehat{U}\widetilde{U}U\widehat{\widetilde{U}})^\triangle$$

$$+ \widehat{U}\widetilde{U}(\widehat{U}\widetilde{U}U)^\triangle + \widehat{U}\widetilde{U}(\widehat{U}\widehat{\widetilde{U}}\widehat{U})^\triangle + \widehat{U}\widetilde{U}(\widehat{U}U\widehat{\widetilde{U}})^\triangle + \widehat{U}\widetilde{U}(\widetilde{U}U\widehat{\widetilde{U}})^\triangle + \widehat{U}(\widehat{U}\widetilde{U}U\widehat{\widetilde{U}})^\triangle$$

$$+ \widetilde{U}(\widehat{U}\widetilde{U}U\widehat{\widetilde{U}})^\triangle, \tag{43}$$

$$C_{(6)} = -(U\widehat{\widetilde{U}}\widehat{U}\widetilde{U}(\widehat{U}\widetilde{U})^\triangle + U\widehat{\widetilde{U}}\widehat{U}\widetilde{U}(\widehat{U}U)^\triangle + U\widehat{\widetilde{U}}\widehat{U}\widetilde{U}(\widehat{U}\widehat{\widetilde{U}})^\triangle + U\widehat{\widetilde{U}}\widehat{U}\widetilde{U}(\widetilde{U}U)^\triangle$$

$$+ U\widehat{\widetilde{U}}\widehat{U}\widetilde{U}(\widehat{\widetilde{U}}\widehat{U})^\triangle + U\widehat{\widetilde{U}}\widehat{U}\widetilde{U}(U\widehat{\widetilde{U}})^\triangle + U\widehat{\widetilde{U}}\widehat{U}(\widehat{U}\widetilde{U}U)^\triangle + U\widehat{\widetilde{U}}\widehat{U}(\widehat{U}\widehat{\widetilde{U}}\widehat{U})^\triangle$$

$$+ U\widehat{\widetilde{U}}\widehat{U}(\widehat{U}U\widehat{\widetilde{U}})^\triangle + U\widehat{\widetilde{U}}\widehat{U}(\widetilde{U}U\widehat{\widetilde{U}})^\triangle + U\widehat{\widetilde{U}}\widetilde{U}(\widehat{U}\widetilde{U}U)^\triangle + U\widehat{\widetilde{U}}\widetilde{U}(\widehat{U}\widehat{\widetilde{U}}\widehat{U})^\triangle$$

$$+ U\widehat{\widetilde{U}}\widetilde{U}(\widehat{U}U\widehat{\widetilde{U}})^\triangle + U\widehat{\widetilde{U}}\widetilde{U}(\widetilde{U}U\widehat{\widetilde{U}})^\triangle + U\widehat{U}(\widehat{U}\widetilde{U}U\widehat{\widetilde{U}})^\triangle + U\widehat{U}\widetilde{U}(\widehat{U}\widetilde{U}U)^\triangle$$

$$+ U\widehat{U}\widetilde{U}(\widehat{U}\widehat{\widetilde{U}}\widehat{U})^\triangle + U\widehat{U}\widetilde{U}(\widehat{U}U\widehat{\widetilde{U}})^\triangle + U\widehat{U}\widetilde{U}(\widetilde{U}U\widehat{\widetilde{U}})^\triangle + U\widehat{U}(\widehat{U}\widetilde{U}U\widehat{\widetilde{U}})^\triangle$$

$$+ U\widetilde{U}(\widehat{U}\widetilde{U}U\widehat{\widetilde{U}})^\triangle + \widehat{\widetilde{U}}\widehat{U}\widetilde{U}(\widehat{U}\widetilde{U}U)^\triangle + \widehat{\widetilde{U}}\widehat{U}\widetilde{U}(\widehat{U}\widehat{\widetilde{U}}\widehat{U})^\triangle + \widehat{\widetilde{U}}\widehat{U}\widetilde{U}(\widehat{U}U\widehat{\widetilde{U}})^\triangle$$

$$+ \widehat{\widetilde{U}}\widehat{U}\widetilde{U}(\widetilde{U}U\widehat{\widetilde{U}})^\triangle + \widehat{\widetilde{U}}\widehat{U}(\widehat{U}\widetilde{U}U\widehat{\widetilde{U}})^\triangle + \widehat{\widetilde{U}}\widetilde{U}(\widehat{U}\widetilde{U}U\widehat{\widetilde{U}})^\triangle + \widehat{U}\widetilde{U}(\widehat{U}\widetilde{U}U\widehat{\widetilde{U}})^\triangle), \tag{44}$$

$$C_{(7)} = U\widehat{\widetilde{U}}\widehat{U}\widetilde{U}(\widehat{U}\widetilde{U}U)^\triangle + U\widehat{\widetilde{U}}\widehat{U}\widetilde{U}(\widehat{U}\widehat{\widetilde{U}}\widehat{U})^\triangle + U\widehat{\widetilde{U}}\widehat{U}\widetilde{U}(\widehat{U}U\widehat{\widetilde{U}})^\triangle + U\widehat{\widetilde{U}}\widehat{U}\widetilde{U}(\widetilde{U}U\widehat{\widetilde{U}})^\triangle$$

$$+ U\widehat{\widetilde{U}}\widehat{U}(\widehat{U}\widetilde{U}U\widehat{\widetilde{U}})^\triangle + U\widehat{\widetilde{U}}\widetilde{U}(\widehat{U}\widetilde{U}U\widehat{\widetilde{U}})^\triangle + U\widehat{U}\widetilde{U}(\widehat{U}\widetilde{U}U\widehat{\widetilde{U}})^\triangle + \widehat{\widetilde{U}}\widehat{U}\widetilde{U}(\widehat{U}\widetilde{U}U\widehat{\widetilde{U}})^\triangle, \tag{45}$$

$$C_{(8)} = -U\widehat{\widetilde{U}}\widehat{U}\widetilde{U}(\widehat{U}\widetilde{U}U\widehat{\widetilde{U}})^\triangle. \tag{46}$$

Proof. We verified the explicit formulas (39) – (46) for $C_1, \ldots, C_8$ using Symbolic Geometric Algebra package for SymPy [25].

We also present an analytical proof of the explicit formula (40) for $C_{(2)}$.

Step 1: Let us denote

$$d_1 := U\widehat{\widetilde{U}} + \widehat{U}\widetilde{U} + (\widehat{U}\widetilde{U})^\triangle + (U\widehat{\widetilde{U}})^\triangle, \quad d_2 := U\widehat{U} + \widehat{\widetilde{U}}\widetilde{U} + (\widehat{U}U)^\triangle + (\widetilde{U}\widehat{\widetilde{U}})^\triangle,$$

$$d_3 := U\widetilde{U} + \widehat{\widetilde{U}}\widehat{U} + (\widehat{U}\widehat{\widetilde{U}})^\triangle + (\widetilde{U}U)^\triangle, \quad d_4 := U\widehat{U}^\triangle + \widehat{\widetilde{U}}\widetilde{U}^\triangle + \widetilde{U}\widehat{\widetilde{U}}^\triangle + \widehat{U}U^\triangle,$$

$$d_5 := U\widetilde{U}^\triangle + \widehat{\widetilde{U}}\widehat{U}^\triangle + \widetilde{U}U^\triangle + \widehat{U}\widehat{\widetilde{U}}^\triangle, \quad d_6 := UU^\triangle + \widehat{U}\widehat{U}^\triangle + \widetilde{U}\widetilde{U}^\triangle + \widehat{\widetilde{U}}\widehat{\widetilde{U}}^\triangle,$$

$$d_7 := U\widehat{\widetilde{U}}^\triangle + \widehat{\widetilde{U}}U^\triangle + \widehat{U}\widetilde{U}^\triangle + \widetilde{U}\widehat{U}^\triangle. \tag{47}$$

Using the properties (10) and (12), we can prove that the projections onto the subspace of the grade 0 of all terms in each of the 7 expressions (47) are equal to each other. For example,

$$\frac{1}{4}\langle d_1 \rangle_0 = \langle U\widehat{\widetilde{U}} \rangle_0 = \langle \widehat{U}\widetilde{U} \rangle_0 = \langle (\widehat{U}\widetilde{U})^\triangle \rangle_0 = \langle (U\widehat{\widetilde{U}})^\triangle \rangle_0.$$

Using (25), (2), (39), and (47), we get

$$C_{(2)} = 4\langle U(U - C_{(1)}) \rangle_0 = -4\langle U(\widehat{\widetilde{U}} + \widehat{U} + \widetilde{U} + \widehat{U}^\triangle + \widetilde{U}^\triangle + U^\triangle + \widehat{\widetilde{U}}^\triangle) \rangle_0$$
$$= -\langle d_1 + d_2 + d_3 + d_4 + d_5 + d_6 + d_7 \rangle_0,$$

which differs from (40) only by the scalar part operation.

Step 2: It follows from (19), (20), and $\widetilde{d_3} = \widehat{d_3}^\triangle = d_3$ that $d_1 \in \mathcal{G}_{p,q}^0$, $d_2, d_3 \in \mathcal{G}_{p,q}^0 \oplus \mathcal{G}_{p,q}^5$. However, using (3) and $\langle UV \rangle_n = \langle VU \rangle_n$ for odd n, we can prove that d_2 and d_3 belong to $\mathcal{G}_{p,q}^0$:

$$\langle d_2 \rangle_5 = \langle U\widehat{U} + \widehat{\widetilde{U}}\widetilde{U} - \widehat{U}U - \widetilde{U}\widehat{\widetilde{U}} \rangle_5 = \langle U\widehat{U} + \widehat{\widetilde{U}}\widetilde{U} - U\widehat{U} - \widehat{\widetilde{U}}\widetilde{U} \rangle_5 = 0,$$
$$\langle d_3 \rangle_5 = \langle U\widetilde{U} + \widehat{\widetilde{U}}\widehat{U} - \widehat{U}\widehat{\widetilde{U}} - \widetilde{U}U \rangle_5 = \langle U\widetilde{U} + \widehat{\widetilde{U}}\widehat{U} - \widehat{\widetilde{U}}\widehat{U} - U\widetilde{U} \rangle_5 = 0.$$

Using (21), we get that the following sum can be represented in the form

$$d_4 + d_5 + d_6 + d_7 = (U + \widehat{U} + \widetilde{U} + \widehat{\widetilde{U}})(U + \widehat{U} + \widetilde{U} + \widehat{\widetilde{U}})^\triangle$$
$$= 16(U_0 + U_4)(U_0 - U_4) = 16(U_0^2 - U_4^2) \in \mathcal{G}_{p,q}^0,$$

because $U_0^2, U_4^2 \in \mathcal{G}_{p,q}^0$. Therefore the expression (40) belongs to $\mathcal{G}_{p,q}^0$. $\qquad \square$

6   Conclusions

In this paper, we present new explicit formulas for all characteristic polynomial coefficients in geometric algebras $\mathcal{G}_{p,q}$ with $n = p+q = 5$. These results generalize the results of the paper [19] for the cases $n \leq 4$. The formulas involve only the operations of geometric product, summation, and operations of conjugation. We actively use the $\triangle$-conjugation in our considerations. Several new properties of the operation $\triangle$ and other operations of conjugation in geometric algebra are presented. Using symbolic computation, we verified that all explicit formulas for the characteristic polynomial coefficients presented in this paper coincide with the known recursive formulas (25). For the first time, we present an analytical proof of the explicit formulas for $C_{(2)}$ and $C_{(3)}$ in the case $n = 4$ and the explicit formula for $C_{(2)}$ in the case $n = 5$. The proof of the coincidence of the proposed explicit formulas with the recursive ones turned out to be rather nontrivial. Different (explicit or recursive) formulas can be used for different purposes. Note that the presented explicit formulas for the characteristic polynomial coefficients in the cases $n \leq 5$ look like elementary symmetrical polynomials (if we ignore the operation $\triangle$) in the variables U, $\widehat{U}$, $\widetilde{U}$, etc. They can be interesting from a theoretical point of view and for different applications of geometric algebra in computer science and engineering.

We plan to present explicit formulas for all characteristic polynomial coefficients in the case $n = 6$ and a method for obtaining the corresponding coefficients in the case of an arbitrary dimension n in the extended version of this paper. The explicit formulas for the case $n = 6$ may be interesting, including for applications of the geometric algebra $\mathcal{G}_{3,3}$ of projective geometry in computer vision and computer graphics [8, 14].[6]

Acknowledgments. The authors are grateful to the four anonymous reviewers for their helpful comments on how to improve the presentation. This work is supported by the grant of the President of the Russian Federation (project MK-404.2020.1).

References

1. Acus, A., Dargys A.: Geometric Algebra Mathematica package (2017). https://github.com/ArturasAcus/GeometricAlgebra
2. Acus, A., Dargys, A.: The inverse of a multivector: beyond the threshold $p+q = 5$. Adv. Appl. Clifford Algebras **28**, 65 (2018)
3. Bayro-Corrochano, E.: Geometric Algebra Applications, vol. I. Springer, Cham (2019). https://doi.org/10.1007/978-3-319-74830-6
4. Cendrillon, R., Lovell, B.: Real-time face recognition using eigenfaces. In: Visual Communications and Image Processing, pp. 269–276 (2000). https://doi.org/10.1117/12.386642
5. Dirac, P.: Wave equations in conformal space. Ann. Math. Second Ser. **37**(2), 429–442 (1936). https://doi.org/10.2307/1968455
6. Doran, C., Lasenby, A.: Geometric Algebra for Physicists. Cambridge University Press, Cambridge (2003)
7. Dorst, L., Fontijne, D., Mann, D.: Geometric Algebra for Computer Science. The Morgan Kaufmann Series in Computer Graphics, San Francisco (2007)
8. Dorst, L.: 3D oriented projective geometry through versors of $R^{3,3}$. Adv. Appl. Clifford Algebras **26**(4), 1137–1172 (2016)
9. Hadfield H, Wieser E., Arsenovic A., Kern R., The Pygae Team: pygae/clifford: v1.3.1 (2020). https://doi.org/10.5281/zenodo.1453978. https://github.com/pygae/clifford
10. Helmstetter, J.: Characteristic polynomials in Clifford algebras and in more general algebras. Adv. Appl. Clifford Algebras **29**, 30 (2019)
11. Hestenes, D.: Space-Time Algebra. Gordon and Breach, New York (1966)
12. Hildenbrand, D.: Foundations of Geometric Algebra Computing. Springer, Heidelberg (2013). https://doi.org/10.1007/978-3-642-31794-1
13. Hitzer, E., Sangwine, S.: Multivector and multivector matrix inverses in real Clifford algebras. Appl. Math. Comput. **311**, 375–389 (2017)

---

[6] One of the anonymous reviewers of this paper also noted that "in physics the conformal space-time algebra or conformal Dirac algebra $\mathcal{G}_{4,2}$ and $\mathcal{G}_{2,4}$ are also of great importance and the direct multivector algebra computation of characteristic polynomials may be very useful there" (see [5,6]).

14. Klawitter, D.: A Clifford algebraic approach to line geometry. Adv. Appl. Clifford Algebra **24**, 713–736 (2014)
15. Lasenby, A., Lasenby, J.: Applications of geometric algebra in physics and links with engineering. In: Corrochano, E.B., Sobczyk, G. (eds.) Geometric Algebra with Applications in Science and Engineering. Birkhauser, Boston (2001)
16. Li, H.: Invariant Algebras and Geometric Reasoning. World Scientific, Singapore (2008)
17. Lounesto, P.: Clifford Algebras and Spinors. Cambridge University Press, Cambridge (1997)
18. Sangwine, S., Hitzer, E.: Clifford multivector toolbox (for MATLAB) (2015–2016). http://clifford-multivector-toolbox.sourceforge.net/
19. Shirokov, D.: On computing the determinant, other characteristic polynomial coefficients, and inverse in Clifford algebras of arbitrary dimension. Comput. Appl. Math. **40**, 173 (2021). https://doi.org/10.1007/s40314-021-01536-0. 29 pp
20. Shirokov, D.: On basis-free solution to Sylvester equation in geometric algebra. In: Magnenat-Thalmann, N., Stephanidis, C., Wu, E., Thalmann, D., Sheng, B., Kim, J., Papagiannakis, G., Gavrilova, M. (eds.) CGI 2020. LNCS, vol. 12221, pp. 541–548. Springer, Cham (2020). https://doi.org/10.1007/978-3-030-61864-3_46
21. Shirokov, D.: Basis-free solution to Sylvester equation in Clifford algebra of arbitrary dimension. Adv. Appl. Clifford Algebras **31**, 70 (2021). https://doi.org/10.1007/s00006-021-01173-0
22. Shirokov, D.: A classification of lie algebras of pseudo-unitary groups in the techniques of Clifford algebras. Adv. Appl. Clifford Algebras **20**(2), 411–425 (2010). https://doi.org/10.1007/s00006-009-0177-0
23. Shirokov, D.: Quaternion typification of Clifford algebra elements. Adv. Appl. Clifford Algebras **22**(1), 243–256 (2012). https://doi.org/10.1007/s00006-011-0288-2
24. Shirokov, D.: Development of the method of quaternion typification of Clifford algebra elements. Adv. Appl. Clifford Algebras **22**(2), 483–497 (2012). https://doi.org/10.1007/s00006-011-0304-6
25. The Pygae Team: pygae/galgebra: v0.5.0 (2020), https://github.com/pygae/galgebra
26. Turk, M., Pentland, A.: Face recognition using eigenfaces. In: Proceedings of IEEE Conference on Computer Vision and Pattern Recognition, pp. 586–591 (1991)
27. Turk, M., Pentland, A.: Eigenfaces for recognition. J. Cogn. Neurosci. **3**(1), 71–86 (1991). https://doi.org/10.1162/jocn.1991.3.1.71

Unified Expression Frame of Geodetic Stations Based on Conformal Geometric Algebra

Zhenjun Yan[1], Zhaoyuan Yu[1,2,3], Yun Wang[1], Wen Luo[1,2,3]($\boxtimes$), Jiyi Zhang[4], Hong Gao[1], and Linwang Yuan[1,2,3]

[1] School of Geography, Nanjing Normal University, Nanjing 210023, China
`09415@njnu.edu.cn`
[2] Key Laboratory of Virtual Geographic Environment, Ministry of Education, Nanjing Normal University, Nanjing 210023, China
[3] Jiangsu Center for Collaborative Innovation in Geographical Information Resource Development and Application, Nanjing 210023, China
[4] College of Geographic Science, Nantong University, Nantong 226019, China

Abstract. Global geodetic stations are the basis for the study of International Terrestrial Reference Frame (ITRF) and crustal plate motion. This paper has collected a total of 288 global geodetic stations calculated by four spatial geodetic technologies. Because different types of geodetic stations use different spatial references, the data of different types of stations can only be used after necessary spatial conversion. And with the motion of the Earth's crust, conversion methods and formulas are constantly being revised. The complexity and dynamics of spatial conversion have greatly hindered the integrated application of different global geodetic stations. This paper proposes a unified expression frame for global geodetic stations. Based on the theory of conformal geometric algebra, the motion operator that uniformly expresses translation, rotation, and scaling in the form of versor product is introduced. From the perspective of the unified expression and calculation of the operator, a unified expression frame and ITRF conversion method for different reference frames of the geodetic station are constructed. The experimental case shows that the ITRF conversion method based on the unified motion operator reduces the complexity of the reference frame conversion, which provides a certain reference for the unified expression and analysis of different frame conversion and crustal plate motion.

Keywords: Conformal geometric algebra (CGA) · Motion operator · Versor product · Unified expression frame · ITRF conversion

1 Introduction

With the continuous development of observation technology and application fields, the space of Geographic Information System (GIS) research objects expands from traditional ground space to underground space, interior space and cosmic space [1, 2]. Thus, types and numbers of space frames keep increasing. And different frames always have

© Springer Nature Switzerland AG 2021
N. Magnenat-Thalmann et al. (Eds.): CGI 2021, LNCS 13002, pp. 682–693, 2021.
https://doi.org/10.1007/978-3-030-89029-2_51

many differences in positioning, orientation and expression scale [3]. According to different requirements of expressing geographic objects, these frames can be divided into spherical frame, orthogonal frame and plane frame (Fig. 1). These frames are all based on Euclidean Geometry, which makes the expression and calculation of GIS objects highly dependent on the coordinate system. There is no uniformity in the expression and analysis of geographical objects under different frames.

Among numerous spatial frames, the International Terrestrial Reference Frame (ITRF) is considered the most accurate and stable reference frame, provided by International Earth Rotation Service (IERS) [4]. ITRF also provides references for other global and regional frames. ITRF contains not only coordinate information of geodetic stations but also their velocity field information [5, 6]. Hence, when transforming ITRF frames, in addition to the conventional spatial conversion, the displacement effect caused by time-varying motion should also be considered.

However, the current methods of ITRF conversion are all based on matrix operation in Euclidean space, which means that spatial objects to be converted are expressed according to coordinate vector [7]. Such method expresses the translation and rotation motions in the form of vector and matrix respectively, resulting in the non-unified expression forms and non-linear mapping operations [8]. It also leads to the fragmentation of conversion integrity. Faced with such a problem, it is difficult for the current method to realize the conversion caused by compound change of motion and gain the unified formal expression in Euclidean space. Hence, to realize the comprehensive application of GIS in different space frames, it is necessary to find a new mathematical method to realize expression and calculation of the conversion process in a concise and unified style.

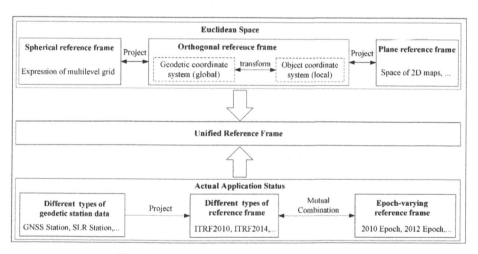

Fig. 1. The demands of a unified reference frame

Geometric Algebra (GA) is an algebraic language for describing and calculating geometric problems, which has the potential to become the theoretical basis of unified spatial frame construction [9, 10]. Conformal Geometric Algebra (CGA) is an algebraic type of GA. Compared with Euclidean geometry, CGA introduces two additional dimensions to establish a unified and compact homogeneous algebraic frame [11]. In CGA, various conversions are uniformly expressed in the form of versor product [12]. Multiple single conversions can be synthesized into a compound conversion based on the associativity of versor product. Due to the unified expression and integrity of motion based on CGA, it has been applied in many research fields, especially for expression and application of rigid body motion [13]. Bayro-Corrochano [14] and Li [15] discussed the solution process of motion parameter based on CGA, and designed different types of motion operators. Zou et al. [16, 17] deduced the generality of rotation operator based on CGA for geometric conversion, which proved that conformal motion operators have a unified expression form for translation, rotation and scaling. Based on the expression form of any motion in CGA, Fan et al. [18] replaced the rotation matrix with the rotation operator in photogrammetry, which proved that the rotation operator and the rotation matrix are the same. Based on the theory of CGA, the operator expression of motion can be realized, which provides a feasible idea for the unified formal expression of different geodetic stations.

In this paper, we introduce a unified expression of rotation, translation and scaling motion by introducing the versor product in CGA into expression of geodetic stations, and construct a unified expression frame of geodetic stations. ITRF conversion method is also constructed based on the unified expression frame. This paper is organized as follows: in Sect. 2, the basic theory and motion operator are introduced. In Sect. 3, the unified expression frame of geodetic stations is constructed based on the motion operator and the ITRF conversions method is also constructed based on the unified frame. Then, the feasibility of the method is venrified by experiment. At last, the conclusion and discussion of this paper are given.

2   Basic Theory and Basic Idea

2.1   Basic Theory

CGA is an algebraic type of geometric algebra, which realizes the conversion between Euclidean space and conformal space by introducing two additional dimensions [11]. Li thoroughly discusses the mapping and conversion between Euclidean geometry and CGA [19]. For Euclidean space E^3, there is a set of 3-dimensional orthogonal basis vectors $\{e_1, e_2, e_3\}$. Compared with Euclidean geometry, a set of two additional independent basis vectors $\{e_0, e_\infty\}$ are introduced in CGA. Thus, a set of normative orthogonal basis vectors $\{e_1, e_2, e_3, e_0, e_\infty\}$ in conformal space are also constituted.

If there exists a point P in Euclidean space E^3, whose coordinate is (x, y, z), the expression formula of point P in CGA [20] is:

$$C(P) = P + \frac{P^2 e_\infty}{2} + e_0. \tag{1}$$

Based on the conformal point, the conformal line can be constructed, and its expression is $L = C(P_1) \wedge C(P_2) \wedge e_\infty$. According to the mapping relationship between Euclidean space and conformal space, here we have **Definition 1:**

For frames expressed by GA, X-axis, Y-axis and Z-axis of a frame in Euclidean space are respectively defined as the basis vectors $\{e_1, e_2, e_3\}$, and the origin of a frame is defined as e_0. According to the formula (1), point P in Euclidean space can be mapped to conformal space, marked as $C(P)$.

2.2 Motion Operator

Through mapping relationship between Euclidean space and conformal space, the motion operators in conformal space are introduced. In CGA, conversions such as rotation, translation and scaling can be uniformly defined in the form of versor product based on the characteristics of associativity of the geometric product [21]. The versor product can achieve uniform formalized expression of various motion, whose expression formula is:

$$o_r = MoM' \tag{2}$$

where o represents moving geometric primitives. M represents universal expression operators for motion, and M' is inverse form of M, then we get $MM' = 1$ [22].

Rotation in Conformal Space. Taking the normal vector of rotation plane as rotation axis, the formalized expression of rotation operator R in CGA can be described as follows:

$$R = e^{\pm \frac{\theta}{2} l} \tag{3}$$

where l is rotation axis bivector. θ is the corresponding rotation angle, such that "+" represents clockwise rotation, and "−" represents anticlockwise rotation.

According to formula (2), rotation operation in Euclidean space can also be applied in CGA, whose expression formula is:

$$RC(P)R' = R\left(P + \frac{P^2 e_\infty}{2} + e_0\right)R' = RPR' + \frac{P^2}{2}Re_\infty R' + Re_0 R'$$

$$= P' + \frac{P'^2 e_\infty}{2} + e_0 = C(RPR') \tag{4}$$

where $P' = RPR'$, which means the application of rotation operator in Euclidean space and CGA is the same. The P is a point in Euclidean space, and its coordinates are (x, y, z). C(P) is the conformal point.

Translation in Conformal Space. In Euclidean space E^3, if translation vector is expressed as $t = t_1 e_1 + t_2 e_2 + t_3 e_3$, translation operator T in CGA can be defined as:

$$T = e^{-\frac{t}{2}e_\infty} = 1 + (-t \wedge e_\infty/2) + \frac{1}{2!}(-t \wedge e_\infty/2)^2 + \ldots = 1 - \frac{t}{2}e_\infty \tag{5}$$

According to formula (2), applying translation operator to a point in CGA, we get:

$$TC(P)T' = \left(1 - \frac{t}{2}e_\infty\right)\left(P + \frac{P^2 e_\infty}{2} + e_0\right)\left(1 + \frac{t}{2}e_\infty\right) = P' + \frac{P'^2 e_\infty}{2} + e_0 = C(P + t) \tag{6}$$

where $P' = P + t$, which means translation in CGA is realized by operator T.

Scaling in Conformal Space. The scaling factor is expressed as μ in Euclidean space, and γ represents scaling parameters. It has conversion relationship as $\gamma = \log \mu$. Then, scaling operator S in CGA can be defined as:

$$S = e^{\frac{\gamma}{2}e_0 \wedge e_\infty} = 1 + \frac{\gamma}{2}e_0 \wedge e_\infty + \frac{1}{2!}\left(\frac{\gamma}{2}e_0 \wedge e_\infty\right)^2 + \ldots = cosh\frac{\gamma}{2} + sinh\frac{\gamma}{2}(e_0 \wedge e_\infty) \quad (7)$$

According to formula (2), applying scaling operator to a point in CGA, we get:

$$SC(P)S' = e^{\frac{\gamma}{2}e_0 \wedge e_\infty}\left(P + \frac{P^2 e_\infty}{2} + e_0\right)e^{-\frac{\gamma}{2}e_0 \wedge e_\infty} = e^{\gamma}\left(P' + \frac{P'^2 e_\infty}{2} + e_0\right) \quad (8)$$

where $P' = e^{-\gamma}P$, that means scaling in CGA is realized by operator S.

2.3 Basic Idea

Based on the theory of geometric algebra, this paper aims to solve the difficulty of integration applications of geodetic stations due to the complex conversion of multiple reference frames. Firstly, we construct the motion operator in CGA, and then the mapping relationship between the operator and process of frame conversion is built. From the perspective of the integration of operator expression and calculation, a unified conversion frame for geodetic stations under different reference frames is constructed based on the motion operator. There are many practical applications of the unified reference frame, such as ITRF conversion. For the ITRF conversion, we construct two translation operators, three rotation operators and a scaling operator, which can realize the conversion between different frames and different epochs, as shown in Fig. 2.

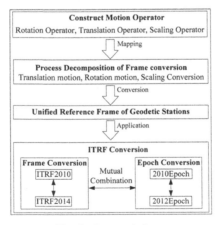

Fig. 2. Research frame

3 Unified Expression Frame and ITRF Conversion

Based on the motion operator, the formal expression of the conversion between different epochs and different reference frames is as follows:

$$G_j(P_1, P_2, \cdots, P_n) = Rot(G_i(P_1, P_2, \cdots, P_n), R(T_i)) \tag{9}$$

Where P_i is the coordinate of geodetic stations on different plates, G_i, G_j respectively represent the state of the reference frame of the geodetic station at time i and j, and $R(T_i)$ is the motion operator that transforms the state of the reference frame at time i to the state of the reference frame at time j. Specifically, $R(T_i)$ is constructed by fine combination of R, T and S operators. When the conversion only involves epoch conversion, $R(T_i)$ and T_e are equivalent. When the conversion only involves reference frames conversion, $R(T_i)$ is constructed by a combination of T_f, R and S. If the conversion involves the overall conversion of epochs and frames, $R(T_i)$ is constructed by a combination of T_e, T_f, R and S.

By mapping an object from Euclidean space to CGA and defining motion operators, the conversion process of ITRF based on CGA can be realized, where the key point is to construct the corresponding motion operator. ITRF conversion involves three rotation operators, two translation operators and one scaling operator.

Rotation conversion among different ITRF frames can be decomposed into three rotation motions around corresponding coordinate axis. According to the operation rules of rotation operator in conformal space, here we have Definition 2: based on rotation parameters and the motion velocity of geodetic stations, rotation angles to construct rotation operators can be obtained. Taking X-axis, Y-axis and Z-axis as rotation axis respectively, and taking $\{\theta_X, \theta_Y, \theta_Z\}$ as rotation angles, rotation operators $\{R_X, R_Y, R_Z\}$ can be constructed according to formula (3).

There are two translation operations in the conversion process of ITRF. According to operation rules of translation operators in CGA, Definition 3 can be defined as: for epoch conversion, moving distance can be obtained based on time and speed of movement, which can form a translation vector (t_e). And translation operator T_e for an epoch conversion can be constructed according to formula (5). For frame conversion, based on translation parameters and their velocity of geodetic stations, moving vector $\{t_X, t_Y, t_Z\}$ can be obtained to construct translation vectors t_f. And translation operator T_f for frame conversion can be established according to formula (5).

According to operation rules of scaling operator in conformal space, Definition 4 can be defined as: based on scaling factor and the velocity of geodetic stations, scaling parameter μ can be obtained. And taking its logarithm, scaling operator S can be constructed according to formula (7).

By considering the unified expression of motion operators and associativity of versor product, formal unified expression of ITRF conversion based on CGA can be realized as:

$$F(P) = T_f R_Z R_Y R_X S T_e P T_e' S' R_X' R_Y' R_Z' T_f' = MPM'. \tag{10}$$

where a subscript of a translation operator T represents its motion vector. And a subscript of rotation operator R represents its rotation axis. The expression method can intuitively reflect geometric meaning of motion, and keep homogeneous mapping and unified expression at the same time.

After the conversion process of ITRF is completed, the error of coordinates conversion is usually used as the index to evaluate the accuracy of conversion. By summarizing frame conversion and epoch conversion of ITRF, the formula of the ITRF conversion and error checking can be represented as:

$$\begin{cases} F(P_i) = (P_i, R, S, T_f, T_e), \\ \quad V = F(P_i) - O(P_i). \end{cases} \tag{11}$$

where P_i is a conformal point of ITRF to be transformed. $\{R, S, T_f\}$ respectively represents rotation, scaling and translation operators of a frame conversion. T_e is the translation operator of epoch conversion. $F(P_i)$ are the coordinates of P_i after complete conversion, and $O(P_i)$ is the coordinate of P_i provided by IERS. The threshold range of V should be determined according to the requirements of the actual application. Under normal circumstances, the centimeter level will be satisfactory [23].

4   Case Study

ITRF frame conversion is divided into epoch conversion and frame conversion. The epoch can be regarded as the moment, and the frame of reference can be understood as the reference datum of the coordinates. Epoch conversion can realize the conversion of geodetic station coordinates at different epochs based on the same frame. Frame conversion can realize the conversion of geodetic station coordinates in different frames based on the same epoch. As for epoch conversion, since the shape of the earth is in the process of slowly changing, the change of the position of the geodetic stations in the frame can be approximately regarded as a uniform motion over time [24]. Thus, the motion conversion of the ITRF frame over time can be converted into a translation motion in space. The formal expression is as follows:

$$(X, Y, Z)_{ITRF_{xx}}^{t_i} \rightarrow^{T_e} (X, Y, Z)_{ITRF_{xx}}^{t_j} \tag{12}$$

where (X, Y, Z) are the coordinates of the geodetic stations, t_i and t_j are the different epochs, $ITRF_{xx}$ is the frame of reference.

Frame conversion is the position change of the ITRF frame in space, involving rotation and translation of the coordinate axis, and scaling between different scales [25]. It requires three translation parameters, three rotation parameters, and one scaling parameters. The parameters are related to the movement rate of the geodetic station. The frame conversion involves translational motion, rotation motion and scaling conversion. The formal expression is as follows:

$$(X, Y, Z)_{ITRF_{xx}}^{t_i} \rightarrow^{T_f, R, S} (X, Y, Z)_{ITRF_{yy}}^{t_i} \tag{13}$$

where (X, Y, Z) is the coordinates of the station, t_i is the epoch time of the geodetic stations, $ITRF_{xx}$ and $ITRF_{yy}$ are the frame of reference.

This paper has collected 232 GNSS stations, 11 ILRS stations, 5 IVS stations and 40 IDS stations as the overall database to verify the CGA-based reference frame conversion method (Fig. 3). Due to a large amount of data, this paper uses the four GNSS stations XIAN, WUHN, SHAO and LHAS as experimental points to verify the feasibility, effectiveness and simplicity of CGA-based ITRF conversion. Based on the CGA conversion method, the coordinates of the four geodetic stations in the 2012 epoch and ITRF2014 frame are converted to the 2010 epoch and ITRF2008 frame. The coordinates and velocities of the four IGS stations in the 2012 epoch and ITRF2014 frame are shown in Table 1, and the conversion parameters from ITRF2014 to ITRF2008 are shown in Table 2.

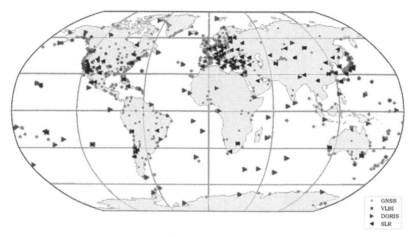

Fig. 3. Global distribution map of GNSS, SLR, VLBI, DORIS geodetic stations

Table 1. Coordinates and velocities of GNSS stations under the frame of ITRF2014 in the 2012 epoch

GNSS station	X/m	Y/m	Z/m	V_x/(m/y)	V_y(m/y)	V_z(m/y)
XIAN	−1735212.932	4976840.032	3580538.241	−0.0320	−0.0059	−0.0097
WUHN	−2267749.575	5009154.221	3221290.632	−0.0318	−0.0080	−0.0100
SHAO	−2831733.662	4675665.891	3275369.377	−0.0306	−0.0113	−0.0109
LHAS	−106938.262	5549269.486	3139215.444	−0.0457	−0.0074	0.0143

Table 2. Conversion parameters from ITRF2014 to ITRF2008

Parameter	T_X/mm	T_Y/mm	T_Z/mm	D/ppb	R_X/.001″	R_Y/.001″	R_Z/.001″	Epoch
	1.60	1.90	2.40	−0.02	0.00	0.00	0.00	2010
Velocity	$\dot{T}_X$/(mm/y)	$\dot{T}_Y$/(mm/y)	$\dot{T}_Z$/(mm/y)	$\dot{D}$/(ppb/y)	$\dot{R}_X$/(.001″/y)	$\dot{R}_Y$/(.001″/y)	$\dot{R}_Z$/(.001″/y)	
	0.0	0.0	0.1	0.03	0.00	0.00	0.00	

The construction parameters of the motion operator are solved based on the above-mentioned original conversion parameters, and the corresponding operators for rotation, scaling and translation are constructed according to the definition of the motion operator. It can be seen from the conversion process of the ITRF frame that the translation operator of the epoch conversion is determined by each geodetic station (Table 3), because the displacement of each station on the coordinate axis is different due to its different movement speed. For the conversion of different reference frames in the same epoch, the geodetic stations are all converted from the same reference frame to another same reference frame. Thus, the conversion parameters are the same, the conversion operator of the frame conversion is shown in Table 4.

Table 3. Conversion parameters and operators of the epoch conversion

GNSS station	tvx/mm	tvy/mm	tvz/mm	Translation operator
XIAN	64	11.8	19.4	$T_{XIAN} = e^{-\frac{64e_1 + 11.8e_2 + 19.4e_3}{2}e_\infty}$
WUHN	63.6	16	20	$T_{WUHN} = e^{-\frac{63.6e_1 + 16e_2 + 20e_3}{2}e_\infty}$
SHAO	61.2	22.6	21.8	$T_{SHAO} = e^{-\frac{61.2e_1 + 22.6e_2 + 21.8e_3}{2}e_\infty}$
LHAS	91.4	14.8	-28.6	$T_{LHAS} = e^{-\frac{91.4e_1 + 14.8e_2 - 28.6e_3}{2}e_\infty}$

Table 4. Conversion parameters and operators of the frame conversion

Velocity	t_X/mm	t_Y/mm	t_Z/mm	γ/ppb	θ_X/.001″	θ_Y/.001″	θ_Z/.001″
	1.60	1.90	2.40	-0.02	0.00	0.00	0.00
Operator	$T_f =$ $e^{-\frac{1.6e_X + 1.9e_Y + 2.4e_Z}{2}e_\infty}$			$S =$ $e^{(1+2*10^{-11})\hat{e}_\infty/2}$	$R_X =$ $e^{-\frac{0}{2}e_1}$	$R_Y =$ $e^{-\frac{0}{2}e_2}$	$R_Z =$ $e^{-\frac{0}{2}e_3}$

Based on the Python language, the operation rules and conversion operators of the conformal geometric algebra are implemented. And the process of converting the coordinates of the four IGS stations from the 2012 epoch ITRF2014 frame to the 2010 epoch ITRF2008 frame is completed through the program. The conversion results are exchanged with the official IERS website. The selected data are compared with, and the accuracy is shown in Table 5.

Table 5. Accuracy of ITRF frame conversion results under conformal geometric algebra

GNSS station	$|\triangle X|/m$	$|\triangle Y|/m$	$|\triangle Z|/m$
XIAN	0.023	0.017	0.009
WUHN	0.002	0.002	0.005
SHAO	0.001	0.004	0.006
LHAS	0.002	0.005	0.502

It can be seen from Table 5 that the accuracy of most of the coordinates of the geodetic stations after conversion is at the millimeter level, which can meet the accuracy requirements of general coordinate conversion. There is insufficient accuracy in the Z direction of the LHAS site, which might be related to the epoch of the site data itself and conversion parameters between ITRF. The experimental results show that the ITRF frame conversion method based on conformal geometric algebra proposed in this paper is feasible and effective. This method is based on operator-based operations, which overcomes the tediousness and complexity of the traditional method based on matrix operation conversion methods. Therefore, the proposed method is conciseness.

5 Conclusion and Discussion

In this paper, we introduce CGA to construct a unified expression frame of geodetic stations. The versor product in CGA can uniformly express conversions, which can express nonlinear vector and matrix operations as conformal operators. Based on the versor product, we constructed three types operators: rotation operator, translation operator and scaling operator. And based on the three types operators, we then construct a unified expression frame of geodetic stations. The ITRF conversion method is established based on the unified expression frame, which realizes the compound conversions and the formal unification of expressions. Through relevant experimental cases, the feasibility of the ITRF conversion is verified. In the process of multiple continuous conversions, such conversion methods can ensure unified expression form and intuitive geometric meaning. And the accuracy of conversion results meets the requirements of daily applications.

The conversion based on CGA has characteristics of uniformity in the expression of geometric objects and motion. However, it still has problems (efficiency needs to be improved) that need to be continuously improved in other research fields like numerical analysis. And future works include two aspects. While the expression of operators based on versor product is unified, the spinor form of expressions is still quadratic and nonlinear, which reduces the efficiency of the algorithm. Twistor expression [10] of CGA can transform motion from parameterized space to vector space and realize linear operations, which can effectively improve efficiency and achieve overall optimization of motion.

Acknowledgment. This work was supported by National Natural Science Fundation for Distinguished Young Scholar (Grant No. 41625004), National Natural Science Foundation of China (Grant No. 42001325, 41976186, 41971404, 42001320).

References

1. Yuan, L., Yu, Z., Luo, W., et al: Geometric algebra for multidimension-unified geographical information system. Adv. Appl. Clifford Algebras. **23**(2), 497–518 (2013). https://doi.org/10.1007/s00006-012-0375-z

2. Hua, Y.: The core problems and key technologies of Pan-Spatial information system. J. Geo. Sci. Tech. **33**(4), 331–335 (2016). https://doi.org/10.3969/j.issn.1673-6338.2016.04.001

3. Crespi, M., Mazzoni, A., Colosimo, G.: Global and local reference frames. Rendiconti Lincei **26**(1), 25–31 (2015). https://doi.org/10.1007/s12210-015-0435-0

4. Altamimi, Z., Collilieux, X., Métivier, L.: ITRF2008: an improved solution of the international terrestrial reference frame. J. Geod. **85**(8), 457–473 (2011). https://doi.org/10.1007/s00190-011-0444-4

5. Böckmann, S., Artz, T., Nothnagel, A.: VLBI terrestrial reference frame contributions to ITRF2008. J. Geod. **84**(3), 201–219 (2010). https://doi.org/10.1007/s00190-009-0357-7

6. Liu, J., Wei, N., Shi, C.: Status and prospects of the international terrestrial reference frame (ITRF). Chinese J. Nat. **35**(4), 243–250 (2013). https://doi.org/10.3969/j.issn.0253-9608.2013.04.002

7. Wang, J.: Correlations among parameters in seven-parameter transformation model. J. Geod. Geadyn. **27**(2), 43–46 (2007). https://doi.org/10.14075/j.jgg.2007.02.008

8. Liu, L., Cheng, Y.: On transform between ITRFS. J. Geod. Geodyn **30**(2), 141–143 (2010). https://doi.org/10.14075/j.jgg.2010.02.003

9. Yuan, L., Yu, Z., Wen, L., et al.: Multidimensional-unified topological relations computation: a hierarchical geometric algebra-based approach. Int. J. Geogr. Inf. Sci. **28**(11–12), 2435–2455 (2014). https://doi.org/10.1080/13658816.2014.929136

10. Yuan, L., Yu, Z., Chen, S., et al.: CAUSTA: clifford algebra-based unified spatio-temporal Analysis. Trans. GIS **14**(s1), 59–83 (2010). https://doi.org/10.1111/j.1467-9671.2010.01221.x

11. Li, H.: Conformal geometric algebra–a new frame for computational geometry. J. Comput. -Aided Des. Comput. Graph. **17**(11), 2383–2393 (2005). https://doi.org/10.1016/j.molcatb.2005.02.001

12. Dorst, L., Daniel, F., Stephen, M.: Geometric Algebra for Computer Science: An Object-Oriented Approach to Geometry. Morgan Kaufmann Publishers, San Francisco (2007)

13. Wareham, R., Cameron, J., Lasenby, J.: Applications of conformal geometric algebra in computer vision and graphics. In: Li, H., Olver, P.J., Sommer, G. (eds.) GIAE/IWMM -2004. LNCS, vol. 3519, pp. 329–349. Springer, Heidelberg (2005). https://doi.org/10.1007/11499251_24

14. Bayro-Corrochano, E., Scheuermann, G.: Geometric Algebra Computing. Springer, London (2010)

15. Li, H.: Conformal geometric algebra for motion and shape description. J. Comput. -Aided Des. Comput. Graph. **18**(7), 895–901 (2006). https://doi.org/10.1016/S1004-4132(06)60027-3

16. Zou, L., Lasenby, J., He, Z.: Pattern analysis of conformal array based on geometric algebra. IET Microwaves Antennas Propag. **5**(10), 1210–1218 (2011). https://doi.org/10.1049/iet-map.2010.0588

17. Zou, L., Lasenby, J., He, Z.: Polarisation diversity of conformal arrays based on geometric algebra via convex optimization. Iet. Radar Sonar Navig. **6**(6), 417–424 (2012). https://doi.org/10.1049/iet-rsn.2011.0293

18. Fan, Y., Liu, W., Shi, G., et al.: A research on method based on the foundation of the theory of rotation matrix described by the CGA [C]. In: The 9th Member Congress of China Photographic Society and the Academic Annual Conference, pp. 307–311. Beijing (2014)

19. Li, H.: Conformal geometric algebra and algebraic manipulations of geometric invariants. J. Comput.-Aided Des. Comput. Graph. **18**(7), 902–911 (2006). https://doi.org/10.1016/S1005-8885(07)60042-9
20. Vince, J.: Geometric Algebra for Computer Graphics. Springer, London (2008)
21. Perwass, C.: Geometric Algebra with Applications in Engineering. Springer, Berlin Heidelberg (2009)
22. Yuan, L., Lv, G., Yu, Z., et al.: Multidimensional Unified GIS Based on Geometric Algebra: Theory, Algorithm. Application. Science Press, Beijing (2012)
23. Cheng, Y.: Brief introduction of ITRF2008 frame. J. Geod. Geodyn. **32**(1), 47–50 (2012). https://doi.org/10.14075/j.jgg.2012.01.011
24. Liu, L., Cheng, Y.: Research on some problems of coordinate frame transformation. GNSS World of China **001**, 20–24 (2010). https://doi.org/10.13442/j.gnss.2010.01.014
25. Peng, X., Gao, J., et al.: Research of the coordinate conversion between WGS84 and CGCS200. J. Geod. Geodyn. **35**(2), 119–221 (2015). https://doi.org/10.14075/j.jgg.2015.02.010

Never 'Drop the Ball' in the Operating Room: An Efficient Hand-Based VR HMD Controller Interpolation Algorithm, for Collaborative, Networked Virtual Environments

Manos Kamarianakis[1,2]([envelope]) [iD], Nick Lydatakis[1,2] [iD],
and George Papagiannakis[1,2] [iD]

[1] University of Crete, Heraklion, Greece
[2] ORamaVR, Heraklion, Greece
{manos,nick,george.papagiannakis}@oramavr.com
http://www.oramavr.com

Abstract. In this work, we propose two algorithms that can be applied in the context of a networked virtual environment to efficiently handle the interpolation of displacement data for hand-based VR HMDs. Our algorithms, based on the use of dual-quaternions and multivectors respectively, impact the network consumption rate and are highly effective in scenarios involving multiple users. We illustrate convincing results in a modern game engine and a medical VR collaborative training scenario.

Keywords: Interpolation · Keyframe generation · Geometric algebra

1 Introduction

Collaborative, shared virtual environments (CVEs) are among the most researched and developed areas of the last decades [1,13,16,18]. The growing need of remote networked communication, further accelerated by the ongoing pandemic, have resulted in great leaps in technological advancements. Head-mounted displays (HMDs) are now capable of supporting intensive resource-demanding Virtual Reality (VR) applications. To further facilitate this support, powerful algorithms are being developed and optimized by VR specialists (Fig. 1).

Part of this research revolves around the efficient relay of synchronized, networked information from the HMD to the VR engine that is responsible for the rendering of the scene [19]. This information typically involves user interactions through the HMD controllers such as *displacement data* (e.g., translation and rotation of the controller) within specific time intervals and button-press events.

Specifically, when the user moves the hand-based controllers of his HMD, the hardware initially detects the movement type and logs it, in various time

© Springer Nature Switzerland AG 2021
N. Magnenat-Thalmann et al. (Eds.): CGI 2021, LNCS 13002, pp. 694–704, 2021.
https://doi.org/10.1007/978-3-030-89029-2_52

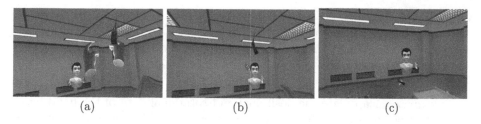

(a)   (b)   (c)

Fig. 1. Catching a tool in a VR collaborative scenario. (a) A user throws a tool (in our case a medical drill) at another. (b) The object's keyframes, sent by the user that threw it, are interpolated using multivector LERP (see Sect. 4.2) on the receiver's VR engine. (c) The receiver manages to catch the tool, as a result of the effective frame generation that is visualized in his/her HMD. This example is just to illustrate extreme hand-based interpolation in collaborative, networked virtual environments and is provided for illustration only. To better understand the significance of this figure, please watch the paper's presentation found in [9]. DO NOT TRY THIS AT HOME.

intervals based on the user's or developer's preferences. This logged movement, that is either a translation and/or a rotation, is constantly transcoded into a suitable format and relayed to the VR application and rendered as a corresponding action, e.g., hand movement, object transformation or some action. The controller's data format to be transmitted to the rendering engine affects the overall performance and quality of experience (QoE) and poses challenges that must be addressed. These challenges involve keeping the latency between the movement of the controller and its respective visualization in the HMD below a certain threshold that will not break the user's immersiveness. Furthermore, the information must be relayed efficiently such that a continuous movement of the controller results in a smooth jitter-less outcome in the VR environment. Such challenges heavily depend on the implementation details regarding the communication channel that handles the way that position and rotation of the controller is relayed, as well as the choice of a suitable interpolation technique. The displacement data are transmitted at discrete time intervals, approximately 20–40 times per second. To maintain a high frame-per-second scenery in the VR, multiple in-between frames must be created on-the-fly by the appropriate tweening algorithm. An efficient algorithm will allow the generation of natural flow frames while requiring fewer intermediate keyframes. Such algorithms will help reduce a) bandwidth usage between the HMD and the rendering engine and b) CPU-strain, resulting in lower energy consumption as well as lower latency issues in bandwidth-restricted networks. Moreover, HMDs with controllers of limited frequency will still be able to deliver the same results as more expensive HMDs.

The current state-of-the-art methods regarding the format used to transmit the displacement data mainly involves the use of 3D vectors for translation and quaternions for rotation data. These representation forms are dominant due to the fact that they involve very few bytes to be represented (3 and 4 respectively) and the fact that they support fast and efficient interpolations. Specifically, 3D vectors are usually linearly interpolated where as the SLERP method is usually used for quaternion blending. In some engines, such as Unity3D, rotations are sometimes provided in terms of Euler angles, but for interpolation needs, they are internally transformed to their quaternion equivalents.

Our Contribution. In this work, we propose the use of geometric algebra (GA) as a means to encapsulate the positional and rotational data of the hand-based VR HMD controllers and to generate the intermediate frames in the rendering engine. Our idea aims to take advantage of the fact that basic geometric entities used in VR, such as points, planes, lines, translations, rotations and dilations (uniform scalings), can be uniformly represented as *multivectors*, i.e., elements of a suitable geometric algebra such as 3D Projective (3D PGA) or 3D Conformal Geometric Algebra (3D CGA). Algebras such as 3D PGA and 3D CGA are showing rapid adaptation to VR implementations due to their ability to represent the commonly used vectors, quaternions and dual-quaternions natively as multivectors. In fact, quaternions and dual-quaternions are contained as a sub-algebra in both these algebras [7]. Therefore, they incorporate all benefits of quaternions and dual-quaternions representation such as artifact minimization in interpolated frames [11]. Furthermore, geometric algebras enable powerful geometric predicates and modules within an all-in-one framework [10], providing, if used with caution, performance which is on par with the current state-of-the-art frameworks [14]. We illustrate convincing results in a modern game engine and a medical VR collaborative training scenario (see the video presentation of this work [9] and Fig. 2).

Fig. 2. Images taken from a modern VR training application that incorporates our proposed interpolation methods for all rigid object transformations as well as hand and avatar movements. It is recommended to see the video presentation of this work [9], to better understand the significance of these figures.

2   State of the Art

The current state-of-the-art for representing the controller's displacement are 3D vectors for the positional data and quaternions for the rotational data. Regarding the position, the controllers log their current position $v = (v_x, v_y, v_z)$ at each time step with respect to a point they consider as the origin. Their rotation is stored as a *unit* quaternion $q = (q_x, q_y, q_z, q_w) = q_x \boldsymbol{i} + q_y \boldsymbol{j} + q_z \boldsymbol{k} + q_w$, i.e., it holds that $q_x^2 + q_y^2 + q_z^2 + q_w^2 = 1$. The use of unit quaternions revolutionized graphics as it provided a convenient, minimal way to represent rotations, while avoiding known problems (e.g., gimbal lock) of other representation forms such as Euler angles [11]. The ways to change between unit quaternions and other forms representing the same rotation, such as rotation matrices and Euler angles, are summarized in [2].

The interpolation of the 3D vectors containing the positional data is done linearly, i.e., given v and w vectors we may generate the intermediate vectors $(1 - a)v + aw$, for as many $a \in [0, 1]$ as needed. Given the unit quaternions q and r the intermediate quaternions are evaluated using the SLERP blending, i.e., we evaluate $q(q^{-1}r)^a$, for as many $a \in [0, 1]$ as needed, like before. If these intermediate quaternions are applied to a point p, the image of p, as a goes from 0 to 1, has a uniform angular velocity around a fixed rotation axis, which results in a smooth rotation of objects and animated models.

3   Room for Improvements

The current state for representing and interpolating positional and rotational data is based on the use of 3D vectors and quaternions as the main VR rendering engines, Unity3D and Unreal Engine, have the respective frameworks already built in. Graphics courses worldwide mention quaternions as the next evolution step of Euler angles; a step that simplified things and amended interpolation problems without adding too much overhead in the process. Despite it being widespread, the combined use of vectors and quaternions does not come without limitations.

A drawback that often arises lies in the fact that the simultaneous linear interpolation of the vectors with the SLERP interpolation of the quaternions applied to rigid objects does not always yield smooth, natural looking results in VR. This is empirically observed on various objects, depending on the movement the user *expects* to see when moving the controllers. Such *artifacts* usually require the developer's intervention to be amended, usually by demanding more intermediate displacements from the controller to be sent, i.e., by introducing more non-interpolated keyframes. This results mainly in the increase of bandwidth required as more information must be sent back and forth between the rendering engine and the input device, causing a hindrance in the networking layer. Multiplayer VR applications, that heavily rely on the input of multiple users on the same rendering engine for multiple objects, are influenced even more, when such a need arises. Furthermore, the problem is intensified if the rendering application resides on a cloud or edge node; such scenarios are becoming increasingly more common as they are accelerated by the advancements of 5G networks and the relative functionalities they provide.

4   Proposing New Approaches

4.1   Proposed Method Based on Dual Quaternions

In the past few years, graphics specialists have shown that dual quaternions can be a viable alternative and improvement over quaternions, as they allow us to unify the translation and rotation data into a single entity. Dual quaternions are created by quaternions if dual numbers are used instead of real numbers as coefficients, i.e., they are of the form $d := A + \epsilon B$, where A and B are ordinary quaternions and ϵ is the *dual unit*, an element that commutes with every element and satisfies $\epsilon^2 = 0$ [12]. A subset of these entities, called *unit dual quaternions*, are indeed isomorphic to the transformation of a rigid body. A clear advantage of using dual quaternions is the fact that we only need one framework to maintain and that applying the encapsulated information to a single point requires a simple sandwich operator. Moreover, the rotation stored in the unit dual quaternion $A + \epsilon B$ can be easily extracted as the quaternion $r := A$ is the unit quaternion that amounts to the same rotation. Furthermore, if $B^\star$ denotes the conjugate quaternion of B, then $t := 2AB^\star$ is a pure quaternion whose coefficients form the translation vector [12].

Taking advantage of the above, we propose the replacement of the current state-of-the-art sequence (see Fig. 3, Top) with the following (see Fig. 3, Middle). The displacement data of an object is again represented as a vector and a quaternion; in this way, only a total of 7 float values (3 and 4 respectively) need to be transmitted. The VR engine combines them in a dual quaternion [12] and interpolates with the previous state of the object, also stored as a dual quaternion. Depending on the engine's and the user's preferences, a number of in-between frames are generated via SLERP interpolation [11] of the original and final data. For each dual-quaternion received or generated, we decompose it to a vector and a quaternion and apply them to the object. This step is necessary to take advantage of the built-in optimized mechanisms and GPU implementations of the VR engine.

A major advantage of the proposed method is that we can obtain similar results with the state-of-the-art method by sending less keyframes per second. As an empirical law, we may send 20 displacement data per second with our method to obtain the same quality of generated frames as if we had sent 30 data per second with the current state-of-the-art method. This 33% reduction of required data applies for each user of the VR application, greatly lowering the bandwidth required as more users join. As an example, if n users participate, the total displacement data required for our method would be $1120n$ bytes per second (20 messages per second X 7 floats per message X 8 bytes per float, assuming a classic implementation) as opposed to $1680n$ bytes per second (20 messages per second X 7 floats per message X 8 bytes per float) with the default method. The numbers of updates per second mentioned above relate to the case of unrestricted-bandwidth network; for the respective results regarding constrained networks Sect. 5 and Table 1. The performance boost of our method

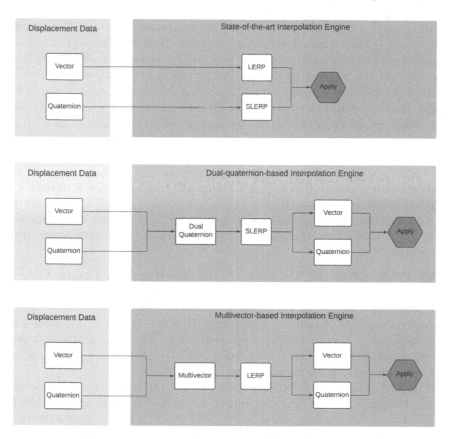

Fig. 3. Algorithm layout of the different interpolation engines used to generate intermediate frames.

is further validated as it is used in the MAGES SDK [17] for cooperative VR medical operations.

The drawbacks of this method is the need to constantly transform dual-quaternions to vector and rotation data after every interpolation step but this performance overhead is tolerable as the extraction of the displacement data is accomplished in a straight-forward way. Also, performing SLERP on a dual quaternion (proposed method) instead of a quaternion (state-of-the-art method) demands more operations per step. The trade-offs between the two methods seem to favor our method, especially in the case of collaborative VR applications.

4.2 Proposed Method Based on Multivectors

The proposed method described in Sect. 4.1 was based on the use of dual quaternions and the fact that interpolating them (using SLERP) produced smooth intermediate frames. In this section, we go one step further and suggest the use of multivectors instead of dual-quaternions (see Fig. 3, Bottom). This transition can be done in a straight-forward way if we use multivectors of 3D Conformal (see [7]) or 3D Projective Algebra (see [4] and its updated Chap. 11 in [3]). The interpolation of the resulting multivectors can be accomplished via LERP [6]; if M_1 and M_2 correspond to two consecutive displacement data, then we can generate the in-between multivectors $(1-a)M_1 + aM_2$, for as many $a \in [0,1]$ as needed (and normalize them if needed). Notice that since we are only applying these displacements to rigid bodies, we may use LERP instead of SLERP (see Fig. 4). For every (normalized) multivector M received or interpolated, we may now extract the translation vector and rotation quaternion. Every multivector received or generated has to be decomposed to a vector and a quaternion in order to be applied to the object, as modern VR Engines natively support only the latter two formats. Assume that $M = T * R$ where T and R are the multivectors encapsulating the translation and rotation, we may extract them depending on the Geometric Algebra used (all products below are geometric unless stated otherwise):

- **3D PGA**: Given M, we evaluate $e_0 M$. Since in this algebra $T = 1 - 0.5e_0(t_1 e_1 + t_2 e_2 + t_3 e_3)$, represents the translation by (t_1, t_2, t_3) and $e_0 e_0 = 0$, it holds that $e_0 M = e_0 T R = e_0 R$. Therefore, if $e_0 Q = e_0 R = ae_0 + be_{012} + ce_{013} + de_{023}$, we obtain the multivector $R = a + be_{12} + ce_{13} + de_{23}$ which corresponds to the quaternion $q = a - di + cj - bk$. We can now evaluate T as it equals $MR^{-1} = M(a - be_{12} - ce_{13} - de_{23}) = 1 + xe_{01} + ye_{02} + ze_{03}$ and extract the translation vector $(-2x, -2y, -2z)$.
- **3D CGA**: Given M, we obtain R by adding the terms of M that contain only the basis vectors $\{1, e_1, e_2, e_3, e_{12}, e_{23}, e_{13}\}$. This derives from the fact that $T = 1 - 0.5 * (t_1 e_1 + t_2 e_2 + t_3 e_3)(e_4 + e_5)$ (which corresponds to the translation by (t_1, t_2, t_3)) and therefore $TR = R + m$ where m necessarily contains basis elements containing e_4 and e_5 (or their geometric product) that cannot be canceled out. After the obtaining of R, we simply evaluate $T = MR^{-1}$, normalize it and extract the translation vector (t_1, t_2, t_3) from the quantity $t = T \cdot (e_5 - e_4) = t_1 e_1 + t_2 e_2 + t_3 e_3$. The conversion of R to quaternions and the evaluation of R^{-1} is identical with the case of 3D PGA above.

The advantage of such a method lies on the fact that we can use LERP blending of multivectors instead of SLERP. This saves as a lot of time and CPU-strain; SLERP interpolation requires the evaluation of a multivector's logarithm, which requires a lot of complex operations [5]. Notice that, LERP is efficient in our case since only rigid objects displacements are transfered via the network; if we wanted to animate skinned models via multivectors it is known that only SLERP can produce jitter-less intermediate frames [11]. Another gain of this proposed method is the ability to incorporate it in an all-in-one GA framework, that will use only multivectors to represent model, deformation and animation data. Such a framework is able to deliver efficient results and embeds powerful modules [10,14,15]. In such frameworks, decomposition of multivectors to vectors and quaternions will be redundant, as we can apply the displacement to the object's multivector form via a simple sandwich operation.

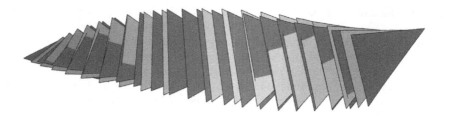

Fig. 4. A triangular object is interpolated via multivectors. A motor including both a translation and a rotation is applied to the triangle via its mass center. Between the extreme positions of the object, we generate 20 intermediate frames using LERP (yellow) and SLERP (green) interpolation of the multivector. Only minimal differences are spotted between the two outcomes. (Color figure online)

The trade-offs of such an implementation are based on the fact that modern VR engines do not natively support multivectors and therefore production-ready modules, with basic functions implemented, are almost non-existent. An exception is the Klein C++ module for 3D PGA, found in www.jeremyong.com/klein; for 3D CGA no such module is available the moment this paper is written. This makes it difficult for GA non-experts to adopt and implement such methods. Furthermore, multivectors require 16 (3D PGA) or 32 (3D CGA) float values to be represented and therefore even a simple addition between two amounts to 16 or 32 float operations respectively. Unoptimized modules, usually running in CPU and not in GPU, may result in slow rendering. On the contrary, optimized ones, such as GAALOP [8], can take advantage of the fact that very few of the multivector coordinates are indeed non-zero, as the multivectors involved are always motors, i.e., represent translations and/or rotations, and therefore have specific form.

5 Our Results

The methods proposed were implemented in Unity3D and applied to a VR collaborative training scenario. The video accompanying this work demonstrates the effectiveness of our methods compared with the current state of the art. Specifically, we compare the three methods under different input rates per second, i.e., the keyframes sent per second to the VR rendering engine. The input rates tested are 5, 10, 15 and 20 frames per second (fps), where the last option is an optimal value to avoid CPU/GPU strain in collaborative VR scenarios. These rates are indicative values of the maximum possible fps that would be sent in a network whose bandwidth rates from very-limited (5 fps) to unrestricted (more than 20 fps). In lower fps, our methods yield jitter-less interpolated frames compared to the state-of-the-art method, which would require 30 fps to replicate similar output. As mentioned before, this reduction of required data that must be transfered per second by 33%–58% (depending on the network quality, see Table 1) is multiplied by every active user, increasing the impact and the effectiveness of our methods in bandwidth-restricted environments.

Table 1. Summary of the metrics of our methods (Ours) versus the state-of-the-art methods (SoA). The first column describes the possible network quality which correlates to the maximum number of updates per second that can be performed. The second column contains the update rate required to obtain the same QoE under the specific network quality limitations. The third column contains the comparison of the bandwidth and the running time difference by our algorithms compared with the SoA algorithm, when using the respective update rates of the second column.

Network quality	How to achieve best QoE	Metrics on our methods
Excellent	SoA: 30 updates/sec	33% less bandwidth
	Ours: 20 updates/sec	16.5% lower running time
Good	SoA: 20 updates/sec	50% less bandwidth
	Ours: 10 updates/sec	16.5% lower running time
Mediocre	SoA: 15 updates/sec	53% less bandwidth
	Ours: 7 updates/sec	16.5% lower running time
Poor	SoA: 12 updates/sec	58% less bandwidth
	Ours: 5 updates/sec	16.5% lower running time

The workflows of the two algorithms, compared with the current state of the art, are summarized in Fig. 3. In Fig. 5 we demonstrate the interpolation of the same object, at specific time intervals, for all methods; the intermediate frames feel natural for both methods proposed.

In Table 1, it is demonstrated that, under various network restrictions, both proposed methods required less data (in terms of updates per sec) to be transmitted via the network to achieve the same QoE. This decrease in data transfer leads to a lower energy consumption of the HMDs by 10% (on average, preliminary result) and therefore enhances the overall mobility of the devices relying on batteries. Our methods provide a performance boost, decrease the required time to perform the same operation, with fewer keyframes but the same number of total generated frames, by 16.5% (on average). The running times were produced in a PC with a 3,1 GHz 16-Core Intel Core i9 processor, with 32 GBs of DDR4 memory. The same percentage of performance boost is expected in less powerful CPUs; in this case, the overall impact, in terms of absolute running time, will be even more significant.

Fig. 5. Different interpolation algorithms yield different, yet jitter-less, intermediate frames. (Top): State of the art: Vector and quaternion separate interpolation. (Middle): Dual-quaternion based interpolation algorithm. (Bottom): Multivector based interpolation algorithm.

6   Conclusions and Future Work

In this work, we proposed two alternative interpolation algorithms based on dual-quaternions and multivectors respectively. These algorithms can be applied in the context of a networked virtual environment to efficiently handle the interpolation of displacement data for hand-based VR HMDs. The amount of displacement data per second that should be transmitted over the network to support a good QoE can be reduced using our methods instead of the state-of-the-art. This results in a performance boost and also lowers device energy consumption. The significance of our proposed methods are further highlighted in bandwidth-restricted networks and when multiple users are involved. Our results are illustrated in a modern game engine and a medical VR collaborative training scenario.

The proposed algorithms and results can be further improved by using optimized C# Geometric Algebra bindings (such as the ones provided in bivector.net). This would allow for efficient SLERP for the multivector interpolation engine and therefore unlock the potential to apply motors for rigged model animation in VR, as in [15]. It is our intention to integrate the algorithms proposed to an all-in-one GA framework that also enables features such as cut, tear and drill, as in [10].

Acknowledgments. This work was co-financed by European Regional Development Fund of the European Union and Greek national funds through the Operational Program Competitiveness, Entrepreneurship and Innovation, under the call RESEARCH - CREATE - INNOVATE (project codes: T1EDK-01149 and T1EDK-01448). The project also received funding from the European Union's Horizon 2020 research and innovation programme under grant agreement No 871793.

References

1. Churchill, E.F., Snowdon, D.: Collaborative virtual environments: an introductory review of issues and systems. Virtual Reality **3**(1), 3–15 (1998)
2. Diebel, J.: Representing attitude: euler angles, unit quaternions, and rotation vectors. Matrix **58**(15–16), 1–35 (2006)
3. Dorst, L.: A guided tour to the plane-based geometric algebra pga. https://bivector.net/PGA4CS.html
4. Dorst, L., Fontijne, D., Mann, S.: Geometric algebra for computer science - an object-oriented approach to geometry. The Morgan Kaufmann series in computer graphics (2007)
5. Dorst, L., Valkenburg, R.: Square root and logarithm of rotors in 3d conformal geometric algebra using polar decomposition. In: Guide to Geometric Algebra in Practice, pp. 81–104. Springer, London (2011). https://doi.org/10.1007/978-0-85729-811-9_5
6. Hadfield, H., Lasenby, J.: Direct linear interpolation of geometric objects in conformal geometric algebra. Adv. Appl. Clifford Algebras **29**(4), 1–25 (2019). https://doi.org/10.1007/s00006-019-1003-y
7. Hildenbrand, D.: Foundations of geometric algebra computing. Springer (2013)
8. Hildenbrand, D., Pitt, J., Koch, A.: Gaalop-high performance parallel computing based on conformal geometric algebra. In: Geometric Algebra Computing, pp. 477–494. Springer (2010)
9. Kamarianakis, M., Lydatakis, N., Papagiannakis, G.: Video presentation of the paper 'Never Drop the Ball' (2021). https://youtu.be/xoXrRU-2gLQ
10. Kamarianakis, M., Papagiannakis, G.: An all-in-one geometric algorithm for cutting, tearing, drilling deformable models. arXiv preprint arXiv:2102.07499 (2021)
11. Kavan, L., Collins, S., Žára, J., O'Sullivan, C.: Geometric skinning with approximate dual quaternion blending. ACM Trans. Graph. **27**(4), 105 (2008)
12. Kenwright, B.: A beginners guide to dual-quaternions: What they are, how they work, and how to use them for 3D character hierarchies. In: WSCG 2012 - Conference Proceedings, pp. 1–10. Newcastle University, United Kingdom, December 2012
13. Molet, T., et al.: Anyone for tennis? Presence: Teleoperators Virtual Environ. **8**(2), 140–156 (1999)
14. Papaefthymiou, M., Hildenbrand, D., Papagiannakis, G.: An inclusive Conformal Geometric Algebra GPU animation interpolation and deformation algorithm. Vis. Comput. **32**(6–8), 751–759 (2016)
15. Papagiannakis, G.: Geometric algebra rotors for skinned character animation blending. In: SIGGRAPH Asia 2013 Technical Briefs, SA 2013, December 2013
16. Papagiannakis, G., Singh, G., Magnenat-Thalmann, N.: A survey of mobile and wireless technologies for augmented reality systems. Comput. Animation Virtual Worlds **19**(1), 3–22 (2008)
17. Papagiannakis, G., et al.: Mages 3.0: Tying the knot of medical vr. In: ACM SIGGRAPH 2020 Immersive Pavilion. Association for Computing Machinery (2020)
18. Ruan, J., Xie, D.: Networked vr: State of the art, solutions, and challenges. Electronics **10**(2), 166 (2021)
19. Vilmi, O.: Real-time Multiplayer Software Architecture. Bachelor thesis, Metropolia University of Applied Sciences, March 2020

The Rules of 4-Dimensional Perspective: How to Implement Lorentz Transformations in Relativistic Visualization

Andrew J. S. Hamilton$^{(\boxtimes)}$ (iD)

JILA and Department Astrophysical and Planetary Sciences, Box 440,
U. Colorado Boulder, Boulder, CO 80309, USA
Andrew.Hamilton@colorado.edu
http://jila.colorado.edu/~ajsh/

Abstract. This paper presents a pedagogical introduction to the issue of how to implement Lorentz transformations in relativistic visualization. The most efficient approach is to use the even geometric algebra in 3+1 spacetime dimensions, or equivalently complex quaternions, which are fast, compact, and robust, and straightforward to compose, interpolate, and spline. The approach has been incorporated into the Black Hole Flight Simulator, an interactive general relativistic ray-tracing program developed by the author.

Keywords: Special relativistic visualization · Lorentz transformations · Complex quaternions

1 Introduction

Einstein's theory of Special Relativity revolutionized space and time, uniting them from the separate 3-dimensional and 1-dimensional entities familiar to everyday experience, into an inextricably entwined 4-dimensional spacetime. The consequences of special relativity are not evident to everyday experience because we move through our surroundings at only a tiny fraction of the speed of light. But if you moved around at near the speed of light, then you would very much notice [1–3].

The positions of objects in 3 dimensions are described by 3-dimensional vectors, or 3-vectors for short. Of primary importance in 3d visualization software is the ability to rotate 3-vectors rapidly and robustly. A rotation in 3 dimensions decomposes into rotations about each of 3 directions. It is well known that the best way to program rotations is using quaternions, invented by William Rowan Hamilton in 1843 [4]. The algebra of quaternions is precisely that of the even Clifford algebra, or geometric algebra, in 3 spatial dimensions.

In relativistic visualization, the perceived position of an object is described by a 4-dimensional vector, a 4-vector. The analog of rotations of a 4-vector are

© Springer Nature Switzerland AG 2021
N. Magnenat-Thalmann et al. (Eds.): CGI 2021, LNCS 13002, pp. 705–717, 2021.
https://doi.org/10.1007/978-3-030-89029-2_53

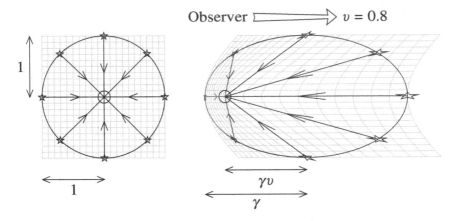

Fig. 1. The rules of 4-dimensional perspective. In special relativity, the scene seen by an observer moving through the scene (right) is relativistically beamed compared to the scene seen by an observer at rest relative to the scene (left). On the left, the observer at the center of the circle is at rest relative to the surrounding scene. On the right, the observer is moving to the right through the same scene at $v = 0.8$ times the speed of light. The scene is distorted into a celestial ellipsoid with the observer displaced to its focus. The arrowed lines represent energy-momenta of photons. The length of an arrowed line is proportional to the perceived energy of the photon. The scene ahead of the moving observer appears concentrated, blueshifted, and farther away, while the scene behind appears expanded, redshifted, and closer.

Lorentz transformations [5]. To the usual 3 spatial rotations of space, Lorentz transformations adjoin 3 rotations between space and time, also known as boosts, a total of 6 spacetime rotations. The 3 boosts represent a change of the observer's velocity along each of the 3 spatial directions. To someone moving through a scene at much less than the speed of light, these boosts have a negligible effect on the appearance of a scene. But if you move at near the speed of light, then the boosts are very evident.

The purpose of this paper is to present a pedagogical introduction to implementing Lorentz transformations in computer visualizations. The paper starts, Sect. 2, by presenting a conceptual picture of how a scene appears distorted to an observer who moves through it at relativistic speed [6]. Then Sect. 3 describes how to implement Lorentz transformations using complex quaternions, also called biquaternions by William Rowan Hamilton. The equivalence of the Lorentz group to complex quaternions was discovered by Silberstein in 1912 [7], and remarked by Dirac [8]; see [9] for further references. The algebra of complex quaternions is precisely that of the even geometric algebra in 3+1 spacetime dimensions.

In relativity, time behaves mathematically as if it were an imaginary spatial dimension. Lorentz transformations rotate spatial and time dimensions among each other. In relativity it is extremely useful to use "natural" units in which the speed of light is one, $c = 1$, since then space and time are measured in the same unit.

2   The Rules of 4-Dimensional Perspective

The conceptual picture presented in this section is from the author's website [6], where animations may be found.

In 3-dimensional perspective, two ideas are fundamental:

- A straight line in 3 dimensions remains a straight line in perspective;
- Parallel lines meet at a vanishing point.

The rules that govern the appearance of a scene when you move through it at near the speed of light can be called the rules of 4-dimensional perspective. These rules can be grasped, much like the rules of 3-dimensional perspective, without needing to understand intricate mathematics. The rules of 4-dimensional perspective can be summarized as follows:

- Paint the scene at rest on the surface of a celestial sphere;
- Stretch the celestial sphere by Lorentz factor γ along the direction of motion into a celestial ellipsoid, and displace the observer to a focus of the ellipsoid;
- Adjust the brightness, color, and clock speed at any point on the ellipsoid in proportion to the length of the radius between the point and the observer.

Figure 1 illustrates the rules of 4-dimensional perspective. On the left, you are at rest relative to the scene. Imagine painting the scene on a celestial sphere around you. The arrows represent the directions of lightrays (photons) from the scene on the celestial sphere to you at the center. Technically, these arrows represent the energy-momentum 4-vectors of the lightrays that you see, Sect. 3.4.

On the right in Fig. 1, you are moving to the right through the scene, at velocity $v = 0.8$ times the speed of light. The celestial sphere is stretched along the direction of your motion by the Lorentz gamma-factor $\gamma = 1/\sqrt{1 - 0.8^2} = 5/3$ into a celestial ellipsoid. You, the observer, are not at the center of the ellipsoid, but rather at one of its foci (the left one, if you are moving to the right). The focus of the celestial ellipsoid, where you the observer are, is displaced from center by $\gamma v = 4/3$. The scene appears relativistically aberrated, which is to say concentrated ahead of you, and expanded behind you.

The lengths of the arrows in Fig. 1 are proportional to the energies, or frequencies, of the photons that you see. When you are moving through the scene at near light speed, the arrows ahead of you, in your direction of motion, are longer than at rest, so you see the photons blue-shifted, increased in energy, increased in frequency. Conversely, the arrows behind you are shorter than at rest, so you see the photons red-shifted, decreased in energy, decreased in frequency. Since photons are good clocks, the change in photon frequency also tells you how fast or slow clocks attached to the scene appear to you to run.

The following table summarizes the four effects of relativistic beaming on the appearance of a scene ahead of you and behind you as you move through it at near the speed of light:

Effect	Ahead	Behind
Aberration	Concentrated	Expanded
Color	Blueshifted	Redshifted
Brightness	Brighter	Dimmer
Time	Speeded up	Slowed down

Figure 2 shows a visualization of passing by a sphere at near the speed of light, in this case $v = 0.97$ (in natural units $c = 1$). The visualization was made using the Black Hole Flight Simulator software [11]. The visualization illustrates how relativistic aberration distorts the appearance of the sphere, concentrating it and blueshifting it towards the direction the oberver is moving, and expanding and redshifting it behind.

A feature of relativistic aberration is that circles transform to circles, and angles are preserved. These facts were first pointed out by [12] and [13], prior to which it had been widely thought that circles would appear Lorentz-contracted and therefore squashed. Lines of latitude and longitude on the surface of a sphere are circles, and they intersect at right angles. Figure 2 illustrates how relativistic aberration preserves these properties. The outline of a sphere is itself a circle, and the outline of a relativistically aberrated sphere remains circular.

 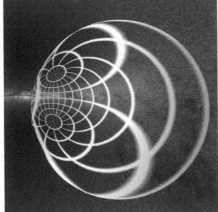

Fig. 2. Passing by a sphere at 0.97 of the speed of light ($\gamma v = 4$), in the general direction of the center of our Galaxy, the Milky Way (left) undistorted, (right) relativistically beamed. The sphere is painted with lines of latitude and longitude. The background is an image of the Milky Way from Gaia Data Release 3 [10]. In the undistorted (left) view, most of the sphere is behind the observer; relativistic aberration (right) brings the sphere behind into view. The sphere and background are colored with appropriately blue- and red-shifted blackbody colors; the unredshifted color temperature is 5,780 K, the color of the Sun. The field of view is 105° across the diagonal. The visualization was made using the Black Hole Flight Simulator software [11].

3 How to Implement Lorentz Transformations on a Computer

The advantages of quaternions for implementing spatial rotations are well-known to 3d game programmers. Compared to standard rotation matrices, quaternions offer increased speed (fewer multiplications) and require less storage, and their algebraic properties simplify composition, interpolation, and splining.

Complex quaternions retain similar advantages for implementing Lorentz transformations. They are fast, compact, and straightforward to interpolate or spline. Moreover, since complex quaternions contain real quaternions, Lorentz transformations can be implemented as an extension of spatial rotations in 3d programs that use quaternions to implement spatial rotations.

At a deeper level, the elegant properties of quaternions and complex quaternions can be traced to the fact that they are the even geometric subalgebras in respectively 3 spatial dimensions and 3+1 spacetime dimensions.

3.1 Real Quaternions

It is useful to start by reviewing basic definitions and properties of ordinary (real) quaternions. Many of these properties carry over to complex quaternions.

A quaternion q is a kind of souped-up complex number,

$$q = w + ix + jy + kz \,, \tag{1}$$

where w, x, y, z are real numbers, and the three imaginary numbers i, j, k, are defined to satisfy

$$i^2 = j^2 = k^2 = -ijk = -1 \,. \tag{2}$$

The convention $ijk = 1$ in the definition (2) allows i, j, k to be identified as bivectors (4) of the 3d geometric algebra, but is opposite to the traditional definition $ijk = -1$ famously carved by William Rowan Hamilton in the stone of Brougham Bridge while walking with his wife along the Royal Canal to Dublin on 16 October 1843 [4]. A consequence of Eqs. (2) is that each pair of imaginary numbers anticommutes:

$$ij = -ji = -k \,, \quad jk = -kj = -i \,, \quad ki = -ik = -j \,. \tag{3}$$

Quaternions are distributive and associative, but not commutative. Similarly to complex numbers, two quaternions are multiplied by multiplying and combining their components.

The algebra of quaternions can be recognized as that of the even geometric algebra in 3 spatial dimensions. The 3d geometric algebra is generated by the $1 + 3 + 3 + 1 = 8 = 2^3$ orthornormal basis multivectors

$$\underset{\text{1 scalar}}{1} \,, \quad \underset{\text{3 vectors}}{\gamma_x \,, \gamma_y \,, \gamma_z} \,, \quad \underset{\text{3 bivectors (pseudovectors)}}{I_3\gamma_x \,, I_3\gamma_y \,, I_3\gamma_z} \,, \quad \underset{\text{1 pseudoscalar}}{I_3 \equiv \gamma_x\gamma_y\gamma_z} \,. \tag{4}$$

The quaternionic imaginaries i, j, k are just the basis bivectors $I_3\gamma_a$ of the 3d geometric algebra.

A quaternion q can be stored as a 4-component object

$$q = \{ w \quad x \quad y \quad z \} . \tag{5}$$

The convention to put the scalar component w in the first position is standard in mathematics and physics.

A basic operation on quaternions is quaternionic conjugation, also called reversal in the geometric algebra, which is analogous to taking the complex conjugate of a complex number. The reverse $\bar{q}$ of a quaternion q is the quaternion obtained by flipping the sign of all 3 imaginary components,

$$\bar{q} \equiv \{ w \quad -x \quad -y \quad -z \} . \tag{6}$$

The modulus $|q|$ of a quaternion q is, similarly to the modulus of a complex number, the square root of the product of itself with its reverse,

$$|q| = \sqrt{q\bar{q}} = \sqrt{\bar{q}q} = \sqrt{w^2 + x^2 + y^2 + z^2} . \tag{7}$$

The modulus $|q|$ of a quaternion is unchanged by any rotation.

One of the advantages of quaternions is that quaternions are easy to invert: the inverse of a quaternion q is, again similarly to the inverse of a complex number, its reverse $\bar{q}$ divided by its squared modulus,

$$q^{-1} = \frac{\bar{q}}{\bar{q}q} . \tag{8}$$

The positions of objects in a 3d scene are described by vectors in the 3d geometric algebra. According to the array (4) of basis multivectors, a basis vector γ_a in the 3d geometric algebra equals minus the pseudoscalar times a bivector, $\gamma_a = -I_3(I_3\gamma_a)$, which implies that a vector in 3d rotates in the same way as a bivector. The result is that a vector in a 3d program can be handled as though it were a bivector, that is, a quaternion with zero scalar component. The 3-vector position $\boldsymbol{r}$ of an object in a 3d scene can be represented by a quaternion

$$\boldsymbol{r} = ix + jy + kz = \{ 0 \quad x \quad y \quad z \} . \tag{9}$$

A 3d rotation is represented by a quaternion of unit modulus, a rotor in the 3d geometric algebra. For example, the rotor R corresponding to a right-handed rotation by angle θ about the x-direction is

$$R = e^{-i\theta/2} = \cos(\theta/2) - i\sin(\theta/2)$$
$$= \{ \cos(\theta/2) \quad -\sin(\theta/2) \quad 0 \quad 0 \} . \tag{10}$$

More generally, if $\boldsymbol{n} = ix + jy + kz$ is a unit vector in the direction $\{x, y, z\}$, then a right-handed rotation by angle θ about the $\boldsymbol{n}$-direction is represented by the rotor

$$R = e^{-\boldsymbol{n}\theta/2} = \cos(\theta/2) - \boldsymbol{n}\sin(\theta/2) . \tag{11}$$

A rotation S following a rotation R is just their quaternionic product SR.

Rotating a 3-vector $\boldsymbol{r}$ by a rotor R is accomplished by taking the quaternionic product

$$\boldsymbol{r} \to R\boldsymbol{r}\overline{R} , \tag{12}$$

a one-line calculation in a language that supports quaternionic operations.

It should be remarked that the sign conventions above are the standard ones in physics. Software implementations of quaternions vary in their conventions.

3.2 Complex Quaternions

Introduce yet another imaginary I which commutes with the 3 quaternionic imaginaries i, j, k,

$$I^2 = -1 , \quad Ii = iI , \quad Ij = jI , \quad Ik = kI . \tag{13}$$

A complex quaternion q is a quaternion with complex coefficients, $w = w_R + I w_I$, etc.,

$$q = w + ix + jy + kz . \tag{14}$$

A complex quaternion q can be stored as the 8-component object

$$q = q_R + I q_I = \begin{Bmatrix} w_R & x_R & y_R & z_R \\ w_I & x_I & y_I & z_I \end{Bmatrix} . \tag{15}$$

The top line contains the real part q_R of the quaternion q, the bottom line the imaginary part q_I. A complex quaternion can be implemented in software as a pair of quaternions.

The algebra of complex quaternions is that of the even geometric algebra in 3+1 spacetime dimensions. The geometric algebra in 3+1 dimensions is generated by the $1 + 4 + 6 + 4 + 1 = 16 = 2^4$ orthornormal basis multivectors

$$\begin{array}{cccccc} 1, & \gamma_t, \gamma_a , & \gamma_a\gamma_b, I\gamma_a\gamma_b, & I\gamma_t, I\gamma_a , & I \equiv \gamma_t\gamma_x\gamma_y\gamma_z , \\ \text{1 scalar} & \text{4 vectors} & \text{6 bivectors} & \text{4 pseudovectors} & \text{1 pseudoscalar} \end{array} \tag{16}$$

where indices a, b run over the 3 spatial dimensions x, y, z. The imaginary I in the complex quaternion (15) is just the pseudoscalar of the geometric algebra. The 6 bivectors of the geometric algebra comprise 3 spatial bivectors $\gamma_a\gamma_b$, along with 3 bivectors $I\gamma_a\gamma_b$ which look like spatial bivectors multiplied by the pseudoscalar. The geometric algebra in 3+1 dimensions is precisely that of Dirac γ-matrices in relativistic physics, which accounts for the notation γ_m.

The reverse $\overline{q}$ of the complex quaternion (15) is, similarly to the reverse (6) of a real quaternion, the quaternion with all quaternionic imaginary components flipped in sign,

$$\overline{q} = \begin{Bmatrix} w_R & -x_R & -y_R & -z_R \\ w_I & -x_I & -y_I & -z_I \end{Bmatrix} . \tag{17}$$

The complex conjugate q^* of the quaternion is the quaternion with all imaginary I components flipped,

$$q^\star = \left\{ \begin{matrix} w_R & x_R & y_R & z_R \\ -w_I & -x_I & -y_I & -z_I \end{matrix} \right\} . \tag{18}$$

The operations of reversal and complex conjugation commute.

The modulus $|q|$ of a complex quaternion is defined, similarly to the modulus (7) of a real quaternion, to be the square root of the product $q\bar{q}$ of the complex quaternion with its reverse, but whereas the modulus of a real quaternion is a real number, the modulus of a complex quaternion is a complex (with respect to I) number,

$$|q| \equiv \sqrt{q\bar{q}} = \sqrt{\bar{q}q} = \sqrt{w^2 + x^2 + y^2 + z^2} . \tag{19}$$

The modulus $|q|$ is complex (with respect to I) because the components w, x, y, z are complex. To obtain a real number, the absolute value $\|q\|$ of the complex quaternion q, it is necessary to take the absolute value of the complex modulus,

$$\|q\| \equiv \sqrt{|q||q|^*} = \left| \sqrt{w^2 + x^2 + y^2 + z^2} \right| . \tag{20}$$

3.3   Lorentz Transformations

A Lorentz transformation, a special relativistic rotation of spacetime, can be represented as a complex quaternion of unit modulus, a Lorentz rotor R, satisfying the unimodular condition

$$R\bar{R} = 1 . \tag{21}$$

The inverse of a Lorentz rotor R is its reverse $\bar{R}$. The unimodular condition (21) is a complex (with respect to I) condition, which removes 2 degrees of freedom from the 8 degrees of freedom of a complex quaternion, leaving the Lorentz group with 6 degrees of freedom, which is as it should be.

Spatial rotations correspond to real unimodular quaternions, and account for 3 of the 6 degrees of freedom of Lorentz transformations. For example, a spatial rotation by angle θ right-handedly about the x-axis is the real Lorentz rotor

$$R = e^{-i\theta/2} = \cos(\theta/2) - i\sin(\theta/2) , \tag{22}$$

or, stored as a complex quaternion,

$$R = \left\{ \begin{matrix} \cos(\theta/2) & -\sin(\theta/2) & 0 & 0 \\ 0 & 0 & 0 & 0 \end{matrix} \right\} . \tag{23}$$

The expression (23) coincides with the earlier expression (10) for a spatial rotation as a real quaternion, which is as it should be.

Lorentz boosts account for the remaining 3 of the 6 degrees of freedom of Lorentz transformations. A Lorentz boost is mathematically equivalent to a rotation by an imaginary angle $I\theta$. Physicists call the boost angle θ of a Lorentz boost its rapidity. The velocity v of the Lorentz boost is the hyperbolic tangent of the boost angle θ,

$$v = \tanh\theta . \tag{24}$$

The Lorentz gamma-factor γ and associated momentum factor γv that appear in Fig. 1 are related to the boost angle θ by

$$\gamma = \cosh\theta , \quad \gamma v = \sinh\theta . \tag{25}$$

A Lorentz boost by boost angle θ along, for example, the x-axis is the complex Lorentz rotor

$$R = e^{-Ii\theta/2} = \cosh(\theta/2) - Ii\sinh(\theta/2) , \tag{26}$$

or, stored as a complex quaternion,

$$R = \left\{ \begin{matrix} \cosh(\theta/2) & 0 & 0 & 0 \\ 0 & -\sinh(\theta/2) & 0 & 0 \end{matrix} \right\} . \tag{27}$$

More generally, a Lorentz boost by boost angle θ along a unit 3-vector quaternion direction $\boldsymbol{n}$ is

$$R = e^{-In\theta/2} = \cosh(\theta/2) - In\sinh(\theta/2) . \tag{28}$$

The most general Lorentz transformation is a Lorentz rotor R, a unimodular complex quaternion. Any such Lorentz rotor can be decomposed into a combination of a spatial rotation and a Lorentz boost, but it is not necessary to carry out such a decomposition. The arithmetic of complex quaternions takes care of itself. The rule for composing Lorentz transformations is the same as the rule for composing spatial rotations: a Lorentz transformation S following a Lorentz transformation R is just the product SR of the corresponding complex quaternions.

A general Lorentz rotor R can be written as the exponential of a complex quaternion angle $\boldsymbol{\theta}$, which is itself the product of a complex (with respect to I) angle θ equal to the modulus of $\boldsymbol{\theta}$, and a unimodular complex 3-direction $\boldsymbol{n}$,

$$R = e^{-\boldsymbol{\theta}} = e^{-\theta n} , \tag{29}$$

with

$$\theta = |\boldsymbol{\theta}| = \theta_R + I\theta_I , \quad \boldsymbol{n} = \boldsymbol{n}_R + I\boldsymbol{n}_I , \quad \bar{\boldsymbol{n}}\boldsymbol{n} = 1 . \tag{30}$$

The complex quaternion 3-direction $\boldsymbol{n}$ is a 6-component object, but the unimodular condition on $\boldsymbol{n}$ removes 2 of the degrees of freedom, leaving $\boldsymbol{n}$ with 4 degrees of freedom. Those 4 degrees of freedom add to the 2 degrees of freedom of the complex angle θ to give 6 degrees of freedom, which is the correct number of degrees of freedom of Lorentz transformations.

3.4   4-Vectors

The positions of objects in a relativistic scene are described by 4-vectors in the geometric algebra in 3+1 dimensions. In much the same way that 3-vectors in

3d can be packaged as quaternions, Eq. (9), 4-vectors in 3+1 dimensions can be packaged as complex quaternions. In any geometric algebra, an odd element of the geometric algebra can be written uniquely as the product of some particular vector (an odd element) and an even element of the algebra. It is convenient to choose the chosen particular vector to be the time basis vector γ_t. In 3+1 dimensions, an odd element of the algebra is a sum of a vector r_1 and a pseudovector Ir_2. Their sum, the odd multivector r, can be written as the product of the time vector γ_t and an element of the even algebra, a complex quaternion q,

$$r \equiv r_1 + Ir_2 = \gamma_t q. \tag{31}$$

The odd multivector r Lorentz transforms under a Lorentz rotor R as

$$r \to R\gamma_t q\overline{R} = \gamma_t R^\star q\overline{R}. \tag{32}$$

The conjugated rotor $R^\star$ appears in the transformation (32) because commuting the time vector γ_t through the rotor R converts the latter to its complex (with respect to I) conjugate, which is true because the time vector commutes with the quaternionic imaginaries i, j, k, but anticommutes with the pseudoscalar I. Equation (32) shows that the complex quaternion q equivalent to the odd multivector r Lorentz transforms as

$$q \to R^\star q\overline{R} . \tag{33}$$

When you are looking at a scene, it is light that carries the image of the scene to your eyes. The perceived position of an object traces back along the energy-momentum 4-vector of the light that the object emits and that you see. The arrowed lightrays in Fig. 1 represent the energy-momentum 4-vectors of the lightrays. When you change your velocity through the scene, the energy-momentum 4-vectors of the lightrays Lorentz-transform accordingly. Light travels at light speed, so the components of the energy-momentum 4-vector p of a lightray (a photon) take the form

$$p = E\{1, v\} \tag{34}$$

in which the magnitude of the velocity v is one, the speed of light, $v \equiv |v| = 1$. The energy of the lightray (photon) is E, and its 3-momentum is Ev. The energy-momentum 4-vector of an object moving at the speed of light is null; in the language of the geometric algebra, the energy-momentum 4-vector p of a lightray satisfies the null condition

$$p\overline{p} = 0 . \tag{35}$$

The positions r of objects in a relativistic scene are thus not just any old 4-vectors, but rather they are null 4-vectors, satisfying the null condition

$$r\overline{r} = 0 . \tag{36}$$

The complex quaternion q equivalent to the 4-vector r, Eq. (31), satisfies the null condition

$$q\overline{q} = 0 . \tag{37}$$

In relativistic visualization, one starts by defining a rest frame, a frame with respect to which (most) objects are not moving. Relative to an observer at rest in the scene, the 3-vector of an object in the scene at distance r and unit 3-direction $\boldsymbol{n}$ is $r\boldsymbol{n}$. The direction $\boldsymbol{n}$ to the object is opposite in sign to the direction $\boldsymbol{v}$ of a lightray from the object to the observer. The null 4-vector position $\boldsymbol{r}$ of the object is encoded in the null complex quaternion

$$q = r(1 + I\boldsymbol{n}) . \tag{38}$$

For example, the null 4-vector position of an object lying in the x-direction relative to the observer is

$$q = r \begin{Bmatrix} 1 & 0 & 0 & 0 \\ 0 & 1 & 0 & 0 \end{Bmatrix} . \tag{39}$$

More generally, if the 3-vector position of the object is $r\boldsymbol{n} = \{x, y, z\}$, then the components of the corresponding null complex quaternion position q are

$$q = \begin{Bmatrix} r & 0 & 0 & 0 \\ 0 & x & y & z \end{Bmatrix} . \tag{40}$$

When the observer rotates spatially or accelerates, the scene appears to the observer Lorentz-transformed by a Lorentz rotor R, which transforms perceived null complex quaternion positions q according to Eq. (33). This is similar to the transformation (12) of a 3d position by a spatial rotation, except that the rotor R^* in the Lorentz transformation (33) is complex-conjugated. A spatial rotation corresponds to a real rotor R, whose complex conjugate is itself, in which case the Lorentz transformation (33) reduces to the spatial transformation (12). The Lorentz transformation (33) of the position q instructs to multiply three complex quaternions R^*, q, and $\overline{R}$, a one-line expression in a language that supports complex quaternion operations.

As an illustration of how the Lorentz transformation (33) works, consider the (simple) example of an object unit distance from the observer in the (say) x-direction, so $q = (1 + Ii)$, and the Lorentz transformation is by boost angle θ in the same x-direction, so the Lorentz rotor is $R = e^{-Ii\theta/2}$, Eq. (27). Then the Lorentz transformation (33) is

$$\begin{Bmatrix} 1 & 0 \\ 0 & 1 \end{Bmatrix} \rightarrow \begin{Bmatrix} \cosh\frac{\theta}{2} & 0 \\ 0 & \sinh\frac{\theta}{2} \end{Bmatrix} \begin{Bmatrix} 1 & 0 \\ 0 & 1 \end{Bmatrix} \begin{Bmatrix} \cosh\frac{\theta}{2} & 0 \\ 0 & \sinh\frac{\theta}{2} \end{Bmatrix}$$
$$= e^{\theta} \begin{Bmatrix} 1 & 0 \\ 0 & 1 \end{Bmatrix} , \tag{41}$$

which says that the Lorentz-boosted position appears farther away by the factor e^{θ}. The exponential factor e^{θ} agrees with the conventional special relativistic Doppler shift formula

$$e^{\theta} = \cosh\theta + \sinh\theta = \gamma(1 + v) = \sqrt{\frac{1+v}{1-v}} . \tag{42}$$

The result also agrees with Fig. 1, which illustrates that the scene directly ahead appears farther away and blueshifted by the Doppler factor $\gamma(1 + v)$.

Lorentz transforming a scene typically involves a large number of Lorentz transformations, one for each point on the scene. A complex quaternion has 8 components, and two position vectors r_1 and r_2 can be transformed for the price of one by treating one of them, r_2, as a pseudovector, and packing the two into a single complex quaternion,

$$q = r_1(1 + In_1) - Ir_2(1 + In_2) . \tag{43}$$

If the 3-vector components of the two positions are $r_i n_i = \{x_i, y_i, z_i\}$, $i = 1, 2$, then the components of the packed complex quaternion q are

$$q = \left\{ \begin{matrix} r_1 & x_2 & y_2 & z_2 \\ -r_2 & x_1 & y_1 & z_1 \end{matrix} \right\} . \tag{44}$$

The same Lorentz transformation formula (33) applies.

4   Conclusion

In the future, children will learn the mysteries of special and general relativity by playing with relativistic flight simulators. Relativity will cease to be something accessible only to the cognoscenti.

The first task in coding a relativistic flight simulator is to implement Lorentz transformations. The right way to do that is with complex quaternions. This paper shows how.

References

1. Kraus, U.: First-person visualizations of the special and general theory of relativity. Eur. J. Phys. **29**, 1–13 (2007). arXiv:0708.3454. https://doi.org/10.1088/0143-0807/29/1/001
2. Kraus, U., Zahn, C.: Relativity visualized (2001–2021). https://www.spacetimetravel.org/
3. Sherin, Z.W., Cheu, R., Tan, P., Kortemeyer, G.: Visualizing relativity: the Open-Relativity project. Am. J. Phys. **84**, 369–374 (2016). https://doi.org/10.1119/1.4938057
4. O'Donnell, S.: Portrait of a Prodigy (Boole Press). Dublin (1983). https://doi.org/10.1163/182539177X01015
5. Lorentz, H.A.: Electromagnetic phenomena in a system moving with any velocity smaller than that of light Proc. Royal Netherlands Academy Arts Sci. **6**, 809–831 (1904)
6. Hamilton, A.J.S.: The Rules of 4-dimensional Perspective (2010). https://jila.colorado.edu/~ajsh/insidebh/4dperspective.html
7. Silberstein, L.: Quaternionic form of relativity. Phil. Mag. **23**, 790–809 (1912). https://doi.org/10.1080/14786440508637276

8. Dirac, P.A.M.: Application of quaternions to lorentz transformations. Proc. Royal Irish Academy. Section A: Math. and Phys. Sci. **50**, 261–270 (1944)
9. Berry, T., Visser, M.: Lorentz boosts and Wigner rotations: self-adjoint complexified quaternions. arXiv:2101.05971
10. https://www.esa.int/ESA_Multimedia/Images/2020/12/The_colour_of_the_sky_from_Gaia_s_Early_Data_Release_32
11. Black Hole Flight Simulator. https://jila.colorado.edu/~ajsh/insidebh/bhfs.html
12. Penrose, R.: The apparent shape of a relativistically moving sphere. Proc. Cambridge Phil. Soc. **55**, 137–139 (1959). https://doi.org/10.1017/S0305004100033776
13. Terrell, J.: Invisibility of the lorentz contraction. Phys. Rev. **116**, 1041–1045 (1959). https://doi.org/10.1103/PhysRev.116.1041

Author Index

Abdulkhaev, Kamron 670
Alanko, Joel 433
Ali, Saba Ghazanfar 421
Aran, Oya 205
Araujo, Victor 548

Baculo, Maria Jeseca C. 205
Bao, Fanyu 621
Beauchamp, Andre 378
Bi, Lei 242, 354

Chang, Jian 621
Chen, Lianggangxu 190
Chen, Nianzhe 339
Chen, Shuangmin 452
Chen, Wentao 151
Chen, Yijing 125
Chen, Ying 276
Chi, Xiaoyu 67, 421
Coelho, R. C. 315
Cordier, Frederic 365
Costa, Angelo 548

da Fontoura, Vladimir Soares 589
Dalmoro, Bruna 548
Ding, Hui 339
Ding, Zhanfeng 89
Dong, Tianyang 89
dos Santos, G. M. 315
dos Santos, V. S. 315
Du, Zhenjiang 217

Er, Lim Hwee 491

Favaretto, Rodolfo 548
Fei, Lunke 264
Fudos, Ioannis 3

Gao, BoYu 608
Gao, Hong 682
Garrofé, Guillem 41
Ge, Chao 621
Godoy, C. C. 315
Godoy, C. M. G. 315

Guo, Hao 327
Guo, Yufei 477
Gutiérrez, Anna 41

Hai, Yongqing 477
Hamilton, Andrew J. S. 705
He, Gaoqi 190
He, Xiangui 242, 354
Hitzer, Eckhard 658
Hu, Ruimin 101
Hu, Wei 276
Huang, Binhao 190
Huang, Dongjin 327
Huang, Enquan 288
Huang, Xuhui 477
Huo, Yuchi 519

Ikkala, Julius 433

Jääskeläinen, Pekka 433
Ji, Penglei 139
Jia, Wei 264
Jiang, Hao 504
Jiang, Luyan 139
Jiang, Shiqi 229
Jiang, Xinghao 80
Jin, Shuo 125
Jung, Hoijoon 633
Jung, Younhyun 633

Kamarianakis, Manos 694
Khoong, Cheng Siok 491
Kim, HyungSeok 608
Kim, Jinman 242, 354, 421
Kim, Minyoung 398
Kim, Seon Tae 633
Kim, Young J. 398
Kivi, Petrus 433

Lee, Euro 633
Lee, Sungmin 633
Li, Chenhui 229
Li, Dan 178
Li, Guiqing 125

Li, Hanchao   139
Li, Hanhui   491
Li, Kaiwen   288
Li, Ping   67, 242, 421
Li, Zhaoxin   113
Li, Zhen   67, 421
Liang, Hui   621
Lin, Feng   167
Lin, Hongwei   568
Liu, Kun   354
Liu, Rui   339
Liu, Shiguang   464
Liu, Shu   288
Liu, Xinguo   139
Liu, Zhitao   217
Long, Xiaoyi   101
Loučka, Pavel   645
Lu, Yujun   608
Luo, Fei   54
Luo, Weiqi   608
Luo, Wen   682
Lydatakis, Nick   694

Ma, Lei   300
Ma, Yitian   151
Ma, Zhe   477
Ma, Zhenwei   190
Maciel, Anderson   589
Mäkitalo, Markku   433
Mao, Lijuan   67, 421
Mi, Zhongjie   80
Miralles, David   41
Mishra, Nidhi   491
Molina, Elena   25
Moutafidou, Anastasia   3
Musse, Soraia Raupp   548

Nie, Yufeng   339
Niu, Qirui   339

Papagiannakis, George   694
Paquette, Eric   378
Parés, Carlota   41
Park, Hunmin   519
Pelechano, Nuria   25
Pellegrin, Florian   378
Peng, Chaoyang   80
Peng, Guoqin   535
Ping, Lee Mei   491

Qi, Yue   252

Rida, Imad   264
Ríos, Alejandro   25
Ruiz Jr, Conrado   41, 205

Sang, Tian   151
Seah, Hock Soon   167
Selusniacki, M. C.   315
Seo, Hyewon   365
Serra, Gerard   41
Shang, Yuanyuan   339
Sheng, Bin   67, 242, 354, 406, 421
Shi, Wuzhen   178
Shirokov, Dmitry   670
Sun, Kewu   477
Sun, Tanfeng   80
Sun, Yusheng   621

Teng, Shaohua   264
Thalmann, Nadia Magnenat   491
Toulatzis, Vasileios   3
Tu, Changhe   452
Tu, Huawei   608
Tulsulkar, Gauri   491

Vašík, Petr   645
Vilanova, Felipe   548

Wang, Beibei   300
Wang, Changbo   229
Wang, Hui   151
Wang, Jihong   67, 421
Wang, Sijia   504
Wang, Wei   276
Wang, Wenping   452
Wang, Yun   682
Wang, Zhaoqi   504
Wei, Lin   54
Wen, Jiawei   113
Wen, Jie   264
Wen, Yang   67, 242, 354

Xian, Chuhua   125
Xiao, Chunxia   54
Xie, Ning   217
Xie, Zhifeng   406
Xin, Shiqing   452
Xu, Chenkai   568

Xu, Dan   535
Xu, Xin   101, 276
Xu, Xun   242, 354
Xu, Yupeng   242, 354
Xue, Zhongmin   300

Yan, Feihu   113
Yan, Zhenjun   682
Yang, Wenjun   288
Yang, Xubo   151
Yang, Yang   217
Yao, Lihong   80
Ying, Wenyuan   89
Yoon, Sung-Eui   519
Yu, Chunpeng   406
Yu, Zhaoyuan   682
Yuan, Linwang   682

Zhang, Guisong   406
Zhang, Hao   535
Zhang, Jiyi   682
Zhang, Xiaohua   217
Zhang, Xinpeng   89
Zhang, Yu   464
Zhang, Yue   327
Zhang, Zheng   452
Zhao, Dapeng   252
Zhao, Junhao   452
Zhao, Kangqiao   167
Zhao, Rongli   477
Zheng, Jiaheng   406
Zheng, Yongmin   264
Zhou, Yuanfeng   452
Zhou, Zhong   113
Zou, Beiji   288
Zou, Kaifeng   365

Printed in the United States
by Baker & Taylor Publisher Services